Rabbinic Culture and Its Critics

Rabbinic Culture and Its Critics

Jewish Authority, Dissent, and Heresy in Medieval and Early Modern Times

Edited by

DANIEL FRANK

and

MATT GOLDISH

Wayne State University Press
Detroit

Manufactured in the United States of America.

12 11 10 09 08 5 4 3 2 1

Library of Congress Cataloging-in-Publication Data

Rabbinic culture and its critics : Jewish authority, dissent, and heresy in medieval and early modern times / edited by Daniel Frank and Matt Goldish.
p. cm.
Includes index.
ISBN-13: 978-0-8143-3237-5 (hardcover : alk. paper)
ISBN-10: 0-8143-3237-4 (hardcover : alk. paper)
1. Rabbinical literature—History and criticism—Congresses. 2. Judaism—History—Medieval and early modern period, 425–1789—Congresses. 3. Dissenters—History—Congresses. 4. Heresy—History—Congresses. I. Frank, Daniel. II. Goldish, Matt.

BM496.6.R33 2007
296.6'7—dc22
2007002353

∞ The paper used in this publication meets the minimum requirements of the American National Standard for Information Sciences—Permanence of Paper for Printed Library Materials, ANSI Z39.48–1984.

Designed and typeset by Keata Brewer, E. T. Lowe Publishing Company
Composed in Palatino and David

Contents

II.
Jews, Conversos, and Heretics
in the Early Modern Period

III.
Sabbateanism and Its Repercussions

Preface and Acknowledgments

Rabbinic culture—its leaders, institutions, and texts—attained a dominant position within Judaism in late antiquity and retained its absolute authority well into the modern period. Though differing significantly in matters of custom, Jewish communities throughout the world adhered to a system of law and a set of doctrines remarkable for their uniformity. And yet there was dissent. Judaism—unlike Christianity—is primarily grounded in practice rather than doctrine, but over the centuries rabbinic leaders frequently attacked specific beliefs for being heretical. Some cases seemed clear-cut: the Karaite movement, for example, denied the authority of the oral tradition and established a new scripturalist law of its own. And the messianic movement of Shabbatai Zvi, in its various manifestations, obviously constituted an extremely serious challenge to rabbinic Judaism. But there were other manifestations of discontent as well: to some scholars, conventional religiosity seemed a poor substitute for true spirituality; others decried the ignorance, superstition, and crude theology of the masses; and there were those whose exposure to contemporary intellectual currents led them to question the very principles of rabbinic culture.

These critics, and the elusive "Judaism" they challenged, have been examined in many contexts. Rarely, however, has a group of scholars sought to investigate dissent from rabbinic Judaism as a category in the history and culture of the Jewish people. The present volume seeks to address this need, by focusing on rabbinic culture in the Middle Ages and early modern period—from the days of the Babylonian *geonim,* who first championed the Talmud, to the *maskilim,* who promoted the Jewish Enlightenment in the eighteenth and nineteenth centuries. The essays discuss Jewish thinkers, famous and obscure: sectarians, conversos, learned critics, and cranks. Taken together, these studies offer a fresh, interdisciplinary perspective on Jewish dissent within a traditional society that cuts across temporal, geographical, and phenomenological boundaries.

In an introductory essay, we define rabbinic culture in literary, practical, ideological, and institutional terms. We then survey the various types of critiques leveled against it within the Jewish world from the early Middle Ages to the Enlightenment. The volume proper comprises three sections: "Rabbinic Judaism and Its Boundaries in the Middle Ages"; "Jews, Conversos, and Heretics in the Early Modern Period"; and "Sabbateanism and Its Repercussions."

Part 1 opens with two papers that discuss the critiques of Andalusian literati and philosophers. Adena Tanenbaum surveys the Sefardic tradition of belletristic satire aimed at indecorous worship, religious hypocrisy, and parochialism. Despite their own connections to the rabbinic elite, Samuel ha-Nagid (11th c.) and Judah Alḥarizi (12th–13th c.) did not hesitate to lampoon the posturing of an ignorant teacher or a pompous cantor who contravened aesthetic and spiritual ideals. Displeased with insular talmudism, Shem Tov Falaquera (13th c.) used belles lettres to advocate a broad curriculum combining religious scholarship with philosophical study. As a critical medium, poetry and rhymed prose appealed to a broader audience, and writers could criticize types in the guise of individuals or vice versa. Although the paper focuses on the eleventh to thirteenth centuries, the author notes that belletristic critiques of this kind remained popular for many centuries.

The leading exponent of the Sefardic intellectual tradition, Moses Maimonides (1138–1204), was also the most important Jewish thinker of the Middle Ages. Menachem Kellner discusses Maimonides' critical attitude toward the rabbinic culture of his time. His consistent nominalism and insistence on God's absolute transcendence often led Maimonides to universalist positions that were at odds with mainstream rabbinic thought. He regularly desacralized subjects that most Jewish thinkers had invested with sanctity, such as the Hebrew language, the concept of holiness, ritual purity and impurity, and the nature of angels. The rationalistic Judaism that he espoused thus stood in sharp opposition to the theologies of contemporary rabbis and the mysticism of the kabbalists who became prominent after his lifetime.

Maimonides soon left his mark on Jewish thinkers outside the Islamic world. The next two papers in the volume are devoted to rabbinic culture in northern Europe. Ephraim Kanarfogel analyzes the reception in Ashkenaz of Maimonides' strong stance against anthropomorphism. Contrary to received wisdom, he shows that a wide range of opinions on the subject prevailed in northern France and Germany: there were those who upheld anthropomorphic beliefs, those who rejected them, and those—like certain German Pietists—who held intermediate positions. Although they lacked a systematic religious philosophy, these northern European rabbis addressed sensitive theological questions with far greater sophistication than has previously been realized. Of course, theological pronouncements of any kind would have been impossible, had they not possessed some definition of faith. In a diachronic study, Joseph Davis considers the very different ways in which Ashkenazic Jews defined belief and unbelief over a period of seven hundred and fifty years. While northern French scholars in the thirteenth century branded as heretics those, like Maimonides, who allegorized *aggadot,* German rabbis in the fifteenth century readily drew upon the great Andalusian for their formulation of a creed. In the seventeenth century, heresy for some meant the rejection of Kabbalah, and in the eighteenth it meant Sabbateanism—unless one subscribed to Mendelssohn's view that "Jewish society, like all societies, must allow freedom of conscience." The essay clearly shows that Ashkenazi rabbis did not maintain some static, anti-rationalist conception of Jewish belief; on the contrary, clashing views competed throughout medieval and early modern times in the struggle to define orthodoxy and dissent.

The last two papers in the section are devoted to Karaites, Jewish sectarians who denied rabbinic authority and rejected the Oral Law. Marina Rustow investigates the Rabbanite ban excommunicating the Karaites that was issued on the Mount of Olives in 1029. While certain Rabbanite leaders recognized the value of making common cause with the sectarians and sought rapprochement between the two groups, the Rabbanite laity stigmatized Karaites as "eaters of meat with milk" and denounced them as heretics. The affair of the ban and its aftermath illustrate the social forces that accompany schism and reveal the importance of the political factor in Rabbanite-Karaite relations. For their part, Karaite scholars studied rabbinic texts closely—and not always with polemical intent. Daniel Frank focuses on a seventeenth-century Karaite, Elijah ben Baruch Yerushalmi, who sought to prevent the assimilation of Crimean sectarians to Rabbanite Judaism on the one hand, while encouraging them to read rabbinic literature on the other, since "their statements are the words of our ancestors." Elijah maintained that Rabbanite luminaries, such as Abraham Ibn Ezra and Moses Maimonides, recognized the truth of Karaite biblical interpretations, but would not admit this publicly because they wished to preserve the authority of the rabbinic tradition within their community. While he tried to show the extent of this alleged duplicity in one treatise, he devoted a separate work to popularizing philosophical notions and dicta that he had culled from Rabbanite authors as well as classic rabbinic literature. Like earlier Karaite scholars in Constantinople, he sought an intellectual rapprochement with rabbinic Judaism that would not compromise the spiritual integrity of his own community.

In part 2, the volume shifts to the Western Sefardi Diaspora in the seventeenth century, comprising communities of Portuguese ex-conversos in Amsterdam, London, Hamburg, Livorno, and southern France. Raised in Iberia as New Christians under the shadow of the Inquisition, these Jews were often ambivalent about the rabbinic tradition that they first encountered in communities of their own construction.

Using Inquisitional documents, Miriam Bodian demonstrates that at least some crypto-Jews living in Spain and Portugal evinced marked anti-ecclesiastical attitudes. She explores the evidence concerning such figures as Luis de Carvajal, Isaac de Castro Tartas, and Diogo da Asumpção, who deliberately antagonized the inquisitors by engaging in doctrinal debates, in which they took "Jewish" or quasi-Protestant positions. Their main thesis was the right of individuals to interpret Scripture independently—a position that was anathema to both Catholic and rabbinic authorities. The debates between these prisoners and their inquisitors afford real insight into the converso mentality that would profoundly affect Jewish society and Western thought.

Amsterdam, of course, became a crucible for early modern Jewish thought. Adam Sutcliffe discusses the doctrinal issues facing the Dutch rabbis and their attempts to regulate interaction between Jews and Christians in the city. Unaccustomed to rabbinic authority, the local Jews were mistrustful of rabbis. The porous social boundaries of the community, moreover, allowed easy interactions with Christians, and some dissatisfied ex-conversos even gravitated toward various Protestant denominations, including the Quakers.

Resorting to communal enactments and anti-Christian polemics, the rabbis of Amsterdam attempted to control the situation, but apparently enjoyed only limited success. Jewish preaching in the city also targeted "heretical views"; Marc Saperstein studies several key sermons by Ḥaham Saul Levi Morteira, chief rabbi of the community for much of the seventeenth century. Although Morteira clearly sought to address the problem within his own congregation, he discusses heresy in veiled, impersonal terms with reference to ancient heresies. At the same time, it is possible to correlate some of his statements with major contemporary issues, such as the question of the soul's immortality or the validity of the Oral Law. Morteira does not mention Uriel da Costa by name, but he is plainly responding to the challenge posed by the famous dissenter.

The most famous and influential of the Portuguese Jewish dissenters in Amsterdam was undoubtedly Baruch Spinoza, who did not stop with a critique of rabbinic authority and teachings, but attacked the very foundations of revealed religion. Excommunicated in 1656, Spinoza was specifically denounced for having denied the soul's immortality. Steven Nadler examines the charge against Spinoza and assesses the importance of the issue in seventeenth-century Amsterdam. The denial of personal immortality would become central for Spinoza, and more generally in the anti-religious discourse of the early Enlightenment. Spinoza's image became ever more influential after his death, in both Western thought and within the European Jewish community. Allan Nadler shows how later proponents of Jewish enlightenment (*maskilim*) manipulated Spinoza's legacy for their own purposes. In the satiric preface to his textual critique of the Bible, *Ha-Ketav ve-ha-Mikhtav,* Abraham Krochmal (1817–88) claims that his proposed emendations were not the product of human reason, but derive from an ancient manuscript unearthed in Poland. The author of this work, asserts Krochmal, was none other than Spinoza, who had decided to burn it before he died. Before he could do so, however, his disciple Rabbi Adam Baal Shem—a mythical character known from early Ḥasidic literature—made a copy that he bequeathed to his son, who taught it in turn to the founder of the Ḥasidic movement, Israel Baal Shem Tov, who subsequently buried it. Nadler explains this bizarre tale and the rhetorical significance of its various figures and motifs; the second part of his chapter is an annotated translation of Krochmal's preface.

The final section of the volume is devoted to the messianic movement of 1665–66 surrounding Shabbatai Zvi, which has often been called a watershed in the history of Jewish mystical dissent. Matt Goldish discusses Gershom Scholem's claims concerning the heretical nature of the Sabbatean movement, and contrasts these with the accusations of heresy leveled by a contemporary, Ḥaham Jacob Sasportas. While both Scholem and Sasportas call the Sabbateans heretics, they mean very different things. For Scholem, the ritualized antinomianism justified on kabbalistic grounds by the movement's leaders constituted a kind of mystical heresy. This trend really began, however, after Shabbatai had converted to Islam. Sasportas, on the other hand, branded the Sabbateans heretics because of their dissent from rabbinic tradition and authority at the movement's crest, before Shabbatai's apostasy. In Sasportas's view, then, the movement should be seen within the context of other contemporary critiques of rabbinic culture.

Nathan of Gaza, the chief Sabbatean theologian of the seventeenth century, and Jacob Frank, the foremost Sabbatean messianic figure of the eighteenth century, played crucial roles in the movement's history. Harris Lenowitz shows how both men tried to fashion the Sabbatean believer into a "new model man" who followed his doubts about traditional rabbinic authority over the abyss and into a new world of belief. The new faith of the believer would be fideistic and heterodox, dedicated to a new authority—that of the messiah. Centered in Poland, the Frankist movement mainly affected the Ashkenazi world. Pace Scholem, Lenowitz finds no evidence to suggest that Frankism exerted a direct influence on the rise of Reform Judaism, the *Haskalah,* and the Ḥasidic movement. Based on his conception of Frank's "new man," however, he concludes that all these movements were part of a common nexus centered on the daring critique of rabbinic authority.

There was another order of Sabbatean believers in eighteenth-century Poland, however, who rejected the radical antinomianism of Frank, while remaining secret adherents of Shabbatai. At mid-century, an enormous controversy erupted within the upper echelons of the Ashkenazi rabbinate when Rabbi Jacob Emden accused Rabbi Jonathan Eibeschuetz of belonging to this heretical underground movement. Sid Z. Leiman considers the role of another highly distinguished leader, Rabbi Jacob Joshua Falk, in this dispute. Taking Emden's side, Falk sought to isolate Eibeschuetz by forcing him either to appear before a rabbinic council and publicly repent of his heresies, or to hold tight to his secret and lose his position in disgrace. Falk's death in 1756, however, foiled this strategy and left the controversy forever unresolved.

We would like to thank the Melton Center for Jewish Studies of the Ohio State University and its longtime director, Professor Tamar

Rudavsky, for sponsoring the conference in October 2001 which inspired this volume, and for the generous subvention which made its publication possible. We are especially grateful to the Schiff family for their generosity in establishing the Schiff Lehrhaus, which funded the conference. Dr. David Malkiel (Bar-Ilan University) kindly offered many judicious comments on our manuscript, for which we are most grateful, and we would like to acknowledge as well two anonymous readers for their considered criticisms and suggestions. We would also like to express our gratitude to Kathryn Wildfong, Kristin Harpster Lawrence, and Carrie Downes Teefey, editors of Wayne State University Press for their help and encouragement throughout this project. And we would like to thank Eric Schramm for meticulously copyediting a long, complex text and Barry D. Walfish for providing the volume with a comprehensive index.

Finally, our thanks to the following presses for permitting us to reprint pieces that have appeared elsewhere in somewhat different form: The Littman Library of Jewish Civilization, for permission to reprint Menachem Kellner's chapter from his book *Maimonides' Confrontation with Mysticism* (2006); Hebrew Union College Press, for permission to reprint Marc Saperstein's chapter from his book *Exile in Amsterdam: Saul Levi Morteira's Sermons to a Congregation Of "New Jews"* (2005); Oxford University Press, for permission to reprint Steven Nadler's chapter from his book *Spinoza's Heresy: Immortality and the Jewish Mind* (2001); Harvard University Press, for permission to reprint Matt Goldish's chapter from his book *The Sabbatean Prophets* (2004).

Rabbinic Culture and Dissent

An Overview

DANIEL FRANK and MATT GOLDISH

Rabbinic Culture

The phrase "rabbinic culture" describes traditional forms of Judaism whose practices, beliefs, values, and social structures are firmly rooted in the Talmud and its interpretation. With a few notable exceptions, the culture of all Jewish communities from late antiquity until the nineteenth century was rabbinic. Naturally, this culture was not monolithic: customs, mores, and aesthetics varied with time and place. Jews also took part in the general culture of the societies in which they lived, and the quality of this participation affected their local Jewish cultures as well. Jewish society, moreover, was stratified: the poor, the wealthy, the learned, and the uneducated were certainly not uniform in all their views. And yet throughout the centuries and the many lands of the Diaspora, Jews maintained a cultural identity remarkable for its coherence, and a pattern of life striking for its consistency.[1]

Rabbinic culture is founded upon a literature—its interpretation, the imperative to study it, and the authority of its leading interpreters. Composed over the course of a thousand years, this literature includes exegetical and homiletical treatments of the Bible (*midrash*), as well as collections of legislation. Its central work, the Babylonian Talmud, defines a religious, textually grounded set of attitudes and behavioral norms. Classical Judaism has rightly been characterized as law-based, for Jewish law (*halakhah*) covers virtually the totality of the human experience, regulating civil, social, and family life as well as every detail of religious practice.[2] This law derives from two canonical sources: the Hebrew Bible (Scripture) and the Talmud (Tradition). In reality, the Talmud is supreme, since it encompasses the rabbinic understanding of Scripture. In the introduction to his comprehensive code, *Mishneh Torah,* the Andalusian polymath Moses Maimonides (1138–1204) describes the nature of this relationship and how it came into being. Drawing upon early rabbinic sources, he explains that God revealed the Torah to Moses together with its authoritative interpretation. While the former was set down in writing, the latter was to be transmitted orally from generation to generation. Ultimately, however, historical circumstances drove the leading scholar of his time, Rabbi Judah the Prince (ca. 135–220), to edit this material, in the form of a code, known as the Mishnah:

> Copies of it were made and widely disseminated, so that the Oral law might not be forgotten in Israel. Why did our teacher, the saint, act so and not leave things as they were? Because he observed that the number of disciples was diminishing, fresh calamities were continually happening, the wicked government was extending its domain and increasing in power, and Israelites were wandering and emigrating to distant countries. He therefore composed a work to serve as a handbook for all, the contents of which could be rapidly studied and not be forgotten. Throughout his life, he and his colleagues were engaged in giving pubic instruction in the Mishnah.[3]

But even this drastic step proved insufficient, for with time, the Mishnah's laconic language and abstruse subject matter demanded explication. The Babylonian Talmud records extended discussions of the Mishnah that took place over several centuries. Redacted in stages, it betrays diverse styles and preserves countless conflicting opinions. If its skeleton, the Mishnah, is codificatory in form, its substance—commonly called the Gemara—is discursive in the extreme.[4]

Talmudic discussion relates primarily to law (*halakhah*) and its interpretation, but much space is also given over to non-legal material (*aggadah*)—legend, ethics, wisdom, history, and the like. Rabbinic Judaism is centered on law, certainly, but it is hardly the dry legalism presented by its severest detractors.[5] Inextricably intertwined, law and lore complement each other in essential ways. As the renowned poet and essayist Ḥayyim Naḥman Bialik (1873–1934) put it, "Halakhah is the crystallization, the ultimate and inevitable quintessence, of Aggadah; Aggadah is the *content* of Halakhah."[6]

Sabbath observance, for example, is closely regulated, with thirty-nine categories of labor explicitly proscribed.[7] At the same time, the day of rest safeguarded by this mass of legislation possesses ineffable qualities: the Sabbath is said, for example, to impart a special fragrance to the delicacies with which it is celebrated—a fragrance that can be savored only by those who keep the day holy![8] Personified as a queen or bride, the Sabbath is a beloved guest welcomed weekly with joy and solicitousness, at home and in the synagogue.[9] The Sabbath demands scrupulous observance of religious law: the avoidance of what is forbidden and the fulfillment of what is commanded. "Whoever delights in the Sabbath," says Rabbi Judah, "is granted his heart's desires. . . . When it is said, 'and you shall call the Sabbath a delight' [Isa. 58:13] you must say that it refers to the delight of the Sabbath."[10] According to the Talmud, this delight consists in special dishes.[11] And according to a midrashic source, it also manifests itself in the lights kindled on Friday at dusk, which inaugurate the holy day and illuminate an evening when lighting fires is prohibited. But kindling these lights is more than a means of getting around an inconvenient biblical prohibition; it constitutes a positive precept with its own accompanying benediction and regulations.[12] As Bialik exclaimed, "Who shall presume to decide whether Halakhah or Aggadah gave [the Sabbath] being and made her what she is?"[13]

Arranged as a running discussion of the Mishnah, the Talmud establishes the pattern of text and interpretation. Obviously a product of the academy, it raises questions, proposes solutions, then challenges them, offering others in their place. Argumentation is rigorous, invoking recognized hermeneutic rules.[14] While practical law is propounded, theoretical problems are considered as well—even when they are outlandish in the extreme. Judah the Prince may betray impatience when he is asked how a two-headed man is to don phylacteries, but the Talmud makes it clear that even hypotheticals of this kind may have practical ramifications.[15]

Digressive, discursive, and frequently obscure, the Talmud demands explication. From the time it received its canonical shape during the sixth century C.E. it has continually been studied both by trained scholars and the Jewish populace at large. During the Middle Ages, different interpretive traditions and schools developed, first in the ancient Babylonian center and later in Andalusia, northern France, and Germany. Talmudic learning was incremental, with later scholars responding to the interpretations of their predecessors. A volume of the famous Vilna edition (1880–86), for example, reproduces the comments of many scholars from different periods and places, from Rashi (Solomon ben Isaac) of Troyes (1040–1105) and Ḥananel ben Ḥushiel of Kairouan (ca. 990–1050) to Isaiah of Trani (thirteenth century), Joel Sirkes of Poland (1561–1640), and Elijah, the Gaon of Vilna (1720–97). Biblical studies followed a parallel course: on a page of a rabbinic Bible, Samuel ben Meir (Rashbam; d. ca. 1174) confronts his grandfather Rashi, while Moses Naḥmanides of Gerona (1194–1270) cites Abraham Ibn Ezra, who wandered Europe during the twelfth century. As certain texts established themselves in the rabbinic canon, they in turn were subjected to endless scrutiny and interpretation. The Torah commentaries of Rashi and Ibn Ezra, for example, spawned numerous supercommentaries.[16]

The same process may be observed in other disciplines. Maimonides' *Guide of the Perplexed* (ca. 1190) called forth responses from every subsequent Jewish philosopher.[17] And among legal works, the *Shulḥan Arukh* (1565–66) of Joseph Karo elicited a succession of responses, commentaries, and supercommentaries.[18] Driving this ceaseless exegetical enterprise was the conviction that divine revelation is timeless and embodies all truth. Legal experts responded to queries with decisions grounded directly in the Talmud.[19] Preachers related the weekly Torah reading firmly to their congregants' experience.[20] Philosophers sought to make sense of the anthropomorphic expressions in the Bible and *aggadah*.[21] Kabbalists uncovered an entire, concealed theosophy in Revelation.[22] Indeed for most readers, a single scriptural text could hold multiple meanings.[23] As we shall see, the possibility of interpreting canonical texts in many different ways provoked considerable debate and dissent.

A potent educational ideal also underlay all this scholarly activity. *Talmud Torah* (lit. "Torah study") designates a religious imperative to meditate upon God's word day and night.[24] According to Maimonides, it forms the eleventh positive injunction of the 613 commandments and merits a special treatise in his *Mishneh Torah*.[25] Of course, *Talmud Torah* encompasses much more than Bible study. Indeed, since the Babylonian Talmud embraces both biblical exegesis and the elucidation of the Mishnah, there are those who argue that it offers an almost self-sufficient course of study.[26] *Talmud Torah* possesses obvious practical benefits. Indeed, a basic knowledge of ritual law remains essential for any Jew. But there is also a religious obligation to study the Torah—in the broadest sense—for its own sake (*Torah li-shemah*). Thus, even legislation that has been held in abeyance since the destruction of the Second Temple in 70 C.E., such as the laws pertaining to sacrifices, forms part of the traditional curriculum. Rabbinic literature itself extols the virtues of *Talmud Torah:* "Four things a man does, and he enjoys their fruits in this world, while the stock is laid up for him in the world to come, to wit: honoring father and mother, acts of loving-kindness, establishing peace between man and his fellow man, and the study of Torah, which is equal to them all."[27] From the time his children begin to speak, writes Maimonides, a father is obligated to teach them Torah; studying the Law will then become a lifelong obligation. Communities must establish and support primary schools where Bible is taught.[28] Before long, pupils are introduced to Mishnah and then Talmud; those who acquire real proficiency may be said to have attained "the crown of the Torah," which, we are told, is more prized than the crowns of kingship or priesthood.[29]

Finally, talmudic scholarship has affected rabbinic culture, by determining Jewish religious and political authority.[30] At the individual level, mastery of the Law promotes personal status and prestige. Rabbinic literature not only preserves the teachings of the ancient sages but also records their erudition, insight, and piety. Numerous sayings and exempla stress their wisdom and saintliness as well as their readiness to suffer hardship for their beliefs and way of life: "The Oral law is not found among those who pursue the pleasures of this world—its passions, its glory, or its greatness, but only among those who deprive themselves for its sake."[31] Again, it is Maimonides who codifies the recognition of these sages: just as there is a religious obligation to study the Law, there is a positive commandment to honor its students, who embody the ideal of *Talmud Torah.*[32] As halakhic experts and repositories of traditional learning, moreover, they directly shape Jewish religious, social, economic, and communal life. The influence rabbis exert may stem from their personal reputations; often it is also of an institutional nature.[33]

Rabbinic literature was created in the academies (*yeshivot*) of the Land of Israel and Babylonia by men who consciously sought to mold Jewish life. Combinations of colleges and high courts, these institutions were organized as rigid hierarchies with powerful *geonim* at their heads. By virtue of their legal authority, the *yeshivot* succeeded in extending their spheres of influence far beyond their immediate geographic areas. During the first centuries of Abbasid rule in the Islamic East (ca. 750–950), there was a struggle for supremacy between the Academy of the Land of Israel and the Babylonian *yeshivot*. Ultimately, the latter triumphed, thereby ensuring the ascendancy of the Babylonian Talmud and many Babylonian customs. But the Babylonian institutions themselves were at odds. The *yeshivot* of Sura and Pumbedita and the office of the Exilarch—who represented the Jewish population at the court of the Abbasid caliph—competed for the allegiance and financial support of Diaspora communities, which looked to Baghdad for the production of authoritative texts, the resolution of complex legal affairs, and even the appointment of local judges. But as these communities in turn developed their own *yeshivot* and produced native scholars, the power of the old Babylonian academies waned. This was certainly the case in Andalusia, where an important new academy emerged in Lucena during the eleventh century.[34] In other parts of Europe, large, enduring *yeshivot* did not always develop. An outstanding scholar would attract disciples, but with his passing they would likely move elsewhere.[35]

Nor was rabbinic authority ever absolute. While rabbinic scholars might seek to normalize Jewish practice and belief, they necessarily remained responsive to the communities they served. Their rulings were tempered by local custom (*minhag*) and usage, which in turn were often shaped by socioeconomic conditions and relations with non-Jewish populations. Attempts to curb certain traditions and to impose others frequently failed. Some of the Babylonian *geonim* strove to suppress local customs they deemed unacceptable, in favor of practices sanctioned by the academies. But more often than not, they could do little more than recommend their own practices. In northern Europe during the early Middle Ages, on the other hand, ancestral custom was extolled, even equated with Scripture. The many instances where local *minhag* prevailed over talmudic norms confirm the force of praxis. Under these circumstances, rabbinic scholars sought to reconcile the two sources of law rather than impose textbook decisions. In this way, neither the Talmud's prestige nor their role as its expert interpreters were weakened in the face of popular usage.[36] What remained true for the entire Diaspora throughout the Middle Ages and early modern period is that religious, juridical, and often communal leadership remained largely in the hands of talmudic scholars: rabbinic culture was controlled by rabbis.[37]

The Karaite Critique

We have considered four salient aspects of rabbinic culture: the literature that defines it, the continuing interpretation of that literature, the scholarly ideal, and the authority wielded by those scholars. The literature, in fact, chronicles its own history through a series of works that date back as far as the Mishnaic tractate Avot and include the *Order of Tannaim and Amoraim* (885), the *Epistle of Sherira Gaon* (986), and Abraham Ibn Daud's *Book of Tradition* (1160–61), as well as such later books as Abraham Zacut's *Book of Genealogies* (1502 or 1504) and Gedaliah Ibn Yaḥya's *Chain of Tradition* (1549–87).[38] As their titles indicate, these compositions celebrate many generations of rabbinic scholarship and leadership, taking the place of a more conventional historiography of dynasties and wars.[39] Ibn Daud's book, for example, continues the narrative two centuries beyond Sherira's *Epistle*, while glorifying in particular the contributions of Andalusian scholars. Typically, it also presents a historical scheme that suggests the messianic age is about to dawn. Strikingly, one of its central aims is also to defend the rabbinic tradition against Karaite attacks.[40]

In its early, scripturalist form, Karaism presented a stark, uncompromising alternative to rabbinic Judaism. The Karaite movement crystallized in the Islamic East during the ninth and tenth centuries, spreading to Byzantium and Spain during the eleventh and twelfth.[41] Since the Karaites explicitly rejected many of the premises and values of the Rabbanites—this is the standard academic term for rabbinic Jews—their criticisms offer a good starting point for any discussion of rabbinic culture and its critics.

Deriving their name from the word for Scripture (*miqra*), the Karaites (Heb. *qara'im*) professedly based their practices and beliefs solely upon the Bible, which they interpreted according to human reason and communal consensus. As for the Talmud, they denied its authority, claiming that rabbinic literature was a fabrication and rabbinic law a "commandment of men learned by rote" (Isa. 29:13)—that is, a human construct which had been perfunctorily transmitted. In a vigorous polemic titled *The Wars of the Lord*, Salmon ben Yerūḥim (mid-tenth century) disputes the authenticity of the Talmud; if it constitutes a God-given Oral Law, why is it riddled with contradictory statements? "This . . . scholar declares a thing to be forbidden to the people of Israel, while that one declares it to be permitted."[42] Rabbinic legislation, moreover, has obviously embroidered upon the Bible's plain meaning. Nowhere, for example, does Scripture specify the length of the ritual fringe or the dimensions of the booth in which the Festival of Sukkot is to be celebrated; and yet these measurements are regulated by the Talmud.[43] He is equally shocked by the anthropomorphisms and anthropopathisms of the *aggadah;* how could stories describing God's weeping, mourning, and praying be anything but blasphemy?[44] In the face of such inconsistencies and absurdities the Karaites naturally concluded that the rabbinic doctrine of the Oral Law was pure invention, and they rejected talmudic law. The rabbinic leadership branded them heretics.

It must be stressed here that the Karaite heresy consisted equally in their denial of a religious principle and in their use of biblical exegesis to create a *halakhah* of their own. The nature of Jewish dogma need not detain us here, and we shall return to the subject of heresy below; but it is worth emphasizing that the Karaite position attacks the validity of rabbinic Judaism with competing, rationally based interpretations of the Law. As we have seen, the rabbis enjoined the kindling of Sabbath lights on Fridays at sunset in order to enhance the day of rest; in doing so, they interpreted Exodus 35:3 (*lo teva'aru esh*) to mean "you shall not light fires in all your dwelling-places on the Sabbath day." Karaite scholars countered that the key phrase means "you shall not have any fires burning"; consequently, they welcomed the Sabbath in darkness, a practice that would become a badge of their dissent and exegetical integrity.[45] An even more striking example relates to the calendar: according to Leviticus 23:15, the Festival of Shavuot is determined by counting off seven full weeks from the Passover Festival, beginning on "the day after the Sabbath." According to rabbinic law, the word *shabbat* in this verse does not actually mean "Sabbath," but refers to the beginning of Passover. The Karaites, on the other hand, always celebrate Shavuot on a Sunday, since they interpret "the day after the Sabbath" literally, applying it to the Sabbath following the beginning of Passover.[46]

In emphasizing Bible study, the Karaites naturally departed from the talmudism of the rabbinic academies. But in their quest to uncover Scripture's original, contextual meaning, they also advocated a broader curriculum that promoted a rigorously philological and rationalistic approach to the text.[47] Here, they were clearly influenced by the Muslims' development of Arabic lexicography and grammar as powerful tools for the study of the Qur'ān. Impressed by the intellectual rigor of Muslim theologians of the Mutazilite school, they adapted Islamic speculative theology (*kalām*) to their own needs as well; Jewish religious beliefs would no longer be conditioned by the awkward *aggadot* of the rabbis.[48] To be sure, there were also Rabbanite authors in the East, such as Saadya Gaon (882–942) and Samuel ben Hophni Gaon (d. 1013), who read widely in many different fields and effectively integrated "alien wisdom" into their works. But the Karaite challenge no doubt helped stimulate these scholars to go beyond the traditional program of the old *yeshivot*.[49]

Finally, the Karaites challenged rabbinic authority, which they regarded as an unjust imposition by a group of interlopers. Japheth ben Eli, the foremost Karaite exegete of the tenth century, complains of the taxes levied by the academies, the rabbis' abuse of their "power to permit, to prohibit, and to scrutinize the people's affairs," and the harsh, overbearing manner in which they treated the Karaites.[50] During the eleventh century, relations between Karaite and Rabbanite Jews improved in certain respects, in part perhaps due to the influence of several Karaite leaders at the Fatimid court in Egypt. Still, there were Rabbanites who called upon the Head of the Academy in Jerusalem to excommunicate the Karaites for defying rabbinic law—a clear attempt to put the schismatics in their place through a show of institutional authority.[51]

Heresy and Dissent

In rejecting the Oral Law, the Karaites excluded themselves from the larger Jewish community. Many Rabbanites tended to identify them with the ancient Sadducees, who likewise had denied the existence of a divinely revealed tradition.[52] From the rabbinic perspective, this type of radical dissent constituted heresy (*minut*). Karaites were to be regarded as "deniers of the Torah" (*koferim ba-torah*) or "dissidents" (Arabic: *khawārij*); as such, Rabbanites were not allowed to count them as part of a prayer quorum or to consume their meat.[53] Until the seventeenth century, no other Jewish group stood in such clear opposition to the rabbinic tradition; indeed, all other communities strictly adhered to laws and rituals firmly grounded in the

Talmud.[54] At the same time, there were challenges to the accepted interpretations of classical texts and movements for curricular reform. Such opposition brought recriminations: charges of heresy recur throughout the medieval period.

The Karaites' staunchest opponent was Saadya Gaon, who tirelessly defended the rabbinic tradition and polemicized against the sectarians. Ironically, Saadya was himself a great innovator who wrote pioneering works in disciplines new to the Jewish literary repertoire. These novel compositions—which include a Hebrew lexicon, a Hebrew grammar, an Arabic translation of Scripture, Bible commentaries, and a theological *summa*—constitute a dramatic expansion of the old literary repertoire (*midrash,* legal digest, and responsum).[55] In the introduction to his *Book of Doctrines and Beliefs,* he defends theological speculation against the charge that it leads to unbelief or heresy. He explains that the Mishnah's ban on inquiring into "what is below and what is above, what came first and what will be last" (Ḥagigah 2:1) is directed only against those who cast Scripture aside in favor of human reason. The proper course is "to have verified in fact what we have learned from the Prophets of God theoretically," that is, to confirm rationally what has been revealed in Scripture and tradition.[56] Philosophically speaking, Saadya is a conservative; most of the positions he espouses align comfortably with aggadic teachings scattered throughout the Talmud and *midrashim.* But by presenting these ideas systematically in Arabic and offering logical demonstrations of their validity, he breaks sharply with the rabbinic literary tradition. He does this for a second reason: to refute those who challenge rabbinic doctrines, or more simply, to prevent heretical notions from taking root.

The Islamic world in which Saadya lived teemed with religious divisions and sects, whose adherents communicated freely in the Arabic lingua franca. A Jew in Iraq would certainly encounter Muslims and Christians of various denominations, but there were also Zoroastrians, pagans, and freethinkers. It is in this context that we must understand Saadya's refutation of a dozen unapproved theories of creation and his discussion of unacceptable theories concerning the soul. The most fantastic of these notions may have been no more than straw men, but the more sophisticated, philosophical theories could well have seemed persuasive to certain susceptible Jews.[57] "The heretic [*al-kāfir*]," says Saadya, "is he who abandons the basic principle of the faith, that is, the belief in the one, all-encompassing God." Some heretics worship a being other than God, while others are atheists. A third group, however, remains outwardly attached to the faith while privately harboring religious doubts, so that when they pray, it is without conviction.[58]

Immersion in the surrounding society could readily trigger heresy, unbelief, or even apostasy. Verbal sparring at special convocations (Arabic: *majālis*) was a popular activity among the intelligentsia of the Islamic world, and some Jews participated enthusiastically out of a desire to partake of the intellectual culture. Debates often centered on philosophical or religious topics, and learned Jews might be asked to defend, for example, the eternal validity of the Law of Moses. A poor showing could give rise to public ridicule while planting doubt in the debater's mind.[59]

The twelfth century brought different problems for North African and Andalusian Jewry. The Almohade invasions led to mass exiles and conversions to Islam. Some uprooted populations sought to reestablish themselves in new communities under Christian rule, but others chose to convert outwardly to Islam while living as crypto-Jews. In his *Epistle on Martyrdom,* Moses Maimonides sought to bolster their resolve, explaining how their external apostasy was not truly blameworthy: an insincere profession of faith without any public violation of Jewish law could not be considered idolatrous.[60] Under the circumstances, there was a real danger that Jews might ultimately acknowledge certain Muslim tenets and even apostasize.[61] It is not surprising, therefore, that Maimonides articulated his famous creed some years later. His well-formulated dogmas were intended to dispel any doubts as to what a Jew was obligated to believe.[62] He presented these articles of the faith at the end of the introduction to his commentary on Mishnah Sanhedrin, chapter 10, "Ḥeleq." The Mishnah begins: "All Jews have a share in the world to come . . . but these have no share in the world to come: one who says that the resurrection of the dead is not taught in the Torah; one who says that the Torah is not from heaven; and the atheist [*apiqoros*]." It is easy to see why Maimonides chose this text for a discourse on fundamental issues: the afterlife, religious motivation, the interpretation of *aggadah,* and dogma.[63]

Matters of Interpretation

Ironically, Maimonides' views on the afterlife would provoke outrage, charges of heresy, and two separate intercommunal controversies. As we might expect, his is a philosophical conception: the souls of the righteous "will become wise out of the knowledge of God the Creator, as the higher physical bodies do, or even wiser." This is the *summum bonum,* in which the soul reaches such an exalted state that it endures eternally, like the Creator, who has caused it to exist so that it perceives Him.[64] Readers uninformed—or unpersuaded—by philosophy will likely find this notion troubling, since it denies anticipated, tangible pleasures, such as physical resurrection followed by a life without care and reunion with the dearly departed. Maimonides sketches five commonly held conceptions of the afterlife at the beginning of his introduction to "Ḥeleq." He deplores the general weakness of human insight and the natural tendency to fret over insignificant forms of recompense; ideally, one should seek to serve God out of love, not in expectation of benefit. While he will permit people their hopes of reward for good works, he emphasizes that the ultimate felicity will consist in the eternal, spiritual delights that come with knowledge of God. He concedes the difficulty in grasping this idea, but emphasizes that it is not alien, for it was expressed by the ancient sages in aggadic parables: "In the world to come there is no eating, drinking, washing, anointing, or sexual intercourse; but the righteous sit with their crowns on their heads enjoying the radiance of the Divine Presence."[65] Passages like this, argued Maimonides, demand allegorization. Since the ancient rabbis were exceptionally wise and could differentiate between the possible and the impossible, their more extraordinary statements must possess hidden as well as obvious meanings: "Thus, whenever the sages spoke of things that seem impossible, they were employing the style of riddle and parable which is the method of truly great thinkers."[66] As he explains in the *Mishneh Torah:* "The phrase 'the righteous sit' is allegorical and means that the souls of the righteous exist there without labour or fatigue. The phrase 'their crowns on their heads' refers to the knowledge they have acquired, and for the sake of which they have attained life in the world to come."[67] By interpreting the *aggadah* allegorically, Maimonides showed that the Sages had been philosophers in their own right; once again, rational and revealed knowledge were seen to concur. But though philosophical allegory had its adherents, it ran counter to the traditional ways in which rabbinic—and biblical—texts were read.

In 1191–92 Maimonides' ideas concerning the afterlife triggered at least one public debate, a flurry of correspondence between Baghdad, Yemen, and Cairo, a treatise by the Gaon, Samuel ben Eli, in Iraq, and a rejoinder by Maimonides' favorite disciple—all dealing with philosophical and exegetical matters alike.[68] Maimonides' own contribution to the debate, his "Essay on Resurrection," represents a painstaking clarification of his position. Alternately exasperated and patient, he reviews his statements in the introduction to "Ḥeleq" and the *Mishneh Torah,* showing how they have been ignored or misunderstood. The problem stems both from his opponents' inability to conceive of a perfectly incorporeal existence, and their failure to recognize that certain *aggadot* must be understood symbolically.[69] Here, as in many of his other writings, he is contending with a rigid, traditionalist mindset. He concedes that people grasp abstractions with difficulty, but deplores their dogged literalism. As a Jewish thinker and exegete he is swimming against the tide.[70] With the wide dissemination of Maimonides' works during the thirteenth century, there developed rationalist and anti-rationalist camps in northern Spain, Provence, and northern France. The great controversy of 1232–35, which climaxed in the burning of *Guide of the Perplexed,* was instigated by scholars in Provence who understood the *aggadah* literally. When they were shown a copy of the *Guide* and the first book of the *Mishneh Torah,* "The Book of Knowledge," the northern French rabbis were horrified by Maimonides' rationalism; consequently, they banned both works, in an attempt to restrict the Jewish course of study.[71]

Curricular Concerns

In Andalusia, where Maimonides was educated, young Jewish gentlemen were taught both sacred and secular subjects. His younger contemporary, Joseph ben Judah Ibn 'Aqnīn (d. 1220), describes a comprehensive, integrated curriculum that starts with penmanship in Hebrew characters and continues with Bible, Mishnah, and Hebrew grammar. Next, students are taught Hebrew poetry, presumably as a means of improving their linguistic proficiency and giving their writing some rhetorical polish.[72] Only at age fifteen does instruction in Talmud begin. After basic skills and fluency have been acquired, students are trained to think independently. Finally, when they have immersed themselves in talmudic studies for many years and have fully internalized its intellectual and ethical values, as well as its halakhic obligations—in other words, when they are secure in their faith—are they introduced to speculative theology with its demonstrations of religious truths and its refutations of heretical teachings.[73] At this point, they commence a second graded syllabus of philosophic studies: first logic, then mathematics, geometry, astronomy, music, and medicine. Finally, they are taught Aristotelian metaphysics, "the first among sciences."[74] Since this scientific syllabus consisted entirely of Arabic works—both original compositions and translations—and since Ibn 'Aqnīn wrote in Judeo-Arabic, it is clear that he expected students to receive a thorough grounding in that language as well. As we learn from Maimonides' *Epistle Dedicatory* to the *Guide,* this is precisely the kind of education that he insisted advanced students have before he would teach them "the secrets of the prophetic books," that is, their true, philosophical meanings.[75] One of his closest readers and his translator, Samuel Ibn Tibbon (ca. 1150–1230), was brought up this way—in Provence. He memorized didactic poetry by Samuel Ibn Nagrela ha-Nagid (993–1056), practiced Hebrew and Arabic calligraphy, and studied medicine, ethics, and physics, alongside Bible and Talmud. His father advised him to keep up his Arabic by reviewing the weekly Torah portion in Saadya Gaon's translation.[76]

The aim of this well-rounded program was to instill piety and spirituality, to develop refined language and behavior, and to cultivate broad learning, since true science and revealed religion are in complete harmony; as Isadore Twersky has remarked, "Rationalism and spirituality are congenial."[77] For the Sefardic Jews who advocated this course of study, traditional talmudism seemed limited, narrow-minded, and conducive to religiosity. The casuistry of the academies, in fact, could easily degenerate into self-serving displays of erudition. A favorite ploy was to raise impossible, hypothetical questions. The eleventh-century judge and moralist Baḥya Ibn Paquda recounts how a scholar responded to a student who had produced a puzzle of this kind:

> O you who ask me about something the ignorance of which cannot harm you at all. Have you already completed the study of those duties which you cannot afford to ignore and must not neglect, that you find leisure to turn to these difficult and complicated problems, the knowledge of which would not add anything to your faith and religion, nor correct any of your soul's vices? As for me, I swear I have devoted thirty-five years to the study of the obligations my religion imposes upon me. You know the scope of my endeavors and the number of books I have read, and still I have no time to spare for the kind of thing you have just questioned me about.[78]

Lamenting misguided erudition as well as mindless praxis, Baḥya seeks to develop spirituality through a heightened awareness of interior obligations, or "duties of the hearts," such as reliance upon God, sincerity, and self-examination. Following Saadya's lead, he provides a rational basis for every duty, together with biblical and talmudic proof texts. Baḥya's tone is reasonable, earnest, cajoling—but never mocking. It was left to the great Andalusian poets—Samuel Ibn Nagrela, Moses Ibn Ezra, Judah Alḥarizi, and others—to ridicule a certain type of talmudist for his narrow mind, uncouth ways, and insincerity.[79]

In eleventh- and twelfth-century Germany and northern France, where Jews did not have ready access to the scholarly culture of Latin Christendom, the curriculum remained narrowly defined by rabbinics. Youngsters learned Bible, Targum, and Mishnah as prerequisites for talmudic studies. In the Tosafist academies, scholars favored a dialectic approach, seeking to resolve apparent contradictions in classic texts. They placed great stock in developing *novellae* (*ḥiddushim*) on talmudic passages, while neglecting biblical studies. The German Pietists (Ḥasidei Ashkenaz) proposed extensive reforms to a system that promoted elitist behavior and haughtiness. Recognizing that not everyone had the makings of a Tosafist, they advocated the study of Bible, Mishnah, and practical *halakhah* by older students, and attacked the pursuit of dialectics by unqualified scholars. For these Ḥasidim, true study and spirituality were inextricably intertwined.[80]

Piety or Power?

In the *Mishneh Torah,* Maimonides underscores the universality of *Talmud Torah:* the obligation devolves upon all Jewish men, bringing with it the proud badge of scholarship, the "crown" of Torah.[81] According to the Talmud, the importance of *Talmud Torah* is such that "a bastard who is a scholar takes precedence over an ignorant High Priest."[82] Indeed, *Talmud Torah* surpasses all other commandments in value.[83] Possessed by such notions, young men might turn to scholarship for the prestige it bestows. Naturally, allowances must be made for imperfect motivations. Maimonides refers to the well-known principle that fulfilling religious commandments out of ulterior motives can lead—through habituation—to observing them for their own sake.[84] But he is alert to the real dangers involved, citing the warning of Avot 4:5, "Do not make a crown of them [one's scholarly accomplishments] with which to aggrandize yourself or a spade with which to dig." In his commentary on the dictum, he censures those who have imposed levies upon individuals and communities, turning rabbinic appointments into tax collection agencies. They are wrong to persuade the masses that supporting scholars and academies is a religious obligation; there is neither biblical nor talmudic justification for such financial impositions. On the contrary, some of the most celebrated sages were hewers of wood and drawers of water.[85] Scholarship must not become professionalized; every man should earn a living of his own, rather than living on public charity. For Maimonides the issue was not in the least theoretical. When Joseph ben Judah Ibn 'Aqnīn, the dedicatee of the *Guide,* sought permission to open a school, Maimonides authorized him to teach Talmud, but admonished him against accepting any payment, since "one zuz earned from sewing, carpentry, or weaving . . . is preferable to the office of the Exilarch; if you take payment from [your students], you shall become contemptible."[86]

Maimonides' statements reflect an ancient view that one may not be paid for teaching Talmud. Even though a loophole existed—the so-called *sekhar battalah* ("lost opportunity costs")—scholars were encouraged to support themselves by other means.[87] Naturally, it was impossible to maintain such standards everywhere. In many communities taxes were levied so that academies, students, and teachers could be maintained.[88] But the rabbinate was becoming professionalized as well, with communities appointing their spiritual leaders.

Nor were rabbis above politics. In Spain and Provence, they possessed the authority to excommunicate and fine those who defied them.[89] The ban, or *ḥerem,* could become a powerful weapon in communal and intercommunal disputes, as we have seen with the Maimonidean Controversies of the thirteenth century. Most of the protagonists in these disputes were eminent rabbinic figures whose scholarly reputations had given them influence which they did not hesitate to use. Since piety and power could not always be separated with ease, the crown of the Torah was not always worn with modesty. Not infrequently, it was used to intimidate opposition.[90]

The Quest for Spirituality

As we have seen, the Talmud betrays the rabbis' self-awareness: in a society shaped by rabbinic culture, the pursuit of learning may turn into status-seeking, "a crown with which to aggrandize oneself or a spade with which to dig." Consequently, the sages urged renunciation of temporal pleasures along with separation from worldly temptations, sources of ritual impurity, and contact with Gentiles. For good reason the fathers of rabbinic culture were known as "Pharisees" (Heb. *perushim*), "those who are separated." While they did not engage in the extreme acts of self-mortification performed by certain early Christians, they did advocate temporary abstinence or a moderate asceticism, even setting forth a sort of spiritual way: "Heedfulness leads to cleanliness, cleanliness leads to abstinence [*perishut*], abstinence leads to purity, purity leads to holiness, holiness leads to modesty, modesty leads to fear of sin, fear of sin leads to saintliness, saintliness leads to the Holy Spirit, the Holy Spirit leads to the revivification of the dead."[91] The Talmud mentions certain "ancient pietists" (*ḥasidim rishonim*) who would devote extra hours to meditation and prayer and engage in other acts of supererogation.[92] In the medieval period, *Ḥasidut* would attract new followers. To no small degree, trends or movements within the surrounding culture spurred Jewish pietists to recover their own authentic forms of spirituality. Baḥya Ibn Paquda's "duties of the hearts" are largely presented in the language of Muslim Sufism, although the author is careful to cite copiously from the Bible and rabbinic literature.[93]

Sufism seems to have attracted at least some Jewish adherents in Egypt.[94] Maimonides, though praising the wisdom and holiness of the "ancient pietists," warns the ordinary Jew against imitating their self-abnegating practices.[95] Curiously, however, his own son Abraham (1186–1237), who served as Head of Egyptian Jewry, led a movement to reform Jewish worship and to reinvigorate Jewish religious life in light of Sufi teachings. According to Abraham Maimuni, the Muslim Sufis of his day perpetuated the ancient practices of the prophets when they donned ragged coats and kept night-vigils.[96] Their orderly prayers, punctuated by numerous prostrations and gestures, also hew more closely to biblical and rabbinic practice.[97] The extant volumes of his *Complete (Guide) for the Servants of God* evince the author's immersion in Sufi writings, as he sought to recast Jewish ethical teachings in a contemporary mode. But unlike Baḥya Ibn Paquda, Abraham was not content to preach an intellectualized spirituality; he and his immediate circle actually attracted a substantial following, which aroused the opposition of the rabbinic establishment, the communal leaders, and the common people. The movement persisted for a considerable time; in Syria, Maimonides' great-great-great grandson, David ben

Solomon (d. 1415), still championed a distinctive ascetic-mystical lifestyle that now incorporated kabbalistic accretions.[98]

As Jewish Sufism developed in Egypt, another pietist movement was emerging in the Rhineland. We have already referred to the German Pietists (Ḥasidei Ashkenaz), whose teachings and literary legacy proved to be quite influential in northern Europe.[99] Samuel ben Kalonymous of Speyer, his son Judah (d. 1217), and Eleazar ben Judah of Worms (ca. 1165–1230) expounded a pietism that emphasized scrupulous treatment of one's fellow and relentless self-examination. Sins could be expiated by means of specific penances prescribed by experts—a system with obvious Christian analogues. Here the "teacher" was as much spiritual advisor as professor. Indeed, these Ḥasidim did not spare scholars who were preoccupied with their own intellectual acumen, at the expense of simple goodness: "'Better is a handful of quietness' [Eccl. 4:6]—that a man know the practical rulings of the halakhah—'than two hands full of toil' [ibid.]—than that he know how to ask difficult questions and to answer them and to turn things about in the Talmud. For it is an evil spirit, to show his breadth of mind, to take pride that he is sharp and clever."[100] The Ḥasid's quest for moral and spiritual perfection was motivated, in part, by a sense of communal responsibility. Only an elite would ever succeed in fulfilling the pietist ideal, but those who maintained the highest standards of behavior, observance, and faith, serving as models to their flocks, might ward off divine punishment.

Kabbalah

As the situation of European Jewry destabilized in the late Middle Ages, the function of rabbinic discourse changed. Many Spanish Jews ceased to care greatly about the problems of anthropomorphism in the Torah, the conundrum of divine attributes, or philosophical proofs for the existence of God. Maimonidean philosophy did not engage them, and they often had only contempt for the dry Aristotelian theology of the intellectual elite. From the mid-thirteenth century, much of European Jewry faced conversionary pressure, false accusations of malfeasance that often led to violence, and expulsions. Their freedom of practice—even their very existence—was threatened. In this atmosphere, Jews looked for new sources of solace. While *halakhah* remained central to rabbinic culture, neither law nor rationalist philosophy fully satisfied their spiritual needs. For many, this was provided by Kabbalah.

Kabbalah was a product of Jewish thought in the Christian environment. It drew heavily on traditions that went back to the talmudic period and the legacy of Jewish Neoplatonism, but its real wellsprings came out of Ashkenaz as well as Sefarad. Medieval mystical contemplation of the divine chariot described in Ezekiel 1, and the early numerical mysteries of the *Sefer Yeṣirah* (Book of Creation), fed the imagination of the authors of the book *Bahir* (Splendor) and other early proto-kabbalistic works. Circles of mystics in twelfth-century Provence (where the *Bahir* may have been edited) developed the first schools of Kabbalah proper, followed by the German Pietists in the early thirteenth century. The pietists' pessimistic, unsystematic thought reflects the fervor of contemporary Christian piety almost as much as it does the influence of the rabbis. Some scholars have argued that the horrors of the Crusades underlie the convictions of this school as well. Asceticism, self-flagellation, martyrdom, and demonology define the worldview of the German Pietists as clearly as Aristotelian rationalism defined that of their Sefardic contemporaries.[101]

From Provence and Germany, Kabbalah made its way to Christian Spain. While the school of ecstatic Kabbalah, formulated by Abraham Abulafia, reflects relationships with Sufi mysticism as well as the *Sefer Yeṣirah* and the *Bahir,* the classic Spanish Kabbalah is expressed in the theurgic writings of the thirteenth-century Castilian and Catalonian Jewish mystics, operating in the Christian milieu. The ideas of these schools culminated with the appearance of *Sefer ha-Zohar* (Book of Illumination) around 1280–86 in the circle of Moses ben Shem Tov de Leon of Guadalajara.[102] The Zohar and contemporary theosophical and theurgic kabbalistic literature tell of a universe that God created by emanating ten aspects, called *sefirot,* from His infinite self. By understanding these *sefirot,* their interrelationships, qualities, and powers, the mystic could learn to influence both God and the world. This is accomplished especially through the intense direction of prayer and commandment-performances toward the aspects of God manifested in particular *sefirot.*[103] Although it took several generations for any of the specifics of this system to reach the common Jew, its general outlook seeped into the Jewish mind relatively quickly through sermons, Torah commentaries like that of Naḥmanides, and the infiltration of kabbalistic elements into other literature read by the educated Jewish public. The immanent God of the kabbalists was surely more meaningful to those generations than the transcendent God of the philosophers.

Another comforting aspect of kabbalistic thought for people beset by persecutions was its glorification of Jewish importance and power, and its negation of temporal Gentile dominion. While rationalist modes of thought often became universalist, stressing the importance of understanding God philosophically over the importance of religious differences between thinkers, the Kabbalah focused on the theurgic power of the individual Jew's ritual observances. Kabbalah presents a mirror image of the world, in which the mighty Gentiles become insignificant, while the impotent Jews uphold the world with their unique righteousness. This particularist trend took a vigorous form with the so-called Circle of the Responding Angel (*ha-mal'akh ha-meshiv*), a radically anti-Christian prophetic group active in Spain, a generation before expulsion.[104]

It is puzzling that there was little vocal opposition to the triumph of Kabbalah over rationalist philosophy. The psychological advantages of the kabbalist's God, after all, come at a price. Maimonides and his fellow rationalists struggled mightily to define God in a way that would avoid the ultimate Jewish heresy: a plurality of divinities. For the philosopher, the kabbalists' theology should immediately stand out as completely heretical—it posits a God who has various aspects, differentiates his qualities into distinct emanations, and can be affected by the actions of people. Indeed, Christian thinkers often saw Kabbalah as closely akin to their own Trinitarian theology. Kabbalah, furthermore, depends on ideas and practices with no discernible antecedents in the known Jewish tradition, thus implicitly threatening the centrality of the rabbinic legacy. There were only minor outcries, however, usually directed against some specific practice such as praying directly to the *sefirot*. The few systematic refutations of Kabbalah remained almost entirely in manuscript until modern times, and circulated in only tiny numbers of copies.[105] Perhaps it was Kabbalah's extravagant emphasis on the observance of commandments that gave it an orthodox image. The mystics stressed the unknowable depths of each action, while rationalist explanations of the commandments gave individuals the impression of understanding, and therefore elective control, of observances.

The kabbalists also developed defenses against their detractors. Jews had always preferred to attach the endangerment of one or more commandments to accusations of heresy and definitions of orthodoxy in order to keep belief within the framework of Jewish law. The most famous example of this tendency is Maimonides' decision to place dogma at the beginning of his code of law, the *Mishneh Torah*. Philosophers, talmudists, and now kabbalists would often couch their criticisms of each other in terms of their opponents' insufficiency in the commandment to know the one God. Here is an example of how one kabbalist from the early eighteenth century, Ḥakham Joseph Ergas, expressed his criticism of the philosophers and talmudists:

> He who studies at the simple level alone will not fulfill this commandment [belief in God] in full measure, for he has no understanding of these matters, so he cannot fulfill the commandment of belief in God properly. Nor do they fulfill the commandment to believe in God's unity properly because they do not know what the unity of God means. . . . But indeed, the philosophers' books also contain several false and heretical opinions, which is why it is forbidden to read them. . . . A heavy burden of guilt falls upon a few people from our nation who wished to make the opinions of the Torah and prophets fit those of the philosophers. . . . See what is written in the Zohar, Portion of Jethro, p. 87: "Rabbi Isaac opened the session by saying . . . How much must a person be careful not to err by deriving from the Bible something he did not know and receive from his teachers. For anyone who interprets the words of the Torah to say things he did not know and receive from his teachers, it is of him that the passage 'Thou shalt not make any idol or graven image' speaks."[106]

Kabbalah thus becomes the only true form of worship in the eyes of its practitioners. While they do not explicitly accuse talmudists and philosophers of false worship (*avodah zarah*), at least a taint of that error is implied in the claim that nobody but the kabbalists truly fulfills the commandments to know God, believe in His unity, and reject false deities.

Kabbalah, then, with all its anthropomorphism and immanence, largely displaced rationalism as the dominant mode of abstract Jewish thought almost without a struggle. Since the last generation of Spanish Jewish life, when many rationalist rabbis converted to Christianity, it would almost always be philosophy rather than mysticism that raised suspicion of heresy in Judaism. This development appears to confirm Gershom Scholem's contention that "there is no way of telling a priori what beliefs are possible or impossible within the framework of Judaism. . . . The 'Jewishness' in the religiosity of any particular period is not measured by dogmatic criteria that are unrelated to actual historical circumstances, but solely by what sincere Jews do, in fact believe, or—at least—consider to be legitimate possibilities."[107]

The Expulsion from Spain

Between 1391, when major anti-Jewish riots initiated a century of rapid decline in Spanish Jewry, and 1497, when the Portuguese Jews were forcibly converted to Christianity, a great many Iberian Jews—perhaps more than half—became Christians. The converted Jews, usually called New Christians or conversos, ran the gamut from sincere or even fanatical Christianity to a perfunctory show of Catholicism covering strong crypto-Jewish impulses. The Catholic Monarchs, Ferdinand and Isabella, along with most of the "Old" Christians, suspected widespread backsliding among these former Jews. For this reason a national Inquisition was established in Spain in 1479–80, with authority to prosecute suspected Judaizers and other heretics. In 1492 Ferdinand and Isabella declared the expulsion of all Jews from their realm, citing the pernicious influence of a living Jewish community on the orthodoxy of conversos. Among those hardy souls who chose exile over conversion, some made their way with great difficulty and suffering to the Ottoman Empire, North Africa, and Italy; but the largest group went to Portugal with promises from the king of a safe haven there. In 1497 those promises were broken in the most barbarous manner.[108]

The expulsion and forced conversion of Iberian Jewry was the last stage in a series of expulsions, beginning at the end of the thirteenth century, that excluded Jews from all but a few isolated locations in western Europe.[109] The impact of these events on rabbinic culture was considerable. We have already noted some of the shifts in the realm of theology. The dispersion of Spanish scholars brought their style of Talmud study, Kabbalah, ethics, and exegesis to diverse parts of the Jewish world, where their impact was immense.[110] The expulsion, however, also brought an apparent crisis of faith among some Jews, who witnessed their family, their friends, and often their rabbis converting to Catholicism, while they themselves suffered the exigencies of exile. It appears that the four volumes by Isaac Abarbanel dealing with redemption and the coming of the messiah were composed in response to a widespread feeling of despondency among Spanish Jews, whose faith in divine salvation was sorely tested.

An excess of faith in imminent redemption could also be a challenge to the stability of rabbinic culture. From the fall of Constantinople to the Ottoman Turks in 1453 until the end of the sixteenth century, the Jewish community, like those of the Christians and Muslims, was deluged with messianic expectations and pretenders. It is difficult to gauge how much of this came from within the Jewish world and how much was influenced by the excitement in the surrounding cultures, but we know for certain that there was interfaith communication on this matter.[111] Several major movements materialized around specific personalities, gathering considerable followings. The immediate problem for the rabbis was whether to support these movements, and how to prevent defection and additional despondency when they failed. In a larger sense, messianism could threaten the entire foundation of rabbinic culture because the Torah, Talmud, and Midrash speak of a radical break in the messianic era: a new Torah will replace the old one, and the entire order of things will change.[112] While the sixteenth-century messiahs did not generally take upon themselves to offer this new Torah, the problem surfaced explosively later on.[113]

Another development, whose impact on rabbinic culture was not so immediately noticeable, but would ultimately be as important as the expulsion itself, was the return of conversos to the Jewish world. In the first generation of life as Catholics, many Spanish and Portuguese Jews sought ways to effect an (illegal) escape to lands where they could return safely to Judaism. They were usually welcomed, and they returned to the practices they had been forced to temporarily abandon. Many more conversos, however, remained longer in Iberia, whether because they were unable to escape, or because they were unwilling to forgo the freedom to compete profitably and receive university education in their new Catholic identities. The process of reintegration became less simple in the second and third generations after the expulsion. Conversos would appear in Jewish communities knowing only what their parents or grandparents had told them of Judaism, which was often sketchy at best. They had never lived as Jews. Their parents and grandparents had remained as Catholics in Spain or Portugal rather than escaping at the first opportunity. They seldom knew the Hebrew language, Jewish prayers, or rituals. They were thus looked down upon by those whose families had taken the hard road of exile. But at the same time, the conversos were often wealthier and better educated than these untainted Jews.

The tension increased over the course of the sixteenth century, as the escaping conversos became further and further removed from their Jewish antecedents. Their presence often created a challenge for the rabbis, who not only had to educate these individuals in the Jewish religion but also had to deal with their often growing resentment of the Jewish establishment.[114]

New Centers in the Sixteenth Century

The Jewish world experienced two major demographic and cultural shifts during this period. The first was the movement of expelled German, Italian, and northern French Jews into Poland-Lithuania. By 1575 this region had more Jews than Spain at the time of the expulsion; it would grow to be by far the largest Jewish community in the world in modern times. Jews were welcomed by the king, and invited by the powerful landowners in the vast eastern area of the country to help manage their holdings. As the demand for Polish timber and grain grew in western Europe, the Jews' ability to conduct commerce on behalf of their employers was at a premium. Jews thus tended to be spread in small towns, which was their typical demographic distribution in those regions up to the twentieth century.[115] Rabbinic culture flourished mightily in Poland-Lithuania because of the stable economic standing of the Jews there, their traditionalism (aided by a distaste for local culture), the need for rabbis to officiate in all the towns holding the swelling Jewish population, an innovative system of *yeshivot,* and the leadership of many great rabbis. Not until the late nineteenth century would skeptical anti-rabbinic trends make significant headway in Poland-Lithuania. Nevertheless, skepticism, rationalist doubters, and radical movements of other sorts were not lacking earlier.[116]

The other great demographic shift was the movement of Sefardic Jews back into the Muslim world, this time to the Ottoman Empire. The Ottomans, who conquered most of Asia Minor, Greece, and the Middle East over the course of the fifteenth and sixteenth centuries, were willing to allow Jewish settlement in their lands. At times they even welcomed these immigrants, for the same reason their Ashkenazic co-religionists were welcomed in Poland-Lithuania: they had no political aspirations, and they often brought desperately needed skills or capital with them. The old Jewish centers of Spain were being replaced by Salonika, Istanbul (still called Constantinople by contemporary Jewish authors), Edirne, Tripoli, Tunis, Oran, Aleppo, and later

Izmir. Again, the Jews were highly successful in trade, and they generally remained quite traditional.[117]

A particularly influential event for rabbinic culture was the capture of Palestine by the Ottomans in 1516. Displaced Jews flocked to the Holy Land, despite the relatively limited economic opportunities it offered. In the early sixteenth century Jerusalem became a major center of rabbinic thought; but by mid-century, when the local government was making Jerusalem less hospitable to Jews, the city of Safed in the Galilee became a greater attraction. Safed had a successful textile trade industry, but it became much more famous subsequently for the coterie of Jewish mystics that gathered there. Joseph Karo, a kabbalist and author of the standard Jewish law code *Shulḥan Arukh,* came from Greece together with his renowned associate, Solomon Alkabetz. Moses Alsheikh, author of an important mystical Torah commentary, and the great Kabbalah synthesizer Moses Cordovero were also among this early group. The most famous figure, however, was Isaac Luria (the AR"I), who only lived in Safed for about two years before his death in 1572, but taught a mystical system whose impact on the Jewish world has been incalculable. The AR"I's student Hayyim Vital organized and wrote the thoughts of his master in the forms in which they later became famous.[118]

Both the image and thought of this community would revolutionize rabbinic culture. It introduced new mystical views that were lapped up by an anxious Jewish public, and it was the springboard (often despite itself) of the popularization of Kabbalah. Its innovations blew new life into the Jewish psyche, but again this came with a hidden price. By promoting the roles of imagination, prophecy, and charisma, the Safed group set the stage for innovations in Jewish thought that could easily short-circuit the authority structure of the rabbinic establishment, leading Judaism in unanticipated directions.

Impact of the Renaissance and Reformation

The Renaissance was a paradoxical era for Italian Jewry, during which intellectual contacts between Jews and Christians intensified, but (or perhaps as a result) new persecutions abounded as well. The Humanist movement gave rise to a long dormant Christian interest in Judaism. As the Humanists investigated the world of classical antiquity in search of long lost truths, Judaism, the "third" ancient culture, attracted occasional interest alongside ancient Greece and Rome. This was particularly manifested in the Christian Kabbalah. Giovanni Pico della Mirandola, one of the philosophical luminaries of the Florentine school, became fascinated by this study, hiring several Jews and former Jewish apostates to translate and learn with him. While Pico and the other Christian kabbalists often justified these investigations as part of a conversionary effort, it is obvious that many of them were at least as interested in Kabbalah for its intrinsic value. This meant the rabbis had to argue about Kabbalah in their disputations now, in addition to Torah and Talmud; but it also gave rabbinic culture a certain prestige, as Christian savants flocked to learn from them.[119]

Kabbalah, however, was not the only Jewish literature of interest to Christians. Around the turn of the sixteenth century, an increasing number of European scholars sought to learn the Bible in its original languages—Greek for the New Testament, Hebrew for the Old Testament. They wanted to know the nuances of meaning in the text, and for this purpose they often sought out Jewish Bible commentaries as well. Before the seventeenth century, it was unusual to attempt any such study without a Jewish (or apostate) tutor. This trend increased dramatically after the Protestant Reformation, when the Torah and Talmud were recognized for their importance in reconstructing the original apostolic Christianity.[120] Occasionally, rabbis debated how much of the Torah might be taught to such people.

The invention of print during the fifteenth century had a direct impact on Christian Hebraism, as well as other areas of Jewish life. With the growth of demand for Hebrew books among Christians as well as Jews, some printers, whose craft was still in its infancy, began creating Hebrew type so they could enter this market. Often, rabbis would be hired to establish standard editions of classic Jewish texts and to proofread for these presses, which were usually owned by Christians. This brought Jews and Christians together in a working environment that included conversionary pressure, but also a modicum of mutual respect. Another effect of print may have been to help standardize Jewish doctrine, as well as practice and prayer rituals, since standard theological texts were distributed all over the Jewish world. Innovations, such as those of the Safed kabbalists, became rapidly familiar to Jews across the Diaspora through print. Printed books brought the ideas of classical and Christian thinkers (Muslims were slower to venture into print culture) into the hands of Jews who might never have had contact with them otherwise. These ideas sometimes influenced the development of skeptical or unorthodox thinking.[121]

Jewish creativity itself had many highlights in Renaissance Italy, both in traditional genres and more innovative areas. Exegesis, belles lettres, grammar, and Kabbalah were among the leading subjects of study. Isaac Abarbanel, a former leader of Iberian Jewry, settled in Italy after the expulsion and composed most of his famous biblical commentaries there. His son Judah Abarbanel (known as Leone Ebreo) became an important figure in the history of Italian literature for his Neoplatonic philosophical work *Dialogues on Love.* Other rabbinic authors composed travel diaries, histories and historical critiques, sermon collections, responsa, exemplary letters, rhetoric primers, mystical works, and medical treatises.[122]

The Renaissance search for truths among the wisdom of the ancients helped inspire a particular style of humanism among the rabbis. Although Jews had often supported the claim of the Church Fathers that the ancient Greeks learned all their wisdom from the biblical Jews, this view took on entirely new implications for Renaissance Jewish scholars. As the wisdom of classical antiquity was uncovered and its arts and sciences revived, a number of Jewish scholars renewed the claim that this was all really ancient Jewish knowledge. Everything written by the Greeks and Romans, including the many newly discovered texts, was taught to them by Moses, Solomon, Abraham, and the prophets. Thus, Jewish antiquity was much more important than classical antiquity, and Jews had proprietary rights on all this recovered knowledge. In practice this approach was a sort of license for Jews to pursue the arts and sciences, which were to be perceived not as foreign to Jewish thought (as they usually were in Ashkenaz), but as part and parcel of the Torah. Indeed, the Italian Renaissance rabbi—the *Rav ha-Kollel* (complete rabbi)—was expected to be expert in all fields of knowledge. The literature of Renaissance rabbis often displays a more worldly and culturally informed perspective than that of most Ottoman and Ashkenazic contemporaries.[123]

More sinister developments were brewing in sixteenth-century Italy as well, however. In 1516, immediately preceding the start of the Protestant Reformation, the first walled ghetto was introduced in Venice. This institution spread throughout Italy in the later part of the century. Every manuscript and printed volume of the Talmud that could be found was burned by papal order in 1553. Other Jewish literature was censored. Italian inquisitions destroyed the community of former conversos at Ancona in 1555 and burned twenty-four of them at the stake. Jewish economic opportunities, which had always been severely limited, were curtailed even more. The rabbis struggled to maintain a semblance of communal normality amid this chaos. Like the conditions of the Spanish Expulsion, there is strong evidence that all this persecution was a backlash against the social and intellectual interaction perceived to be occurring between Christians and Jews.[124]

The Reformation affected Jews in other ways as well. Some Jews, observing their Christian neighbors removing and destroying church icons, concluded that the Christians had abandoned their religion. This could only mean that they were about to embrace Judaism, which must prove that the messiah had come.[125] A more subtle impact of the Reformation on rabbinic culture was the atmosphere of radical change and abandonment of tradition that permeated the European religious atmosphere after 1517. As the Catholics and Protestants squared off for over a century of religious warfare (some of which devastated Jewish communities along the way), rabbinic culture could not but be touched by this aura of instability undermining its already uncertain footing. The feeling was compounded by the changing view of the world engendered by the voyages of discovery and the scientific revolution.

The seaports bringing people to Italy from every part of the known world, its atmosphere of humanism and scientific study, and the many former conversos who made their homes there all created an atmosphere fertile for diverse ideas that were not always amenable to rabbinic culture. The most striking example is a Hebrew manuscript that turned up in Venice in 1622, called *Qol Sakhal* (Voice of the Fool) by its rabbinic detractors. This book constituted a highly learned, scathing critique of rabbinic culture—so striking, in fact, that one modern author referred to it as the *Shulḥan Arukh* of the *apiqorsim* (heretics). The purported author was Amitai bar Yedaiah Ibn Raz, an obvious pseudonym, and the book's claim to have been composed in Alcalá in the year 1500 is almost certainly spurious. An enormous scholarly debate lasting over a century about the real authorship of the book has yielded suggestive but inconclusive results. Clues in the language of the book strongly suggest that it is a product of early-seventeenth-century Italy. The most likely candidate for author is the distinguished but quirky Leon Modena, in whose hands the manuscript first appeared, and who wrote a weak, incomplete refutation of it.[126]

Conceptually, *Qol Sakhal* is close to the Karaite tradition; the work sets out to critique rabbinic culture and law while still upholding the essential value of the Torah and Jewish peoplehood. But the book diverges from Karaism in ascribing merit to Jewish traditions, insofar as they are not codified or legislated by rabbinic fiat. Unlike the Karaites, the author does not seek to undermine the entire Jewish legal tradition; rather, he proposes a truly "reformed" law system reflective of ancient Judaism before generations of power-hungry rabbis burdened it with accretions. In contrast to the contemporary critiques of conversos, *Qol Sakhal* is clearly a work composed from deep within rabbinic culture.

The importance of *Qol Sakhal* as a critique of rabbinic culture goes far beyond its own almost negligible influence. What is most important is that the early seventeenth century spawned a figure deep within the rabbinic tradition who was capable of thinking and writing down this brilliant, carefully conceived criticism. If one Jew from that background could write *Qol Sakhal,* others must have harbored similar doubts—perhaps vaguer and uncommunicated, but real nonetheless. In other words, in the same period that the world of European Christendom began to see the first recorded glimmerings of fideism, Deism, and even atheism, rabbinic Judaism suffered a parallel assault from within.

The Western Sefardic Diaspora

It appears that toward the end of the sixteenth century, many conversos escaping from Spain and Portugal and wishing to practice Judaism were no longer prepared to tolerate second-class religious status in established Sefardic communities.[127] They were also interested in the burgeoning mercantile trade then shifting toward northern Europe, where Jews could not live openly. It thus came about that conventicles of crypto-Jewish conversos, still outwardly professing Catholicism, settled in Antwerp, Amsterdam, London, Hamburg, Bayonne, and other cities that still excluded Jews. When their secret Jewish practice became known, as it almost always did in the end, each city had to decide whether it preferred to remain free of Jews, or to benefit from the important trade networks and wealth of these Spanish and Portuguese merchants. Antwerp sent them packing; Bayonne and Bordeaux refused to acknowledge them as Jews for many decades, thus sidestepping the problem. But Amsterdam, London, Hamburg, Livorno, and several smaller towns chose to allow the enclaves to remain and practice Judaism openly. These communities of former conversos are known collectively as the Western Sefardic Diaspora, and they had certain unique characteristics critical to the changes in seventeenth-century rabbinic culture.

The challenges to rabbinic culture from the Western Sefardim all derived from the fact that these former conversos (at least in the early stages) grew up as Catholics and many had never experienced life in a Jewish community except the one they created themselves. Three specific types of challenges developed: those from the center of the community, built into its very makeup; those from individuals who chose to remain at the margins of Jewish identity; and those from radical thinkers. The challenges from the center, oddly, have drawn little scholarly notice until the present generation. The very core of these communities, their wealthiest and most dedicated lay leaders, created communal identity (in the form of synagogue regulations, societal bylaws, and the like) that were more cultural and ethnic than religious in nature. Their focus was on the collective formed by conversos and former conversos, rather than with the religious collectivity of Jews. Their self-designation as the *Nação* (Nation) was often of superior importance in their minds to membership in the Jewish people. This attitude privileged cultural and ethnic Jewish identity over religious identity, a subtle but important break with rabbinic tradition.

Another aspect of the lives of even the most observant Western Sefardim was their tendency to separate their existence into the sacral areas—activities that took place in synagogue, school, and home (to a degree), over which the rabbis properly dictated the law; and areas exterior to religious control—business and "neutral" cultural activities. This bifurcation reflects something of a Catholic approach rather than the view of Jewish legal tradition, whose legislation extends to every aspect of life. Thus, for example, the Ashkenazic and Levantine rabbis struggled mightily with the halakhic problem of credit as interest in the context of mercantile trade, whereas the Western Sefardim showed little concern about it. There was also the matter of reeducating returning conversos in the ways of Jewish life, a challenge to their rabbis, who could never honestly hope to remove all vestiges of Christian thought from their charges. More generally, the former conversos simply tended to be lax in observing the commandments, without articulating a rationale for it.[128]

Marginal conversos were a mixed group of people who had returned to Judaism officially but refused to live according to communal and rabbinic dictates, and those who had never returned openly but enjoyed cultural contact with the community. These individuals were a ceaseless challenge to rabbinic authority. They often influenced members of the congregations to relax their observance and take liberties with communal rules as they themselves did. In a larger sense, their ability to enjoy the positive identity of the *Nação* while flitting between Judaism, Catholicism, and some non-partisan individuality tended to blur the boundaries of both congregational membership and Judaism itself. While the radical thinkers have made a bigger historiographical splash, the identity-bending proclivities of ordinary Western Sefardim may have had an equally deep impact on the future of rabbinic culture.[129]

Several former conversos who rejoined Judaism in western Europe made the claim that they were unprepared for contemporary Jewish communal life because their knowledge of Judaism came only from the Bible.[130] While the truth of that assertion is somewhat doubtful, there was certainly a heavy streak of anti-rabbinism among this group. Others, having learned to hate the domination of the Catholic Church, became skeptical about all religious authority, and arrived at an even more critical position. Most of the time such views remained a private matter, but there were several men who brought their skepticism into the public eye. Among these was a group who styled themselves Karaites and separated themselves from the Amsterdam community; the physician David Farar, whose criticism of rabbinic exegesis caused a split in the Amsterdam Beth Jacob synagogue in 1619; Juan de Prado and Daniel Ribera, expelled from the Amsterdam community for anti-rabbinic views in 1656; Uriel da Costa, whose attacks on rabbinic tradition caused him a series of devastating excommunications; and by far the most famous, Baruch Spinoza, whose opinions on religious authority threatened all religious establishments.[131]

The skeptical journey of da Costa is worth examining further because its trajectory is almost a microcosm of the larger critical trends in seventeenth-century religion. In his autobiography, da Costa tells of his attraction to Judaism as an alternative to Catholic doctrine, and his disappointment with the living rabbinic Judaism he found in Amsterdam. "I had not been there many days, before I observed, that the customs and ordinances of the modern Jews were very different from those commanded by Moses. Now if the law was to be strictly observed, according to the letter, as it expressly declares, it must be very unjustifiable in the Jewish doctors to add to it inventions of a quite contrary nature. This provoked me to oppose them openly."[132] Da

Costa's open opposition to the rabbis' prerogative to interpret scriptural law brought upon him dire sanctions by the *Mahamad*, the lay board of community leaders that worked with the rabbis. Da Costa's first fusillade was apparently not launched in Amsterdam, but in Hamburg, where he stopped for a period on his journey. In 1616 he sent a challenge to the Venice rabbis, a series of eleven theses on rabbinic tradition that he felt contradicted Torah precepts. The spirit of this work was close enough to that of *Qol Sakhal* that some scholars took them to be from the same author. The theses acknowledged the place of tradition, but attacked the rabbis' claim to be the sole authoritative interpreters of Scripture.

In 1624, in Amsterdam, da Costa published a treatise called *Examination of Pharisaic Traditions* in which he systematically argued against the rights of the rabbis to interpret Scripture authoritatively, and denigrated the claims of the Talmud to represent God's explication of biblical law. Here da Costa laid particular stress on the lack of foundation for the rabbinic belief in immortality of the soul, a question then under heated debate in both Jewish and Protestant communities. This new work was received with bitter fury on the part of the rabbis and communal leaders. Not only was its author excommunicated but all copies of the work were destroyed, with the exception of one that almost miraculously survived and was recently rediscovered through determined detective work. Finally, broken and inconsolable, da Costa committed suicide in 1640, leaving behind his autobiography. This work goes beyond Karaite-style claims about the Oral Law and leans toward a much more radical, almost deist position.[133] Looking at da Costa and the series of responses to his challenge, it is easy to see how dangerous even one such thinker was to the foundations of rabbinic culture. It is also possible to follow the intellectual path from the views of da Costa that stop short of denigrating religious authority altogether, to those of Spinoza, who not only claimed Scripture was of human authorship but also called for an end to all temporal authority of churches. Spinoza, however, had been expelled from the Jewish community by the time he wrote these devastating critiques.[134]

Shabbatai Zvi

The Christian religious establishment of the seventeenth century was discovering that skeptical rationalists like Spinoza were not the only threat to its authority—prophetic "enthusiasm" was equally dangerous. Visionary and millenarian movements like the Collegiants, Quakers, Fifth Monarchists, and French Prophets undercut the power of the established churches by claiming direct access to God's word without ecclesiastical mediation. In 1665–66, the rabbis came to the same realization. It was then that a kabbalist from Izmir named Shabbatai Zvi made his public claim to be the messiah, convinced most Jews to believe it (including many major rabbis), then plunged the Jewish world into crisis by converting to Islam under threat of execution. The shards of this movement, including the development of numerous heterodox ideas, books, and sub-movements, continued to plague Jewish communities for over a century.

The news that the messiah had arrived was initially promoted by Nathan of Gaza, a young rabbi who was already famous as a seer and doctor of the soul at the age of twenty-two. Nathan said he had experienced divine prophecies that told him Shabbatai was to be the messiah. Shabbatai, who appears to have been a manic depressive, did not take long to invoke the rabbinic tradition of a new Torah in the messianic age. In his manic states he would publicly break laws of the Torah or declare changes in the order of the calendar, often reciting a traditional blessing to God "who frees the imprisoned," but playing on the sense of an alternate translation, "who permits the forbidden." Shabbatai and Nathan demanded that the Jews believe in their prophecy and mission without any demonstration of a sign or wonder, citing Maimonides' dictum that the messiah could not be identified by his performance of miracles.[135]

Perhaps the most telling aspect of this entire situation was not the rise of a mystical messianic pretender, something not at all unknown in Jewish history, but the fact that the rabbis did not detect enough danger in the movement to oppose it actively. With the exception of one or two stalwart opponents, the bizarre behavior and lack of confirmatory evidence demonstrated by Shabbatai and his prophets either failed to raise a red flag or did not sufficiently concern the rabbis to make them vocally oppose the tide of support. This demonstrates the degree to which the foundations of rabbinic culture had already become debased at this time—Shabbatai's habit of flouting Jewish law, had it occurred in the generation of Maimonides or Naḥmanides, would surely have been the end of anyone's messianic pretensions (as indeed it was in Yemen). The only evidence that Shabbatai and Nathan offered was based on prophecies, popular visions, and kabbalistic reasoning. Against this, the new messiah transgressed Jewish law in public, claiming a special prerogative because of his visionary insight into the new age. This appears to be a moment when rabbinic culture suffered the consequences of the Kabbalah's hidden peril.

If mysticism was central to the rise of the Sabbatean movement, it became even more pivotal at the next stage, after Shabbatai Zvi was hauled before the sultan and chose to convert to Islam rather than die. While this final bizarre act of Shabbatai's turned most Jews against him, and the Jewish world began to return to its diasporic normality, a sizeable group refused to believe it was all a failure. Nathan of Gaza and Abraham Miguel Cardoso, the major ideologues of Sabbateanism, produced mystical explanations for why Shabbatai had to convert in order to fulfill his messianic mandate. While Shabbatai did not subscribe to all their views of his actions, neither did he renounce his messianic role and put an end to the faith. Cells of Sabbatean believers, some secret and some relatively open, created a sect of the faithful in the Ottoman Empire and Europe. Kabbalistic prophecy became their stock in trade, and various records have been preserved of their visions, dreams, and predictions concerning the final act of Shabbatai's messianic manifestation. A group of several hundred families in Greece, called Dönme, chose to convert to Islam in the 1680s in imitation of Shabbatai's act. Their secret faith in him remained intact up to the twentieth century. Among the larger group that remained within Judaism, it was not uncommon to find otherwise very observant secret Sabbateans deliberately transgressing some commandment in a ritualized act of antinomianism like those of Shabbatai.[136]

The sect did not disappear even after Shabbatai's death in 1676. Despite the clear decision of the rabbis to hunt down the believers and treat them as absolute heretics, the campaign against them had only limited success. It appears that many Jews did not see the continued threat and chose to act as if the whole episode had never occurred rather than revive its memory. This attitude was encouraged by the faithful, who communicated their Sabbatean theology in kabbalistic terms so obscure that they were unrecognizable as such even to most experienced kabbalists. Opponents like Moses Ḥagiz and Jacob Emden often failed to convince the Jewish world that the extremely subtle indications of Sabbateanism in abstruse mystical works could in fact threaten Judaism. In several cases their anti-Sabbatean zeal backfired and they themselves suffered for their efforts.[137] Meanwhile, in 1700, believers mounted an amazingly unconcealed mission to the Land of Israel, designed to help speed the messianic advent. Rabbis from among the secret believers officiated in several Jewish communities. The most striking case was that of Solomon Aailion, who kept his Sabbatean belief (including, apparently, a stint among the Dönme) concealed throughout a long, distinguished career as rabbi in London and Amsterdam. Aailion came close to ruinous exposure when he supported the machinations of Neḥemiah Ḥiyya Ḥayon, a more radical Sabbatean adventurer with a pseudo-trinitarian Sabbatean theology.[138] The common feature of this entire underground movement was its willingness to dissemble and commit certain transgressions as an integral part of the faith.

The danger of Sabbateanism redoubled in the eighteenth century with the appearance of Jacob Frank, a Polish Jew who claimed the messianic mantle as Shabbatai's heir. Frank made great show of being a *prostak,* an uneducated Jew whose messianism was predicated on his personal relationship with God rather than some obscure rabbinic tradition. While this image was not entirely accurate, Frank succeeded in attracting thousands of followers and thus severely troubling the rabbinic establishment for decades. His group was fairly open about flouting Jewish law; they were even reputed to swap wives and hold orgies (as were earlier Sabbateans). Frank challenged the Polish rabbis and Karaites to a theological debate before church officials in 1757, and afterward he and a group of followers converted to Catholicism. A larger group of Frankists remained within Judaism but kept up their faith in Frank.[139] In the meantime, Emden had publicly accused the great scholar Jonathan Eibeschuetz of being a secret Sabbatean. This controversy rocked Ashkenazi Jewry, again demonstrating both the continued threat of the Sabbatean issue and the brittle state of rabbinic culture in that age. While rabbinic conflicts were common throughout history, the status of the chief figures, the seriousness of the charges, the aggressiveness with which they were pursued, and the wide dissemination of the fight make it qualitatively different from the commonplace squabbles between scholars.[140] This is not to say that the traditionalism of most Jews was in any immediate danger, but that serious cracks inhered in the seemingly sturdy structure of rabbinic authority. Notwithstanding the attacks of recent scholars on Scholem's famous claim that Sabbateanism was at the root of the Jewish Enlightenment (*Haskalah*) and the Reform movement, it would be erroneous to disregard the fallout of these antinomian and heretical movements as factors, for the *Haskalah* and Reform did not materialize out of nowhere.[141]

Radical Changes in Eighteenth-Century Ashkenaz

After the many remarkable threats to rabbinic culture during the sixteenth and seventeenth centuries, and with epochal changes so soon to come, the relative placidity of early-eighteenth-century Jewish life may seem somewhat peculiar. It is only well beneath the surface of the communities that the shape of past and future metamorphoses might be detected. The economic fortunes of the Western Sefardic and Italian congregations were slowly waning. The Sabbateans were pursued, sometimes half-heartedly and other times with alacrity. Eastern European Jews were struggling with financial and social stresses within the community as well as without. Kabbalah was spreading rapidly among ordinary Jews with the help of aids written for this purpose by rabbis. Some western European Jews were becoming decreasingly scrupulous in their observance as surrounding cultures became increasingly appealing, but this was hardly uncommon in Jewish history.[142] In general, Jewish law remained highly sensitive to the ordinary living needs of Jews in this setting, as it had always done, so there was no sudden tension over legal problems.[143]

Most of Ashkenaz, like the Jews of Ottoman lands, continued to be highly traditional until at least the middle of the eighteenth century. The doctrinal critiques that did appear there, while fascinating, were few and far between.[144] Thus, when the enormous rifts of the later eighteenth century occurred in Ashkenaz, they seemed almost inexplicable. They did not burst forth in any of the centers of seventeenth-century anti-rabbinism, nor among the most acculturated Jews. This was partly because well-acculturated Jews felt little real tension between their own society and that of their Christian or Muslim neighbors. They did not see themselves as outsiders seeking a way in, but as participants. Many assimilated or even converted, but few tried to change Judaism itself.

A desire for change in rabbinic culture, however, was precisely what characterized the two great movements of later eighteenth-century Judaism. One of these was the Ḥasidic movement of eastern Europe, led by the charismatic Israel ben Eliezer, called Baal Shem Tov ("Master of the Good Name" or "Good Master of Names" [i.e., secret names of God], ca. 1700–1760), which encompassed over half of

Polish Jewry at its peak. Ḥasidism emphasized the ability of every Jew to be close with God through kabbalistic intensity in prayer and ritual, and in many branches by a close relationship with a *ṣaddiq* or *rebbe* who was on a high spiritual plane.

The challenges Ḥasidism posed to the rabbinic establishment were many, some immediately evident and others only revealed over time. The power of the *rebbe* went far beyond that of traditional Jewish leaders who criticized his role, akin to a medium between Jews and God, as nearly idolatrous. His qualifications were typically based on spiritual magnetism and dynastic considerations rather than talmudic prowess. The Ḥasidic deemphasis of Torah study in favor of other activities for spiritual enrichment struck at the very core of rabbinic values. Ḥasidim created serious social rifts as well, forming their own synagogues to pray in the mystical style of Rabbi Isaac Luria. Certain *rebbes* (including the Baal Shem Tov) gyrated and tumbled wildly in the ecstasy of prayer, detracting from its dignity in the eyes of traditionalists. Some Ḥasidim took liberties with the law, establishing their own practices for matters such as the ritual slaughter of kosher meat, thus alarming a rabbinic culture still reeling from the Sabbatean debacle. Indeed, there was a period in which it was altogether unclear whether Ḥasidism could remain within the rabbinic Jewish world at all.[145]

A much smaller movement, in a far corner of the Ashkenazi world, was the *Haskalah* or *Aufklärung,* the Jewish Enlightenment, based in Germany. The *Haskalah* has often been privileged in Jewish historiography over similar developments elsewhere in Europe at the same time because the structures of Jewish life and religion today (e.g., the concept of "Orthodox" Judaism; the Reform movement; the belief that Jewish modernity is essentially different from traditional Jewish life) can be traced directly back to Germany. While the Jewries of England, Holland, France, Italy, and other Western countries underwent radical social and cultural shifts in the eighteenth century, the crisis of rabbinic culture in all those lands was tied to the ideology of the German *Haskalah.* German rabbis and their ideas were the hub to which liberal scholars from everywhere connected.[146]

The *Haskalah* began among a circle of Jews (for the most part originally from eastern Europe) who were deeply attracted by the brilliant culture of the German Enlightenment and sought to adjust Judaism to be palatable within that culture. The alterations sought by *Haskalah* figures such as Hartwig Wessely (né Naphtali Herz Weisel) were meant to make Judaism feel a part of German society as much as

Lutheranism and Catholicism. These men were encouraged by German intellectuals who spoke of the possibility of Jewish emancipation if only the Jews could give up their repulsive, alien ways.[147] In the next generation, many products of this environment chose to convert to Christianity. Some of those who chose to remain Jewish sought to reengineer Judaism itself to German Enlightenment standards. They selected rabbis who were involved in the new intellectual approach of *Wissenschaft des Judentums,* the (historical) "science" of Judaism that sought to prove that the Jews, like other nations, had a great epochal history of creativity even after the biblical period. These rabbis and their acculturated congregants created the Reform movement, whose original goal was to amalgamate Judaism and Germanism in a way that would allow Jews full participation in both worlds.[148]

Needless to say, the *Haskalah* and Reform movements aroused great consternation among traditionalist rabbis. The challenge to rabbinic power was open, and there was no mistaking the ideology of deliberate change; the prayer service, rituals, and laws that had defined rabbinic culture for many centuries were being drastically modified. An interesting facet to this debate is the fact that the *maskilim* (proponents of *Haskalah*) and early Reform leaders usually avoided the underlying theoretical issue that had been at the forefront of earlier critiques of rabbinic culture: the status of the Talmud and the Torah. It was clear to everyone that the innovations practiced could only be undertaken if the rabbinic tradition was understood to have lost all or part of its authority. This, however, was not a point that was argued from principles or defended historically until later. Theology and dogma were not the battleground of *Haskalah* and Reform—their adherents were only interested in a Judaism that would serve their needs. This turned out to be true for most western European Jews, and over the course of the nineteenth and twentieth centuries it became almost universal in the Jewish world. As the training of rabbis and the definition of rabbinic roles shifted under the impact of these movements, so did the entire meaning of rabbinic culture.

A separate, external factor combined with these internal movements to signal the death knell of traditional rabbinic authority in Germany. This was the decline of Jewish communal autonomy, as the absolutist German state began unprecedented levels of interference in rabbinic affairs. The change was represented as a positive result of Enlightenment natural law theory—it was the right of the individual to relate directly to the government rather than through some mediating institution. In practice, however, meaningful authority of the rabbis over the Jewish community could not endure the dual assault from within and without.[149] Under Napoleon, the state dissolution of Jewish communal autonomy spread through most of western Europe, and the parameters of rabbinic culture were forever altered. In the nineteenth and twentieth centuries, these religious and political trends that began largely in Germany had spread throughout the Jewish world. The only vestige of medieval rabbinic culture still retaining any recognizable temporal authority may now exist in the rooms of the Israeli Rabbinate where marriage and divorce documents are issued.

Rabbinic culture is a protean phenomenon. In the pages above, we have attempted to describe its salient features while sketching some of its diverse manifestations. There were, in truth, many different rabbinic cultures, some of them competing directly with each other. For Jews, there was never any single, centralized authority, no institutional hierarchy, no councils to determine practice or belief. While such institutions as the Babylonian *yeshivot* or an individual scholar like Maimonides could exert lasting influences, no one could finally decree what all Jews must do or believe. Dissent within the main fold of rabbinic Judaism always remained a possibility. In this essay, therefore, we have tried to show how rabbinic culture and its critics have developed and confronted each other historically in the medieval and early modern periods.

The quest for spirituality led learned Jews to seek fulfillment in diverse disciplines. Some scholars successfully compartmentalized the disparate fields in which they excelled. Others sought to harmonize them. Judah Ibn Waqqar (mid-fourteenth century), for example, attempted an ambitious synthesis of philosophy and Kabbalah.[150] Not infrequently, however, the advocates of one branch of learning sought to elevate its position at the expense of another. As Profiat Duran (fl. ca. 1400) explained, halakhists, philosophers, and kabbalists in his day each claimed their particular field as the true path to the *summum bonum*—cavalierly sweeping aside the course of biblical studies and grammar that he advocated.[151] Sharp critiques of talmudism warn against a preoccupation with *halakhah* at the expense of spiritual development—what Isadore Twersky has called "the kabbalistic claim than an unreflective observance of commandments, not plugged into kabbalistic concepts and intentions, misses the mark and that a merely 'literalist' approach to Talmud is deficient."[152] Philosophy, on the other hand, ultimately struck some scholars as, at best, a futile exercise, which cannot definitively answer vital, metaphysical questions.[153] At worst, of course, both philosophy and Kabbalah could lead the unwary to entertain beliefs perceived as heretical.

Heresy figures prominently in many of the studies collected here, which explore, inter alia, the rabbinic terminology for heterodoxy, specific beliefs that were labeled heretical, and the social or political dynamics leading to excommunication. As we have made clear, Judaism has always emphasized doctrine, though without ever offering a unified theology that gained widespread acceptance. Even the definitions of heresy found in tannaitic literature are far from ambiguous.[154] Not surprisingly, although Maimonides' creed has been widely adopted during the past two centuries by Orthodox Jews, in earlier times all attempts at formalizing the articles of faith failed to win universal approval.[155] And as the resurrection controversy of the 1190s would show, even Maimonides' own doctrinal statements were subject to intense scrutiny and debate.[156]

Lacking a central authority and a monolithic theology, rabbinic Judaism developed organically. The culture sustaining this complex of diverse ideas and practices was similarly variegated and bore within it a vigorous tradition of self-criticism and dissent. As we have stressed and as this volume shows, various factors contributed to this self-critique. The rival curricular ideals described above reflected competing theological and teleological ideas. But they could also be bound up with personal struggles for authority and power, at the root of which often lay economic and demographic issues. External forces were also at work: it was impossible to turn a blind eye to surrounding, non-Jewish cultures and their approaches to faith.

The Maimonidean Controversies of the thirteenth century illustrate the interplay between several disparate factors.[157] The widely diverging attitudes toward philosophy among Jews in northern Spain, Provence, and northern France set the disputes in motion. But there were also social and political dimensions to these struggles. In Barcelona, for example, the assault on Maimonides' works took place against the background of a struggle between the aristocratic lay leadership and members of the rabbinic elite—a contest the rabbis ultimately won.[158] The complex relationships between communities and the elite groups that governed them were also played out through the bans, the correspondences, and the missions of leading figures to enlist support for their various positions.[159] But the rabbis' opposition to philosophy and their imposition of a ban against its study can only be understood within the wider context of the Church's reaction to rationalism and campaign against heresy.[160] The assault on Maimonides' *Guide* and *Book of Knowledge* must be viewed against the backdrop of the Church's ban on Aristotle. Nor is it any accident that Jews were accusing each other of heterodoxy in the south of France, not far from the heartland of the Albigensians.

The anti-rabbinism of some conversos also exemplifies the ways in which different social and historical elements could produce challenges to rabbinic authority. Ferdinand and Isabella forced the choice of expulsion or conversion on Spanish Jewry in 1492 for religious, social, and political reasons. King Manoel of Portugal forcibly converted the Jews who had fled to his realm in 1497. Later generations of conversos grew up in a religious and social minefield in which they were forced to practice Catholicism, even as they were suspected of Judaizing—an environment that led many of them to deprecate all religion. A number of these disaffected individuals came in contact with Erasmians, free-thinkers, fideists, and other religiously dangerous types in Iberian universities. When groups of conversos returned to the Judaism of their ancestors in the early modern period, they often brought with them a skepticism and anticlericalism born of bitter experience. For some this resentment was further piqued by unpleasant experiences with rabbinic authority in their own lives.[161]

Both of these cases illustrate the close connection between rabbinic culture and authority. In rabbinic culture talmudic knowledge has always meant power, a power that the advocates of talmudism have sought to preserve and extend. As the essays collected here show, there have always been dissenters from within the fold and without who have sought to resist or temper the dominance of the Talmud and its champions. These are the critics of rabbinic culture.

Notes

1. On Jewish culture in general and rabbinic culture in particular, see Louis Finkelstein, ed., *The Jews*, 4th ed., 3 vols. (New York: Schocken, 1970), esp. Judah Goldin, "The Period of the Talmud," in vol. 1; G. D. Cohen, "The Talmudic Age," in *Great Ages and Ideas of the Jewish People*, ed. L. Schwarz (New York: Random House, 1956); E. E. Urbach, *The Sages: Their Concepts and Beliefs* (Cambridge, Mass.: Harvard University Press, 1979); S. W. Baron, *A Social and Religious History of the Jews*, 2nd ed., 18 vols. (New York: Columbia University Press; Philadelphia: Jewish Publication Society, 1952–83), 6:3–151 ("Reign of Law"); H. H. Ben-Sasson and S. Ettinger, eds., *Jewish Society through the Ages* (New York: Schocken, 1971); A. Green, ed., *Jewish*

Spirituality: From the Bible through the Middle Ages (New York: Crossroad, 1986); L. Fine, ed., *Judaism in Practice: From the Middle Ages through the Early Modern Period* (Princeton: Princeton University Press, 2001); D. Biale, ed., *Cultures of the Jews: A New History* (New York: Schocken, 2002); and J. Wertheimer, ed., *Jewish Religious Leadership: Image and Reality,* 2 vols. (New York: Jewish Theological Seminary, 2004).

2. In this connection, Isadore Twersky coined the term "halakocentricity"; see "Religion and Law," in *Religion in a Religious Age,* ed. S. D. Goitein (Cambridge, Mass.: Association for Jewish Studies, 1974), 70.
3. Maimonides, *Mishneh Torah: The Book of Knowledge,* trans. M. Hyamson (Jerusalem: Boys' Town, 1962; reprint, New York: Feldheim, 1981), 2b. On the Mishnah's redaction, see D. Weiss Halivni, *Midrash, Mishnah, and Gemara* (Cambridge, Mass.: Harvard University Press, 1986), chap. 2. Saul Lieberman has argued convincingly that the Mishnah was published orally and only committed to writing in the post-talmudic period; see *Hellenism in Jewish Palestine,* 2nd ed. (New York: Jewish Theological Seminary, 1962), 83–99.
4. On the term *gemara,* which became current as a result of Christian censorship, see H. L. Strack and G. Stemberger, *Introduction to the Talmud and Midrash* (Minneapolis: Fortress Press, 1996), 165.
5. For a passionate response to charges of "Pharisaic legalism," see I. Abrahams, "Professor Schürer on Life under the Jewish Law," *Jewish Quarterly Review* o.s. 11 (1899): 626–42. See also S. Schechter, *Aspects of Rabbinic Theology* (New York: Macmillan, 1909), chap. 11, and R. Goldenberg, "Law and Spirit in Talmudic Religion," in Green, *Jewish Spirituality: From the Bible through the Middle Ages,* 232–52.
6. H. N. Bialik, "Halachah and Aggadah," trans. L. Simon, in *An Anthology of Hebrew Essays,* ed. I. Cohen and B. Y. Michali (Tel Aviv: Institute for the Translation of Hebrew Literature, 1966), 2:368.
7. Apart from the ban on kindling fire (Exodus 35:3), these prohibitions do not occur in the Pentateuch. They are set forth in BT Shabbat 73a–76a.
8. BT Shabbat 119a.
9. Ibid. The metaphor of the Sabbath bride or queen has been popularized by the hymn "Lekha Dodi," composed by Solomon Alkabetz (1505–76) and recited on Friday evenings; see L. Fine, *Safed Spirituality* (New York: Paulist Press, 1984), 33–34, 38–40.
10. BT Shabbat 118b.
11. Ibid., where a dish of beets, fish, and garlic is mentioned. Jewish communities the world over have developed many different delicacies especially for the Sabbath; meat, wine, and fish figure prominently. On the ritual and mystical significance of these three foods, see Isaiah Horowitz, *Shenei luḥot ha-berit,* "Massekhet shabbat," "Ner miṣvah," sec. 36.
12. The basis for the prohibition is Exodus 35:3. The practice of lighting Sabbath lamps or candles is the subject of Mishnah Shabbat, chap. 2. For the identification of Sabbath light with Sabbath delight, see Midrash Tanḥuma, *Parashat Meṣora,* sec. 9. On Sabbath lights as a positive commandment, see Maimonides, *Mishneh Torah,* "Hilkhot Shabbat," 5:1. On the ceremony's ritual significance, see F. Gottlieb, *The Lamp of God: A Jewish Book of Light* (Northvale, N.J.: Jason Aronson, 1989), 227–36.
13. Bialik, "Halachah and Aggadah," 371.

14. See Strack and Stemberger, *Introduction to the Talmud and Midrash,* 15–30.
15. See BT Menaḥot 37a.
16. Among the best-known supercommentaries on Rashi are those of Elijah Mizraḥi (1455–1526), Maharal of Prague (d. 1609), and Mordecai Jaffe (1530–1612). In the fourteenth century, Judah Moskoni claims to have seen twenty-eight supercommentaries on Ibn Ezra; see S. B. Bowman, *The Jews of Byzantium, 1204–1453* (University: University of Alabama Press, 1985), 133–34, 283–84. See also U. Simon, "Interpreting the Interpreter: Supercommentaries on Ibn Ezra's Commentaries," in *Rabbi Abraham Ibn Ezra: Studies in the Writings of a Twelfth-Century Jewish Polymath,* ed. I. Twersky and J. M. Harris (Cambridge, Mass.: Harvard University Center for Jewish Studies, 1993), 86–128.
17. See C. Sirat, *A History of Jewish Philosophy in the Middle Ages* (Cambridge: Cambridge University Press, 1985), chaps. 7–9.
18. See I. Twersky, "The Shulhan 'Aruk: Enduring Code of Jewish Law," *Judaism* 16 (1967): 141–58; E. Fram, "Jewish Law from the Shulhan Arukh to the Enlightenment," in *An Introduction to the History and Sources of Jewish Law,* ed. N. S. Hecht et al. (Oxford: Clarendon Press, 1996), 359–77; and M. Elon, *Jewish Law: History, Sources, Principles* (Philadelphia: Jewish Publication Society, 1994), vol. 3, chaps. 36–38.
19. For a characterization of the responsa literature, see Elon, *Jewish Law,* chap. 39, esp. 1473–82.
20. See M. Saperstein, *Jewish Preaching, 1200–1800: An Anthology* (New Haven: Yale University Press, 1989), esp. 44–63.
21. See, e.g., Sirat, *A History of Jewish Philosophy in the Middle Ages,* 180–85.
22. See, e.g., G. Scholem, *On the Kabbalah and Its Symbolism* (New York: Schocken, 1965).
23. Cf. the well-known dictum, "the Torah has seventy aspects"; see Midrash Numbers Rabbah 13:16, fol. 54, col. c. On the character of allegorical interpretation by medieval Jews, see F. E. Talmage, "Apples of Gold: The Inner Meaning of Sacred Texts in Medieval Judaism," in Green, *Jewish Spirituality from the Bible through the Middle Ages,* 313–55.
24. See Joshua 1:8.
25. Maimonides, *Sefer ha-Miṣvot,* ed. Y. Qafiḥ (Jerusalem: Mossad Harav Kook, 1971), 65.
26. Tosafot on BT Avodah Zarah 19b, s.v. *yeshallesh adam shenotav,* citing Rabbi Jacob ben Meir Tam. Cf. *Shulḥan Arukh,* Y.D. 246:4.
27. *The Fathers According to Rabbi Nathan,* trans. J. Goldin (New Haven: Yale University Press, 1955), chap. 40, 163; cf. parallels in Mishnah Pe'ah 1:1, BT Shabbat 127a, BT Qiddushin 39b–40a, etc.
28. Maimonides, *Mishneh Torah,* "Hilkhot Talmud Torah," chaps. 1–2.
29. Ibid., 3:1, citing Exodus Rabbah 34:2. Cf. *The Fathers According to Rabbi Nathan,* trans. Goldin, chap. 41, 169 and BT Yoma 72b.
30. See M. S. Berger, *Rabbinic Authority* (New York: Oxford University Press, 1998), and M. Walzer et al., eds., *The Jewish Political Tradition* (New Haven: Yale University Press, 2000), 1:244–306.
31. *Midrash Tanḥuma-Yelammedenu,* "Noaḥ," sec. 3, trans. S. A. Berman (Hoboken, N.J.: Ktav, 1996), 42. Cf. Maimonides, *Mishneh Torah,* "Hilkhot Talmud Torah," 3:6.
32. Maimonides, *Mishneh Torah,* "Hilkhot Talmud Torah," chaps. 5–6.

33. See Urbach, *The Sages*, esp. 603–20, and Urbach, "The Talmudic Sage, Character and Authority," in *Jewish Society through the Ages*, ed. H. H. Ben-Sasson and S. Ettinger (New York: Schocken, 1971), 116–48.
34. See, e.g., the semi-mythic account of the process in Abraham Ibn Daud's *Sefer ha-Qabbalah*, analyzed by G. D. Cohen, "The Story of the Four Captives," in *Studies in the Variety of Rabbinic Cultures* (Philadelphia: Jewish Publication Society, 1991), esp. 178–79. On the academy in Lucena, see E. Ashtor, *The Jews of Moslem Spain* (Philadelphia: Jewish Publication Society, 1979), 2:143–49.
35. See E. Kanarfogel, *Jewish Education and Society in the High Middle Ages* (Detroit: Wayne State University Press, 1992), chap. 4.
36. On custom in Jewish law, see S. W. Baron, *A Social and Religious History of the Jews*, 2nd ed. (New York: Columbia University Press, 1958), 6:121–30, and M. Elon, *Jewish Law: History, Sources, Principles* (Philadelphia: Jewish Publication Society, 1994), 2:880–944. On the situation in northern Europe, see I. M. Ta-Shma, *Early Franco-German Ritual and Custom* (Hebrew) (Jerusalem: Magnes Press, 1992), esp. 27–35, and H. Soloveitchik, "Religious Law and Change: The Medieval Ashkenazic Example," *AJS Review* 12 (1987): 205–21. On the modification of talmudic law in the face of early medieval practice, see J. Katz, *The "Shabbes Goy": A Study in Halakhic Flexibility* (Philadelphia: Jewish Publication Society, 1989), 19–34. For an important case study, see H. Soloveitchik, *Principles and Pressures: Jewish Trade in Gentile Wine in the Middle Ages* (Hebrew) (Tel Aviv: Am Oved, 2003).
37. See M. Breuer, *Oholei Torah (The Tents of Torah): The Yeshiva, Its Structure and History* (Hebrew) (Jerusalem: Zalman Shazar Center, 2003); S. Schwarzfuchs, *A Concise History of the Rabbinate* (Oxford: Basil Blackwell, 1993); and Wertheimer, *Jewish Religious Leadership.*
38. G. D. Cohen, *The Book of Tradition (Sefer ha-Qabbalah) by Abraham Ibn Daud* (Philadelphia: Jewish Publication Society, 1967), l–lvii. On Sherira's *Epistle*, see R. Brody, *The Geonim of Babylonia and the Shaping of Medieval Jewish Culture* (New Haven: Yale University Press, 1998), 20–25, 341–43. On Zacut, see J. Chabás and B. R. Goldstein, *Astronomy in the Iberian Peninsula* (Philadelphia: American Philosophical Society, 2000), esp. 6–15; on Gedaliah Ibn Yaḥya, see A. David, "R. Gedalya Ibn Yahya's Shalshelet Hakabbalah (Chain of Tradition): A Chapter in Medieval Jewish Historiography," *Immanuel* 12 (1981): 60–76.
39. See L. Kochan, *The Jew and His History* (New York: Schocken, 1977), 19–20, 39–49, and Y. H. Yerushalmi, *Zakhor: Jewish History and Jewish Memory* (Seattle: University of Washington Press, 1982), 31–40.
40. G. D. Cohen, *The Book of Tradition*, xliii–xlii. On Karaism in Andalusia, see D. J. Lasker, "Karaism in Twelfth-Century Spain," *Journal of Jewish Thought and Philosophy* 1 (1992): 179–95.
41. See L. Nemoy, *Karaite Anthology* (New Haven: Yale University Press, 1952); Baron, *A Social and Religious History of the Jews*, 5:209–85; Z. Ankori, *Karaites in Byzantium: The Formative Years, 970–1100* (New York: Columbia University Press, 1959); and M. Polliack, ed., *Karaite Judaism: A Guide to the History and Literary Sources of Medieval and Modern Karaism* (Leiden: Brill, 2003).
42. Nemoy, *Karaite Anthology*, 76.
43. Ibid., 80–81. For the ritual fringe or tassel, see Numbers 15:37–41; for the booth, see Leviticus 23:42–44. On the rabbinic regulation of their dimensions, see respec-

tively BT Menaḥot 41b–42a and Mishneh Sukkah 1:1. On Karaite-Rabbanite polemics about the fringes, see D. Frank, *Search Scripture Well: Karaite Exegetes and the Origins of the Jewish Bible Commentary in the Islamic East* (Leiden: Brill, 2004), chap. 2.

44. *The Book of the Wars of the Lord,* ed. I. Davidson (New York: Jewish Theological Seminary, 1934), 108–9. Note also Salmon's incredulous remarks about the *Shi'ur Qomah,* a mystical text detailing the Lord's physical dimensions, 114–24.
45. On the polemic over Sabbath lights, see D. Frank, "Karaite Ritual," in Fine, *Judaism in Practice* (Princeton: Princeton University Press, 2001), 250–52, 260–64.
46. Ankori, *Karaites in Byzantium,* 275–80.
47. See D. Frank, "Karaite Exegesis," in *Hebrew Bible/Old Testament: The History of Its Interpretation,* vol. 1/2, ed. M. Saebø (Göttingen: Vandenhoeck and Ruprecht, 2000), 110–28, and Frank, *Search Scripture Well.*
48. See H. Ben-Shammai, "Kalām in Medieval Jewish Philosophy," in *History of Jewish Philosophy,* ed. D. H. Frank and O. Leaman (London: Routledge, 1997), 115–48, esp. 127–34.
49. See D. Sklare, *Samuel b. Ḥofni Gaon and His Cultural World* (Leiden: Brill, 1996), esp. 37–141.
50. Frank, "Karaite Commentaries on the Song of Songs from Tenth-Century Jerusalem," in *With Reverence for the Word,* ed. J. D. McAuliffe, B. D. Walfish, and J. W. Goering (Oxford: Oxford University Press, 2003), 59.
51. On this episode, see Marina Rustow's chapter in this volume. The Karaite attitude toward rabbinic literature changed substantially over the following centuries; see Daniel Frank's contribution to this collection.
52. Later Karaites regarded this label as a slander, since unlike the Sadducees they uphold the doctrine of resurrection; see Baron, *A Social and Religious History of the Jews,* 5:254–55.
53. On the label *min* for Karaites, see M. Gil and E. Fleischer, *Yehuda Ha-Levi and His Circle* (Hebrew) (Jerusalem: World Union of Jewish Studies, 2001), 182–83 and n. 46. For *khawārij,* see Judah Halevi, *Al-Kitāb al-Khazarī,* ed. D. H. Baneth (Jerusalem: Magnes Press, 1977), 1:1, p. 3. Maimonides' definition of a *kofer ba-torah* would certainly apply to Karaites; see *Mishneh Torah,* "Hilkhot Teshuvah," 3:8. See also G. Blidstein, "Maimonides' Attitude Towards the Karaites" (Hebrew) *Techumin* 8 (1987): 501–10.
54. To be sure, there were also isolated communities, such as the Beta Israel of Ethiopia or the Benei Israel of India, who were unfamiliar with rabbinic Judaism and followed their own rituals. For obvious reasons, they will not be considered here.
55. Though dated, the best overview of Saadya's life and works remains H. Malter, *Saadia Gaon: His Life and Works* (Philadelphia: Jewish Publication Society, 1921). See now Brody, *The Geonim of Babylonia,* index, s.v. "Se'adyah Gaon."
56. Saadia Gaon, *The Book of Beliefs and Opinions,* trans. S. Rosenblatt (New Haven: Yale University Press, 1948), 27–28. On the book's title, see Saadya Gaon, *The Book of Doctrines and Beliefs,* trans. A. Altmann (Oxford: East and West Library, 1946), 19–20.
57. See Saadia Gaon, *The Book of Beliefs and Opinions,* I:3, 50–83 (creation); VI:1, 235–39 (the soul). For discussions, see H. A. Wolfson, *Repercussions of the Kalam in Jewish*

Philosophy (Cambridge, Mass.: Harvard University Press, 1979), 124–62, and H. Davidson, "Saadia's List of Theories of the Soul," in *Jewish Medieval and Renaissance Studies,* ed. A. Altmann (Cambridge, Mass.: Harvard University Press, 1967), 75–94.

58. See Saadia Gaon, *The Book of Beliefs and Opinions,* V:4, 219. Rosenblatt translates *kāfir* "renegade," changed here to "heretic."
59. See S. Stroumsa, "On Jewish Intellectuals Who Converted in the Early Middle Ages," in *The Jews of Medieval Islam,* ed. D. Frank (Leiden: Brill, 1995), 179–97; M. R. Cohen and S. Somekh, "Interreligious *Majālis* in Early Fatimid Egypt," in *The Majlis: Interreligious Encounters in Medieval Islam,* ed. H. Lazarus-Yafeh et al. (Wiesbaden: Harrassowtiz Verlag, 1999), 128–36; and, in the same volume, D. Sklare, "Responses to Islamic Polemics by Jewish Mutakallimūn in the Tenth Century," 137–61.
60. See A. Halkin and D. Hartman, *Crisis and Leadership: Epistles of Maimonides* (Philadelphia: Jewish Publication Society, 1985), 13–90, esp. 30.
61. It is instructive to compare the *Epistle on Martyrdom* with Maimonides' later *Epistle to Yemen* which also addresses the problem of forced conversion to Islam; see Halkin and Hartman, *Crisis and Leadership,* 91–207, esp. 95–114. In Yemen, at least one twelfth-century Jewish scholar acknowledged that Muhammad was a real prophet, though only to his own people; see D. Levine, *The Bustan al-Ukul by Nathanael Ibn al-Fayyumi* (New York: Columbia University Press, 1908), 108–9.
62. On Maimonides' creed, see M. Kellner, *Dogma in Medieval Jewish Thought: From Maimonides to Abravanel* (Oxford: Littman Library and Oxford University Press, 1986), esp. chap. 1. For a much earlier list of dogmas, see H. Ben-Shammai, "Saadya Gaon's Ten Articles of Faith" (Hebrew), *Da'at* 37 (1996): 11–26.
63. See I. Twersky, *A Maimonides Reader* (New York: Behrman House, 1972), 401–23. For the Arabic original and a modern Hebrew translation, see Y. Shailat, *Haqdamot ha-Rambam la-Mishnah* (Ma'aleh Adumim: Ma'aliyot, 1992), 126–223, 360–74.
64. Twersky, *A Maimonides Reader,* 411–12; Shailat, *Haqdamot,* 366.
65. Twersky, *A Maimonides Reader,* 411, citing BT Berakhot 17a; Shailat, *Haqdamot,* 366.
66. Twersky, *A Maimonides Reader,* 409; Shailat, *Haqdamot,* 366.
67. Maimonides, *Mishneh Torah,* "Hilkhot Teshuvah," 8:2; see fols. 90a–b in the Hyamson trans., cited in note 3.
68. On this episode, see S. Stroumsa, "Twelfth-Century Concepts of Soul and Body: The Maimonidean Controversy in Baghdad," in *Self, Soul and Body in Religious Experience,* ed. A. I. Baumgarten et al. (Leiden: Brill, 1998), 313–34.
69. For Maimonides' *Essay,* see Halkin and Hartman, *Crisis and Leadership,* 209–92, and Ralph Lerner, *Maimonides' Empire of Light: Popular Enlightenment in an Age of Belief* (Chicago: University of Chicago Press, 2000), 42–55, 154–77. Ten years later, a new controversy concerning the same issues erupted in northern Spain and Provence, where philosophical studies had found an eager Jewish readership, while theological conservatives like Meir ha-Levi Abulafia (Ramah) still exercised considerable influence. On this second "resurrection controversy," see B. Septimus, *Hispano-Jewish Culture in Transition: The Career and Controversies of Ramah* (Cambridge, Mass.: Harvard University Press, 1982), chap. 3.
70. On Maimonides' critique of traditional rabbinic culture, see Menachem Kellner's contribution to this volume.

71. For the controversy of 1232–35, see J. Sarachek, *Faith and Reason: The Conflict over the Rationalism of Maimonides* (New York, 1935; reprint, New York: Hermon Press, 1970), and D. J. Silver, *Maimonidean Criticism and the Maimonidean Controversy, 1180–1240* (Leiden: Brill, 1965). On the various attitudes of northern French rabbis toward biblical and talmudic anthropomorphisms, see Ephraim Kanarfogel's contribution to this volume. On the northern French and Ashkenazic understanding of heresy, see Joseph Davis's essay.
72. On the cultural value of Hebrew poetry for Andalusian Jewry, see R. P. Scheindlin, *Wine, Women, and Death: Medieval Hebrew Poems on the Good Life* (Philadelphia: Jewish Publication Society, 1986), esp. 3–11. Note that Ibn 'Aqnīn specifies liturgical poetry (*piyyut*) for its edifying qualities; much secular verse would have been considered unsuitable for teenagers.
73. It is instructive to compare this portion of the curriculum with the first eight classes of men described by Baḥya ben Joseph Ibn Paquda in *The Book of Direction to the Duties of the Heart,* trans. M. Mansoor (London: Routledge and Kegan Paul, 1973), 3:4, 192–94.
74. Jacob Rader Marcus, *The Jew in the Medieval World, A Source Book, 315–1791,* rev. ed. M. Saperstein (Cincinnati: Hebrew Union College Press, 1999), 428–32, no. 77.
75. Twersky, *A Maimonides Reader,* 234–35.
76. See "A Father's Admonition by Judah Ibn Tibbon," in I. Abrahams, *Hebrew Ethical Wills* (Philadelphia: Jewish Publication Society, 1926), 1:51–93. Samuel translated both Maimonides' *Guide* and his introduction to "Ḥeleq" into Hebrew.
77. Twersky, "Religion and Law," 78n6.
78. Baḥya Ibn Paquda, *The Book of Direction to the Duties of the Heart,* "Introduction," 93. Unlike the story of the fellow who wondered about the phylacteries of a two-headed man (see above), the student does not seem to have been vindicated by subsequent developments. In his comment on Genesis 25:27, Rashi illustrates the young Esau's sanctimoniousness with a midrashic story: "He would ask [Isaac], 'Father, how does one tithe salt and straw?' Accordingly, his father believed that he observed the commandments very strictly."
79. On Andalusian belletristic critiques of rabbinic culture, see Adena Tanenbaum's contribution to this volume.
80. See H. Soloveitchik, "Three Themes in the 'Sefer Hasidim,'" *AJS Review* 1 (1976): 339–54, and Kanarfogel, *Jewish Education and Society,* esp. chaps. 5 and 6.
81. Maimonides, *Mishneh Torah: The Book of Knowledge,* "Hilkhot Talmud Torah," 3:1 (fol. 59a in the Hyamson trans. = Twersky, *Maimonides Reader,* 66). For halakhic reasons that cannot be elaborated here, women, slaves, and minors are exempt from the obligation; see Maimonides, "Hilkhot Talmud Torah," 1:1 (Hyamson trans., 57a).
82. Mishnah Horayot 3:8, cited by Maimonides, "Hilkhot Talmud Torah," 3:2 (Hyamson trans., fol. 59a).
83. Mishnah Pe'ah 1:1, cited by Maimonides, 3:3 (Hyamson trans., fol. 59a).
84. See BT Pesaḥim 50b, *she-mitokh she-lo li-shmah ba li-shmah,* cited by Maimonides, "Hilkhot Talmud Torah," 3:5 (Hyamson trans., fol. 59a). See also Maimonides' parable near the beginning of the introduction to "Ḥeleq," in Twersky, *A Maimonides Reader,* 404–5.
85. *Massekhet Avot im Peirush Rabbenu Mosheh ben Maimon,* ed. Y. Shailat (Jerusalem: Ma'aliyot, 1994), 4:6(7), 70–75, 152–54.

86. See ibid., 74. See also Maimonides, "Hilkhot Talmud Torah," 3:9 (Hyamson trans., fol. 59b), and cf. *Mishneh Torah*, "Hilkhot Mattenot Aniyim," 10:18.
87. The *sekhar battalah* represents compensation for earnings the teacher would have had from another form of gainful employment; see Kanarfogel, *Jewish Education and Society*, 43–45.
88. See, e.g., the "Book of the Statutes of the Torah," trans. E. Kanarfogel, in Fine, *Judaism in Practice*, 191–202, esp. 196.
89. S. W. Baron, *The Jewish Community: Its History and Structure to the American Revolution*, 3 vols. (Philadelphia: Jewish Publication Society, 1942), 2:228–36.
90. On a related communal dispute involving bans and counter-bans, see B. Septimus, "Piety and Power in Thirteenth-Century Catalonia," in *Studies in Medieval Jewish History and Literature*, ed. I. Twersky (Cambridge, Mass.: Harvard University Press, 1979), 197–230.
91. See S. Fraade, "Ascetical Aspects of Ancient Judaism," in Green, *Jewish Spirituality: From the Bible through the Middle Ages*, 253–88, esp. 269–77; for the dictum cited—attributed to Phineas ben Jair—see 270, citing BT Avodah Zarah 20b.
92. See BT Berakhot 32b; BT Nedarim 10a; BT Baba Qama 30a; and BT Niddah 38a.
93. On Baḥya's sources, see *The Book of Direction to the Duties of the Heart*, trans. M. Mansoor, 18–39; on the Islamic background, see esp. G. Vajda, *La Théologie ascétique de Bahya Ibn Paquda* (Paris: Imprimerie Nationale, 1947).
94. See S. D. Goitein, *A Mediterranean Society* (Berkeley: University of California Press, 1988), 5:470–74, reprinted as "An Egyptian Woman Seeks to Rescue Her Husband from a Sufi Monastery," in Fine, *Judaism in Practice*, 186–90.
95. Maimonides, "Eight Chapters," chap. 4, in Twersky, *A Maimonides Reader*, 370–71.
96. On Abraham Maimuni, see Goitein, *A Mediterranean Society*, 5:474–96, and S. Rosenblatt, ed. and trans., *The High Ways to Perfection of Abraham Maimonides*, 2 vols. (New York: Columbia University Press, 1927, and Baltimore: Johns Hopkins University Press, 1938). For Abraham's laudatory comments concerning the Sufis, see Rosenblatt, 1:50, 2:266–67, 2:320–23, and 2:422–23.
97. See D. Frank, Review of Nissim Dana, ed., *Abraham Maimonides: Kifāyat al-Abidīn*, part 2, vol. 2, *Journal of Jewish Studies* 40 (1989): 253–58.
98. On the Jewish Sufis of eleventh- and twelfth-century Egypt, see P. B. Fenton, "Devotional Rites in a Sufi Mode," in Fine, *Judaism in Practice*, 364–74; Fenton, "Judaism and Sufism," in *History of Islamic Philosophy*, ed. S. H. Nasr and O. Leaman (London: Routledge, 1996), 755–68; Fenton, "Abraham Maimonides (1187–1237): Founding a Mystical Dynasty," in *Jewish Mystical Leaders and Leadership in the 13th Century*, ed. M. Idel and M. Ostow (Northvale, N.J.: Jason Aronson, 1998), 127–54; and Fenton, *The Treatise of the Pool, al-Maqala al-Hawdiyya by Obadyah Maimonides*, 2nd ed. (London: Octagon, 1995).
99. On the German Pietists, see Y. F. Baer, "The Socioreligious Orientation of 'Sefer Hasidim,'" in *Binah*, vol. 2, *Studies in Jewish Thought*, ed. J. Dan (New York: Praeger, 1989), 57–95; I. Marcus, *Piety and Society: The Jewish Pietists of Medieval Germany* (Leiden: Brill, 1981); Marcus, "The Devotional Ideals of Ashkenazic Pietism," in Green, *Jewish Spirituality: From the Bible through the Middle Ages*, 356–66; Marcus, "Judah the Pietist and Eleazar of Worms: From Charismatic to Conventional Leadership," in *Jewish Mystical Leaders and Leadership in the 13th Century*, ed. M. Idel and M. Ostow (Northvale, N.J.: Jason Aronson, 1998), 97–126; A.

Cronbach, "Social Thinking in the *Sefer Hasidim*," *Hebrew Union College Annual* 22 (1966): 1–149; H. Soloveitchik, "Three Themes in the *Sefer Hasidim*," *AJS Review* 1 (1976): 311–57; and K. Stow, *Alienated Minority* (Cambridge, Mass.: Harvard University Press, 1992), 121–34.

100. Baer, "The Socioreligious Orientation of 'Sefer Hasidim,'" 65, citing *Sefer Hasidim*, sec. 648.
101. See *The Early Kabbalah* ed. Joseph Dan, texts trans. R. C. Kiener (New York: Paulist Press, 1986); J. Dan, *The Ancient Jewish Mysticism* (Tel Aviv: Ministry of Defense, 1993); Elliot Wolfson, *Through a Speculum That Shines: Vision and Imagination in Medieval Jewish Mysticism* (Princeton: Princeton University Press, 1994).
102. For a new translation in progress, see D. C. Matt, *The Zohar: Pritzker Edition* (Palo Alto: Stanford University Press, 2003).
103. See Gershom Scholem, *Major Trends in Jewish Mysticism* (New York: Schocken, 1946); Scholem, *Origins of the Kabbalah* (Princeton: Princeton University Press, 1987); Moshe Idel, *Kabbalah: New Perspectives* (New Haven: Yale University Press, 1988).
104. See Moshe Idel, "Inquiries into the Doctrine of 'Sefer ha-Meshiv'" (Hebrew), *Sefunot* 17 [= N.S. 2] (1983): 185–266.
105. See *Wisdom of the Zohar*, 3 vols., ed. I. Tishby and F. Lachower, trans. D. Goldstein (Oxford: Littman Library, 1989), vol. 1, introduction.
106. Joseph Ergas, *Shomer Emunim* (reprint, Jerusalem: n.p., 1965), 23–27.
107. Gershom Scholem, *Sabbatai Ṣevi: The Mystical Messiah*, trans. R. J. Z. Werblowsky (Princeton: Princeton University Press, 1973), 283.
108. See Yitzhak Baer, *History of the Jews in Christian Spain*, 2 vols. (Philadelphia: Jewish Publication Society, 1961–66); Elie Kedourie, ed., *Spain and the Jews: The Sephardi Experience, 1492 and After* (London: Thames and Hudson, 1992); H. Beinart, ed., *Moreshet Sepharad: The Sephardic Legacy*, 2 vols. (Jerusalem: Magnes Press, 1992).
109. See Jonathan I. Israel, *European Jewry in the Age of Mercantilism, 1550–1750*, 3rd ed. (Oxford: Littman Library, 1998), chap. 1.
110. See Beinart, *Moreshet Sepharad;* Kedourie, *Spain and the Jews;* Hava Tirosh-Rothschild, *Between Worlds: The Life and Thought of Rabbi David ben Judah Messer Leon* (Albany: State University of New York Press, 1991).
111. See David A. Ruderman, "Hope Against Hope: Jewish and Christian Messianic Expectations in the Late Middle Ages," in *Exile and Diaspora: Studies in the History of the Jewish People Presented to Professor Haim Beinart* (Jerusalem: Ben-Zvi Institute and Consejo Superior de investigaciones científicas Madrid, 1991), 185–202, reprinted in *Essential Papers on Jewish Culture in Renaissance and Baroque Italy*, ed. D. B. Ruderman (New York: New York University Press, 1992), 299–323.
112. See R. Patai, *The Messiah Texts* (Detroit: Wayne State University Press, 1979).
113. On this entire issue see M. Goldish and R. H. Popkin, eds., *Millenarianism and Messianism in Early Modern European Culture*, vol. 1, *Jewish Messianism in the Early Modern World* (Dordrecht: Kluwer, 2001); H. Lenowitz, *The Jewish Messiahs, from the Galilee to Crown Heights* (Oxford: Oxford University Press, 1998); G. Scholem, *The Messianic Idea in Judaism* (New York: Schocken, 1971); M. Idel, *Messianic Mystics* (New Haven: Yale University Press, 1998).
114. See Z. Ankori, *From Lisbon to Salonica and Constantinople* (Hebrew) (Tel Aviv: Tel Aviv University Press, 1988).
115. See Israel, *European Jewry*, chaps. 2–3.

116. See, e.g., J. Davis, "The *Ten Questions* of Eliezer Eilburg and the Problem of Jewish Unbelief in the 16th Century," *Jewish Quarterly Review* 91, nos. 3–4 (2001): 293–336; J. Elbaum, *Openness and Insularity: Late Sixteenth-Century Jewish Literature in Poland and Ashkenaz* (Hebrew) (Jerusalem: Magnes Press, 1990).
117. See Kedourie, *Spain and the Jews;* Beinart, *Moreshet Sepharad.*
118. See R. J. Z. Werblowsky, *Joseph Karo: Lawyer and Mystic* (Oxford: Oxford University Press, 1962; reprint, Philadelphia: Jewish Publication Society, 1977), and L. Fine, *Physician of the Soul, Healer of the Cosmos: Isaac Luria and His Kabbalistic Fellowship* (Palo Alto: Stanford University Press, 1993).
119. See J. Dan, ed., *The Christian Kabbalah: Jewish Mystical Books and Their Christian Interpreters* (Cambridge, Mass.: Harvard College Library, 1997); J. Blau, *The Christian Interpretation of the Cabala in the Renaissance* (Port Washington, N.Y.: Kennikat Press, 1944); C. Wirszubski, *Pico della Mirandola's Encounter With Jewish Mysticism* (Cambridge, Mass.: Harvard University Press, 1989).
120. See S. G. Burnett, *From Christian Hebraism to Jewish Studies: Johannes Buxtorf (1564–1629) and Hebrew Learning in the Seventeenth Century* (Leiden: Brill, 1996); F. Manuel, *The Broken Staff: Judaism Through Christian Eyes* (Cambridge, Mass.: Harvard University Press, 1992).
121. See E. Eisenstein, *The Printing Press as an Agent of Change* (Cambridge: Cambridge University Press, 1979); A. Raz-Krakotzkin, "Censorship, Editing, and the Reshaping of Jewish Identity: The Catholic Church and Hebrew Literature in the Sixteenth Century," in *Hebraica Veritas? Christian Hebraists and the Study of Judaism in Early Modern Europe,* ed. A. P. Coudert and J. S. Shoulson (Philadelphia: University of Pennsylvania Press, 2004), 125–55; S. Baruchson, *Books and Readers: The Reading Interests of Italian Jews at the Close of the Renaissance* (Hebrew) (Ramat Gan: Bar-Ilan University Press, 1993); R. Bonfil, *Jewish Life in Renaissance Italy,* trans. A. Oldcorn (Berkeley: University of California Press, 1994); S. W. Baron, *A Social and Religious History of the Jews,* vol. 13 (New York: Columbia University Press, 1969).
122. See D. B. Ruderman, ed., *Essential Papers on Jewish Culture in Renaissance and Baroque Italy* (New York: New York University Press, 1992); Bonfil, *Jewish Life;* C. Roth, *The Jews in the Renaissance* (Philadelphia: Jewish Publication Society, 1984); D. B. Ruderman and G. Veltri, eds., *Cultural Intermediaries: Jewish Intellectuals in Early Modern Italy* (Philadelphia: University of Pennsylvania Press, 2004).
123. See R. Bonfil, *Rabbis and Jewish Communities in Renaissance Italy* (Oxford: Littman Library, 1993); Ruderman, *Essential Papers,* chap. 1.
124. See Ruderman, *Essential Papers;* K. Stow, *Theater of Acculturation: The Roman Ghetto in the Sixteenth Century* (Seattle: University of Washington Press, 2001).
125. H. H. Ben-Sasson, "The Reformation in Contemporary Jewish Eyes," *Proceedings of the Israel Academy of Sciences and Humanities* 4 (Jerusalem: Israeli Academy, 1970), 239–326; J. Friedman, "The Reformation in Alien Eyes: Jewish Perceptions of Christian Troubles," *Sixteenth Century Journal* 14 (1983): 23–40.
126. On the *Qol Sakhal,* see T. Fishman, *Shaking the Pillars of Exile: 'Voice of a Fool,' an Early Modern Jewish Critique of Rabbinic Culture* (Palo Alto: Stanford University Press, 1997).
127. On this see the essays of R. Cohen and Z. Ankori in *From Lisbon to Salonica and Constantinople,* ed. Z. Ankori (Hebrew) (Tel Aviv: Tel Aviv University Press, 1988).

128. On the Western Sefardi Diaspora see Y. Kaplan, *From Christianity to Judaism: The Story of Isaac Orobio de Castro,* trans. R. Loewe (Oxford: Littman Library, 1989); Y. Kaplan, *An Alternative Path to Modernity: The Sephardi Diaspora in Western Europe* (Leiden: Brill, 2000); Y. H. Yerushalmi, *From Spanish Court to Italian Ghetto: Isaac Cardoso, a Study in Seventeenth-Century Marranism and Jewish Apologetics* (Seattle: University of Washington Press, 1981); M. Bodian, *Hebrews of the Portuguese Nation: Conversos and Community in Early Modern Amsterdam* (Bloomington: Indiana University Press, 1997); D. Swetschinski, *Reluctant Cosmopolitans: The Portuguese Jews of Seventeenth-Century Amsterdam* (Oxford: Littman Library, 2000). The communal record books and personal letters of rabbis from these communities contain extensive evidence of the common laxity in practice.
129. See Kaplan, *An Alternative Path;* Matt Goldish, "Jews, Christians, and Conversos: The Struggles of Solomon Aailion in the Converso Community of London," *Journal of Jewish Studies* 45, no. 2 (1994): 227–57.
130. On this see Yosef Hayim Yerushalmi, "The Re-Education of Marranos in the Seventeenth Century," Third Annual Rabbi Louis Feinberg Memorial Lecture, Judaic Studies Program (Cincinnati: Studies Program, University of Cincinnati, 1980). See also the Hebrew version, with considerable differences, in *Proceedings of the Fifth World Conference of Jewish Studies,* vol. 2 (1969), 201–9.
131. See Kaplan, *An Alternative Path;* S. Rosenberg, "Emunat Hakhamim," in *Jewish Thought in the Seventeenth Century,* ed. I. Twersky and B. Septimus (Cambridge, Mass.: Harvard University Press, 1987), 285–342; J. I. Israel, *The Radical Enlightenment: Philosophy and the Making of Modernity* (Oxford: Oxford University Press, 2001); S. Nadler, *Spinoza: A Life* (Cambridge: Cambridge University Press, 1999); I. S. Révah, *Spinoza et le Dr. Juan de Prado* (Paris: Mouton, 1959); Uriel da Costa, *Examination of Pharisaic Traditions,* trans., notes, and introduction by H. P. Salomon and I. S. D. Sassoon (Leiden: Brill, 1993).
132. Da Costa, *Examination,* autobiography in appendix.
133. Ibid.
134. See S. Nadler, *Spinoza's Heresy: Immortality and the Jewish Mind* (Oxford: Oxford University Press, 2002).
135. See Scholem, *Sabbatai Ṣevi;* Matt Goldish, *The Sabbatean Prophets* (Cambridge, Mass.: Harvard University Press, 2004).
136. See G. Scholem, "Redemption Through Sin," in Scholem, *The Messianic Idea;* Y. Liebes, *Studies in Jewish Myth and Jewish Messianism,* trans. B. Stein (Albany: State University of New York Press, 1993).
137. See E. Carlebach, *The Pursuit of Heresy: Rabbi Moses Hagiz and the Sabbatian Controversies* (New York: Columbia University Press, 1990); J. J. Schacter, "Rabbi Jacob Emden: Life and Major Works" (Ph.D. diss., Harvard University, 1988).
138. See Carlebach, *Pursuit of Heresy;* M. Goldish, "An Historical Irony: The Court of Hakham Solomon Aailion Tries the Case of a Repentant Sabbatean," *Studia Rosenthaliana* 27, nos. 1–2 (1993): 5–12.
139. Scholem, "Redemption Through Sin"; Jacob Frank, *Sayings of the Lord . . . ,* ed. and trans. H. Lenowitz (New York: Scholar's Press, forthcoming); A. Kraushar, *The End to the Sabbataian Heresy,* ed. H. Levy (Lanham, Md.: University Press of America, 2000).

140. See Schacter, "Rabbi Jacob Emden." For comparison, see, e.g., the rabbinic controversies described in E. Zimmer, *Fiery Embers of the Scholars: The Trials and Tribulations of German Rabbis in the Sixteenth and Seventeenth Centuries* (Hebrew) (Be'er Sheva: Ben-Gurion University Press, 1999). On the widespread nature of this controversy, see Sid Z. Leiman's chapter in this volume.
141. See Scholem, "Redemption Through Sin," in *The Messianic Idea,* 140–41; H. Levine, "Frankism as a 'Cargo Cult' and the Haskalah Connection: Myth, Ideology, and the Modernization of Jewish Consciousness," in *Essays in Modern Jewish History in Honor of Ben Halperin,* ed. F. Malino and P. C. Albert (London: Associated University Presses, 1982), 81–94; J. Katz, "On the Question of a Connection Between Sabbateanism, Haskalah, and Reform" (Hebrew), in *Studies in Jewish Religious and Intellectual History Presented to Alexander Altmann,* ed. S. Stein and R. Loewe (University: University of Alabama Press, 1979), 83–100; S. Werses, *Haskalah and Sabbateanism: The Story of a Controversy* (Hebrew) (Jerusalem: Shazar Center for Jewish History, 1988).
142. Israel, *European Jewry;* J. Katz, *Tradition and Crisis: Jewish Society at the End of the Middle Ages,* trans. B. D. Cooperman (New York: New York University Press, 1993).
143. See E. Fram, *Ideals Face Reality: Jewish Law and Life in Poland, 1550–1655* (Cincinnati: Hebrew Union College Press, 1997).
144. See Katz, *Tradition and Crisis;* Davis, "The Ten *Questions* of Eliezer Eilburg."
145. See G. D. Hundert, ed., *Essential Papers on Hasidism: Origins to Present* (New York: New York University Press, 1991); Hundert, *New Perspectives on the Beginning of Hasidism* (New York: Hunter College, 2002); A. Rapoport-Albert, ed., *Hasidism Reappraised* (London: Vallentine Mitchell, 1996).
146. In reaction to Jacob Katz and *Wissenschaft* historiography, scholars today have largely rejected the Germanocentric view of *Haskalah* and change in the eighteenth century. At least in the religious sphere, however, Germany holds a special place, for it was disproportionately influential in the "modernization" of Judaism, if not the Jewish people. This will be manifest from the networks of communication between liberal Jewish thinkers all over western Europe at the time.
147. See A. Arkush, *Moses Mendelssohn and the Enlightenment* (Albany: State University of New York Press, 1994); D. Sorkin, *The Transformation of German Jewry, 1780–1840* (Detroit: Wayne State University Press, 1999); R. Jospe and S. M. Wagner, eds., *Great Schisms in Jewish History* (Denver: Center for Jewish Studies, University of Denver; New York: Ktav, 1981).
148. See M. A. Meyer, *Response to Modernity: A History of the Reform Movement in Judaism* (Detroit: Wayne State University Press, 1995); M. A. Meyer, *The Origins of the Modern Jew: Jewish Identity and European Culture in Germany, 1749–1824* (Detroit: Wayne State University Press, 1979).
149. See M. Breuer, "The Gradual Decline in Jewish Communal Autonomy," and "Internal Weakening of Rabbinical and Communal Authority," in *German Jewish History in Modern Times,* vol. 1, ed. M. A. Meyer and M. Brenner (New York: Columbia University Press, 1996), 251–60.
150. See H. Tirosh-Samuelson, "Philosophy and Kabbalah: 1200–1600," in *The Cambridge Companion to Medieval Jewish Philosophy,* ed. D. H. Frank and O. Leaman (Cambridge: Cambridge University Press, 2003), esp. 236–41, and G. Vajda,

Recherches sur la philosophie et la kabbale dans la pensée juive du Moyen Age (Paris and La Haye: Mouton, 1962), 115–297.

151. See Twersky, "Religion and Law," 69–77.
152. See I. Twersky, "Talmudists, Philosophers, Kabbalists: The Quest for Spirituality in the Sixteenth Century," in *Jewish Thought in the Sixteenth Century,* ed. B. D. Cooperman (Cambridge, Mass.: Harvard University Center for Jewish Studies, 1983), 441, and J. Katz, "Halakhah and Kabbalah as Competing Disciplines of Study," in Green, *Jewish Spirituality,* 2: 34–63.
153. One such figure was Jehiel Nissim da Pisa (sixteenth century), who was deeply versed in the Aristotelian tradition; see Twersky, "Talmudists, Philosophers, Kabbalists," 443–47, and Bonfil, *Rabbis and Jewish Communities in Renaissance Italy,* 284–89.
154. See, e.g., Mishnah Sanhedrin 10:1 and *Maimonides' Commentary on the Mishnah* ad loc., trans. Fred Rosner (New York: Sepher-Hermon Press, 1981), 134–88.
155. See Menachem M. Kellner, *Dogma in Medieval Jewish Thought, From Maimonides to Abravanel* (Oxford: Littman Library, 1986); Kellner, "Heresy and the Nature of Faith in Medieval Jewish Philosophy," *Jewish Quarterly Review* 77, no. 4 (1987): 299–318; Kellner, *Must a Jew Believe Anything?* (London: Littman Library, 1999); Marc B. Shapiro, *The Limits of Orthodox Theology: Maimonides' Thirteen Principles Reappraised* (Oxford: Littman Library, 2004).
156. On the resurrection controversy of the 1190s in the East, see Stroumsa, "Twelfth-century Concepts of Soul and Body." On the controversy a decade later in the West, see B. Septimus, *Hispano-Jewish Culture in Transition,* 39–60. See, in general, the material assembled in J. Dienstag, ed., *Eschatology in Maimonidean Thought: Messianism, Resurrection, and the World to Come* (New York: Ktav, 1983).
157. See Sarachek, *Faith and Reason;* Silver, *Maimonidean Criticism and the Maimonidean Controversy, 1180–1240;* R. Jospe, "Faith and Reason: The Controversy Over Philosophy," in *Great Schisms in Jewish History,* ed. R. Jospe and S. M. Wagner (New York: Ktav, 1981), 73–117; I. Dobbs-Weinstein, "The Maimonidean Controversy," in *History of Jewish Philosophy,* ed. D. H. Frank and O. Leaman (London: Routledge, 1997), 331–49; and R. Ben-Shalom, "The Ban Placed by the Community of Barcelona on the Study of Philosophy and Allegorical Preaching—A New Study," *Revue des études juives* 159 (2000): 387–404.
158. See B. Septimus, "Piety and Power in Thirteenth-Century Catalonia," 197–230.
159. See R. Ben-Shalom, "Communication and Propaganda Between Provence and Spain: The Controversy Over Extreme Allegorization (1303–6)," in *Communication in the Jewish Diaspora,* ed. S. Menache (Leiden: Brill, 1996), 171–224.
160. See, e.g., R. Ben-Shalom, "The Ban Placed by the Community of Barcelona on the Study of Philosophy and Allegorical Preaching—A New Study," *Revue des études juives* 159 (2000): 387–404.
161. See da Costa, *Examination of Pharisaic Traditions* and the bibliography in notes 128–31 above.

I

Rabbinic Judaism and Its Boundaries in the Middle Ages

1

Arrogance, Bad Form, and Curricular Narrowness

Belletristic Critiques of Rabbinic Culture from Medieval Spain and Provence

ADENA TANENBAUM

On October 14, 1663, the curious Samuel Pepys visited a London synagogue. As luck would have it, it was the festival of Simḥat Torah when, as Cecil Roth put it, "The Jew traditionally allowed himself some license even in the synagogue."[1] Unaware that he had witnessed anything out of the ordinary, Pepys confided to his diary, "Lord! to see the disorder, laughing, sporting, and no attention, but confusion in all their service, more like brutes than people knowing the true God, would make a man forswear ever seeing them more: and indeed I never did see so much, or could have imagined there had been any religion in the whole world so absurdly performed as this."[2] Like his seventeenth-century English namesake, Samuel ha-Nagid (993–1056) was appalled by worship lacking in decorum. But the Nagid was hardly a stranger to the synagogue: master poet, seasoned statesman, and soldier, Samuel b. Joseph Halevi Ibn Nagrela was also a respected and powerful communal leader and one of the foremost talmudic authorities of his day.[3] Nevertheless, as an Andalusian courtier and aesthete, with a passion for elegance and eloquence, he expected communal prayer and study to adhere to a certain etiquette. Uncouth devotees became the object of his patrician disdain. In his satirical "Ha-yirhav ha-zeman bi-rvi ve-rava" (Will fate be cruel to Rabbi and

Rava?), Samuel (here identified with the poem's speaker) vents his contempt for a talmudist and his students whose coarse manner and unseemly ways affront the poet's refined sensibilities.

Will fate be cruel to Rabbi and Rava?
  Does it have a quarrel with the Talmud—
To place it in the hands of fools,
  men of girth and gowns and gray hair?
And every boor who asserts, "I am
  Mephiboshet, and Rav Hai is like Ziba my steward"
thinks that with fringes and beard
  and turban he will head the Academy!
Remember, my brother, when we both went
  to the synagogue on Hoshana Rabba
and heard close by a donkey bray,
  cows shrieking and lowing?
And I asked, "Who has turned the house of God
  into a cow-shed? It's a sin and a scandal!"
And they said, "No asses or fatlings are in the house of the Lord—
  they're simply studying Talmud."
So I cried, "You've changed the instruction and Law;
  now what am I to do?"
Angry, we came to the house of God
  (I wish we had strayed from the path!)
We saw teacher and students swaying their heads
  like a tamarisk tree in the desert.
Their mouths reviled Hillel and Shammai;
  they were cheeky to Rabbi Akiva.
The teacher drew out his discourse,
  and pried a few words from their mouths.
I sat there, irate at the sight;
  my soul grew grievously sad.
I respectfully asked how he was,
  but he answered with malice and hate.
He started reciting the blessings
  in a coarse voice, like an army or swarm.
He praised God, who'd not made him a woman
  but a man—and I answered him thus:
Do you count yourself among men?
  By God, you're only a female![4]

Samuel's indignation is kindled by a combination of arrogance, bad form, and religious posturing. The boorish, self-aggrandizing talmudist and his awkward students are, in Peter Cole's translation, "stuffed old fools in robes" (*peta'im, metei beten ve-adderet ve-seivah*), whose scholarly pretensions are an insult to the illustrious Rav Hai (the last of the Babylonian *geonim;* d. 1038), and a slap in the face to the tannaitic giants Hillel, Shammai, and Rabbi Akiva. They place undue emphasis on externals, expecting their ritual fringes, beards, and turbans to carry religious weight with their contemporaries. Much of the poet's critique is stylistic and directed at their deportment: during study, the scholar and his students bray like asses and sway furiously.[5] The poem's one homonymic rhyme, *aravah,* links Hoshana Rabba (here called *yom aravah,* lit. "the Day of Willows") with their lurching to and fro (*ke-ar'ar ba-aravah;* "like a tamarisk in the wilderness"), suggesting that their movements are especially violent when performing the Hoshana Rabba ritual of circling the synagogue with a bunch of willow sprigs which are then beaten against the ground.[6] (Like Pepys, Samuel happened upon the indecorous worshipers on a holiday that occurs once a year, though in contrast with Simḥat Torah, it is quite a solemn day.) The teacher's exposition is interminable, his pedagogic approach overly forceful. He prays in a coarse, bellowing voice, and lacks social graces. Confronted with such shameless indelicacy and clumsiness, the poet becomes enraged. His aristocratic sense of propriety is offended, and his repulsion is palpable. As a member of the cultural elite, Samuel had thoroughly assimilated the Arabic *adab* ideal of the gentleman-scholar, for whom the cultivation of superb style—in conversation, composition, and comportment—was de rigueur.[7] Clearly, the uncouth talmudist and his gauche disciples have not absorbed the Andalusian courtier-rabbis' exemplary elegance and élan. Though they appear to belong to the same broad cultural orbit, the poem's protagonists are locked in a socially conditioned clash of behavioral norms and scholarly expectations.

Admittedly, the encounter described might be imaginary. The poetic genre afforded the Nagid a literary vehicle for vaunting his cultivated tastes and deploying his sharp tongue, while indulging his creative powers. Since Hebrew poets had appropriated the poetic lampoon (*hijā'*) from Arabic letters, where it was a standard part of the repertoire, one might argue that "Ha-yirhav ha-zeman" is merely a clever literary exercise. But the poem—like many in Samuel's *dīwān*—has an editorial superscription that conveys the circumstances of its composition.[8] Written in Judeo-Arabic, these headings are generally thought to preserve some kernel of historicity. We are told that this piece is "about people he came upon and heard studying Talmud in an extremely distorted fashion (*'alā ghāya min al-taḥrīf*), and he described them and their teacher."[9] The term *taḥrīf* would have resonated with Samuel's medieval readers, for it was the technical term used in Muslim polemics to charge that the Jews had falsified their Scriptures in order to remove all allusion to Muhammad's advent.[10] While Muslims accused Jews (and Christians) of *deliberate* scriptural corruption, our poetic study group distorts their Talmud because they are too ignorant to read it properly. Bungled readings have also led to their inadvertent alteration of Scripture, hence Samuel's accusation, "You have changed the instruction and Law" (*hamirotem te'udah ve-torah*). His criticisms, then, are not only stylistic or cosmetic, for the group's slovenly study habits have substantive halakhic—or perhaps theological—ramifications.

No one in his generation had done more than the Nagid to encourage serious halakhic study in Spain, based on correct, authoritative texts. A generous patron of scholars, he amassed a vast library, employing scribes to copy previously unavailable works, and charging agents throughout the Middle East and North Africa with acquiring collections of geonic responsa and other halakhic writings. A critical scholar in his own right, Samuel composed the first influential legal code in Spain. Though these activities enabled Hispano-Jewry to grow ever more independent of the Babylonian *geonim*, his poetic eulogies and encomia voice the utmost respect and affection for the outstanding halakhic authorities of his day in the Land of Israel, Babylonia, and North Africa.[11] Rather than a critique of rabbinic culture from without, his is an informed censure from within the Andalusian tradition, driven by an intolerance of scholarly amateurishness and uncultivated religious conduct.

The sanctimony of boors is also denounced by Moses Ibn Ezra (ca. 1055–after 1138) in "Leshon dim'o yegalleh sod ṣefuno" (His tear's tongue betrays his heart's hidden woe), one of a series of poems lamenting the poet's exile to Christian Spain following the Almoravid conquest of his native Granada in 1090.[12] Ibn Ezra complains that fate has thrust him among a brutish people—contrary, deceitful, proud, and self-satisfied. Invoking a motif familiar from the Nagid's poem, he deplores these men who consider themselves more learned than the foremost sages of earlier generations. Playing on *ya'shim* and *Shammai, Hillel* and *yeholel*, Ibn Ezra reproaches them for condemning

Shammai's words and dismissing Hillel's teachings as so much foolishness (v. 14). Their pretensions also extend to the realm of worship: they draw out their prayer to prove their piety, attempting to deceive not only their fellows but their Maker as well (v. 15). At midnight they cry out (in penitential devotion) until they are hoarse, yet they pray with their mouths, not with their hearts (v. 16). Ibn Ezra seems to be referring to the custom of rising before dawn to recite *seliḥot,* or supererogatory penitential prayers, during the High Holiday season. His critique of the worshipers' superficiality echoes Baḥya Ibn Paquda's pietistic distinction between external "Duties of the Limbs" and internal "Duties of the Heart." In his *Book of Direction to the Duties of the Heart* (*Kitāb al-hidāya ilā farā'iḍ al-qulūb*), Baḥya writes: "When a man prays only with his tongue, his heart preoccupied with something other than the meaning of the prayer, then his prayer is like a body without a soul, or a shell without contents, for only his body is present; his heart is absent from his prayer."[13] Thus Ibn Ezra's poetic subjects go through the motions of prayer and repentance to affect a pious façade, without true devotion or inwardness, or even rational contemplation—for the heart is also the seat of reason according to philosophically informed thinkers like Baḥya and Moses Ibn Ezra.

The poet's alienation from his coreligionists in Christian Spain is due, in large part, to the cultural chasm that separates them. Like Samuel ha-Nagid, Ibn Ezra was the product of a broad Judeo-Arabic education that combined secular learning with classical Jewish scholarship. He had studied at the rabbinical academy in Lucena under the headship of the Nagid's protégé, Isaac Ibn Ghayyat, a first-rate talmudist and accomplished liturgical poet, whose receptivity to a wide range of ideas is manifest in his philosophical commentary on Ecclesiastes.[14] The urbane scion of an influential Granadan family, Ibn Ezra was thoroughly versed in the *adab* skills required of an Andalusian gentleman. His *Sefer ha-Anaq* is the first book of Hebrew *tajnīs* (homonymic) rhymes in the tradition of Arabic manneristic verse, and his prose works are peppered with maxims attributed to Greek and Islamic philosophers and citations of Hebrew grammarians and Arabic littérateurs.[15] Ibn Ezra was a consummate and prolific poet who cultivated the full range of Andalusian genres, from elegant nature songs to playfully scandalous erotic poems to poignant liturgical pieces. He was also a distinguished literary theorist, whose *Kitāb al-muḥāḍara wa'l-mudhākara* (The Book of Conversation and Discussion) is the only extant book of Hispano-Hebrew poetics. A nuanced endorsement of Arabic-style Hebrew poetry, *Kitāb al-muḥāḍara* draws its illustrative quotes from the Qur'ān and a wide range of Arabic poetry as well as from the Bible and Hebrew verse.[16] His other major prose work, *Maqālat al-ḥadīqa fī ma'na 'l-majāz wa'l-ḥaqīqa,* is devoted to "the meaning of figurative and literal language" in the Bible. Motivated by aesthetic as well as theological concerns, it applies contemporary Arabic literary theory to the scriptural text in an effort to elucidate difficult expressions. That *Maqālat al-ḥadīqa* is also informed by Neoplatonic thought and *kalām* speculations testifies to its author's comprehensive cultural and intellectual commitments.[17]

Ibn Ezra thrived in the company of similarly cosmopolitan thinkers and men of letters. Forced to abandon his intimate circle of friends and familiar milieu, he bemoans his loss. In many prose passages and poems reflecting on his "exile" in northern Spain, he voices a keen sense of displacement and isolation, as well as estrangement from those around him, whom he often derides as uncivilized knaves.[18] These complaints figure in "Leshon dim'o," but the attack on poseurs who pray "with their mouths, not with their hearts" appears motivated by more than a general social and cultural malaise. It reflects extreme distaste for religious hypocrisy, but also a profound dissatisfaction with religious life that is unenlightened and unthinking. The poet's interest in penitential prayer was more than casual: renowned for his poems of contrition, Moses Ibn Ezra became known to history as *Ha-sallaḥ,* the author of *seliḥot* par excellence.[19] His preoccupation with individual spirituality is evident in many of his devotional poems, which integrate contemplative themes drawn from Neoplatonic thought.[20] For a scholar quite so immersed in the life of the mind and the spirit, it was hard to fathom Jews whose religious life seemed devoid of real intellectual or spiritual content. Indeed, in "Leshon dim'o" and similar laments, Ibn Ezra fears that their shallow, common, and culturally impoverished society will dull his own rational faculties and cause him to lose his acute intelligence, polish, and cleverness.[21] His critique, like Samuel ha-Nagid's, though from within rabbinic Judaism, is fueled by a sense of cultural superiority, or perhaps chauvinism, in the face of philistine insolence and religious insincerity. Similarly, the threat he perceives is not to rabbinic authority per se, but rather to his cherished Andalusian brand of broad-minded, sophisticated, and cerebral Judaism.

Communal leaders who postured piously, but actually lacked erudition, made an excellent target for satire. In the twenty-fourth chapter of his rhymed prose narrative, the *Taḥkemoni,* Judah Alḥarizi (1165–1225) turns his attention to a cantor in the city of Mosul in Iraq. Heber the Kenite, the ubiquitous hero of the *Taḥkemoni,* recounts his experiences in a palatial synagogue in that thriving Eastern metropolis. He arrives on the eve of the Sabbath, "in perplexed spirit," and seats himself "in the midst of the throng."[22] Beside him sit "two elderly gentlemen with long beards. . . . They were tall and their bellies were like heaps of wheat. They had despicable souls and their eyes were haughty. . . . When I asked them about their great men and the rest of their community and their ḥazzan, they replied: 'We have a ḥazzan, a preacher. He is meek and shy and bashful; rotund and sleek as the rams of Bashan. His prayer is sweet, his company is loved, and his chanting is beautiful. He instructs in the Torah, is versed in the Scriptures, and gives many fine interpretations of the Prophets. He knows precious *piyyutim* [liturgical poems] and is a singer of songs.' "

Upon hearing this description, Heber offers thanks to God for "deeming [him] worthy to behold" such a distinguished and learned religious leader. While he is engrossed in reverie, the ḥazzan makes his entrance. His appearance bespeaks excessive religiosity, and the net effect is rather ridiculous: on his head is "a shining white turban, two hundred cubits high." He is wearing phylacteries—something not done either at night or on the Sabbath. His beard reaches down to his navel.[23] He is covered with a prayer shawl, which is described as a "blanket." He drags its ritual fringes along the ground and almost trips over them.

Alḥarizi exploits to comical effect the glaring discrepancy between the cantor's farcical conduct and the esteem with which the community regards him.[24] In the presence of such an imposing figure, the congregation trembles in silent awe as they await the opening of the prayer service. Heber the Kenite counts more than one hundred "clear and evident mistakes" in the ḥazzan's prayer, "besides the other [errors] which it is not fitting to mention." Nevertheless, Heber grants him the benefit of the doubt, allowing that he may be preoccupied, or exhausted.

The next morning Heber returns to the synagogue. Enter the ḥazzan, who seats himself "in the place of honor." He begins to recite the morning blessings in a loud, shrill voice, and here too he makes egregious errors, which prove to be an extraordinarily clever parody of portions of the fixed liturgy, achieved through the change of only a word, letter, or vowel:[25] "Blessed art Thou, O Lord, who has created man a beast" (*behemah,* instead of *be-ḥokhmah,* "in wisdom").[26] Instead of "Spare Thy servant also from willful sins" (or: arrogant men; *mi-zedim ḥasokh*)[27] he says, "Train Thy servant also away from olives" (*mi-zeitim ḥanokh*). Instead of "He guards all his bones" (*shomer kol aṣmotav*),[28] he says (*shover kol aṣmotav*), "He breaks all his bones." Instead of "He gives you in plenty the fat of wheat" (*ḥelev ḥittim*),[29] he says, "He gives you in plenty a sharp sword" (*ḥerev ḥaddim*). Instead of "Who covers the heavens with clouds" (*ha-mekhasseh shamayim be-avim*),[30] he says "Who covers the heavens with clothes" (*ha-mekhasseh shamayim begadim*). Instead of "Let Israel rejoice in his Maker" (*yismaḥ yisra'el be-osav*),[31] he says, "Let Ishmael rejoice in Esau" (*yismaḥ yishma'el be-esav*). Instead of "Praise Him with stringed instruments and the pipe" (*halleluhu be-minnim ve-ugav*),[32] he says, "Praise Him with cheeses and cake" (*be-gevinim ve-ugah*). And instead of "In Your power it is to make all [creatures] great and strong" (*u-ve-yadekha le-gaddel u-leḥazzeq la-kol*),[33] he says, "In Your power it is to defame and do injury to all" (*le-gaddef u-lehazzeq la-kol*).

Needless to say, Heber is horrified by this performance which borders on sacrilege and, incidentally, reflects the grotesque precentor's obsession with food.[34] He goes on to describe the arrogant cantor's uncouth movements during prayer: "He covered his face, but not out of humility. He stood haughtily and increased his swaying motions. He shook his shoulders, lifted his right leg and lowered his left, then moved backward slightly." According to David Segal, Alḥarizi's criticism is leveled not just at wild, spasmodic motions that are completely out of place, but also at the cantor's exaggerated and showy rendition of movements that had become customary during prayer, such as the three steps backward taken at the close of the silent *Amidah*.[35] The ḥazzan then begins to recite liturgical poems. He drags out his recitation so long that people start to flee the synagogue, even though the statutory prayers are not yet done. Those who remain are all asleep. By noon the entire hall is empty of worshipers. Like Samuel ha-Nagid, Alḥarizi uses animal imagery to convey the ignorance, boisterous clumsiness, ill-breeding, and downright asininity of his subjects. Describing the congregants' flight, Heber says, "The oxen scattered from the shepherd; the cattle and flocks fled until there were only four asses left, braying and bellowing with the ḥazzan—and they fancied themselves a choir!" As Segal has noted, this motif is foreshadowed when the two elders of the congregation tell Heber their beloved cantor is like a fatted ram, and particularly when the ḥazzan makes his first blasphemous morning blunder, praising God for creating man "a beast" (*behemah*) instead of "in wisdom" (*be-ḥokhmah*).[36]

Alḥarizi's splendid lampoon is humorous, at times even hilarious, yet it is not merely meant to amuse. In his introduction to the *Taḥkemoni,* he signals that the goals of this imaginative work are didactic as well as delightful, edifying as well as entertaining.[37] A rhymed prose narrative interspersed with metrical poems, the *Taḥkemoni* is modeled on the Arabic *maqāma* and consists of fifty self-contained episodes recounting its wandering hero's adventures. Such belletristic works developed primarily in Christian Spain during the post-classical period of Hispano-Hebrew literature (mid-twelfth to fifteenth centuries). They aimed at a broader, socially more diverse audience than Andalusian courtly poetry and treated a correspondingly wide range of subjects.[38] Withering satires of recognizable—and often elite—social types and professions featured prominently. The cantor is an object of ridicule in two slightly earlier belletristic works, Joseph Ibn Zabara's *Sefer Sha'ashu'im* (late twelfth century) and Judah Ibn Shabbetai's *Divrei ha-Alah ve-ha-Niddui* (early thirteenth century), both of which highlight the officiant's moral turpitude and, hence, unsuitability for his official communal post.[39] Scholars have noted that rabbinic tradition set impossibly rigorous standards for the ḥazzan: he should be learned, humble, pious, and have a sweet voice. His public recitation of the liturgy should be letter-perfect, so as to fulfill the obligation of a worshiper who did not have a text before him, or who may not have understood the prayer.[40] Ḥazzanim who had dulcet voices but questionable morals, or who were too free with the text of the set prayers, were denounced in medieval responsa.[41] Baḥya Ibn Paquda (fl. late 11th c.) had censured precentors who flaunted their melodious voices in public prayer and chanted new liturgical poems (*aṣḥāb al-ḥizūn fī 'l-aqwāl al-muḥdatha*) in order to impress their audiences rather than to please God.[42] The manifest disparity between the ideal and reality seems to have fed the Spanish satirists' fascination with the failings and vices of the precentor.[43]

Alḥarizi's ḥazzan is a travesty of the profession: a poseur and an ignoramus whose chanting lacks all musical appeal. Those who nevertheless revere him are themselves described as crass philistines. Effectively, then, the author's low opinion extends to the entire Jewish community of Mosul and its cultural values, such as they are. The chapter ends with a dispute over the propriety of reciting *piyyutim* during the synagogue service, a question long debated in medieval halakhic literature.[44] Angry objections are raised to the ḥazzan's unrestrained interpolation of worthless poems that are not only unintelligible to the congregants but also so lengthy that the worshipers—who only come to synagogue on the Sabbath—leave before they have fulfilled their obligation to hear the statutory prayers. An advocate retorts that "the essence of prayer is praise," and that the most effective and desirable vehicles of worship are the sung *piyyutim,* which most closely approximate the songs of the Levites in Temple times. Alḥarizi gives the opponent of payyetanic embellishment the upper hand, yet his own opposition is motivated by an Andalusian aesthetic disdain for the unruly, bloated Eastern tradition rather than a wholesale repudiation of *piyyut*.[45] Unlike the Andalusians' carefully crafted liturgical poems, the *piyyutim* recited by the ḥazzan in Mosul are "broken, lame, and blind. Their way was crooked, without meter or rhyme, matter or form." A play on the word *meshorer* suggests that the handful of congregants who stay behind to bray and bellow with the cantor fancy themselves not only singers but poets as well! When the advocate of *piyyut* asserts that they in Mosul will not abandon the custom of all congregations—in Spain, the Maghreb, Byzantium, and France—his opponent counters that no other community is so entirely made up of fools and ignoramuses as this one, where not a soul—not even the cantor—understands the words recited in synagogue: "Therefore I say that *qerovot* and poems are permissible everywhere but here." Both disputants repeatedly refer to the *qerovah,* a versified version of the *Amidah* prayer that developed in Byzantine Palestine but fell largely into disuse in medieval Spain, where *piyyutim* no longer replaced portions of the fixed liturgy. Such *piyyutim* of the older, Eastern variety conformed in neither genre, style, nor linguistic texture to the Andalusian poetic principles of balance, symmetry, and eloquence. As an heir to the Andalusian Jewish intellectual and cultural tradition, Alḥarizi measured his Eastern coreligionists against its cultivated and refined standards. Judging from the *Taḥkemoni's* enchanting blend of fiction and realism, he found religious leaders and congregants alike sorely lacking in their poetic and aesthetic sensibilities as well as in their synagogue literacy and decorum.

Religious hypocrisy, insincerity, and ineptitude were not the only aspects of rabbinic culture pilloried in literary sources. Poetry and rhymed prose narratives also served to address questions of curricular priorities and intellectual ideals.[46] Authors steeped in philosophical learning used these belletristic media to criticize the insularity and parochialism of scholars interested solely in Talmud study. Solomon Ibn Gabirol (1021/22–ca. 1057/58), an accomplished man of letters and the first Jewish philosopher in Spain, composed biting poetic responses to nameless opponents of his metaphysical studies. In "Nefesh asher alu she'oneha" he describes his antagonists as benighted anti-rationalists, complaining, "My soul thirsts for a man of intellect, but she can find no one to slake her thirst" (v. 9).[47] Disparaging his detractors as "thorns and thistles," he asks why they object to his pursuit of philosophical wisdom (v. 21), and vows to persevere until he attains knowledge of the Lord (v. 31). In "Niḥar be-qor'i geroni" he laments his isolation amidst the Jews of Saragossa, who quarrel with him "as with a Greek" (v. 26)—in an apparent allusion to the Greek origin of his philosophical theories—and who relate to his quest for metaphysical knowledge as though it were magic or divination (v. 34).[48] Since Ibn Gabirol provides few clues to his adversaries' commitments, we cannot clearly establish that they are provincial talmudists opposed to any sort of intellectual inquiry that does not directly further religious observance. As Bernard Septimus has observed, his critics "need not have been obscurantists"; Ibn Gabirol had contemporaries in Saragossa who were engaged in scientific disciplines such as logic and philology, yet still considered philosophical rationalism corrosive of faith.[49]

But among the Andalusian Jewish intelligentsia there was a recurrent critique of excessive talmudism. Ibn Gabirol's younger contemporary and fellow Saragossan, Baḥya Ibn Paquda, was both a *dayyan* and a thinker whose magnum opus shows strong affinities with Islamic speculative, ascetic, and mystical teachings.[50] In his *Hidāya* Baḥya censures those who devote themselves to the study of Torah out of impure motives—i.e., in order to win acclaim—and are so single-minded in their goal that they neglect their religious obligation to investigate rationally the fundamentals of their faith. He goes on to criticize scholars who immerse themselves in halakhic minutiae at the expense of improving their moral qualities and honing their spiritual sensibilities.[51] The multifaceted career of Abraham Ibn Ezra (1089/92–1064/67) encompassed biblical exegesis, poetry, Hebrew grammar, philosophy, and science. Small wonder, then, that in his *Yesod Mora,* a work devoted to the rationale for the biblical commandments, Ibn Ezra deplores the curricular narrowness of those Talmud scholars who have no interest or grounding in any complementary discipline because the Talmud furnishes them with all they need to know in order to observe the *miṣvot*.[52] This sort of tunnel vision was directly at odds with the paideia of

Andalusian intellectuals, whose curriculum combined propaedeutic and religious sciences and culminated in philosophical study.[53] For these thinkers, knowledge grasped by the mind through rational demonstration was qualitatively superior to received knowledge, even though they accepted the ultimate authority of revelation. Thus, in his introduction, Baḥya adduces biblical verses that give "priority to knowledge by demonstration (*'ilm al-istidlāl*) over knowledge acquired through tradition (*'ilm al-khabar wa 'l-naql*)."[54] It was imperative to investigate philosophically the authoritative teachings of religious tradition.[55]

The premium placed on rational verification of truths known through religious tradition even found expression in synagogue poetry. Baḥya's contemporary, Levi Ibn Altabban, tellingly extols reason alongside revelation in a *piyyut* for the morning service of Shavuot, the festival marking the giving of the Torah. Opening with the words "Ha-sekhel ve-ha-dat shenei me'orot," the poem describes reason and religion as two luminaries that enlighten man and teach him God's ways. The preponderance of light imagery is characteristic of the *me'orah* genre, composed for recitation before the blessing praising the Creator of the heavenly lights (*yoṣer ha-me'orot*). Ibn Altabban skillfully fuses traditional descriptions of the enlightening properties of the Torah with the Neoplatonic metaphor of the intellect's illumination of the soul. Here is the first half of the poem in Raymond Scheindlin's translation:

Reason and religion are two luminaries,
Restoring man's soul, enlightening his eyes.

  Philosophers, the wise, have taught
  That reason sheds its light over the soul,
  Ever revealing to it whatever is hidden,
Wandering around it, teaching it
To go in God's straight paths.

  So too those who keep the Torah's law,
  Dearer than all things, in truth;
  It brings out to light all who walk in darkness;
An adornment of grace, a diadem for your head,
For God's words are words of truth . . . [56]

As Scheindlin has observed, there is a certain ambiguity in Ibn Altabban's treatment of reason and revelation. At first glance, they seem to be complementary, equally weighty sources of divine truth. But the poet's use of the term *me'orot* (luminaries) has associations for the reader: according to a rabbinic homily on the biblical creation story, the sun and the moon, although initially equal in stature, did not long remain on the same footing.[57] There is thus a subtle suggestion that, as the second luminary—the *ma'or ha-qaton*—revelation is epistemologically inferior to reason, the *ma'or ha-gadol*. Read in this way, the poem contains an implicit critique of those who rely on religious tradition without exercising their reason to substantiate its truths.

The depiction of reason and religion as two lights recurs in a series of treatises on the relationship between philosophy and revelation from the fifteenth century on.[58] In the thirteenth century it occurs in a slightly different guise, in the introductory poem to Shem Tov Falaquera's *Epistle of the Debate* (*Iggeret ha-vikkuaḥ*). A rhymed prose disputation between a philosopher and a Torah scholar, the *Epistle* was intended to convince a pious, philosophically unsophisticated audience of the permissibility of rational inquiry and of "the Agreement That Exists Between the Law and Wisdom" (as per the tract's subtitle).[59] Adumbrating the work's spirited apology for philosophy, the prefatory poem features the following lines:

> Fools think that between the Law
> And Thought there is at all times war.
>
> They think that the hatred of wisdom
> Is posited by the Law.
>
> They say that all her foundations
> She completely destroys.
>
> They do not understand that wisdom
> Is a twin sister of the Law.[60]

In the body of the text, the philosopher paints an unflattering picture of believers with obscurantist instincts:

> There are men who are lacking in their intellect, who see themselves as the believers in the Law and observers of its commandments, and yet, when they hear a word of the sciences from a scholar, they hasten to spread the report that he is among the infidels, without

> examining whether it is true or not. . . . Even though this [scientific teaching] may be obligated by our Law and among the things that strengthen our faith, they will out of their stupidity deny it and reproach him who has said it, just because it is mentioned in the philosophical books.[61]

In the course of the debate, the philosopher touches on several fundamental cruxes of medieval Jewish philosophy.[62] By the end, he succeeds in convincing the Torah scholar that philosophers are not infidels who deny the existence of the Creator; that Scripture contains profound philosophical truths which must be elicited through speculation; and that one's faith will be stronger if attained through intellect than if attained through tradition.

Not much is known of Falaquera's biography, though he seems to have moved between northern Spain and Provence, a geographic and intellectual crossroads where the Andalusian scientific and philosophical tradition met—and at times collided with—the rabbinic culture of northern France.[63] By Falaquera's time (ca. 1225–95), Provence had been home to several generations of Andalusian emigré translators rendering influential philosophical, exegetical, and scientific works from Arabic into Hebrew.[64] Throughout the thirteenth century, Provençal Jewry was embroiled in a series of bitter controversies over Maimonides' rationalistic teachings. Notwithstanding their different foci and complex intercommunal alliances, these were at base curricular battles over the acceptability of studying rationalist works. At the time of Falaquera's birth, the repercussions of the resurrection controversy were still keenly felt, and the first Maimonidean Controversy was about to erupt. It is against this background that Falaquera's oeuvre must be read and his mission understood.[65]

Written during the author's youth, the *Epistle of the Debate* makes purely didactic use of poetry and rhymed prose; the work has none of the belletristic brilliance, rhetorical flair, or linguistic virtuosity of Alḥarizi's *Taḥkemoni*. Yet Falaquera had been a prolific and gifted poet in the Andalusian style who toward middle age renounced poetry and belles lettres for the pursuit of philosophy.[66] His *Book of the Seeker* (*Sefer ha-Mevaqqesh,* 1264) reflects this reorientation of curricular priorities with its narrative of a young man in quest of true wisdom and man's ultimate felicity.[67] Determined to identify the most important of all disciplines in life, the Seeker embarks on a journey reminiscent of the Islamic *ṭalab al-'ilm,* or search for knowledge.[68] Along the way he encounters representatives of various social classes and professions, allowing the author to voice sharp social criticism through satirical portrayals of types drawn from contemporary Jewish society. The Seeker's sixteen interlocutors include a wealthy man, an artisan, a doctor, a pious and morally virtuous man, a grammarian, a poet, two types of Torah scholar, an astronomer, and finally a philosopher. He questions and challenges each in turn about his calling, and apprentices himself to each for an extended period. The meeting with the philosopher marks the climax of the search; his is the only exposition that satisfies the Seeker.

Sefer ha-Mevaqqesh is divided into two parts; the first is composed in lively rhymed prose interspersed with clever metrical poetry, while the second is written in straight prose. The meeting with the poet concludes the first section of the work. Much of the exchange with the poet is devoted to a moral condemnation of poetry, accomplished through a parody of the elevated language of the Bible. Like other thirteenth-century critics, the Seeker insists that falsehood is integral to poetry, since poets are expected "to lie explicitly," flattering miserly patrons by calling them generous. He expresses an Aristotelian scorn for poetry's metaphorical language, the product of man's imaginative faculty, which is inferior to the rational faculty. The Seeker advises the poet to abandon the vanities of his art for the pursuit of true philosophical wisdom. Eventually, the poet recants, but just to drive home his point, Falaquera as narrator steps in and informs us that "these are my final poems. From this day on I have no share in poetry and no part in songs."[69] The second part of *Sefer ha-Mevaqqesh* will be supported exclusively "upon pillars of prose."[70] Still, Falaquera had a complex relationship with the Andalusian literary tradition. His ostensible repudiation of poetry may not be as straightforward as it appears at first glance. By his time there was a well-established convention of mature Hebrew poets renouncing the frivolous compositions of their youth. Classical poets such as Moses Ibn Ezra and Judah Halevi had paid lip service to this penitential motif some two centuries earlier. Moreover, the fact that Falaquera uses poetry to discredit the first seven professions the Seeker encounters would seem to imply that the art has a useful if circumscribed function to fulfill in society. Because of its appeal for the educated lay reader, poetry could be profitably employed to guide a thinking person toward the ultimate goal of perfection through philosophical study.[71]

Falaquera's treatment of the Torah scholar is also complex; both the "Believer" in the Torah (*ma'amin ba-torah*) and the man learned in

Torah *and* philosophical wisdom (*ḥakham ba-torah u-ve-ḥokhmah*) have valuable lessons to teach, which correspond to two stages in Falaquera's graduated curriculum.[72] Although the Seeker is not fully satisfied with either encounter, neither portrait is openly satirical, nor remotely as ridiculous as some of the vignettes in part 1. The Seeker's meeting with the *ma'amin* inaugurates part 2 of the work, which showcases the genuinely important disciplines leading to the attainment of true wisdom. Predictably, the Believer holds that the key to man's ultimate felicity is complete devotion to Torah study and observance of the commandments. But Falaquera does not simply perpetuate this stereotype. To further his didactic goal of making philosophy palatable to his readers, he subtly injects elements of philosophical discourse into the Torah scholar's presentation. Though the Believer is hostile to the idea of rational demonstration and reliance on human reason, he outlines the principles of the Torah with terminology and categories drawn from contemporary religious philosophy: belief in the existence of the Creator, in His unity, in creation *ex nihilo,* etc. The Seeker disparages exclusive dependence on received tradition for these fundamental beliefs, but the Believer vehemently denies any need for validation through rational demonstration. The encounter ends with a heated exchange.[73]

The Seeker then moves on to the Torah scholar who is also a philosophical adept.[74] He too insists that man attains true felicity through observance of the Torah, but unlike the insular scholar, he endorses philosophical study as the sole means of rationally supporting and comprehending the Torah's root principles and profound mysteries. He exercises caution, lest he disclose esoteric knowledge to the uninitiated, and recommends immersion in Maimonides' *Guide of the Perplexed,* but only after proper preparatory study.[75] He outlines a graded curriculum that corresponds fairly closely to the Seeker's progressive studies, and which includes a critique of excessive preoccupation with halakhic matters: One should start with the written Torah and then proceed to the Oral Law, in conjunction with Alfasi's *Halakhot* and Maimonides' *Mishneh Torah* and Mishnah commentary. These should be adequate for one who wants to know the law's practical application or *pesaq,* although it is useful to examine the talmudic give-and-take in order to sharpen one's mind. However, it is not appropriate to spend all one's days working out difficult talmudic cruxes, as do some who exhaust themselves puzzling over a single *halakhah* during the course of an entire night, yet in the morning still have no definitive solution. After adequate Torah study, one should advance to natural sciences and metaphysics; then one will find knowledge of God. But one must take care not to forget the words of the Torah. The scholar warns the Seeker not to believe anything the philosophers say that contradicts Scripture, for God's revelation is superior to rational inquiry, and it alone leads to knowledge of the truth. Most of the philosophers' metaphysical opinions are untrue, and their knowledge of natural science is a mixture of falsehood and truth. Despite the scholar's ambivalent attitude toward philosophy, the Seeker stays with him for five years, profitably studying Torah and commentaries. Only then does he seek out experts in the various secular sciences, ending his quest with the philosopher.

A confirmed Maimonidean, Falaquera was committed to disseminating the Master's thought and defending his reputation. Steeped in Arabic learning, he advanced the transmission of the Maimonidean corpus to readers beyond the Islamic cultural orbit through translation, consolidation, and commentary. His *Moreh ha-Moreh,* considered one of the most significant medieval commentaries on the *Guide,* includes Falaquera's own translations of difficult passages.[76] By rendering extracts from the Arabic original of *Meqor Ḥayyim* (*Fons Vitae*) into Hebrew, he also helped to preserve the Neoplatonic thought of Solomon Ibn Gabirol in Jewish circles.[77] A consummate intellectual, he controlled highly abstruse speculative works by Muslim Aristotelians as well.[78] Yet he is best known as a popularizer whose several encyclopedias and literary works such as the *Epistle of the Debate* and *Book of the Seeker* were intended to facilitate access to philosophical learning and to disprove the accusation that philosophy corrodes faith and undermines the Torah.[79] For Falaquera, rabbinic learning and observance untouched by—or, worse, hostile to—rational inquiry was intellectually impoverished. Only philosophy could lead to the fullest appreciation of Torah and to true wisdom.

Though our select literary critiques span almost three centuries, they are representative rather than exhaustive. The trend would continue into the fourteenth century, with Kalonymus ben Kalonymus's scathing exposure of degenerate Torah scholars in his *Even Boḥan* (Touchstone) and Isaac Polgar's trenchant debate between a divine and a philosopher in his polemical defense of Judaism, *Ezer ha-Dat.*[80] Despite the chronological and contextual diversity of these pieces, their shared medium sets them apart from other responses or challenges to rabbinic culture. The belletristic genre had many advantages:

it could be light-hearted and enjoyable to read, and thus might reach a broader audience than ponderous prose denunciations or humorless diatribes. Though it often aspired to verisimilitude, it allowed for poetic license and artful blending of fiction with reality. One could take aim at recognizable types while seeming to engage in ad hominem attacks. And one could entertain and educate at the same time. But our texts have more in common than their poetic or belletristic genres. The men who authored them were prominent polymaths, productive in diverse fields. Strong personalities, they did not hesitate to express their likes and dislikes or their aesthetic and intellectual preferences. All were products of a broad Judeo-Arabic education combining secular and religious studies, though not all were proficient in each and every discipline of its rich curriculum. Courtiers, literati, translators, and travelers, our critics moved with ease between the Jewish and Islamic cultural worlds, remaining faithful to the one while appropriating the most appealing elements of the other. There is nothing particularly heterodox about their critiques: all were insiders to rabbinic culture who acknowledged the authority of Scripture and rabbinic law. But their cosmopolitanism led to dissatisfaction with religious leaders, scholars, and community members whose prayer and study struck them as graceless, pretentious, insincere, insular, or parochial. Samuel Pepys might have had to concede that they were fairly civilized.

Notes

1. Cecil Roth, *A History of the Jews of England,* 3rd ed. (Oxford: Oxford University Press, 1964), 174.
2. H. B. Wheatley, ed., *The Diary of Samuel Pepys,* vol. 1 (New York: Random House, 1893), 745.
3. Samuel bore the title *Nagid* ("Prince") as regional head of the Maghrebi community and its supreme representative before the government. The most recent biography of the Nagid is Ḥayyim Schirmann, *The History of Hebrew Poetry in Muslim Spain* (Hebrew) (Jerusalem: Magnes Press and Ben-Zvi Institute, 1995), 183–256. The most comprehensive biography in English is still Schirmann, "Samuel Hanagid, The Man, The Soldier, The Politician," *Jewish Social Studies* 13 (1951): 99–126. See also the introduction to Leon Weinberger, *Jewish Prince in Moslem Spain* (University: University of Alabama Press, 1973), 1–17.
4. In preparing my translation I have consulted Peter Cole, *Selected Poems of Shmuel HaNagid* (Princeton: Princeton University Press, 1996), 33–34, and Weinberger, *Jewish Prince in Moslem Spain,* 98. For the Hebrew text see Ḥayyim Schirmann, *Ha-Shirah ha-Ivrit bi-Sefarad u-vi-Provans* [Hebrew Poetry in Spain and Provence;

henceforth *HPSP*] (Jerusalem and Tel Aviv: Bialik Institute and Dvir Company, 1954–56; 2nd ed., 1960–61), 1:147–48, and Samuel ha-Nagid, *Diwan,* vol. 1: *Ben Tehilim,* ed. Dov Jarden (Jerusalem: Hebrew Union College Press, 1966), 228–29.

5. This is one of the earliest Andalusian references to movement during prayer and study; see Eric Zimmer, *Society and Its Customs: Studies in the History and Metamorphosis of Jewish Customs* (Hebrew) (Jerusalem: Zalman Shazar Center, 1996), 72–111, esp. 99, and Yehuda Ratzaby, *Migginzē Shirat Hakkēdem* (Jerusalem: Misgav Yerushalayim, 1991), 256–61. In the twelfth century, Judah Halevi seemed less troubled by Jewish swaying during study, which he traced back to a time when the many members of a study group all bent over one book; see *Kuzari* 2:79–80.
6. The Nagid's halakhic work alludes to a legal disagreement over the implementation of the ritual: the Babylonian rite used a *lulav* (palm frond), while the Palestinian-Italian rite of Samuel's teacher, Rabbi Ḥanokh of Bari, used only willow; see *Hilkhot ha-Nagid,* ed. Mordecai Margalioth (Jerusalem: American Academy for Jewish Research, 1962), Introduction, 22, and sec. 14, 112–13. In its original biblical context (Jer. 17:6), the simile *ke-ar'ar ba-aravah* evokes the barrenness and isolation awaiting the man "who turns his thoughts from the Lord." The Nagid's allusion thus intimates that the objects of his scorn are not only physically awkward but religiously insincere as well.
7. On the various uses of the term *adab* in the Middle Ages, see S. A. Bonebakker, "*Adab* and the Concept of *Belles-Lettres,*" in *The Cambridge History of Arabic Literature: 'Abbasid Belles Lettres,* ed. Julia Ashtiany et al. (Cambridge: Cambridge University Press, 1990), 16–30, and Gustave von Grunebaum, *Medieval Islam: A Study in Cultural Orientation,* 2nd ed. (Chicago: University of Chicago Press, 1961), 250–57.
8. Samuel's son Joseph edited his father's *dīwān.*
9. For the Arabic superscription see Samuel ha-Nagid, *Diwan,* 1:228.
10. The Nagid was long thought to have authored an imprudently bold critique of the Qur'ān whose sole surviving fragments were quoted in a polemical response by the eminent Muslim theologian Ibn Ḥazm. However, Sarah Stroumsa has convincingly shown that the passages Ibn Ḥazm quotes were not penned by the Nagid; they are from a lost treatise by the infamous ninth-century Muslim heretic Ibn al-Rāwandī. See Sarah Stroumsa, "From Muslim Heresy to Jewish-Muslim Polemics: Ibn al-Rāwandī's *Kitāb al-Dāmigh,*" *Journal of the American Oriental Society* 107, no. 4 (1987): 767–72, and Sarah Stroumsa, *Freethinkers of Medieval Islam* (Leiden: Brill, 1999), 201–13.
11. See Abraham Ibn Daud, *Sefer ha-Qabbalah,* ed. and trans. Gerson D. Cohen (Philadelphia: Jewish Publication Society, 1967), Hebrew, 56, English, 74–75; and *Hilkhot ha-Nagid,* Introduction, 1–67.
12. For the text of the poem see Moses Ibn Ezra, *Secular Poems,* ed. H. Brody and D. Pagis, 3 vols. (Jerusalem: Schocken, 1935–77), 1:144–46 (no. 142).
13. Baḥya ben Joseph Ibn Paqūda, *Kitāb al-hidāya ilā farā'iḍ al-qulūb (Torat ḥovot ha-levavot),* ed. and trans. J. Qafiḥ (Jerusalem: n.p., 1973), 8:3, p. 343; trans. Menahem Mansoor, *The Book of Direction to the Duties of the Heart* (London: Routledge and Kegan Paul, 1973), 365.
14. See Moses Ibn Ezra, *Kitāb al-muḥāḍara wa'l-mudhākara (Sefer ha-Iyyunim ve-ha-Diyyunim),* ed. and trans. A. S. Halkin (Jerusalem: Mekize Nirdamim, 1975), 39a

(p. 72). For the commentary on Ecclesiastes see *Kitāb al-zuhd,* in *Ḥamesh Megillot im Peirushim Attiqim,* ed. and trans. J. Qafiḥ (Jerusalem: Ha-Aguddah le-Haṣṣalat Ginzei Teiman, 1962) [misattributed to Saadya Gaon].

15. For the full text of *Sefer ha-Anaq* (also known as *Tarshish* and in Arabic as *Kitāb zahr al-riyāḍ*) see Moses Ibn Ezra, *Secular Poems,* 1:295–404; for excerpts with English translation see *Selected Poems of Moses Ibn Ezra,* ed. H. Brody and trans. S. Solis-Cohen (Philadelphia: Jewish Publication Society, 1934), 66–92.
16. On the work's fundamental ambivalence toward Andalusian Hebrew poetry see Raymond Scheindlin, "Rabbi Moshe Ibn Ezra on the Legitimacy of Poetry," *Medievalia et Humanistica* n.s. 7 (1976): 101–15, and Ross Brann, *The Compunctious Poet: Cultural Ambiguity and Hebrew Poetry in Muslim Spain* (Baltimore: Johns Hopkins University Press, 1991), 59–83. For the range of Ibn Ezra's quotations from non-Jewish sources see *Kitāb al-muḥāḍara wa'l-mudhākara,* 314 and 332.
17. See Paul Fenton, *Philosophie et exégèse dans* Le Jardin de la métaphore *de Moïse Ibn 'Ezra, philosophe et poète andalou du XIIe siècle* (Leiden: Brill, 1997).
18. See Brann, *The Compunctious Poet,* 61–68.
19. See the Introduction to Moses Ibn Ezra, *Selected Poems,* xxxii. See also Adena Tanenbaum, "The Andalusian *Seliḥah* and Its Individualistic Conception of Penitence," in *Be'erot Yitzhak: Studies in Memory of Isadore Twersky,* ed. Jay Harris (Cambridge, Mass.: Harvard Center for Jewish Studies and Harvard University Press, 2005), 377–98.
20. On Neoplatonic themes in Ibn Ezra's *piyyut* see Adena Tanenbaum, *The Contemplative Soul: Hebrew Poetry and Philosophical Theory in Medieval Spain* (Leiden: Brill, 2002), 106–31.
21. For additional expressions of longing for his Andalusian intimates and alienation from his northern Spanish coreligionists, whose obscurantism threatens to erode his own prodigious intellect, see, e.g., the following in Ibn Ezra, *Secular Poems:* "Shavti ve-taltalei zeman lo shavu," 1:24–27 (no. 20, to his friends in the West [= Andalusia]), vv. 31–32; "Nadu yemei ha-shaḥarut," 1:116–17 (no. 114), vv. 11–14; "Aḥar yemei ha-shaḥarut," 1:149 (no. 145), vv. 5–6; "Be-rishpei ha-bekhi nafshi serufah," 1:175–77 (no. 176, to Isaac Ibn Barun, requesting a copy of his *Book of Comparison Between the Hebrew and Arabic Languages*), vv. 11, 32–33; "Rikhvei nedodim," 1:195–98 (no. 195), v. 20; and "Yerivi ba'adi yerev amarav," 1:215–19 (no. 214), vv. 52–54.
22. Because it is quite faithful to the original, I have chosen to cite (with slight modification) the translation of V. E. Reichert, *The Tahkemoni of Judah Al-Harizi,* vol. 2 (Jerusalem: Raphael Haim Cohen Ltd., 1973), 110–21. Those interested should also consult David S. Segal's marvelous rhyming translation, *Judah Alḥarizi: The Book of Taḥkemoni* (Oxford: Littman Library, 2001), 215–23, and his insightful analysis, 534–40. For the Hebrew text see Schirmann, *HPSP* 2:161–69, and Judah Alḥarizi, *Taḥkemoni,* ed. I. Toporowsky (Tel Aviv: Maḥbarot le-Sifrut and Mossad Harav Kook, 1952).
23. On attitudes toward beards, see Elliot Horowitz, "On the Significance of the Beard in Jewish Communities in the East and Europe in the Middle Ages and Early Modern Times" (Hebrew), *Pe'amim* 59 (1994): 124–48. In medieval Hebrew satire, excessively long beards often suggest religious hypocrisy; see Judith Dishon, *The Book of Delight by Joseph Ben Meir Zabara* (Hebrew) (Jerusalem: Rubin Mass, 1985),

192n44 (cited by Horowitz, "Significance of the Beard," 136n42). See also the discussion above of Samuel ha-Nagid's disdain for the boorish talmudist who "thinks that with fringes and beard / and turban he will head the Academy!"

24. See Judith Dishon, "Ha-Ḥazzan ba-Maqāma ha-Ivrit bi-Sfarad," *Sinai* 74/5–76 (1974): 242–51, esp. 248, and Segal, *The Book of Taḥkemoni,* 540.
25. See Israel Davidson, *Parody in Jewish Literature* (New York: Columbia University Press, 1907; reprint, New York: AMS Press, 1966), xv. Dishon points out that the ḥazzan regularly exchanges certain pairs of letters; see "Ha-Ḥazzan ba-Maqāma ha-Ivrit," 249. In this connection it is interesting to note that the rabbis of the Talmud prohibited a priest who habitually interchanged certain letters from reciting the priestly blessing before the congregation; see BT Megillah 24b.
26. The introductory blessing, *asher yaṣar et ha-adam be-ḥokhmah,* is recited as part of *Birkhot ha-shaḥar.*
27. Ps. 19:14; the phrases parodied here are all from the section of the service known as *Pesuqei de-zimra* or *Zemirot.*
28. Ps. 34:21.
29. Ps. 147:14.
30. Ps. 147:8.
31. Ps. 149:2.
32. Ps. 150:4.
33. I Chron. 29:12.
34. See Segal, *The Book of Taḥkemoni,* 535, and Dishon, "Ha-Ḥazzan ba-Maqāma ha-Ivrit," 249n49.
35. See Segal, *The Book of Taḥkemoni,* 536–37. This custom goes back to talmudic times; its symbolism and performance are discussed in Saadya Gaon's *Siddur.* See N. Wieder, *The Formation of Jewish Liturgy in the East and the West* (Hebrew), 2 vols. (Jerusalem: Ben-Zvi Institute, Yad Izhak Ben-Zvi, and the Hebrew University of Jerusalem, 1998), 1:172–77.
36. See Segal, *The Book of Taḥkemoni,* 536. Segal notes that Alḥarizi's humorous *asher yaṣar et ha-adam behemah* actually echoes a blessing found in the Italian rite, praising God "who did not make me a beast." On this lesser-known member of the group of morning blessings, "who did not make me a heathen/a slave/a woman," see Wieder, *The Formation of Jewish Liturgy,* 1:206–12.
37. For Alḥarizi's playful reworking of a longstanding penitential genre, see Tanenbaum, *The Contemplative Soul,* 195–217. Alḥarizi's blend of entertainment and moral instruction was much admired by the author of a sixteenth-century Hebrew rhymed prose narrative from Yemen; see Adena Tanenbaum, "Of a Pietist Gone Bad and Des(s)erts Not Had: The Fourteenth Chapter of Zechariah Alḍahiri's *Sefer hamusar,*" *Prooftexts* 23, no. 3 (2003): 297–319.
38. See Dan Pagis, "Variety in Medieval Rhymed Narratives," *Scripta Hierosolymitana* 27 (1978): 79–98.
39. See Dishon, "Ha-Ḥazzan ba-Maqāma ha-Ivrit," 244–48, and Yehuda Ratzaby, "Ḥazzanim in the Literature of the Middle Ages" (Hebrew), *Tatzlil* 5 (1965): 80–83. Also noteworthy is a remarkable, fragmentary *maqāma* relating the story of a cantor who brings a court case against a young man who had rejected his advances despite the cantor's offer to pay him for his services by selling books from the synagogue library. See Matti Huss, "*The Maqama of the Cantor:* Its Possible Sources and

Relation with Medieval Hebrew Homoerotic Literature" (Hebrew), *Tarbiz* 72 (2002–3): 197–244.

40. BT Ta'anit 16a, discussing Ta'anit 2:2, specifies that the ḥazzan must not only be conversant with the prayers but also one "whose youth was unblemished, who is meek and is acceptable to the people; who is skilled in chanting, who has a pleasant voice, and possesses a thorough knowledge of the Torah, the Prophets and the Hagiographa, of the Midrash, *Halachoth* and *Aggadoth* and of all the Benedictions" (trans. *The Babylonian Talmud,* ed. I. Epstein [London: Soncino Press, 1935–52]). BT Ḥullin 24b requires the representative of the community (*sheliaḥ ṣibbur*) to have a fully grown beard as a sign of his maturity. BT Rosh Hashanah 34b mentions the precentor's duty to "clear from his obligation" one who is not familiar with the prayers; see also Maimonides, *Mishneh Torah,* "Tefillah," 8:9–10, and *Shulḥan Arukh: Oraḥ Ḥayyim* 124:1. These sources are cited by A. Z. Idelsohn, *Jewish Music in Its Historical Development* (New York: Schocken, 1975), 101–9; Leo Landman, *The Cantor: An Historic Perspective* (New York: Yeshiva University Press, 1972), 3–8; Segal, *The Book of Taḥkemoni,* 534 and nn. 1–3; and Dishon, "Ha-Ḥazzan ba-Maqāma ha-Ivrit," 242–43. See also Leo Landman, "The Office of the Medieval *Ḥazzan,*" *Jewish Quarterly Review* 62, no. 3 (1972): 156–87 and 62, no. 4 (1972): 246–76.
41. See Dishon, "Ha-Ḥazzan ba-Maqāma ha-Ivrit," 244, and Landman, *The Cantor,* 58–64.
42. Baḥya, *Kitāb al-hidāya,* 5:5, 263; trans. Mansoor, 290. I am grateful to Professor Sid Leiman for calling my attention to this passage.
43. Segal views the two elders' exaggerated claims for their cantor as a parody of the unrealistic rabbinic requirements; see *The Book of Taḥkemoni,* 534.
44. On this debate and its rabbinic antecedents see Ruth Langer, *To Worship God Properly: Tensions Between Liturgical Custom and Halakhah in Judaism* (Cincinnati: Hebrew Union College Press, 1998), 110–87; Ratzaby, *Migginzē Shirat Hakkēdem,* 249–55; and Judith Dishon, "Judah Alharizi and the Dispute about Reciting *Piyyutim* on the Sabbath" (Hebrew), in *Massoret ha-piyyut,* vol. 2, ed. Binyamin Bar-Tikva and Ephraim Hazan (Ramat Gan: Bar-Ilan University Press, 2000), 97–110.
45. In this respect, his condemnation is reminiscent of Abraham Ibn Ezra's censure of Qallirian *piyyut*: as the author of Arabic-style Hebrew poetry, Ibn Ezra had little patience for the compositions of pre-Spanish liturgical poets; see both his comments on Eccles. 5:1 and Joseph Yahalom, "The Poetics of Spanish *Piyyut* in Light of Abraham Ibn Ezra's Critique of Its Pre-Spanish Precedents," in *Abraham Ibn Ezra and His Age,* ed. F. Díaz Esteban (Madrid: Asociación de Orientalistas, 1990), 387–92. Alḥarizi's thorough internalization of Andalusian poetic ideals is evident in his Hebrew poetry, most of which is non-liturgical, and his evaluations of the Andalusian school in chapters 3 and 18 of the *Taḥkemoni.* Arabic-style quantitative verse had made inroads among Eastern Jewish literati in Alḥarizi's day—witness Elazar ben Jacob's treatise on poetics (Judaeo-Arabic text and Hebrew translation edited by Joseph Yahalom [Jerusalem: Ben-Zvi Institute, Yad Izhak Ben-Zvi, and the Hebrew Univerity of Jerusalem, 2001])—but does not seem to have affected the *piyyutim* recited in Mosul. On the state of *piyyut* during what Ezra Fleischer calls the "Late Eastern period" (ninth–eleventh centuries), see his *Hebrew Liturgical Poetry in the Middle Ages* (Hebrew) (Jerusalem: Keter, 1975), 277–330.

46. Of course, these questions were not restricted to belletristic genres. Two of the best-known Jewish plans of study reflecting the impact of the Arabic paideia are set forth by Joseph Ibn 'Aqnīn in his ethical work *Tibb al-nufūs* (ca. 1180) and by Judah Ibn Tibbon in the "ethical will" he wrote for his son Samuel (second half of the twelfth century). See J. R. Marcus, *The Jew in the Medieval World* (New York: Atheneum, 1983), sec. III D, no. 77, 374–77, and Israel Abrahams, ed. and trans., *Hebrew Ethical Wills* (Philadelphia: Jewish Publication Society, 1948), 1:51–92. See also S. Assaf, *Meqorot le-Toledot ha-Ḥinnukh be-Yisra'el*, new edition, ed. Shmuel Glick, vol. 2 (New York: Jewish Theological Seminary, 2001), 39–155 passim. It is worth noting that Ibn Tibbon, "the father of translators," urges his son to emulate the manifold accomplishments of Samuel ha-Nagid, and repeatedly buttresses his advice with citations of the Nagid's gnomic poetry.
47. For the text see Schirmann, *HPSP* 1:189–90. On the poem's depiction of metaphysical wisdom see Tanenbaum, *The Contemplative Soul*, 140–41.
48. Schirmann, *HPSP* 1:207–10.
49. See Bernard Septimus, *Hispano-Jewish Culture in Transition: The Career and Controversies of Ramah* (Cambridge, Mass.: Harvard University Press, 1982), 61, and Jefim Schirmann, "Salomon Ibn Gabirol, sa vie et son oeuvre poétique," *Revue des études juives* 131 (1972): 334–35.
50. See Georges Vajda, *La théologie ascétique de Baḥya Ibn Paquda* (Paris: Imprimerie Nationale, 1947).
51. Baḥya, *Kitāb al-hidāya*, Introduction, 23–24; trans. Mansoor, 92–93; cited from the translation of Moses Hyamson in Isadore Twersky, "Religion and Law," in *Studies in Jewish Law and Philosophy* (New York: Ktav, 1982), 205–6. Of course, Baḥya also depicts courtier culture as spiritually bereft, attacking it for its exclusive preoccupation with the rhetorical arts as a means to social and political advancement. See *Hidāya* 5:5 and Bezalel Safran, "Baḥya ibn Paquda's Attitude toward the Courtier Class," in *Studies in Medieval Jewish History and Literature* vol. 1, ed. I. Twersky (Cambridge, Mass.: Harvard University Press, 1979), 154–96.
52. *Yesod mora* 1:4 in *Abraham Ibn Ezra Reader* (Hebrew), ed. Israel Levin (New York/Tel Aviv: Israel Matz Hebrew Classics and I. Edward Kiev Library Foundation, 1985), 318; cited from the Prague 1833 printing in Twersky, "Religion and Law," 204–5.
53. See, e.g., *Yesod mora* 1:9.
54. Baḥya, *Kitāb al-hidāya*, Introduction, 27; trans. Mansoor, 95–96.
55. See Herbert A. Davidson, "The Study of Philosophy as a Religious Obligation," in *Religion in a Religious Age*, ed. S. D. Goitein (Cambridge, Mass.: Association for Jewish Studies, 1974), 53–68.
56. Raymond P. Scheindlin, *The Gazelle: Medieval Hebrew Poems on God, Israel, and the Soul* (Philadelphia: Jewish Publication Society, 1991), 140–41. For the Hebrew original see Dan Pagis, *The Poems of Levi Ibn Al-Tabbān* (Jerusalem: Israel Academy of Sciences and Humanities, 1967), 125–27; see also his discussion, 175–78.
57. Cited in Rashi's comment on Gen. 1:16.
58. See Pagis, *The Poems of Levi Ibn Al-Tabbān*, 175–78.
59. See Steven Harvey, ed. and trans., *Falaquera's Epistle of the Debate* (Cambridge, Mass.: Harvard University Press, 1987), ix–xii.
60. Ibid., 13–14; for the Hebrew original see p. 55, ll, 13–16.

61. Ibid., 21.
62. For a summary see ibid., xi.
63. See the dated but still valuable article by Henry Malter, "Shem Tob Ben Joseph Palquera: A Thinker and Poet of the Thirteenth Century," *Jewish Quarterly Review* n.s. 1 (1910): 151–81; Raphael Jospe, *Torah and Sophia: The Life and Thought of Shem Tov Ibn Falaquera* (Cincinnati: Hebrew Union College Press, 1988), 1–30; and Ḥayyim Schirmann, *The History of Hebrew Poetry in Christian Spain and Southern France* (Hebrew) [henceforth *HPCS*] (Jerusalem: Magnes Press and Ben-Zvi Institute, 1997), 330–45. On the cultural ties between the communities of northern Spain, Provence, and northern France in the early thirteenth century see Septimus, *Hispano-Jewish Culture in Transition,* 26–38.
64. See James T. Robinson, "The Ibn Tibbon Family: A Dynasty of Translators in Medieval 'Provence,'" in *Be'erot Yitzhak: Studies in Memory of Isadore Twersky,* 193–224.
65. The literature on the Resurrection and Maimonidean Controversies is vast; for treatments see Septimus, *Hispano-Jewish Culture in Transition,* 39–74; Ram Ben-Shalom, "Communication and Propaganda Between Provence and Spain: The Controversy over Extreme Allegorizaton," in *Communication in the Jewish Diaspora: The Pre-Modern World,* ed. Sophia Menache (Leiden: Brill, 1996), 171–225; and Ram Ben-Shalom, "The Ban Placed by the Community of Barcelona on the Study of Philosophy and Allegorical Preaching—A New Study," *Revue des études juives* 159 (2000): 387–404 and the bibliography cited there. Poetry and rhymed prose were exploited for polemical purposes during the controversies; see, e.g., James H. Lehmann, "Polemic and Satire in the Poetry of the Maimonidean Controversy," *Prooftexts* 1 (1981): 133–51.
66. See Harvey, *Falaquera's Epistle of the Debate,* 128–32.
67. For the complete Hebrew text (of which there is no critical edition), see *Sefer ha-Mevaqqesh,* ed. M. Tamah (The Hague, 1772); reprinted in *Kitvei r. shem tov falaquera,* vol. 3 (Jerusalem: Sifriyat meqorot, 1970). Part 1 trans. by M. Herschel Levine, *Falaquera's Book of the Seeker* (New York: Yeshiva University Press, 1976). For selections from the Hebrew see Schirmann, *HPSP* 2:331–42.
68. On the Arabic echoes of the protagonist's title see B. Klar, *Meḥqarim ve-Iyyunim* (Tel Aviv: Maḥbarot le-Sifrut and Mossad Harav Kook, 1954), 338–56, esp. 355–56. See also Brann, *The Compunctious Poet,* 126 and 214n33, who refers the reader to I. Goldziher, *Muslim Studies,* trans. C. R. Barber and S. M. Stern (London: George Allen and Unwin, 1971), 2:165ff. (primarily a discussion of journeys to obtain *ḥadīth* materials).
69. *Sefer ha-Mevaqqesh,* 63; trans. Levine, 91.
70. *Sefer ha-Mevaqqesh,* 10; trans. Levine, 3.
71. For a compelling interpretation of the arguments for and against poetry in *Sefer ha-Mevaqqesh* see Brann, *The Compunctious Poet,* 129–37. On Ibn Ezra and Halevi as "compunctious poets," see 59–118.
72. See Jospe, *Torah and Sophia,* 147–48.
73. *Sefer ha-Mevaqqesh,* 64–70.
74. Ibid., 70–73.
75. Cf. Maimonides' introductory letter to his disciple Joseph ben Judah Ibn 'Aqnīn in *The Guide of the Perplexed,* trans. S. Pines (Chicago: University of Chicago Press, 1963), 1:3–4 ("Epistle Dedicatory").

76. For a critical edition of the text see Shem Tov ben Joseph Ibn Falaquera, *Moreh ha-Moreh,* ed. Yair Shiffman (Jerusalem: World Union of Jewish Studies, 2001). See also, by Yair Shiffman, "Falaquera and Ibn Tibbon as Translators of *Guide of the Perplexed*" (Hebrew), *Da'at* 32–33 (1994): 103–41, and "The Differences Between the Translations of Maimonides' *Guide of the Perplexed* by Falaquera, Ibn Tibbon and Al-harizī, and their Textual and Philosophical Implications," *Journal of Semitic Studies* 44 (1999): 47–61.
77. Falaquera's Hebrew epitome made possible Solomon Munk's 1845 identification of Ibn Gabirol as the author of the *Fons Vitae,* a work that for centuries had been ascribed to a Latin author called Avicebron; see Isaac Husik, *A History of Mediaeval Jewish Philosophy* (New York: Atheneum, 1969), 60–63.
78. See Jospe, *Torah and Sophia,* 31–76 passim.
79. See Schirmann, *HPCS,* 331, and Malter, "Shem Tob Ben Joseph Palquera," 169–73.
80. See Kalonymus ben Kalonymus, *Even Boḥan,* ed. A. M. Habermann (Tel Aviv: Maḥbarot le-Sifrut and Mossad Harav Kook, 1956), 55–57, and Isaac Polgar, *Ezer ha-Dat,* ed. J. Levinger (Tel Aviv: Chaim Rosenberg School of Jewish Studies, Tel Aviv University, 1984), 68–104.

2

Maimonides' Critique of the Rabbinic Culture of His Day

MENACHEM KELLNER

Moses Maimonides (1138–1204) expressed a vision of Judaism as a remarkably naturalist religion of radical responsibility, a religion in which concrete behavior serves the needs of abstract thought, and a religion in which that abstract thought is to be understood as the deepest layer of the Torah and is a system of thought that, at least in Maimonides' day, could be most clearly and accurately expressed in the vocabulary of the Neoplatonized Aristotelianism that Maimonides accepted as one of the highest expressions of the human spirit. This Judaism was at one and the same time deeply elitist and profoundly universalist. Maimonides was brought to crystallize and express this vision of Judaism because the Jewish world in his day was, in his view, debased and paganized.

In terms of his contributions to the Jewish tradition, Maimonides may be fairly characterized as one of the most influential Jews who ever lived. Aside from the first Moses and Judah the Prince, it is hard to think of any individual whose career impacted so dramatically on the history of Judaism as a body of laws and traditions. His law code, the *Mishneh Torah,* had a profoundly democratizing effect upon Judaism (giving direct and relatively easy access to the entire body of Jewish law to anyone who could read the extremely clear Hebrew in which the book was written) and made possible the composition of subsequent codes, preeminently the *Shulḥan Arukh* of Joseph Karo (1488–1575). As a philosopher, Maimonides' closest competitor for prominence is Judah Halevi (d. 1141), but while Maimonides has been influential in all generations and in all circles, Halevi's influence, while very deep in certain sectors, was barely felt in others, and was certainly intermittent. If we consider Maimonides the halakhist and Maimonides the philosopher as one individual (as we should), then the oft-repeated saying, "From Moses to Moses there arose none like Moses" looks less like popular hagiography and more like a restrained evaluation of the facts.[1]

But, despite this, not long after his death a composition appeared that, for contrary impact and influence in the realms of thought and practice, can be seen as a worthy competitor to the works of Maimonides. I refer, of course, to the *Sefer ha-Zohar.* The world of the Zohar is so unlike that of Maimonides that at times it appears impossible that it and Maimonides' *Guide of the Perplexed* should both be accepted as authoritative in the same religious tradition. It is to one aspect of the complex relationship between the worlds of the Zohar and of the *Guide* that I wish to devote this study. That aspect was well summarized by the late Isadore Twersky, who, apropos Maimonides' unusual views concerning the nature of the Hebrew language, noted that "Maimonides' desacralization of language should be seen as an expression of his consistent opposition to hypostasized entities endowed with intrinsic sanctity."[2]

Twersky is surely correct. Among the entities that Maimonides seeks to "de-hypostasize" are the Hebrew language, the land of Israel, the people of Israel, the divine glory (*kavod*), the divine presence (*shekhinah*), angels, and sin.[3] Consistent with this approach, he seeks to present distinctions fundamental to Judaism, such as holy/profane, ritually pure/ritually impure, permissible/impermissible, and, especially, Jew/Gentile as institutional, sociological, and historical issues, and not as ontological matters.[4]

In each of these issues Maimonides implicitly (and sometimes explicitly) criticizes important elements of the regnant rabbinic culture of his day.[5] Focusing our attention on that critique allows us to understand that Maimonides' overall aim in his writings was not simply the harmonization of philosophy and Torah, as is often thought to be the case, but, rather, the use of philosophy to purify a corrupted and paganized Torah.

Attending to the historiography of Moshe Idel will make this point clearer. Idel has argued persuasively that Kabbalah crystallized out of preexisting materials in response to the challenge posed by Maimonides. He has also noted that Maimonides' views themselves crystallized in response to "proto-kabbalistic" elements in Judaism. The Maimonides who emerges from this interpretation is thus something of a tragic figure: seeking to purify Judaism from "proto-Kabbalah," what he actually succeeded in doing was to force up to the bright light of day these currents of thought from the subterranean depths in which they had hitherto flowed. In that light they flourished, grew, and ultimately became dominant. Kabbalah has long since become the mainstream of Judaism, relegating Maimonideanism to the status of a largely ignored backwater.

Maimonides was a religious reformer, but he was also a proud and loyal Jew. He realized that were he to formulate his vision of Judaism as a series of theses and nail them onto the synagogue door in Fostat, he either would be ignored or would foment schism, neither of which would accomplish his ends. He therefore decided to express his vision of Judaism in a way that would not harm those incapable of accepting it, while helping those who were capable.[6] With very few exceptions, Maimonides does not openly attack Jewish positions which he rejects. He ignores the opposition wherever he can, stating or at least hinting at the truth as he sees it. This may have been a matter of personality or a matter of policy, or both, but it certainly seems to be a consistent mode of operation throughout his writings.[7]

Maimonides did not wait till he wrote *Guide of the Perplexed* in order to express his vision of Judaism. All his writings express this vision to one extent or another. In writings addressed to ordinary Jews *and* their rabbis, he subtly refashions the Judaism of his readers into one closer to the austere and demanding faith that he believed was revealed at Sinai.[8]

In order to see how he does this, we shall have to embark upon a short tour of elements of the Judaism Maimonides found in North Africa and in Egypt when his family was forced to flee its ancestral Andalusia.[9] This tour will enable us to discover that there are underlying unities in Maimonides' religious and philosophical thought, deeper than those detected in the past.

As noted, Moshe Idel has propounded a two-part thesis concerning the relationship between Maimonides and the Kabbalah. According to Idel, Maimonides crystallized his views in reaction to what we may call "proto-kabbalistic" tendencies in pre-Maimonidean Judaism. By unearthing an ancient tradition, Maimonides, Idel argues, "implicitly indicated than any existing train of Jewish esotericism consisted of distortions of ancient esoteric truth. . . . [This was] an attempt to change the prevalent understanding of the ultimate essence of Judaism. . . . Instead of an overt confrontation, he chose a silent opposition."[10] Maimonides' opposition was not actually "silent," something Idel himself notes in a fuller statement of his position:

> Maimonides' conception of the history of the *Sitre Torah* (mysteries of the Torah) and their content is, in my opinion, revolutionary. According to him, the peculiar meaning of *Ma'aseh Bereshit* and *Ma'aseh Merkavah* was lost soon after the Tannaitic period. Maimonides implicitly discredited the corpus of mystical literature which included, inter alia, long discussions concerning the nature of these two subjects. Even treatises overtly titled *Beraita de- Ma'aseh Bereshit* or *Ma'aseh Merkavah* passed unmentioned by him. No one who is aware of Maimonides' wide range of Jewish knowledge can imagine that Maimonides was ignorant of this brand of literature. Moreover, another important treatise belonging to the Hekhalot corpus, *Sefer Shi'ur Qomah,* was openly rejected by Maimonides, who regarded it as a Jewish Byzantine forgery. *It seems that he was the first important Jewish theologian who dared oppose most ancient types of Jewish mystical theology, either by ignoring their existence, or by an overt attack.*[11]

Thus far the first prong of Idel's account of Maimonides and Kabbalah: Maimonides was aware of proto-kabbalistic elements in Judaism and formulated his vision of Judaism in conscious opposition to them.

The second and better-known prong of Idel's thesis maintains that, in an ironic twist of fate, it was Maimonides' struggle against what I have called proto-Kabbalah that called forth Kabbalah itself:

> Kabbalah emerged in the late twelfth and early thirteenth centuries as a sort of reaction to the dismissal of earlier mystical traditions by Maimonides' audacious reinterpretation of Jewish esotericism and his attempt to replace the mystical traditions with a philosophical understanding. Kabbalah can be viewed as part of a restructuring of those aspects of rabbinic thought that were denied authenticity by Maimonides' system. Far from being a total innovation, historical Kabbalah represented an ongoing effort to systematize existing elements of Jewish theurgy, myth, and mysticism into a full-fledged response to the rationalistic challenge. Indeed, we can consider

> Kabbalah as part of a silent controversy between the rationalistic and mystical facets of Judaism. It was "silent" in that the main organon of the kabbalistic response took the form not of open attacks on Maimonides—an extremely rare phenomenon in early Kabbalah—but of an ongoing building of an alternative to his system on the basis of earlier materials.[12]

The two prongs are summarized in the following statement: "But just as the purification of Jewish literature caused a relocation of the mysterious, mystical, or magical elements in midrash, so the rationalistic reconstructions of Judaism prompted, in turn, a powerful reaction wherein an amalgam of older traditions, including the same mystical, mythical, and magical elements, came to the surface in more overt and crystalized forms."[13] The first part of Idel's thesis depends upon the existence of "proto-kabbalistic" elements in pre-Maimonidean Judaism. Much of *Kabbalah: New Perspectives* is given over to providing evidence of such elements. Idel has been criticized for the nature of the evidence he adduced in that book.[14] It is not my place, nor am I particularly competent, to involve myself in that dispute. What I do want to argue, however, is that Maimonides agrees with Idel. To put the point in historically more acceptable terms, reading Maimonides as if he agrees with Idel enables us to understand the entire Maimonidean corpus in a new, integrative fashion. This is the burden of what I will be trying to do in this essay. To the extent that I succeed, I will not only be making claims about Maimonides but will also be supporting Idel in an important fashion.

Idel's view that Maimonides was fighting a battle against important spiritual trends in the Judaism of his day should be contrasted with that of Harry Austryn Wolfson: "In point of time, Halevi preceded Maimonides. Yet in comparing them we must treat Halevi as the critic of the tendency which Maimonides represented, the tendency which began long before Halevi and reached its climax in Maimonides. Maimonides may be considered as swimming with the stream, he was the expression of his age; Halevi was swimming against the stream, he was the insurgent, the utterer of paradoxes."[15] Wolfson, I believe, misunderstood what Maimonides was doing, largely because he was unaware of the materials unearthed by scholars like Gershom Scholem, Moshe Idel, and their colleagues. Maimonides was confronted with a form of Judaism which found, perhaps, its most sophisticated exponents in Judah Halevi, who preceded Maimonides,[16] and in Naḥmanides

(1194–1270), who followed him.[17] Pace Wolfson, the Judaism of Halevi and Naḥmanides dominated the Jewish world before and after Maimonides and continues to dominate it today. If anyone was swimming against the stream, it was Maimonides, not Halevi.

Maimonides was forced to swim against the mainstream of important elements in the regnant rabbinic culture of his day because of his consistent nominalism and his insistence on the absolute transcendence of God. With respect to the first, he writes: "After what I have stated about providence singling out the human species alone among all the species of animals, I say that it is known that no species exists outside the mind, but that the species and the other universals are, as you know, mental notions and that every existent outside the mind is an individual or group of individuals."[18] The implications of this position are far-reaching. Intrinsic holiness cannot inhere in the people of Israel, for example, since there is no such thing as the people of Israel—there are only individual Jews. There can furthermore be no such thing as sanctity as such; at most there can be sacred objects, places, times, and perhaps individuals. Nor can there be ritual purity as such, only ritually pure or impure objects, places, and individuals.

Maimonides combines philosophical nominalism with religious nominalism: halakhic entities and distinctions are precisely that, halakhic. *Halakhah,* for Maimonides, does not *describe* preexisting reality; rather, it *constitutes* or *constructs* a social reality. This point is important for Maimonides since it assists him in protecting God's transcendence. The Torah, for example, obligates Jews to be holy, because God is holy (Lev. 19:2). Were that interpreted to mean that Jews (or sacred objects, times, and places) are or can be intrinsically holy, we would be saying that God and certain created entities share the characteristic of holiness, an approach which Maimonides repeatedly disallows.[19] Holiness must be *institutional,* a matter of halakhic definition, not intrinsic, somehow actually in the world.

The connection between Maimonides' nominalism and his emphasis on the transcendence of God may be made clearer by taking advantage of an insight of Mary Douglas. At the beginning of *Leviticus as Literature* Douglas emphasized the radical nature of biblical monotheism:

> All the other religions were polytheistic in one sense or another; only Israel's religion was severely monotheistic. There were no subsidiary or rival deities at all, only one true God who forbade any

> cult to be paid to any others. This does not mean that the existence of other spirits was denied. In fact the Bible has a role for angels as messengers of God or as manifestations of God; Satan figures as an independent agent in Zechariah, the angel of God appears in the Book of Numbers to rebuke Balaam. The wicked thing was to pay cult to the spiritual beings around.[20] Only the one God has any power,[21] and it is pointless to apply to lesser spiritual beings, as well as an unpardonable insult to the majesty of the one God. Everything else flows from this. It is hard to realize how completely their strict monolatry separated the religion of Israel from the others in the region.[22]

This last sentence of this otherwise very Maimonidean paragraph helps us to understand what Maimonides is all about: biblical Judaism surely can appear as monolatry, and there were many texts circulating in Maimonides' day attributed to talmudic rabbis that clearly lent themselves to this interpretation (to put the matter mildly). But true Judaism, Maimonides was convinced, was absolute and pure monotheism, not monolatry.

The purer the monotheism, the more transcendent is God. But the more God is understood as transcendent, the greater the need and impulse to posit quasi-divine intermediaries, to bridge the gap between God and ourselves. But such intermediaries turn monotheism into monolatry. There is ample evidence that much of the Judaism that Maimonides knew had succumbed to this dangerous impulse. Maimonides was faced with an exquisitely difficult dilemma: he had to protect the absolutely unique and hence wholly transcendent God of true Judaism from all attempts at humanization and personification, while at the same time not making God's transcendence so blatant as to invite the positing of intermediaries.

Maimonides' nominalism and emphasis on divine transcendence lead him to adopt positions that today would be called universalist,[23] and which were certainly unusual in his day. In his view, all human beings are created with the same general potential; there is nothing inherent that distinguishes Jews from Gentiles. The processes leading to human perfection must thus be open in principle to all human beings—Maimonides cannot (nor does he wish to) make it impossible for non-Jews to achieve perfection without the Torah.[24]

As is evidenced by his esotericism, Maimonides clearly realized that his vision of Judaism was not widely accepted in his day.[25]

Indeed, it might be fair to say that his great Iberian predecessor, Judah Halevi, wrote his *Kuzari* precisely in order to refute the kind of Judaism that was soon to find its classic expression in the works of Maimonides. But, while Maimonides realized that his views were unusual, he was also convinced that they were correct. Judaism, he thought, was in desperate need of reform in order to return to its pristine purity. The question facing him was how best to effect that reform.

Guide of the Perplexed is an avowedly esoteric work. By its very nature, an esoteric work is one addressed to more than one audience. In that sense, I am convinced that all, or almost all, of Maimonides' writings must be understood as esoteric, addressed simultaneously to several audiences. That does not mean that works other than *Guide of the Perplexed* contain contradictions or that any of his works contained teachings that Maimonides thought were Jewishly heterodox. He was convinced, however, that his writings contained teachings which many of his contemporaries would find to be Jewishly heterodox.

To my mind, Maimonides' esotericism is directly linked to his elitism.[26] Convinced that he and very few like him truly understood the truths taught by Judaism, he chose to hide this truth from the masses. He may have done this out of disdain for the masses, out of fear of persecution, or—and this, I think, is the truth—out of a sense of *noblesse oblige*. Revealing the truths of the Torah to people incapable of or unwilling to accept them would benefit no one. Rather, Maimonides chose to write such that his true opinions could be teased out of his writings, but not by everyone. Maimonides did this so well that his writings to this day function as a kind of Rorschach test: people very often find in them what they expect to find in them.[27]

We now turn to an examination of a number of issues that illustrate the general claims made to this point. In each of these I show that Maimonides' positions were "Jewishly unusual" in his day, that they reflect his "religious nominalism," and give expression to what Twersky called "his consistent opposition to hypostasized entities endowed with intrinsic sanctity." This brief survey also shows that Maimonides would have agreed with Moshe Idel: many views that were later systematized, crystallized, and made prominent in Kabbalah were prevalent in the Judaism of Maimonides' day. Finally, this survey helps us to appreciate Maimonides the Jewish thinker in his battle against the corrupted, paganized Judaism that seemed to prevail in his time and place.

Hebrew Language

Maimonides' effort to dethrone the prevailing vision of Judaism and replace it with another vision altogether was a conscious project on his part, but one carried out without any explicit announcements. Maimonides was fighting what he took to be a debased and ultimately corrupt version of Judaism and appears to have thought that the best way to wage this war was by not declaring it.[28] Let us begin our survey with the issue that prompted the statement quoted from Twersky above, Maimonides' desacralization of language in general and of Hebrew in particular.

Maimonides is well known, even notorious, for having denied that there is anything intrinsically unique about Hebrew.[29] He maintained, in effect, that the sanctity of Hebrew has nothing to do with the facts that the Bible was written in it, that God said *Let there be light* in it and in so doing created the universe, that it is the language of prophecy, that it was the "ur-language" of humankind, or that it is the most exalted language, spiritually and poetically, on earth. No, Maimonides maintained that Hebrew is called holy simply because it is a language without words for foul and disgusting matters, especially concerning sex and defecation. Maimonides thus claims that Hebrew is holy because of one of its characteristics, a characteristic that could, in principle, be shared by other languages. Hebrew is a language like other languages, only more refined.

In staking out this position, Maimonides seems to be taking clear issue with the dominant understanding of the Jewish tradition as it had developed to his day, and certainly as it found expression in the views of Judah Halevi. In the context of the Judaism he inherited from his forebears and teachers, Maimonides' views on Hebrew are surely unusual.[30] The very first verses of the Bible teach that the cosmos was created through a Hebrew utterance. Hebrew is the language with which God addresses humankind and is the language in which the Torah was couched. It is hardly surprising, therefore, that many Jewish thinkers attached special significance to the Hebrew language and saw in it a tool that not only reflects reality at its deepest level but creates realities as well.[31] This is certainly the view of *Sefer Yeṣirah,* as Moshe Idel notes: *Sefer Yeṣirah* "contributed the theory that the letters of the Hebrew alphabet entered the process of creation not only as creative forces but as the elements of its material structure."[32] *Sefer Yeṣirah* was seen as a legitimate expression of talmudic Judaism by most of Maimonides' philosophic predecessors and successors.

Sefer Yeṣirah is both influential and enigmatic. Attributed in the tradition to the patriarch Abraham, scholars are deeply divided over the question of its place and time of composition.[33] In some ways, it is hard even to call it a book, since it has reached our hands in three different recensions.[34] There are dramatic differences of opinion concerning the very nature of the book. Saadya Gaon (882–942) saw it as a scientific work,[35] while Halevi emphasized its teachings concerning what may be called Hebrew language mysticism.[36] It has been treated as an astrological treatise,[37] and as having astronomical import.[38] It was read by Ḥasidei Ashkenaz as a mystical text, and many scholars find in it the source of the kabbalistic doctrine of the *sefirot*.[39] Three prominent students of Jewish mysticism have recently proposed three very different views of *Sefer Yeṣirah:* Joseph Dan harks back to a variant of the view of Saadya, and sees the author of *Sefer Yeṣirah* as primarily a scientist, who was, withal, also a mystic.[40] Moshe Idel finds in *Sefer Yeṣirah* guidance for the creation of a golem.[41] Yehuda Liebes has recently devoted an entire book to *Sefer Yeṣirah,* in which he argues that it is fundamentally a meditation on creativity, divine and human.[42]

Maimonides, it is safe to say, knew *Sefer Yeṣirah.* Shlomo Pines has given good grounds to making this assertion.[43] Y. Tzvi Langermann has recently supported this view in convincing fashion.[44] If so, why does Maimonides never mention the book in any of his extant writings? Moshe Idel is convinced that Maimonides purposely ignored *Sefer Yeṣirah.*[45] The case of *Sefer Yeṣirah* appears to be a good example of Maimonides' penchant for attacking objectionable texts and positions from the flanks, not frontally.

However we interpret *Sefer Yeṣirah,* it is clear that the doctrine of language contained in the book had to have appeared as dangerous to Maimonides. Helpful in this regard is the following comment of the historian of magic and science, Brian Vickers, who notes that one of the ways of distinguishing the occult from the scientific is "the relationship between language and reality. In the scientific tradition, I hold, a clear distinction is made between words and things and between literal and metaphorical language. The occult tradition does not recognize this distinction: Words are treated as if they are equivalent to things and can be substituted for them. Manipulate the one, and you manipulate the other."[46] Maimonides' approach to the nature of Hebrew is but a reflection of his deeper adherence to the scientific culture of his day, and of his rejection of the occult. But more than that, attributing objective power to the Hebrew language, maintaining that its letters are the elements out of which the cosmos was created, and so on, are all ways, Maimonides seems clearly to have held, of limiting the power and awesome uniqueness and transcendence of God.

God's Names and Magic

Related to the issue of the special character of the Hebrew language are the issues of the manipulation of God's name and the use of amulets and charms, either to ward off evil or to promote some desired end. The writing of amulets containing holy names and the manipulation of divine names (*shemot* in Hebrew, *al-shemot* in Maimonides' Judeo-Arabic) were common forms of magical praxis in antiquity, widely accepted among the Jews.[47] Maimonides gives short shrift to these practices.[48]

Seeing God's name as something powerful which may be used is not only typical of clearly magical works like *The Sword of Moses*,[49] but it also has rabbinic sources.[50] The apparent orthodoxy of the notion may explain the fervor with which Maimonides attacks it in *Guide of the Perplexed* I:61–62.

Many readers today will have a hard time understanding Maimonides in this connection, since few are aware of the extent to which magic infiltrated the very warp and woof of Jewish life in antiquity. An example of the sort of writing Maimonides attacks is the *Sefer ha-Razim* (Book of Mysteries). This book is a compilation of magical texts, including many bizarre names meant to be invoked in magical formulae, which was, according to Ithamar Gruenwald, compiled in the sixth or seventh centuries out of much earlier elements, not all of which were understood by the compiler.[51] Lee I. Levine dates the work to the fourth century, and characterizes it as a "Jewish handbook of popular magic that was heavily indebted to popular pagan (later Christian) traditions and practices that were ubiquitous throughout the ambient Roman-Byzantine world."[52] Baruch Levine dates the book even earlier, opining that it may have been written in the first century.[53] The work was reconstructed on the basis of genizah texts and published in its entirety for the first time by Mordecai Margalioth in 1967.[54] The book is representative of a great number of similar books[55] and represents a kind of literature with important connections to the world of the Talmud.[56] For our purposes the book is important not only because it is representative of a large class of similar works, and not only because—its heterodoxy notwithstanding[57]—it was a work widely accepted as normative in Jewish antiquity,[58] but because it was apparently known to Maimonides. As Margalioth points out in the introduction to his edition of the work (40), Maimonides makes reference in "Laws of Idolatry" 6:1 to the custom of holding a sceptre made of myrtle. This, according to Margalioth, is a detail of magical praxis found only in *Sefer ha-Razim.*

The question of the nature of these connections in particular, and of the place of magic in rabbinic culture in general, is hotly disputed. With respect to *Sefer ha-Razim,* Margalioth sees it as entirely outside the rabbinic mainstream. P. S. Alexander, on the other hand, holds that "there is good evidence to suggest that such [magical] material circulated at the very heart of rabbinic society."[59] Alexander is supported by Peter Schaefer, who holds that "the Talmud is more lenient toward magic than Margalioth, and *Sefer ha-Razim* is a wonderful example of how plain magic could well be integrated into the theological framework of rabbinic Judaism."[60] The connections between *Sefer ha-Razim* and Hekhalot literature are also not well understood.[61]

Sefer ha-Razim and works like it explain, perhaps, the fervor of Maimonides' statements in *Guide of the Perplexed* I:61–62, and surely explain why he found it of such pressing importance to undermine the theory of Hebrew which makes these works possible.[62]

Holiness

Thus far we have seen that Maimonides denies any special sanctity to the Hebrew language and attacks magical use of God's name in particular and magic in general. Underlying these positions is a deeper and more fundamental issue, the nature of holiness. In a separate context I have analyzed Maimonides' approach to the holiness of persons, of the people of Israel, of the Land of Israel and Jerusalem, of Torah scrolls, *tefillin,* and *mezuzot,* and of special times (Sabbath and holy days).[63] In each case Maimonides was faced with three different possibilities. The holiness of persons, nations, places, objects, and times could be something having ontological standing that inheres in them from the time of creation, something having ontological standing that was added to them at some point in history, or a name for their institutional standing within the halakhic framework.[64]

Before explaining further this tri-partite distinction, an introductory comment is necessary. The question of what holiness is has been very rarely asked of Jewish texts, perhaps because the notion of holiness is so pervasive in Judaism that asking Jewish texts about the nature of holiness is like asking fish about the nature of water.[65] Thus, with the exception of the *Kuzari,* it is hard to pinpoint pre-Maimonidean texts that take a stand, explicitly or implicitly, on this issue.[66]

The first two notions of holiness stated above share in common the idea that however it becomes holy, a holy place, person, nation, time, or object is, once holy, objectively different from profane places, persons, nations, times, and objects. On both these views, sanctity is real, it inheres in sacred places, etc., it is intrinsic to them; it is, one might say, part of their metaphysical make-up; it has ontological standing. Holy places, persons, nations, times, and objects are ontologically distinct from (and religiously superior to) profane places, persons, nations, times, and objects. This distinction is part of the universe, whether from the time of creation or, say, from Sinai.

Let me try to make this point clearer with an analogy. Radioactivity existed before Geiger discovered a way to measure it. Similarly, holiness can be thought objectively to inhere in holy places, persons, nations, times, and objects, even though there is no way for us (presently) to measure it. It is "out there," a feature of the objectively real world, even if not part of the world susceptible to laboratory examination.

I find a different, third view of holiness in the thought of Maimonides. In his view holiness cannot be characterized as ontological or essentialist since holy places, persons, nations, times, and objects are in no objective way distinct from profane places, persons, nations, times, and objects; holiness is a status, not a quality of existence. It is a challenge, not a given; normative, not descriptive. It is institutional (in the sense of being part of a system of laws) and hence contingent. This sort of holiness does not reflect objective reality; it helps constitute social reality. In this view, holy places, persons, nations, times, and objects are indubitably holy, and must be treated with all due respect, but they are, in and of themselves, like all other places, persons, nations, times, and objects. What is different about them is the way in which the Torah commands that they be treated. Holy places, persons, nations, times, and objects derive their sanctity from the uses to which they are put.[67]

Maimonides could not adopt any variant of the ontological, essentialist interpretation of holiness: the Torah obligates Jews to be holy, because God is holy (Lev. 19:2). Were that interpreted to mean that Jews (or sacred objects, times, and places) are or can be essentially holy, we would be saying that God and certain created entities share a characteristic, namely, the characteristic of holiness. This is something that, as noted above, Maimonides repeatedly disallows. Holiness, it follows, must be *institutional,* a matter of halakhic definition, not ontological, somehow actually in the universe.[68]

Ritual Purity and Impurity

With respect to the issue of holiness, it takes an intricate and extended argument to demonstrate Maimonides' position, and it is hard to point out clear texts to which he may have been responding. But with respect to an issue intimately related to the nature of holiness, that of ritual purity and impurity, the situation is very different. Biblical and rabbinic texts, when taken together, allow for a wide variety of approaches to the meaning of ritual purity and impurity (*tohorah, tum'ah*). Here I focus on two such approaches. Maimonides was familiar with them both; he adopted one and consciously rejected the other. By this point it should be clear that Maimonides' position is part of a much broader orientation, one that helps us to understand the sort of religious sensibility he sought to inculcate in his readers, and the sort of religious sensibility against which he sought to inoculate them.[69]

Maimonides made a conscious choice between two competing views of the nature of ritual purity and impurity; one he accepted, the other he rejected. What are these two views? They are well captured by a pair of texts. *Hekhalot Rabbati* reports that the students of Rabbi Neḥunya ben ha-Kanah wished to recall him from what appears to have been a mystical experience without endangering him. The text reports as follows:

> Immediately I took a very fine woolen cloth[70] and gave it to Rabbi Akiba, and Rabbi Akiba gave it to a servant of ours saying: "Go and lay this cloth beside a woman who immersed herself a second time.[71] For if that woman will come and declare the circumstances

of her menstrual flow[72] before the company, there will be one who forbids her to her husband and the majority will permit. Say to that woman: 'Touch this cloth with the end of the middle finger of your hand, and do not press[73] the end of your finger upon it, but rather as a man who takes a hair which had fallen therein from his eyeball, pushing it very gently.'" They went and did so, and laid the cloth before Rabbi Ishmael. He inserted it into a bough of myrtle full of oil [of foliatum] that had been soaked in pure balsam[74] and they placed it upon the knees of Rabbi Neḥunya ben ha-Kanah; and immediately they dismissed him from before the throne of glory where he had been sitting and beholding:

> Wonderful loftiness and strange dominion,
> Loftiness of exaltation and dominion of majesty,
> Which come to pass before the throne of glory,
> Three times each day, in the height,
> From the time the world was created and until now, for
> praise.[75]

As Lawrence Schiffman points out, the principle operating here seems to be that of the least possible impurity.[76] The real, objective power of menstrual impurity is such that if a woman who is ritually pure halakhically, but about whom a minority of authorities would hold that she might still be ritually impure, were to touch glancingly a clean cloth, and that cloth was wrapped around a myrtle bough full of oil which had been soaked in an extremely valuable spice (balsam), and the bough then placed upon the knees of a person engaged in a heavenly ascent, this would be enough to shatter the connection between the person making the heavenly ascent and his or her heavenly partners. Ritual impurity, according to the evidence of this text, is a powerful force in the universe.[77] This force exists independently of *halakhah,* or, perhaps better, prior to *halakhah.* The force can effect real changes in the world of objective reality.[78] In this view found in this text, ritual impurity is hypostasized, seen as a force or substance having objective reality, a force or substance that can harm and which must be resisted, subdued, overcome. In what follows, for lack of a better term, I call this the "ontological" view of ritual impurity.

There are good reasons to think that Judah Halevi adopted this "ontological" view of ritual purity.[79] It appears to be the view of Naḥmanides[80] and is certainly the mainstream view of Kabbalah. It is a view Maimonides explicitly rejects.[81] It is also a view Maimonides must reject. There are a number of reasons for this. First, to attribute some sort of actual existence to ritual impurity is to offend what I take to be Maimonides' very fundamental nominalist sensibility. More important, it is to attribute the power to do actual spiritual harm to a class of entities that, once created, are, in effect, independent of God. This clearly offends Maimonides' monotheistic sensibilities. Third, such an understanding runs counter to Maimonides' conception of the nature of halakhah. He was, after all, the person who wrote explicitly: "Know that all the practices of the worship, such as reading the Torah, prayer, and the performance of the other *commandments,* have only the end of training you to occupy yourself with His commandments, may He be exalted, rather than with matters pertaining to this world."[82] The practices of Judaism, I take Maimonides to be teaching here, were ordained *only* for purposes of training. To play on Maimonides' words, the commandments do not relate to matters pertaining to any objectively existent entities and distinctions in this world.

Angels

Despite their prominence in the Bible and in rabbinic literature (outside of the Mishnah),[83] Maimonides denies the existence of angels as ordinarily understood.[84] Howard Kreisel puts this point well:

> The separate intellects, together with the celestial spheres and the natural existents and forces of the sublunar world, are the "angels" spoken of in the Bible and in rabbinic literature according to Maimonides. The only existents not considered by him to be angels are the "angels" as they are literally depicted. Such creatures do not exist in his ontology. Maimonides considers the biblical and rabbinic descriptions of the angels to be imaginative representations, primarily of the separate intellects.[85]

But if Maimonides has no problems with the existence of separate intellects,[86] why is he so troubled by the existence of winged intermediaries between God and humans, carrying harps or not?

While Maimonides could not have been happy with rabbinic personification of angels, with rabbinic doctrines of fallen angels,[87] and with some talmudic texts that present the angel Meṭaṭron as a kind of vice-regent to God, none of these present more difficulties than biblical anthropomorphisms. It is the prominent place of angels in extra-rabbinic literature that was probably the focal point of Maimonides' concern.

The role of angels as intermediaries between humans and God is one of the central features of Hekhalot literature.[88] Characteristic of this literature is the myriads of angels thought to exist, their power to help or hinder human beings, and a failure to keep sharp boundaries between the angels and God.[89] The blurring of distinctions between God and angels is particularly clear in the case of the angel Meṭaṭron, sometimes called the *Sar ha-Panim,* who is often presented as a kind of assistant God.[90] Since the angels are thought to have power to help or harm, much of Hekhalot literature is given over to adjurations addressed to the angels.[91]

Rachel Elior explains that "mysticism, magic, and angelology are founded upon a shared cosmological view which assumes continuity between the upper realms and the terrestrial world, allowing a reciprocal relationship between them." This confusion of boundaries had to be galling to a person like Maimonides, whose view of God is resolutely transcendent and who staunchly affirms the Aristotelian distinction between the natures of the sub- and superlunar worlds.[92]

Was Maimonides familiar with this literature? It stretches credulity to think that he was not. The vast amount of this material found in the Cairo Genizah, for one thing, makes it unlikely that Maimonides was unfamiliar with it. Furthermore, he claims to have read every idolatrous text he could find;[93] is it possible that he read Gentile idolatrous texts and ignored Jewish ones? Moreover, he himself cites at least one Hekhalot text, *Shi'ur Qomah,*[94] and there is indirect evidence that he was familiar with *Sefer ha-Razim.* Several scholars have also found indications of Maimonidean familiarity with Hekhalot themes and texts in his writings.[95]

Maimonides' depersonification of angels seems to be a clear attempt to distance himself from the regnant Jewish culture of his day, that is, the Judaism apparently taught as normative by many, perhaps all, of his rabbinic colleagues in North Africa and the Middle East.[96]

Other Issues

The issues raised to this point by no means exhaust the matters on which Maimonides rejected, refined, or reworked the rabbinic Judaism of his day. There are many others that need to be researched.

These include the nature of *shekhinah,* God's presence, and of *kavod,* God's glory. It can be shown that Maimonides "de-ontologizes" the two notions.[97] But to say that he "de-ontologizes" them is to imply that they had been understood before him as having ontological standing. Many biblical and rabbinic texts[98] invite this interpretation, as do key Hekhalot texts.[99] This is clearly the case with Saadya Gaon, who sees the *kavod* as a created entity.[100]

The existence of demons (as noted above), the impact of sin upon the soul, the theurgic impact of the commandments, talismans, spiritual powers of astral bodies, and so on are all topics that must be examined in this context. So, too, a detailed examination of Maimonides' bête noire, the Sabians, would be valuable in this arena.[101] I suspect that he attacks the Sabians in places where it would be impolitic to attack directly the true objects of his ire. Much can also be learned about the Judaism Maimonides criticized by studying *piyyutim,* liturgical poems. Maimonides' disdain for *piyyutim* is not simply a halakhic matter, nor is it only because of the sometimes audacious anthropomorphisms found in them. Many of the *piyyutim* embody those elements of the rabbinic Judaism of his day that Maimonides found most offensive. Examination of this literature will give us a fuller picture of the Judaism he sought to purify.[102]

An issue which I have discussed briefly elsewhere will have to come into play: the nature of the relationship between *halakhah* and reality. Does *halakhah* reflect a preexisting ontological reality, or does it constitute a social, institutional reality? If the former, *halakhah* could not be other than it is; if the latter, *halakhah* could have been different. If the former, the this-worldly consequences of sin can be seen as objective and actual; if the latter, the this-worldly consequences of sin can only be in the social realm. Connected to this is the interesting fact that for Maimonides, the consequences of mistakes made with respect to halakhic matters are relatively benign, while those made with respect to some metaphysical matters are fatal and final. I hope to address all these matters in the near future.

Concluding Remarks

In the foregoing discussion I have tried to show that many of Maimonides' Jewishly unusual positions can be understood as consequences of his philosophic and religious nominalism and of his insistence on the absolute transcendence of God.[103] In formulating the Jewish consequences of his positions, he was forced to make (often implict, but nonetheless emphatic) criticisms of the Judaism of his day. Examining that Judaism, as we have begun to do in this essay, gives us a new, fuller picture of what Maimonides was trying to accomplish.

In scholarly circles, Maimonides is often depicted as if he should be understood primarily against the background of Greek, Hellenist, and Arabic philosophy. Lawrence V. Berman summarized this view in the title of his classic article, "Maimonides, the Disciple of Alfarabi."[104] In traditionalist Jewish circles, by contrast, Maimonides is often depicted as if he should be understood exclusively in the context of the Jewish tradition, as it existed before him, and as it continued to exist after him. For the last twenty-five years, following the lead of scholars like Isadore Twersky and David Hartman, I have sought to argue that Maimonides is best understood against both these backgrounds and that he stood at the intersection of two vectors, one beginning with the first Moses and the second beginning with Plato.

It now appears to me that in searching for rabbinic and philosophical antecedents to his thought, I have paid too little attention to the Judaism against which Maimonides was reacting. True, much of what he wrote appears to have been written as if he were trying to refute Judah Halevi, but it is the way in which Halevi is representative of the Jewish culture of his day that has been insufficiently noted.

Maimonides did not simply sift through the rabbinic and philosophical literature available to him in order to find raw materials for his highly naturalistic account of Judaism. He also read carefully the literature attributed to the talmudic rabbis, and the literature written by their successors, in order to find elements that needed to be refined or even rejected altogether.

Notes

A revised version of this essay appears in my book, *Maimonides' Confrontation with Mysticism* (Oxford: Littman Library, 2006). I would like to thank Mordechai Pachter and Jolene S. Kellner for commenting on an earlier draft.

1. See Yiṣḥak (Isadore) Twersky, "Maimonides' Image: An Essay on His Unique Stature in Jewish History," *Asufot* 10 (1997): 9–35 (Hebrew).
2. *Introduction to the Code of Maimonides* (New Haven: Yale University Press, 1980), 324n.
3. Gad Freudenthal pointed out to me that I am misusing the word "de-hypostasize" here, since, strictly, one can only hypostasize or de-hypostasize notions, not entities. But that is precisely my point: Maimonides was convinced that certain notions had

been illegitimately hypostasized; he sought to correct that state of affairs by showing that these matters were "only" notions, not entities.

4. Relevant also is the fact that in Maimonides' view the narratives and commandments of the Torah appear to be historically conditioned, not absolute.
5. Maimonides presents what might be called a statement of the main textual components of the rabbinic orthodoxy of his day toward the end of his introduction to the *Mishneh Torah,* where he lists the books summarized in his own work: geonic commentaries, halakhic monographs and responsa, as well as the following talmudic works: the Babylonian Talmud and the Jerusalem Talmud, the Sifra, the Sifri, and the Tosefta. But in addition to these sources, I hope that my present work will show that in order to understand Maimonides fully, we must also take note of less formal aspects of the regnant Jewish culture of his day: *piyyutim* (liturgical poetry), Hekhalot literature, the writings of figures like Judah Halevi and Abraham Ibn Ezra, and even magical writings.
6. A good example of this approach is Maimonides' famous statement in the introduction to his "Eight Chapters": "Know that the things about which we shall speak in these chapters and in what will come in the commentary are not matters invented on my own nor explanations I have originated. Indeed, they are matters gathered from the discourse of the Sages in the Midrash, the Talmud, and other compositions of theirs, as well as from the discourse of both the ancient and modern philosophers and from the compositions of many men. Hear the truth from whoever says it. Sometimes I have taken a complete passage from the text of a famous book. Now there is nothing wrong with that, for I do not attribute to myself what someone who preceded me said. We hereby acknowledge this and shall not indicate that 'so and so said' and 'so and so said,' since that would be useless prolixity. *Moreover, the name of such an individual might make the passage offensive to someone without experience and make him think it has an evil inner meaning of which he is not aware. Consequently, I saw fit to omit the author's name, since my goal is to be useful to the reader.* We shall explain to him the hidden meanings in this tractate." I cite the text from the introduction to "Eight Chapters" as it is translated in Raymond Weiss and Charles Butterworth, *Ethical Writings of Maimonides* (New York: Dover, 1983), 60 (emphasis added).
7. With respect to Maimonides' apparent propensity to fight positions without specifying what he is fighting against, Alfred Ivry ("Isma'ili Theology and Maimonides' Philosophy," in *The Jews of Medieval Islam: Community, Society, and Identity,* ed. Daniel Frank [Leiden: Brill, 1995], 271–99), argues that part of Maimonides' motivation in writing *Guide of the Perplexed* was to counter teachings of Isma'ilism. His response is not direct, but "oblique" (280). "A good deal of the *Guide of the Perplexed,*" Ivry argues, "should thus be seen as a response to, and implicit rebuttal of, various Isma'ili themes and assertions, as well as a qualified, tacit endorsement of others" (282).
8. See M. Kellner, "The Literary Character of the *Mishneh Torah:* On the Art of Writing in Maimonides' Halakhic Works," in *Me'ah She'arim: Studies in Medieval Jewish Spiritual Life in Memory of Isadore Twersky,* ed. E. Fleischer, G. Blidstein, C. Horowitz, and B. Septimus (Jerusalem: Magnes Press, 2001), 29–45.
9. On Maimonides' pride in his Andalusian background, and concomitant reservations about the Judaism he found in North Africa and Egypt, see Joshua Blau, "Maimonides, Al-Andalus, and the Influence of the Spanish-Arabic Dialect on His Language," in *New Horizons in Sephardic Studies,* ed. Yedida K. Stillman and George

K. Zucker (Albany: State University of New York Press, 1993), 203–10; Joel Kraemer, "Maimonides and the Spanish Aristotelian School," *Christians, Muslims, and Jews in Medieval and Early Modern Spain: Interaction and Cultural Exchange,* ed. Mark D. Meyerson and Edward D. English (Notre Dame, Ind.: University of Notre Dame Press, 1999), 40–68; and Kraemer, "The Life of Moses ben Maimon," in *Judaism in Practice from the Middle Ages through the Early Modern Period,* ed. Lawrence Fine (Princeton: Princeton University Press, 2001), 413–28. For Maimonidean reservations concerning the level of Judaic learning and understanding in contemporary Babylonia, see the introduction to Sarah Stroumsa, *On the Beginnings of the Maimonidean Controversy in the East: Yosef ibn Shim'on's Silencing Epistle Concerning the Resurrection of the Dead* (Jerusalem: Makhon Ben-Zvi, 1999) (Hebrew), and Y. Tzvi Langermann, "The Letter of R. Shmuel ben Eli on Resurrection," *Koveṣ al Yad* 15 (2000): 41–92 (Hebrew). Maimonides also peppers his writings with uncomplimentary comments about the level of true understanding of Torah displayed by his rabbinic contemporaries. For some examples, see Menachem Kellner, *Maimonides on the "Decline of the Generations" and the Nature of Rabbinic Authority* (Albany: State University of New York Press, 1996), 37–54. See further Ḥaim Kreisel, "The Torah Commentary of R. Nissim ben Mosheh of Marseilles: On a Medieval Approach to Torah u-Madda," *Torah u-Madda Journal* 10 (2001): 20–36, who notes that Maimonides "did not hide his negative opinion of most of the rabbinic scholars of his generation due to their ignorance of the truths of philosophy" (33). Kreisel cites as representative sources *Guide of the Perplexed* II:6 (263), the parable of the palace in III:51 (on which, see M. Kellner, *Maimonides on Human Perfection* [Atlanta: Scholars Press, 1990], chap. 3), and the opening of the "Treatise on Resurrection."

10. Moshe Idel, "*Sitre 'Arayot* in Maimonides' Thought," in *Maimonides and Philosophy,* ed. Shlomo Pines and Yirmiyahu Yovel (Dordrecht: Kluwer Academic, 1986), 79–91, 86.
11. Moshe Idel, "Maimonides and Kabbalah," in *Studies in Maimonides,* ed. Isadore Twersky (Cambridge, Mass.: Harvard University Press, 1990), 31–81, 34 (emphasis added). On the change in Maimonides' attitude toward *Shi'ur Qomah* (from authoritative text to Byzantine forgery) see Joseph Qafiḥ, "Fragment from an Ancient Yemenite Composition Concerning Shi'ur Qomah," *R. Joseph Qafiḥ—Ketavim,* ed. J. Tobi, vol. 1 (Jerusalem: General Council of Yemenite Communities in Israel, 1989), 475–78 (Hebrew).
12. Moshe Idel, *Kabbalah: New Perspectives* (New Haven: Yale University Press, 1988), 253. As Idel notes, H. Graetz was the first scholar to express this idea. For discussion, see Gershom Scholem, *Origins of the Kabbalah* (Princeton: Princeton University Press, 1987), 7.
13. Moshe Idel, "Infinities of Torah in Kabbalah," in *Midrash and Literature,* ed. Geoffrey H. Hartman and Sanford Budick (New Haven: Yale University Press, 1986), 141–57, 143. For a parallel view, see Josef Stern's concluding sentence in his *Problems and Parables of Law: Maimonides and Naḥmanides on Reasons for the Commandments (Ta'amei ha-Mitzvot)* (Albany: State University of New York Press, 1998), 160: "Maimonides' explanation of the *ḥuqqim* attempted to bring about the fall of myth in Judaism. Instead it led, through its formative influence on Naḥmanides just one generation later, to the resuscitation of the same myths."

14. See, e.g., Robert Alter, "Jewish Mysticism in Dispute," *Commentary* (September 1989): 53–59.
15. Harry Wolfson, "Maimonides and Halevi: A Study in Typical Jewish Attitudes Towards Greek Philosophy in the Middle Ages," in *Studies in the History of Philosophy and Religion,* ed. I. Twersky and G. Williams (Cambridge, Mass.: Harvard University Press, 1977), 120–61.
16. Howard (Ḥaim) Kreisel convincingly argues for the position that Maimonides was familiar with Halevi's work. See his "Judah Halevi's Influence on Maimonides: A Preliminary Appraisal," *Maimonidean Studies* 2 (1991): 95–122. In the same issue of *Maimonidean Studies* Joel Kraemer takes it as a given than Maimonides knew the *Kuzari,* and cites texts which prove that Maimonides was also familiar with some of Halevi's poetry; see "Six Unpublished Maimonides Letters from the Cairo Genizah," 82. In "Parallels Between the *Kuzari* and the Non-Philosophical Treatises of Maimonides (Appendix VII to 'Shi'ite Terms and Conceptions in Judah Halevi's *Kuzari*')," in his *Studies in the History of Jewish Thought,* vol. 5, ed. Warren Zev Harvey and Moshe Idel (Jerusalem: Magnes Press, 1997), Shlomo Pines writes: "The foregoing observations assume that Maimonides, having read the *Kuzari,* adapted various texts in that work—those discussed above and perhaps also others—for his own purposes. The hypothesis that he and Judah Halevi had a common source is, of course, also possible. But it is unnecessary, given the practical certainty that Maimonides was familiar with the *Kuzari;* an important apologetic and theological work written by a celebrated member of the Jewish community of Spain would hardly have escaped his notice" (51). See further Pines, "On the Term Ruḥaniyyut and Its Origin, and on Judah Halevi's Doctrine," *Tarbiz* 57 (1988): 511–34 (Hebrew); on 533 Pines takes it as obvious that Maimonides knew Halevi's work well. Most recently, Moshe Gil and Ezra Fleischer, *Yehudah Ha-Levi and His Circle* (Jerusalem: World Union of Jewish Studies, 2001), 199–203 (Hebrew), discuss Halevi's prominence in Egypt in the generation before Maimonides. Indeed, the poet Elazar ben Ḥalfon ha-Cohen lived long enough to write poems of praise of both Halevi and Maimonides. Given the excitement among Egyptian Jewish intellectuals at Halevi's visits to Alexandria and Cairo in 1140–41, it seems hardly credible that Maimonides, who reached Egypt in 1165, was unfamiliar with the man and his work.
17. By citing Halevi and Naḥmanides together I mean only to imply that much of what they share in common distinguishes them sharply from Maimonides. Mordechai Pachter says that Naḥmanides may be considered the disciple of Halevi. See his "The Root of Faith is the Root of Heresy in the Teaching of R. Azriel," *Kabbalah* 4 (1999): 315–41, 337n70 (Hebrew). See further David Novak, *The Theology of Naḥmanides Sytematically Presented* (Atlanta: Scholars Press, 1992), 34–35, and Moshe Idel, "Abulafia's Secrets of the Guide: A Linguistic Turn," *Revue de métaphysique et de morale* 4 (1998): 495–528. In the latter Idel notes that Naḥmanides was "quite critical, though only rarely mentioning names, toward allegorical exegesis and philosophical intellectualism; he is much more in concert with those forms of thought found in some of the Jewish philosophers who preceded Maimonides, like Yehudah ha-Levi or Abraham bar Ḥiyya, for example. He was more open toward magic and had a positive view of the perception of Hebrew as a natural language. Maimonides' stand on this issue consists, however, in

weakening the importance of the sacred language by attenuating its special status" (516). Further on the connection between Halevi and Naḥmanides, compare Isadore Twersky's comment: "In many respects, R. Judah Halevi, Naḥmanides, and the Maharal constitute a special strand of Jewish thought—threefold, yet unified," in his "Maimonides and Eretz Israel: Halakhic, Philosophic, and Historical Perspectives," in *Perspectives on Maimonides: Philosophical and Historical Studies,* ed. Joel Kraemer (Oxford: Oxford University Press, 1991), 261n. On Halevi's influence on Naḥmanides, see the studies listed by Ephraim Kanarfogel in "On the Assessment of R. Moses ben Naḥman (Naḥmanides) and His Literary Oeuvre," *Jewish Book Annual* 54 (1997): 78.

18. *Guide of the Perplexed* III:18. Here and throughout I cite from the translation of Shlomo Pines (Chicago: University of Chicago Press, 1963), with occasional slight emendations. The text cited here is on 474. Maimonides repeats the point at the end of the same chapter (476): "It would not be proper for us to say that providence watches over the species and not the individuals, as is the well-known opinion of some philosophic schools. For outside the mind nothing exists except the individuals; it is to these individuals that the divine intellect is united. Consequently providence watches only over these individuals." Maimonides immediately continues: "Consider this chapter as it ought to be considered; for through it all the fundamental principles of the Law will become safe for you and conformable for you to speculative philosophic opinions; disgraceful views will be abolished." Elisheva Oberman and Josef Stern first drew my attention to these passages. Alfred Ivry comments perceptively: "Maimonides, as a good Aristotelian and would-be nominalist, would like to 'save the phenomena' and not add to them immaterial entities of a conjectural and ultimately redundant sort." See his "Strategies of Interpretation in Maimonides' *Guide of the Perplexed,*" *Jewish History* 6 (1992): 116. Maimonides' nominalism affects other aspects of his thought. See Yochanan Silman, "Halakhic Determinations of a Nominalistic and Realistic Nature: Legal and Philosophical Considerations," *Dine Israel* 12 (1986): 249–66 (Hebrew).
19. See the second and third of Maimonides' "Thirteen Principles"; *Mishneh Torah,* "Laws of the Foundations of the Torah," 1:8; and *Guide of the Perplexed* I:54.
20. Compare Maimonides' natural history of idolatry in "Laws of Idolatry," chap. 1.
21. Compare the fifth of Maimonides' "Thirteen Principles" in which this point is emphasized.
22. Douglas, *Leviticus as Literature* (Oxford: Oxford University Press, 1999), 2–3.
23. In *Maimonides on Judaism and the Jewish People* (Albany: State University of New York Press, 1991) I argue that Maimonides maintained that Jews as such were in no way intrinsically different from any other people. I did not connect that issue to his nominalism, as I do here. I hope to issue a revised and greatly expanded Hebrew translation of my book, in which the point made here will be taken up at much greater length. In the meantime, see "On Universalism and Particularism in Judaism," *Da'at* 36 (1996): v–xv; "Chosenness, Not Chauvinism: Maimonides on the Chosen People," in *A People Apart: Chosenness and Ritual in Jewish Philosophical Thought,* ed. Daniel H. Frank (Albany: State University of New York Press, 1993): 51–76, 85–89; "Overcoming Chosenness," in *Revelation and Redemption in Judaism and Mormonism,* ed. Raphael Jospe and Seth Ward (Madison, N.J.: Farleigh Dickinson University Press, 2001), 147–72; and "Was Maimonides Truly Universalist?"

Trumah: Beitraege zur juedischen Philosophie 11 (*Festgabe zum 80. Geburtstag von Ze'ev Levy*) (2001): 3–15.

24. This claim depends upon an interpretation of "Laws of Kings," 8:11, which I present and defend in *Maimonides on Judaism and the Jewish People,* 75–79. I take up the issue in much greater detail in "Steven Schwarzschild, Moses Maimonides, and 'Jewish Non-Jews,'" in *Moses Maimonides (1138–1204)—His Religious, Scientific, and Philosophical Wirkungsgeschichte in Different Cultural Contexts,* ed. Görge K. Hasselhoff and Otfried Fraisse (Wuerzburg: Ergon, 2004).
25. Maimonides was an esoteric writer for a number of reasons. There were some matters that could not in principle be expressed clearly—they could only be apprehended intuitively. There were other matters about which he could not make up his mind. There were yet other matters which were too dangerous to reveal clearly. I do not believe that he was motivated by fear of danger to himself, but rather by fear of endangering the simple faith of non-philosophical Jews. It is this last sense that I have in mind in this sentence. Further on this sort of esotericism, see my "The Literary Character of the *Mishneh Torah*" (above, note 8). For a valuable study of the whole issue, see Sara Klein-Braslavy, *Shelomoh Ha-Melekh ve-ha-Ezoterizm ha-Filosofi be-Mishnat ha-Rambam* (Jerusalem: Magnes Press, 1996).
26. For examples of Maimonides' elitism see the end of his introduction to *Guide of the Perplexed,* before the list of contradictions (16). For another emphatic example, see II:36, 372. See further his comments in his introduction to *Ḥelek,* the tenth chapter of Mishnah Sanhedrin, where he speaks of a group whose "members are so few in number that it is hardly appropriate to call them a group." I cite the translation from I. Twersky, *A Maimonides Reader* (New York: Behrman House, 1972), 408. "Laws of the Foundations of the Torah," 4:11, would be another good example, as is Maimonides' commentary on Mishnah Ḥagigah 2:1. For an English translation, see "Maimonides' Commentary on *Mishnah Ḥagigah* II.1: Translation and Commentary," in *From Strength to Strength: Lectures from Shearith Israel,* ed. Marc D. Angel (New York: Sepher-Hermon Press, 1998), 101–11.
27. I owe this arresting image to Jolene S. Kellner.
28. Compare Maimonides' explanation of the purpose of *ḥuqqim* as fighting an undeclared war against idolatry. For details, see Josef Stern, *Problems and Parables of Law,* throughout, and esp. 109–60.
29. For details, see my "Maimonides on the 'Normality' of Hebrew," in *Judaism and Modernity: The Religious Philosophy of David Hartman,* ed. Jonathan Malino (Jerusalem: Shalom Hartman Institute, 2001), 435–71.
30. See, for example, BT Berakhot 55a: "Rab Judah said in the name of Rab: Bezalel knew how to combine the letters by which the heavens and earth were created. It is written here, *And He hath filled him with the spirit of God, in wisdom [ḥokhmah] and in understanding [tevunah], and in knowledge [da'at]* (Ex. 35:31) and it is written elsewhere, *The Lord by wisdom [ḥokhmah] founded the earth; by understanding [tevunah] He established the heavens* (Prov. 3:19) and it is also written, *By His knowledge [da'at] the depths were broken up* (Prov. 3:20)." See further BT Avodah Zarah 3a, Genesis Rabbah XVIII, and Ephraim Urbach, *The Sages* (Jerusalem: Magnes Press, 1975), 197–213. For another interesting text, this one from merkavah literature, see Gershom Scholem, *Jewish Gnosticism, Merkabah Mysticism, and Talmudic Tradition* (New York: Jewish Theological Seminary, 1960), 79.

31. On the "ontological" status of Hebrew in *Sefer Yeṣirah,* see further Alexander Altmann, "Saadya's Theory of Revelation: Its Origin and Background," in *Saadya Studies,* ed. E. I. J. Rosenthal (Manchester: Manchester University Press, 1943), 4–25; Joseph Dan, "The Religious Meaning of Sefer Yeṣira," *Jerusalem Studies in Jewish Thought* 11 (1993): 7–36 (Hebrew); Moshe Idel, "Midrashic versus Other Forms of Jewish Hermeneutics: Some Comparative Reflections," in *The Midrashic Imagination: Jewish Exegesis, Thought, and History,* ed. Michael Fishbane (Albany: State University of New York Press, 1993), 45–58. It is surely worthy of note that while Halevi included a commentary on *Sefer Yeṣirah* in the Kuzari (IV:25), Maimonides, so far as is known to us, never mentioned the work. It is hardly credible that he never heard of it.
32. See his "Reification of Language in Jewish Mysticism," in *Mysticism and Language,* ed. Steven Katz (New York: Oxford University Press, 1992), 42–79, 47.
33. For discussions of the issue, see Nehemiah Allony, "The Date of the Composition of *Sefer Yeṣirah,*" *Temirin* 2 (1981): 41–50 (Hebrew), and, more recently, Steven M. Wasserstrom, "Sefer Yesira and Early Islam: A Reappraisal," *Journal of Jewish Thought and Philosophy* 3 (1993): 1–30.
34. See Peter Hayman, "The 'Original Text': A Scholarly Illusion?" in *Words Remembered, Texts Renewed: Essays in Honor of John F. A. Sawyer,* ed. G. Harvey, Jon Davies, and W. Watson (Sheffield: Sheffield Academic Press, 1995), 434–49, and Y. Tzvi Langermann, "A New Redaction of Sefer Yesira?," *Kabbalah* 2 (1997): 49–64. For the book itself, see Ithamar Gruenwald, "A Preliminary Critical Edition of *Sefer Yeṣira,*" *Israel Oriental Studies* 1 (1971): 132–77.
35. See Raphael Jospe, "Early Philosophical Commentaries on the *Sefer Yeṣirah:* Some Comments," *Revue des études juives* 149, no. 4 (1990): 369–415; Shlomo Pines, "Appendix III: Quotations from Saadya's Commentary on Sefer Yeṣira in Maimonides' *Guide of the Perplexed* (Appendix to: Points of Similarity between the Exposition of the Doctrine of the Sefirot in the *Sefer Yeṣira* and a Text of the Pseudo-Clementine *Homilies:* The Implications of this Resemblance," in his *Studies in the History of Jewish Thought,* ed. Warren Zev Harvey and Moshe Idel (Jerusalem: Magnes Press, 1997), 158–63; Colette Sirat, *A History of Jewish Philosophy in the Middle Ages* (Cambridge: Cambridge University Press, 1985), 10; and Irene Zwiep, *Mother of Reason and Revelation: A Short History of Medieval Jewish Linguistic Thought* (Amsterdam: Gieben, 1997), 54. See also Alexander Altmann, "Saadya's Theory of Revelation: Its Origin and Background," in *Saadya Studies,* ed. E. I. J. Rosenthal (Manchester: Manchester University Press, 1943), 4–25. In "Saadya's Goal in his *Commentary on Sefer Yeṣira,*" in *A Straight Path: Studies in Medieval Philosophy and Culture . . . in Honor of Arthur Hyman,* ed. Ruth Link-Salinger (Washington, D.C.: Catholic University of America Press, 1988), 1–9, Haggai Ben-Shammai argues that in his commentary, Saadya sought to detach *Sefer Yeṣirah* from mythical, mystical, and magical interpretations proposed by earlier interpreters of the book.
36. Halevi's view has recently been championed by Irene Zwiep, *Mother of Reason,* 54. In this, Zwiep follows Moshe Idel; see "Reification of Language in Jewish Mysticism," in *Mysticism and Language,* ed. Steven Katz (New York: Oxford University Press, 1992), 42–79, and "Midrashic versus Other Forms of Jewish Hermeneutics: Some Comparative Reflections," in *The Midrashic Imagination: Jewish Exegesis,*

Thought, and History, ed. Michael Fishbane (Albany: State University of New York Press, 1993), 45–58.

37. Ronald Kiener, "Astrology in Jewish Mysticism from the *Sefer Yesira* to the *Zohar,*" *Jerusalem Studies in Jewish Thought* 6 (1987): 1–42.
38. Y. Tzvi Langermann, "Hebrew Astronomy: Deep Soundings from a Rich Tradition," in *Astronomy Across Cultures: The History of Non-Western Astronomy,* ed. Helaine Selin (Dordrecht: Kluwer, 2000), 555–84.
39. See, for example, Elliot Wolfson, "The Theosophy of Shabbetai Donnolo, with Special Emphasis on the Doctrine of *Sefirot* in *Sefer Ḥakhmoni,*" *Jewish History* 6 (1992): 281–316 (*Frank Talmage Memorial Volume*).
40. Joseph Dan, "The Religious Meaning of *Sefer Yeṣira*" (above, note 31).
41. Moshe Idel, *Golem: Jewish Magical and Mystical Traditions on the Artificial Anthropoid* (Albany: State University of New York Press, 1990), 9–26.
42. Yehuda Liebes, *Torat ha-Yeṣirah shel Sefer Yeṣirah* (Jerusalem: Schocken, 2000).
43. Pines, "Quotations from Saadya's Commentary on Sefer Yeṣira" (above, note 35).
44. Y. Tzvi Langermann, "On Some Passages attributed to Maimonides," in *Me'ah She'arim: Studies in Medieval Jewish Spiritual Life in Memory of Isadore Twersky,* ed. G. Blidstein E. Fleischer, C. Horowitz, B. Septimus (Jerusalem: Magnes Press, 2001), 223–40 (Hebrew). See also Liebes (above, note 42), 94, who finds footprints of *Sefer Yeṣirah* in Maimonides' language in "Laws of the Foundation of the Torah," 2:10.
45. See Moshe Idel, "Maimonides and Kabbalah," in *Studies in Maimonides,* ed. Isadore Twersky (Cambridge, Mass.: Harvard University Press, 1990), 34, and Idel, "Jewish Thought in Medieval Spain," in *Moreshet Sepharad: The Sephardi Legacy,* ed. Haim Beinart (Jerusalem: Magnes Press, 1992), 264.
46. See "Analogy vs Identity: The Rejection of Occult Symbolism, 1580–1680," in *Occult and Scientific Mentalities in the Renaissance,* ed. Brian Vickers (Cambridge: Cambridge University Press, 1984), 95.
47. The question of how best to define "magic" has become a major issue in recent scholarship. For a recent discussion, see Yuval Harari, "Religion, Magic, and Adjurations: Methodological Reflections Aimed at a New Definition of Early Magic," *Da'at* 48 (2002): 33–56 (Hebrew). For our purposes, the behaviors forbidden by Maimonides in "Laws of Idolatry," chap. 11, can serve to delimit the parameters of magical praxis. See also *Guide of the Perplexed* III:37 and the discussion of that text in Dov Schwartz, *Astral Magic in Medieval Jewish Thought* (Ramat Gan: Bar-Ilan University Press, 1999), 108–10 (Hebrew).
48. That he knew about them cannot be doubted. Alexander Altmann, "Maimonides' Attitude Towards Jewish Mysticism," in *Studies in Jewish Thought: An Anthology of German Jewish Scholarship,* ed. Alfred Jospe (Detroit: Wayne State University Press, 1981), 207, notes that *Guide of the Perplexed* I:26 shows that Maimonides "was acquainted with the mystical writings about the permutations of the Divine Name."
49. See the edition of Yuval Harari, *Ḥarba de-Mosheh: Mahadurah Ḥadashah u-Meḥkar* (Jerusalem: Akademon, 1997), and the critical comments of Meir Bar-Ilan in his review in *Da'at* 43, 125–40. The "sword" in this book is a list of holy names that can be used for magical purposes. Harari (52) shows that the work was known to Hai Gaon (939–1038) while Bar-Ilan (140) argues that it goes back to the sixth century. There is no evidence that Maimonides knew this work, but it was hardly atypical. *Ḥarba de-Mosheh* was originally edited by Moses Gaster, *Studies and Texts* (New

York: Ktav, 1971), 3:69–103. Gaster's translation of that text may be found in vol. 1, 312–37; he comments on the text on 288–311. On the use of God's name in other texts, see Karl Erich Groezinger, "The Names of God and the Celestial Powers: Their Function and Meaning in the Hekhalot Literature," *Jerusalem Studies in Jewish Thought* 6 (1987): 53–70, and Rachel Elior, "The Concept of God in Hekhalot Literature," *Binah: Studies in Jewish History, Thought, and Culture,* ed. Joseph Dan, vol. 2 (New York: Praeger, 1989), 97–120.

50. See, e.g., BT Kiddushin 71a, BT Makkot 11a, BT Menaḥot 29b, and BT Pesaḥim 50a.
51. Ithamar Gruenwald, *Apocalyptic and Merkavah Mysticism* (Leiden: Brill, 1980), 225–34.
52. Lee I. Levine, *Judaism and Hellenism in Antiquity: Conflict or Confluence?* (Seattle: University of Washington Press, 1998), 10.
53. See Baruch Levine, "Appendix: The Language of the Magical Bowls," in *A History of the Jews in Babylonia,* ed. Jacob Neusner (Leiden: Brill, 1970), 344.
54. Mordecai Margalioth, *Sefer ha-Razim* (Jerusalem: American Academy for Jewish Research, 1967). On this edition, see Joseph Dan, "Margolioth's Edition of *Sefer ha-Razim,*" *Tarbiz* 37 (1968): 208–14. The work was translated into English by Michael Morgan in *Sepher ha-Razim: The Book of the Mysteries* (Chico, Calif.: Scholars Press, 1983).
55. On this, see Gruenwald, *Apocalyptic and Merkavah Mysticism,* 225, and, importantly, the discussion in Scholem, *Jewish Gnosticism,* 66–74, 81–84, and 94–100.
56. Dan, "Margalioth's Edition of *Sefer ha-Razim,*" 212, and Peter Schaefer, "Jewish Magic Literature in Late Antiquity and Early Middle Ages," *Journal of Jewish Studies* 41 (1990): 75–91.
57. See Gruenwald, *Apocalyptic and Merkavah Mysticism,* 230: "Conjuration of the angels is frequently connected with ritual performances which, according to traditional standards, are downright idolatry. One is expected to offer libations to the angels and incense to the astral bodies. In one case one even has to sacrifice a white cock to the moon and stars. Most surprising is the prayer to Helios, which one has to say if one desires to see the sun rising in its chariot."
58. Margalioth, *Sefer ha-Razim,* 41.
59. See P. S. Alexander, "Incantations and Books of Magic," in *The History of the Jewish People in the Age of Jesus Christ (175 B.C.–A.D. 135) By Emil Schuerer,* ed. Fergus Millar, Martin Goodman, and Geza Vermes (Edinburgh: T. and T. Clark, 1986), 349.
60. See Peter Schaefer, "Magic and Religion in Ancient Judaism," in *Envisioning Magic: A Princeton Seminar and Symposium,* ed. Peter Schaefer and Hans G. Kippenberg (Leiden: Brill, 1997), 38.
61. See Rachel Elior, "Mysticism, Magic, and Angelology—The Perception of Angels in Hekhalot Literature," *Jewish Studies Quarterly* 1 (1993): 41. Further on *Sefer ha-Razim,* see Judah Goldin, "The Magic of Magic and Superstition," in *Studies in Midrash and Related Literature,* ed. Barry L. Eichler and Jeffrey H. Tigay (Philadelphia: Jewish Publication Society, 1988), 353–55.
62. For further background on the magical and theurgic uses of Hebrew in rabbinic texts and culture, see Ithamar Gruenwald, "*Ha-Ketav, ha-Mikhtav,* and the Articulated Name—Magic, Spirituality and Mysticism," in *Massu'ot: Meḥqarim . . . le-Zikhro shel Prof. Ephraim Gottlieb,* ed. Michal Oron and Amos Goldreich (Jerusalem: Mossad Bialik, 1994), 75–98 (Hebrew). For evidence that the magical and theur-

gic uses of divine names were widespread in the generations immediately after Maimonides, see the text of Abraham Abulafia (b. 1240) cited in Moshe Idel, "Judaism, Jewish Mysticism, and Magic," *Jewish Studies* 36 (1996): 35–36 (Hebrew).

63. In an as yet unpublished study.
64. I am deeply grateful to Prof. Joshua Golding of Bellarmine University for helping me to think through this issue; he is in no way responsible for the use to which I put his insights here!
65. Compare Louis Jacobs, "Holy Places," *Conservative Judaism* 37, no. 3 (1984): 4–16, who points to "the absence of anything like a systematic treatment of the topic [of holiness in Judaism]" (4). My claim here is well illustrated in a fascinating study by F. E. Peters, *Jerusalem and Mecca: The Typology of the Holy City in the Near East* (New York: New York University Press, 1986). The question of how Judaism and Islam understand the nature of holiness is nowhere addressed in this important book.
66. Even Halevi, who clearly sees the distinctions between the Land of Israel and all other lands, and between the Jewish people and other peoples, as reflecting something real in the universe (i.e., as having what I have been calling here ontological standing), nowhere speaks clearly and explicitly about the nature of holiness.
67. A good example of the ambiguity on the subject of holiness in pre-Maimonidean Judaism may be found in the language of the opening formula of blessings ordinarily recited before the fulfillment of any positive commandment: "Blessed are You, Lord our God, king of the universe, Who has sanctified us with His commandments and commanded us to. . . ." One can understand this language as affirming that the imposition of the commandments has made Israel intrinsically holy, or, on the other hand, as affirming, as I claim Maimonides to do, that holiness is a consequence of fulfilling the commandments and that it means nothing more than that.
68. I have written a separate and as yet unpublished study proving the claims made in this section of the paper. My thinking on holiness was greatly helped by Warren Zev Harvey, "Holiness: A Command to Imitatio Dei," *Tradition* 16 (1977): 7–28; Kenneth Seeskin, "Holiness as an Ethical Ideal," *Journal of Jewish Thought and Philosophy* 5 (1996): 191–203; Yochanan Silman, "Commandments and Transgressions in Halakhah—Obedience and Rebellion, or Repair and Destruction?" *Dine Israel* 16 (1991): 183–201 (Hebrew); and Yochanan Silman, "Introduction to the Philosophical Analysis of the Normative-Ontological Tension in the Halakha," *Da'at* 31 (1993): v–xx. For useful studies of some of the many texts which give expression to a distinctly non-Maimonidean understanding of holiness, see the studies collected in Joseph Dan, *Al Ha-Qedushah* (Jerusalem: Magnes Press, 1997).
69. I am, of course, not the first student to take note of the unusual character of Maimonides' views on the subject of ritual purity and impurity (see, for example, the very important comments of David Henshke, "On Judicial Reality in the Teachings of Maimonides," *Sinai* 92 [1982–83]: 228–39 [Hebrew]), but I am not aware of other attempts to see in these views a reflection of a much broader religious orientation on the part of Maimonides, as I do here.
70. A soft, white cloth, appropriate for intimate examinations of menstrual purity.
71. Niddah 67a.
72. I.e., a minor question concerning her ritual purity persists.
73. From the root *d-r-s,* which indicates a form of contact which imparts ritual impurity.

74. I.e., the myrtle bough had been soaked in pure balsam and was itself full of oil of foliatum; the fine white cloth was wrapped around this bough.
75. I cite the translation of Morton Smith brought in Scholem, *Jewish Gnosticism,* 10.
76. See Lawrence Schiffman, "The Recall of Rabbi Neḥunya ben ha-Kanah from Ecstasy in the *Hekhalot Rabbati,*" *AJS Review* 1 (1976): 274. Seth Kadish pointed out to me that one of the matters at issue here is that an entity held to be ritually impure only by minority opinion can still have an extremely minor but actual ritual impurity. In other words, in this view the power of ritual impurity is greater than or at least independent of established *halakhah.*
77. For a clear expression of ritual purity thus understood, see Mary Douglas, *Purity and Danger: An Analysis of the Concepts of Pollution and Taboo* (London: Routledge, 1984), 114.
78. Further on this text, see Saul Lieberman, "The Knowledge of the Halakhah by the Author (or Authors) of the Heikhaloth," in *Apocalyptic and Merkavah Mysticism,* ed. Ithamar Gruenwald (Leiden: Brill, 1980), 241–44, and Michael D. Swartz, *Scholastic Magic: Ritual and Revelation in Early Jewish Mysticism* (Princeton: Princeton University Press, 1996), 170–72.
79. I base this claim on an analysis of *Kuzari* 2:14, 2:60, 3:21, and 3:53 in my "Maimonides on the Nature of Ritual Purity and Impurity," *Da'at* 50–52 (2003): i–xxx.
80. Naḥmanides seems to follow Halevi, not Maimonides, in his view of the nature of ritual impurity. For an indication of this, see his commentary to Leviticus 16:4 (near the end). Further indication of this may be found in his commentary to Leviticus 19:2, especially as explicated by José Faur, *In the Shadow of History: Jews and Conversos at the Dawn of Modernity* (Albany: State University of New York Press, 1992), 12–13. See further the comment of Alan J. Yuter, "Positivist Rhetoric and Its Functions in Haredi Orthodoxy," *Jewish Political Studies Review* 8 (1996): 156: "A third critique of Maimonides stems from Naḥmanides, who does not believe that Jewish normativity can be defined solely on the basis of the absolute, hard, cold statute."
81. Most emphatically in "Laws of Immersion Pools," 11:12, "Laws of the Ritual Impurity of Foodstuffs," 16:12, and *Guide of the Perplexed* III:47 (595–96). For these and many other texts, see my "Maimonides on the Nature of Ritual Purity and Impurity."
82. *Guide of the Perplexed* III:51, 622. Compare "Laws of Substituted Offerings" (*Temurah*) IV:13. See the translation of this text and discussion in Twersky, *Introduction to the Code of Maimonides,* 416–17. See also the following sentence in *Guide of the Perplexed* III:52 (630): "The end of the actions prescribed by the whole Law is to bring about the passion of which it is correct that it be brought about. . . . I refer to the fear of Him . . . and the awe before His command." The commandments, Maimonides goes on to explain, bring one to awe of God, while the doctrines taught in the Torah bring one to love of God. The commandments are all means to an end external to them. My concern here is with the question of ritual purity and impurity; on how the passage adduced here fits into Maimonides' doctrine of the reasons for the commandments (*ta'amei ha-miṣvot*), see Stern, *Problems and Parables of Law,* chaps. 4 and 6.
83. Given the prominence of angels in rabbinic *aggadah,* it is quite remarkable to note that angels do not appear at all in the Mishnah. See Judah Goldin, *Studies in Midrash*

and Related Literature, ed. Barry L. Eichler and Jeffrey H. Tigay (Philadelphia: Jewish Publication Society, 1988), 375.

84. For studies on Maimonides' understanding of the nature of angels, see Zvi (Harry) Blumberg, "The Separate Intelligences in Maimonides' Philosophy," *Tarbiz* 40 (1971): 216–25; and Lenn Evan Goodman, "Maimonidean Naturalism," in *Maimonides and the Sciences,* ed. R. S. Cohen and H. Levine (Dordrecht: Kluwer, 2000), 57–85. Relevant to our theme also are Joseph Elias Heller, "The Essence and Purpose of the Active Intellect According to Maimonides," in *Sefer Yovel Li-Shemvél Kalman Mirsky,* ed. S. Bernstein and G. Churgin (New York: Mirsky Jubilee Committee, 1958), 26–42 (Hebrew), and Y. Tzvi Langermann, "Maimonides' Repudiation of Astrology," *Maimonidean Studies* 2 (1991): 123–58.

85. Howard (Ḥaim) Kreisel, "Moses Maimonides," in *History of Jewish Philosophy,* ed. Daniel H. Frank and Oliver Leaman (London: Routledge, 1997), 255.

86. For background on the notion of the separate intellects in general, see the studies of Harry Austryn Wolfson: "The Problem of the Souls of the Spheres, from the Byzantine Commentaries on Aristotle through the Arabs and St. Thomas to Kepler," in *Studies in the History and Philosophy of Religion,* ed. Isadore Twersky and George H. Williams (Cambridge, Mass.: Harvard University Press, 1973), 22–59, and, in the same collection, "The Plurality of Immovable Movers in Aristotle, Averroes, and St. Thomas," 1–21. Maimonides' identification of the angels of Scripture with the separate intellects did not go unchallenged. Shem Tov Ibn Shem Tov (ca. 1380–1441) was the author of a kabbalistic critique of philosophy called *Sefer ha-Emunot* (Ferrara, 1556; photoedition, 1969). In the first chapter of the fourth part (*sha'ar*) of this work (24b–26b), Shem Tov acknowledges that Maimonides identified the angels of the Bible with the separate intellects of the philosophers, and goes on to criticize him mightily for it. For an important discussion, see Erez Peleg's recently completed doctoral dissertation, "Shem Tov ibn Shem Tov's Critique of Philosophy," University of Haifa, 2003 (Hebrew).

87. For background on rabbinic anthropomorphizing of angels, see Leo Jung, *Fallen Angels in Jewish, Christian, and Mohammedan Literature* (New York: Ktav, 1974); Joseph Schultz, "Angelic Opposition to the Ascension of Moses and the Revelation of the Law," *Jewish Quarterly Review* 61 (1970/71): 282–307; and Alexander Altmann, "The Gnostic Background of the Rabbinic Adam Legends," in *Essays in Jewish Intellectual History* (Hanover, N.H.: University Press of New England, 1981), 1–16. For a general survey on angels in rabbinic texts, see Ephraim Urbach, *The Sages: Their Concepts and Beliefs* (Jerusalem: Magnes Press, 1975), 1:134–83.

88. Rachel Elior maintains: "The three primary characteristics, which together create the uniqueness of the Hekhalot tradition, are *mysticism, angelology,* and *magic*" ("Mysticism, Magic, and Angelology," 6). See also Swartz, *Scholastic Magic,* 20. Summarizing a huge body of research, Swartz identifies "three prevailing elements of Jewish magical texts: (1) the emphasis on the power of the name of God; (2) the intermediacy of the angels in negotiating between divine providence and human needs; (3) the application of divine names and ritual practices for the needs of specific individuals." The magical texts Swartz speaks of are all part of the Hekhalot literature.

89. Apropos *merkavah* texts, Gershom Scholem makes reference to "the frequent use of secret or mystical names of God, the difficulties arising from such use, and the consequent blurring, in some instances, of the borderline between these names of God and the names of angels." See his *Jewish Gnosticism,* 10. See also Elior, "Mysticism, Magic, and Angelology," 34: "The abundance of angels and the appropriation of the uniqueness of the name of God indicate an essential change in religious conception . . . from a single God to a complex of divine forces, nullifying the uniqueness of the single divine entity."
90. For an extended study of Meṭaṭron texts, see Nathaniel Deutsch, *Guardians of the Gate: Angelic Vice Regency in Late Antiquity* (Leiden: Brill, 1999), and the important study of Moshe Idel, "Enoch is Meṭaṭron," *Jerusalem Studies in Jewish Thought* 6 (1987): 151–70 (Hebrew).
91. For an extended discussion of this phenomenon, see Rebecca M. Lesses, *Ritual Practices to Gain Power: Angels, Incantations, and Revelation in Early Jewish Mysticism* (Harrisburg, Pa.: Trinity Press International, 1998). Compare also Elior ("Mysticism, Magic, and Angelology," 39), who points out that in the Hekhalot literature angels "are served, adored, praised, and worshiped."
92. Elior, "Mysticism, Magic, and Angelology," 12. Elior goes so far as to see the "perception of angels of the Hekhalot literature, [as] reflecting the continuation of the process of mythologization which began in post-Scriptural literature, [and which] was consolidated . . . in a period when polytheism, paganism, occult, and magical traditions were pre-eminent in the surrounding cultures" (29). Lesses agrees, characterizing the vision of Hekhalot literature as "polytheistic" and as resembling "the profusion of deities and angels whom the Greco-Egyptian adjurations address" (*Ritual Practices to Gain Power,* 276). On the distinction between the sub- and superlunar worlds, see *Guide of the Perplexed* II:22–24.
93. See Maimonides' comment in his "Letter on Astrology" to the effect that he did not think that a single Arabic language text on idolatry had escaped his notice. See Y. Shailat, ed. and trans., *Iggerot ha-Rambam* (Jerusalem: Ma'aliyot, 1988), vol. 2, 481. Compare statements in the same vein in *Guide of the Perplexed,* III:29, 518, and III:49, 612. The apparent contradiction between this claim and Maimonides' statement in "Laws of Idolatry," II:2, that God has forbidden us to read these books has generated considerable discussion.
94. See above, note 11.
95. In a cleverly argued discussion, Steven Harvey suggests "the possible influence of merkavah terminology and symbolism on Maimonides." See his "Maimonides in the Sultan's Palace," in *Perspectives on Maimonides* (above, note 17), 64. In the same volume of studies, in an essay titled "Maimonides' Quest Beyond Philosophy and Prophecy" (141–57), Ithamar Gruenwald notes that "there are good reasons for believing that Maimonides was familiar with some of the mystical writings of the *merkavah* mystics" (142). In "Some Forms of Divine Appearance in Ancient Jewish Thought," in *From Ancient Israel to Modern Judaism . . . Essays in Honor of Marvin Fox,* ed. Jacob Neusner (Atlanta: Scholars Press, 1989), 261–70, Michael Fishbane argues that some of Maimonides' religious language is derived from texts of "mystical theosophy." The point I am urging here is different from that made by Harvey and Fishbane: not only did Maimonides use lan-

guage and symbolism derived from *merkavah* texts but he purposefully did so in order to quietly undermine the teachings of those texts and replace them with what was in his mind a more refined and truer version of Judaism. Compare Alfred Ivry, "Isma'ili Theology and Maimonides' Philosophy," 285: "Accordingly, Maimonides may be seen, in much of the first part of the *Guide*, and elsewhere, as engaged in a prolonged struggle not merely or even essentially with a primitive Jewish fundamentalism, but rather with a highly imaginative theosophy. This theosophical approach, while nourished by earlier Jewish sources, could well have been encouraged by certain parallel religious formulations in Shi'i literature. . . . It may well be that Maimonides is inveighing against a traditional but growing religious fashion in his day, one current among Jews and Muslims alike; a fashion that was temporarily stalled with the political defeat of the fatimids and with the success of Maimonides' own efforts, but which, in the form of Kabbalah and later Persian theosophy, was not to be denied much longer in either faith."

96. If Maimonides was unenthusiastic about angels, he was downright antagonistic to demons. I plan to address the subject in a separate study. In the meantime, see his commentary to Mishnah Avodah Zarah 4:6, "Laws of Idolatry," 11:20, *Guide of the Perplexed* I:7 and III:29 and 46, and the discussions in Marc Shapiro, "Maimonidean Halakhah and Superstition," *Maimonidean Studies* 4 (2000): 69–70; Bezalel Safran, "Maimonides' Attitude to Magic and to Related Types of Thinking," *Porat Yosef: Studies Presented to Rabbi Dr. Joseph Safran*, ed. B. Safran and E. Safran (New York: Ktav, 1992), 92–110; and Y. Tzvi Langermann, "A New Source Concerning Samuel ibn Tibbon's Translation of the *Guide of the Perplexed* and His Comments on It," *Pe'amim* 72 (1997): 51–74 (Hebrew). While he may have never explicitly denied their existence, he was certainly thought to have done so. The Gaon of Vilna, as is well known, attacked him fiercely for having denied the existence of demons. See the latter's commentary to Yoreh De'ah 179:13 and the discussion in Jacob Dienstag, "The Relation of R. Elijah Gaon to the Philosophy of Maimonides," *Talpioth* 4 (1949): 253–68. An amusing sidelight to this issue is the position attributed to Menaḥem Mendel of Kotzk, who, it is said, tried to reconcile Maimonides' denial of the existence of demons with the many rabbinic texts that accept their existence as factual. When Maimonides declared that demons did not exist, the Kotzker is said to have maintained, Heaven accepted his position, and demons ceased to exist. I found this in Yeḥezkel Bransdorfer, *Lekket me-Oṣar ha-Ḥasidut* (Jerusalem, 1976), 22.

97. The argument has not yet been made, nor is this the place to make it. Key texts include *Guide of the Perplexed* I:10, 22, 23, 25, 27, 28; II:41, 42, 45; III:45, 52; and especially Maimonides' commentary to Mishnah Ḥagigah 2:1. Relevant studies include Hannah Kasher, "Maimonides' Interpretation of the Story of the Divine Revelation in the Cleft of the Rock," *Da'at* 35 (1995): 29–66, and Klein-Braslavy, *Shelomo ha-Melekh*, 203–10.

98. For representative biblical verses see Exodus 33:18, 24:17, 16:10, 40:34; Leviticus 9:6, 9:23; Numbers 14:10, 14:22, 17:7; 1 Kings 8:11; Isaiah 6:3, 40:5, 60:1; Ezekiel 1:28, 3:23, 10:19, 43:5; and 2 Chronicles 7:1. For a representative rabbinic text, see Genesis Rabbah XIX:7; for discussion, see Michael Fishbane, "The Measure and

Glory of God in Ancient Midrash," in *The Exegetical Imagination: On Jewish Thought and Theology* (Cambridge, Mass.: Harvard University Press, 1998), 56–72.

99. For details, see Elior, "The Concept of God in Hekhalot Literature," above, note 49; Scholem, *Jewish Gnosticism,* above, note 30; Scholem, *On the Mystical Shape of the Godhead: Basic Concepts in the Kabbalah,* trans. Joachim Neugroschel (New York: Schocken, 1991); Shlomo Pines, "God, the Divine Glory, and the Angels According to a 2nd Century Theology," *Jerusalem Studies in Jewish Thought* 6:3–4 (1987): 1–14 (Hebrew); Elliot Wolfson, "Merkavah Traditions in Philosophical Garb: Judah Halevi Reconsidered," *Proceedings of the American Academy for Jewish Research* 57 (1990/91): 179–242; and Wolfson, "Theosophy of Shabbetai Donnolo," above, note 39.

100. On this issue in Saadya, see Alexander Altmann, "Saadya's Theory of Revelation: Its Origin and Background," *Saadya Studies,* ed. E. I. J. Rosenthal (Manchester: Manchester University Press, 1943), 4–25; Gad Freudenthal, "Stoic Physics in the Writings of R. Saadia Ga'on al-Fayyumi and Its Aftermath in Medieval Jewish Mysticism," *Arabic Sciences and Philosophy* 6 (1996): 113–36; and Ronald C. Kiener, "The Hebrew Paraphrase of Saadiah Gaon's *Kitab al-amanat wa'l-i'tiqadat,*" *AJS Review* 11 (1986): 1–25.

101. For a recent study on the Sabians, with references to earlier literature, see Frances E. Peters, "Hermes and Harran: The Roots of Arabic-Islamic Occultism," in *Intellectual Studies on Islam: Essays Written in Honor of Martin B. Dickson,* ed. Michael M. Mazzaoui and Vera B. Moreen (Salt Lake City: University of Utah Press, 1990), 185–215, esp. 188 and 193–206. On Maimonides' use of the Sabians, see Stern, *Problems and Parables of Law,* 111–25, and Sarah Stroumsa, "'Ravings': Maimonides' Concept of Pseudo-Science," *Aleph* 1 (2001): 141–63.

102. For aspects of the *piyyutim* that Maimonides had to have found objectionable, see Alexander Altmann, "Sacred Poetry in Early Hekhalot Literature," *Melilah* 2 (1946): 2–24 (Hebrew); Ithamar Gruenwald, "Yannai's Piyyutim and the Literature of Yordei ha-Merkavah," *Tarbiz* 36 (1967): 257–77 (Hebrew); and, especially, the following two studies by Michael D. Swartz: "Ritual about Myth about Ritual: Towards an Understanding of the *Avodah* in the Rabbinic Period," *Journal of Jewish Thought and Philosophy* 6 (1997): 135–55, and "Place and Person in Ancient Judaism: Describing the Yom Kippur Sacrifice," International Rennert Guest Lecture Series (Ramat Gan: Bar-Ilan University Faculty of Jewish Studies, 2001). For studies on Maimonides on *piyyutim,* see Ya'akov Blidstein, *Ha-Tefillah be-Mishnato he-Hilkhatit shel ha-Rambam* (Jerusalem: Mossad Bialik, 1994), 123–25; Seth Kadish, *Kavvana: Directing the Heart in Jewish Prayer* (Northvale, N.J.: Jason Aronson, 1997), 397–400; and Zvi Zohar, "Umi Metaher Etkhem? Avikhem Shebashamayim—The Prayer, 'Seder ha-Avodah' on the Day of Atonement: Content, Purpose, Meaning," *AJS Review* 14, 1 (1989): 1–28 (Hebrew section).

103. I am aware of the fact that some of the positions I attribute to Maimonides in this essay were also attributed to him (always with great force, but often without sufficient care) by the late Yeshayahu Leibowitz. I arrived at my understanding of Maimonides largely thanks to my studies with the late Steven Schwarzschild and my discussions with Kenneth Seeskin, *yibbadel le-ḥayyim arukkim ve-tovim.* I person-

ally find as much Leibowitz as I do Maimonides in Leibowitz's readings of Maimonides. For my reservations concerning Leibowitz's approach to Maimonides, see my review of his *Judaism, Human Values and the Jewish State in New York Times Book Review,* July 19, 1992, 7, and my "Torah and Science in Modern Jewish Thought: Steven Schwarzschild vs. Yeshayahu Leibowitz," in *Torah et science: Perspectives historiques et théoriques: études offertes à Charles Touati,* Collection de la Revue des études juives, ed. Gad Freudenthal, Jean-Pierre Rothschild, and Gilbert Dahan (Paris/Louvain: Peeters, 2001), 229–37.

104. *Israel Oriental Studies* 4 (1974): 154–78.

3

Varieties of Belief in Medieval Ashkenaz

The Case of Anthropomorphism

EPHRAIM KANARFOGEL

Samuel b. Mordekhai of Marseilles, a little-known Provençal scholar writing in defense of Maimonides and against his detractors (in light of the Maimonidean Controversy of the 1230s), records in an epistle that "the majority of the rabbinic scholars in northern France [accept] anthropomorphism."[1] Naḥmanides (Ramban), in his better-known letter of 1232 to the rabbis of northern France, notes that Ashkenazic scholars leveled the charge that Maimonides was mistaken in insisting (in his *Sefer ha-Madda*) that God has no form or shape. These rabbinic scholars apparently believed that God did have some kind of physical form.[2] Rashi is singled out by a Provençal rationalist, Asher b. Gershom (perhaps of Beziers), as maintaining, in consonance with the view of Maimonides but against the general tenor within the rabbinic circles of northern France, that the physical or anthropomorphic descriptions of God reported by the prophets were products of their (prophetic) imagination rather than actual images.[3] This study will argue that the range of beliefs found in twelfth- and thirteenth-century Ashkenaz with respect to anthropomorphism was broader than these particular (polemical) passages suggest, and was more varied and nuanced than we have become accustomed to thinking.

In considering anew the specific question of anthropomorphism in Ashkenazic rabbinic thought, two related issues that have clouded earlier perceptions must be addressed. The first concerns the interpretation of talmudic and rabbinic *aggadah* generally, and its place within medieval Ashkenazic rabbinic scholarship. Literal versus non-literal interpretation of *aggadah* was a core issue of the Maimonidean Controversy.[4] The approach to aggadic interpretation in medieval Ashkenaz was relatively uniform. E. E. Urbach has shown that the Tosafists (who were the leading talmudic scholars, interpreters, and halakhists in northern France and Germany and, to a lesser extent, in England, Austria, and Italy during the twelfth and thirteenth centuries) brought proofs to their talmudic interpretations from works that were essentially aggadic. Indeed, there are extensive citations from these works in Tosafist literature.[5] The Tosafists took talmudic *aggadah* seriously (even investing it with halakhic valence)[6] and, as legalists, they tended to interpret this material literally or according to its plain sense (following the approach of Rashi in his talmudic commentary).[7] Nonetheless, the fact that the Tosafists (and Rashi) do not seem to have been particularly troubled in their talmudic commentaries by anthropomorphic statements in the *aggadah* should not be taken as proof that they endorsed this position.[8] As Urbach suggests, the Tosafist approach to *aggadah* and to *midrash* was akin to their approach to *halakhah* in another respect as well. The Tosafists (perhaps taking their cue from Rashi once again) did not often pursue the spiritual dimensions or the religious significance of aggadic texts when they interpreted them.[9] Only the Ḥasidei Ashkenaz (German Pietists) composed what Urbach characterizes as "a kind of theological *Tosafot*."[10]

Moreover, although *Tosafot* passages gather and compare aggadic statements to each other and attempt to resolve contradictions between them,[11] Urbach maintains that these comparisons and conclusions should be viewed as typical specimens of Tosafist interpretation of the talmudic corpus, rather than as possible evidence for Tosafist religious thought or beliefs. In order to argue that something is an actual theological position or belief of the Tosafists, one must be able to demonstrate that a belief that emerges from an interpretation of *Tosafot* is not simply a part of the resolution of the talmudic contradiction or textual problem at hand.[12] The fact that Urbach devotes less than a handful of pages in his work to this issue further supports the sense that aggadic interpretation was not, in any event, a major scholarly activity or concern of the *Ba'alei ha-Tosafot*.[13] In sum, despite the tendency in medieval Ashkenaz to understand talmudic *aggadah* according to its literal or plain sense, uniformity of position with respect to anthropomorphism should not automatically be assumed.

The second issue that should be raised at this point emerges from the polemical literature of the kind cited at the beginning of this study. This literature maintains that groups of French rabbis espoused various anti-Maimonidean positions, including anthropomorphism. These views are presumed without offering any significant corroboration from the writings or statements of the French rabbis themselves. Although no one questions the reliability per se of the Provençal or Spanish rabbinic writers who made these assertions, it is nonetheless problematic to learn about the positions that northern French anti-Maimunists or anti-rationalists allegedly held primarily from the pens of those whose mission it was to defend Maimonides.[14]

Accusations in the Maimonidean Controversy were never made to or about a particular Tosafist or Ashkenazic rabbinic scholar. Naḥmanides does not mention the names of any northern French rabbinic figures in his letter to them in which he asks that their ban on the study of *Sefer ha-Madda* (Book of Knowledge) and *Moreh Nevukhim* (Guide of the Perplexed) be lifted or modified. At one point, Naḥmanides refers to the *ḥerem* as having been agreed upon by "all the land of northern France, its Rabbis and Torah leaders."[15] The letter sent by Asher b. Gershom is titled אגרת שלוחה מאת הרב ר' אשר בר' גרשום על אודות מורה הנבוכים לרבני צרפת.[16] Similarly, when the anti-Maimunist, Rabbi Solomon b. Abraham of Montpellier, wished to bring his case against Maimonides and his philosophical writings to the rabbis of northern France for their opinion (in Solomon's words, חשבנו בלבנו להראות צרותינו לרבני צרפת וגדוליה . . . גם הגיע אליהם ספר מורה נבוכים וחרה אפם מאד) he did so without designating a particular rabbinic figure as the addressee. Rabbi Solomon sent Rabbi Yonah of Gerona (who had studied in northern France at the Tosafist academy at Evreux) to carry out this mission. Here, too, there is no record of any specific rabbinic figures with whom Rabbenu Yonah interacted.[17]

Who then were the French rabbis in question? From all the evidence that we have (and despite the lofty titles and designations found in the various letters to the rabbis of northern France), recognized French or German Tosafists (with one exception) were not openly involved in this phase of the Maimonidean Controversy, certainly not in the *ḥerem* that was promulgated against *Sefer ha-Madda* and *Moreh Nevukhim* in the early 1230s.[18] There were, of course, many non-Tosafist rabbinic scholars and students in northern France, and it may well have been this level of the intelligentsia that was more heavily involved.[19] The only known Tosafist to have penned a letter during this phase of the Maimonidean Controversy seems to have been Rabbi Samuel b. Solomon of Falaise.[20] Rabbi Samuel's brief document, however, focuses mostly on the importance of the literal interpretation of *aggadah* (and the negative influences of Maimonides' works) and does not refer to the issue of anthropomorphism at all.[21]

Moreover, Samuel's leading Tosafist contemporaries and colleagues in northern France, Rabbi Yeḥi'el of Paris and Rabbi Moses of Coucy, can hardly be characterized as anti-Maimonidean in the way that Rabbi Samuel was.[22] Rabbi Moses makes extensive use of *Mishneh Torah* in his *Sefer Miṣvot Gadol*. Indeed, *Sefer Miṣvot Gadol* appears to be dependent on *Mishneh Torah* in many ways. To be sure, Rabbi Moses plays down and even ignores many of the philosophical aspects of *Mishneh Torah*.[23] This pattern is not surprising, however, given that the Tosafists (and Ashkenazic rabbinic scholars on the whole) received neither legacy nor training in the formal discipline of philosophy, and displayed no real interest in its study.[24] Although Maimonides' philosophical teachings and *Moreh Nevukhim* were certainly not part of the curriculum of the Tosafists,[25] our inability to identify leading rabbinic figures who were involved in the Maimonidean Controversy should cause us to resist the temptation and the tendency to lump all Tosafists and Ashkenazic rabbinic figures together when it comes to the issues that surrounded this controversy, such as anthropomorphism. The picture that has emerged to this point in our study, which has focused only on developments in northern France, is already much more complex and variegated than has been assumed.[26]

Indeed, contrary to the impression given by the defenders of Maimonides (that has been perpetuated by modern scholarship), a number of Tosafists and rabbinic figures in both northern France and Germany plainly assert that the divine form cannot be characterized or defined accurately through anthropomorphic terms or physical dimensions. Nonetheless, these rabbinic scholars also had to contend with the various biblical and talmudic passages that suggest that God appeared in different modalities and forms to prophets and certain rabbinic figures. Although one might not be inclined to attribute actual physical (or human) dimensions to God, the Bible and the Talmud certainly seem to suggest that God has the ability to appear to human beings in various guises that they can apprehend.

In an effort to reconcile these disparate conceptions, Rabbi Joseph b. Isaac *Bekhor Shor*, a late-twelfth-century northern French *peshat* exegete and Tosafist (who studied with Rabbenu Tam, and is known in the literature of the *Tosafot* as Rabbi Joseph of Orleans),[27] offers the following as the first of two interpretations to Genesis 1:26, "Let us make man in our image" (נעשה אדם בצלמנו כדמותנו). "Let us create man in such a way that (through intimidation) he will rule and dominate all (on earth), just as the Almighty and other heavenly beings dominate in their realms." *Bekhor Shor* cites several biblical verses that suggest that God cannot be described in physical terms or compared with physical beings. The biblical phrases that refer to the eyes or hands of God and so on are merely a convention devised to convey divine actions to man (*le-sabber et ha-ozen*), who can comprehend intelligent existence and functions only in human terms. The vision reported by Ezekiel in which God appears to the prophet in human form is only in the prophet's mind's eye. "For God and the Heavenly entourage can make themselves appear in any form that they would like man to see." The same holds true for the various rabbinic figures (as reported by the Talmud) and other prophets to whom the Almighty appeared. Thus, the comparison of forms in Genesis 1:26 is made (only) with respect to the ability to intimidate other beings, even though in this case as well, the comparison is imprecise.[28]

One is tempted to suggest that Joseph of Orleans had access to Maimonides' *Mishneh Torah.* In "Hilkhot Yesodei ha-Torah" 1:8, Maimonides writes that Scripture explicitly indicates that God has no body or bodily form. Two of the three verses which Maimonides cites to prove his contention are Deuteronomy 4:15 and Isaiah 40:25, the key proof texts adduced by *Bekhor Shor.* In "Yesodei ha-Torah" 1:9, Maimonides goes on to explain (just as *Bekhor Shor* does) that the Torah's phrases which describe the various limbs and parts of God are meant only as illustrations, expressed in human terms that are the only ones which man can appreciate and understand (הכל לפי דעתן של בני אדם הוא שאינן מכירין אלא הגופות), and are not meant to be taken literally. On the other hand, since Joseph of Orleans probably died before Maimonides' death in 1204, and the earliest citation of *Mishneh Torah* by French Tosafists does not occur before the turn of the twelfth century,[29] it is unlikely that Joseph derived his formulation from this work.[30] To be sure, Joseph *Bekhor Shor* is known as one of the more "rationalistic" Tosafists and *peshat* exegetes.[31] He attempted, in a number of verses (and almost systematically), to eliminate anthropomorphic references.[32] Joseph had access to works of Spanish biblical exegesis and thought, including those of Judah Ḥayyuj, Abraham bar

Ḥiyya, and Baḥya Ibn Paquda, if not to the commentaries of Abraham Ibn Ezra.[33] Nonetheless, *Bekhor Shor* does not express himself here in philosophical terms,[34] and cannot be characterized as anything more than a rationalistic rabbinic scholar who had to confront the vexing but obvious dilemma outlined above: How can God, who is essentially non-corporeal, appear to man in seemingly human form? *Bekhor Shor*'s solution appears similar to that of Maimonides in *Mishneh Torah* (as noted) and in *Guide of the Perplexed* as well.[35] Good Tosafist that he was, *Bekhor Shor* was also concerned with identifying and explaining relevant talmudic sources, and he marshals them to support his claim that God appears to man in physical form only via some type of mental imagery (*medammeh/idmei*).

The notion of a paranormal or psychologistic revelation, directed by God, through which a vision appears in the mind of the prophet without anything actually happening in the external world, is also held by Rabbi Hai Gaon, Rabbi Ḥanan'el b. Ḥushi'el of Kairouan, and Rabbi Nathan b. Yeḥi'el of Rome, author of the *Arukh*.[36] Clearly, the Tosafist Rabbi Joseph (*Bekhor Shor*) of Orleans cannot be included among those rabbis of northern France who wished to attribute forms of corporeality or anthropomorphism to God. To be sure, Joseph's view also dovetailed with his second interpretation of Genesis 1:26, an overtly polemical refutation of this verse as a Trinitarian proof text.[37]

Rabbi Moses Taku, a German Tosafist writing (ca. 1220) in his rather idiosyncratic treatise of Jewish thought titled *Ketav Tamim*,[38] describes the Almighty in terms that are, at first blush, strikingly similar to those of Joseph *Bekhor Shor*. Moreover, Taku's underlying concerns are the same as those of *Bekhor Shor*. Nonetheless, Taku reaches a conclusion that is decidedly different.[39]

Although Rabbi Moses Taku begins, as *Bekhor Shor* did, with an assertion that God cannot be accurately characterized by or compared to any particular physical form (*lo yidmeh lo shum demut*),[40] Taku adds that when God decides to show himself in a particular form to angels or to prophets, he actually adopts that form. He does not create a separate form (often referred to as the *kavod ha-nivra*) to represent Him (which is the view held by Saadya Gaon and, with modification, by the leaders of the German Pietists, as we shall see). Moreover, while God sometimes does adopt a well-defined form, in other instances He does not, appearing instead as "an unusual light without form,"[41] or even through a voice, without any visual imagery.[42] In addition, Rabbi Moses asserts that God has the power of movement (נידה וניעה), an assessment that once again puts him at odds with both Maimonides and Saadya (who believe that this compromises God's infinitude).[43]

In the course of this passage then, Rabbi Moses Taku rejects almost all other contemporary Jewish approaches toward eliminating or minimizing anthropomorphism, a contrarian approach taken throughout his *Ketav Tamim* for which Rabbi Moses is well known in modern scholarship.[44] It must be pointed out and emphasized, however, that Rabbi Moses himself does not believe that God is simply or consistently anthropomorphic.[45] Rather, just as God has the ability or possibility of appearing in various forms, He has the ability to move in certain ways and vice versa. This observation explains the somewhat perplexing fact that Rabbi Moses (unlike several other Ashkenazic thinkers, including Eleazar of Worms and members of the Ḥug ha-Keruv ha-Meyuḥad) denies completely the authority of the highly anthropomorphic *Shi'ur Qomah* on any plane (even the non-literal or symbolic).[46] Some have understood this as a function of Taku's respect for the canonical (biblical and) talmudic corpus, and his concomitant discounting of conflicting rabbinic traditions or interpretations outside of that corpus.[47] Although this may be so (and we will see another example of this attitude below, in Taku's interpretation of Genesis 1:26), the more compelling ideological reason for Taku's view, to my mind, is based on the notion that God does not have a singular, permanent form that can be precisely traced or described (as the work *Shi'ur Qomah* attempts to do). What God does have, according to Taku, is the possibility of adopting different forms as the situation warrants. As Israel Ta-Shma put it, Taku's approach "does not reject the anti-anthropomorphic conception [*ha-tefisah ha-mufshetet*] which is also not exclusive but only one possibility. The Godhead can choose for itself the type of appearance that is most appropriate at a particular time and does not require the approval of the philosophers in order to adopt for itself the option of anthropomorphism, [which can be done] as warranted or desired."[48]

For this reason, in my view, Rabbi Moses is equally unhappy with the more "permanent" solutions proposed by Saadya (that God appears through the created *kavod*), Rabbi Judah he-Ḥasid (that God appears through an emanated *kavod*), and Maimonides (that God appears to the prophet in a vision that is in the prophet's mind).[49] For Rabbi Moses, God actually appears to the prophet in a particular form at a specific point and time, even though He has no fixed, permanent form that can be sketched or described. Indeed, Rabbi Moses distinguishes elsewhere in *Ketav Tamim* between a *ṣelem,* which God has, and a fixed *demut,* which He does not have. *Ṣelem* for Rabbi Moses denotes the fact that a being (in this case the Almighty) actually exists, as opposed to *demut,* which conveys the notion of a fixed form for that being (which does not apply to God).[50] This distinction, between the physical appearance of God at a particular point in human history even though God does not have a fixed form, is found in Taku's interpretation of Genesis 1:26 (where he presents additional examples of God's ability to appear in different forms).[51] Rabbi Moses Taku (and a northern French predecessor, Rabbi Jacob b. Samson,[52] whose view Rabbi Moses cites approvingly in this passage), could certainly have been a target of the Maimunists' critique. Nonetheless, it should be noted that while Rabbi Moses Taku was not completely atypical in his view, he does not represent a monolithic position within medieval Ashkenaz, as we shall continue to see.[53] Moreover, Moses is not arguing for absolute divine corporealism, nor does he believe that God can be fairly and accurately characterized in crude anthropomorphic terms. Indeed, if we look purely from the standpoint of methodology, the distance between Taku and *Bekhor Shor* is not all that great.[54]

Rabbi Solomon Simhaḥ b. Eliezer of Troyes (c. 1235–1300), a descendant of Rashi and student of Rabbi Meir of Rothenburg and Rabbi Pereẓ of Corbeil, flourished well after the Maimonidean Controversy of the 1230s.[55] Nonetheless, given his keen interest in maintaining an anti-allegorical approach to Scripture, Rabbi Solomon analyzes and addresses the dilemma of divine anthropomorphism in his *Sefer ha-Maskil.* Solomon utilizes terms and texts found in both *Bekhor Shor* and Taku, but ultimately stakes out a unique position somewhere in between their approaches. In two places in his work, Solomon criticizes the view held by (rabbinic) scholars and philosophers that when the Torah asserts that God spoke, it is merely a *mashal* (allegory), since speech only emanates from a being that has a body. According to this view, God's words were not heard at Sinai, but rather they were apprehended and understood by the intellects of Moses and the Jewish people. Solomon rejects this possibility, arguing that it is not the physical mouth that gives a human being the power of speech but rather the *ruaḥ,* the essential being or existence of the person. Similarly, God's existence gives Him the ability to speak (although the speech of God is obviously produced in a different manner). Thus, even though God is incorporeal, He did actually speak to the Jewish people.[56]

In another passage, Solomon chides those who go astray by presuming that God actually revealed Himself in the various physical forms and imageries that the Torah intimates and that are described by the prophets. Rather, Solomon insists, God has no image or form (*ein leha-Shem yitbarakh demut ve-ṣurah*). Solomon cites the verses in Isaiah 40 to this effect, and he also notes that the biblical descriptions of various divine limbs are simply to facilitate their understanding, *le-sabber et ha-ozen mah she-hi yekholah lishmoa'*. Moving forward, Solomon characterizes the physical forms that the prophets saw in their prophetic visions in a different way. What they saw was a temporary image (*demut she-hu lefi sha'ah*), "For God does not have a standing (permanent) form or shape."[57]

Gad Freudenthal notes that one of the verses cited by *Sefer ha-Maskil* is found in Maimonides' treatment of anthropomorphism in "Hilkhot Yesodei ha-Torah" 1:8 (and both are found in Shabbetai Donnolo's treatment of Genesis 1:26, in his *Sefer Ḥakhmoni*).[58] More significantly, however, both verses are also found in *Bekhor Shor*'s commentary to Genesis 1:26, as is the phrase *le-sabber et ha-ozen*.[59] The question here is whether Solomon's use of the concept of *demut le-fi ṣorekh ha-sha'ah* (even though, at the same time, "*ein lo demut omedet*") signifies that God actually adopted the temporary physical form (in line with the view of Moses Taku), or whether Solomon, in accordance with the view of *Bekhor Shor,* means that God has no real image or form (*demut omedet*) and that the temporary prophetic image that he refers to is not a corporeal manifestation of God.

Freudenthal holds that as opposed to Taku, Solomon was not a *magshim* (even though Solomon, like Taku, was strongly against allegorical interpretation).[60] Indeed, Freudenthal demonstrates that *Sefer ha-Maskil* also developed a unique approach to angelology that informs his view. According to Solomon, there are three classes of angels who do the will of the Almighty. The "permanent" or "existing" ones (*mal'akhim qayyamim*) are those such as Mikha'el, Refa'el, and Gavri'el. The second and third classes are called the "temporary angels" (*mal'akhim le-sha'ah*) and the "separate air" (*ruaḥ nifrad*). The temporary angels are appointed for a particular mission or activity. When their mission is completed, they are consumed by fire. This type of angel is also described as "a separate air from the secret source, from the mysterious (divine) air, blessed be He" (*ruaḥ ha-mufla barukh Hu*). Similarly, the members of the third class (the *ruaḥ nifrad*) were also mobilized specially in order to do His bidding, but following their missions they are returned to their place. As opposed to the "permanent angel," the latter two classes of angels are derived from the essence of the Almighty (*ruaḥ ha-iqqar*). While the "permanent" angels have set responsibilities, the latter two groups do not, serving in limited capacities and particular one-time situations.[61]

Most important for our purposes, however, is Solomon's view that the divine essence (*ha-E-l ha-iqqar*), which in Solomon's cosmological scheme is to be identified with the cosmic Air that fills the entire world (*ha-E-l ha-avir/ha-avir ha-mufla*),[62] can be manifested through various physical forms. The different "separate airs," each of which has a unique and finite mission, do not compromise divine corporeality on the one hand, but are responsible, on the other hand, for the many forms through which the Almighty reveals Himself to the prophets and to others.[63] It is these groups of angels who are responsible for the "temporary manifestations" (*demut she-hu lefi sha'ah*) of God that appeared to the prophets as needed (*le-ṣorekh ha-sha'ah*), but who then receded. As Solomon concludes, אין להקב"ה גוף וצורה עומדת—all of these various representations of God are angelic, and are therefore not permanent.

Although Solomon's solution to the problem of anthropomorphism in situations where God appeared to prophets and others seems to be closer empirically to the approach of Joseph *Bekhor Shor* than to the position of Moses Taku, there is one additional factor that must be considered. The identification made by Solomon between God and the cosmic Air is itself at least partly anthropomorphic. Saadya's comparisons between God and the *avir* that fills the entire world (found especially in his commentary to *Sefer Yeṣirah*) were figurative and were meant only as metaphor. Solomon invested this comparison, however, with real, physical properties (the substance of God is to be found in the air and in the light above the firmament), moving him closer overall to the position of Taku.[64]

There were, however, a number of other leading scholars in northern France and Germany during the twelfth and thirteenth centuries whose views are more closely in line with the position of *Bekhor Shor.* The German Pietists were quite interested in eliminating anthropomorphism by distinguishing between the hidden essence of God and the divine glory (*kavod*) that was created or emanated, and therefore distinct from God. Beginning with Rabbi Judah *he-Ḥasid* himself, and employing ideas of Saadya Gaon,[65] as well as other earlier medieval rabbinic figures such as Rabbi Nathan b. Yeḥi'el, Rabbi Ḥanan'el b.

Ḥushi'el, Rabbi Shabbetai Donnolo, and Rabbi Abraham Ibn Ezra (and, to a lesser extent, Abraham bar Ḥiyya), the pietists were thus able to explicitly and repeatedly reject anthropomorphism, and to assert that God has no material or representable form.[66]

In a treatise attributed to Rabbi Judah he-Ḥasid, three approaches are presented as to which manifestation of God the prophets saw: (1) they saw the created Glory (following Saadya); (2) they saw a vision in their own mind, directed by God, but which never actually occurred (*aḥizat enayim;* this position is held by Rav Hai and by Maimonides); (3) they saw an emanated divine power, the Divine Glory (*kavod*). The upper aspect of this emanation cannot be seen, but the lower aspect is the subject of prophetic vision. This is the position that Rabbi Judah *he-Ḥasid* prefers, although he was not unalterably opposed to the others. Judah's preferred position follows the approach of Abraham Ibn Ezra.[67]

The phrase אין שייך בו [לבורא] לא צלם ולא דמות and its variants are found repeatedly in the treatise titled *Sha'arei ha-Sod ve-ha-Yiḥud ve-ha-Emunah,* composed by Judah's leading pupil, Rabbi Eleazar of Worms. Eleazar also decries those who insisted on radical anthropomorphism by attributing various limbs to the Almighty (אין לבורא לא גוף וגושם/אין לו איברים / אין לו מידת הגושמ[נים]/ אין לדמותו לבריותיו), categorizing them as grave sinners (חוטאים בנפשם). Biblical phrases that describe God's actions in anthropomorphic terms were formulated only so that human beings would be able to grasp their meaning (ומה שנאמר מילות בקרייה ענייני גושמנים לא נכתבו כי אם להבין לבני אדם.)[68] Rabbi Eleazar mentions those earlier rabbinic authorities (including Saadya Gaon, Rabbenu Ḥanan'el, Rabbi Nissim Gaon, and Rabbi Nathan b. Yeḥi'el) who agreed that God has no physical image or form. Like Rabbi Judah he-Ḥasid, Rabbi Eleazar is fundamentally comfortable with their views, even as he, like Rabbi Judah, advocates the model of the emanated (or revealed) *kavod* that appeared to the prophets in various forms (including human ones) as needed (כפי צורך שעה).[69]

In this same treatise, Rabbi Eleazar also offers a related interpretation of Genesis 1:26–27 that blunts the possible anthropomorphic reference suggested by these verses. According to Eleazar, these verses do not imply that the Creator has the form or image of His creations. Rather, the meaning of making man "in our image" is that "we [the angels who are implied in the plural form of the verse] wish to be revealed to the prophets in the most desirable countenance, which is the human face." Thus, man was created in the cherished human-like countenance or image of the angels, which is the image that God shows to the prophets.[70]

Naḥmanides, in his letter of 1232 to the *rabbanei Ṣarefat* (French rabbis), cites extensively from this treatise by Rabbi Eleazar of Worms in an effort to show that the view of a leading Ashkenazic scholar (and sometime Tosafist as well) is compatible with that of Maimonides.[71] He also notes that this work of Rabbi Eleazar was readily available to the rabbis of northern France.[72]

In his commentary to *Sefer Yeṣirah,* Eleazar states unequivocally that God has no bodily image and cannot be seen. Nonetheless, God "appears to the prophets by means of the presence of His glory through many images (נראה לנביאים על ידי שכינת כבודו בדמיונות הרבה), according to His desire and will." The prophets, according to Eleazar, did not simply see a figurative image of God in their minds. Rather, the Divine Glory assumed a concrete shape or form in the mind of the one seeing the vision.[73]

It must be noted, however, as this last example intimates, that the German Pietists also had to deal with earlier esoteric materials which tended to support anthropomorphic descriptions. Within their more exoteric writings (such as the treatise of Rabbi Eleazar of Worms cited by Naḥmanides, which was part of the so-called *sifrut ha-Yiḥud*),[74] the pietists were able to firmly maintain their commitment to eliminating anthropomorphism. In their esoteric writings, however, the pietists developed strongly mythical formulations in accordance with the symbolism of the earlier esoteric material. Thus, anthropomorphic speculations can be found in the esoteric writings of Eleazar of Worms and others, especially with respect to the prophetic and visionary experiences that were cultivated and achieved in connection with pronouncing and understanding certain divine names. Anthropomorphic beliefs can also perhaps be found within the intentions of prayer (*kavvanot ha-tefillah*) of a related mystical circle, the Ḥug ha-Keruv ha-Meyuḥad. All these various mystical practices and experiences were, however, highly private and deeply secret, and were taught and shared only in limited ways.[75]

In the same vein, a leading member of the Ḥug ha-Keruv ha-Meyuḥad, Rabbi Elḥanan b. Yaqar, included in his *Sod ha-Sodot* (a mystical treatise on creation and cosmology) one formulation concerning the way that God appeared to the prophets that is markedly different from his other treatments of this subject, even those within the same work. Although Elḥanan does not mention Rabbi Moses Taku or his

Ketav Tamim by name, the more radical formulation of Rabbi Elḥanan contains several close similarities and parallels to anthropomorphic passages in *Ketav Tamim*.[76]

Rabbi Eleazar of Worms's pietist student, Rabbi Abraham b. Azri'el of Bohemia (who composed his *Arugat ha-Bosem* ca. 1234), in commenting on a liturgical poem that refers to the Divine *kavod,* reviews and briefly describes the theories that were known to him with respect to the forms through which God revealed himself to man.[77] Abraham begins by stating that God never revealed His essence, about which one cannot make comparisons or offer formulations. The talmudic passages in the first chapter of tractate *Berakhot* that refer to God putting on *tefillin* and the like speak about the manifest form of God, the *shekhinah* (the *kavod*). Indeed, one Gaon (a reference to Rav Hai) understands the talmudic passages in *Berakhot* to mean that God showed the *kavod* to His prophets and adherents (and indeed to Moses) and they perceived it, through an understanding of the heart (*ovanta de-libba*). That is, they received a mental image of a seated person (or any other vision that was meant to represent God) but did not see it with their eyes (*lo re'iyyah be-ayin*). Rabbi Abraham related (with approval) the approach of this Gaon to the manner in which God appeared to Moses following the sin of the golden calf, and also mentions the similar approach of his teacher Rabbi Eleazar of Worms and of a Rabbi Neḥemyah b. Solomon.[78]

Abraham next presents the view of Maimonides on this issue, as it is found in "Hilkhot Yesodei ha-Torah," 1:8–9. God cannot possibly have any anthropomorphic form. The anthropomorphic phrases found in the Torah are written in this way only so that human beings can have a proper understanding of God's functions and powers. A proof for this approach is that one prophet saw a vision of God dressed in pristine clothing, another prophet saw God in soiled clothes, Moses saw God at the crossing of the Red Sea as a fighting warrior, and God appeared at Sinai as a prayer leader wrapped in a *tallit*. All of these diverse visions show that God has no (physical) image or form, only the non-physical manifestations that are seen in prophetic visions.

Rabbi Abraham turns next to Saadya Gaon. Saadya stresses that the divine form that appears to the prophets, the form that speaks to them and that sits on the throne and so on, is a created, distinct form (*ha-ṣurah beru'aḥ hi va-ḥadashah*). This created luminous form is the Divine *kavod,* also known as the *shekhinah.* At times, the light (of the *shekhinah*) shines without embracing any image or form, and the divine voice is heard from the luminous form. Abraham then distinguishes between the way that Moses and other prophets heard this voice. He cites Rabbi Ḥanan'el b. Ḥushi'el who held (like Rav Hai) that prophetic visions were mental images (*avna de-libba*) and not actual ones, since God has no real, physical form. Rabbenu Nissim Gaon and Shabbetai (Donnolo) ha-Rofe also held this view. Moving to a related issue, Rabbi Abraham describes a tradition of his teacher Rabbi Judah he-Ḥasid on the way that Moses more clearly perceived the *kavod* (*be-ispaqlarya ha-me'irah*) than did all other prophets (*be-ispaqlarya she-einah me 'irah*) and he also cites a passage from Rabbenu Ḥanan'el on this issue.

Finally, Rabbi Abraham cites a passage from Moses Taku's *Ketav Tamim* on the same subject. As Urbach notes,[79] this passage is not found in the version of *Ketav Tamim* that is extant, a fact that is not particularly troubling since we know that there are sections of the original work that have not survived.[80] More suggestive, however, is the fact that Rabbi Abraham, who cites *Ketav Tamim* with some frequency in his work and without fanfare, omits Rabbi Moses' anthropomorphic approach to the appearance of God in prophetic visions.[81] Rabbi Abraham chose not to present it in this survey that, in accordance with the somewhat eclectic style of his pietist teachers in this matter, is otherwise quite thorough and complete. Indeed, Abraham had no difficulty including the rationalistic position of Maimonides.[82]

Rabbi Isaac b. Moses of Vienna, author of the Tosafist halakhic compendium *Sefer Or Zarua'*, was a student of Rabbi Judah Sirleon, Rabbi Simḥah of Speyer, Rabiah, and Rabbi Samson of Coucy, among other Tosafists in northern France and Germany. He also studied with Rabbi Judah he-Ḥasid and with others associated with the German Pietists, including Rabbi Abraham b. Azri'el of Bohemia.[83] In the course of his (halakhic) commentary to tractate *Berakhot*, Rabbi Isaac cites at length the explanation and approach of Rabbenu Ḥanan'el (which was mentioned briefly by Rabbi Abraham in his *Arugat ha-Bosem*) to two talmudic passages that seemingly attribute physical forms to God. In light of the fact that God does not project an actual physical image (according to the verses in Isaiah and others), Rabbenu Ḥanan'el interprets the claim that the Almighty wears *tefillin* in accordance with the concept that God provides a mental or psychologistic image of Himself (as represented by the lower *kavod*) to the prophets (בראיית הלב ולא בראיית העין). Similarly, when the Talmud maintains that

God prays, the reference is to a mental image of God (ראיית הלב) represented by the *kavod.* Rabbi Isaac also ratifies the view of Rabbenu Ḥanan'el that the figure of Akatri'el, who appeared to Rabbi Ishma'el the High Priest in the Holy of Holies, was a manifestation of the *kavod* (seen by Rabbi Ishma'el in his mind's eye), and was not merely an angelic figure.[84]

Rabbi Isaac b. Judah ha-Levi, the northern French compiler of the Tosafist biblical commentary *Pa'neaḥ Raza* that appeared in the late thirteenth century, was strongly influenced by the Torah commentary of Rabbi Joseph *Bekhor Shor.* Rabbi Isaac ha-Levi also included much exegetical (and pietistic) material from the German pietists.[85] According to one of the comments to Genesis 1:26 found in *Pa'neaḥ Raza,* God's intention to create man in "our image" refers to the image of the angels (who have a human form). God appears to the prophets via this (angelic human) form, so that the prophets will not become disoriented or terrified. *Pa'neaḥ Raza* emphasizes that all intelligent people must understand that the Creator Himself has no structure or form (as the verses in Isaiah 40 indicate). He sees but is not seen, just as the human soul, which is infused with His spirit but has no form, allows a person to see but is itself not seen, even as it fills the entire human body. Similarly, there is no finitude to the greatness of God. He is unlimited and has no limbs, but He fills everything. All references to the hands and ears and heart and mouth (of God) are merely representations (*mashal*) of His ability to hear, think, and speak in order that the (human) ear hear what it is capable to understand. The prophets saw only the splendor of (the lower) part of the *kavod.* Moses saw this through a clear speculum (as Rabbenu Ḥanan'el explains in tractate *Yevamot*), but no one ever saw the (upper) *kavod.* Furthermore, Rabbenu Ḥanan'el and Rabbenu Nissim, among others, wrote that the Creator has no form, and they castigated anyone who claims that He does. One who believes that the Creator has no form is fortunate and one who does not believe thusly will be afflicted and is close to being a heretic. In the work of Maimonides, it is stated that whoever posits a form for the Creator is among those who will be severely punished. The comparable forms (of God and man), alluded to in Genesis 1:26, only establish the comparison with respect to the ability to intimidate others, so that their fear will extend to created beings.[86]

This passage in *Pa'neaḥ Raza* (like the passage in Abraham b. Azri'el's *Arugat ha-Bosem*) includes virtually every one of the approaches that we have encountered in medieval Ashkenaz to address the problem of anthropomorphism. It begins with the interpretation of Rabbi Eleazar of Worms, that the human image adopted by those angels who are sent by God to appear to the prophets constitutes the "common image" between the divine and the human realms. The passage refers to the Saadyanic theory of the *kavod,* and mentions by name the early medieval talmudists who subscribed to a form of this view. Maimonides' position is cited directly, and the verses and principles gathered to explain the references to anthropomorphic characteristics in the Torah follow both the specifics in *Mishneh Torah* and in the commentary of Rabbi Joseph *Bekhor Shor*.[87] Interestingly, *Pa'aneaḥ Raza* (again like *Arugat ha-Bosem*) found no need or opportunity to include the approach of Rabbi Moses Taku. In a comment to Exodus 20:3 (לא יהיה לך אלהים אחרים על פני), *Pa'neaḥ Raza* rejects completely the possibility that God possesses an actual physical form.[88]

To be sure, *Pa'neaḥ Raza* was composed well after the Maimonidean Controversy of the 1230s, and was perhaps influenced in its interpretation of Genesis 1:26 by that complex of events as well. Nonetheless, there are other, earlier Ashkenazic interpretations of Genesis 1:26 (aside from that of Rabbi Eleazar of Worms) that express their rejection of anthropomorphism in this verse by invoking a comparison to the images of the angels, using even simpler terms. The earliest example is the commentary of Rashbam, "in our image [means] in the image of the angels." Similarly, Rashbam interprets that the divine image in which man was created (in Genesis 1:27) refers to (the image of) the angels.[89] Rashbam makes his comment from the standpoint of rationalistic *peshat* exegesis, without any recourse to formal philosophical (or mystical) concepts or terms.[90]

The views of Rashbam and Maimonides (as well as *Bekhor Shor*) are brought together in an interpretation of the northern French Tosafist Torah commentary *Sefer ha-Gan* (compiled by Aaron b. Joseph ha-Kohen ca. 1240) to Genesis 1:26.[91] *Sefer ha-Gan* begins by presenting (without attribution) the essence of *Bekhor Shor*'s interpretation of this verse. It is inappropriate to refer to the form of the Creator as various biblical verses indicate. The references to divine eyes or speech is an allegory to convey the notion that God can communicate, just as Scripture compares the voice of God to the sound of deep, rushing water. The claim that man is made in God's image refers only to the ability to intimidate, that man's fear (like God's) will be placed over other creatures.[92] *Sefer ha-Gan* describes the punishment for one who believes that God has a physical image according to Maimonides (בספר הר"ר משה אבן מיימון), in what appears to be a paraphrase of "Hilkhot Teshuvah," 3:6–7.

Sefer ha-Gan then links Rashbam's interpretation of Genesis 1:26 (that the form attributed to man is the unique form of the angels) to Maimonides' description of the category of angels in "Yesodei ha-Torah" 2:7 called אישים (anthropos), who appear in prophetic visions.[93] This is the sense of the verse that God created man in the image of the Divine (*be-ṣelem E-lohim*), meaning in the image of the angels (*be-ṣelem mal'akhim*), since in many (biblical) contexts, angels are referred to as *elohim.* These passages from Maimonides are also cited in several subsequent Tosafist Torah commentaries from the mid- and late thirteenth century.[94]

Rabbi Isaiah di Trani (RiD, ca. 1170–1240) was an Italian hakakhist who apparently studied in his youth with the German Tosafist Rabbi Simḥah of Speyer. Israel Ta-Shma has reviewed Rabbi Isaiah's large corpus, and has sketched the contours of his scholarship.[95] RiD was especially familiar with the talmudic writings of Rashi, Rashbam, and Rabbenu Tam (and those of one of Rabbenu Tam's leading students, Rabbi Isaac b. Mordekhai of Regensburg). He also cites leading earlier authorities from the Sefardic world such as *Halakhot Gedolot,* Rabbenu Ḥanan'el, and Rabbi Isaac Alfasi (RiF), as well as several important rabbinic figures from his homeland in southern Italy. In terms of overall methodology, however, RiD behaves, for the most part, like an Ashkenazic scholar, as indicated not only by his extensive *Tosafot* but also in his *pesaqim* and other halakhic compositions as well.[96]

One of RiD's first compositions, written according to Ta-Shma before any of his *Tosafot* and talmudic novellae (and in all probability shortly after he returned to Italy from his studies in Germany, somewhere in the early years of the thirteenth century), was his commentary to the Pentateuch titled *Nimmuqei Ḥumash.*[97] Not surprisingly, this work betrays a heavy dose of Ashkenazic influence. Virtually all the rabbinic figures that RiD cites in this work (which comports with the overall genre of Tosafist Torah commentary and includes halakhic and talmudic material, as well as *gematria* and the like) are from either northern France or Germany,[98] with one notable exception. In three places, Rabbi Isaiah reproduces passages from Maimonides' *Moreh Nevukhim.*[99] Indeed, Ta-Shma notes (and explains) the rather curious phenomenon that RiD hardly quotes Maimonides' *Mishneh Torah* in his vast halakhic corpus (and this is true for RiD's successors in Italy for quite a while), but does quote *Moreh Nevukhim* at length on these three occasions. Thirteenth-century Ashkenazic halakhists and rabbinic figures quoted from *Mishneh Torah* but tended to ignore *Moreh Nevukhim.* RiD's unusual pattern of citation shows that Maimonides' philosophy was not what kept RiD away from his halakhic writings (as it did for some other rabbinic figures). Rather, Ta-Shma argues, the rejection or displacement of Maimonidean *halakhah* in Italy was due to the dominance of the Franco-German halakhic tradition in Italy during this time. Nonetheless, RiD's use of *Moreh Nevukhim* stands out, and is suggestive.[100]

Assessing the availability of *Moreh Nevukhim* (in its Hebrew translation) in thirteenth-century Ashkenaz is difficult at best. It seems from the various letters mentioned earlier in connection with the Maimonidean Controversy that parts (if not all) of *Moreh Nevukhim* were shown to groups of *rabbanei Ṣarefat* (some of whom voiced specific criticisms) and were therefore available in some form to Ashkenazic rabbinic scholars who wished to use it.[101] Nonetheless, Tosafists in northern France and Germany, including those who were supportive of *Mishneh Torah,* do not cite *Moreh Nevukhim.*[102] Included in this pattern are figures such as Rabbi Moses of Coucy and Rabbi Isaac *Or Zarua',*[103] and even the more philosophically inclined Rabbi Eleazar of Worms[104] and Rabbi Abraham b. Azri'el of Bohemia (author of *Arugat ha-Bosem*),[105] as well as the eclectic *Sefer ha-Maskil.*[106] Although it is possible that Rabbi Isaiah di Trani received a copy of *Moreh Nevukim* through Italian channels,[107] it would appear that he is (given the point in his career when he wrote *Nimmuqei Ḥumash*) the first Tosafist and rabbinic scholar trained in Ashkenaz to cite *Moreh Nevukhim* with authority and consistency.

RiD's use of *Moreh Nevukhim* must therefore be closely studied. Ta-Shma maintains that RiD, as reflected in his commentary to Genesis 1:26, encountered some radical Ashkenazic *magshimim* (anthropomorphists), who believed that God had a corporeal form in the literal or simplest sense. Given the inability until now to identify and pinpoint such groups, this would appear to be a discovery of great significance. RiD does not espouse this position, and he seeks to diffuse it using a lengthy citation from *Moreh Nevukhim,* while not rebuking its adherents too sharply or too directly. Indeed, it would appear that RiD also wished to explain how these *magshimim* (mistakenly) came to embrace their position. Owing to the importance of this passage, which Ta-Shma considers to be the first instance of a leading rabbinic scholar looking from the "outside" into a group of this type of committed *magshimim,* Ta-Shma reproduces the opening lines of the passage that, in his view, are a record or reflection of this encounter.[108]

In fact, however, this entire passage is a faithful, virtually verbatim reproduction of the Hebrew translation of *Moreh Nevukhim* I:1 (although RiD does not note this source in his commentary, nor does he indicate that this is a citation). Thus, there is no exchange of any kind taking place here between RiD and Ashkenazic *magshimim.* Rather, RiD is presenting only the words of Maimonides, explaining why some Jews (presumably not from Ashkenaz) incorrectly felt that they must attribute a physical form to God (in order to have certain biblical verses make sense). To be sure, RiD, in citing this passage may have sought to undercut the view that existed in Ashkenaz as well among those who believed in pronounced anthropomorphism, but their voices are not being heard here. The main point of *Moreh Nevukhim* I:1 is to distinguish philosophically between *ṣelem,* which denotes the essential existence of a being (in this instance the Divine Being and Intellect) without signifying corporeality and *demut,* a comparative term that does imply a measure of similarity between God and man in Genesis 1:26. Maimonides' (and RiD's) conclusion is that the similarity is to be found in the intellects of God and man, and not in the physical realm.[109] Nonetheless, despite the fact that RiD has not helped us to pinpoint an identifiable group of Ashkenazic *magshimim,* we have in RiD another important Ashkenazic thinker who is supportive of the Maimonidean position on anthropomorphism, citing it for the first time not from *Mishneh Torah,* but from *Moreh Nevukhim.*

RiD copies extensively from *Moreh Nevukhim* in two additional instances. In his commentary on Genesis 19:1, "And the Almighty tested Abraham," RiD reproduces Maimonides' unique interpretation of the test that the binding of Isaac presented to Abraham, and he lists where this chapter is found in *Moreh Nevukhim.*[110] In his commentary to Exodus 32:16, RiD again refers his reader to a specific (albeit brief) chapter in *Moreh Nevukhim* (and reproduces it faithfully), in which Maimonides explains the biblical phrase (and connotation) that the tablets containing the Ten Commandments were the product of the Almighty (*ma'aseh E-lohim*). This issue has an anthropomorphic tinge as well, and RiD again seems to be endorsing the Maimonidean view by citing in full the appropriate chapter from *Moreh Nevukhim.*[111]

The commentary to Ezekiel attributed to RiD (which was probably composed by his grandson, Rabbi Isaiah the younger) expresses an anti-anthropomorphic view as well, although in this case it is closer to the *kavod ha-ne'eṣal* found in *Sha'arei ha-Sod ha-Yiḥud ve-ha-Emunah* (and in other exoteric writings) of Rabbi Eleazar of Worms (while also harking back to the *kavod ha-nivra* of Saadya Gaon) than it is to the view of Maimonides. Commenting on Ezekiel's description of the *Merkavah* (chariot), at the point where a form or image that appears to be human is seen above the image of the throne (Ezekiel 1:26, *ve-al demut ha-kisse demut ke-mar'eh adam alav mi-le-ma'alah*), Rabbi Isaiah asserts that this refers to the *shekhinah* (the *kavod*). It is inappropriate, however, to ascribe any form or image to the Creator himself. Rather, this form that is seen is a temporary one by which the Creator appears to his prophets. Indeed, we find the Creator appearing in a number of different forms to his prophets, and each of these forms is created for a particular instance. He appeared to Moses as the burning fire within the bush. And at Mount Sinai as well, the appearance of the Divine Glory was as a consuming fire. Nonetheless, a person should not say that any of these are His actual form, nor should he spend a lot of time pondering these issues since one cannot fully grasp the properties of God and the glory of the *shekhinah.* In conclusion, a person should fully believe that the Creator has no form and no image. What appeared to the prophets is a form that was developed specifically for that moment, so that the prophet could say that God sent him and the voice of the Divine came directly to the prophet.[112]

This study has shown that the impression created by the Maimunists' letters to northern France during the Maimonidean Controversy of the 1230s, that many or most of the *rabbanei Ṣarefat* believed in divine anthropomorphism, was rather exaggerated, certainly with respect to the leading scholars or the rabbinic elite of the period.[113] We have seen instead a wide range of positions within the rabbinic literature of medieval Ashkenaz during the twelfth and thirteenth centuries, from the relatively anthropomorphic views of Rabbi Moses Taku and Rabbi Solomon Simḥah of Troyes, to the essentially Maimonidean view held by Rabbi Joseph *Bekhor Shor* of Orleans and *Sefer ha-Gan* (and other Tosafist Torah commentaries). Other Tosafists, especially those with connections to the German Pietists, were somewhere in the middle, espousing different versions of the doctrine of the (derivative) Divine Glory (*kavod*) that appeared to the prophets and others in real or imagined form. We have found these positions expressed in a number of different Tosafist genres (and contexts) as well, an important factor when trying to determine the personal beliefs and positions of the Tosafists.

If the criteria set forth by Naḥmanides in his letter are used as a measuring stick, only those Ashkenazic scholars who held positions more anthropomorphic than the non-esoteric (*sifrut ha-Yiḥud*) view(s) of Rabbi Eleazar of Worms and Rabbi Judah he-Ḥasid could be considered believers in divine corporeality (*magshimim*), although, to be sure, fully committed Maimunists (or Jewish Aristotelians) might have had a lower threshold for measuring anthropomorphism than Naḥmanides did.[114] Indeed, we have been unable to positively identify any Ashkenazic rabbinic scholars who espoused radical (or crude) forms of anthropomorphism. The positions of Rabbi Moses Taku and *Sefer ha-Maskil* did not include overt or fixed divine corporeality and, in any case, these positions do not seem to have had much of an impact on subsequent Ashkenazic rabbinic literature.

David Berger has suggested that the question sent by Rabbi Abraham Klausner of Vienna to Rabbi Menaḥam Agler of Prague in the late fourteenth century concerning which characterization of God's nature is more correct, the corporeal or the non-corporeal, means that this basic question had never been fully resolved in Ashkenaz, and that the anthropomorphic view had at least remained current.[115] As Rabbi Abraham indicates, however, he raised his question on the basis of having read the writings of Rabbi Saadya Gaon and Rabbi Abraham Ibn Ezra, as well as the (pietistic) *Shir ha-Yiḥud* (which all held the non-anthropomorphic view), followed by Rabbi Moses Taku's *Ketav Tamim*, which challenges this view. Abraham was impressed by the array of biblical and talmudic texts that Taku cites and, as a result, posed his question. It would seem that Abraham became aware of the anthropomorphic view mainly from his reading of this unusual and erudite book (which was not often cited in the thirteenth century). Troubled by the impressive argumentation of this work against such luminaries as Saadya Gaon and Maimonides, Abraham sends his query to his colleague Rabbi Menaḥem Agler, who was partial to philosophy. Rabbi Menaḥem rejects *Ketav Tamim*'s view on anthropomorphism out of hand in favor of the view of Maimonides, referring to Taku's work derisively as *ketav tame* (an impure text). As this instance demonstrates as well, the view of *Ketav Tamim* on anthropomorphism was not widely accepted within medieval Ashkenaz, even as the existence of *Ketav Tamim* and the position on anthropomorphism that it represents were known to some rabbinic scholars.[116]

Formulations of Rabbi Eleazar of Worms and other German Pietists seem to assume that there were individuals in Ashkenaz who did support the more radical position.[117] Paradoxically, the more esoteric writings of the German Pietists and associated mystical circles (such as the Ḥug ha-Keruv ha-Meyuḥad) do convey a greater inclination toward anthropomorphism, at least on the symbolic level, but this position, held by a small, inner group of pietist followers, was hidden from non-Ashkenazic Jewry and probably from the bulk of Ashkenazic Jewry as well.[118] Rabbi Isaiah di Trani (and any of those Tosafists who held a middle position) may have been writing to bring people away from the edge, but there is no evidence for direct interaction with any individuals who actually held the more radical anthropomorphic position.

Perhaps there were members of the intelligentsia, who qualified as scholars of some note but were not represented by or did not contribute to the writings of the Tosafists, who believed in radical anthropomorphism (if not the position advocated by Taku).[119] As was the case for Rabbi Samuel of Falaise, these scholars may have been less aware of Spanish and Sefardic (rationalistic) sources, as compared to those Ashkenazic authors who presented non-anthropomorphic views. To be sure, there may also have been a degree of simple or crude anthropomorphism present within the less educated and less learned strata of Ashkenazic society. Alas, the paucity of sources that record popular religious beliefs in medieval Ashkenaz does not allow us, at this time, to assess the situation in this part of Ashkenazic society in more concrete terms.

From the larger perspective of medieval Jewish intellectual history, the range of views in Ashkenaz that we have traced with regard to anthropomorphism helps to diminish the "backward" image that has sometimes been assigned to the talmudic scholars of this region (as compared, for example, to Maimonides). Without benefit of a sustained philosophical tradition, the Tosafists (not to mention the German Pietists) were able nonetheless to respond to the important theological questions that stood before them, against the backdrop of the full corpus of talmudic and rabbinic literature. The positions that they developed are interesting and even innovative, and they speak to a more varied and sophisticated rabbinic culture in medieval Ashkenaz than has been imagined until now.

Notes

1. Vatican Library MS Neofiti 11, fol. 219v: כי רוב חכמי צרפת מגשימים. See Gershom Scholem, *Origins of the Kabbalah* (Princeton: Princeton University Press, 1987),

406–7. On Rabbi Samuel b. Mordekhai and his epistle, cf. Scholem, *Origins of the Kabbalah,* 224–26, and Moshe Idel, "Qeta Iyyuni le-R. Asher b. Meshullam mi-Lunel," *Qiryat Sefer* 50 (1975): 148–53.

2. See the text of Naḥmanides' letter published in *Kitvei ha-Ramban,* ed. C. B. Chavel (Jerusalem: Mossad Harav Kook, 1968), 1:345–46 [= *Qoveṣ Teshuvot ha-Rambam* (Leipzig, 1859), sec. 3. fols. 9d–10b]. Cf. Bernard Septimus, *Hispano-Jewish Culture in Transition: The Career and Controversies of Ramah* (Cambridge, Mass.: Harvard University Press, 1982), 79: "Not only rationalist polemicists but even an anti-rationalist like Nahmanides indicates that anthropomorphism played an important role in the condemnation of Maimonides' works [in Ashkenaz]." Naḥmanides cites extensively from a treatise of Rabbi Eleazar of Worms to show that Eleazar did not subscribe to the anthropomorphic view. Naḥmanides indicates that there were some right-minded (but unnamed) *Hakhmei Ṣarefat* who agreed with the non-anthropomorphic view. E. E. Urbach, *Sefer Arugat ha-Bosem,* vol. 4 (Jerusalem: Mekize Nirdamim, 1963), 74–81, suggests that the goal of Eleazar in composing his treatise and, indeed, the broader purpose of the German Pietists in developing their *torat ha-kavod,* was to counter those around them who insisted on radical anthropomorphism. See below, notes 66, 68, 70.

3. See MS Cambridge Add. 507. 1, fols. 75r–v, transcribed in Joseph Shatzmiller, "Les Tossafistes et la premiere Controverse Maïmonidienne," in *Rashi et la culture juive en Fance du Nord au moyen age,* ed. G. Dahan et al. (Paris: E. Peeters, 1997), 75. Later in his letter (fol. 78–v; Shatzmiller, 79–80), Asher claims that the rabbis of northern France decreed that the Bible and the Talmud must be studied only according to the commentaries of Rashi, ostensibly because Rashi tends to interpret in accordance with rabbinic teachings and the plain sense meaning of *aggadah.* (This claim is also found in the letter to the rabbis of northern France sent by Samuel b. Abraham Saporta; see B. Septimus, *Hispano-Jewish Culture in Transition,* 78.) And yet, Asher notes, there are instances in which Rashi interprets a biblical verse according to its context, unlike Onkelos and without any support from talmudic literature. Moreover, Rashi maintains in "many instances" that Scripture is phrased in a manner that "appeases the ear" (לשכך את האוזן) so that it can be understood in a way "which comports with the words of our teacher (Maimonides)." Shatzmiller (note 229) suggests that an example of this can be found in Rashi's commentary to Exodus 15:8, "And with a blast of Thy nostrils the waters [of the Red Sea] were piled up." Rashi's comment is that "Scripture speaks as if this were possible of the Divine Presence in the way of a king of flesh and blood, only in order to let the ears of people hear in accordance with what usually happens, in order that they will be able to understand the matter. When a person is angry, his breath emerges from his nostrils." See also Shatzmiller, note 167.

4. This is evident throughout the studies of the Maimonidean Controversy (with special emphasis on the events of the 1230s) that have appeared over the last four decades. See, e.g., D. J. Silver, *Maimonidean Criticism and the Maimonidean Controversy, 1180–1240* (Leiden: Brill, 1965), chaps. 8–9; Joseph Shatzmiller, "Li-Temunat ha-Maḥloqet ha-Rishonah al Kitvei ha-Rambam," *Zion* 35 (1969): 126–44; Shatzmiller, "Iggarto shel R. Asher b. Gershom le-Rabbanei Ṣarefat mi-Zeman ha-Maḥloqet al Kitvei ha-Rambam," in *Meḥqarim be-Toledot Am Yisra'el ve-Ereṣ Yisra'el le-Zekher Ṣevi Avneri,* ed. A. Gilboa et al. (Haifa: University of Haifa Press, 1970),

129–40; Shatzmiller, "Les Tossafistes," 54–82; Azriel Shohat, "Berurim be-Farashat ha-Pulmus ha-Rishon al Sifrei ha-Rambam," *Zion* 36 (1971): 26–60; Septimus, *Hispano-Jewish Culture in Transition,* chaps. 4–5; David Berger, "Judaism and General Culture in Medieval and Early Modern Times," in *Judaism's Encounter with Other Cultures,* ed. J. J. Schacter (Northvale, N.J.: Jason Aronson, 1997), 85–100. See also Moshe Halbertal, *Bein Torah le-Ḥokhmah* (Jerusalem: Magnes Press, 2000), 114, and below, at n. 21.

5. E. E. Urbach, *Ba'alei ha-Tosafot,* 4th ed. (Jerusalem: Magnes Press, 1980), 2:713–15.
6. Thus, for example, both Avraham Grossman, "Shoroshav shel Qiddush ha-Shem be-Ashkenaz ha-Qedumah," in *Qedushat ha-Ḥayyim ve-Ḥeruf ha-Nefesh,* ed. Isaiah Gafni and Aviezer Ravitzky (Jerusalem: Merkaz Zalman Shazar, 1992), 99–130, and Israel Ta-Shma, "Hit'abdut ve-Rezah ha-Zulat al Qiddush ha-Shem: Li-She'elat Meqomah shel ha-Aggadah be-Massoret ha-Pesiqah ha-Ashkenazit," in *Yehudim Mul ha-Ṣelav,* ed. Y. T. Assis et al. (Jerusalem: Magnes Press, 2000), 150–56, have argued with respect to preemptive acts of martyrdom (including suicide and the killing of others) that Ashkenazic rabbinic leaders decided these difficult matters of Jewish law on the basis of aggadic passages within the talmudic corpus. Without undermining in any way the validity of this approach, I have demonstrated that medieval Ashkenazic martyrdom was justified by leading rabbinic decisors on the basis of precise halakhic grounds and categories as well. See my "Halakhah and *Mezi'ut* (Realia) in Medieval Ashkenaz: Surveying the Parameters and Defining the Limits," *Jewish Law Annual* 14 (2003): 193–224.
7. Note, e.g., the comment of Rabbi Samson of Sens (*Kitab 'al Rasa'il,* ed. Yeḥiel Brill [Paris, 1871], 136): ואיך יעלה על לב [איש] לומר שלא נקח דברי ה[א]גדה כפשטה, cited and briefly discussed by Septimus, *Hispano-Jewish Culture in Transition,* 57–58, and see below, note 18. Cf., however, *Shitah Mequbbeṣet to Bava Meṣi'a* 85b. The Talmud recounts an incident in which Elijah showed a rabbinic scholar the members of the heavenly academy in their heavenly abode, with the proviso that this scholar not look at the throne on which Rabbi Ḥiyya sat. The scholar could not restrain himself and his eyes were injured. Although the standard *Tosafot* (B.M. 86a, s.v. *itsei*) appears to understand this passage in literal terms, *Shitah Mequbbeṣet* records a passage from *Tosafot Shanṣ* in which "our teacher" (*rabbenu*), ostensibly Rabbi Samson himself, maintained that Elijah showed this sight to the rabbinic scholar only in a dream.
8. See Marc Saperstein, *Decoding the Rabbis* (Cambridge, Mass.: Harvard University Press, 1980), 7–8, and Israel Ta-Shma, *Ha-Sifrut ha-Parshanit la-Talmud,* vol. 2 (Jerusalem: Magnes Press, 2000), 193–94, and cf. above, note 3. In one instance, Ta-Shma contrasts Rashi's silence on the aggadic sections that present anthropomorphic challenges early in the first chapter of *Berakhot* (fols. 6–7) with the vigorous anti-anthropomorphic interpretation of his North African predecessor Rabbenu Ḥanan'el. It should be noted, however, that Rabbi Eliezer b. Nathan (Raban), an early German Tosafist from the mid-twelfth century, reproduces a significant part of Rabbi Ḥanan'el's commentary in his own interpretation (*Sefer Raban, massekhet Berakhot* [reprint; Jerusalem, 1975], sec. 126). Rabbenu Ḥanan'el's passage is also cited at the end of the twelfth century by Rabbi Judah b. Qalonymus of Speyer, in his *Sefer Yiḥusei Tanna'im va-Amoraim* (see Urbach, *Ba'alei ha-Tosafot,* 1:376–77), and in the thirteenth century (in even greater detail) by Rabbi Isaac b. Moses of Vienna,

in his *Sefer Or Zarua'*; see below, note 84. Ta-Shma also notes Rashi's relatively uncritical acceptance of Rabbi Yishma'el's heavenly journey and conversation with the angel Ṣuri'el (*Berkahot* 51a), which Rashi suggests, citing the *Beraita de-Ma'aseh Merkavah*, was achieved by adjuring a Divine Name. As I have described elsewhere, however, Rashi interprets several other heavenly journeys mentioned by the Talmud in the same manner. These interpretations reflect Rashi's familiarity with Hekhalot literature and other mystical practices and procedures, and are not the result of a simple, literal, or unsophisticated approach to the talmudic passage. See my *Peering through the Lattices: Mystical, Magical, and Pietistic Dimensions in the Tosafist Period* (Detroit: Wayne State University Press, 2000), 144–53, and my "Hekkeruto shel Rashi be-Sifrut ha-Hekhalot uve-Torat ha-Sod," *Sefer Bar Ilan* 30–31 (2006): 491–500. At the same time, *Tosafot Ḥagigah* 14b, s.v. *nikhnesu la-pardes*, interprets another of these heavenly journeys (which in Rashi's view occurred again by means of an adjured divine name) as happening only in the minds of the sages involved, an interpretation consonant with the (anti-anthropomorphic) approach of Rabbi Ḥanan'el referred to above. For this passage and other relevant *Tosafot* variants, see my *Peering through the Lattices*, 189n2.

9. As I have noted in *Peering through the Lattices*, 4–5, 217–18, even those Tosafists who were interested in mysticism and other forms of spirituality hardly expressed themselves within the genre of *Tosafot*. These ideas found their expression, for the most part, in other kinds of compositions and Tosafist literature. This is not surprising, given the decidedly halakhic nature of the talmudic corpus. Indeed, Naḥmanides, who was a leading kabbalist and whose Torah commentary is replete with kabbalistic material, barely refers to kabbalistic issues in his talmudic commentaries. See also Judah Galinsky, "Ve-Lihyot Lefanekha 'Eved Ne'eman kol ha-Yamim': Pereq be-Haguto ha-Datit shel R. Mosheh mi-Coucy," *Da'at* 42 (1999): 13–14.
10. Within Ashkenaz, only the German Pietists were consistently committed to a level of allegorical interpretation as well. See Joseph Davis, "Philosophy, Dogma, and Exegesis in Medieval Ashkenazic Judaism: The Evidence of *Sefer Hadrat Qodesh*," *AJS Review* 18 (1993): 216–18. At the trial of the Talmud held at Paris in 1240, Rabbi Yeḥi'el b. Joseph of Paris asserted that *aggadah* does not have the same binding force as talmudic law (and need not be taken as literally), although the polemical pressure of the trial was undoubtedly a factor in his formulation. See Davis, 217n80, and Berger, "Judaism and General Culture," 97–98. Israel Ta-Shma's interesting theory, that Nicholas Donin prior to his apostasy was part of a group that wished to rebel against the "Talmudism" of the Tosafists, in part by reading the written Torah allegorically, has not been sufficiently demonstrated. See Ta-Shma, "R. Yehiel de Paris: L'homme et l'oeuvre, religion et société," *Annuaire de l'École pratique des hautes etudes* 99 (1990–91): 215–19. The (Jewish) allegorists referred to by Rabbi Joseph b. Isaac *Bekhor Shor* in his biblical commentary (Leviticus 17–11, Numbers 12:8, Deuteronomy 6:9, and by Rabbi Solomon Simḥah of Troyes in his *Sefer ha-Maskil*), noted by Ta-Shma, were in all likelihood from a Spanish or Sefardic milieu, with which *Bekhor Shor* (and Solomon Simḥah) were familiar. See below, notes 33, 55; my "Rabbinic Attitudes Toward Non-Observance in the Medieval Period," in *Jewish Tradition and Nontraditional Jews*, ed. J. J. Schacter (Montvale, N.J.: Jason Aronson, 1992), 3–35 (and esp. 10n17); Berger, "Judaism and General Culture," 119n107; Judah Galinsky, "Mishpat ha-Talmud bi-Shenat 1240

be-Paris," *Shenaton ha-Mishpat ha-Ivri* 22 (2001–3): 45–48, 65–69; and cf. Martin Lockshin, *Rashbam's Commentary on Exodus* (Atlanta: Scholars Press, 1997), 129n10.

11. For example, Urbach (*Ba'alei ha-Tosafot,* 714n79) notes *Tosafot Bava Meṣi'a* 58b, s.v. *ḥuẓ,* which presents a fairly systematic treatment of the order of the punishments that are meted out in *gehinnom.* For a similar treatment concerning the locale of *gan eden,* see *Tosafot Bava Batra* 84a, s.v. *be-ṣafra; Tosafot Bekhorot* 55b, s.v. *mitra;* and *Tosafot Qiddushin* 71b, s.v. *ad.*
12. On rare occasions, Tosafists do give us systematic glimpses into their beliefs. See, e.g., my "Medieval Rabbinic Conceptions of the Messianic Age: The View of the Tosafists," in *Me'ah She'arim: Studies in Medieval Jewish Spiritual Life in Memory of Isadore Twersky,* ed. Ezra Fleischer et al. (Jerusalem: Magnes Press, 2001), 147–70. My methodological contention there is that by detecting repetitive phrases and conceptions in different genres and contexts that cannot be attributed purely to the resolution or interpretation of talmudic texts, it is possible to discover an authentic "personal" position of Tosafist thought. The Tosafists' material on the messianic age contains characteristics and constructs that are diametrically opposed to those of Maimonides. Nonetheless, the Tosafists developed and presented their material in an equally consistent and nuanced way.
13. A comparison to the first edition of Urbach, *Ba'alei ha-Tosafot* (Jerusalem, 1956), 551–53, shows that little was added or changed on this topic for the revised edition. See also Yonah Frenkel, *Darkhei ha-Aggadah ve-ha-Midrash* (Giv'atayim: Yad la-Talmud, 1991), 2:512–23.
14. The fact that the position of the northern French anti-rationalists on anthropomorphism is not found explicitly in any of their writings, but is recorded only in documents written by the Maimunists, is noted in several of the studies cited above, note 4. See, e.g., Septimus, *Hispano-Jewish Culture in Transition,* 79, and Shatzmiller, "Iggarto shel R. Asher b. Gershom," 134–35. As noted (above, note 2), the treatise of Rabbi Eleazar of Worms cited by Naḥmanides in his letter implies that there were those who believed that God is corporeal, although in this case as well, no names are mentioned and it is impossible to determine whether Eleazar had any specific individuals in mind (greater or lesser rabbinic scholars or laypersons) and where they were located (within the Rhineland or even beyond).
15. *Kitvei ha-Ramban,* ed. Chavel, 1:338. Cf. above, note 2. To be sure, Naḥmanides throughout his talmudic *ḥiddushim* frequently refers to the interpretations of *rabboteinu ha-Ṣarefatim/ḥakhmei ha-Ṣarefatim* (not to mention [*ba'alei ha-*]*Tosafot*), titles that often denote specific and recognized Tosafist authors and compositions. These designations, however, do not represent Tosafists beyond the era of Ri (Isaac b. Samuel of Dampierre) (d. 1189) and Rabbi Samson of Sens (d. 1214). See, e.g., *Ḥiddushei ha-Ramban le-Massekhet Ketubbot,* ed. Ezra Chwat (Jerusalem: n.p., 1993), editor's introduction, 31–38. As Chwat notes, Naḥmanides also had access to *Tosafot* and talmudic interpretations from the study halls of the brothers of Evreux and Rabbi Yeḥi'el of Paris through his cousin Rabbenu Yonah. These rabbinic figures, however, are never mentioned in connection with the *ḥerem* and, indeed, do not seem to have had any involvement in the Maimonidean Controversy. See below, notes 17, 18, 22. On Naḥmanides' goals and strategy in writing his letter, see David Berger, "How Did Nahmanides Propose to Resolve the Maimonidean Controversy?" in *Me'ah She'arim* (above, note 12), 135–46.

16. For the title of Asher's letter, see Shatzmiller, "Les Tossafistes," 63. In the body of the letter, Asher refers to רבותי רבני צרפת וחכמיה, and he mentions passages and ideas in both *Mishneh Torah* and *Moreh Nevukhim;* cf. Shatzmiller, 62, 72, 74–78. (On 79, however, Asher refers to a group of *rabbanei Ṣarefat* who were able to see Samuel Ibn Tibbon's Hebrew translation of *Moreh Nevukhim* only after they arrived in Marseilles. Cf. Simon Schwarzfuchs, *Yehudei Ṣarefat Bimei ha-Benayim* [Tel Aviv: Hakibbutz Hameuchad, 2001], 186.) Similarly, the letter sent by Samuel Saporta is titled כתב אשר שלח הרב ר׳ שמואל ב״ר אברהם [ספורטא] לרבני צרפת וקנאתו על מה שהשיגו על הרב רבינו משה ז״ל. This letter contains a strong critique of the anthropomorphic view that was supposedly held by these rabbis, and refers to passages in *Moreh Nevukhim* that were apparently available to them. See *Yeshurun* (ed. Joseph Kobak) 8 (1875): 132–39, 152–53.
17. See A. Shohat, "Berurim be-Farashat ha-Polmos ha-Rishon," 30–31, and D. J. Silver, *Maimonidean Criticism and the Maimonidean Controversy,* 159n1. On Rabbenu Yonah's student days at Evreux, see my *Peering through the Lattices,* 27, 63–64, 70–72. It should be noted that the study hall at Evreux was linked in a number of respects to the German Pietists, whose anti-anthropomorphic views will be discussed below. Whether Rabbenu Yonah would have found this academy particularly receptive to his mission is therefore questionable. Cf. Septimus, *Hispano-Jewish Culture in Transition,* 64: "It would seem that Rabbi Jonah, a former student at the French academies, personally brought the case before those old teachers," and below, note 20.
18. In the so-called resurrection controversy that took place in the early years of the thirteenth century (the anti-Maimunist) Rabbi Meir *ha-Levi* Abulafia (Ramah) sent Maimonidean material to Rabbi Samson b. Abraham of Sens (and his Tosafist brother Rabbi Isaac b. Abraham [Riṣba] of Dampierre) among other rabbinic figures, and received a relatively mild response composed by Rabbi Samson. Although the letter of Ramah ultimately reached Rabbi Eleazar of Worms, three of the other five northern French figures to whom Ramah addressed his letter, Samson of Corbeil, David of Chateau Thierry, and Abraham of Touques, are otherwise unknown to us. See Septimus, *Hispano-Jewish Culture in Transition,* 48–50, and Norman Golb, *The Jews in Medieval Normandy* (Cambridge: Cambridge University Press, 1998), 402n75. Of the remaining two, Solomon (*ha-Qadosh*) b. Judah of Dreux was a Tosafist who had studied with Ri (see Urbach, *Ba'alei ha-Tosafot,* 1:337–40; Golb, *The Jews in Medieval Normandy,* 400–403; and my *Peering through the Lattices,* 97–98), and Eliezer b. Aaron of Bourgogne apparently authored a treatise on *issur ve-heter* titled *Sha'arei ha-Panim,* that is cited (once) by two late medieval halakhic compendia. Cf. Simcha Emanuel, "*Sifrei Halakhah Avudim shel Ba'alei ha-Tosafot*" (Ph.D. diss., Hebrew University, 1993), 255–56.

The letter of Asher b. Gershom makes reference to the anti-Maimonidean stance taken by the rabbinic scholars in Orleans (וחכמי אורלינגש אשר כתבו כי יש לאל ידם למסרנו למלכות), without mentioning a single scholar by name. Asher also refers to an unidentified French anti-Maimonidean rabbinic figure by the derogatory epithet והרב ר׳ משה רב לציון. Moreover, Asher alleges that no fewer than thirty-six *rabbanei Ṣarefat* set out to defame (the Maimunist) Rabbi David Kimḥi (Radak). Needless to say, we cannot name even one of these rabbis. See Shatzmiller, "Iggarto shel R. Asher b. Gershom," 135–37, and Shatzmiller, "Les Tossafistes," 60–61.

(Shatzmiller's suggestion in his French article that the derisively characterized רב משה רב לציון referred to by Asher may perhaps be a relative of the Tosafist Rabbi Joseph of Clisson [קליצון] is interesting but improbable; in any event, there is no known Tosafist from Clisson by this name.) Corbeil and Orleans were important locales during the Tosafist period and each produced a number of Tosafists. The fact that no known scholars from these places can be identified as an anti-Maimunist heightens the dilemma. In short, there were obviously some northern French talmudic scholars who held this position, but none have been identified as leading Tosafists. And yet, a number of contemporary scholars refer consistently to the anti-Maimonidean stance of "the Tosafists." Indeed, Shatzmiller titled his French article "The Tosafists and the First Maimonidean Controversy" (and see esp. 55–57), and Septimus writes (63–64) that "Solomon [of Montpellier]'s circle turned for support to the Tosafist schools of northern France. . . . Discoveries by Joseph Shatzmiller have shown that at least some of the Tosafists responded with sharp condemnation of Provençal rationalism." See also Jeffrey Woolf, "Maimonides Revisited: The Case of the *Sefer Miswot Gadol,*" *HTR* 90 (1997): 178, 189. The absence of leading Ashkenazic rabbinic (Tosafist) names associated with the purported northern French *ḥerem* against *Sefer ha-Madda* and *Moreh Nevukhim* is noted by Berger, "Judaism and General Culture," 109n107 (in the name of Haym Soloveitchik), and by Schwarzfuchs, *Yehudei Ṣarefat Bimei ha-Benayim,* 196. I have heard this from Israel Ta-Shma as well. See also Dan, "Ashkenazi Hasidism and the Maimonidean Controversy," *Maimonidean Studies* 3 (1992–93): 31.

19. See Moritz Güdemann, *Ha-Torah ve-ha-Ḥayyim,* vol. 1 (Warsaw, 1897), 56n4, and cf. Moshe Idel, "Kabbalah and Elites in Thirteenth-Century Spain," *Mediterranean Historical Review* 9 (1994): 5–19, and Boaz Hus, "Hofa'ato shel Sefer ha-Zohar," *Tarbiz* 70 (2001): 532–42. On the relatively small size of the Tosafist academies (especially in northern France), and the distinction between Tosafist academies and other (lesser) *battei midrash* (and Torah scholars) within medieval Ashkenaz, see my *Jewish Education and Society in the High Middle Ages* (Detroit: Wayne State University Press, 1992), 16–18, 49–51, 66–68. See also the above note, and below, notes 26, 117.

20. The letter was published by Shatzmiller, "Li-Temunat ha-Maḥloqet ha-Rishonah al Kitvei ha-Rambam," 139, from British Library MS Add. 27131, and cf. Shatzmiller, 127–30. The preamble begins with the phrase, וזאת אגרת אחת מאגרות רבני צרפת אשר נתקבצו כולם והסכימו לנדות כל מי שקורא בספר מורה הנבוכים וספר המדע אשר חבר הרב הגדול רבינו משה בן מיימון זצ"ל. The letter is signed by שמואל בן הנדיב ר' שלמה שיחיה, who is presumed to be the Tosafist of this name, and by (his brother?) יצחק בן הנדיב ר' שלמה שיחיה. Falaise is proximate to Evreux and perhaps Samuel was in touch with Rabbenu Yonah, although, as indicated, there is no evidence for any such contact.

21. Samuel's father, Rabbi Solomon b. Samuel ha-Ṣarefati, traveled to Germany where he was a student of both Rabbi Samuel and Rabbi Judah he-Ḥasid. He authored a Torah commentary in the style of the German Pietists, replete with *gematria* and *sod* interpretations, and he also composed interpretations of difficult passages in Abraham Ibn Ezra's biblical commentaries, especially those dealing with divine names. Among the *sodot* that Rabbi Solomon explains is the notion mentioned cryptically by Ibn Ezra that Moses did not write all the verses in the Torah himself

and several phrases or expressions were added by others (a concept also found in the biblical commentaries of Rabbi Judah he-Ḥasid and other members of his circle). He also preserved various *sodot ha-tefillah.* See my *Peering through the Lattices,* 94–96, 100–102.

Samuel b. Solomon studied with the Tosafist Rabbi Solomon *ha-Qadosh* of Dreux (one of the recipients of the letter from Ramah to northern France; see above, note 18) and with others who were known for their piety or who had an awareness of mystical concepts. Samuel cites two *gematria* interpretations from his father but otherwise displays no overt tendencies toward *ḥasidut* or *perishut,* except that he was much more hesitant than his colleague Rabbi Yeḥi'el of Paris in declaring accepted stringencies invalid, even those that were found not to be well based. See my *Peering through the Lattices,* 96–100, and cf. N. Golb, *The Jews in Medieval Normandy,* 396–407, 463–74, and Gavriel Zinner, *Oṣar Pisqei ha-Rishonim al Hilkhot Pesaḥ* (Brooklyn: n.p., 1985), 14–15, 31. On the tendency toward *ḥumra* in the writings of Rabbenu Yonah, see, e.g., Israel Ta-Shma, *Ha-Sifrut ha-Parshanit la-Talmud,* vol. 2, 28–29; Ta-Shma, "Ḥasidut Ashkenaz bi-Sefarad: Rabbenu Yonah Gerondi—ha-Ish u-Fo'olo," *Galut Aḥar Golah,* ed. A. Mirsky et al. (Jerusalem: Ben-Zvi Institute, 1988), 180–91, and my *Peering through the Lattices,* 66–67.

22. On Rabbi Yeḥi'el of Paris, see above, notes 10, 21, and E. E. Urbach, "Ḥelqam shel Ḥakhmei Ashkenaz ve-Ṣarefat ba-Polmos al ha-Rambam ve-al Sefarav," *Zion* 12 (1947): 158–59. Rabbi Yeḥi'el had a particular interest in the biblical teachings of Ibn Ezra. See my *Peering through the Lattices,* 96n8, 235n43; and cf. Berger, "Judaism and General Culture," 119n107; I. Ta-Shma, "Mashehu al biqqoret ha-Miqra be-Ashkenaz Bimei ha-Benayim," *Ha-Miqra bi-Re'i Mefarshav,* ed. Sara Japhet (Jerusalem: Magnes Press, 1994), 456n21; and Abraham Lifshitz, "R. Avraham Ibn Ezra be-Ferushei Ba'alei ha-Tosafot al ha-Torah," *Hadarom* 28 (1968): 202–21. On the brothers of Evreux, see above, note 17. On Rabbi Moses of Coucy, see Urbach, *Ba'alei ha-Tosafot,* 1:471–73, and the next note.

23. See Woolf, "Maimonides Revisited," 175–203; Judah Galinsky, "Ve-Lihyot Lefanekha 'Eved Ne'eman kol ha-Yamim,'" 16–22; and cf. Urbach, *Ba'alei ha-Tosafot,* 1:468–69 (and in the above note); and Zev Harvey, "She'elat I-Gashmiyyut ha-E-l Eṣel Rambam, Rabad, Crescas u-Shpinozah," in *Meḥqarim be-Hagut Yehudit,* ed. S. O. Heller Wilensky and M. Idel (Jerusalem: Magnes Press, 1989), 69–74. Urbach points out that there is not the slightest reference to the Maimonidean Controversy in *Sefer Miṣvot Gadol* (in addition to noting Moses' effusive praise of Maimonides' scholarship in the introduction to *Sefer Miṣvot Gadol;* cf. below, note 103), although the pitfalls of allegorical interpretation may have been behind Moses' vigorous sermons and exhortations to ensure the performance of various precepts. Cf. Dan, "Ashkenazi Hasidism and the Maimonidean Controversy," 33–34, 46–47, and Urbach (below, note 26), 154. Galinsky (16n19) notes the veneration for *Mishneh Torah* demonstrated by associates of Rabbi Moses of Coucy in Paris (ca. 1240), who seem to have been unmoved and unaffected by the development of the Maimonidean Controversy. In the absence of a clear and direct statement by Rabbi Moses about anthropomorphism, Galinsky (20n41) is unsure as to where Rabbi Moses stands on this issue. It should be noted, however, that in *Sefer Miṣvot Gadol,* in both the (second) introduction to the positive commandments and in the third positive commandment (citing extensively from an introductory passage in Shabbetai Donnolo's

Sefer Ḥakhmoni that interprets the phrase in Genesis 1:26, נעשה אדם בצלמנו; see Shraga Abramson, "Inyanut be-Sefer Miṣvot Gadol," *Sinai* 80 [1977]: 210–14, and cf. below, note 41), Rabbi Moses characterizes in detail the pronounced physicality of the human being, as compared to the presumed non-corporeal existence of the Almighty.

24. See Berger, "Judaism and General Culture," 117–19, and my *Peering through the Lattices,* 19n1, 161n70, and 208n40 (and the literature cited). There was, however, an awareness and interest in certain natural and scientific phenomena, especially on the part of the German Pietists. The pietists were also more aware of and involved with philosophical teachings and trends. Cf. above, note 10. Woolf (in the above note) suggests that Rabbi Moses of Coucy handled the philosophical material in *Mishneh Torah* in the way that he did in order to render the halakhic material in *Mishneh Torah* more suitable and acceptable to his audience.
25. Cf. below, notes 102–3.
26. Rabbi Yeḥi'el of Paris, Rabbi Moses of Coucy, and Rabbi Samuel b. Solomon of Falaise are mentioned and linked together in a passage from Qreshbiyahu (Crespia) *ha-Naqdan* b. Isaac *ha-Sofer* concerning the writing of bills of divorce in Paris; see, e.g., *Teshuvot u-Fesaqim,* ed. Efraim Kupfer (Jerusalem: Mekize Nirdamim, 1973), 325–26. A fourth rabbinic scholar, Rabbi Judah b. David of Melun (or Metz), is also mentioned by Qreshbiyahu as having been involved in this process. As E. E. Urbach notes (*Ba'alei ha-Tosafot,* 1:461), however, Judah is referred to only once in the literature of the *Tosafot* (although these four scholars were also invited to participate in the Disputation of Paris in 1240; see Galinsky, "Mishpat ha-Talmud be-Paris," n. 26). There is no way, therefore, of knowing Judah's view (or the view of other lesser-known scholars like him) on anthropomorphism. Urbach, "Ḥelqam shel Ḥakhmei Ashkenaz ve-Ṣarefat ba-Polmos al ha-Rambam ve-al Sefarav," 149–59, also attempts to document the stance of German Tosafists during the Maimonidean Controversy of the 1230s. The matter requires further elucidation, however, in light of the numerous documents and studies that have appeared in the half-century since this article was published.
27. See Urbach, *Ba'alei ha-Tosafot,* 1:132–40.
28. See *Perushei R. Yosef Bekhor al ha-Torah,* ed. Yehoshafat Nevo (Jerusalem: Mossad Harav Kook, 1994), 6: כי אין לתת דמיון ודמות ותמונה למעלה . . . אינו אלא לשבר את האוזן . . . שהקב"ה ופמליא של מעלה מדמין עצמו . . . בכל עניין שירצו להראות לאדם.
29. See Ephraim Kanarfogel and Moshe Sokolow, "Rashi ve-Rambam Nifgashim ba-Genizah ha-Qahirit: Hafnayah el Sefer 'Mishneh Torah' be-Miktav Me'et Eḥad mi-Ba'alei ha-Tosafot," *Tarbiz* 67 (1998): 411–16.
30. The Tosafist exegetical comment to Genesis 1:26 (*Tosafot ha-Shalem,* ed. Jacob Gellis, vol. 1 [Jerusalem: Mif'al Tosafot Ha-Shalem, 1982], 65–66), which Israel Ta-Shma has claimed (in his *Ha-Sifrut ha-Parshanit la-Talmud,* vol. 2 [Jerusalem: Magnes Press, 2000], 106n22) demonstrates *Bekhor Shor*'s use of *Mishneh Torah* is, in fact, an addendum or interpolation made by *Sefer ha-Gan* (MS Nuremberg 5) to *Bekhor Shor*'s core comment on this verse (see below, note 91). *Sefer ha-Gan,* written by Aaron b. Josef ha-Kohen, was completed ca. 1240, when *Mishneh Torah* was already more widely available in northern France. For the heavy influence of *Bekhor Shor*'s commentary on *Sefer ha-Gan,* see J. Mitchell Orlian, "Sefer ha-Gan: Text and Analysis of the Biblical Commentary" (Ph.D. diss., Yeshiva University, 1973), 54–61. Pro-

fessor Orlian was kind enough to inform me that the text of *Sefer ha-Gan* found in MS Vienna Heb 28 (19/5) cites *Mishneh Torah* in a comment to Leviticus 21:4. Cf. Gellis, *Tosafot ha-Shalem,* vol. 8 (Jerusalem: Mif'al Tosafot Ha-Shalem, 1990), 119.

31. See my *Peering through the Lattices,* 160–61n69, 166–67n86, and the literature cited.
32. See, e.g., S. A. Poznanski, *Mavo al Ḥakhmei Ṣarefat Mefarshei ha-Miqra* (reprint, Jerusalem: n.p., 1965), 66, and Urbach, *Ba'alei ha-Tosafot,* 1:234. With regard to the literary conventions (*le-sabber et ha-ozen*) noted by *Bekhor Shor* in Genesis 1:26, see also his commentary to Numbers 23:22.
33. See, e.g., Nevo's introduction to his edition of *Bekhor Shor*'s Torah commentary, 3; *Tosafot ha-Shalem,* ed. Gellis, 1:115; Moshe Idel, "Perush Mizmor Yod Tet bi-Tehillim le-Rav Yosef Bekhor Shor," *Alei Sefer* 9 (1981): 63–69; Avraham Grossman, "Ha-Qesharim bein Yahadut Sefarad le-Yahadut Ashkenaz Bimei ha-Benayim," *Moreshet Sefarad,* ed. Ḥaim Beinart (Jerusalem: Magnes Press, 1992), 176–77; Avraham Grossman, *Ḥakhmei Ṣarefat ha-Rishonim* (Jerusalem: Magnes Press, 1995), 472–73; and cf. Lifshitz (above, note 22), 219–21.
34. Cf. Galinsky, "Ve-Lihyot Lefanekha 'Eved Ne'eman kol ha-Yamim,'" 20–22.
35. See *Moreh Nevukhim* I:46, II:44–45.
36. See, e.g., Elliot Wolfson, *Through a Speculum That Shines* (Princeton: Princeton University Press, 1994), 144–48, and cf. below, note 69. Wolfson characterizes what the prophets saw, according to this theory, as a mental image (*dimyon*). A text of Rabbi Judah *he-Ḥasid* defines this conception of a prophetic vision as an *aḥizat enayim* (illusion). See Joseph Dan, "Ashkenazi Hasidism and the Maimonidean Controversy," 38–39; Dan, *Iyyunim be-Sifrut Ḥasidei Ashkenaz* (Ramat Gan: Masadah, 1975), 165; and cf. below, note 67.
37. The first northern French Tosafist and biblical exegete (and polemicist) to deny divine anthropomorphism was actually Rashbam; see below, note 89. Since Naḥmanides was certainly aware of the Torah commentary of *Bekhor Shor* (see Hillel Novetzky, "The Influence of Rabbi Joseph Bekhor Shor and Radak on Ramban's Commentary on the Torah" [M.A. thesis, Yeshiva University, 1992], 6–33), perhaps *Bekhor Shor* is to be counted as part of the "minority position" among northern French rabbis to whom Naḥmanides alludes in his letter. See above, note 2.
38. On Rabbi Moses as Tosafist and halakhist, see Urbach, *Ba'alei ha-Tosafot,* 1:420–23. See also J. N. Epstein, "R. Mosheh Taku b. Ḥisdai ve-Sifro Ketav Tamim," in *Meḥqarim be-Sifrut ha-Talmud uvi-Leshonot Shemiyyot,* vol. 1 (Jerusalem: Magnes Press, 1983), 294–302; and my "The Development and Diffusion of Unanimous Agreement in Medieval Ashkenaz," in *Studies in Medieval Jewish History and Literature,* vol. 3, ed. Isadore Twersky and Jay M. Harris (Cambridge, Mass.: Harvard University Press, 2000), 29–31.
39. *Ketav Tamim* [facsimile edition of MS Paris H711 with an introduction by Joseph Dan] (Jerusalem: Dinur Center, 1984), 53–55 (fols. 27a–28a): ולא ידמה לו שום דמות . . . וכשרצונו להראות עצמו למלאכים מראה עצמו בקומה זקופה . . . ופעמים מראה להם אור משונה בלא דמות . . . וכשרוצה הקב"ה לדבר עם נביא יוצא קול במקום שזורחת שכינתו.
40. Cf. M. M. Kasher, *Torah Shelemah,* 16:315–19. Because of the similarities in terminology between *Bekhor Shor* and Taku, Kasher posits that they share the same overall view (that God, despite the fact that He has no physical form *per se,* can choose different guises to adopt including physical ones), against the view of Maimonides that God cannot have any corporeal characteristics whatsoever.

41. Saadya, in the second section (*ma'amar ha-yiḥud*) of his *Emunot ve-De'ot* (Leipzig, 1859), 62, writes that the *kavod* sometimes appears as "a (great) light, and not in a human form." Shabbetai Donnolo, the tenth-century Byzantine scholar whose *Sefer Ḥakhmoni* was available in medieval Ashkenaz, interprets the *demut ha-Elohim* of Genesis 1:26 as "light that has no measure or [dimension of] greatness." According to Donnolo, however, the boundless light is to be identified with the invisible "upper glory," and is not the divine manifestation that was revealed to created beings, prophetic or angelic. See my *Peering through the Lattices,* 127–34.
42. Texts from the *Circle of the Special Cherub* (*Ḥug ha-Keruv ha-Meyuḥad*) identify the revealed (or emanated) Divine Glory as having "neither form nor image, only voice, spirit and speech." See Joseph Dan, "The Emergence of Mystical Prayer," in *Studies in Jewish Mysticism,* ed. Dan and Frank Talmage (Cambridge, Mass.: Association for Jewish Studies, 1982), 93–99. See also *Sefer ha-Maskil,* below, note 56. Again, however, the reference here is to the Divine Glory and not to a direct appearance of the Almighty himself.
43. For Maimonides, see, e.g., *Perush ha-Mishnayyot le-Sanhedrin,* chap. 10, "Yesod shelishi"; *Mishneh Torah,* "Yesodei ha-Torah" 1:11, and *Moreh Nevukhim* I:54. For Saadya, see his *Emunot ve-De'ot,* ed. Yosef Qafiḥ (Jerusalem: Sura Institute, 1970), 108.
44. See, e.g., Joseph Dan's introduction to the facsimile edition of *Ketav Tamim* (above, note 39), 11–27, and the studies cited in the next note.
45. Because of Rabbi Moses' negative attitude toward *Shi'ur Qomah* (see the next note), Urbach, *Ba'alei ha-Tosafot,* 423–24, argues that Taku did not advocate a pronounced or extreme version of divine anthropomorphism (as does D. J. Silver, *Maimonidean Criticism and the Maimonidean Controversy,* 138–40). Similarly, David Berger, "Judaism and General Culture in Medieval and Early Modern Times," 93, suggests that Taku "affirmed a moderate kind of anthropomorphism" (that was nonetheless corporeal by Maimonidean standards). Joseph Dan, "Ashkenazi Hasidism and the Maimonidean Controversy," 43, writes that Taku "most probably . . . did not believe in an anthropomorphic God." According to Joseph Davis, "Philosophy, Dogma, and Exegesis in Medieval Ashkenazic Judaism," 213, "to suppose that the Ashkenazic rabbis, even Rabbi Moses Taku, the author of *Ketav Tamim* and the most vocal opponent of philosophy, held a corporealist view of God's nature is to credit him and them with a doctrinal or dogmatic approach to theology that they did not in fact take." On the other hand, Ḥaim Hillel Ben-Sasson, in his review of Urbach's *Ba'alei ha-Tosafot* in *Behinot be-Viqqoret ha-Sifrut* 9 (1956): 51–52, characterized Taku as an outright *magshim,* as did J. N. Epstein (above, note 38), 298–99; Septimus, *Hispano-Jewish Culture in Transition,* 79; Gad Freudenthal, "Ha-Avir Barukh Hu u-Varukh Shemo be-Sefer ha-Maskil" (part one), *Da'at* 32–33 (1994): 193; and M. Saperstein (above, note 8).
46. Rabbi Moses expresses his opinion on *Shi'ur Qomah* in *Ketav Tamim,* 5 (fol. 3a). For the views of Ḥasidei Ashkenaz and the associated Ḥug ha-Keruv ha-Meyuḥad and their contemporaries, see, e.g., Alexander Altmann, "Moses Narboni's 'Epistle on *Shi'ur Qomah,*'" in *Jewish Medieval and Renaissance Studies,* ed. A. Altmann (Cambridge, Mass.: Harvard University Press, 1967), 225–39, and Moshe Idel, "Olam ha-Malakhim bi-Demut Adam," *Meḥqerei Yerushalayim be-Maḥashevet Yisra'el* 3 [1–2] (1984): 1–2, 8–11, 15–19; Wolfson, *Through a Speculum That Shines,* 214–34; and cf. below, note 72.

47. See Urbach, Dan, and Davis, above, note 45.
48. See Ta-Shma, *Ha-Sifrut ha-Parshanit la-Talmud,* vol. 2, 194n8, and cf. J. Davis, "Philosophy, Dogma, and Exegesis in Medieval Ashkenazic Judaism," 213, and M. M. Kasher, *Torah Shelemah,* 16:319, 321. Ta-Shma implies, however, that this approach to anthropomorphism is virtually ubiquitous within Ashkenaz, an assessment that the present study argues should be qualified. Cf. below, note 53, and at note 108.
49. *Ketav Tamim,* 17–18 (fols. 9a–b). Cf. below, note 67.
50. Note the similar distinction between these terms made by Maimonides in *Moreh Nevukhim* I:1, in support of his diametrically opposed position with respect to anthropomorphism. Cf. Zev Harvey, "Qeṣad le-Hathil Lilmod et Moreh ha-Nevukhim 1:1," *Da'at* 21 (1988): 5–23, and Yair Lorberbaum, "'Al Da'atam shel Ḥakhamim z"l lo Altah ha-Hagshamah me-Olam' (Moreh ha-Nevukhim 1:46): Antropomorfhiyut be-Sifrut Ḥazal—Seqirat Meḥqar Biqqortit," *Madda'ei ha-Yahadut* 40 (2000): 41–45.
51. *Ketav Tamim,* 7–11 (fols. 4a–6a), and cf. Kasher, *Torah Shelemah,* 16:310–11: וראוהו על הים כבחור ... נלחם ובסיני כזקן מלא רחמים ...וכן כשבא לבראות העולם נראה בדמות ובקומה שהרי בדיבור בראו ... ואם תאמר בהקב"ה שכתוב בו הלא את השמים ואת הארץ אני מלא כיצד היה מתראה בצימצום קומת אדם. On the changeable forms assumed by the angels that Taku describes toward the end of this passage, see below, note 70.
52. On Rabbi Jacob b. Solomon (1070–1140) and his commentary to *Avot,* see Grossman, *Ḥakhmei Ṣarefat ha-Rishonim,* 412–16. From this passage in *Ketav Tamim,* we learn that Jacob was a student of Rashi and a teacher of Rabbenu Tam in northern France. Grossman also sees this passage as proof for Jacob's authorship of the *Avot* commentary found in *Maḥzor Vitry,* because there is a parallel passage in *Maḥzor Vitry* (cited by Grossman, 414n215): כי בצלם א־להים עצמו עשאו המקום. ואית דלא גרסי הא, דכיון דאין לצור דמיון ולא תמונה מי שאומר כזה חיישינן שמא מין הוא. The passage in *Maḥzor Vitry* continues: ואף כי בצלם אית דמתרגם ארי בצלמא ה' עבד ולא בצלמא דה' ובעברי היקף [הזקף] גדול בצדין של בצלם לפיס[ו]ק הטעם להבין פתרונו. For variants of the *Maḥzor Vitry* passage and their implications, see Kasher, *Torah Shelemah,* 16:310n3, and *Arugat ha-Bosem,* ed. Urbach, 4:80–81. On the author of the *Avot* commentary in *Maḥzor Vitry,* cf. Ta-Shma, "Al Perush Avot shebe-Maḥzor Vitry," *Qiryat Sefer* 42 (1967): 507–8, and Urbach, *Arugat ha-Bosem,* n. 50.
53. See Davis, "Philosophy, Dogma, and Exegesis in Medieval Ashkenazic Judaism," 212–13n65 (citing M. Saperstein, who describes Taku as "anachronistic and isolated"), and Dan (with whom Davis fundamentally agrees), who argues that Taku was unexceptional (as does Ta-Shma, above, note 48). Septimus (above, note 45) writes, "It would perhaps be rash to assert that R. Moses was fully representative of mainstream Franco-German tradition." Berger (above, note 45), 93, characterizes Taku as "not entirely a marginal figure" (although on 118, he calls *Ketav Tamim* an unusual work). Dan (in the introduction to the fascsimile edition of *Ketav Tamim,* 8–11, and in "Ashkenazi Hasidism and the Maimonidean Controversy," 40–47), stresses that Taku's *Ketav Tamim* predates the Maimonidean Controversy and reflects none of its actual struggles (even as Taku does argue strongly against the "heretical" views of Saadya, Maimonides, Ibn Ezra, and the German Pietists), and that *Ketav Tamim* does not seem to have caused any stir within Ashkenaz. Urbach maintains (*Arugat ha-Bosem,* 4:80), specifically with regard to anthropomorphism, that Taku saw himself as fighting against a "new heresy" within Ashkenaz

that wished to label those who supported the "incumbent" position of anthropomorphism as heretics. Urbach bases his formulation on a passage in *Ketav Tamim* (facsimile ed., 61, = fol. 31a): כי זו הדת החדש וחכמתם חדשה מקרוב באו ויאמרו מה שראו נביאים הם צורות הברואים. As we have seen, Taku himself insists that wherever the biblical corpus, as explicated by the rabbis of the talmudic period, indicates that God appeared, it was God Himself who appeared, rather than a figure that He created and dispatched הבורא ולא הברואים.

54. See above, note 40. The extent to which Provençal anti-Maimunists (such as those in the circle of Rabbi Solomon Montpellier) held a crude or simplistic form of anthropomorphism is also a matter of conjecture. See, e.g., Scholem, *Origins of the Kabbalah,* 204–16, 404–8; Isadore Twersky, *Rabad of Posquieres,* 2nd ed. (Philadelphia: Jewish Publication Society, 1980), 282–86 (and the addendum on 358); Septimus, *Hispano-Jewish Culture in Transition,* 80–81, and esp. n. 45; Berger, "Jewish and General Culture in Medieval and Early Modern Times," 94–95; Silver, *Maimonidean Criticism and the Maimonidean Controversy,* 156–63; and Moshe Halbertal, *Bein Torah le-Ḥokhmah,* 125–29, 183–89. Scholem and Urbach (see the above note) attempt to correlate the events and positions in Ashkenaz during the Maimonidean Controversy with the oft-cited gloss of Rabad on anthropomorphism ("Hilkhot Teshuvah," 3:7). Cf. Harvey, above, note 50.

55. See Israel Ta-Shma, "'Sefer ha-Maskil'—Ḥibbur Yehudi Ṣarefati Bilti-Yadua' mi-Sof ha-Me'ah ha-Yod Gimmel," *Meḥqerei Yerushalayim be-Maḥashevet Yisra'el* 2:3 (1983): 417–19; my *Peering through the Lattices,* 239–40; and Susan Einbinder, *Beautiful Death: Jewish Poetry and Martyrdom in Medieval France* (Princeton: Princeton University Press, 2002), 126–48. Rabbi Solomon Simḥah was interested in the powers and use of divine names and mentions his teacher Rabbi Meir of Rothenburg and Rabbi Judah he-Ḥasid as the greatest authorities in this area. He displays clear familiarity with the *torat ha-kavod* of the German Pietists (as well as that of Saadya Gaon), and with a form of the doctrine of the ether (referred to by Solomon as אויר מופלא ברוך הוא וברוך שמו) that was akin to versions of *torat ha-avir* found in the writings of these and other medieval Jewish thinkers, and in Stoic thought as well. See Freudenthal, "Ha-Avir" (part one), 208–9, and Freudenthal, "Stoic Physics in the Writings of R. Sa'adyah Gaon al-Fayyumi and Its Aftermath in Medieval Jewish Mysticism," *Arabic Science and Philosophy* 6 (1996): 133–36. Although Solomon did not have access to Maimonides' writings (see the next note), Freudenthal shows that he was aware of non-Ashkenazic sources such as Ibn Gabirol's *Keter Malkhut* and various Provençal philosophical writings (in addition to Saadya's *Sefer Emunot ve-De'ot* and Donnolo's *Sefer Ḥakhmoni*). Einbinder notes Solomon's awareness of Sefardic *piyyut;* see *Beautiful Death,* 132.

56. See the introductory section to *Sefer ha-Maskil,* MS Moscow 508, fol. 1v (transcribed in Gad Freudenthal, "Ha-Avir Barukh Hu u-Varukh Shemo be-Sefer ha-Maskil" [part two], *Da'at* 34 [1995]: 87–88): וראיתי דברי בני אדם אשר נקראו בשם גדולים חכמים ופילוסופים אשר יצאתה מהם שגגה. . . . באמרם 'ויאמר ה'', 'וידבר ה'' אין זה אלא משל שאין מאמר ודבור יוצא אלא ממי שיש לו פה ובקב"ה אין לנו לומר שום גשמות וחיתוך איברים ודמו הדבר למשל ואמרו כי לא היה בזה רק דעה של משה ודעה של ישראל. ומי הוא אשר לא ימצא בזה עקירת נפש מן האמונה השלימה . . . .ועוד כי כבר ידענו שאין הפה מדבר ואין העין רואה. אבל הרוח כל זמן שהוא בתוך הלב [האדם] רואה דרך עינים ומדבר דרך הפה. וכל זה גורם לו הרוח, כי לאחר שמת האדם מי מעכבו מלדבר - הלא יש לו פה! וכן בהמות וחיות ועופות שיש להם פה מי מעכבן מלדבר? אלא הרוח הוא

שמדבר. Cf. Rashi's commentary to *Niddah* 31a, s.v. *mar'eh ha-ayin* (noted by Freudenthal, "Ha-Avir" [part one], 221n120): שאע"פ שנבראת העין מן האב והאם, אינו רואה [בלא הקב"ה שנותן לו רוח ונשמה וכו']. תדע שהרי המת יש לו עינים ויש לו שפתים ויש לו אזנים ואינו רואה ולא שומע ולא מדבר. On this section in *Sefer ha-Maskil,* see also Ta-Shma, "Sefer ha-Maskil," 420. Ta-Shma argues, correctly in my view, that those scholars who hold the position rejected by Solomon are Jewish thinkers. Indeed, Freudenthal, "Ha-Avir" (part one), 192–93, suggests that Solomon is criticizing the view of Maimonides himself, although he also maintains that Solomon does not seem to have had *Mishneh Torah* in front of him. Rather, Solomon became aware of Maimonides' views on anthropomorphism (as they appear in *Mishneh Torah*) from another Ashkenazic source that had this work (such as Abraham b. Azri'el's *Arugat ha-Bosem*). Solomon certainly did not have a copy of *Moreh Nevukhim.* Cf. Freudenthal, "Ha-Avir" (part one), 205, and see below, note 106. A more detailed version of the passage just cited (which further supports the notion that Rabbi Solomon Simḥah is arguing against learned Jewish allegorists) is found in *Sefer ha-Maskil* on fols. 48a–b. See Freudenthal, "Ha-Avir" (part one), 195, and (part two), 121–22.

57. MS Moscow 508, fol. 9a (Freudenthal, "Ha-Avir" [part two], 89): העקר להעשיר את עניי הדעת אשר לבם פונה והולך אנה ואנה . . . וכבר ידענו כי אין להש"י דמות וצורה כמה שנ' ואל מי תדמיוני ואשוה ואל מי תדמיון א־ל ומה דמות תעלכו לו כי אעפ"י שנא' עיני ה', פני ה', יד ה' . . . והארץ הדום רגלי, לשבר את האזן מה שהיא יכולה לשמוע נכתב. כי ודאי אין להקב"ה דמות וצורה עומדת. ומה שנגלה ליחזקאל ולישעיהו לא נגלה להם בדמות אמתית עומדת אלא בדמות שהוא לפי שעה ובאספקלריא שאינה מאירה היו רואים ולא היו יכולין לכוין להשיג אמיתת עצמותו והמראה ההיא לא היתה אלא לפי צורך השעה כי ודאי אין להקב"ה דמות וצורה עומדת. (Phrases in this passage are reminiscent of formulations by Rabbenu Ḥanan'el in his talmudic commentary. See Wolfson, *Through a Speculum That Shines,* 147–48, and above, note 36). See also the introductory section of *Sefer ha-Maskil,* cited by Ta-Shma, 420–21: עוד נפלאו כי עמדו הנביאים ואמר אחד מהם 'ראיתי את ה' יושב על כסאו וכל צבא השמים עומדים עליו מימינו ומשמאלו' אם כן נראה כמייחס להם לו גבול שיש לו ימין ושמאל וכן נאמר ביחזקאל . . . וכל העולם יודעים כי אין לו חקר וקצבה ברוך הוא, and MS Moscow 508, fol. 12a (Freudenthal, "Ha-Avir" [part two], 90).
58. See Freudenthal, "Ha-Avir" (part one), 195n19, and above, note 41.
59. Freudenthal, "Ha-Avir" (part one), 193–94n15a, also notes that the phrase אין להש"י דמות וצורה used by Rabbi Solomon Simḥah has parallels in *Mishneh Torah,* Saadya's *Emunot ve-De'ot,* and works of Rabbi Eleazar of Worms (including his *Sefer Roqeaḥ*). In this instance, however, there are also parallels to the passage by Rabbi Joseph *Bekhor Shor* (see above, note 28), and in Moses Taku's *Ketav Tamim* (above, note 39).
60. Freudenthal, "Ha-Avir" (part one), 193.
61. MS Moscow 508, fol. 9b (Freudenthal, "Ha-Avir" [part two], 89–90).
62. Freudenthal, "Ha-Avir" (part one), 189–92. See also Ta-Shma, "Sefer ha-Maskil," 429: האויר המופלא ברוך הוא וברוך שמו הוא הקב"ה והוא הממלא את הכל והנמצא בכל.
63. Freudenthal, "Ha-Avir" (part one), 196.
64. See Ta-Shma, "Sefer ha-Maskil," 427–31; Berger, "Jewish and General Culture in Medieval and Early Modern Times," 95, and cf. above, note 55.
65. On the availability of a Hebrew paraphrase of Saadya's *Emunot ve-De'ot* in Medieval Ashkenaz, see, e.g., Ronald Kiener, "The Hebrew Paraphrase of Sa'adiah Gaon's *Kitab 'al Amanat wa'l-I'tiqadat,*" *AJS Review* 11 (1986): 1–25, and cf. my *Peering through the Lattices,* 219n68.

66. See, e.g., Gershom Scholem, *Major Trends in Jewish Mysticism* (New York: Schocken, 1941), 110–16; J. Dan, *Torat ha-Sod shel Ḥasidut Ashkenaz* (Jerusalem: Mossad Bialik, 1968), 104–16, 129–30; Wolfson, *Through a Speculum That Shines,* 134n30, 193–94, 214–15; Daniel Abrams, "Ha-Shekhinah ha-Mitpalelet Lifnei ha-Qadosh Barukh Hu—Maqor Ḥadash li-Tefisah Te'osofit eṣel Ḥasidei Ashkenaz," *Tarbiz* 63 (1994): 510–11; and cf. above, note 36.
67. See Joseph Dan, *Iyyunim be-Sifrut Ḥasidei Ashkenaz,* 165–73, and Dan, "Ashkenazi Hasidism and the Maimonidean Controversy," 38–39. As Dan notes (42–43), Rabbi Moses Taku was aware of this treatise, referring to it as *Sefer ha-Kavod.* See also above, note 49.
68. See Joseph Dan, "Sefer Sha'arei ha-Sod ha-Yiḥud ve-ha-Emunah le-R. Eleazar mi-Worms," *Temirin* 1 (1972): 141–56; Gad Freudenthal (above, note 59); *Arugat ha-Bosem,* ed. Urbach, 4:74; *Sefer Ḥasidim,* ed. Bologna, sec. 2.
69. Dan, "Sefer Sha'arei ha-Sod ha-Yiḥud," esp. 146–47, 151. Cf. D. Abrams, "'Sod Kol ha-Sodot': Tefisat ha-Kavod ve-Khavvanat ha-Tefillah be-Khitvei R. Eleazar mi-Worms," *Da'at* 34 (1995): 61–72, and Abrams, "From Divine Shape to Angelic Being: The Career of Akatriel in Jewish Literature," *Journal of Religion* 76 (1996): 50–55. It is important to note that *Bekhor Shor,* Moses Taku, and *Sefer ha-Maskil,* like the German Pietists, were all very much aware of the various approaches to anthropomorphism held by Spanish (Sefardic) rationalists. See above, notes 33, 41, 49, 55, and see Dan, "Ashkenazi Hasidism and the Maimonidean Controversy," 34–38. The awareness of these materials is perhaps one of the elements that distinguishes these figures (including Moses Taku) from those Ashkenazic Jews who may have been simple *magshimim.*
70. Dan, "Sefer Sha'arei ha-Sod ha-Yiḥud," 146: ומה שכתב 'ויאמר א־להים נעשה אדם בצלמינו כדמותינו . . . ויברא את האדם בצלמו בצלם א־להים ברא אותו . . . כי בצלם א־להים עשה את האדם', לא שיש לבורא ית' דמות וצלם בריותיו, אלא פיר' בצלמינו שאנו חפיצים להתראות לנביאים בפרצוף אדם החמוד הוא פני אדם צלם המיוחד לנו דמות דמיון הנראה לנו מכובד ויקר זהו בצלמו המכובד בעיניו בצלם מלאכים נראים בו שהוא יקר. Wolfson, *Through a Speculum That Shines,* 210–11, also records another instance of this interpretation in Eleazar's writings. He notes (n. 89) that Eleazar follows the interpretation of Ibn Ezra to Genesis 1:26 ("the expression 'in God's image' refers to an angel"). This is the interpretation of Rashbam as well; see below, note 89. Wolfson mentions the view of the German Pietists (and others) implied in their interpretation of Genesis 1:26 (and against the philosophical view of Maimonides), that the angels (like man) are composed of both matter and form. Cf. Moses Taku (above, note 51); *Tosafot Bava Meṣi'a* 85b, s.v. *nir'in ke-okhlin; Perushei R. Yosef Bekhor Shor al ha-Torah* to Genesis 18:1 (ed. Nevo, 30); *Tosafot ha-Shalem,* ed. Gellis (Jerusalem: Mif'al Tosafot Ha-Shalem, 1983), 2:110. Not surprisingly, Rashbam and *Bekhor Shor* (and *Sefer ha-Gan;* see below, note 93) are closer to the Maimonidean view, but without the philosophical dimension. Cf. below, note 90.
71. *Kitvei ha-Ramban,* ed. Chavel, 1:346–47: כי אין קץ ותכלית לכל אשר יש בו ואין לו גבול ולא אברים לבורא העולמים . . . וכתבו שאין דמות וגשם לבורא וקללו המאמין בזה . . . לא יהיה כוונתם בדבר הנראה לעין מלאכים או לעין נביאים לקרותו א־ל כי אם ביוצר הכל אשר אין לו דמות ואין לו קץ.
72. Ibid., 1:348 (וידעתי כי הספר ההוא מצוי אצלכם). On the diffusion of this work, see Urbach, "Ḥelqam shel Ḥakhmei Ashkenaz ve-Ṣarefat ba-Polmos al ha-Rambam ve-al Sefarav," 151; Urbach, *Ba'alei ha-Tosafot,* 1:408–9; and my *Peering through*

the Lattices, 19–20. On the understanding and use of *Shi'ur Qomah* by *Ḥasidei Ashkenaz* as referring to the *kavod ha-nir'eh* (in a manner similar to that of Saadya Gaon), see above, note 46.

73. See *Perush Sefer Yeṣirah le-R. Eleazar mi-Worms,* cited and analyzed in Wolfson, *Through a Speculum That Shines,* 207–8. *Dimyon(ot)* in this context denotes that the invisible is made visible. Cf. Moshe Idel, "Le-Gilguleha shel Tekhniqah Qedumah shel Ḥazon Nevu'i Bimei ha-Benayim," *Sinai* 86 (1980): 1–3.
74. See J. Dan, "'Sifrut ha-Yihud' shel Ḥasidei Ashkenaz," *Qiryat Sefer* 41 (1966): 533–44; Dan, *Torat ha-Sod shel Ḥasidut Ashkenaz,* 164–68.
75. See Wolfson, *Through a Speculum That Shines,* 192–95, 234–69; Moshe Idel, "Gazing at the Head in Ashkenazi Hasidism," *Journal of Jewish Thought and Philosophy* 6 (1997): 280–94; Arthur Green, *Keter: The Crown of God in Early Jewish Mysticism* (Princeton: Princeton University Press, 1997), 106–20; Dan, "Ashkenazi Hasidism and the Maimonidean Controversy," 31–32; Dan, *Torat ha-Sod shel Ḥasidut Ashkenaz,* 156–64; Dan, "*Pesaq ha-Yirah ve-ha-Emunah* and the Intention of Prayer in Ashkenazi Esotericism," *Frankfurter Judaistische Beitrage* 19 (1991–92): 185–215, although cf. D. Abrams, "The Evolution of the Intention of Prayer to the 'Special Cherub,'" *FJB* 22 (1995): 1–14. Naḥmanides also appears to be anti-anthropomorphic in his letter to the *rabbanei Ṣarefat* (and in several passages in his biblical commentary); see, e.g., Bernard Septimus, "'Open Rebuke and Concealed Love': Nahmanides and the Andalusian Tradition," in *R. Moses Nahmanides (Ramban): Explorations in His Religious and Literary Virtuosity,* ed. Isadore Twersky (Cambridge, Mass.: Harvard University Press, 1983), 24–29, and esp. n. 45. In certain kabbalistic contexts, however, his stance becomes more complex as well, and he becomes more supportive of an anthropomorphic orientation. See Yair Lorberbaum, "Qabbalat ha-Ramban 'al Beri'at ha-Adam be-Ṣelem E-lohim," *Kabbalah* 5 (2000): 287–326.
76. See J. Dan, "Seridei Polmos al Torat ha-E-lohut be-Sefer 'Sod ha-Sodot' le-R. Elḥanan b. Yaqar mi-London," *Tarbiz* 61 (1992): 249–71. The passage under discussion is published by Dan on 265–67 (from MS JTS 8118, fols. 53a–b): על דברתי בני אדם האומרים כי שכינה בכל מקום. פתרון דבריהם, בכל מקום טהור שרצונו לזרוח שם שכינתו. כי השמש בשמים זורח בכל מקום נקלה ונכבד, ועל בתי האלילים ועל מקומות מטונפים בכל. הבורא יתברך שמו וזכרו אינו כן, כי זריחתו בכל מקום אשר יבחר לשכן שמו שם . . . כן אינו מתראה במקדש העליון בזריחתו בכל עת כי אם בעת הצורך . . . ומראיו מתהפכים ברצונו לעינינם רבים כאשר קבלו מפי רבותינו ע"ה. Cf. above, notes 39, 51, and see Dan's analysis, esp. 267, 270–71. On Elḥanan b. Yaqar, see also my *Peering through the Lattices,* 191–92.
77. See *Arugat ha-Bosem,* ed. Urbach, 1:197–201.
78. On the identity of this scholar, see Urbach, "Sefer Arugat ha-Bosem le-R. Avraham b. Azri'el," *Tarbiṣ* 10 (1939): 50–51.
79. *Arugat ha-Bosem,* ed. Urbach, 1:201n8.
80. See, e.g., J. Dan's introduction to the facsimile edition of *Ketav Tamim,* 7.
81. See Urbach, "Sefer Arugat ha-Bosem," 47–49, and Dan, "Ashkenazi Hasidism and the Maimonidean Controversy," 46–47.
82. Cf. Urbach, "Sefer Arugat ha-Bosem," 49–50.
83. See Urbach, *Ba'alei ha-Tosafot,* 1:436–39, and cf. my *Peering through the Lattices,* 111–13.
84. *Sefer Or Zarua',* vol. 1, "Hilkhot Qeri'at Shema," secs. 7–8. Cf. I. Ta-Shma, *Ha-Sifrut ha-Parshanit la-Talmud,* 2:191–92. Moritz Güdemann (above, note 19) notes this

material from *Sefer Or Zarua'* as part of the specific evidence for his broad contention that no leading Ashkenazic rabbinic figures supported any form of anthropomorphism. A less elaborate version of the interpretation of Rabbenu Ḥanan'el, as recorded by Isaac *Or Zarua'* in sec. 7, is found already in the commentary of the mid-twelfth-century German Tosafist Rabbi Eliezer b. Nathan (*Sefer Raban* [reprint; Jerusalem, 1975], *massekhet Berakhot,* sec. 126). The material in sec. 8 on Rabbi Ishma'el and the identity of Akatri'el is found in the *Seder Tanna'im va-Amora'im* of Rabbi Isaac b. Moses' German predecessor, Rabbi Judah b. Qalonymus (Rivaq) of Speyer (d. ca. 1200); see Urbach, *Ba'alei ha-Tosafot,* 1:376–77. Like Isaac, Rivaq offers talmudic proofs for Rabbi Ḥanan'el's claim that Akatri'el represents the *kavod* (and is not an angel), although Isaac's proofs are somewhat different. Cf. my *Peering through the Lattices,* 163–64n75, and Wolfson, *Through a Speculum That Shines,* 261–62. On Isaac *Or Zarua'*s tendencies toward pietism and mysticism, see my *Peering through the Lattices,* 128–30, 221–25 (and in the above note), and Uziel Fuchs, "Iyyunim be-Sefer Or Zarua' le-R. Yishaq b. Mosheh me-Vienna" (M.A. thesis, Hebrew University, 1993), 18–19, 29, 33–40.

85. See my *Peering through the Lattices,* 248–49n79 and the literature cited, and Joy Rochwarger, "Sefer Pa'neah Raza and Biblical Exegesis in Medieval Ashkenaz" (M.A. thesis, Touro College, Jerusalem, 2000), chap. 4. Cf. Sara Japhet, "The Nature and Distribution of Medieval Compilatory Commentaries in Light of Rabbi Joseph Kara's Commentary on the Book of Job," in *The Midrashic Imagination,* ed. Michael Fishbane (Albany: State University of New York Press, 1993), 98–122, and Japhet, "Perush ha-Ḥizzequni la-Torah: Li-Demuto shel ha-Ḥibbur ule-Mattrato," *Sefer ha-Yovel le-Rav Mordekhai Breuer,* ed. Moshe Bar-Asher (Jerusalem: Academon, 1992), 91–111.

86. This passage is included in Gellis, *Tosafot ha-Shalem,* 1:61–62, from MS Warsaw 260 and MS Bodl. 2344. Cf. Wolfson, *Through a Speculum That Shines,* 211. A transcription of this passage is also found in Rochwarger, "Sefer Pa'neah Raza and Biblical Exegesis in Medieval Ashkenaz," 79, from MS Bodl. 2344, fol. 8a.

87. Cf. Rochwarger, "Sefer Pa'neah Raza and Biblical Exegesis in Medieval Ashkenaz," 80.

88. Cited in Gellis, *Tosafot ha-Shalem,* 8:84 (and see also *Moshav Zeqenim,* ad loc.): פי׳ לא תחשבו שום דמות להב״ה, והא דכתיב בצלם א־להים [בר׳ ט:ו] ר״ל בצלם חשוב שהיה לו, ולכן יש אתנחתא תחת בצלם.

89. Cf. M. Lockshin, *Rabbi Samuel b. Meir's Commentary on Genesis* (Lewiston, N.Y.: Edwin Mellen Press 1989), 53–54. A similar comment (to 1:26) is recorded anonymously, in a manuscript variant (MS Paris 260) of the Tosafist Torah commentary, *Moshav Zeqenim* (published by Y. S. Lange in *Ha-Ma'ayan* 12 [1972]: 81, and also in Gellis, *Tosafot ha-Shalem,* 1:65): כדמותנו - ר״ל דמות המלאכים דאין לומר דמות הבורא יתברך דהא כתיב ואל מי תדמיוני ואשוה יאמר קדוש.

90. On Rashbam's rationalism (including his awareness of aspects of Spanish biblical exegesis), and his rejection of mystical teachings, see my *Peering through the Lattices,* 159–61, and cf. Davis, "Philosophy, Dogma, and Exegesis in Medieval Ashkenazic Judaism," 213n67, and above, note 33. Sara Japhet has noted in her *Perush Rashbam le-Sefer Iyyov* (Jerusalem: Magnes Press, 2000), 127–35, that in his commentary to Job as well, Rashbam attempted to eliminate or reinterpret anthropomorphic depictions of God. Japhet notes, however, that Rashbam is not fully consistent in this

effort. As Mordechai Cohen notes in his review of Japhet's book (*AJS Review* 27 [2003]: 128–32), this is because Rashbam does not have the rigorously philosophical outlook that Maimonides did. Cf. Lockshin, *Rabbi Samuel b. Meir's Commentary,* 338–39n3, and above, note 24. A good example of the similarities (and differences) between the exegetical/philosophical approaches of Rashbam and Maimonides can be seen in their interpretations of Genesis 18, the story of the three angels who came to visit Abraham. Coming mostly from the exegetical (*peshat*) perspective, but reflecting a degree of rationalism as well, Rashbam puts forward (in his commentary to Genesis 18:1, against the view of Rashi) the fairly radical interpretation that the appearance of the three angels (in physical form, as the Torah describes) constitutes the appearance of God mentioned by the Torah at the beginning of this episode. In *Moreh Nevukhim* II:42, Maimonides, like Rashbam, maintains that God appeared to Abraham in the guise of the angels. A philosophical issue, however, rather than an exegetical one was at the core of Maimonides' interpretation. In Maimonides' rigorous philosophical model, angels, like God, do not have corporeal form. Thus, they appeared to Abraham, as representatives of God, in a prophetic dream. See also *Mishneh Torah,* "Yesodei ha-Torah," 2:7.

91. MS Nuremberg 5, cited in Gellis, *Tosafot ha-Shalem,* 1:65–66: אין נכון לומר בדמות הבורא כי אין לו לאדם לתת לו דמות ותמונה דכתיב כי לא ראיתם כל תמונה וכתיב אל מי תדמיוני ואשוה, ואל מי תדמיון א־ל. ומה שמצינו גבי הבורא עינים ולשון, אין זה כי אם דרך משל להשמיע לאזנים כמו שכתוב קולו כקול מים רבים. והא דאמר בצלמינו כדמותינו אין זה כי אם על האיום, כלומר שתהיה אימתו מוטלת על הבריות. ובספר הר"ר משה אבן מיימון מצאתי כל העורך דמות לבורא, הוא מאותם שגיהנום כלה ואינם כלים. וביסודו של רבי שמואל ראיתי בצלמו בצלם המיוחד לנו, כדמותינו כדמות. ועוד ראיתי בספר הר"ר משה אבן מיימון כי עשה מיני משמשין של הקב"ה לכדמותינו של מטה, הקרובים אלינו הנזכרים בפסוק גבי הגר, גבי יהושע וגבי מנוח, ובהרבה מקומות אותם המלאכים משווים כדמותנו נדמים בדמות כדמותנו, והיינו דכתיב בצלם א־להים ברא אותם פירוש <u>בצלם מלאכים</u> ובהרבה מקומות נקראו מלאכים אלהים. See above, note 30, for another citation of Maimonides by the author of *Sefer ha-Gan.*
92. See above, note 28.
93. The examples that are given in *Sefer ha-Gan,* from the angels that appeared to Hagar, Joshua, and Manoaḥ, are not specifically mentioned in this passage in *Mishneh Torah,* but are mentioned in *Moreh Nevukhim* II:42. See above, note 90. This suggests that the author of *Sefer ha-Gan* had access to *Moreh Nevukhim* as well. See below, note 103.
94. Gellis, *Tosafot ha-Shalem,* 1:65, records two other Tosafist Torah commentaries, MS Bodl. 271 and ms. Paris 48, which cite the first reference to Maimonides found in *Sefer ha-Gan* (on the punishment for believing God is corporeal), together with Rashbam's comment. Both these collections were put together after *Sefer ha-Gan,* and one of them cites material directly from *Sefer ha-Gan.* See Gellis's introduction, 22–23, 34. The second Maimonides passage found in *Sefer ha-Gan,* on the angels who appear in human form in prophetic visions, is cited in *Perushei ha-Torah le-R. Ḥayyim Palti'el,* ed. Y. S. Lange (Jerusalem: Hafaṣah Rashit Ben Arza, 1981), 4. Lange notes in his introduction (10–11) that this commentary contains a significant amount of material from both Joseph *Bekhor Shor* and *Pa'neaḥ Raza.* Ḥayyim Palti'el was a student of Rabbi Meir of Rothenburg, who ultimately settled in eastern Germany. His collection of *minhagim* followed those of Rabbi Judah he-Ḥasid,

including a number that reflect earlier practices in northern France rather than those of Rhineland Germany. Rabbi Ḥayyim Palti'el appears to have spent some time in northern France himself, and is also referred to as R. Ḥayyim of Falaise. Indeed, somewhat ironically, he may have been the son-in-law of R. Samuel of Falaise (see above, note 21). See Lange in *Alei Sefer* 8 (1980): 142–45, Eric Zimmer, *Olam ke-Minhago Noheg* (Jerusalem: Merkaz Zalman Shazar, 1996), 271, 277, 283, 286, 296–97, and my *Peering through the Lattices,* 113. Maimonides' statement of the principle of divine incorporeality (based on *Mishneh Torah*) is quoted by Jacob b. Judah *Ḥazzan* of London in his *Eṣ Ḥayyim,* ed. Israel Brodie (Jerusalem: Mossad Harav Kook, 1962), 1:5–6 (אינו גוף וגויה). Cf. Davis, "Philosophy, Dogma, and Exegesis in Medieval Ashkenazic Judaism," 217–18. On the increased use of *Mishneh Torah* in Ashkenaz in the mid- and late thirteenth century, see, e.g., my "Preservation, Creativity, and Courage: The Life and Works of R. Meir of Rothenburg," *Jewish Book Annual* 50 (1992–93): 250–52.

95. See Ta-Shma, "Ha-Rav Yeshayah di Trani ha-Zaqen u-Qesharav im Bizantiyyon ve-Ereṣ Yisra'el," *Shalem* 4 (1984): 409–16; Ta-Shma, "Ha-Sefer Shibbolei ha-Leqet u-Khfilav," *Italia* 11 (1994): 39–51; Ta-Shma, "R. Yeshayah di Trani u-Mif'alo ha-Sifruti," *Meḥqerei Talmud* 3 [Prof. E. E. Urbach Memorial Volume 2]: 916–43. The synopsis presented here follows primarily Ta-Shma's treatment of Rabbi Isaiah in his *Ha-Sifrut ha-Parshanit la-Talmud,* 2:174–87. See also my *Peering through the Lattices,* 223, and my "Progress and Tradition in Medieval Ashkenaz," *Jewish History* 14 (2001): 287–92.

96. Indeed, as noted by Ta-Shma, *Ha-Sifrut ha-Parshanit la-Talmud,* 2:185, Ritva and other Spanish scholars refer to him as Rabbi Yesha'yah *ha-Ashkenazi.*

97. See Ta-Shma, "Sefer 'Nimmuqei Ḥumash' le-R. Yesha'yah di Trani," *Qiryat Sefer* 64 (1992–93): 751–75. According to Ta-Shma, the most complete version of this work is preserved in MS Moscow 303.

98. See ibid., 752. See also Ta-Shma, "The Acceptance of Maimonides' *Mishneh Torah* in Italy," *Italia* 13–15 (2001): 82. Among the northern French and German rabbinic figures cited by RiD are Rabbi Joseph Qara (fol. 77r), Rabbi Joseph *Bekhor Shor,* Rabbi Judah *he-Ḥasid* and Rabbi Eleazar of Worms, Rabbenu Tam, Ri, Rabbi Eliezer of Metz' *Sefer Yere'im,* Rabbi Samson of Coucy, RiD's long-standing correspondent Rabbi Isaac, *Or Zarua'* (and Rabbi Isaac's teacher Rabbi Jonathan b. Isaac of Wurzburg), as well as eastern European scholars such as Rabbi Moses Fuller. In addition, one or two Italian scholars are mentioned. See also below, note 112.

99. MS Moscow 303, fols. 59v, 64r, and 80r.

100. Ta-Shma, "The Acceptance of Maimonides' Mishneh Torah in Italy," 79–90. Cf. Jacob Dienstag, "Yaḥasam shel Ba'alei ha-Tosafot leha-Rambam," in *Sefer ha-Yovel le-S. K. Mirsky,* ed. Simon Bernstein and Gershon Churgin (New York: Va'ad ha-Yovel, 1955), 365.

101. See above, notes 16, 17, 20.

102. See Davis, "Philosophy, Dogma, and Exegesis in Medieval Ashkenazic Judaism," 210n58, and Dienstag, "Yaḥasam shel Ba'alei ha-Tosafot leha-Rambam," 350–79.

103. On the citation of *Mishneh Torah* by Tosafists in the mid-thirteenth century, see Ta-Shma in *Italia* (above, note 98), and cf. above, notes 2, 23, 28, 94. (On Rabbi Moses of Coucy's possible awareness of the existence of *Moreh Nevukhim,* see Woolf, "Maimonides Revisited: The Case of *Sefer Miswot Gadol,*" 186.) The so-called *perushei*

Ba'alei ha-Tosafot al ha-Torah (with the exception of the passage in *Sefer ha-Gan,* above, note 91, which betrays an awareness of *Moreh Nevukhim*) also follow this pattern for the most part. Indeed, these commentaries do not even cite *Mishneh Torah* with much frequency. See, e.g., Gellis, *Tosafot ha-Shalem,* 1:61–62, 65–66 (the pieces from *Mishneh Torah* cited in connection with Genesis 1:26; see above, notes 86, 91, 94); 121 (a possible parallel to *Moreh Nevukhim* on the angelic powers of the primordial snake); 183 (a possible parallel to *Moreh Nevukhim* from a passage in *Bekhor Shor,* cf. above, note 35); 6 (1986): 42 (*Mishneh Torah* on the laws of inheritance); 9 (1993): 101 (a citation from *Mishneh Torah,* "Hilkhot Avodah Zarah"); 172 (the making of the *ḥoshen* based on *Mishneh Torah,* "Hilkhot Kelei ha-Mikdash").

104. Rabbi Eleazar of Worm's pietistic introductory section to his halakhic work, *Sefer Roqeaḥ* ("Hilkhot Ḥasidut"), was patterned, to some extent, after Maimonides' *Sefer ha-Madda;* cf. Urbach, *Ba'alei ha-Tosafot,* 1:393. Maimonides' "Hilkhot Teshuvah" is also cited extensively in the so-called *Sefer Ḥasidim* I (ed. Bologna, secs. 1–152); see, e.g., Ivan Marcus, "The Recensions and Structure of 'Sefer Hasidim,'" *Proceedings of the American Academy for Jewish Research* 45 (1978): 131–53. Cf. Dan, *Torat ha-Sod shel Ḥasidut Ashkenaz,* 31. And yet, the German Pietists do not cite *Moreh Nevukhim* as far as I can tell.

105. *Arugat ha-Bosem* cites liberally from *Mishneh Torah,* including the theological portions of *Sefer ha-Madda;* see Ta-Shma (above, note 100), and Urbach, *Arugat ha-Bosem,* 4:166, 177. Moses Taku, somewhat surprisingly, does not refer to *Moreh Nevukhim* in his attack on Maimonides' philosophy, but works only with material found in *Mishneh Torah.* Cf. Dan, "Ashkenazi Hasidism and the Maimonidean Controversy," 31–34, 40–41; Silver, *Maimonidean Criticism and the Maimonidean Controversy,* 138; and cf. above, notes 51, 55. Reference is made to a passage in *Moreh Nevukhim* in a gloss found in the Paris manuscript of *Ketav Tamim* (see the facsimile edition, 43–44 [=fol. 22a-b]). Although the identity of the author of this gloss is unclear, it does not appear to have been Rabbi Moses himself.

106. See Freudenthal, "Ha-Avir" (part one), 193. Cf. above, note 23.

107. To be sure, however, there are no Italian halakhists prior to Rabbi Isaiah who can be positively identified as the conduits. Note that the kabbalist Abraham Abulafia apparently taught or explained pieces of *Moreh Nevukhim* in Rome to RiD's grandson (and namesake), Rabbi Isaiah the younger (Ri'az), and to the Italian halakhist, Rabbi Zedekiah b. Abraham ha-Rofe (author of *Shibbolei ha-Leqet,* d. ca. 1260), who had a strong literary connection with RiD (although he did not actually study with him). See Ta-Shma, "Ha-Rav Yesha'yah di Trani," 411; Moshe Idel, *R. Menaḥem Reqanati ha-Mequbbal* (Tel Aviv: Schocken, 1998), 36; and my *Peering through the Lattices,* 228n21.

108. Ta-Shma, "Sefer Nimmuqei Ḥumash," 752: צלם ודמות, כבר חשבו בני אדם כי צלם בלשון העברי יורה על תמונת הדבר ותואר והביא זה אל הגשמה גמורה לאומ׳ נעשה אדם בצלמנו כדמותנו וחשבו שהשם על צורת האדם ר״ל תמונתו ותוארו, והתחייבה להם ההגשמה הגמורה והאמינו בה וראו שאם הם יפרדו מזאת האמונה יכזיבו הכתוב, וגם ישימו את השם נעדר אם לא יהיה לו גוף בעל פנים ויד כמותם בתמונה ובתואר, אלא שהוא יותר גדול ויותר בהיר לפי סברתם וחומר שלו גם כן אינו בשר ודם, וזהו תכלית מה שיחשבוהו רוממות בחוק השם. Cf. Ta-Shma, *Ha-Sifrut ha-Parshanit la-Talmud,* 2:194. After citing Ta-Shma's "Sefer Nimmuqei Ḥumash," Yair Lorberbaum, "Al Da'atam shel Ḥakhamim z"l lo Altah ha-Hagshamah me-Olam," 6nn17–18, 42n170, notes that the passage in *Nimmuqei Ḥumash* is taken word for word from

Moreh Nevukhim I:1, but maintains nonetheless that it helps to demonstrate that "many rabbis" in Ashkenaz took anthropomorphism literally.

109. נאמר [בצלמינו כדמותינו] באדם מפני זה הענין ר״ל מפני השכל הא־להי המודבק בו שהוא בצלם א־להים ובדמות[ו], לא שהשם ית׳ גוף שיהיה [א״כ] בעל תמונה. This kind of distinction between *ṣelem* and *demut* was taken to a very different conclusion by Rabbi Moses Taku and Rabbi Jacob b. Samson. See above, notes 51–52.

110. MS Moscow 303, fol. 64r: רבי׳ משה בן מיימון ז״ל דבר על זה הפסוק וייסד עליו פרק כ״ד בחלק שלישי לספר מורה הנבוכים, ענין הנסיון גם כן מסופק מאוד וכו׳. The rest of RiD's commentary to *Va-Yera* consists of the full citation of this chapter, ending on fol. 65v.

111. MS Moscow 303, fols. 80r–v, citing from *Moreh Nevukhim* I:66: רבינו משה דבר על זה הפסוק בחלק הראשון פרק ס״ו וכו׳.

112. See RiD to Ezekiel 1:26, in *Miqra'ot Gedolot 'Haketer': Ezekiel,* ed. M. Cohen (Ramat Gan: Bar-Ilan University Press, 2000). וחלילה חלילה שנתאר דמות או תמונה לבורא, אלא זו הצורה ברואה היא לפי שעה שהבורא מדבר לנביאיו. ובכמה צורות משונות מצינו שנדמה לנביאיו, והכל הם נבראים לפי שעה . . . כמה יסמוך ויאמין כל אדם כי אין דמות לבורא, לא דמות ולא תמונה, ואין לו חקר מרוב דקותו והעלמו. ומה שנדמה לנביאיו הוא דמיון נוצר לפי שעה . . . [partially cited in E. Z. Melammed, "Le-Ferush Nakh shel R. Yesha'yah mi-Trani," in *Meḥqarim ba-Miqra uva-Mizraḥ ha-Qadmon Muggashim li-Shemu'el Loewenstamm bi-Melot lo Shiv'im Shanah,* ed. Yitzhak Avishur and Joseph Blau (Jerusalem: A. Rubenstein, 1978), 292]. RiD is referring here to a form of the כבוד הנברא. RiD's last sentence is also quite similar to a formulation of Saadya Gaon in *Emunot ve-De'ot,* ed. Qafiḥ, 103. For a similar notion of a lower divine form that is created (or emanated) for a short period of time in order to be shown to a prophet in a particular situation, see, e.g., Dan's edition of Rabbi Eleazar of Worms's *Sefer Sha'arei ha-Sod ha-Yiḥud ve-ha-Emunah,* 147, 151, and see above note 69. Cf. the analysis of the German Pietists' *Shir ha-Kavod* in Green, *Keter,* 111 (to line 11), "God's appearance changes as is appropriate to human need in a particular situation." RiD cites a pietistic biblical interpretation of Rabbi Eleazar in his *Nimmuqei Ḥumash,* MS Moscow 508, fol. 81v, and interpretations of Rabbi Judah he-Ḥasid (fols. 63r, 68v, 85r, 98r). Moreover, Naḥmanides noted the availability of Eleazar's *Sha'arei ha-Sod* within Ashkenaz; see above, note 72. Note also *Tosafot* RiD to *Ḥagigah* 16a, where RiD refers to man's inability to ponder and to ascertain a full understanding and description of the *shekhinah.* In the final section of that discussion (s.v. *di-khtiv ke-maer'eh ha-qeshet*), RiD concludes, כך מראה השכינה אינם יכולים לכוין בבירור מה הוא.

113. A letter written from Narbonne to Spain in the 1230s severely ridiculed the "great men of Israel among the *Ṣarefatim* and their scholars, their heads and men of understanding," for their magical uses of divine names, angels, and demons through conjuration, referring to them as "madmen full of delusions" and the like. See, e.g., Septimus, *Hispano-Jewish Culture in Transition,* 86–87; Halbertal, *Bein Torah le-Ḥokhmah,* 115. As I have demonstrated throughout my *Peering through the Lattices,* these practices, found among many (but certainly not all) of the Tosafists in Ashkenaz, were undertaken with the same kind of care and precision that typified the talmudic scholarship of Ashkenaz.

114. In addition, the unique version of the *kavod* theory held by the Ḥug ha-Keruv ha-Meyuḥad might have been considered closer to anthropomorphism than the other versions of this theory that we have seen. See Scholem, *Origins of the Kabbalah,* above, note 54, and cf. above, note 76.

115. Berger, "Judaism and General Culture in Medieval and Early Modern Times," 95–96. The correspondence between Rabbi Abraham and Rabbi Menahem Agler was published by Efraim Kupfer, "Li-Demutah ha-Tarbutit shel Yahudut Ashkenaz ve-Ḥakhameha ba-Me'ot ha-Yod-Dalet—Tet-Vav," *Tarbiz* 42 (1972–73): 114–15. See also Y. Y. Yuval, *Ḥakhamim be-Doram* (Jerusalem: Magnes Press, 1989), 301.
116. Cf. above, notes 53, 76, 81, 88. On the limited reception of *Ketav Tamim* during the early modern period in eastern Europe, see, e.g., *She'elot u-Teshuvot ha-Rema,* ed. Asher Siev (New York: Yeshiva University Press, 1971), no. 126, sec. 3; and cf. Jacob Elbaum, *Petiḥut ve-Histaggerut* (Jerusalem: Magnes Press, 1990), 166n46.
117. See Urbach, *Sefer Arugat ha-Bosem,* above, note 2.
118. See above, note 75.
119. See above, notes 19, 26. Cf., e.g., *Tosafot ha-Shalem,* ed. Gellis, 1:262. Unknown and unnamed Ashkenazic rabbinic figures expressed and implemented their views with regard to a complex, highly charged (and tragic) application of the precept of *qiddush ha-Shem.* Interestingly, the lives and achievements of those who wrote the letters to *Rabbanei Ṣarefat* on behalf of the Maimonidean corpus, with the obvious exception of Naḥmanides, are also barely known to us. See also my essay, "Bein Yeshivot Ba'alei ha-Tosafot le-Battei Midrashot Aḥerim be-Ashkenaz Be-yimei ha Benayim," in *Yeshivot u-Battei Midrashot,* ed. I. Etkes (Jerusalem: Merkaz Shazar, 2006), 85–108.

4

Drawing the Line

Views of Jewish Heresy and Belief among Medieval and Early Modern Ashkenazic Jews

JOSEPH DAVIS

Introduction

How did medieval and early modern Ashkenazic Jews define heresy? What types of villainy or error were depicted in the Ashkenazic heresiographical imagination? How did they interpret the rabbinic heritage, at once complex and vague, of images and definitions of heresy (in rabbinic Hebrew, *minut* or *apiqorsut* or *kefirah*)? How did they draw the line between what is not Judaism and what is, between unbelief and belief?[1] The definition of heresy among medieval Ashkenazic Jews is important, not because there were so many heretics within the Ashkenazic Jewish communities—there weren't—but because of what the question implies. What did Ashkenazic Jews in the Middle Ages think that Judaism is?

In a somewhat different context, Morton Smith remarks: "[There is] a continuous interplay between behavior and vocabulary. Society presents the vocabulary. . . . Individuals produce a constant supply of new behavior which both constitutes the social types and, so far as it differs from the previous norms, changes the types. The society struggles to describe and categorize these changes, using old words in new senses, making up new terms to fit new behavior, and so producing a new vocabulary . . . which a new generation will, in its turn, begin to imitate, reject, and alter."[2] Within medieval and early modern Ashkenazic Judaism, the need to categorize new groups of heretics brought about new interpretations of the older talmudic vocabulary of heresy. At the same time, however, new understandings of Jewish belief produced ever new categories of heretics.

Our story has five acts. The first act begins about 1100 with Rashi and continues through the Maimonidean Controversy of 1232, when the rabbis of northern France defined belief in Judaism as literal belief in talmudic *aggadot,* and heresy as misinterpretation. In the second act, fifteenth- and sixteenth-century Ashkenazic Jews accepted the Thirteen Maimonidean Principles, and the notion that they define Jewish belief; heresy is the rejection of dogma. In the third act, during the seventeenth century, Kabbalah became a crucial element of Ashkenazic Judaism and rejection of kabbalistic doctrines such as *gilgul* (transmigration) was seen as a sort of heresy. During the eighteenth-century controversies over Sabbateanism—the fourth act, as it were—the focus of discussions of heresy shifted toward accusations of immorality and evil kabbalistic heretics. The fifth and final act is the early *Haskalah,* and Mendelssohn's rejection of the notions of dogma, required belief, and Jewish heresy.[3]

The Rule of Talmudic Literalism

In 1232, a question was brought to the rabbis of northern France. Are Maimonides' teachings the teachings of Judaism or are they heresies? These rabbis answered that Maimonides' views are heretical because they disagree with the words of talmudic *aggadot.*[4] Two rabbis, Samuel b. Solomon of Falaise and his brother Isaac b. Solomon, wrote,

> Those who read [Maimonides'] *Sefer ha-Madda* are heretics [*minim*], schismatics [*apiqorsim*] who reject their teachers, and who deny the words of the Sages. How do they dare to question the rewards of Gan Eden, and other *halakhot* and *aggadot*? . . . And if, Heaven forfend, a man were to reject this on account of [reading] the words of Rabbi Moses [Maimonides], he would be as one who rejects the words of the Tannaim and Amoraim, and similarly the other *aggadot,* the speaking of [Balaam's] ass [Num. 22:28], and the Leviathan that [the righteous] will eat [in the hereafter] [BT Bava Batra 75a], which our rabbis have interpreted literally [*ki-feshutan*]. . . . And one should not speculate on what is above and what is below.[5]

The Tosafists of northern France rejected Maimonides' notion of a metaphysical Aristotelian Heaven. Indeed, they distrusted the study of metaphysics altogether. Most of all, however, they rejected Maimonides' allegorization of talmudic legends. The rabbis of northern France insisted that when the righteous Jews of all the ages return to life, and they are given the Leviathan to eat as their reward at the eschatological feast, the Leviathan is not going to be an allegorical fish. It is going to be a real fish, no doubt a supernatural fish, but in any case a real one.

But is it a heresy to interpret talmudic *aggadot* allegorically? What is a heretic, according to Jewish law? The word "heretic" (in Hebrew, *min, kofer,* or *kofer ba-iqqar,* or *apiqoros*) appears in a few places in the Mishnah and in many places in the Talmud and ancient *midrashim.* In one place, the Babylonian Talmud offers two definitions of *min;* in another, two of *apiqoros.* (*Kofer* is left undefined.) The Talmud defines a *min* as either one who worships *avodah zarah,* that is, a polytheist or an idolater, or else "one who eats forbidden meat for spite" and not for the pleasure of the food.[6] And an *apiqoros* is either one who "shames Torah scholars" or one who "shames his colleagues before Torah scholars."[7]

There is some debate among modern talmudic interpreters concerning the identity of the talmudic *minim,* and especially concerning the question of whether the *minim* were Christians.[8] Regardless of this, the term *min* became one of the standard medieval Hebrew names for a Christian, whether a born Christian or a Jew who converted to Christianity.[9] From the point of view of medieval Jews, Christians fit several of the talmudic definitions that we have mentioned. Medieval Jews tended to consider Trinitarianism a form of polytheism, and they often took the veneration of images to be idol worship and medieval Christians to be idolaters.[10] Furthermore, Christians eat foods forbidden by biblical law out of theological conviction—not out of spite, perhaps, but not out of mere appetite either; and finally, Christians were not seen to give conspicuous deference to Torah scholars.

But followers of Maimonides were not any sort of Christians, and they were certainly not accused of eating forbidden meat. Given this talmudic background, how could they be called *minim,* heretics? The crucial interpretive step had been taken by Rashi in his Talmud commentary. In several places, Rashi's glosses on *min* and *apiqoros* focused on the issue of interpretation of Scripture. An *apiqoros* "is one who changes the meanings of the Torah with mistaken and idolatrous interpretations," Rashi wrote in one place.[11] Rashi did not invent the category of "the one who changes the meanings of the Torah"—*megalleh panim ba-torah.* He took it from a saying in Pirqei Avot (3:21), where it is one of five categories of persons who are denied a place in the world to come. The same category appears again in the talmudic discussion of the definition of *apiqoros.* The Talmud debates the exact relation of the two categories, which are evidently quite close, but concludes clearly that the two are not identical. Elsewhere in his commentaries, despite this talmudic passage, Rashi emphasized the notion of misinterpretation, and identified the *apiqoros* and the *min* with such misinterpreters.

The definition of the heretic as one who rejects rabbinic interpretations of Scripture, or more narrowly defined as one who rejects the Talmud, recurred in many Ashkenazic writings of the twelfth and thirteenth centuries. In the early thirteenth century, Moses of Coucy, author of the *Sefer Miṣvot Gadol,* listed as the fifteenth negative commandment of the Torah the prohibition on entertaining thoughts that lead one toward heresy. Unfazed by the questions concerning Maimonides' orthodoxy, Rabbi Moses relied heavily on Maimonides' *Mishneh Torah,* and revised a list of theological doubts that he found there. Rabbi Moses added to Maimonides' list "Pondering whether the Oral Torah is from Heaven or not." With such thoughts, Rabbi Moses wrote, "does Satan attack a man and tempt him towards heresy."[12]

Although there were few if any Karaites in the immediate vicinity of France and Germany, Ashkenazic Jews were aware of Karaism as a heresy.[13] The emphasis on heresy as rejection of rabbinic interpretation is no doubt a continuation of anti-Karaite polemic; it also may reflect the importance of scriptural interpretation within the culture as a whole.

Fifty years earlier, before Maimonides' views were ever attacked, or even expressed, the great twelfth-century Tosafist Rabbi Jacob Tam suggested in passing, in a letter to his student Meshullam of Melun, that it is heresy to reject any work of rabbinic literature. Rabbi Jacob criticized certain halakhic views that his student had expressed. Rabbi Meshullam's views, Rabbi Jacob wrote, although they do not contradict any passage in the Talmud, do contradict the rulings of the Tosefta and the tractate *Soferim.* Although, Rabbi Jacob punctiliously remarked, we do not follow all of the rulings of *Soferim,* there are passages from that work that lie at the basis of many of our customs. One who rejects *Soferim,* Rabbi Jacob Tam warned his student ominously, one who relies on the Talmud and on no other ancient rabbinic text, is a heretic.[14] Rabbi Jacob did not, of course, actually accuse Rabbi Meshullam of being a heretic. But only in the culture of the Tosafists, perhaps, could such a Jewish heretic be imagined—one whose heresy is that he rejects the authority of tractate *Soferim.*

Moses b. Ḥasdai Taku, in his polemical work *Ketav Tamim,* took precisely the reverse approach. Writing about 1220, he drew very narrowly the circle of authoritative rabbinic writings. He too, however, insisted fiercely on the literal interpretation of *aggadot.*[15] The ultimate sources of error, Taku averred, together with the pagan philosophers, were "the *minin,* the followers of Jesus, who treat the commandments of the Torah as parables, and among [the Jewish] people, the Karaites, who walk in darkness and deny the Oral Torah." Taku accused the Karaites of forging ancient texts (they then claimed to have found them in caves, he remarked), and he cast doubt on the authority and authenticity of ancient Jewish texts such as *Shi'ur Qomah* and *Pereq Shirah.*

The scholar who allowed these heresies to enter rabbinic Judaism, in Taku's view, was Saadya Gaon. Like the two rabbis of Falaise, who were careful not to attack Maimonides himself or to impugn his orthodoxy but only that of his followers, Taku was careful not to refer to his Rabbanite opponents as *minim* themselves. But he traced Saadya's teachings back to what he claimed were their Christian and Karaite origins, and forward into his own time and place. From Saadya, these deplorable errors spread to Maimonides and to Abraham Ibn Ezra, and from them finally (and closest to home) to the Ḥasidei Ashkenaz (German Pietists). The common thread of all of these—Christians, Karaites, Saadya, Ibn Ezra, Maimonides, Ḥasidei Ashkenaz—was, for Moses Taku, their willingness to ignore the plain meaning of the Talmud and the *midrashim.* He wrote, "I have seen that they interpret the 'river of fire' (Daniel 7:10) as the sphere of the fixed stars. If so, they are outside of the Talmud of our rabbis. Is it right for any believer in the Torah to say that . . . a teaching of the Torah is . . . a parable?"[16]

The Rise of Dogma

The Ashkenazic Jews about the year 1200 had no special allegiance to Maimonides' Thirteen Principles. As we have seen, Maimonides himself was regarded with suspicion. The Ashkenazic rabbis naturally accepted some of the articles of faith, for instance, that God exists and that He is One. The third principle, on the other hand, belief in divine incorporeality, was a doubtful point.[17] But even if they could have accepted all of Maimonides' creed in its entirety, Ashkenazic Jews did not define Judaism by a set of basic tenets.[18]

Gradually, however, over the course of the Middle Ages, Maimonides' principles became a part of Ashkenazic Judaism and came to define its limits.[19] Take, for instance, *Sefer Hadrat ha-Qodesh,* written in 1400 by a Jew in Regensburg. The author, Simeon ben Samuel, had accepted the Thirteen Principles, accepted that God is incorporeal, and so on; *Sefer Hadrat ha-Qodesh* is a commentary on the Thirteen Principles. Likewise, Simeon ben Samuel accepted that allegorical interpretation—both of *aggadah* and of Scripture—is not heresy. What is heresy, then? Heresy for Simeon ben Samuel was the denial of one of the Thirteen Principles.[20]

Other Ashkenazic texts from about the same time also expressed a commitment to Maimonidean dogma.[21] In Prague, Yom-Tov Lipmann Muehlhausen wrote a poetic version of the principles, and endorsed them once again in his anti-Christian polemic, *Sefer Niṣṣaḥon.*[22] Muehlhausen took a more cautious view of allegory than did Simeon ben Samuel. In *Sefer Niṣṣaḥon,* Muehlhausen followed Maimonides in suggesting that *aggadah* should not generally be interpreted literally. Scripture, however, may and indeed must be interpreted literally, although it too may be given allegorical and other non-literal interpretations in addition to its literal interpretation. "Those who follow either philosophy or kabbalah," Muehlhausen wrote, "and say that the Torah means only one of them and not the *peshat* . . . and who have doubts concerning this, have strayed into heresy."[23]

A century later, in the mid-sixteenth century, the leading light of Polish Jewry, Rabbi Moses Isserles, took a view similar to that of Muehlhausen. Isserles identified the core of Jewish belief with a set of dogmas. He defended the allegorical interpretation of both *aggadah* and Scripture, and did not accept the literal interpretation of all *aggadot.* He did, however, insist on the literal truth of all of Scriptural narrative, while accepting additionally the validity of allegorical or other interpretations.[24] One of Isserles's students, Abraham Horowitz, went further. He argued that literal interpretation of Scripture is not a dogma of Judaism, and hence that rejection of the literal sense, for instance, of the story of Balaam and his donkey is not a heresy. He quickly added, however, that he personally did accept the story of Balaam in its literal sense.[25]

The controversy in the 1570s over Azariah de' Rossi's *Me'or Einayim* again raised the question of skepticism with regard to *aggadah.* Maharal (Judah Loew, ca. 1520–1609), the great sage of Prague, stated, perhaps with some hyperbole, that *Me'or Einayim* ought to be burnt, on account of de' Rossi's rejection of certain talmudic *aggadot,* or truly certain details of certain *aggadot.* Yet Maharal stopped short of explicitly calling de' Rossi a heretic; nor did Maharal actually affirm the literal truth of all talmudic *aggadot,* but only (like his predecessor in the Prague rabbinate centuries before, Yom-Tov Muehlhausen) their copious meaningfulness.[26]

In Isserles's system of theology, the dogma of Creation *ex nihilo* took central place. By the same token, the arch-heresy in his view was the Aristotelian belief in the eternity of the world.[27] Isserles's students and his students' students continued this emphasis. One telling example is a remarkable comment by Issachar Ber ha-Kohen of Szczebrzeszyn, a disciple of Isserles. Commenting on the extraordinary statement in Genesis Rabbah that the serpent in the Garden of Eden was a heretic (*min*), Rabbi Issachar explained that like Aristotle, it had believed in the eternity of the world, and rejected belief in Creation.[28]

At the same time that these scholars regarded Creation as the Jewish arch-dogma, there were others who argued that Creation *ex nihilo* is not a dogma of Judaism at all, not one of Maimonides' Thirteen Principles. Writing in 1618, Gedaliah b. Solomon Lipschuetz, a young student of the talmudist Meir of Lublin, was careful not to question the truth of Creation *ex nihilo,* but argued that it is no more central to Judaism than any other miracle, for instance the miracle of Balaam's donkey.[29] Similarly, the skeptic Eliezer Eilburg had argued about 1575, in his unpublished work "Ten Questions," that Creation *ex nihilo* is not one of the Thirteen Principles. But then Eilburg, who argued that there can be no physical resurrection, and made many other controversial claims as well, may very well have been regarded as a heretic himself. He spent years in prison and was put into *ḥerem,* perhaps on account of his beliefs.[30]

Commitment to talmudic literalism did not disappear quickly in Ashkenazic Judaism, if indeed it ever disappeared at all. In 1559, Abraham Horowitz debated the young, brilliant, very pious scholar Joseph Ashkenazi concerning Maimonides and *Guide of the Perplexed.* "There is not a chapter in the *Guide,*" Ashkenazi declared, "in which there is not heresy." Echoing quite consciously the position of the Tosafist masters in the Maimonidean Controversies three hundred years before, Joseph Ashkenazi insisted on literal interpretation of the Talmud. But when Joseph Ashkenazi restated his objections to Maimonides and Jewish philosophy a few years later, he chose to recast them in a dogmatic form. The root error of the philosophers and those who follow them, he declared, is their belief in the incorporeality of God and his unchangeable nature. Their denial of miracles flows from this root error, and in consequence of their rejection of miracles, the denial of divine providence and, finally, of belief in reward and punishment.[31]

The notion of dogma also did not win immediate acceptance in the fifteenth or even the sixteenth century. Maharil (Rabbi Jacob Moellin [Maharil], d. 1432), for instance, objected that the public recitation of a credo might be seen, in a Christianizing way, as a substitute for the performance of *miṣvot* such as *ṣiṣit, tefillin,* and the study of Torah.[32] About 1560 Isserles's cousin, Solomon Luria, still objected to "Yigdal," a prayer based on Maimonides' Thirteen Principles whose recitation had by then become common, on the grounds that all of the Torah consists of necessary beliefs, not merely these few principles.[33] But Ashkenazic Jewish culture in the sixteenth century was very different than it had been in the thirteenth century, at the time of the original Maimonidean Controversies. In 1559, the *Guide* was not successfully banned, nor was "Yigdal" successfully kept out of Ashkenazic siddurim. By 1612, Shabbetai Sofer, a student of Solomon Luria's students, did not even understand the objections to "Yigdal." He thought that they were perhaps on account of the uncertainty, which we have discussed, regarding certain of the dogmas. It did not occur to him that anyone might reject dogmas as such.[34]

There is another difference between Ashkenazic Jews of the thirteenth and the sixteenth centuries. In the earlier centuries, the limits of the heresiographical imagination of the Ashkenazic Jews had been a skeptic "who throws off the yoke of the commandments completely." In the sixteenth century, Elijah Levita, an Ashkenazic Jewish scholar living in Italy, could define *min* as "a man who has no religion"; and he imagined Mani, the founder of Manicheanism, for whom (he claimed, following the lead of the philosopher Joseph Albo) *minim,* or perhaps more properly Manim are named, as "a man spoken in the books of the Greeks, who was not a member of any religion."[35] Heresy as religious neutrality lurks in the wings.[36]

Toward the very end of the sixteenth century, a Yiddish folk tale revisited the thirteenth-century controversies over Maimonides. In one of the stories in the *Maysebukh* (Basel, 1602), Rabbi Meir is sent from Germany to visit Maimonides and investigate the charges made against him. Maimonides raises Rabbi Meir's suspicion with some unconventional behavior, but in the end, he is shown to be innocent. The author of the story, glossing in Yiddish the Hebrew term *min,* combined a new definition of *min* in the spirit of Levita with the old one of Rashi. "There were many rabbis who did not agree with [Maimonides], and considered him a heretic, i.e., an unbeliever, one who is neither a Jew nor a Christian, and who interprets the Law according to his own opinion and not in accordance with the interpretation of the sages."[37]

Kabbalah as Orthodoxy

The first great shift in medieval Ashkenazic theology was the rise of dogma. The second was the rise of Spanish Kabbalah. Beginning in the late sixteenth century, and continuing in the following centuries, kabbalistic beliefs were sometimes seen as necessary to orthodoxy.[38] The great halakhic scholar of the early seventeenth century, Joel Sirkes, rabbi of Brest-Litovsk and later of Cracow, author of the *Bayit Ḥadash,* penned a stark attack on those who reject Kabbalah. The occasion was provided in 1618 by the case of a Jewish doctor in Amsterdam, a converso lately returned to Judaism, a man named David Farar, who scandalized parts of the Amsterdam Jewish community through his skeptical remarks concerning miracles and other topics. The Amsterdam community, founded just a few years before, turned for help from outside in deciding the case. Rabbis in the Ottoman Empire wrote letters to condemn Farar; from Venice, Leon Modena wrote to the contrary that Farar's opinions were within the purview of permissible Jewish rationalism.

But the affair had also come to the ears of Sirkes, who wrote from Brest-Litovsk that Farar should be excommunicated, and declared him to be a heretic. Sirkes had two arguments. First of all, he wrote, Farar is a follower of philosophy, and philosophy, Sirkes wrote, is "heresy itself" (*ha-minut be-aṣmah*). Second of all, Sirkes argued, Farar rejects Kabbalah, and Kabbalah is "the essence of the Torah" (*iqqar ha-torah*); that is, Sirkes identified unbelief with philosophy, and he identified true Jewish belief with Kabbalah. Sirkes treated the authority of Kabbalah as an extension of the rule that the writings of the ancient rabbis must be accepted. "It is obvious that such a person deserves excommunication," wrote Sirkes in his condemnation, "for there can be no greater mockery of Torah . . . than this."[39]

Sirkes was not alone in identifying opposition to Kabbalah as heresy. For instance, in the previous generation, Joseph Ashkenazi, whose 1559 polemic against Maimonides we have remarked on above, in his later polemic (the same work in which he attacked the root belief in God's incorporeality) wrote that ancient kabbalistic works such as (he listed) the Zohar, the *Hekhalot,* and the *Shi'ur Qomah* were among the ancient rabbinic writings whose authority cannot be questioned.[40] Similarly, in the generation after Sirkes, the kabbalist Naphtali Bacharach wrote in his book *Emeq ha-Melekh* that "it is unquestionably proper to call [a Jew who disagrees with the Zohar—more specifically, who disagrees with the doctrine of *gilgul* (cycles of reincarnation)] a heretic (*min*)."[41] In the same passage, Bacharach discussed a potential objection to his own position. If Kabbalah is an esoteric teaching, and if *gilgul* is a secret, hidden doctrine, then how can anyone be blamed for not believing in it? If Kabbalah is not taught publicly, then it is at most one sort of Jewish belief. It may be a higher or truer type of belief, but it cannot be the only type. Bacharach replied that just on this account, it is necessary that Kabbalah should be made available to everyone.[42]

In this vein, we should contrast the interpretation of the famous story of Jacob wrestling the angel (Gen. 32:21–32) by the great late-sixteenth-century preacher Ephraim of Luntshits in his well-known commentary, *Keli Yeqar*.[43] The comment brings together the theme of heresy with the theme of Maimonidean rationalism, and the theme of kabbalistic belief. Following a midrashic and medieval line of interpretation, Luntshits identified the angel who wrestled Jacob as Samael, that is, the evil inclination. The name Samael, Luntshits noted, is from the root *samekh-mem-alef,* the Blinder, for the evil inclination draws its victims into blindness. Since Jacob was now a wealthy man, Luntshits argued, Samael wished to blind Jacob, so to speak; that is, he wished to fill him so entirely with greed "that he would forget God entirely . . . and deny God above." But when the morning rose, Luntshits continues, Samael's scheme was defeated by the light of the sun, which represents knowledge of God's existence, knowledge that is based (by the medieval philosophers) on the movement of the heavenly spheres. Jacob, in Luntshits's interpretation, is saved from heresy by his rational apprehension of God's existence, and hence His Providence. (While endorsing the literal meaning of the passage as well, Luntshits's treatment is allegorical.) But the blinding angel, Luntshits concluded, was partly successful. The angel made Jacob lame in the thigh; that is (Luntshits suggests), Samael deprived Jacob of the understanding of kabbalistic mysteries.

Like many or perhaps all medieval Jews, Luntshits subscribed to the view of Judaism as a dual religion, revealed and concealed, exoteric and esoteric. For Luntshits, however, the revealed religion is rationalistic, based on philosophic proofs, while Kabbalah is to remain concealed, hidden even from the patriarch Jacob. For Luntshits, to deny the revealed religion, to deny the Maimonidean doctrines, is to deny God, and to embrace heresy. Jacob defeated the blinding angel and escaped from heresy. But even Jacob did not—according to Luntshits's interpretation of the story—escape the more subtle denial, which was denial of Kabbalah.

A different view of Jacob and the angel, a different view of Kabbalah and its relation to heresy, was taken in the 1630s by the kabbalist Nathan ben Solomon Spira, author of *Megalleh Amuqot,* Sirkes's colleague in the Cracow rabbinate. In Spira's interpretation, the story of Jacob and the angel is woven tightly together into a web-like biblical and post-biblical history of conflict and antagonism. Spira's story, which is never told in full, runs from Adam and the snake, through Cain and Abel, Jacob and Esau, Moses's slaying of the Egyptian (Exod. 2:11–12), Jeroboam and the division of the Israelite kingdom, the Maccabees and Antiochus, Rabbi Akiva and the Romans, until its conclusion at the end of time when the Messiah son of Joseph will fight the nations and die. The roots of heresy, for Spira—indeed, the roots of experience generally, both positive and negative—are the spiritual repercussions of the sins and good deeds of these biblical heroes and villains, these souls and their *gilgulim,* their cycles of transmigration. In this vein, Spira claimed that the infamous ancient heretic Elisha ben Avuyah was a reincarnation (*gilgul*) of the prophet Elisha's sinful servant Geḥazi. Therefore his sin was the result or recurrence of the sin of Geḥazi, which was itself, however, a recurrence and variation of the other root sins that we have mentioned.[44] As the root of heresy is mystical, so must its cure be mystical. Spira described the blessing against the *minim* in the weekday *Amidah* not only as a *taqqanah,* a rabbinic ordinance, but as a *tiqqun,* an act of mystical repair. Spira placed heresy within a kabbalistic framework of *gilgulim,* sins and their mystical repercussions, each of which awaits its proper kabbalistic *tiqqun.*[45]

The most influential kabbalistic text within Ashkenazic Judaism of the seventeenth and early eighteenth centuries, more influential than those of Bacharach or even Spira, was the *Shenei Luḥot ha-Berit*, the magnum opus of the great kabbalistic and ethical writer Isaiah Horowitz, son of Abraham Horowitz, whom we have mentioned, and a fellow student of Joel Sirkes. One of the many parts of this work, written about 1620, is a commentary to Maimonides' Thirteen Principles. Horowitz's commentary to the first three principles is explicitly kabbalistic; he rephrased Maimonides' statements of divine unity and incorporeality as doctrines of the Ten *Sefirot* and the *Ein Sof*.[46] Horowitz's commentary, and his work generally, treads a fine line between the position of Luntshits, that Kabbalah is esoteric and hence not strictly normative, and that of Bacharach, that Kabbalah is in principle normative and denial of it is prohibited. The Thirteen Principles of Maimonides are normative for Horowitz. In his eyes, was the kabbalistic interpretation that he offered equally normative or was it merely optional?

Certainly, Horowitz's commentary went far to render acceptable (or possibly even normative, as we have suggested) certain radical kabbalistic theories that might otherwise seem heretical. Consider, for instance, the Ninth Principle of Maimonides, the eternity and immutability of the Torah. As his father had remarked before him, literal interpretation of Scripture is not a Jewish dogma. Isaiah Horowitz commented that in the messianic future, the Torah, which is now material, will become spiritual. "In the future, the commandments will be observed according to their meaning at that time. This is our belief. It will be the same Torah, but more luminous, just as man will then be more luminous. This is our belief."[47] After the coming of the messiah, Horowitz might easily be interpreted to say, what has been sin will no longer be sin, and what has been commanded will no longer be commanded in the same sense. The text, while maintaining in a formal or verbal sense the authority of the Maimonidean Principles, provided a sort of charter, half a century later, for Sabbatean antinomianism.[48]

Sabbateanism and the Heretic as Antinomian

The only extended effort at the persecution of heretics within Ashkenazic Jewish society in the Middle Ages and early modern period was the campaign against Sabbateanism in the eighteenth century, and its aftermath, the campaign against Ḥasidism. Over the preceding three centuries, from the beginning of the fifteenth century through the end of the seventeenth, there had been isolated cases of the persecution of heretics within Ashkenazic communities. In the mid-fifteenth century, for instance, in the Jewish community of Wiener Neustadt, opponents of the communal leadership had prevented the rabbi of the city from leading prayers on Rosh Hashanah. Indeed, they had caused him to be removed from the synagogue. The Talmud, we have mentioned, defines an *apiqoros* as one who "shames the sages." Jacob Weil, rabbi of Erfurt, declared that these men who had shamed a scholar were *apiqorsim,* heretics.[49] In the late sixteenth century, Maharal of Prague extended the category of heretic to include anyone who set himself against the organized Jewish community. "To depart from the ways of the community is heretical, for one who does so leaves the community [*ha-kelal*] and shames the community, and so he has no share in the community."[50] In the early seventeenth century, to take a final example, Joel Sirkes branded his own cantor as an *apiqoros* for refusing to read from a *sefer torah* that Sirkes had declared permissible. The cantor had also made disparaging remarks (Sirkes claimed) concerning the Talmud and various medieval rabbis (significantly or not, all opponents of Maimonides and philosophy): the Ba'alei ha-Tosafot, Rabbi Asher b. Yeḥiel, and Rabad.[51]

But cases such as these were exceptional. Although early modern Ashkenazic Jewish communities were often riven by dissension, charges of heresy were rarely used as a tool of social discipline. Those who opposed the leadership in early modern Ashkenazic Jewish communities were generally called names that denoted sin or rebelliousness, such as "trouble-makers," "wicked ones," "sons of Belial," and so on.[52] It should not surprise us, then, that the Ashkenazic campaign against Sabbateans as heretics took many years to begin. For fifty years after Shabbatai Zvi's brief messianic reign, Ashkenazic Jews mostly took a moderate view of Sabbateanism, and did not press accusations of heresy.[53]

Five years after Shabbatai Zvi's apostasy, in 1671, the Council of Four Lands publicly condemned the Sabbateans, calling them "sinners and worthless people." But the document did not use the word "heretic," and offered no specific criticisms of the Sabbateans. The social motives that required Sabbateanism to be suppressed seem to have outrun the thinking that would justify such a policy.[54] Much milder in its tone is the famous diary of Glikl bat Judah ("Glückel of Hameln"), written in 1691. She spoke of Shabbatai Zvi with disappointment and a certain nostalgia, but without the slightest mark of disapproval.[55]

At about the same time, the well-informed doctor Tobias Cohen was a vocal opponent of Sabbateanism. He argued, however, that belief in the coming of the messiah is not a dogma of Judaism. Reward and punishment is a dogma, Cohen argued, following the lead of Albo, but the coming of the messiah is not. By this logic, neither belief nor disbelief in Shabbatai Zvi can in itself make one a heretic.[56] Cohen's brother-in-law, Jair Bacharach, a talmudist in Worms, wrote poignantly on the topic of Jewish belief in his generation. Kabbalah is the root, the source of all Jewish belief, the essence of Judaism, he wrote, but it is so deeply hidden in this generation that we cannot rely on it. What we must rely on, Bacharach argued, is Maimonides' Thirteen Principles. Bacharach, who in 1665 had joined fervently in the messianic expectations of that year, made no special animadversion to Sabbateanism.[57]

From the point of view of the Sabbateans, it was they who were the believers—"Believers" (*ma'aminim*) was the name the Sabbateans used most often for themselves. Their opponents, in their eyes, were the heretics. Ber Perlhefter, a Sabbatean scholar in Prague in the late seventeenth century, called the opponents of Sabbateanism "deniers" (*koferim*); another Sabbatean after the turn of the eighteenth century disparaged his persecutors as *minim*.[58] Sabbateanism, on account of its kabbalistic rationale, had a substantive claim to be regarded as orthodox. If anything, the burden of proof was on the non-believers to show that belief in Sabbateanism was not required by Judaism.

Opponents of Sabbateanism thus needed to activate the category of heretical Kabbalah, *qiṣṣuṣ ba-neti'ot*, a medieval or even a talmudic notion, but until this time, mainly a hypothetical category rather than a concrete one.[59] To do this, they needed to distinguish between orthodox Kabbalah and heretical Kabbalah.[60] They pursued two main avenues of criticism. First, they condemned the Sabbateans for their rejection of Jewish dogma. This approach centered mainly on texts. Second, relying less on text analysis and more on testimony, rumor, and narrative, they condemned the Sabbateans for their immorality. Combined with both of these was the condemnation of the popularization of Kabbalah, and an attempt to reinstitute the policy of kabbalistic esotericism that had so effectively been challenged in the seventeenth century. The overall image of the Sabbateans, combining these three separate lines of attack, was one of evil, kabbalistic unbelievers.

The beginning of the eighteenth-century campaign of persecution of Sabbateans among Ashkenazic Jews was the *ḥerem* issued against the Sabbatean kabbalist Neḥemiah Ḥayon by the chief Ashkenazic rabbi of Amsterdam, Zvi Hirsch Ashkenazi (Ḥakham Ṣevi). Joining Zvi Hirsch was, among others, Naphtali Katz, lately the rabbi of Frankfurt. Zvi Hirsch and Naphtali Katz condemned Ḥayon's publication of kabbalistic secrets. Furthermore, they declared that the version of Kabbalah in Ḥayon's book had crossed the lines of Jewish belief, and had antinomian implications. Katz wrote: "He is of the sect that . . . denies our faith and all of the Thirteen Principles, for they deny the principle on which all others are based, that there is One God and no other . . . but this evil man believes in dualism. . . . Woe to the eyes that have seen . . . that they explain [Shabbatai Zvi's] apostasy on the basis of the Holy Zohar. . . . And certain men transgress all of the commandments in the Torah, and justify it on the basis of a book called The Secret of the Godhead."[61] Four years later, Leib ben Ozer, the *shammes* ("beadle") of the Ashkenazic synagogue in Amsterdam, wrote a Yiddish history of Shabbatai Zvi and the Sabbatean movement. Rather than the theological unorthodoxy of the Sabbateans, Leib ben Ozer emphasized the demonic and immoral aspect of the Sabbateans' kabbalistic endeavors. He wrote, "In Saloniki, there is a large sect of those wicked men. . . . And they still study everything according to the Kabbalah, but they commit every abomination of the Lord. They have sex with menstruating women intentionally, and they commit adultery and homosexual intercourse, and they desecrate Sabbath in public, and they say that they are doing these things in order to subdue the unclean *qelippot,* so as to bring the redemption. . . . Behold the power of the Other Side to lead believers so far astray as to do great sins, thinking that they were *miṣvot*."[62] Are kabbalists who commit adultery necessarily heretics? In an earlier section, we said that the Talmud distinguishes one who sins "for spite" (*le-hakh'is*) from one who sins "for pleasure" (*le-te'avon*). The former is a *min,* a heretic, while the latter is merely a sinner. (Jair Bacharach, for instance, invoked this distinction for the benefit of a Jewish bandit. Although the bandit is surely a bad man, he has not forfeited his place in the community, Bacharach argued.)[63] This definition might seem designed for use against antinomian Sabbateans. In fact it was rarely used. Instead, perhaps surprisingly, the opponents of Sabbateanism returned to Rashi's definition of the heretic as the one who misinterprets the Torah. The Sabbatean leader Ḥayyim Mal'akh, wrote Leib ben Ozer, "began in holiness, but then the *qelippot* and the Other Side attached themselves to him, until he read Shabbatai Zvi into passages from the Holy Zohar."[64]

The anti-Sabbatean offensives of the mid-eighteenth century repeated these elements: esotericism, a defense of dogma, the attack on kabbalistic antinomianism, the charge of heretical misinterpretation. In 1725, Ezekiel Katzenellenbogen, rabbi of Hamburg-Altona, together with the anti-Sabbatean leader Moses Ḥagiz, spearheaded a movement in the German rabbinate to suppress "all kabbalistic works written and published after 1666."

The sins of the Saloniki Sabbateans were also retold. "A few years ago," said the Jewish community of Altona in its official condemnation, "sects of wicked men and scoundrels arose in the land of Turkey, who revived the belief in Shabbatai Zvi, and added foolish things and vanities and evil deeds, so that many were captured by the Primeval Serpent who tempts and leads astray, and, for our sins, they left the community (*minaklal aroys gingn*) and denied Judaism (*koyfer ba'iker gevezn*)."[65] A few years later, Jacob Cohen Poppers in Frankfurt and others accused Moses Ḥayyim Luzzatto of joining the mystical and the evil. Luzzatto's attackers were uncertain whether to class him as a Sabbatean, but they agreed that Luzzatto's claims of angelic revelation must be turned on their head. They argued (not without a certain circularity) that since the revelations are not angelic, they must be demonic.[66] In 1751, the Jews of Metz called the Sabbateans "a group of sinners who tend towards heresy . . . and sent forth their hands against the Prophets and the midrashim of the Rabbis, dressing them in garments of filth through their interpretations."[67]

The climax of the anti-Sabbatean campaigns of the eighteenth century, certainly one of the greatest of all heresiographical efforts in the entire Jewish tradition, was the campaign to denounce and expose the Sabbatean rabbi of Altona-Hamburg, Jonathan Eibeschuetz. The campaign was led by Jacob Emden, the son of Neḥemiah Ḥayon's nemesis, Zvi Hirsch Ashkenazi. Emden's kabbalistic writings hint at the apocalyptic dimensions within which he saw this continued struggle, in his eyes a veritable battle of Good and Evil.[68]

Emden's long series of heresiographical writings—he published more than a dozen works attacking Sabbateanism and Eibeschuetz—were remarkable and unprecedented, at least within Ashkenazic Judaism. What was most novel, perhaps, was the biographical and autobiographical focus of so much of Emden's writings against Eibeschuetz. Neither biography nor autobiography was a major genre in medieval Judaism. Emden's storytelling echoes the work of Leib ben Ozer (whom he had surely known as a young man in Amsterdam), whose biography of Shabbatai Zvi he translated into Hebrew. But in the extent and in the virulence of his writings, Emden left Leib ben Ozer far behind.

Emden ardently collected and published stories, sworn testimony, rumors, scandals, letters, and documents of all kinds about Eibeschuetz and his children. Once, someone saw Eibeschuetz eat some food before the morning prayers, without washing hands, and without saying the blessing. On another occasion, Eibeschuetz is said to have cheated a servant out of some money. (According to Emden, the servant later came back as a ghost to haunt Eibeschuetz.)[69] According to yet a third rumor, an orphan for whom Eibeschuetz had collected money was actually his own illegitimate grandchild. Eibeschuetz later embezzled the money, Emden charged.[70] Eibeschuetz himself, Emden alleged, had many affairs, as did his wife, his daughter, and his sons. Emden accused Eibeschuetz of using rabbinic office for private gain, of coarse table manners, and (this was of course the central accusation) of writing heretical magical amulets that did not work. Emden is a malign Boswell to Eibeschuetz's heretical Johnson.

Intertwined with all of these stories is the story that Emden told and retold of his own opposition to Eibeschuetz. He eventually wrote a full autobiography, centering largely on his clash with Eibeschuetz. That autobiograpy has a twin, a sort of a biography of Eibeschuetz titled *Sefer Hit'abbequt*, "The Book of Wrestling," evoking Jacob's struggle with the angel. Emden's autobiography is a work that is distinctively modern in its scope, detail, and candor: the chatty and obscene *Sefer Hit'abbequt* shares some of the same features.[71]

In the 1760s, as the failure of his earlier campaign against Eibeschuetz was becoming clearer, and as he turned his attention to a new wave of Sabbateanism, namely Frankism, Emden sharpened two of the previous lines of criticism that we have seen. In 1769, he reinforced the image of Sabbateans as evil kabbalists by publishing a wild tale of magic and counter-magic in the rise of Frankism and the Frankist-Rabbanite disputation in Lvov, spun by a certain Abraham of Shargorod.[72] Furthermore, in the previous year, Emden had actually dared to attack the Zohar itself, or at least the authenticity of certain sections of the Zohar. He likened the Zohar to the bronze serpent of Moses that King Hezekiah righteously destroyed when it became an idol.[73]

Both in the biographical approach that he pioneered, and in his resolute focus on bad behavior (and relative lack of interest in Sabbatean doctrine), Emden's approach contrasts sharply with the dogmatic and textological approach taken by many of the other leading opponents of Sabbateanism. For instance, it contrasts, as we have seen, with the approach taken by Emden's father.

The attacks on Ḥasidism in Lithuania and Poland from the 1770s echoed in some respects the earlier condemnations of the Sabbateans, emphasizing kabbalistic esotericism, kabbalistic heresy, and antinomianism. (Emden's biographical approach had no real echo.) In 1772, the Vilna Gaon examined certain kabbalistic writings of the Ḥasidim and declared them to contain "heresy and very evil mystical acts of unification [*yiḥudim*]." The rabbis of Brody declared that Ḥasidim were unqualified as kabbalists and had "cut the shoots." They compared them to the Sabbateans, and accused them, like the Sabbateans, of sexual misconduct.[74]

After the 1770s, other elements of anti-Ḥasidic polemic came to the fore. The Vilna Gaon's anti-Ḥasidic letter of 1796 focused on the charge that the Ḥasidic leaders teach heretical misinterpretations of Scripture (*megallim panim ba-torah she-lo ke-halakhah*).[75] Many opponents of Ḥasidim accused them of disrespect for Torah scholars, one of talmudic definitions of an *apiqoros*, as we have seen. The most characteristic element of anti-Ḥasidic polemic in the 1780s, however, were the long lists of objectionable Ḥasidic ritual and behavioral innovations, such as wild gestures during the prayer service, the liturgical use of Yiddish, the use of the Sefardic prayer rite rather than the Ashkenazic one, the demand that slaughterers used polished blades, and many others.[76] The most striking example of this emphasis may be the 1786 *ḥerem* of the Cracow Jewish community against the Ḥasidim. The Cracow *ḥerem* treated Ḥasidism simply and purely as a ritual innovation and an anti-social sort of sectarianism, to be rejected on the basis of ritual conservatism, communalism, and traditionalism.[77]

As we have seen, and will see again, Ashkenazic Jews in the late eighteenth century, in spite of their large and increasing differences, or perhaps on account of those differences, frequently preferred to debate issues of behavior, not belief.

Divine Providence, Heresy, and the Early *Haskalah*

In the early decades of the seventeenth century, an Alsatian Jew named Alexander b. Isaac Pfaffenhofen wrote a long bilingual poem in Yiddish and Hebrew in which he presented the complaints of the rich against the poor, and of the poor against the rich. In the introduction to his poem, Pfaffenhofen explained that both the wicked ways of the wealthy and the bitterness of the poor can lead to heretical denial of divine providence: "The arrogance of the wealthy who rule over the poor . . . can make the poor hot-headed, so that [the poor man] will ask, why did God decree this? And on that account, he will suppose that everything is random, and that there is no Judge and no Judgment. . . . At the same time, the wicked man will say . . . my hard work and my cleverness have brought me all of the delicacies that men wish for. . . . Thus both of them deny divine providence."[78] For Pfaffenhofen, denial of divine providence was a pervasive heresy, hidden, however, in the recesses of the private conscience. By the eighteenth century, denial of miracles, special Providence, and divine reward had changed, in the view of Ashkenazic Jews, from being a temptation, or a private heretical doubt, to a sectarian option.

The question of orthodox and heretical views of providence was on the minds of many Jewish leaders of the eighteenth century, no doubt on account of the rise of Deism, naturalism, and modern science. In 1705, Rabbi David Nieto in London had been accused of leaning toward heresy and Spinozism in his views concerning providence and nature. Zvi Hirsch Ashkenazi, the same rabbi who would shortly persecute Neḥemiah Ḥayon, defended Nieto. At about the same time, however, Zvi Hirsch Kaidanover warned against the heresy of naturalism and the denial of divine providence. So would a contemporary of Eibeschuetz, the Ḥasidic leader Dov Ber of Mezhirech; while during the heat of the Emden-Eibeschuetz controversy, Ezekiel Landau, in his condemnation of the Sabbatean tract *Va-avo ha-Yom el ha-Ayin,* attributed to Eibeschuetz, accused that work of a denial of divine providence "more atrocious than that of Aristotle."[79]

In his many perfectly orthodox sermons, Jonathan Eibeschuetz gave no hint of any denial of Providence, nor did he refrain from attacking heresy. One heretical view, in fact, against which he warned, a view that he attributed to "those who deny religion," was the denial of supernatural miracles, particularly the denial that the Jewish people have been the subjects of God's special Providence.[80]

Emden too, in a fiery sermon that he delivered in 1775, denounced naturalism, its inroads into the German Jewish community, and its antinomian consequences, such as reading novels and sexual promiscuity. Philosophy is the arch-heresy, Emden preached, the root of all the misfortunes of Jewish history, the root of the heretical sects whose quarrels led to the destruction of the Second Temple, the sin that led to the exile of Jews from Spain, the sin of the sixteenth- and seventeenth-century Jews that led to the Chmielnitsky massacres of 1648.[81]

As is well known, the storm over the *Haskalah* broke in 1781–82 during the conflict over the Edict of Tolerance in the Habsburg Empire, when Naftali Herz Wessely published *Divrei Shalom ve-Emet,* a pamphlet that, like the Habsburg decree itself, called for major reforms in Jewish education. Wessely's piety did not save him from attack. David (Tevele) ben Nathan of Lissa (Leszno) declared him a heretic—a *min,* an *apiqoros.* David mentioned in passing Wessely's naturalism (David used the French word, *naturaliste*); indeed, he accused Wessely of not believing in the Torah at all, of regarding it merely as a book of stories. Mainly, however, David had been offended by Wessely's critical and somewhat patronizing tone toward rabbis both ancient and modern. David's central accusation was that Wessely fit the talmudic definition of an *apiqoros:* he "shamed Torah scholars."[82]

At nearly the same time, Raphael Kohen in Hamburg and Phineas Horowitz in Frankfurt attacked another major work of the Jewish Enlightenment, the Torah translation project of Moses Mendelssohn, the *Bi'ur,* which had been published in 1780. The accusations they directed against the *Bi'ur* were very similar to those of David against Wessely: "It is a new book, a work of heresy, that mocks the words of our sages of blessed memory. . . . [The author says] accept my opinion and my interpretation of the Torah . . . and get rid of all of the words of the sages of blessed memory, the Talmud and midrashim and the commentaries."[83] While David had focused his attack on Wessely as an individual, Raphael Kohen had no doubt that he was dealing with a heretical group. As he put it in his writ of *ḥerem* against a certain Samuel Marcus, they are "a sect of wicked men and wicked deeds, Sabbath-breakers, obscene speakers of heresies . . . who mock the words of our holy Torah."[84]

On Shabbat ha-Gadol, 1782, the same day that David denounced Wessely from the pulpit in Lissa, Ezekiel Landau, the chief rabbi of Prague and one of leading talmudists of his generation, also preached against Wessely, accusing him of heresy.[85] Unlike the others, Landau focused his attack on doctrinal heresy, and more particularly on naturalism. He went very much beyond David in his attention to this theme. He associated Wessely with those who deny "individual Providence, the revelation of the Torah, and supernatural miracles, [and] who say that religion was not given by the Creator."[86] Like Raphael Kohen, Landau asserted that such men formed a "sect." Going beyond Kohen as well, Landau asserted that the sect of the Enlightenment was allied in some sense to the other "strange sects" that had recently appeared within Judaism, Ḥasidism, and Sabbateanism/Frankism. Landau now saw the Jewish world as divided into competing sects. He saw, one could say, as Mendelssohn perhaps also did, the new world of Jewish denominations.[87]

In 1783, just about a year after Landau's and David's sermons, Moses Mendelssohn wrote his *Jerusalem.* In it, he offered a solution to the tangled question of heresy, whose history we have traced. Mendelssohn cut the Gordian knot. Jewish society, he wrote, like all societies, must allow freedom of conscience. Hence, there cannot be any required beliefs, nor any heresies.[88] The irony of events, of course, is that Mendelssohn and the Enlightenment did not end Jewish debates over heresy, but instead breathed new life into those debates. Shortly after *Jerusalem* appeared, Ezekiel Landau wrote from Prague (privately, to be sure), that Mendelssohn's call to abolish *ḥerem* and religious coercion was itself heretical, and Mendelssohn himself a heretic, a *min.*[89] The history of modern Jewish heresiography lies, however, outside the confines of this article.[90]

There is no question—everything that we have seen has shown—that Mendelssohn's approach was a radical shift in Ashkenazic views of Jewish heresy. Kant sarcastically remarked that he had not known Judaism to be so tolerant.[91] Certainly, we have seen a long history of heresy-hunting; the Jews of the eighteenth century were particularly involved in this field of activity. Mendelssohn's position called for far-reaching changes in the legal status and political position of the Jewish community, and opened the door for enormous changes in theology and even Jewish practice.

From a somewhat different point of view, however, Mendelssohn did not veer too far from the consensus of German Jews in his generation. Observance of Jewish law was demanded within the German Jewish communities, at least in a general way, and Mendelssohn, in a general way, endorsed that demand, sanctioning the shared observance, although not the coercive imposition, of Jewish law. The German Jewish communities were not, however, overly particular in matters of belief. Men of Mendelssohn's generation were perhaps less impressed by the zeal of a man like Jacob Emden than by Emden's utter failure to remove Jonathan Eibeschuetz from rabbinic office in Hamburg-Altona. Moreover, Emden's attack on Eibeschuetz, as we have noted, already focused as much on issues of behavior than on their competing interpretations of orthodox or heretical kabbalistic belief. Eibeschuetz too was quoted by Wessely as claiming that beliefs concerning Kabbalah need not be insisted upon.[92]

This consensus of German Jewish opinion can be seen again in the condemnations of the pietist leader Nathan Adler of Frankfurt during the 1770s and 1780s. Adler's kabbalistic theology was not brought under debate. The ire of the community was aroused, rather, by Adler's strict views on Jewish law, and by the unsociable attitude of Adler's group. "[Adler] treats us as Samaritans or Karaites," someone complained. Phinehas Horowitz—the same scholar who condemned Mendelssohn's *Bi'ur*—joined hands with Jewish Enlighteners in Frankfurt in condemning the special stringencies, the kabbalistic practices, the rebelliousness, and the sectarianism—the schismatism or heresy (*afqeruta*)—of Adler.[93]

Whether in Frankfurt or in Cracow, where we have seen a similar trend in the definition of Ḥasidim as heretics, Mendelssohn could not have endorsed the coercive use of the *ḥerem*. The impetus to maintain traditional practices while avoiding theological polemics, however, was one that Mendelssohn shared. Furthermore, he suggested in one place that while the Jewish *kehillah* ought to have no means of coercion, the state was permitted to discourage "atheism and Epicureanism." Other Enlighteners criticized this concession to intolerance. Indeed, Mendelssohn's proposed target of state action was the same denial of divine providence (a position he associated, as Maimonides did, with Epicurus) of which he and the other *maskilim* were accused by Ezekiel Landau and the other opponents of the Enlightenment.[94]

Mendelssohn's argument against required Jewish beliefs had two parts. First, he argued that Judaism, as a religion, ought not to punish, still less to exclude anyone. The purpose of religion being educational in the broadest sense—"to transfer truth from the mind to the heart, to vivify . . . the concepts of reason"—its doors must be open to all. Thus, *ḥerem* must be abolished. Second, he argued against reliance—even voluntary reliance—on formulas of faith, creedal statements, or fixed written texts of any kind. A fixed text, he claimed, will inevitably become an idol, a barrier to the true worship of God, "an empty vehicle . . . turned into a pernicious poison."[95]

Mendelssohn did not deny the existence of Jewish dogmas, in the sense of necessary beliefs without which there can be no Judaism. He did not even argue against the content of Maimonides' Thirteen Principles, which, he noted, "have been accepted by the greater part of the nation." But though he even translated the Thirteen Principles into German for use in the new, enlightened *Freyschule,* he was not committed to them as the only, or necessarily the best, statement of Jewish faith; in *Jerusalem,* he also recommended the minimal three principles of the medieval Jewish philosopher Joseph Albo (the existence of God, revelation of Torah, and reward and punishment). Emphasizing the limitations of all such fixed formulae, Mendelssohn maintained that belief is private. Written texts may inspire belief, but they cannot command it; indeed, they cannot fully express it. In one sense, then, Mendelssohn wished to move away from the question of the interpretation of normative texts, such as, for instance, talmudic *aggadot.* "Without disfiguring them, we cannot force our concepts into words which remain forever the same, for all men and all times, amid all the revolutions of language, morals, manners, and conditions."[96]

In another sense, however, Mendelssohn made the process of interpretation once again central. All theology in Judaism, Mendelssohn argued, must be rooted in "living, spiritual instruction, which can keep pace with all the changes of time and circumstances, and can be varied and fashioned according to a pupil's needs." Every law and each ritual, interpreted generously and yet passionately, points to an eternal truth. In this light, even Mendelssohn could praise the view, which he attributed to "[Isaac] Luria and his disciples, the latter-day kabbalists," that "in our teaching, everything is fundamental."[97]

Notes

Versions of this article were delivered as lectures at Gratz College, Spertus College, Boston University, and the Ohio State University. I thank my audiences and hosts in all of these places. I thank David Ruderman and Joel Hecker, and the librarians at Gratz College, the Jewish Theological Seminary, and the Center for Advanced Judaic Studies at the University of Pennsylvania, for bibliographical assistance.

1. On medieval views of heresy, see John Henderson, *The Construction of Orthodoxy and Heresy: Neo-Confucian, Islamic, Jewish, and Early Christian Patterns* (Albany: State University of New York Press, 1998).
2. Morton Smith, "Messiahs: Robbers, Jurists, Prophets, and Magicians," *Proceedings of the American Academy for Jewish Research* 44 (1977): 185.
3. Ashkenazic Jews in the medieval and early modern periods were not, of course, isolated from the larger world. Many of the intellectual currents discussed in this essay came to Ashkenazic Judaism from Spanish and Mediterranean Judaism, for instance, the notion of dogma, the conception of Kabbalah as orthodoxy, and both the Sabbatean movement and the reaction against it; while Mendelssohn's liberalism

echoed Spinoza's. Ashkenazic Judaism was also influenced by conceptions of heresy within western Christian culture, but there was no close correspondence between Christian trends in the definition of heresy and Ashkenazic Jewish trends. The attitudes of medieval Christian society toward heresy were in general quite different from medieval Jewish attitudes. The violence of Christian attacks on heretics and heretical groups, the institutions established for this purpose, the rich Christian polemical and heresiographical literature—none of these have close parallels in medieval Jewish society, least of all in Ashkenazic Jewish society.

4. Note also the involvement of Samson of Sens in the 1202 resurrection controversy: see his letter in Meir Abulafia, *Kitāb al-rasā'il* (Paris, 1871; reprint, Jerusalem, 1967), 136–37. Samson also defended aggadic literalism, but did not make any accusations of heresy. See Bernard Septimus, *Hispano-Jewish Culture in Transition: The Career and Controversies of Ramah* (Cambridge, Mass.: Harvard University Press, 1980), 49–51, 57–59, 82–83; Ephraim E. Urbach, *Ba'alei ha-Tosafot,* 5th ed. (Jerusalem: Bialik Institute, 1986), 1:272. The secondary literature on the controversies in general is cited in Menachem Kellner's article in this volume.
5. The letter is published in Joseph Shatzmiller, "Li-temunat ha-maḥaloqet ha-rishonah al kitvei ha-Rambam," *Zion* 34 (1969): 139. On Samuel b. Solomon, see the literature cited by Shatzmiller, and also Ephraim Kanarfogel, *Peering through the Lattices: Mystical, Magical, and Pietistic Dimensions in the Tosafist Period* (Detroit: Wayne State University Press, 2000), 96–99. Asher ben Gershom in southern France, responding to the rabbis of northern France, suggests a wider variety of charges than those in the letter of Samuel and Isaac, including objections to Maimonides' denial of resurrection and his view of the purposes of the commandments. The rabbis of northern France are also said to have demanded that the Bible and Talmud be interpreted only in accordance with the commentary of Rashi. See Shatzmiller, "Les Tossafistes et la première Controverse Maïmonidienne: La témoignâge du rabbin Asher ben Gershom," in *Rashi et la culture juive en France du Nord au moyen âge,* ed. Gilbert Dahan et al. (Paris: E. Peeters, 1997), 68, 77, 79. Cf. also the passage on aggadic interpretation in the later thirteenth century, in *Viqquaḥ R. Yeḥi'el,* ed. R. Margaliyot (Lvov, n.d.), 13.
6. BT Avodah Zarah 26b.
7. BT Sanhedrin 99b.
8. See e.g. Stuart Miller, "The Minim of Sepphoris Reconsidered," *Harvard Theological Review* 86 (1993): 377–402; Richard Kalmin, "Christians and Heretics in Rabbinic Literature of Late Antiquity," *Harvard Theological Review* 87 (1994): 155–69.
9. Jewish attitudes toward apostates and definitions of apostasy are not discussed in this article. See Jacob Katz, "Af al pi she-ḥata, Yisra'el hu," *Tarbiz* 27 (1957): 203–17; Benzion Netanyahu, *The Marranos of Spain: From the Late XIVth to the Early XVIth Century according to Contemporary Hebrew Sources* (New York: American Academy for Jewish Research, 1966), 17–21; Bernard Rosensweig, "Apostasy in the Late Middle Ages in Ashkenazic Jewry," *Dine Israel* 10–11 (1983): 43–80 (Eng. sect.); Edward Fram, "Perception and Reception of Repentant Apostates in Medieval Ashkenaz and Premodern Poland," *AJS Review* 21 (1996): 319–39.
10. See Jacob Katz, *Exclusiveness and Tolerance: Studies in Jewish-Gentile Relations in Medieval and Modern Times* (Oxford: Oxford University Press, 1961), 22–36; cf. Frank Talmage, "Mavo," in his edition of *Sefer Niṣṣaḥon* (Jerusalem: Merkaz Dinur, 1984), 32–33; David

Berger, *The Jewish-Christian Debate in the High Middle Ages: A Critical Edition of the Nizzaḥon Vetus* (Philadelphia: Jewish Publication Society, 1979), 263, 331.

11. Rashi on BT Rosh Hashanah 17a. Cf. his comments on Berakhot 12b, Sanhedrin 38b, Proverbs 2:12 and 2:19. See also the commentary on Avot in *Maḥzor Vitry,* ed. Simon Hurwitz (Nuremburg, 1923), 2:504, 512. Misinterpretation of Scripture is also one of the medieval Christian categories of heresy: see Othmar Hageneder, "Die Häresiebegriff bei den Juristen des 12. und 13. Jahrhunderts," in *The Concept of Heresy in the Middle Ages (11th–13th c.),* ed. W. Lourdaux and D. Verdelst (Leuven: Katholieke Universiteit te Leuven, 1976), 45–47. Ashkenazic talmudists did not interpret the definition of *min* given in BT Avodah Zarah 26b to include a believing Jew who transgresses, or even habitually transgresses, Jewish legal norms. See Ephraim Kanarfogel, "Rabbinic Attitudes toward Non-Observance in the Medieval Period," in *Jewish Tradition and the Non-Traditional Jew,* ed. Jacob J. Schacter (Northvale, N.J.: Jason Aronson, 1992), 3–35.
12. *Sefer Miṣvot Gadol,* negative commandment 15, which revises the language of *Mishneh Torah* Avodah Zarah 2:3. The language of the *Sefer Miṣvot Gadol* is repeated in Rabbi Isaac b. Joseph of Corbeil's *Sefer Miṣvot qatan,* commandment 13. Cf. Jeffrey Woolf, "Maimonides Revised: The Case of the Sefer Miswot Gadol," *Harvard Theological Review* 90 (1997): 175–203. Similarly, about the same time, Eleazar of Worms, author of the *Sefer ha-Roqeaḥ,* defined the *minim,* against whom one of the blessings of the *Amidah* is directed, as "the Jewish *minim,* who reject the Talmud, and the Gentile *minim.*" By the former, he presumably meant Karaites; by the latter, Christians; see *Peirush Siddur ha-Tefillah la-Roqeaḥ,* ed. Yehudah and Moshe Hershler (Jerusalem: Mekhon Harav Hershler, 1992), 1:342.
13. See Judah Rosenthal, "Qara'im ve-Qara'ut be-Eiropah ha-Ma'aravit," in *Sefer Yovel le-Rabbi Ḥanokh Albeck* (Jerusalem: Mossad Harav Kook, 1963), 425–43. But note Pethaḥiah of Regensburg's amiable description of Karaites in *Jewish Travelers,* 2nd ed., ed. and trans. Elkan Adler (New York: Hermon Press, 1966), 66.
14. *Sefer ha-Yashar,* ed. Shraga Feivush Rosenthal (Berlin, 1898), 100 (responsum no. 48, sec. 8). The correspondence is discussed in Urbach, *Ba'alei ha-Tosafot,* 1:71–84.
15. *Ketav Tamim,* ed. R. Kirchheim in *Oṣar Neḥmad* 3 (1860): 58–99. Cf. Joseph Dan, "Ashkenazi Hasidism and the Maimonidean Controversy," *Maimonidean Studies* 3 (1993): 40–47.
16. *Ketav Tamim,* 76–77. The text at this point is somewhat unclear. Why does Taku use the example of the "river of fire"? Is it because the existence of Hell is thought to be denied by some of its eventual denizens?
17. See e.g. *Ketav Tamim,* 59–60; *Maḥzor Vitry,* 514. Cf. Martin Lockshin, "Tradition or Context: Two Exegetes Struggle with Peshat," in *From Ancient Israel to Modern Judaism . . . Essays in Honor of Marvin Fox,* ed. Jacob Neusner et al. (Atlanta: Scholars Press, 1989), 2:181.
18. At the beginning of the fourteenth century, Meir ha-Kohen, the author of *Hagahot Maimoniyot,* a commentary to Maimonides' *Mishneh Torah,* felt impelled to remind his readers of the talmudic definitions of *min* and *apiqoros,* and implicitly to reject Maimonides' definitions: see his comments on "Hilkhot Teshuvah" 3:7–8. Contrast the defense of Maimonides' definition of the *apiqoros* in the mid-fifteenth century by Rabbi Jacob Moellin (Maharil) in his responsa, no. 194, ed. Yiṣḥaq Satz (Jerusalem: Mif'al Torat Ḥakhmei Ashkenaz, Mekhon Yerushalayim, 1980), 310–11.

19. On dogma in Judaism, see Solomon Schechter, "The Dogmas of Judaism," in his *Studies in Judaism* [First Series] (Philadelphia: Jewish Publication Society, 1896), 147–81; Menachem Kellner, *Dogma in Medieval Jewish Thought: From Maimonides to Abravanel* (Oxford: Oxford University Press, 1986).
20. See Joseph Davis, "Philosophy, Dogma, and Exegesis in Medieval Ashkenazic Judaism: The Evidence of *Sefer Hadrat Qodesh*," *AJS Review* 18 (1993): 195–222.
21. A document from 1467, published by Ephraim Kupfer in *Qobez Al Yad* 21 (1985): 221–22, expresses the mixed feelings of Ashkenazic Jews of the period toward the *Guide*. Moses b. Isaac Zart of Lichtenfels vows that having "carefully examined . . . the *Guide of the Perplexed*," he accepts "the exalted intention" of the *Guide* and "most" of what it says. But he "flees entirely" from those matters that contradict "the true tradition, the words of our holy rabbis of blessed memory . . . the authors of the Talmud, which they received in an unbroken tradition from Moses our Teacher [who received it] from the Almighty. And in particular I flee from," (he swears), "the opinion of the book in the matter of the angels [who appeared to Abraham] at the terebinths of Mamre [Gen. 18:2], and the sacrifices, and the speaking of [Balaam's] ass, and the reasons for the commandments, together with other matters that do not have to be mentioned." Cf. Abraham Horowitz's defense of Maimonides on the question of the angels and Balaam's ass: *Monatsschrift für Geschichte und Wissenschaft des Judentums* (henceforth *MGWJ*) 47 (1903): 264.
22. Talmage, "Mavo," in his edition of *Sefer Niṣṣaḥon*, 21–23, discusses Muehlhausen's listing of principles. Muehlhausen's colleague Avigdor Kara wrote a poetic version of the Thirteen Principles in Yiddish. See Chone Shmeruk, *Sifrut Yiddish: Peraqim le-Toldoteha* (Tel Aviv: Mif'alim Universita'iyim le-Hoṣa'ah le-Or, 1978), 43–47. Note also the poetic version of the principles in the fifteenth-century Ashkenazic manuscript Oxford-Bodleian Heb. 1114.
23. Muehlhausen, *Sefer ha-Eshkol*, in Judah Kaufman, *R. Yom Tov Lipman Muehlhausen* (New York, 1927), 143. For Muehlhausen's view of aggadic interpretation, see *Sefer Niṣṣaḥon*, para. 305. Cf. para. 112, where Muehlhausen also defended *aggadah*, arguing that there is exaggeration even in the Bible, and also in Christian legend (!), and that *aggadah*, unlike *halakhah*, should not be made the subject of dispute. The latter passage echoes a section of *Vikkuaḥ R. Yeḥi'el* (see above n. 5). Cf. Frank Talmage, "Mavo," to *Sefer Niṣṣaḥon*, 27–29.
24. See Isserles, *Meḥir Yayin* on Esther 4:7 vs. BT Ta'anit 23b. Note also the comments on Esther 1:4 and 2:2, where Isserles quotes Maimonides' remark in the preface to the *Guide* that not every detail of a narrative need have allegorical meaning. Note also his claim that "every word of the Talmud has both manifest and hidden meanings"; see *Torat ha-'Olah*, 3:55, quoted and discussed in Yonah Ben Sasson, *The Philosophical System of R. Moses Isserles* (Hebrew) (Jerusalem: Israel Academy of Sciences and Humanities, 1984), 249, 312. Cf. the position of Isserles's student Mordechai Jaffe, analyzed by Lawrence Kaplan, "Rationalism and Rabbinic Culture in Sixteenth Century Eastern Europe: R. Mordecai Jaffe's Levush Pinat Yikrat" (Ph.D. diss., Harvard University, 1975). N.B. also Alan Cooper, "An Extraordinary Sixteenth-Century Biblical Commentary: Eliezer Ashkenazi on the Song of Moses," in *Frank Talmage Memorial Volume*, ed. B. D. Walfish (Haifa: University of Haifa Press, 1993), 1:131–32.
25. Phillip Bloch, "Der Streit um den Moreh des Maimonides in Posen," MGWJ 47 (1903): 276. On the 1559 Horowitz-Ashkenazi controversy, see below, note 31.

26. Maharal, *Be'er ha-Golah* (New York: Talpiyot, 1952), 125–41. The suggestion of book-burning is on 126. Cf. Jacob Elbaum, "R. Judah Loewe's Attitude to Aggadah," *Scripta Hierosolymitana* 22 (1971): 28–47.
27. See Ben Sasson, *The Philosophical System of R. Moses Isserles,* 60. On creation as an arch-dogma in the sixteenth century, see Hava Tirosh-Rothschild, *Between Worlds: The Life and Thought of Rabbi David ben Judah Messer Leon* (Albany: State University of New York Press, 1991), 164–73.
28. Genesis Rabbah 19:1 and *Mattenot kehunah* ad loc. in *Midrash Rabbah* (Vilna, 1878). Similarly, Jacob Koppelman, a student of Isserles's student Mordechai Jaffe, argued that one who denies Creation *ex nihilo* is "a complete heretic." See note 29 below.
29. See Gedaliah b. Solomon Lipschuetz, *Eṣ Shatul* (Venice, 1618), a commentary on Joseph Albo's *Sefer ha-Iqqarim,* on *Iqqarim* 1:3 and 1:15. Gedaliah disputes Jacob Koppelman there. On Lipschuetz, see *Encyclopaedia Judaica (Berlin)* (article by Samuel Horodezky); note also the approbation to *Eṣ Shatul* by Isaiah Horowitz. On the place of the doctrine of creation in Maimonides' dogmas, see Kellner, *Dogma in Medieval Jewish Thought,* 53–55.
30. Jewish Theological Seminary MS 2323, fol. 75b–77a (the tenth question). See Joseph Davis, "The 'Ten Questions' of Eliezer Eilburg and the Problem of Jewish Unbelief in the Sixteenth Century," *Jewish Quarterly Review* 91 (2001): 293–336.
31. Gershom Scholem, "Yedi'ot Ḥadashot al R. Yosef Ashkenazi ha-tana mi-Ṣefat," *Tarbiz* 28 (1958): 71–72, 207, 225. On the Horowitz-Ashkenazi controversy, see also Bloch, "Der Streit um den Moreh" (above, note 25); Ephraim Kupfer, ed., "Hasagot min ḥakham eḥad al divrei ha-ḥakham R. Yosef . . . neged ha-Rambam," *Qobeṣ al Yad* 21 (1985): 213–88; Haim Hillel Ben Sasson, *Hagut ve-hanhagah: hashqafoteihem ha-ḥevratiyot shel Yehudei Polin be-shilḥei yemei ha-beinayim* (Jerusalem: Mossad Bialik, 1959), 34–54; Jacob Elbaum, *Openness and Insularity: Late Sixteenth Century Jewish Literature in Poland and Ashkenaz* (Hebrew) (Jerusalem: Magnes Press, 1990), 302–24; Elhanan Reiner, "The Attitude of Ashkenazi Society to the New Science in the Sixteenth Century," *Science in Context* 10 (1997): 589–603.
32. See the *liqqutim* at the end of *Sefer Maharil.* Cf. Chone Shmeruk, *Sifrut Yidish,* 45–46; Israel J. Yuval, *Scholars in Their Time* (Hebrew) (Jerusalem: Magnes Press, 1989), 317.
33. "Hanhagat Maharshal," ed. Isaac Raphael, in *Sefer Yovel Li-khvod ha-Rav . . . Shim'on Federbush,* ed. J. L. Fishman-Maimon (Jerusalem: Mossad Harav Kook, 1961), 326. Cf. below, note 97. "Yigdal" was printed first in the 1578 Cracow edition of the siddur: see Israel Davidson, *Thesaurus of Mediaeval Poetry* (New York: Jewish Theological Seminary, 1924–1933), 2:266.
34. *Siddur m[oreinu] ha-rav Shabbetai Sofer mi-Przemysla,* ed. Y. Satz (Baltimore: Ner Israel Rabbinical College, 1986–87), 2:2–5. In a 1607 writ, the Council of Four Lands, seeking to regulate the printing of siddurim, suggested that siddurim printed in Basel or Moravia (?) ought to be checked for "heresy" (*minut*) and errors. See *Pinqas Va'ad Arba' Araṣot,* ed. Israel Hailperin (Jerusalem: Bialik Institute, 1946), 17, no. 55. Hailperin ad loc. discusses the problematic reference to Moravia (no Moravian siddurim are known from this period), and suggests that the term "heresy" refers to unacceptable kabbalistic doctrines. It is more likely to be a reference to unintended heretical or polytheistic expressions, introduced inadvertently through grammatical errors in the vocalization of prayers. See Stefan Reif, *Shabbethai Sofer and His Prayer*

Book (Cambridge: Cambridge University Press, 1979), 39–41; *Siddur . . . R. Shabbetai Sofer,* 2:2.

35. *Sefer ha-Tishbi,* s.v. *min;* cf. Albo, *Iqqarim,* 2:13, ed. Husik, 2:74; Alan Lazaroff, *The Theology of Abraham Bibago* (Tuscaloosa: University of Alabama Press, 1981), 81. Heretical religious relativism was associated with Jewish rationalism by another German Jew in early-sixteenth-century Italy, Asher Lemlein: "From the study of philosophy, heretics (*minim*) have increased among the Jewish people . . . who say that all religious beliefs are only the consensus of the common people [*haskamat hamon am*]"; see Ephraim Kupfer, "Ḥezyonotav shel R. Asher be-R. Meir ha-mekhuneh Lemlein Reutlingen," *Qobeṣ Al Yad* 18 (1976): 406–7.
36. The notion of the heretic as religious neutral is expressed by Muehlhausen in *Sefer Niṣṣaḥon,* no. 348 (ed. Talmage, 193). In his report of a religious disputation held in 1389, Muehlhausen gives his answer to the Christian charge that the Jews curse Christians in *birkat ha-minim* (cf. above n. 13). Muehlhausen responded that the *minim* in the prayer are not Christians in general but only insincere converts who have left Judaism and are not true Christians either. See Israel J. Yuval, "Kabbalisten, Ketzer, und Polemiker: Das kulturelle Umfeld des Sefer ha-Nizachon von Lipman Mühlhausen," in *Mysticism, Magic, and Kabbalah in Ashkenazi Judaism,* ed. Karl Erich Grözinger and Joseph Dan (Berlin: Walter de Gruyter, 1995), 155–71. Note also the religious relativism of the kabbalist Abraham ben Samuel of Worms, discussed by Yacov Guggenheim, "Meeting on the Road: Encounters between German Jews and Christians on the Margins of Society," in *In and Out of the Ghetto,* ed. R. P. Hsia and H. Lehmann (Cambridge: Cambridge University Press, 1995), 134–36.
37. *Ma'aseh Book,* trans. Moses Gaster (Philadelphia: Jewish Publication Society, 1934), 2:461 no. 201; cf. 1:85, "an infidel, a man of no belief, who is neither a Jew nor a Christian."
38. Gershom Scholem, *Kabbalah* (Jerusalem: Keter, 1974), 79, contested by Moshe Idel, "'One from a Family, Two from a Clan': The Diffusion of Lurianic Kabbalah and Sabbatianism: a Reexamination," *Jewish History* 7 (1993): 83. See also Boaz Huss, "Sefer ha-Zohar as a Canonical, Sacred, and Holy Text: Changing Perspectives on the Book of Splendor between the Thirteenth and Eighteenth Centuries," *Journal of Jewish Thought and Philosophy* 7 (1998): 257–307. Note Eliezer Eilburg's remark that "anyone who denies [the teachings of Abraham Abulafia's book] *Imrei shefer,* is either a fool or a heretic" (Jewish Theological Seminary MS 2324, fol. 101a). On Eilburg, see above note 30. Cf. (from outside of the Ashkenazic realm) the conclusion of *Derekh Emunah* by the sixteenth-century kabbalist Meir Ibn Gabbai, where kabbalistic beliefs are called "necessary" (*meḥuyyavim*).
39. See *She'elot u-Teshuvot ha-BaḤ,* no. 5. The responsum is translated in E. J. Schochet, *Rabbi Joel Sirkes: His Life, Works, and Times* (New York: Feldheim, 1971), 250–53; cf. 44, 48, 55. On the Farar case, see Marc Saperstein, *"Your Voice Like a Ram's Horn": Themes and Texts in Traditional Jewish Preaching* (Cincinnati: Hebrew Union College Press, 1996), 367–410, and the literature cited there, 375n25. Note especially Moshe Idel, "Differing Conceptions of Kabbalah in the Early Seventeenth Century," in *Jewish Thought in the Seventeenth Century,* ed I. Twersky and B. Septimus (Cambridge, Mass.: Harvard University Press, 1987), 142–52.
40. Gershom Scholem, "Yedi'ot Ḥadashot al R. Yosef Ashkenazi," 85.

41. Naftali Bacharach, *Emeq ha-Melekh* (Amsterdam, 1648), 7b. Cf. Moses Ḥagiz's remark in the early eighteenth century that "belief in transmigration has been . . . transmitted from the earliest generation. . . . Therefore, anyone who questions it is, in my eyes, as one who denies the existence of God and His judgment." Quoted in Elisheva Carlebach, *The Pursuit of Heresy: Rabbi Moses Hagiz and the Sabbatian Controversies* (New York: Columbia University Press, 1990), 68.
42. "Without kabbalah," Shabbetai b. Isaiah Horowitz wrote, "there is no fear of Heaven"; see Israel Abrahams, *Hebrew Ethical Wills* (Philadelphia: Jewish Publication Society, 1926), 256.
43. *Keli Yekar* on Genesis 32:25–26, in the standard rabbinic Bible, *Miqra'ot Gedolot.* On Luntshits, see Haim Hillel Ben Sasson, "Osher ve-Oni be-Mishnato shel ha-Mokhiaḥ R. Efrayim Ish Lenczyc," *Zion* 19 (1954): 142–66; Ben Sasson, *Hagut ve-Hanhagah,* 90–110.
44. *Megalleh Amuqot; 252 ofanim* (Jerusalem: Y. Goldman, 1981), no. 217. On Spira, see Samuel Abba Horodezky, *Ha-Mistorin be-Yisra'el* (Tel Aviv: N. Tversqi, 1961), 4:129–40; Yehuda Liebes, "Jonah as the Messiah ben Joseph," *Jerusalem Studies in Jewish Thought* 3 (1983–84): 274–311. Contrast Isaiah Horowitz's discussion of Elisha ben Avuyah in *Shenei Luḥot ha-Berit* (Warsaw, 1862; reprint, Jerusalem: n.p., 1980), 2:59a.
45. *Megalleh Amuqot,* no. 81, 186–87. Cf. Moshe Idel, "Jewish Magic from the Renaissance Period to Early Hasidism," in *Religion, Science, and Magic: In Concert and in Conflict,* ed. Jacob Neusner et al. (Oxford: Oxford University Press, 1989), 95–100. As an instance of Spira's influence, note the Sabbatean Ber Perlhefter's repetition of Spira's claim that the Messiah son of Joseph repairs the sin of Jeroboam son of Nebat; see "Peraqim Apoqaliptiyim u-Meshiḥiyim al R. Mordekhai me-Eisenstadt," in Gershom Scholem, *Researches in Sabbateanism* (Hebrew), ed. Yehuda Liebes (Tel Aviv: Am Oved, 1991), 545, 548, 561.
46. See Isaiah Horowitz, *Shenei Luḥot ha-Berit,* 1:42b–43a ("Sha'ar ha-Otiyot," alef). Cf. Yeḥiel Mikhel Epstein, *Qiṣṣur Shenei Luḥot ha-Berit* (Fürth, 1695), 7b–8a. Shabbetai Sofer considers and rejects a kabbalistic interpretation of the hymn "Yigdal" in *Siddur . . . R. Shabtai Sofer,* 3. Note also the vast commentary on the Thirteen Principles by Benjamin Wolf of Litomerice (MS Oxford-Bodleian Heb. 1309), written about 1640, which includes a miscellany of midrashic, philosophic, and kabbalistic material.
47. Cf. Mendel Piekarz, *The Beginning of Hasidism: Ideological Trends in Derush and Musar Literature* (Hebrew) (Jerusalem: Magnes Press, 1978), 211, 354; Zeev Gries, *Conduct Literature* (Hebrew) (Jerusalem: Bialik Institute, 1989), 193–97.
48. Compare the Sabbatean credo from Izmir, published by Gershom Scholem in "Seder Tefillot ha-'Donme' mi-kat ha-Izmirim," in *Studies and Texts Concerning the History of Sabbetianism and Its Metamorphoses* (Hebrew) (Jerusalem: Bialik Institute, 1974), 385: "I believe with perfect faith that the Torah will not be superseded . . . but the *miṣvot* will be annulled." Note also the "Ani ma'amin" of Nathan of Gaza, published in Ḥayyim b. Moses Lipschuetz, *Derekh Ḥayyim* (Sulzbach, 1703), referred to by Isaiah Tishby in *Paths of Faith and Heresy* (Hebrew) (Tel Aviv: Agudat ha-Sofrim be-Yisra'el le-yad Hoṣa'at Masadah, 1964), 44, 206.
49. *She'elot u-Teshuvot Mahari Weil,* no. 140 and no. 152. These new charges of heresy may be related to the professionalization of the Ashkenazic rabbinate. See Israel J. Yuval, *Scholars in Their Time,* 388–90, 404–23. Cf. Dean P. Bell, *Sacred Communities:*

Jewish and Christian Identities in Fifteenth-Century Germany (Leiden: Brill, 2001), 171–83. In other instances, rabbis themselves were called *apiqorsim*. See Yuval, *Scholars in Their Time,* 394, quoting from the responsa of Moses Mintz, no. 76; responsa of Moses Isserles no. 91, ed. Asher Siev (Jerusalem: n.p., 1971), 394, 398. Jewish communities in central Europe in the fifteenth century may have been influenced by the new self-conception of the German cities as sacred communities, and by the willingness of municipal courts in Germany, beginning in the fourteenth century, to try heresy cases. See Bell, *Sacred Communities,* 45–53, 123–25; Richard Kieckhefer, *Repression of Heresy in Medieval Germany* (Philadelphia: University of Pennsylvania Press, 1979), 75–82; Yuval, "Kabbalisten, Ketzer, und Polemiker" (above, note 36).

50. Maharal, *Ḥiddushei Aggadot* on BT Rosh Hashanah 17a. Cf. *Tosafot Yom Tov* on Mishnah Avot 3:11, by one of Maharal's disciples, Yom-Tov Lipmann Heller. Heller asks why "one who shames his neighbor in public" is listed in Avot among those who "have no share in the world to come." Why is the punishment so severe? Heller answered that because mankind is created in the divine image, shaming one's neighbor is tantamount to denial of God.
51. *She'elot u-Teshuvot ha-BaḤ ha-Ḥadashot,* no. 42. See Schochet, *Rabbi Joel Sirkes,* 40–43, 166, 171.
52. See Benzion Dinur, "Reshitah shel ha-Ḥasidut vi-Yesodoteha ha-Soṣi'aliyim veha-Meshiḥiyim," *Zion* 9 (1944): 39–40. Note also, however, Shabbetai Kohen's comment concerning *apiqorsin* in *Siftei kohen* on *Shulḥan Arukh,* Yoreh De'ah 159; cf. Jacob Reischer, *She'elot u-Teshuvot Shevut Ya'aqov,* part 3, no. 97.
53. Cf. Gershom Scholem, "Ha-Tenu'ah ha-Shabta'it be-Folin," in *Studies and Texts Concerning the History of Sabbetianism,* 79–100. Scholem emphasizes the radicalization of Sabbateanism after the turn of the eighteenth century.
54. *Pinqas Va'ad Arba Araṣot,* 495–96. Cf. Gershom Scholem, "Ha-Tenu'ah ha-Shabta'it be-Folin," 78–79. During the height of the messianic excitement, in 1665, Simeon Spira, chief rabbi of Prague, wrote to the anti-Sabbatean organizer Jacob Sasportas and casually hinted that he regarded the Sabbateans as *minim,* but that on account of their piety, he could not criticize the Sabbateans publicly. Jacob Sasportas, *Ṣiṣat Novel Ṣevi,* ed. Isaiah Tishby (Jerusalem: Bialik Institute, 1954), 120–21. Cf. Gershom Scholem, *Sabbatai Ṣevi: The Mystical Messiah,* trans. R. J. Zvi Werblowsky (Princeton: Princeton University Press, 1975), 561–62.
55. Yiddish text in David Kaufmann, ed., *Die Memoiren der Glückel von Hameln 1645–1719* (Frankfurt am Main, 1896), 81–82; Eng. trans. in *The Life of Glückel of Hameln 1646–1724: Written by Herself,* trans. Beth-Zion Abrahams (London: East and West Library, 1962), 45–46. Cf. Elisheva Carlebach, "The Sabbatian Posture of German Jewry," *Jerusalem Studies in Jewish Thought* 17 (2001): 1–29 (English section).
56. *Ma'aseh Toviyah* (Cracow, 1908), part 1, sec. 6, chap. 1. Cf. David Ruderman, "Medicine and Scientific Thought: The World of Tobias Cohen," in *The Jews of Early Modern Venice,* ed. Robert Davis and Benjamin Ravid (Baltimore: Johns Hopkins University Press, 2001), 200–202.
57. *She'elot u-Teshuvot Ḥavvot Ya'ir,* no. 210. See Isadore Twersky, "Law and Spirituality in the Seventeenth Century: A Case Study in R. Yair Hayyim Bacharach," in Twersky and Septimus, *Jewish Thought in the Seventeenth Century,* 447–67.
58. Scholem, "Peraqim Apoqaliptiyim Eisenstadt," 545; Jacob Emden, *Sefer Hit'abbequt* (Lvov, 1877), 22b.

59. See Isaiah Tishby, *Mishnat ha-Zohar,* 3rd ed. (Jerusalem: Bialik Institute, 1982), 1:222. Solomon Luria (Responsa no. 98) had warned against it in the mid-sixteenth century. Note also the characterization of Christians as evil kabbalistic magicians in the late seventeenth century, "Hagahot al Sefer Eṣ Ḥayyim le-R. Yiṣḥaq b. Shmu'el mi-Pozna," *Moriah* 13, 1–2 (1984): 37. The professionalization of Jewish magic at the turn of the eighteenth century may have made magicians a more visible target for accusations of heresy. Cf. Immanuel Etkes, "Meqomam shel ha-Magiyah u-Va'alei ha-Shem ba-Ḥevrah ha-Ashkenazit be-Mifneh ha-Me'ot ha-17–ha-18," *Zion* 60 (1995): 69–104. Cf. above, note 49.
60. At the close of the eighteenth century, Eleazar Fleckeles still noted the difficulty of making this distinction. See the quote in Samuel Werses, *Haskalah and Sabbatianism* (Hebrew) (Jerusalem: Shazar Center, 1988), 68. Abraham Horowitz accused Joseph Ashkenazi of preaching a version of Kabbalah that was heretical on account of its rejection of the Maimonidean doctrine of incorporeality, *MGWJ* 47 (1903): 266.
61. David Kaufmann, "La lutte de R. Naftali Cohen contre Hayyoun," *Revue des études juives* 36 (1898): 273–78. On the Ḥayon case, see Elisheva Carlebach, *The Pursuit of Heresy,* 75–159. The charge of "denying all thirteen principles" is repeated in the letter of Gabriel Eskeles of Nikolsburg; see Menahem Friedman, "Iggerot be-Farashat Polmos Neḥemyah Ḥiyya Ḥayon," *Sefunot* 10 (1966): 533. The charge of dualism is also repeated later in the eighteenth century; see, e.g., the letter from Prague (1725) concerning the Sabbatean work "Va-avo ha-Yom el ha-Ayin" cited in Scholem, *Researches in Sabbateanism,* 351n100. Jacob Cohen Poppers found a "slight weakening of the Unity of God" in "Va-avo ha-Yom el ha-Ayin," attributed to Rabbi Jonathan Eibeschuetz; see Moshe Perlmuter, *R. Yehonatan Eibeschuetz ve-Yaḥaso el ha-Shabta'ut* (Jerusalem, 1947), 40. Later critics of Sabbateanism would add the charge of incarnationism. "Sabbatians are undoubtedly worse and lower than any other *apiqorsim,*" wrote Rabbi Eleazar Fleckeles in 1794. "They make [Shabbatai Zvi] into a Godhead, and they even make more Godheads in every generation, as is well known"; see *She'elot u-Teshuvot, Teshuvah me-ahavah* no. 69. On Fleckeles's anti-Sabbatean polemics, see Werses, *Haskalah and Sabbatianism,* 63–74.
62. Leib ben Ozer [Rosenkrantz], *Sippur ma'aseh Shabbetai Ṣevi/Bashraybung fun Shabsai Ṣevi,* ed. and trans. Zalman Shazar (Rubashov) (Jerusalem: Ben Zvi Institute, 1978), 190. On the passage, see Gershom Scholem, "Berukhyah, rosh ha-Shabta'im be-Saloniqi," in *Researches in Sabbateanism,* 348. Cf. Paul Ira Radensky, "Leyb ben Ozer's Bashraybung fun Shabsai Tsvi: an Ashkenazic Appropriation of Sabbatianism," *Jewish Quarterly Review* 88 (1998): 43–56.
63. *She'elot u-Teshuvot Ḥavvot Ya'ir,* no. 146.
64. Leib ben Ozer, *Sippur Ma'aseh Shabbetai Ṣevi,* 191.
65. See Gershom Scholem and J. D. Wilhelm, "Keruzei 'Ḥivya de-Rabbanan' Neged kat Shabbetai Ṣevi," in *Researches in Sabbateanism,* 600, and Jacob Emden, *Torat ha-Qena'ot* (Amsterdam, 1752), 37a–38b. On the anti-Sabbatean campaign of 1725–26, see Carlebach, *The Pursuit of Heresy,* 167–94.
66. Simon Ginzburg, *Rabbi Mosheh Ḥayyim Luzzatto u-Venei Doro: Osef Iggerot u-Te'udot* (Tel Aviv: Bialik Institute, 1937), 2:319, 375–76, 380. Cf. Carlebach, *The Pursuit of Heresy,* 242–55.
67. *Pinqas Va'ad Arba Araṣot,* 341, no. 668. Cf. the *ḥerem* of Brody against the Sabbateans, "Who make the Torah of Moses and the Talmud of Ravina and Rav Ashi a filthy

thing." Likewise, Abraham Broda, in a letter from 1715, accused Ḥayyim Malakh of "study[ing] a Torah of falsehood and lies . . . an atheist [*kofer ba-iqqar*] who expounds a Torah of emptiness [*Torah shel dofi*]"; see Leib ben Ozer, *Sippur Ma'aseh Shabbetai Ṣevi,* 195–96. Similarly in the 1725 affidavit from Kanitz (Dolní Kounice in Moravia), quoted in Gershom Scholem, *Researches in Sabbateanism,* 332n35: "They invent a pretend kabbalah . . . and do not believe the words of the Sages."

68. See Yehuda Liebes, "Meshiḥiyuto shel R. Ya'aqov Emden ve-yaḥaso le-Shabta'ut," *Tarbiz* 49 (1980): 122–65. On Emden and the Emden-Eibeschuetz controversy in general, see Mortimer Cohen, *Jacob Emden: A Man of Controversy* (Philadelphia: Jewish Publication Society, 1937), and Jacob J. Schacter, "Rabbi Jacob Emden: Life and Major Works" (Ph.D. diss., Harvard University, 1988). Gershom Scholem's essays on Eibeschuetz—including his devastating critique of Cohen—are collected in *Researches in Sabbateanism,* 653–735, and an updated bibliography is provided there by Liebes (679–80, 705–6). See also Sid Z. Leiman, "When a Rabbi Is Accused of Heresy: The Stance of the Gaon of Vilna in the Emden-Eibeschuetz Controversy," in *Me'ah She'arim: Studies in Medieval Jewish Spiritual Life in Memory of Isadore Twersky,* ed. Ezra Fleischer et al. (Jerusalem: Magnes Press, 2001), 251–64.
69. Emden, *Sefer Hit'abbequt* (Altona, 1762; reprint, Lvov, 1877), 2b–3a. Cohen, *Jacob Emden,* 132–36, 168–79, 268–77, discusses Emden's presentation of Eibeschuetz with many examples and excerpts. Although many of Cohen's theses are not at all convincing, his comments on Emden are frequently perceptive.
70. Emden, *Sefat Emet* (Altona, 1758; reprint, Lvov, 1877), 10a–11a, 24a.
71. See Marcus Moseley, "Jewish Autobiography in Eastern Europe: The Pre-History of a Literary Genre" (Ph.D. diss., Oxford University, 1990), 365–98, on the modern literary features of Emden's autobiography.
72. See Majer Balaban, *Le-Toledot ha-Tenu'ah ha-Franqit* (Tel Aviv: Dvir, 1935), 2:294–305.
73. Cf. 2 Kings 18:4. See Emden's introduction to his *Mitpaḥat Sefarim* (Altona, 1768; reprint, Jerusalem, 1995). Cf. Emden, *Sefat Emet,* 10b.
74. Mordecai Wilensky, *Ḥasidism and Mitnaggedim: A Study of the Controversy between Them in the Years 1772–1815* (Hebrew), 2nd ed. (Jerusalem: Bialik Institute, 1990), 1:63–64; cf. 1:46 and 2:179. An example of the charge of sexual misconduct appears in the documents on 1:65.
75. Ibid., 1:187–90.
76. See Norman Lamm, *Torah Lishmah: Torah for Torah's Sake in the Works of Rabbi Ḥayyim of Volozhin and His Contemporaries* (Hoboken, N.J.: Ktav, 1989), 333–37; Haim Hillel Ben Sasson, "Ishiyyuto shel ha-GeRA ve-Hashpa'ato ha-Historit," *Zion* 31 (1966): 204–12. Note particularly the stereotyped beginning of the writs of *ḥerem* and polemical writings of the 1770s and 1780s, from Vilna and elsewhere, which accuse the Ḥasidim of separatism and changes in the prayer service. See the documents in Wilensky, *Ḥasidism and Mitnaggedim,* 1:111–21. The documents that include polemics against Ḥasidic belief, as distinct from behavior, are the Vilna *ḥerem* of 1781 and the accompanying "Qol qore," and the Shklov *ḥerem* of 1787. The 1781 Vilna ban singled out belief in the miracle stories of Ḥasidic *ṣaddiqim* as "complete falsehood." See Wilensky, *Ḥasidism and Mitnaggedim,* 1:102–7, 151–59. In addition, part two of *Shever Posh'im,* attributed to David of Makow, and written (according to Wilensky) in the mid-1780s, includes a long rebuttal of Ḥasidic the-

ories of prayer. See Wilensky, *Ḥasidism and Mitnaggedim,* 2:144–80. Wilensky himself argues (1:17–19) that the central and essential elements of early anti-Ḥasidic polemic were the charges of neglect of Torah study and disrespect for Torah scholars. But one should distinguish the motivation of the opponents of Ḥasidism from the main charges that they brought. While it may be that prayer innovations in themselves would not have aroused such opposition, prayer innovations, not neglect of study, was the issue on which the Mitnaggedim chose to make their stand.

77. Wilensky, *Ḥasidism and Mitnaggedim,* 1:137–41.

78. Pfaffenhofen, *Sefer Massah u-Merivah,* ed. Chava Turniansky (Jerusalem: Magnes Press, 1985), 201. Pfaffenhofen was influenced by his teacher Rabbi Ephraim of Luntshits, and this passage resembles the comment on Jacob and the angel from Luntshits's *Keli Yekar* quoted above in sec. 3. The association of Jewish poverty in Germany in the sixteenth century with insincere apostasy is discussed in Guggenheim, "Meeting on the Road" (above n. 36), 130–31.

79. Zvi Hirsch Ashkenazi, Responsa no. 18; Eng. trans. in Solomon Freehof, *A Treasury of Responsa* (Philadelphia: Jewish Publication Society, 1963), 176–81. Cf. David Ruderman, "Jewish Thought in Newtonian England: The Career and Writings of David Nieto," *Proceedings of the American Academy for Jewish Research* 58 (1992): 202–28. Kaidanover, *Qav ha-Yashar,* chap. 53. Dov Ber of Mezhirech, *Maggid Devarav le-Ya'aqov,* no. 133, ed. Rivka Schatz-Uffenheimer (Jerusalem: Magnes Press, 1990), 233. Landau's condemnation of "Va-avo ha-Yom el ha-Ayin" is a section of his letter on the Eibeschuetz case, published by Perlmuter, *R. Yehonatan Eibeschuetz* (above, note 61), 48–51, and previously by David Kahana, "Emet le-Ya'aqov," *Ha-Shilloaḥ* 6 (1899): 338–39.

80. Eibeschuetz, *Ahavat Yehonatan* (Hamburg, 1764), 43a; cf. 45a. The passage is discussed in Azriel Shochat, *Beginnings of the Haskalah among German Jewry* (Jerusalem: n.p., 1960), 214.

81. Emden had already characterized philosophic rationalism as the root of all heresy in 1747 before his attacks on Eibeschuetz. For Emden's attacks on rationalism, see Schacter, "Rabbi Jacob Emden," 550–68; note that Emden's image of Maimonides as inevitably tainted by rationalism through his efforts—in themselves praiseworthy—to combat rationalist antinomianism and heresy (577–78) may suggest his attitude toward Mendelssohn.

82. Louis Lewin, "Aus dem jüdischem Kulturkampfe," *Jahrbuch der Jüdisch-Literarischen Gesellschaft* 12 (1918): 188–89.

83. Markus Horovitz, *Rabbanei Frankfurt,* ed. Joseph Unna, trans. Joshua Amir (Jerusalem: Mossad Harav Kook, 1972), 159–61; Heinrich Graetz, "Wessely's Gegner," *MGWJ* 20 (1871): 465–69.

84. See Alexander Altmann, *Moses Mendelssohn* (Philadelphia: Jewish Publication Society, 1973), 478–86; Jacob Katz, "R. Rafa'el Kohen, Yerivo shel Mendelssohn," *Tarbiz* 56 (1986): 261–62.

85. The sermon is translated in Marc Saperstein, *Jewish Preaching,* 361–73. On Landau, see Sharon Flatto, "Prague's Rabbinic Culture: The Concealed and the Revealed in Ezekiel Landau's Writings" (Ph.D. diss., Yale University, 2000); his attitude toward the *Haskalah* is discussed there, 69–99.

86. Besides the Maimonidean dogmas, Landau (in another sermon) demanded faith in two non-Maimonidean dogmas: supernatural miracles and free will. See Landau,

Derushei ha-Ṣelaḥ (Warsaw, 1920), sermon for Passover [no. 43], 58b; Flatto, "Prague's Rabbinic Culture," 77–78. Isserles also made free will a dogma of Judaism, as did some minor medieval Jewish thinkers; see Ben Sasson, *The Philosophical System of R. Moses Isserles,* 196; Kellner, *Dogma in Medieval Jewish Thought,* 74–76.

87. Cf. Kenneth Hart Green, "Moses Mendelssohn's Opposition to the Herem: The First Step toward Denominationalism?" *Modern Judaism* 12 (1992): 39–60.
88. See generally Altmann, *Moses Mendelssohn,* 463–74, 489–552.
89. See the letter of Landau, discussed extensively in Flatto, "Prague's Rabbinic Culture," 80–95. Flatto argues convincingly against Altmann's view (*Moses Mendelssohn,* 835n84) that the letter is a forgery.
90. Note, for instance, the spate of writings against Sabbateanism from around 1800: Aaron Chorin, Ber Birkenthal (Ber of Bolochow), Eleazar Fleckeles, and Baruch Jeiteles, as well as Solomon Dubno's Hebrew translation of Leib ben Ozer.
91. Altmann, *Moses Mendelssohn,* 517; note also the comments of Mendelssohn's friend August Hennings, 491. Cf. Alan Arkush, "Kant's View of Mendelssohn," in *Perspectives on Jewish Thought and Mysticism,* ed. Alfred Ivry et al. (Amsterdam: Harwood, 1998), 416–20.
92. Quoted in Werses, *Haskalah and Sabbatianism,* 31, and in Cohen, *Jacob Emden,* 254. The gradual onset of attitudes associated with the Enlightenment among eighteenth-century German Jews is the thesis of Azriel Shochat, *Beginnings of the Haskalah among German Jewry.* On the decline of the institution of *ḥerem* among German Jews in the eighteenth century, see David Sorkin, *Moses Mendelssohn and the Religious Enlightenment* (Berkeley: University of California Press, 1996), 115.
93. See Rachel Elior, "Rabbi Nathan Adler of Frankfurt and the Controversy Surrounding Him," in Grözinger and Dan, *Mysticism, Magic, and Kabbalah,* 223–42; Elior, "Natan Adler ve-ha-Edah ha-Ḥasidit be-Frankfurt: ha-Ziqqah bein Ḥavurot Ḥasidiyot be-Mizraḥ Eiropah u-ve-Merkazah ba-Me'ah ha-18," *Zion* 59 (1994): 48.
94. Moses Mendelssohn, *Jerusalem,* trans. Allan Arkush (Hanover, N.H.: University Press of New England, 1983), 73, 62–63. See also Altmann, *Moses Mendelssohn,* 529; Sorkin, *Moses Mendelssohn and the Religious Enlightenment,* 115–26. Besides the educational purpose of religion, Mendelssohn presents several arguments for religious liberty: he argues that religious coercion is intrinsically ineffective and that it violates an inalienable human right. Cf. Allan Arkush, *Moses Mendelssohn and the Enlightenment* (Albany: State University of New York Press, 1994), 113–21.
95. Mendelssohn, *Jerusalem,* 115.
96. Ibid., 100–102. Cf. 137 against a new enlightened credo; see Sorkin, *Moses Mendelssohn,* 134–35. Note that Mendelssohn, searching for support for his own Enlightenment conception of Judaism, offers a very liberal reading of Albo. Cf. Kellner, *Dogma in Medieval Jewish Thought,* 151–55. For reliance on Albo in the seventeenth century, cf. Gedaliah ben Solomon, Tobias Cohen (above, notes 29, 56).
97. Mendelssohn, *Jerusalem,* 101–2. Altmann (in his commentary to *Jerusalem,* 217) suggests that Mendelssohn's source is Abarbanel, not Luria and the kabbalists. Note Mendelssohn's emphasis (in his discussion of the Indian cosmology of turtles and elephants, *Jerusalem,* 114–15) on the need for generous interpretation. See also Arnold Eisen, "Divine Legislation as 'Ceremonial Script': Mendelssohn on the Commandments," *AJS Review* 15 (1990): 239–67.

5

Laity versus Leadership in Eleventh-Century Jerusalem

Karaites, Rabbanites, and the Affair of the Ban on the Mount of Olives

MARINA RUSTOW

Medievalists have long known that every year for more than a century preceding the Crusader conquest of Jerusalem in 1099, when the Fatimid caliphs still held Palestine, the gaon of the Palestinian *yeshivah* would excommunicate the Karaites en masse in a solemn assembly on the Mount of Olives. One imagines the scene unfolding cinematically, compressing into a single moment of liturgical cursing one of the central and ongoing debates of medieval Judaism: that between the rabbinic heirs to talmudic tradition and the Karaites, who challenged the rabbinic claim to a monopoly on authoritative interpretations of biblical law.[1]

The Karaites stood charged in the rabbinic mind with a transgression perhaps more general than the specific infractions that normally brought about bans of excommunication. Lest this lack of specificity seem an obstacle to the ban's declaration, it hung on a Karaite infringement that, by synecdoche, stood for the entire theological aberration: it was worded "against the eaters of meat with milk"—a formulation intended to imply that by violating the rabbinic extension of the biblical dietary laws, the Karaites had done violence to the entirety of Jewish tradition. And so the Karaites were made to suffer the humiliation of being placed under a severe ban of excommunication that—had it been observed—would have forbidden every rabbinic Jew in the Near

East from conducting any social or commercial intercourse with them whatsoever.

But to judge by documentary evidence of Rabbanite-Karaite social relations during this period, the ban of excommunication was hardly ever observed. The ritual in which it was declared therefore assumes even greater symbolic significance precisely because it failed to erect a barrier between the two communities. It therefore also serves as grounds on which to test literary evidence—accounts of the ban by medieval chroniclers and exegetes—against documentary sources from the Cairo Genizah, which paint a very different picture of how the annual excommunication ritual unfolded.

In what follows, I shall argue that standard depictions of the excommunication ritual are the legacy of a medieval polemical construct. They overlook the broad tenor of medieval Rabbanite-Karaite relations, which were far more irenic than the literary sources would have us believe, and they downplay the paradoxically central role Karaites played in the functioning of rabbinic institutions in the eastern part of the medieval Islamic world. In its drama and details, the excommunication ritual does indeed convey a microcosmic compression of rabbinic Judaism's relationship to the Karaites, but of a sort different from the one we have come to imagine. Far from effecting a final social schism between Rabbanites and Karaites, the ritual and the various controversies attending it demonstrated just how closely and inextricably intertwined the two groups were.

"Like Two Little Flocks of Goats"

The most famous rendering of the excommunication ritual appears in *Sefer ha-Qabbalah* (*Book of Tradition,* 1160–61) by the twelfth-century Iberian talmudist, chronicler, and philosopher Abraham Ibn Dāwūd. The description is only a few lines long, but has cast a long shadow over the annals of medieval Jewish sectarianism. "When the Jews used to celebrate Sukkot on the Mount of Olives, they would encamp on the mountain in groups and greet each other warmly. The heretics would encamp 'before them like two little flocks of goats' [I Kings 20:27]. Then the rabbis would take out a scroll of the Torah and pronounce a ban on the heretics right to their faces, while the latter remained silent like 'dumb dogs' [Isaiah 56:10]."[2]

Ibn Dāwūd composed *Sefer ha-Qabbalah* three generations after the Jews had ceased holding public convocations in Jerusalem.[3] He therefore never knew the ceremony he described at first or even second hand: Jewish pilgrims from Iberia continued to reach the Latin Kingdom of Jerusalem during Ibn Dāwūd's lifetime, but on private pilgrimages, and to the mere handful of Jews they found in the city—four according to Benjamin of Tudela in 1170, only one according to Pethaḥiah of Regensburg a few years later—the mass convocations were at best a distant memory transmitted to them in childhood by their elders.[4]

Sefer ha-Qabbalah is remarkably and famously economical in its inclusion of verifiably correct historical information. This is lamentable, since it is one of very few medieval Jewish chronicles. But the liberties Ibn Dāwūd took with details render his account all the more valuable as a record of twelfth-century polemic. His purpose in *Sefer ha-Qabbalah* was to demonstrate the continuity of rabbinic legal interpretation in an unbroken chain of transmission from God's revelation to Moses on Sinai until the rabbis of his own time. The work is therefore suffused with anti-Karaism: the element of unbroken continuity itself constituted an argument, for if the tradition stretched back to Sinai both continuously and exclusively via the rabbinic line, then Karaite claims on behalf of individual interpretation were invalid since they fell outside this recognized succession.[5]

In his conclusion, Ibn Dāwūd sharpened his claims against the Karaites by leveling a number of accusations designed to demonstrate their putative disfavor in the eyes of God. First, he claimed that the founder of Karaism, Anan b. David, was nothing but an embittered renegade pupil of a great Babylonian rabbi. Next, he claimed that Karaite legal conclusions were utterly counterfeit since they derived from human argumentation rather than divine dispensation. Neither of these arguments was new, both having made their appearance as far back as the tenth century. But then he added a decidedly new claim, asserting that the Karaites were "disqualified by the sheer meagerness of their number"—disqualified, that is, from religious legitimacy. Even if one were to forgive their suspect origins and rationalist methods, Ibn Dāwūd argued, their error is demonstrable *eo ipso* from their lack of a widespread following.[6]

To support this point, Ibn Dāwūd offered an exaggeratedly paltry representation of Karaite demography, claiming that Karaites had effectively ceased to exist "except in one city in the Maghrib, in the desert, called Warjalān, a handful of them in Egypt, and a handful in Palestine," and that his own Iberian Peninsula was fully devoid of

Karaites—claims that contradict what we know from other sources.[7] For Ibn Dāwūd, the legitimacy of Jewish tradition was supported by a consensus of believers, equivalent to the Islamic concept of *ijmā'*, and therefore it included the Rabbanite majority but not the Karaites.[8] Karaite demographic weakness was therefore central to the larger thesis of his work.

Immediately following the section on comparative demographics, Ibn Dāwūd tells us that every autumn during the week-long festival of Sukkot, the Rabbanites would ascend the Mount of Olives and excommunicate the Karaites. The juxtaposition was not accidental: his rendering of the scene drew heavily for its effect upon the theme of Rabbanite numerical supremacy.

Several dramatic embellishments in Ibn Dāwūd's description of the excommunication ceremony invite closer examination. First, it is doubtful whether the Karaites ever "encamped" before the Rabbanites on the hillside during the ritual. Although tenth- and eleventh-century Karaites did ascend the Mount of Olives to offer up private prayers, they did so at various times of the liturgical year rather than on any particular day; although they circumambulated the walls of Jerusalem in mourning for its destruction by the Romans in the first century, the Mount of Olives never appears as a part of these rituals.[9] The Karaites therefore probably never attended the yearly ceremony in which they were excommunicated "right to their faces." But taking this small liberty with the mise-en-scène allows Ibn Dāwūd to borrow the simile of the "two little flocks of goats" from the book of Kings.

That biblical reference is not the most obvious one he might have chosen. In Kings, it is not heretics who encamp like little flocks of goats, but rather the Israelite heroes of the tale, who in their sparseness stand contrasted with the mighty Arameans, whom they have little chance of defeating in battle. The Israelites finally vanquish the enemy only because God delivers them into their hands. By conjuring up this passage Ibn Dāwūd implicitly raises the question of divine providence; only in his scenario, it works in the reverse manner from Kings, where God sides with the weak. For Ibn Dāwūd, God sides with the mighty. This reversal is in keeping with one of the major innovations of his work: the application of triumphalist historicism to anti-Karaite polemic. If the Rabbanites outnumbered the Karaites, it was only further proof of their correctness and favor in God's eyes.[10]

But for Ibn Dāwūd, the Karaites were not only weak in numbers; they were also silent in the face of humiliating treatment: "dumb dogs" who in the verse from Isaiah "cannot even bark." At first blush, it might seem that for Ibn Dāwūd the Karaites were "dumb dogs" merely because they failed to defend themselves against the charges—again, manifest proof of their error. But in fact, the verse Ibn Dāwūd now hurled at the Karaites had a long pedigree in sectarian polemic. In its original context in Isaiah, it stood as an indictment of the post-exilic Israelite leadership, and this is how it was used in the Karaite-Rabbanite debate. It had made its first appearance ca. 900, but from the other side, when an anonymous Karaite halakhist warned his fellow Jerusalemites against consuming meat and wine "even while the city of your holy mount lies destroyed, without an altar and without your priests; dumb and blind dogs are watching you; and menstruating women, ritually impure men, lepers, and uncircumcised Christians enter the shrine of the elevated Ofel."[11] Our anonymous polemist intended the "dumb and blind dogs" to refer to the negligent watchmen and shepherds of the Israelite flock, the Rabbanite Jews, a common trope in Karaite polemics of the period. The late-ninth-century Persian Karaite immigrant to Jerusalem Daniel al-Qūmisī, in his commentary on Hosea (5:1), also compared Rabbanite leaders to inattentive watchmen, although he did not call them dumb dogs, and roughly a century later Japheth ben Eli filled his commentary on Song of Songs with attacks on the Rabbanites as negligent guardians.[12] The Byzantine Karaite Judah Hadassi shot the same arrow at the Rabbanites only twelve years before Ibn Dāwūd shot it back, although it is unknown whether Ibn Dāwūd knew Hadassi's work.[13]

Ibn Dāwūd used the metaphor of the "dumb dogs" to much the same effect as his adversaries—only now it was the Karaites who were the negligent guardians of the flock. He reapplied the verse closer to the end of his work, claiming that the Karaites "never did anything of benefit for Israel, nor produced a book demonstrating the cogency of the Torah or a work of general knowledge or even a single poem, hymn, or verse of consolation. 'They are all dumb dogs who cannot even bark.' If one of them finally did produce a book, he reviled, blasphemed, and spoke insolently against heaven."[14] With this Ibn Dāwūd gives away his chief concern: what bothers him about the Karaites even more than their passivity is their failure as leaders. And implicit in that failure for Ibn Dāwūd is Karaite readiness to break ranks with the rest of Israel.

Of all Ibn Dāwūd's inventions in the service of his *tendenz,* the notion that the Karaites "never did anything of benefit for Israel" is howlingly inaccurate precisely as a description of the period in question. In fact the Jewish communities of tenth- and eleventh-century Egypt and Syria could not have survived without the aid, financial and political, bestowed on them uncomplainingly by Karaite grandees who acted in a manner far less sectarian than Ibn Dāwūd suggests. The rabbinic leaders who cultivated Karaite political patrons never allowed their theological scruples to prevent them from doing so—quite the contrary. From the moment we have enough genizah documents to offer a well-rounded picture of Jewish communal life, the Karaites emerge as mediators in various rabbinic causes. In the early eleventh century, *geonim* of Baghdad cultivated warm relations with Egyptian Karaites who helped them with the central geonic function of collecting donations and disseminating responsa. *Geonim* in Jerusalem relied on Egyptian Karaite support when the politics of Diaspora loyalty made them wary of relying on Babylonian congregants. The gaon and other leaders of the Jerusalem *yeshivah* came to rely increasingly upon Karaite donations to the *yeshivah* and intercession before the caliph's chancery. Nor was this cooperation limited to the upper ranks of the rabbinic leadership. During the same period, both individuals and the Rabbanite collectivities of Alexandria, Ascalon, and Tripoli (Syria) appealed to Karaite grandees in Cairo for fiscal and political aid. The chief Karaite patrons were David ha-Levi ben Isaac, whom al-Ẓāhir appointed chief of taxation in 1023, and the brothers Ḥesed and Abraham al-Tustarī, who ran a major mercantile firm and purveyed luxury items and rendered banking services to the Fatimid court. These men were not only fabulously wealthy but courtiers, poised to ferry Jewish communal appeals to the caliph's chancery. Moreover, as grandees, they needed to act the patron to their clients as much as their clients needed them. Rabbanite reliance on Karaite grandees only intensified over the course of the eleventh century, and at key points the Karaites emerged as kingmakers in internal Rabbanite struggles for both the Jerusalem gaonate and the headship of the Jews.[15] In fact, the argument Ibn Dāwūd made was perhaps more about Karaite intellectual and spiritual leadership, particularly in defending Judaism from attack by other religions; but even here, it is evident that he exaggerated for polemical purposes.

This brings us to a final liberty Ibn Dāwūd takes in his description: he writes that the Jerusalem gaon declared the excommunication "when the Jews used to celebrate Sukkot on the Mount of Olives"—the implication being that they did so annually. Of the various medieval authors—Jewish and Muslim alike—who describe the ascent of the Jews to the Mount of Olives on Sukkot, Ibn Dāwūd is the only one who mentions the Karaite excommunication as a regular and annual part of the ceremony. The earliest description dates only to 1000 and does not mention the Karaites at all, while the first firm reference to the excommunication appears in a late-tenth-century Karaite polemical treatise but is not connected to the public convocation.[16] Ibn Dāwūd can hardly be blamed for what he might not have known. But as historians we must avoid the temptation to accept his singular and synchronic depiction of the excommunication ceremony as bearing anything more than a tangential relationship to how it actually unfolded in real time. From genizah sources, it emerges that the excommunication was indeed, as Ibn Dāwūd tells us, declared on the Mount of Olives on the last day of Sukkot, but—at least during the eleventh century, which the genizah documents much more abundantly than the tenth—it was declared precisely twice: in 1029 and in 1038.[17] On both occasions, it served political purposes that had more to do with internal Rabbanite divisions than with the kind of anti-Karaite sentiment Ibn Dāwūd describes.

The first affair of the ban, in 1029–30, unfolds in remarkable detail in letters exchanged among the curia of the Jerusalem *yeshivah*—thus rendering it one of the very few single events of which the genizah has preserved a large number of eyewitness accounts. From the letters it emerges that it was neither the Jerusalem gaon nor the other high-ranking leaders of the Rabbanite community who agitated for the ban, but rather a nameless faction of their followers whose deeds are known to us only through the lucky accident of preservation in their leaders' correspondence. Differences between Rabbanites and Karaites over the proper observance of *halakhah* had been easily surmounted in other circumstances, as when they married one another, entered into commercial partnerships together, and cultivated each other's patronage. We must therefore ask not merely how the affair of the ban unfolded, but why it broke out precisely when it did. I shall argue in what follows that it was the chief symptom of a backlash against a new style of rabbinic realpolitik that had created tensions within the very structure of the Rabbanite community. Although Ibn

Dāwūd cast the ceremony as sufficient evidence of Karaite defeat, the actual circumstances of its proclamation hardly paint a picture of Rabbanism triumphant.

On the Mount of Olives: Invidious Distinctions

The excommunication affair of 1029 began on Hoshana Rabba, the seventh day of Sukkot, when the ranks of pilgrims to Jerusalem were at their most swollen. Barring war, famine, and other obstacles, the autumn pilgrimage often brought Rabbanites from as far away as Khurasan in the east and the Iberian Peninsula in the west.[18] The curia of the Jerusalem *yeshivah* would take advantage of the occasion to exercise ritual functions that required for their effect a maximum number of worshipers: proclamation of the calendar for the upcoming year; solicitation of contributions earmarked for the upkeep and maintenance of the *yeshivah;* announcing ordinations, granting honorific titles and confirming the positions of the *yeshivah*'s members; and, finally, declaring the blessings and bans. All these agenda items were redolent of the kinds of hierarchical distinctions that lent this mass assembly its ritual meaning.[19]

The self-legitimating rhetoric and methods the Palestinian curia deployed represented, in part, a response to the assemblies regularly held by the rabbinate of the two Iraqi *yeshivot:* the investiture of the new exilarch and the semiannual study convocations during the months of Adar and Elul (*yarḥei kallah*). Each of these three ceremonies iterated symbolic ties between the rabbinic centers and the outlying communities, and in that sense they were pitched against one another in competition for mass loyalties.[20] During the tenth century, the Jerusalem *yeshivah* had used its calendrical proclamations as a method of reinscribing and reinforcing its authority against that of the *yeshivot* in Baghdad.[21] By the 1020s, the Palestinian curia's key issue had metamorphosed into competition for a body of followers all too ready to shift their loyalties away from them.

Because affiliations within the system of rabbinic learning in the medieval Near East were fluid, people whose families hailed from any region were as likely to join either congregation, or, for that matter, to transfer to the local Karaite synagogue. The total enmeshment of Palestinian and Babylonian social networks on the one hand and Karaite and Rabbanite ones on the other forced leaders from both Rabbanite congregations to do their utmost to hold on to their acolytes. The distribution of titles of honor by all three *yeshivot* therefore functioned among other things as a way of persuading scholars from outlying communities, such as Fustat in Egypt and Kairouan in the Maghrib, to secure fealty to one or another center, and the *yeshivot* made frequent (and frequently shameless) use of titles for this purpose. In one telling admission, a rabbinic leader in Ramla, Palestine, in the second quarter of the eleventh century wrote to the head of the Palestinian-rite congregation in Fustat, confessing his worry that because of the latter's haughtiness and high-handed behavior, members of his synagogue would defect to those of the Babylonians or the Karaites.[22] He found it completely unworthy of remark that his followers were as likely to transfer to either congregation: people shifted their religious loyalties for reasons of social affiliation and personal politics as much as theological commitment.

The kinds of distinctions effected in the granting of titles, then, were socially sectarian in the narrow sense: they were intended to reinforce the loyalty of the flock through attachments based on granted honors and thereby to harden boundaries between groups. This, in part, explains the importance of the ritual dispensation of titles on Hoshana Rabba.

After the titles and honorifics, the gaon distributed the blessings and bans, and both sets of declarations continued in the vein of socially sectarian distinctions. All the communities of the Diaspora, the members (*ḥaverim*) of the *yeshivah* and, especially, anyone who had made a financial contribution to the *yeshivah* received the honor of public blessing. In 1029 contributors to the Jerusalem *yeshivah* included a number of Egyptian Karaites, David ha-Levi ben Isaac among them.[23] This resulted in the supreme irony that Karaites were objects of both the blessings and the bans—a contradiction not remarked upon in the sources, but one that encapsulates the role the Karaites played in the ritual symbolism and social drama of the ceremony as it unfolded in 1029.

"Against the Eaters of Meat with Milk"

Since talmudic times, various types of excommunication had served rabbinic leaders, at least in principle, as a form of social anathema against those who refused to submit to the penalty for an infraction they had committed, or else those who had undergone the prescribed punishment and still refused to comply with the law. Someone under a ban was barred from social contact with other Jews—not just members of his immediate local community, but (in theory) Jews everywhere—and, depending on the severity of the ban, from commercial contact as well, until he repented of his rebellious ways.[24] Actual instances of excommunication in genizah documents include husbands who married a second wife without court permission, litigants who made resort to Islamic courts instead of relying upon Jewish ones, defaulted debtors, renters in arrears, those who withheld their tax monies from the communal coffers, and anyone who had failed to comply with a court decision or communal ruling.[25] The rabbinic ban of excommunication was aimed, then, not only against those who had violated some rabbinic precept but also against anyone who infringed indirectly upon the power of the rabbis by subverting their ability to regulate communal affairs. Although the stated purpose of the ban was to enforce specific halakhic injunctions, one of its latent functions was to bolster rabbinic authority itself by binding people more closely to the social structure it regulated.

There was therefore good reason to use it sparingly. As a legal instrument, excommunication was liable to be emptied of force without proper observance. Its enforcement depended, first, upon its wide dissemination—this is why the bans were publicly announced on Hoshana Rabba, at the best attended ceremony of the liturgical cycle—and, second, upon the will of the community to adhere to it, that is, to refrain from interaction with the banned party. Under ideal circumstances, a perfectly observed ban would excise the transgressor from the body of Israel until, under pressure from the majority, he reversed his erroneous behavior. But a ban that went unobserved might also have the reverse effect—acting not upon the transgressor but upon the rabbis, whose authority it implicitly weakened.[26] It is significant for our purposes that medieval people considered excommunication an appropriate measure only against those with a certain degree of social power. On others, a ban was wasted.[27] This in part explains the controversy that the ban against the Karaites provoked in 1029: the Palestinian gaon opposed it; the faction who lobbied for its renewal tacitly acknowledged the social power the Karaites held. It was this, more than their transgression of rabbinic law, that bothered them.

This is our first indication that the ban against the Karaites was not quite the legal procedure of enforcement that it normally constituted. Moreover, it was worded against the Karaites collectively, a fact that decreased its chances of being observed. It was common knowledge that rabbinic Jews conducted regular relations with Karaites—their leaders corresponded with them, entire communities appealed to them, their court functionaries willingly wrote legal documents according to Karaite specifications, Rabbanites married into Karaite families, and Rabbanite family firms developed mercantile partnerships with Karaite ones. Given the total entanglement of the two groups at every level of society, observance of the ban was practically hopeless. That suggests strongly that the social meaning of its declaration lay not in its manifest legal content but in its ritual setting—not in its observance, but in the circumstances of its imposition.[28]

The First Rabbanite Rumor

Genizah letters describing the ban begin to multiply in the late autumn of 1029, in the aftermath of the ceremony. The most prolific correspondent was Solomon ben Judah, gaon of the Jerusalem *yeshivah* from late 1025 until 1051, who addresses many of his letters to Ephraim ben Shemariah, the leader of the Palestinian Rabbanite congregation in Fustat. In his letters, Solomon appears to be a trustworthy narrator. Although his complaints of physical frailty cannot always be taken at face value—they generally come as excuses for failing to go on at greater length, usually after a lengthy letter—on several occasions he candidly describes his own failures of leadership, some of them egregious, and excoriates his own followers and their misdeeds.[29] He can therefore hardly be accused of self-serving distortion, since any aspersions he casts on his flock make him appear to be the more negligent a shepherd. With his first letter in the series, we are already in the thick of the controversy.

According to Solomon's first letter, throngs of Rabbanite pilgrims ascended the Mount of Olives on Hoshanna Rabba in 1029. In the hubbub prior to the ceremony, a faction of pilgrims went about pressuring their leaders to proclaim the ban. The gaon, whose sole prerogative it was to decide upon bans, had no intention of declaring it and, one imagines, had made that clear to them before the ceremony. To air their dissatisfaction, the Rabbanite throng began circulating a rumor that the Karaites had bribed the gaon to omit the ban from the ceremony. The letter has been torn at the top; its legible portion begins as follows: "Many of the common folk were provoking a quarrel. It was [the day of] Hoshana Rabba, and the people had ascended the Mount of Olives, as is their custom. The [defamers] were saying to the people,

'The Karaites have bribed this man [so that] the ban (against the eaters) of meat with milk will [not] be pronounced, and (they say) that he has assured them of this. Therefore gather arou[nd and tell] him not to alter our tradition, and if he refuses (to comply), do not listen to him, and gat[her against him] together.' "[30] According to the Rabbanite rumor, the gaon had fallen under the sway of Karaite power, and in the minds of the faction circulating it, they were the ones who must uphold tradition and see the ban declared. They therefore pressed for what they insisted was an old custom of excommunicating the Karaites and used its hoary antiquity to justify its perpetuation.

The significance of rumors in small-scale societies should not be underestimated—particularly where an individual's influence derived from his place in a hierarchical network of social relationships. Moreover, rumors do not spread unless they give voice to something at least vaguely plausible. Several circumstances might have lent this rumor some extra verisimilitude—and some extra mileage.

First, Solomon ben Judah was widely perceived to be conciliatory toward the Karaites. Indeed, several months earlier, in May of 1029, Solomon had written a letter to his son Abraham in Fustat urging caution and delicacy in mediating conflicts, for he had heard from Sahlān ben Abraham, leader of the Iraqi Rabbanite congregation of Fustat and a close correspondent of both son and father, "that in Fustat there is a dispute between the Rabbanites and the Karaites and among the Rabbanites (themselves; the letter is fragmentary). . . . O my son, I want you not to become involved in that (matter). Rather, write to me . . . , for the people today are ailing and in need of delicate treatment, just as an ailing person is treated delicately."[31] In another letter Solomon wrote upon his appointment as gaon in 1025, he offered lavish praise for the Karaite *nasi* Hezekiah ben David; and in an undated letter to Ephraim, Solomon described himself as leading prayers for the Rabbanite and Karaite communities of Ramla on alternate days.[32]

Another element of verisimilitude was the implication, in the charge of bribery, that the Karaites exercised undue influence in Rabbanite affairs. It was probably no secret that in 1025 the caliph al-Ẓāhir had ratified Solomon's predecessor in the gaonate in office through Karaite mediation, and it is likely that on his accession half a year later Solomon himself sought a caliphal confirmation through the same channels.[33] We shall see further on that his attitude emerged from the exigencies of patronage rather than actual sympathy. But in the minds of the Rabbanite crowd, the difference between political prudence and ideological laxity was a nicety, for what bothered them was the structural need to curry favor with the Karaites in the first place. In that sense, the Rabbanite "defamers" were not entirely wrong in imagining the Karaites as blocking the ban with money and influence.

Rumors give voice not only to plausibilities and anxieties but also to politically unspeakable discourse.[34] This one partook of a chiastic structure of substitutions: in protesting Karaite patronage, the Rabbanite faction leveled their complaint against the gaon instead, who thereby became a symbol of Karaite power. And yet the rumor they spread, by insisting that the gaon had bent to Karaite wishes through bribery rather than in the normal course of affairs, was a discursive means of imagining that he was independent from the Karaites, for if bribery was all that stood between him and the ban, then without it he might have heeded their insistence on declaring it. The rumor of bribery, then, served the Rabbanite imaginary simultaneously as an expression of rabbinic involvement with the Karaites as a political force and as a means of separation from them. Both these elements—deeper enmeshment and increasingly urgent social separation—would recur throughout the affair of 1029.

Finally, the rumor was a way for the gaon's followers to imagine his authority as based solely on internal rabbinic sources such as his place in the *yeshivah* hierarchy, but the ground was shifting under their very feet, for the ban heeded a logic according to which rabbinic ideals and their expression in ritual fiat translated into daily practice. But rabbinic politics heeded a different logic: that of utility and compromise with strange bedfellows. The authority of Jewish communal leaders in the late tenth and eleventh centuries owed as much to their political connections at court and their broad social networks as it did to their learnedness and claims to represent tradition. The rumor therefore shows the fault lines between the rabbinic leaders and their followers: while the *yeshivah* hierarchy recognized that the necessities of patronage trumped those of theology, their followers persisted in the belief that denominational differences must lead to social separation.

Rabbanites and Karaites "Saying Things That Aren't True"

The provocateurs therefore milled about in the throng, spreading the rumor and encouraging the crowd to pressure and even threaten the gaon ("therefore gather against him") to reverse his position. The gaon, for his part, understood that the brewing public spectacle threatened to commandeer the entire ceremony:

> After the sermon, I was saying sweet words to the people for the s[ake of] the contributions to be thrown on the robe, and lo and behold, only a few people were making donations. These were the ones who had come in order to pray. The majority of those who had ascended the mountain (had done so) for the sake of the slander of the defamers (and were) talking insolently, gloating, and being impudent, saying to me: "You say in your sermons, 'I accept (rabbinic tradition) as the rest of you.' Just as you have received [the commandments] and the customs, do not alter the custom of our forefathers. For if you alter (it), everyone will follow and there will be Karaites saying things that aren't true!"

As was his usual practice on Hoshana Rabba, the gaon used his sermon to work the crowd for financial support for the *yeshivah,* and those who turned out sincerely and decorously for the ritual offered contributions. He also used the sermon to defend himself against his detractors' charges: breaking with long-established rabbinic tradition by refusing to declare the ban, and Karaite leanings—as we gather from his brief apologia, "I accept rabbinic tradition just as the rest of you do." The confluence of these two accusations points to the ideological excesses of his Rabbanite accusers, for whom breaking the bonds of custom (refusing to declare the ban) was tantamount to Karaism (which rejected rabbinic tradition). They therefore warned him that if he failed to declare the ban, others might follow his example of ideological compromise and allow the Karaites to go around "saying things that aren't true."

But of course it was the Rabbanites in this instance who were "saying things that aren't true," spreading rumors about the gaon. What were the Rabbanite masses afraid the Karaites would say to slander *them*?

It is tempting to speculate that they feared the accusation—repeated in tenth- and eleventh-century Karaite polemics—that the mere existence of internal Rabbanite dispute proves rabbinic tradition to be a human fabrication rather than revelation from Sinai.[35] If you alter our traditions, they told the gaon, there will be yet another crack in the edifice at which the Karaites have been chipping with their arguments for the mutability, and therefore human fabrication, of rabbinic tradition. Don't preach to *us* about tradition, they told the gaon; tradition dictates declaring the ban!

The gaon continues: "When I saw that no one was listening or paying attention, I stood on the chair and said, 'It is your choice. Do as you wish.' Our master the Third, may God keep him, was also speaking in their ears, saying, 'It is not a commandment that you should fight over it! Why should we concern ourselves with this dispute?!' But they did not listen to him, and the people's quarrel on the mountain increased greatly." It bears noting that the chair on which the gaon was standing and addressing the crowd—the spot from which Jerusalem *geonim* customarily delivered their sermons on pilgrimage festivals, referred to in various genizah documents as the cantors' chair (*kisse' ha-ḥazzanim*)—was believed to occupy the exact site from which the Divine Presence had alighted in Ezekiel 11:23, the proof text for the sanctity of the Mount of Olives.[36] Later the same year, Eli ha-Kohen ben Ezekiel, *parnas* or social services officer of the Jerusalem Rabbanite community, would write to Ephraim ben Shemariah with the news that the Karaites had smashed the chair to bits, more on which below.

The fracas had escalated to the point where the gaon gave up and allowed the throng to do as it chose.

At that point, Tobiah ben Daniel, third in rank in the *yeshivah,* intervened and attempted to convince the crowd that the ban was not a matter of *halakhah* proper but of custom ("It is not a commandment that you should fight over it!")—an argument directed against the crowd's plea not to alter what they insisted was ancient tradition.[37] Tobiah thereby aligned himself with his Iraqi contemporary Hayya bar Sherira, Gaon of Pumbedita (r. 1004–38), who ridiculed his tenth-century predecessor Saadya Gaon's attempts, in the rhetorical war against Karaism, to raise rabbinic traditions to the level of unalterable commandments.[38] Tobiah, Solomon, and others in the *yeshivah* hierarchy, like Hayya, represented a new approach to Karaism. For them, the ideological boundaries between the two positions had hardened, and the social boundaries between those who espoused them could therefore soften. But their followers aligned themselves with the zealously traditionalist camp.

At this point the breach was beyond repair. The gaon continues: "Then some elders came with the governor of the city and they said, 'Please rise and announce the order of the festivals of the Lord,' and I stood up and announced (them), as is the custom. Then they (the Rabbanite masses) cried: 'Declare the ban!' I told them, 'I have already said that I shall not declare it!'" The elders were leaders of the synagogue who were responsible for running the rabbinical court, supporting the head of the community in his efforts to enforce religious commandments, and generally protecting public morality.[39] They were understandably eager for the event to unfold without incident, the Fatimid governor of Jerusalem having materialized as monitor of *dhimmī* public ritual, and therefore took it upon themselves to move the proceedings along.[40] But the crowd waxed intransigent.

Under the watchful eye of the Fatimid authorities, the gaon announced the calendar. The younger members of the curia then took matters into their own hands. "At that, the two brothers, *ḥaverim* (of the *yeshivah*), may God keep them, stood up—my son was with them—and they declared it. But they (only) appeased the crowd with their words: it seemed to them (the crowd) that they (the three men) had mentioned 'meat with milk.' They then descended the mountain." Solomon's letter is frustratingly murky here. It seems that Joseph and Elijah ha-Kohen ben Solomon, the sons of Solomon ben Judah's predecessor to the gaonate, and a third member of the *yeshivah,* Solomon ben Judah's own son Abraham (who was their cousin), attempted to mollify the crowd with a ruse: they uttered the ban of excommunication in such a way that it *appeared* that they had included the traditional formula against "the eaters of meat with milk."[41] One imagines the two men (or perhaps all three of them—Solomon may have been protecting his son by obscuring the question of his participation) mouthing the formula without actually declaring it in full voice, thereby rendering the utterance halakhically ineffective.[42] But the fine distinction between utterance and non-utterance was lost on the governor, who acted swiftly and decisively. Before Solomon ben Judah had even returned home, the government's minions were already in pursuit of the three younger men. "I had not yet reached my house when there came soldiers of the governor of the land, known as Mu'tazz al-Dawla, may God preserve him." The fragment breaks off here. The governor in question—not the governor of Jerusalem but of all of Syria—was Abū Manṣūr Anushtekīn ibn 'Abdallāh al-Duzbarī (r. 1023–ca. 1042, with interruptions), who would reemerge over the course of the affair as the Fatimid official charged with keeping the peace between the two Jewish denominations.[43] The gaon explains in a subsequent letter that the two brothers were found and carted off to Damascus, where they were thrown into prison. His own son was spared punishment.[44]

The conflict between laity and leadership now entered decisively into the realm of high politics: the only way to extract the brothers from their Damascene dungeon would be via the Fatimid chancery, a road that led straight back to Karaite mediation. The Rabbanite throng thereby succeeded in subverting its own intention. That was perhaps inevitable: their protests against the gaon were attempts to shore up the foundations of a communal structure under which the very ground now shifted.

The Gaon's Objections to the Ban

Why did the gaon oppose the ban? Was he merely exercising diplomatic caution so as not to alienate his Karaite patrons at the Fatimid court? Was he loath to embroil the Jews in an internal controversy that would provoke government intervention? Or was he, as his followers claimed, soft on heretics?

In an undated letter to an unidentified party, the gaon expounds upon his opposition to the ban.[45] The upper left corner is torn, making it difficult to reconstruct the first few lines: "To mention . . . we find in the midrash . . . 'Ephraim is addicted to images—let him be' (Hosea 4:17) . . . this is not one of the (infractions) for which lashes . . . // they forbid //, and they say, 'You are permitting the forbidden and transgressing and violating most of the commandments!'" As far as one can tell, Solomon is objecting that his flock has gone too far in trying to punish Karaite offenders for infractions normally not deserving of lashes (a punishment for which excommunication was the usual substitute). The rest of the letter is better preserved. Why, the gaon inquires rhetorically, should we Rabbanites trouble ourselves with the sins of others when our own are great enough?

> (For Karaites who commit those sins,) there should suffice for us the curses written (in the Torah): "Cursed be he who does not uphold (the terms of this Torah and observe them)" (Deut. 27:26). (This means that) everyone who, because of our sins, does not uphold (these commandments) will enter into a curse. Should we excommunicate everyone who desecrates God's Sabbaths?! But the majority desecrate (the Sabbath)! Who is he who keeps the Sabbath as ordained?! And (should we excommunicate) everyone who desecrates the festivals of the Lord?! But they (the Karaites) say that we are the ones who desecrate (it)!

Were we to excommunicate all those who commit the sins of which we accuse the Karaites, the gaon warns, as many Rabbanites as Karaites would have to be placed under a ban. He adds, in a remarkable moment of medieval religious pluralism, that to the Karaites, we are Sabbath and festival desecrators as much as they are to us.

"And (should we excommunicate) everyone who pursues cases in Islamic courts, and who takes inheritances according to Islamic law?! But many who have a legal case go to Islamic courts![46] (Should we excommunicate) those who spread gossip?! But most (engage) in gossip! (Should we excommunicate) anyone who performs magic?! But many—both men and women—do it![47] And (eating) meat with milk is included (among these transgressions). 'That is why a curse consumes the earth' (Isa. 24:6)." The gaon admonishes his followers for accusing the Karaites of eating meat with milk when, as he hints in the penultimate sentence, it is among the transgressions of which Rabbanites are also guilty—although in imputing to his followers the violation of a biblical commandment he phrases the accusation delicately. But the masses require their bread and circus, he continues, and therefore insist upon the ban. "As for those who (merely) seek a quarrel, it seems to them that with the mention of meat with milk the Torah will be upheld! Let us not mention our own evil deeds, our enormous guilt, the abominations and disgraces on our own part. Are there no commandments left for us to uphold except the mention of 'meat with milk,' which has caused us these troubles?! People have nearly been destroyed and the hand of the government has entered into (our affairs) and troubled itself on our account." The gaon complains that his flock has raised the ban to the level of a God-given commandment. The pursuit of heresy, he argues, should not be conflated with the observance of religious precepts.

Like Tobiah ben Daniel on the Mount of Olives, the gaon here displays the new eleventh-century spirit of rebuking his followers for tenth-century zealotry. In the process, he reminds them that they hardly live up to the lofty standards to which they hold their enemies.

The Karaite Response to the Ban: Symbolic and Political Revenge

We learn about how Fatimid agents captured Joseph and Elijah, the *ḥaverim* who pretended to declare the ban, in a letter written by Eli ha-Kohen ben Ezekiel, the Jerusalem *parnas,* also addressed to Ephraim ben Shemariah in Fustat.[48] Eli had probably attended the excommunication ceremony and, like Solomon ben Judah, took it upon himself to keep Ephraim informed of unfolding developments. Eli's letter dates from late 1029 or early 1030, that is, slightly less than two months after the ban had been declared, and has survived in a fragmentary state; it is torn on the left side, so that only disconnected phrases are legible.

After a few lines of greetings and honorifics, Eli describes the Fatimid agents' pursuit of the two brothers: Elijah had fled to Nablus to escape imprisonment, but the authorities apprehended Joseph in Ramla. In the midst of this confusion, Eli writes, the Karaites exacted a violent revenge upon the Rabbanites for declaring the ban: "They went up to the Mount of Olives and broke the chair. . . . They said, 'Let no Rabbanite come up to Jerusalem!' "[49] This was the first but not the only time during the affair of the ban when the Karaites would take matters into their own hands and—at least according to Rabbanite account—perpetrate some act of vengeful violence. The Karaite popular reaction, by returning to the sacred site from which the excommunication had been declared and breaking the cantors' chair, invoked precisely the ritual symbolism deployed by the Rabbanite instigators of the ban.

The Karaites also expressed their vengeance in a different idiom—that of diplomacy and politics. (Was Ibn Dāwūd, in depicting the Karaites as "silent like 'dumb dogs,' " protesting too much?) We learn about the Karaite mobilization of political channels in a letter Solomon ben Judah addressed to Sahlān ben Abraham, the leader of the Babylonian congregation in Fustat, also in late 1029 or early 1030.[50] Joseph and Elijah had been languishing for some time in prison in Damascus. Solomon had attempted to have them freed, but his efforts met with little success and an ever-tightening web of complications binding Rabbanite fate to Karaite communal power. This letter is fragmentary precisely where the greetings end and the content begins. Solomon commences by complaining to Sahlān:

> You [so]ught . . . before the caliph and the vizier, may they live eternally, about freeing the prisoners, may God bri[ng] them out into the light. . . . We were hoping for their release from darkness and shadows and for their bonds to be sundered, but lo and behold, letters came from Damascus (saying) that they are still in prison, although their chains and yokes have been removed. But their jailers are punishing them daily, and they are ailing; may the King of

> Glory send his word, heal them, and take them out into the light, and may they (the rulers) see their righteousness.

The gaon had evidently enlisted various Jewish notables to beseech the Fatimid court for the prisoners' release. He seems to have asked Sahlān to find channels through which to access the caliph al-Ẓāhir and the vizier, al-Jarjarā'ī.[51] Notable in his absence as mediator is David ha-Levi ben Isaac. In 1024, David had helped free Ephraim ben Shemariah from imprisonment on some slanderous charge, and in the spring of 1029, Solomon had petitioned David to have a mixed group of Jerusalem Jews freed from debtors' prison. When David failed to respond to Solomon's entreaties, he asked Ephraim to meet with him personally.[52] Solomon evidently hesitated to seek David's intercession here—presently we shall have reason to speculate why. Meanwhile, Solomon asked two respected members of the Jerusalem Rabbanite community, Abu l-Barakāt Nethanel ha-Kohen and Abu l-Faḍl Mevorakh ben Eli, for their help. Of the former, little is known beyond his role in mediating the affair, including whether he was Rabbanite or Karaite; the latter was a wealthy and respected Rabbanite elder in Fustat.[53] But those interventions had yielded nothing. Solomon received letters from Damascus attesting to the fact that the brothers were still in prison and to their deteriorating state of physical health. Although the jailers had removed the prisoners' chains, they were no closer to being released.

Even in avoiding the Karaite courtiers, by approaching the caliph, Solomon inadvertently invited perhaps more Karaite intervention than he had bargained for. He also failed to anticipate the response of a major Karaite official, the Fatimid military commander of Syria, Adayah ben Manasseh Ibn al-Qazzāz. Solomon's phrasing here employs a web of pronouns that I have attempted to untangle between parentheses. He tells Sahlān:

> And it is written there (in the letters from Damascus) that a document was sent to them (the prisoners) from Adayah ben Manasseh, known as Ibn al-Qazzāz. Written in it (Adayah's document) is a stipulation that they (the prisoners) will swear by God and by the life of the caliph, may he live eternally, that they will never again be called by the title of *ḥaver* and never serve the house of Israel in all of Palestine, in greater or lesser service, neither in law nor in any other matter; and (the letters from Damascus continue) that they

(the prisoners) answered, "We want to hear the words of this document from the mouth of its author (Adayah) and we will answer according to what." (A lacuna follows.)

Adayah imposed harsh stipulations on the imprisoned brothers as a condition of their release: that they relinquish the title of *ḥaver,* be disbarred from the *yeshivah,* and renounce all communal functions for the rest of their lives. And yet his response cannot be seen as motivated merely by Karaite partisanship. As military commander of Syria, he worked directly under the governor, al-Duzbarī, who sent soldiers after the brothers in the first place, and so the orders to punish the ban's declarers must have come from al-Duzbarī himself. Moreover, Adayah was not personally opposed to rabbinic authority, for he had on at least one occasion served as witness in the rabbinical court in Tyre—to a transaction involving the betrothal of David ha-Levi ben Isaac's daughter; David's other daughter happened to be Adayah's wife.[54] We should marvel at the presence of so many Karaites in a rabbinical court only as much as we marvel that rabbinic judges, ordained members of the Jerusalem *yeshivah,* wrote their documents for them.[55] And yet in this instance, Adayah brought the full weight of government authority down on the instigators of the ban. Given that Adayah was David's son-in-law, it is understandable that Solomon avoided seeking the latter's intervention before the caliph: it would have been stretching the bonds of patron-client relationships to the breaking point to importune a grandee to oppose his own relative. The imprisoned brothers were left no choice but to demand a private audience with Adayah. Indeed, they seem to have imagined that in direct conversation they might convince him to retract the harsh stipulations.

Solomon ben Judah, for his part, was horrified at the sour turn his attempts at advocacy had taken and disappointed by the failure of Sahlān's efforts to have the prisoners released, as well as those of Abu l-Barakāt and Abu l-Faḍl.

And when we grasped what he had said (the gaon continues), suffering was added to pain, and I said, "Woe is me! The Lord has added grief" to my grief (Jer. 45:3). "We hope for light, and lo! there is darkness" (Isa. 59:9). I am still weeping over this piece of news! We were hoping that from Damascus they would bring answers to the letters written by the elder dignitary Rav Nethanel ha-Kohen,

> called Abū l-Barakāt, may his Rock preserve him and may God be his aid, and from Rav Mevorakh ha-Sar ben Eli, may the latter's soul be at rest, called Abū l-Faḍl, since they saw that the letters came from Damascus.

Solomon saw that he had no choice but to go to Damascus himself, but complained that the cold Damascene winter would do him in, given his frail physical state. He seems also to have feared some other impediment—whether common banditry or other difficulties traveling we are not told.

> One of the elders (wished to have) brought me in these times, in the days of autumn and frost and cold, but I am old and no longer have the strength even to go from my house to the [mark]et, because—alas and alack!—"my strength fails because of my iniquity" (Ps. 31:11). And even if I am brought to Damascus, I don't know whether "some disaster will befall" me (Gen. 42:2). If our (biblical) patriarch Jacob, peace be upon him, feared for Benjamin the Right[eou]s (his son, and did not send him to Egypt lest some disaster befall him, Gen. 42:2), and both of them have great merit before God, all the more so (should) we who have sinned (not risk travel).

Eventually, the gaon did travel to Damascus—the Jerusalem *parnas* Eli ben Ezekiel, in the letter cited above, speaks of the *rayyis* (i.e., the gaon) going down to Damascus and apologizes to Ephraim ben Shemariah for not having traveled with him himself, since he had been ill.[56]

In the meantime, the gaon divulges to Sahlān the contents of the letters from Damascus, which contained a set of demands that seem to be separate from those Adayah imposed:

> [Lo and behold,] there arrived (in the letters) answers that seemed like . . . about my going (the sentence is obscure). There are also harsh conditions written in them—even our overlords (the caliph and vizier?) would not make conditions for us as they (the Karaites?) have done. And their essence is that the ban not be proclaimed again on the Mount of Oliv[es]; that the Karaites separate out for themselves one shop in the market of the Jews to slaughter and sell m[ea]t without (Rabbanite) inspection or supervision; that the rest of the butchers (i.e., the Muslim and Christian meat-

> sellers), if they have a pregnant ewe or cow, not sell i[t to one of] the Jews; that if it is a [holiday] for them (the Karaites), the Rabbanites not come and try to desecrate it by opening their shops; that the Rabbis [not exercise authority] over them; that the imprisoned [*ḥaverim*] come neither to the Holy City nor to Ramla; and that he write documents . . . (the sentence is interrupted by a lacuna).

The Karaites of Syria, in short, attempted to benefit from the temporary array of forces against the Rabbanites to gain further advantage over them: the *ḥaverim* were in prison and their *yeshivah* colleagues were beholden to Adayah for their release; they therefore campaigned for administrative separation from their coreligionists. The seven conditions fully preserved—an injunction against the ban of excommunication, the disbarring of the *ḥaverim,* and a set of stipulations pertaining to commercial and religious supervision in the meat markets of Palestine—all speak to Karaite resentment of Rabbanite dominance in religious communal affairs.[57]

On the face of things, this was a power struggle plain and simple: installing separate stalls for Karaite butchers in the Jewish market was designed to avoid Karaite meat having to pass rabbinic inspection and to obviate Rabbanite control over the supply of meat to the Jews. Not only that, the Karaites thereby made a bid not merely for independence but for control of the shared food economy by trying to prevent all purveyors of livestock from selling pregnant animals (consumption of which is forbidden according to Karaite law) to Jewish butchers.[58] And by requiring the Rabbanites to close their shops on Karaite festivals and fast days, the Karaites wished to force them to observe the Karaite calendar. One wonders whether the Karaites had any reasonable hope of success in these demands.

But on the symbolic level, these stipulations mirrored the Rabbanite ban for which they were intended as revenge: both attempted to impose a separation between two groups that were otherwise intertwined in the course of daily affairs. The only difference between the challenge and the riposte was one of method: to the ceremonial excommunication of the Rabbanites, the Karaites responded with a political and administrative one. Each group used its own currency against the other. The Rabbanites resented what they perceived as the Karaite stranglehold over Jewish political affairs and sought to free themselves from the web of Karaite and Fatimid power through the medium of religious ritual. The Karaites, for their part, objected to Rabbanite dominance in Jewish communal affairs, especially those tied to public ritual and public commerce, and attempted to extricate themselves by exploiting their political and governmental ties.

The gaon refused to heed the Karaite stipulations. In his praise for Sahlān, he revealed the principle driving his leadership. He expatiated especially upon Israel's enmeshment with one another and responsibility for the whole, themes that resurface in his subsequent correspondence. And yet Solomon's rhetoric could not differ more from Ibn Dāwūd's. Rather than lodge the latter's accusations that the Karaites "never did anything of benefit for Israel," Solomon instead confesses his hope that Karaites will come to his aid by influencing the government to cancel Adayah's stipulations—regardless of their ties of kinship and denomination.

> Every *ḥaver* and the notab[les] "stand surety" (Gen. 43:9), and they will testify about me and about the elders that we stand surety for these matters. "Has the like of this happened in your days. . . . Tell your children about it" (Joel 1:2–3). "Proclaim in the fortresses of Ashdod and in the fortresses of the land of Egypt! (Say: gather on the hill of Samaria and witness the great outrages within her and the oppression in her midst, Amos 3:9)" . . . [Has there been se]en a thing like this or has there been heard like unto it? I have already compromised as much as I can. (He adds above the line, to make certain that his position is clear:) //And I will not agree to even one of their conditions, and nor will the *ḥaverim*.//
>
> I have placed my trust in the Creator. Perhaps He will perform His wonders for us. It is fitting for you, our dear one (Solomon addresses Sahlān), to pray to God and to be fortified and strong and to gird your strength (so that) everyone you know may grasp it.
>
> Perhaps they will take letters for us to the government, may God defend it, in Ramla and Damascus (asking) that they not force us to agree to this stipulation. And the letters that I have mentioned and that our brothers have mentioned do not seem disadvantageous. Time is short, for it is not hidden from you that the el[der]s in Ra[mla] and in Damascus . . . (a lacuna interrupts the sentence).
>
> We rely upon the Lord our God, and what you and yours do in this matter will be for all Israel, near and far, and your well-being [and the well-being of] your brothers, and the well-being of your uncle and your entire community, the young and the old.

Solomon's claim to place his trust solely "in the Creator" is slightly disingenuous: in the very same breath, he expresses the hope that "they will take letters for us to the government in Ramla and Damascus." It is unclear who he was hoping would influence the Syrian governors, but it stands to reason that he means the Karaite elders of Syria, who had probably issued the stipulations in the first place. In closing, the gaon complains of exhaustion, saying, "Because of my sins, I have become weak, and there is no strength left in me to write, nor to read that which I might ask to be written in my name." The letter is in the handwriting of a scribe.

The Rabbanite Resort to Politics

Solomon made good on his promise to Sahlān to engineer an appeal directly to the caliph, and his appeal was successful. Some time in 1030, al-Ẓāhir issued a decree to his Syrian governor, Anushtekīn al-Duzbarī, ordering him (and through him, one assumes, Adayah Ibn al-Qazzāz) to refrain from partiality in his treatment of "the two sects" (Arab. *al-ṭā'ifatayn*).

The decree has survived only in a Judeo-Arabic copy of a lost Judeo-Arabic transcription of the (also lost) Arabic original presented to the caliph for ratification. In the surviving document, the section containing the date has been torn away—but from the contents of the decree it seems virtually certain that it was issued in response to the events described here and that the caliph ratified a set of stipulations the Rabbanites had composed in order to counter the Karaite demands.

> To his majesty, Commander of the Faithful: A petition was submitted in the name of the community of the Rabbanite Jews asking that they be treated according to the most high edict (*sijill*) issued on their behalf, namely, that their *ḥaverim* should be able to fulfill the commandments of their religion and their ancient customs in their synagogues and to serve their communities in Jerusalem, Ramla, and other places; and that those who interfere with them should be stopped, as this is not compatible with the justice of the government; and that they should not be given a free hand to do what is not in accordance with established usage; and that they should not be disturbed on their holidays and in particular while they hold their services on them (a reference to some Karaite act of disruption

> not preserved in other letters, or to the destruction of the cantors' chair?); and that those of their adversaries who do such things should be checked.
>
> Therefore the commander of the Faithful has ordered that decrees should be issued to the effect that each of the Jewish communities, the Rabbanites and the Karaites,[59] should not interfere with one another; and that all who belong to one of the two schools[60] should be allowed to conduct themselves according to the customs taught in their religions, without the harassment of one of the two sects against the other. . . .
>
> In particular the Karaites should not harass the leaders of the Rabbanites by exiling them from the districts of Jerusalem and Ramla, and the businessmen of the two sects should conduct themselves according to their customs with regard to transactions of buying and selling or abstaining from such according to their wishes on the days of their feasts. Each of the communities shall beware of acting against the provisions of this order. Let everyone know that he who disobeys and trespasses will receive heavy punishment, which will check him and deter others.[61]

Here, too, one must ask whether the gaon relied upon his Karaite connections at court to shepherd this rescript through the chancery. Indeed, several of the rescripts pertaining to the Jews from the beginning of al-Ẓāhir's reign of which direct or indirect evidence has survived had been expedited through the mediation of the Karaite courtiers. In fact, as we shall see, al-Ẓāhir and al-Duzbarī came around to the Rabbanite cause without the intervention of the Karaite courtiers.

That same year, Ephraim ben Shemariah wrote a letter, only a scrap of which has survived, to an unknown recipient. What little text remains indicates that he was experiencing sectarian disturbances in the capital on the Nile, and making every effort to resolve the situation without involving Fatimid authority.[62] The principal schism in Fustat, as in Jerusalem and Ramla, was not between Karaites and Rabbanites but between laity and leadership. "The Karaites on Yom Kippur, and they desecrated and profaned (it) . . . between them and some of our brothers the Karaites . . . in anger. They cried, 'We want the ban (against the eaters) [of meat] with milk!' I told them it was not fitting to . . . their breaches in front of the government." As far as one can tell, Ephraim seems to be referring to the fact that the Karaites, by dint of their calendar, observed Yom Kippur on a different day from the Rabbanites and publicly desecrated the Rabbanite holiday. This angered some Rabbanites in Fustat, who demanded that a ban be issued against the Karaites—the same ban "against the eaters of meat with milk" that had been proclaimed in Jerusalem. The Karaites of Fustat provoked the ban "against the eaters of meat with milk" not by eating meat with dairy but by desecrating the Rabbanite calendar—which confirms that like that of the Karaites of Jerusalem, their offense was less halakhic than theological. In Fustat as in Jerusalem, the ban was a means of social vengeance rather than a behavioral corrective. Ephraim, for his part, was reluctant to declare the ban lest this call attention to internal Jewish strife and risk the government authorities entering yet again into the affair—and perhaps also compromise his relationship with his patron David ha-Levi ben Isaac. Ephraim may also have been directing some implicit criticism toward the faction of Karaites he describes (he is careful to refer to "*some of* the Karaites"), who did not hesitate to seek government intervention in their quarrels with the Rabbanites.

Confrontation in Ramla

We learn of the continuation of the affair in a third letter written by Solomon ben Judah some time in 1030, this one in Judeo-Arabic.[63] The letter is torn at the top, where the addressee's name once appeared, and in the body of the letter Solomon addresses him only as "*yā shaykhī*" ("O my lord," written as one word). His correspondent may have been some member of rank in the Palestinian synagogue in Fustat, and had perhaps attended the pilgrimage festival on the Mount of Olives the previous year. This letter differs markedly in style and tone from his Hebrew letters to rabbinic colleagues, in which he rarely strays from a distanced description of events, with an occasional health-related complaint and some stylized sentiments that he expresses through biblical quotations. In this letter, by contrast, his tone is remarkably candid: he shares his feelings with less resort to stereotype and does not hesitate to air complaints against the Karaites. With the veil of diplomacy lifted, it becomes clear that Solomon's generally friendly relations with the Karaites were conditioned not by sympathy but by the necessities of communal governance.

The degree of intimacy the letter displays is also the historian's vexation: the events and main characters were so well known to both parties that Solomon rarely pauses to specify what or whom he means. The primary event he describes, as far as one can tell, is a meeting between Rabbanites and Karaites in the "market of the Jews" (the *majlis* or meeting hall in Ramla) before some arbitrating body that had been called upon to mediate the conflict. The brothers accused of declaring the ban were still languishing in prison and their release remained, for the moment, contingent on the Rabbanites accepting their demands as specified in the writ from Damascus. The gaon begins: "There was presented before us (a version) from them (the Karaites) of what happened (between the two sects); it was asked that the matter be resolved without a stipulation (being placed) either upon us or against us. I consented to this, but they (the Karaites) did not accept (it). Rather, they said, 'Our time has come! This is the day we hoped for; we have lived to see it!'" (Lamentations 2:16). The gaon refused the Karaite demands, and the mediators supported him by asking the Karaites to retract their conditions and requesting that the two sides resolve the affair amicably themselves. But the Karaites instead pressed their demands and, according to the gaon's description, attempted to exploit their temporary advantage over the Rabbanites.

At that point, Fatimid officers entered the fray—although we are not told why, or who exactly they were; they were evidently charged with enforcing the writ from Damascus and so punishing the Rabbanites for their refusal to heed the Karaite stipulations. "They (the officers) struck (with lashes) pitilessly; both priests and scholars were struck. They were carried off, and Israel was weeping and crying, but they (the Karaites) rejoiced until (the verse) was intoned to them: 'Israel was a laughingstock for you, though he was not caught among thieves; but whenever they spoke of him they shook their heads' (in mockery; cf. Jer. 48:27)." The Karaite onlookers openly rejoiced while Rabbanite scholars were dragged off in manacles. The Rabbanite crowd wept and wailed, and their leaders rebuked the Karaites for their open display of *schadenfreude.*

Before we hear further what transpired between the two groups, Solomon voices several complaints about the Karaites' leaders. "Would that those (Karaite) elders, who supported them in frivolity, would see us as making as great an effort in the interpretation of law as their followers, each of whom follows a differing school (of interpretation). But (even though the Karaites differ in law) if there is a dispute between them and the Rabbanites, they all agree with one voice to cut off their names from the land (Josh. 7:9; cf. Ps. 34:17) and they say, 'Fallen not to rise again (is maiden Israel)'" (Amos 5:2; cf. Isa. 24:20). With bitter irony, Solomon notes that though the Karaites cannot agree with one another on a single point of law, they are unanimous in their hatred of the Rabbanites. Indeed, interpretive mayhem was a defining feature of Karaite exegetical and halakhic production in Jerusalem in the tenth and eleventh centuries; the Karaite scholars' Rabbanite contemporaries were aware of the degree of internal Karaite dissent and perhaps somewhat mystified by it.

The term Solomon used to describe the Karaites in their exegetical efforts, *mujtahidīn* (which I have rendered "making an effort in the interpretation of law"), is borrowed from Islamic legal theory, in which it means "exerting oneself" in the search for the correct law. In Karaite as in Islamic jurisprudence, *ijtihād* is the opposite of relying upon tradition, or *taqlīd*. Karaites since Daniel al-Qūmisī had charged that rabbinic law and exegesis, in resorting uncritically to intellectual mimesis and handed-down tradition, reproduced erroneous human interpretations of the biblical text and was therefore nothing more than "a commandment of men, learned by rote" (Isa. 29:13).[64] Karaite exegesis, in contrast, by attending to grammatical and other linguistic details of the biblical text, aimed to cut through centuries of accreted misunderstanding (what the Rabbanites called tradition). The gaon responded pointedly to Karaite anti-Rabbanite polemic: you say that the strength of your method consists in scholarly independence, and indeed it is as if every Karaite scholar has his own school of thought—and yet you have no difficulty agreeing when it comes to despising the Rabbanites.

The gaon's complaints also bear a hint of criticism aimed at what he saw as Karaite lack of fellow feeling—in marked contrast to the hopes he had expressed in his Hebrew letter. And yet on the very next line, he returns the sentiment in kind, chiding the Karaites: gloat to your hearts' content; God has intervened on our behalf, thereby proving the justice of our cause. The Rabbanites had evidently succeeded in preventing the Karaites' demands from being imposed on them (under circumstances alas too familiar to author and reader to bear elaboration).

> That bunch has forgotten the saying of the sage: "God seeks the pursued" (Eccl. 3:15) and that He, may He be praised, has not withheld his mercy from this nation. "The kindness of the Lord has not ended (his mercies are not spent). They are renewed

> every morning" (Lam. 3:22–23). And when we despaired we sought the help of the Merciful. How many women and children were fasting and were not eating anything slaughtered (in penitence)?! How many let their hair grow (also in penitence) until (there came) "mercy, for God first afflicts and then shows mercy" (cf. Lam. 3:32)?!

By order of the caliph and the vizier, the Rabbanite brothers had been freed.

But how? The gaon continues:

> As for me, every time I think about what happened, I wonder how this miracle occurred, and I say: "This is the Lord's doing" (Ps. 118:23). I render thanks to God: "Blessed is the Lord God of our fathers, who put it into the mind of" our lord "the king" (i.e., the caliph, cf. Ezra 7:27), may he live forever, and into the mind of our lord the vizier, may God save him, to speak on our behalf and to seek what is good for us, may His name be elevated for all eternity. "Who ever heard the like? Who ever witnessed such events?" (Isa. 66:8). Say to God, "How awesome are your deeds!" (Ps. 66:3).

The gaon's string of biblical quotations reveals little about the Rabbanites' route to the chancery. Instead he attributes their success to divine providence while excoriating the Karaites for their political tactics. "They trusted in their courtiers and ministers and wealthy ones and those close to the government, 'but we call on the name of the Lord our God' (Ps. 20:8). 'How can [we] repay the Lord for all his bounties towards' us? (Ps. 116:12)." The gaon probably intended these "courtiers, ministers, wealthy ones, and those close to the government" as an indirect reference to the Tustarīs, who were courtiers, and David ha-Levi ben Isaac and Adayah Ibn al-Qazzāz, both "ministers" (*kātibs*). In contrast to the Karaites, the gaon insists disingenuously, the Rabbanite miracle came about not through the intercession of our operatives in Fustat, but through divine intervention.

But the Karaites' diplomatic tactics do not exhaust the gaon's complaint. Here his harangue turns to their sanctimoniousness in religious and intellectual matters. "O my lord," he addresses his correspondent, "in my heart a fire burns (Isa. 25:5) because of the people who hastened to our calamity. They see themselves as 'lilies' (Heb. *shoshanim*) and everyone else as thorns; they consider themselves 'wise ones' (Heb. *maskilim*), but they disagree as to who among them is wise. They should be ashamed! Which of us is obligated to his followers concerning the many laws of Israel that are not written, we or they?" The Karaites have failed to use their power to the advantage of all Israel, the gaon writes, while we Rabbanites spend our time in apprenticeship of the oral tradition ("the many laws of Israel that are not written") and attend to the needs of the collectivity.

It was a staple of Karaite self-conception during this period that the Karaites were the "lilies" (*shoshanim*) and the rest of Israel "thorns" (after Song of Songs 2:2), and Karaites since al-Qūmisī and his school in the early tenth century had referred to themselves as "*maskilim*," wise ones (after Dan. 11:33, 11:35, and 12:3).[65] Salmon ben Yerūḥīm, in his polemical *Book of the Wars of the Lord* (ca. 950), had also called the Karaite community "the congregation of the Lily" (*adat ha-shoshana*), and Japheth ben Eli connected the two concepts along the lines of messianic prognostication, commenting (on Song of Songs 2:1) that the earlier *maskilim* were like the narcissus that blossoms briefly in winter, while his generation of Karaite *maskilim* were lilies flowering in the spring of Israel's salvation.[66] The precise contents of the Karaite polemical arsenal were evidently not unknown in the Rabbanite camp. The gaon returned fire by mocking the Karaites' elitism: the Karaite self-conception as "roses" among thorns and a select group of "wise ones" speaks to religious and intellectual strength in small numbers but, offers the gaon, it runs contrary to pan-Jewish loyalty.

Karaite elitism was no doubt one reason Ibn Dāwūd would turn those numerical arguments on their head and use triumphalist reasoning on behalf of the more numerous Rabbanites. Solomon ben Judah, for his part, was not tempted by triumphalist argumentation, for he had seen the Karaites turn to it first: "Weren't they satisfied with what is between them and their Lord?! But when one mentions it to them, they feel ashamed and say: 'If God, may He be exalted, gave us a high position in service of the king, it was so that we may tell our fellowmen about their negligence toward others.'" When one raises the subject of Karaite success in politics, the gaon claims, they answer that God has granted them this success the better to spread their teachings and "tell our fellows about their negligence" toward the collectivity. While the tenth-century Karaite exegetes had purveyed the elitism of a small community of religious ascetics, the more cosmopolitan Karaites in the caliph's entourage, according to the gaon, deployed the same elitism shorn of the element of material renunciation. In response, the gaon quotes Ecclesiastes' warning against the simplistic attribution of worldly success to divine favor: "'(In my own brief span of life, I have seen both these things: sometimes a good man perishes in spite of his goodness, and sometimes a wicked one endures in spite of his wickedness. So don't overdo goodness and don't act the wise man to excess.) . . . It is best that you grasp the one without letting go of the other' (Eccl. 7:15–18)."

Then the gaon divulges a salient detail of what irks his constituency about the Karaites. "We do not feel safe from the evil prayer of others, and moreover, they make us out to be one whose prayer God does not accept. But if to them we appear thus, why should they procreate with us or intermarry with us? This is forbidden to them!" If the Karaites think of us as evildoers whose prayers God rejects, asks the gaon, then why do they take our daughters in marriage? (One should note here that the gaon never asks why the Rabbanites, from the rank and file up to the very *ḥaverim* who ran the rabbinical courts, accepted those intermarriages as legal and valid.) "As for me, God knows what I would have said to our people when I heard them say, 'We want to separate from those people because of the enmity they show toward us.' I would have said: My brothers, this thing is not good between us. We have found that the house of Judah did not refrain from marrying even the tribes that were worshipping idolatrously. They are our brothers. If we are not bound by any decree, then we should not exact retribution on them for what they inflicted upon us. This is my argument." Even when the tribes of Israel were prostrating themselves to Baal, the gaon argues, they were still marrying from among the daughters of Judah; how can we refuse the Karaites ours? Given that the stipulations have been canceled, he argues, we have no reason to avenge their actions through social separation. As in the episode of the ban more generally, here again we see the Rabbanites arguing for social separation from the Karaites while the gaon restrains them in the name of moderation.

Solomon's comparison of Rabbanite-Karaite intermarriage with unions between Judah and Israel again mobilizes a common trope of Rabbanite-Karaite polemic likening the schism to the split of the united monarchy under Jeroboam, with each side vying for the role of Judah. In the 930s, the Karaite heresiographer Abū Ya'qūb Yūsuf al-Qirqisānī had traced the rise of the various Jewish sects back to the tenth century

B.C.E., writing: "From this time on—that is, the time when Jeroboam committed the aforementioned acts (e.g., maintaining idolatrous shrines)—dissent arose among the children of Israel, and similar practices were planted in their midst, one generation inheriting them from the other." For al-Qirqisānī, the Karaites were the true descendants of Judah while the Rabbanites had followed the straying path of the tribes of Israel.[67] Salmon ben Yerūḥīm, ca. 950, ended his lengthy anti-Rabbanite polemic *The Book of the Wars of the Lord* with a fervent prayer for the day when God would "restore the glory of the tents of Judah and Israel as of old; may they become one. No longer will they be divided into two nations, but rather will be one nation, the chosen people."[68] We have become two kingdoms, the gaon also admitted, but we are still one people, and the Karaites are still our brothers.

The Second Rabbanite Rumor: Symbolic Violence

The second part of the gaon's letter describes the aftermath of the meeting in the *majlis* in Ramla. Like the episode on the Mount of Olives several months earlier, the meeting revolved around Rabbanites spreading a rumor and insisting upon a ban of excommunication.

Some Rabbanites in Jerusalem spread another calumny about the Karaites, this time that they had burnt three Rabbanite figures in effigy on Purim. (It was a time-honored tradition, at least among Rabbanites, to burn one's enemies in effigy on Purim.)[69] Whom the effigies were supposed to have represented we do not know, but S. D. Goitein ingeniously suggests that the libel had them depicting none other than the three Rabbanite leaders who had pronounced the ban on the Karaites—the imprisoned brothers Joseph and Elijah and Solomon's son Abraham.[70] To find out the truth about the accusations, Solomon again called upon the diplomatic services of Abu l-Barakāt Nethanel ha-Kohen, who along with Abu l-Faḍl Mevorakh ben Eli had attempted to have the brothers released from their Syrian prison cell. In the end, it was Abu l-Barakāt who unraveled the Rabbanite libel: "Our people (the Rabbanites) slandered them (the Karaites, saying) that on Purim they had created three effigies and burnt them. They (the Rabbanites) testified against them (the Karaites). But then Shaykh Abu l-Barakāt, may blessing come to him, called in those who had declared (the libel) and they denied (having uttered?) it. He denounced them and said to them: 'If this is the nature of your testimony, surely you will bring destruction upon the world.'" Realizing now that the slanderers were lying, the elders advised the gaon to punish them. "And then came his (Abū l-Barakāt's) colleague Abū 'Alī Muḥsin, may he be remembered well, and he told me and told the elders (what had transpired in his meeting with the Rabbanite offenders). He advised me that I had no way out of this libel but to announce a ban on whoever did what was said and on whomever spread slander of nonexistent things in order to endanger people." Abū 'Alī Muḥsin, or Muḥsin Ibn Ḥusayn, was the scion of a Rabbanite trading family from the northern Syrian coast, a merchant in his own right, and *parnas* and representative of the merchants in the Palestinian Rabbanite community in Fustat—in short, an influential and respected elder who was called upon for his moral stature and, perhaps, for his expertise in negotiation.[71] Abū 'Alī Muḥsin advised the gaon to declare a ban upon the Rabbanites who had spread the rumor, and the gaon complied. "It was done on a fast day in the *majlis* in the Jewish market (in Ramla); the group assembled and I said before them what I could: 'Is the sin of Peor such a small thing to us' (Josh. 22:17; cf. Num. 25:1–9) and what was done against us, so that now the affair will continue because of us, and we will renew the dispute?" The three who renewed the ban on Hoshana Rabba have already suffered imprisonment, the gaon reminded his followers. Was that not enough for us? Must we now risk provoking the anger of the government by spreading this libel against the Karaites? The Rabbanite throng, convinced by the gaon's reasoning, sought to distance themselves from the libel and those who had spread it. "The assembly answered: 'Cast the ban and cast the ban! Behold, we are suffering mightily from their speech, even though the thing happened against our will. (Cast the ban) so that responsibility for what happened isn't thrown back on us!' (The page is torn here; after a lacuna, the gaon continues on verso: And so, as the crowd demanded,) we cast the ban and we ended (the affair), but it troubled many of them, since they knew that they were bringing this about." Just as on the Mount of Olives the Rabbanite masses had demanded that the ban be declared against the Karaites, here they insist that the gaon excommunicate the libelers, whose slander had forced the Rabbanites to suffer at the hands of both the Karaites and the government.[72] Banning them seemed the only way to exonerate the rest of the Rabbanites, but apparently some in the room felt lingering remorse knowing that, after all, they had helped spread the libel. On a bitter and defeated note, the gaon turns to other matters, and that is the last we hear of the excommunication affair of 1029.

"To Be Separated from the Other Sect, So That They Might Not Mingle with Them in Any Matter"

The following year, naturally the question arose as to what would unfold at the pilgrimage gathering on the Mount of Olives. We learn of a second round of disturbances—and some instructive details about the first—in a letter Solomon ben Judah wrote in Hebrew to Ephraim ben Shemariah in Fustat after the pilgrimage season in late 1030.[73] "It is not hidden from you, may your Rock preserve you, that the common people are de[li]ghting in the dispute of sch[olars]. Your witnesses will determine what happened on this festival, but in sum, most of those who made the pilgrimage came only for the sake of the dispute and to seek to be separated from the other sect, so that they might not mingle with them in any matter."[74] Here the gaon issues a remarkably candid statement confirming what I have been arguing above: the ban against the Karaites was intended not as a form of punishment for infringement upon rabbinic dietary (and other) laws, but first and foremost as a means of seeking "to be separated from the other sect."

But the Rabbanite masses' desire for separation was not exhausted by their insistence on the ban. In the letter's continuation, we learn that they went further than this, attacking anyone who in their view harbored pro-Karaite leanings. In his first letter, Solomon painted the Rabbanite throng as imputing Karaite sympathies to him; in his sermon, he defended himself by proclaiming, "I accept rabbinic tradition as the rest of you." Now we learn that the Rabbanites were enlarging the scope of their witch hunt to include not only the gaon but anyone who opposed the ban. "And they (the Rabbanite 'common people') waged war with any person who did not listen to them and defamed him (saying) that he is one of them (the Karaites), and made him 'the butt of gossip in every language and of ridicule from all people'" (Ezek. 36:3). The gaon then describes how the festival of 1030 unfolded, from the beginning of Sukkot until the end. "On the first day of the festival, the people were hardly hearing or listening to the words of the preacher, until an edict came in the name of the government and the military commander to the governor of Ramla to warn (us) not to declare the ban, and that anyone who contravened (the order) would be punished. He wrote to the governor of Jerusalem to come up to the mountain on Hoshana Rabba with instruments of punishment, and anyone who mentioned the ban would be whipped and sent to prison." On the first day of the festival, there was a buzz in the air in anticipation of the ban, as there had been the previous year. Perhaps the preacher himself (whether Solomon or another high-ranking *yeshivah* official, we do not know) began the festival by admonishing the people toward peace. It was only when the government issued a warning against declaring the ban that the people began to listen. Remembering the previous year's imprisonments, they were loath to contravene Fatimid orders.

It must be remembered, however, that the laissez-faire Fatimid administration likely issued the edict only at the behest of some party of Jews who lobbied them for it. Untangling the skein of officials in this letter is a speculative business—by "military commander," does the gaon intend Adayah Ibn al-Qazzāz? Was the "governor of Ramla" the governor of Syria, al-Duzbarī, apparently the official in charge of enforcing and policing Jewish sectarian strife?[75] Either way the edict was drafted in the name of the caliph in Cairo ordering the governor of Ramla (the provincial seat of Palestine) to warn the Rabbanites not to excommunicate the Karaites on penalty of lashes and imprisonment. The governor of Ramla in turn ordered the governor of Jerusalem—who had attended the festival the previous year accompanied by the elders of the *yeshivah*—to ascend the Mount of Olives to supervise the festival proceedings, just as he had the year before. Only this time he came prepared with lashes and prisoners' chains in hand.

Upon learning this news, the Rabbanites considered canceling altogether the ceremony scheduled for the week's end—not only for fear of punishment but because to perform the ceremony without the ban might set a precedent for years to come.

> When this thing was heard, it was not permitted to go up to the mountain because, it was said, if it was established this year not to follow ancient custom, the matter would be rendered permanent for generations to come. And when it was said that the present writer was also advised not to go up lest there be deceit and artifice against him and the festival turn into sorrow and sighing (cf. Est. 9:22, Isa. 35:10, and Amos 8:9–10), most of the people were crying and some of them were moaning and groaning and complaining:

> How did the present writer not gird his loins and separate these from those?

The gaon was advised (perhaps by the elders) to cancel the festival for fear of violent reprisals against him should he omit the ban. To this, the rest of the people objected, accusing the gaon of cowardice in his unwillingness to "separate these from those," that is, to continue the previous year's work of driving the ban like a wedge between the two camps. To the charges of cowardice the gaon retorted by arguing that excommunication was not the only means to separation: "And it was said to them, 'Before the ordained ones were imprisoned, did not the people of Ramla separate themselves from one another since they eat (meat) without inspection? Why should we renew [the ban]?' " Before last year's events, asked the gaon—that is, before we tried to revive the excommunication ritual—did we not possess other means of social separation from the Karaites? The Karaites and Rabbanites of Ramla had obtained separate butcher stalls—through halakhic legislation, he argued, we can achieve the same results as the ban, but without government intervention and without imprisonments. There may also be a hint in his statement that it is politically prudent to place the onus of separation on the Karaites: why should we be the ones to insist on separation, the gaon asked? Let them do so by plying their governmental connections—and let them also assume the risks of doing so. "But the people were not satisfied with this answer, and insisted upon the ban. And (then) they suggested writing a signed document (declaring the ban) and bringing it to every place. But it is not right in my eyes to do so, for he said (?) lest there be a reason (to take action against us)." Here some part of the crowd (or perhaps the elders?) suggested that Solomon declare the ban in written form: if the government objects to the public fracas, then why not decree it silently or even clandestinely in writing? But the gaon still refused, fearing that even a written ban could serve as a pretext for lashings and imprisonments. "And were they (the elders?) to allow (the Rabbanite masses) to behave as before, that excommunication would nearly bec[ome] the people's rupture. But they saw (fit) not to concede it, and the people went out with their complaints. But by the mercy of the Merciful One, there is peace here, and no one was harmed, and blessed be God, and all [the people] ascended [for] (Shemini) Aṣere[t] just as all . . ." (The fragment breaks off here.) The gaon therefore emerged as cooperating with Fatimid supervision, which in this case furthered his goal of building unity among the people. The Jews ascended the Mount of Olives on Hoshana Rabba after all, the ban was not declared, and they ascended a second time the day after Hoshana Rabba, on Shemini Aṣeret.

The Renewal of the Ban in 1038

The next we hear of the ban is in 1038, by which time several crucial changes had taken place in the array of forces.

In 1036, a new caliph ascended the throne, al-Mustanṣir, who was only seven years old at the time of his accession. His mother effectively ran the government during his minority; she had been a slave of Abraham al-Tustarī whom he gave to al-Ẓāhir as a concubine during the 1020s. As regent, she maintained her loyalty toward her former patron, and ultimately two of the three Tustarī brothers would be offered high positions in the Fatimid administration. Interestingly, with the caliph's accession, Abraham al-Tustarī nearly disappears from the genizah, while Ḥesed emerges in a new capacity: while before 1036, he was contacted in time of communal need, now his presence lurks in the background of rabbinic power struggles as patron and kingmaker. Three times between 1038 and 1082, Karaite patronage would prove decisive in rabbinic battles for high leadership posts. We also begin to hear for the first time of Rabbanite leaders cultivating the loyalties of the Karaite rank and file. The first to do so was a pretender to the Palestinian gaonate, Nathan ben Abraham, who for a four-year period between 1038 and 1042 managed to usurp all manner of geonic prerogatives from Solomon ben Judah, including the jealously guarded right to declare bans of excommunication. In part, it was Nathan's successful manipulation of Karaite support that helped him hold the geonic chair as long as he did.

The geonic schism erupted during the Sukkot pilgrimage festival of 1038. The only source we have describing the beginning of the affair is a letter written by a follower of Nathan ben Abraham according to which Solomon ben Judah's son Abraham—one of the three who had appeased the crowd by declaring the ban in 1029—stood up and excommunicated the Karaites on the Mount of Olives.[76] According to the letter, Abraham ben Solomon "excommunicated all those who desecrate the Lord's festivals as they have been passed down through tradition"—a formula that Nathan's follower sanctimoniously notes was "a thing normally unheard of." Abraham then returned the next day and declared the traditional ban "against the eaters of meat with milk." His purpose seems to have been to curry favor with the Rabbanite masses on his father's behalf by offering them the bread and circus they had demanded in 1029. He was perhaps also eager to ensure that declaring bans remained the exclusive purview of the legitimate gaon.

But the strategy backfired horribly. Nathan had meanwhile busied himself courting the Karaite grandees of Cairo, to whom he wrote a series of remarkably self-aggrandizing letters. Several months later he would declare himself leader of the Karaites of Ramla by holding a joint convocation on Purim in 1039, and promptly wrote to his Karaite patrons in Fustat, describing how the congregation had declared with one voice, "Blessed be the Lord who has united the two sects by your hand and in your *majlis*!"[77] Nathan's follower was therefore at pains to point out that in declaring the ban, Solomon's party had intended "to renew dissension among Israel, to multiply evil and to extol themselves. They were successful in this as long as people believed them to be pious, but now God has exposed their utter lack of piety. A great fracas ensued on the mountain, and no one enjoyed the pilgrimage."

Unfortunately, the letter offers too few details for us to know precisely how the crowd responded to Abraham's declaration of the ban. The letter would have us believe that Abraham's tactical error only served to alienate the large mass of Rabbanites from his father's camp—in marked contrast to what transpired in 1029, when declaring the ban had been the way to curry their support. But the letter makes one thing clear: by 1038, writer and addressee alike regarded the excommunication of the Karaites as a transparently self-serving mechanism, a measure of last resort that the rabbinic leadership used only to enhance its own status. As in 1029, the ban against the Karaites was declared only as a result of internal conflicts within the Rabbanite camp.

Conclusion: The Reorganization of Rabbinic Authority in the Eleventh Century

The excommunication affairs of 1029 and 1038 unfolded against the backdrop of harmonious dealings, close social ties, and even kinship relations between Rabbanites and Karaites in Egypt and Syria. One must therefore ask why tensions erupted when they did.

Anthropologists and sociologists have argued on the one hand that ritual creates social cohesion and on the other that it is a setting particularly conducive to communal strife and sectarian violence.[78] The rabbinic curia usually used the set of rituals constituting the ceremony on the Mount of Olives, in the holy city during the largest pilgrimage gathering of the year, to reinscribe its own *communitas,* with both the internal hierarchies and external ruptures that entails. The ceremony created conditions in which both the coherence of the collectivity and some essential fissures traversing it were on display as if in a vitrine or on a proscenium.

This is a phenomenological description, and brings us a certain distance toward understanding why the affair of the ban transpired as it did in 1029. But a diachronic and causal understanding of why the ceremony became a matter of contention both within and without the Rabbanite camp now in particular requires a consideration of the longer trajectory of Jewish politics over the course of the eleventh century. When the Rabbanites suddenly expressed their urgent desire to stake out the limits of their own terrain against the Karaites on the one hand and to oppose the political tactics of their leaders on the other, what motivated them to do so?

Over the course of the 1020s, the Karaite courtiers in Cairo had proven themselves increasingly indispensable to the Rabbanite leadership in Fustat, Jerusalem, Ramla, and even Baghdad. In the first decade of the eleventh century, Hayya Gaon enlisted the Tustarī trading partnership to convey responsa and donations to and from Baghdad, Fustat, and Kairouan; four decades later, he impressed upon his appointees in Fustat the indispensability of Tustarī patronage. From the 1020s through the 1050s at least, in Tyre and Fustat, Karaites and Rabbanites married one another; Karaites brought their business to the rabbinical courts; the scribes who ran them uncomplainingly wrote documents in conformity with their specifications; Karaites served as witnesses in Rabbanite contracts, and invited Rabbanites to witness theirs. Throughout the 1020s the Rabbanite communities of Alexandria, Ascalon, Jerusalem, and Tripoli supplicated the Karaite courtiers for aid, and the Jerusalem *geonim* availed themselves of the Karaite route to the chancery, particularly when it found it necessary to freeze out the Babylonian faction in Fustat. By the late 1020s, the Karaites had become essential allies of the Jerusalem *yeshivah;* by the late 1030s, they had become its kingmakers.

The Rabbanite laity, though perhaps only dimly aware of these shifts in communal operations, acted in such a way as to express their dissatisfaction with their leaders' growing enmeshment with the

Karaite courtiers. The excommunication affair therefore revealed a chasm between the leaders' eager cultivation of the Karaite grandees and their followers' resistance to such an idea.

But it was not merely the grandees who counted. As the century wore on, savvy rabbinic leaders became increasingly aware that it was necessary to bring the Karaite masses of Syria and Egypt aboard the new structure of governance. The groundwork had already been laid in the important communities: Tyre and Fustat boasted a history of easy mingling between denominations; in Jerusalem and Ramla, close quarters and high ideological stakes had bred a tense intimacy that was finally parlayed into willing cooperation. Over the course of the 1030s, the masses mingled with ever more frequency, planting seeds that took root at the *majlis* in Ramla on Purim in 1039, when Nathan ben Abraham presided as anti-gaon over Rabbanites and Karaites alike. Those stalks finally flowered in the second half of the eleventh century. In 1051, the gaon Daniel ben Azariah stood accused of acceding to the geonic chair with Karaite help. In 1082, his son, David ben Daniel, usurped the newly established office of head of the Jews in Fustat by breaking off his engagement to a Rabbanite woman in order to marry the daughter of a Karaite grandee. Only thus could he be assured of the support of the tripartite Jewish community: Babylonians, Palestinians, and Karaites alike.[79]

A certain style of politics—one characteristic of medieval Near Eastern societies in general—contributed to cooperation among the three Jewish congregations under Fatimid rule, from their merchant-courtiers and religious functionaries to their faceless masses. Among the Jews, patronage relationships used congregational differences to their advantage not because political utility rendered denominational commitments secondary, but because under particular conditions, the alliances that reached out across congregations proved to be the stable ones. The Rabbanite leadership had already begun moving toward a new model in which the local Jewish collectivity, regardless of rite or denomination, constituted the primary building block of the Jewish community under Islamic rule. That meant that the Jews of the Fatimid realm, whether they belonged to Iraqi, Syrian, or Karaite congregations, acted increasingly as one transdenominational organization, a development that culminated in the establishment of the office of head of the Jews in the 1060s. By 1029, the leadership had begun to adjust to a context in which the high-ranking members of those central institutions were untroubled by the need to garner Karaite support: they recognized the possibility and even the necessity of identifying sources of authority outside the immediate sphere of the *yeshivah.*

But in the 1020s, the Rabbanite masses were still wedded to an old congregational style of Jewish communal politics—what Goitein has called the "ecumenical" model, according to which loyalties divided according to which rite one followed (Syrian-Palestinian, Babylonian-Iraqi, or Karaite), regardless of where one actually lived. That is why during the ceremony of 1029 the masses unwittingly echoed the zealous champions of rabbinic hegemony of previous centuries: the fight against Karaism was one means of internal consolidation and self-differentiation.

The Karaites, for their part, were the quintessential exemplars of the new model of patronage, and this, perhaps more than anything, irked the Rabbanite masses. Even Karaite exogamy began to symbolize to the Rabbanites a kind of diffuse social structure that seemed part and parcel of the new model of authority. The struggles between the Karaite and Rabbanite communities and between the Rabbanite elite and the Rabbanite masses, then, were struggles over differing models of authority. One found its idiom in ritual, the other in politics.

Karaite participation was essential to this new model. This was so for two reasons: first, the Karaite functionaries in the Fatimid court and administration served the role that the Iraqi Rabbanites had before them—that of the Palestinian Rabbanites' main intercessors before the caliph. Second, the Rabbanite leaders who propounded the new model expressed ideals according to which Jewish communal unity was to be pursued even at the price of forgetting sectarian differences.

For the Rabbanite laity, there was the rub: they resented the new politics, which transcended sectarian difference, and chafed against the notion that they were now expected to join ranks with the Karaites for overarching communal purposes. They chafed even more against the idea that their leadership was now beholden to outside political forces for its survival. They sensed their leaders' dependence on exogenous power structures, that is, upon Karaite operatives at the Fatimid court. They had seen their leaders beseech the Karaites for help. For the vast majority, dependence on forces outside the immediate sphere of the Palestinian rabbinic hierarchy filled them with anxiety: were they to understand that their leaders lacked power in ways that made them dependent upon the very Karaites who for the past century in Jerusalem had set about demarcating a version of Judaism quite different from their own?

The Karaites' rejection of fundamental tenets of rabbinic law was an excellent pretext under which the masses could advocate for social separation from the "heretics"—but a pretext nonetheless. Except for the wording of the ban of excommunication itself, all of the tensions and resentments the Rabbanites expressed throughout the course of the ceremony and its aftermath were social and political rather than religious. The Rabbanite crowd wanted to have the Karaites banned less out of disagreement with their ways of practicing Judaism—religious differences had easily been surmounted in other circumstances—but as a response to the new prominence of Karaites in Jewish communal politics.

The excommunication controversy of 1029–30 shows the Jewish community in a transitional moment between the old model of ecumenical leadership with relative independence among local communities, on the one hand, and a new sort of territorial community that by the 1080s would combine Babylonians, Palestinians, and Karaites. It also shows that in 1029–30, the question of whether the Karaites would be included in the newly emerging body was still an open one. The Karaites were proving themselves to be as instrumental to Palestinian Rabbanite politics in Fustat as the Babylonians had been during the earlier part of the Fatimid period, and the leadership had accepted the fact of Karaite inclusion in the new structures of political authority. The Rabbanite crowd, by contrast, reacted to this shift with deep mistrust of the ties of dependence their gaon was forced to foster with Karaite bureaucrats and courtiers. Their efforts to deepen the distinction between themselves and the Karaite "heretics" demonstrates their wish to return to the old model of the tenth century wherein their political power over the Karaites—and their independence from them—was assured. All this manifested itself in the microcosm of the excommunication ceremony and its aftermath.

Excommunication is intended as a form of social death, but one cannot help noticing that those who lobbied for the excommunication succeeded only in becoming more embroiled with those they wished to cut off from the body of Israel. The excommunication ritual was in that sense a hopeful fiat, an act of wishful thinking, and an utter failure. In both the eleventh-century epistolary sources and Ibn Dāwūd's twelfth-century account, what emerges as a central theme and, to some extent, an open question is the place of the Karaites within a redefined rabbinic orthodoxy. In fact, all excommunicators are symbolically intertwined with the excommunicated, since both parties are vital to the maintenance of a religious orthodoxy. That is why the Karaites appear discursively, if not literally, at the heart of the Rabbanite ritual. That is also why the Karaites appear throughout Ibn Dāwūd's monument of traditionalist polemic as the accursed share, the condemned part on which the system rests—and why his fictionalized representation of the excommunication ceremony has the Karaites physically present to hear the ban declared "right to their faces."

Notes

My thanks to Albert I. Baumgarten, Menahem Ben-Sasson, Mark R. Cohen, Daniel Frank, Arnold Franklin, Ramzi Rouighi, Seth Schwartz, Michael Stanislawski, and Yosef Hayim Yerushalmi for their comments on earlier versions of this article, and to the fellows of the Center for Advanced Judaic Studies at the University of Pennsylvania who offered illuminating comments on an oral version I presented to them in October 2003.

1. See the painting of the scene by John Frazer, based on the literary and epistolary accounts cited below, at the Tower of David Museum, Jerusalem, reproduced in Eli Barnavi, *A Historical Atlas of the Jewish People: From the Time of the Patriarchs to the Present* (New York: Knopf, 1992), 89. The caption there erroneously states that the Karaites were "required to attend" the ceremony.
2. Gerson D. Cohen, *A Critical Edition with a Translation and Notes of the Book of Tradition (Sefer ha-Qabbalah) by Abraham Ibn Daud* (Philadelphia: Jewish Publication Society, 1967), 68 (Hebrew), 94 (English); I have altered Cohen's translation slightly. Like other twelfth-century Iberian authors—Judah Halevi and Judah Alḥarizi among them—Ibn Dāwūd refers to the Karaites merely as "heretics" (Heb. *minim*). For references, see Cohen, *Book of Tradition,* xxxviii, note 110, and Moshe Gil and Ezra Fleischer, *Yehuda ha-Levi and His Circle: Fifty-five Genizah Documents* (Hebrew) (Jerusalem: World Union of Jewish Studies, 2001), 183n46.
3. Around the time of the Saljūq conquest of Jerusalem in 1073, the *yeshivah* moved to Tyre; the pilgrimage convocations were held there and, by 1082, in Haifa. See Moshe Gil, *A History of Palestine, 634–1099,* 3 vols. (Hebrew) (Tel Aviv: Tel Aviv University and the Ministry of Defense, 1983); vol. 1 appears in English as *A History of Palestine, 634–1099,* trans. Ethel Broido (Cambridge: Cambridge University Press, 1993), sec. 899. (I cite the first volume of this work by section rather than page number to facilitate cross-referencing the Hebrew and English.)
4. Joshua Prawer, *The History of the Jews in the Latin Kingdom of Jerusalem* (Oxford: Clarendon, 1988): 46–49 (on the Jewish population of Crusader Jerusalem); see also chap. 6 (on Jewish pilgrims) and chap. 7 (on travel accounts).
5. Cohen, *Book of Tradition,* xv.
6. Ibn Dāwūd in ibid., 67 (Hebrew), 92 (English).
7. Ibid., 68 (Hebrew), 93 (English). I have deviated slightly from Cohen's translation. For a valuable survey of medieval Karaite habitations based on toponymic and

other data see Judith Olszowy-Schlanger, *Karaite Marriage Documents from the Cairo Geniza: Legal Tradition and Community Life in Mediaeval Egypt and Palestine,* Etudes sur le judaïsme médiéval 20 (Leiden: Brill, 1998), 46–68.

8. Cohen, *Book of Tradition,* xliii–lxii.
9. Ezra Fleischer, "Pilgrims' Prayer at the Gates of Jerusalem" (Hebrew), in *Mas'at Moshe: Studies in Jewish and Islamic Culture Presented to Moshe Gil* (Hebrew), ed. Fleischer, M. A. Friedman, and J. A. Kraemer (Tel Aviv: Tel Aviv University Press, 1998), 298–32; Sahl ben Maṣliaḥ, *Sefer ha-Miṣvot,* in A. Harkavy, *Me'assef Niddaḥim* 1 no. 13 (St. Petersburg, 1879; reprint, Jerusalem, 1969), 198, 203; Haggai Ben-Shammai, "A Unique Lamentation on Jerusalem by the Karaite author Yeshuah ben Judah" (Hebrew), *Mas'at Moshe,* 93–102; H. Z. Hirschberg, "On the Mount of Olives in the Geonic Period" (Hebrew), *Bulletin of the Jewish Palestine Exploration Society* 13 (1947): 156–64; Moshe Gil, "Migration to Palestine and Pilgrimage during the First Period of Islamic Occupation (634–1099)" (Hebrew), *Cathedra* 8 (1978): 124–33, with responses by S. Safrai, A. Grossman, and Ben-Shammai; Gil, *A History of Palestine,* 1: secs. 831–34, and doc. 290 (T-S 10 J 9.19); the memorial list in Jacob Mann, *Texts and Studies in Jewish History and Literature* (Cincinnati: Hebrew Union College Press, 1931–35; reprint, New York: Ktav, 1972), 2:260, ll. 50–54; Prawer, *History of the Jews in the Latin Kingdom,* 138; Elchanan Reiner, "Pilgrims and Pilgrimage to Eretz Yisrael, 1099–1517" (Hebrew) (Ph.D. diss., Hebrew University, 1988); and Y. Rozenson, "'While the People Ascended to Celebrate Three Times': On the Pilgrimage to the Mount of Olives in Ancient Liturgical Poetry from the Land of Israel" (Hebrew), *Sinai* 117 (1996): 176–85.
10. Because both Christians and Muslims had aimed similar quantitative argumentation against the Jews, for a Jew to turn it against a minority within his own religion was an audacious step with potentially grave consequences: it legitimized the method of argument while shifting its target to a different minority. See Cohen, *The Book of Tradition,* introduction, lix–lx.
11. JTS Schechter Geniza, 17r–18v; cited in Gil, A *History of Palestine,* 1: sec. 930; cf. citations in sec. 837.
12. Daniel ben Moses al-Qūmisī, *Pitron Sheneim-asar* (Commentary on the twelve minor prophets), ed. I. Markon (Jerusalem: Mekize Nirdamim, 1957), 8. Cf. al-Qūmisī's epistle, Mann, "A Tract by an Early Karaite Settler in Jerusalem," 280. On Japheth, see Daniel Frank, *Search Scripture Well: Karaite Exegetes and the Origins of the Jewish Bible Commentary in the Islamic East* (Leiden: Brill, 2004), 162–63.
13. Judah Hadassi, *Eshkol ha-Kofer* (The cluster of henna blossoms), alph. 123. Cited in Naphtali Wieder, *The Judean Scrolls and Karaism* (London: East and West Library, 1962), 203n2 and 260–61n3.
14. Ibn Dāwūd in Cohen, *Book of Tradition,* 72 (Hebrew), 99–101 (English).
15. For a detailed elaboration of this argument, see Marina Rustow, "Rabbanite-Karaite Relations in Fatimid Egypt and Syria: A Study Based on Documents from the Cairo Geniza" (Ph.D. diss., Columbia University, 2004).
16. The Palestinian *yeshivah* had been holding its convocations on the Mount of Olives since the late ninth century (Hirschberg, "On the Mount of Olives," 158–61). The chronographer al-Bīrunī (973–1048) writes ca. 1000 that "on the last day of the holiday of Tabernacles, which is its seventh day and the twenty-first day of the month called Arava, when there were clouds over the heads of the Israelites in the Sinai wilderness—on this day is Hoshana Rabba, for the Jews gather on the Mount of

Olives [Arab. *fī hārharā,* probably a scribal corruption of Heb. *har ha-zeitim*] in Jerusalem and pilgrims circumambulate with the ark, which in their synagogues is like the *minbar*." For all this ethnographic detail, al-Bīrunī makes no mention of the ban (Muḥammad Ibn Aṃad al-Bīrunī, *al-Āthār al-bāqiya 'an al-qurūn al-khāliya* [The remaining traces of bygone ages], ed. E. Sachau as *Chronologie orientalischer Völker* [Leipzig, 1923], 277; cf. idem, *The Chronology of Ancient Nations* [London, 1879], 270, from which my translation differs; cf. Gil, *A History of Palestine,* 1: sec. 832). The Karaite treatise: Sahl ben Maṣliaḥ vituperates against the enemies of the Karaites because they "make themselves mighty and exhibit excessive pride and lord it over them [the Karaites] with anathema and ban of excommunication and [resort to] the government." This is as clear an indication of Rabbanite excommunication of the Karaites as one might hope for from tenth-century literary sources, but we are not told how and when the ban was imposed (S. Pinsker, *Lickute Kadmoniot: Zur Geschichte des Karaismus und der karäischen Literatur* [Vienna, 1860] 2:31, bottom). Mann connects this passage with Japheth's commentary on Song of Songs 5:7, where he accuses the Rabbanites of inviting government intervention in their conflict with the Karaites, but there is no reference to the excommunication in this passage (*Texts and Studies,* 2:89–90 [and see n. 117], edited there from MS 2 Firk. Heb.-Arab. 3869, but without attribution to Japheth; for a full edition of Japheth's commentary, see J. J. L. Bargès, ed., *In Canticum canticorum commentarium arabicum* . . . [Paris, 1884], this passage on 73–74; and see Frank, *Search Scripture Well,* 162–63). See also the eleventh-century interpolations to the fifteenth-century manuscript of a *midrash* on Ecclesiastes (JTS mic. 5592/2), cited in M. Hirshman, "The Priest's Gate and Elijah ben Menaḥem's Pilgrimage: Medieval Interpolations in Midrash Manuscripts" (Hebrew), *Tarbiz* 55 (1986): 217–26 and *Tarbiz* 60 (1991): 275–76.

17. On the earlier end, this may have owed to extenuating circumstances: during the period of al-Ḥākim's persecutions of *dhimmīs* (ca. 1011–20), public assemblies were probably prohibited, and shortly thereafter the Jarraḥid rebellion against Fatimid rule in 1024–29 brought pilgrim traffic to a near standstill and, one imagines, suspended the ceremony temporarily. For the remainder of the eleventh century, references to the Karaites are conspicuously absent from descriptions of the pilgrimage ceremony.
18. Gil, *A History of Palestine,* 1: secs. 828–32.
19. Cf. S. Poznanski, "Éphraim b. Schemariah de Fostat et l'académie palestinienne," *Revue des études juives* 48 (1903): 153; Gil, *A History of Palestine,* 1: secs. 831–34. For a brief reference to the ceremony on Hoshana Rabbah and the confirmation of members of the *yeshivah* in their positions, see T-S NS 320.42, in Arabic and Hebrew, first ed. (attributed to Solomon ben Judah before he acceded to the gaonate), S. D. Goitein, "New Sources on the Palestinian Gaonate," in *Salo Wittmayer Baron Jubilee Volume on the Occasion of His Eightieth Birthday,* ed. S. Lieberman and A. Hyman (Jerusalem and New York: American Academy for Jewish Research; distributed by Columbia University Press, 1974), 1:503–37, here 529 (shelf-mark incorrectly listed as T-S 320.16), with translation and commentary, 507–15; 2nd ed., with substantially different readings in Gil, *A History of Palestine,* 2: doc. 141 (who attributes the letter to Abraham ben Solomon ben Judah, ca. 1045).
20. Menaḥem Ben-Sasson, seminar presentation at the Center for Advanced Judaic Studies, University of Pennsylvania, October 2003. See also Ben-Sasson, "The

Structure, Goals, and Content of the Story of Nathan ha-Bavli," in *Culture and Society in Medieval Jewish History: Studies Dedicated to the Memory of Haim Hillel Ben-Sasson* (Hebrew), ed. Menaḥem Ben-Sasson, R. Bonfil, and J. Hacker (Jerusalem: Zalman Shazar Center, 1989), 137–96; and Ben-Sasson, "Varieties of Inter-Communal Relations in the Geonic Period," in *The Jews of Medieval Islam: Community, Society, and Identity,* ed. Daniel Frank (Leiden: Brill, 1995), 17–31.

21. The question of when the *geonim* declared the calendar for the upcoming year has occasioned some confusion: a geonic commentary states that the decision about intercalating the year was reached during the month of Av, but according to genizah documents, the senior members of the *yeshivah* agreed upon it during the pilgrimage season in Tishrei and announced it formally on Hoshana Rabba. Goitein, "New Sources," 510–11, note to line 3; cf. Mann, *Texts and Studies,* 1:316n11, and Gil, *A History of Palestine,* 1: sec. 784.
22. Cambridge University Library, T-S 10 J 29.13, in Judeo-Arabic, line 23; first edition in Gil, *A History of Palestine,* 2: doc. 205. See also Goitein, *A Mediterranean Society: The Jewish Communities of the Arab World as Portrayed in the Documents of the Cairo Geniza,* 6 vols. (Berkeley: University of California Press, 1967–93), 2:555n44, and Gil, *A History of Palestine,* 1: sec. 936.
23. Rustow, "Rabbanite-Karaite Relations," chap. 6.
24. A ban therefore had to be made known as widely as possible if it was to be effective—especially since Jews in the Islamic-Mediterranean orbit were so geographically mobile. Those punished with a ban often attempted to escape its purview by fleeing to another town, and the law caught up with some but not all of them, as genizah documents attest. See Goitein, *A Mediterranean Society,* 2:333, especially T-S 13 J 26.6v, a fragment of a letter about a polygamous husband who had been placed under a ban in Fustat and Dammūh for taking a second wife, and then fled to Qūṣ in Upper Egypt; published in M. A. Friedman, *Jewish Polygyny: New Sources from the Cairo Genizah* (Hebrew) (Jerusalem: Bialik Institute, 1986), 267–69. Cf. also Mann, *The Responsa of the Babylonian Geonim as a Source of Jewish History* (Philadelphia: Dropsie College, 1917; reprint, New York: Arno Press, 1973), 348.
25. Mann, *The Responsa of the Babylonian Geonim,* 351–57 (note that the examples Mann cites on 363–64 refer rather to judicial imprecations); Goitein, *A Mediterranean Society,* 2:331–33; Gil, *A History of Palestine,* 1: secs. 757–60; and Elinoar Bareket, *Fustat on the Nile: The Jewish Elite in Medieval Egypt,* The Medieval Mediterranean 24 (Leiden: Brill, 1999), 66–68. See also Goitein, *A Mediterranean Society,* 1:259 (a late debtor), 2:114–15 (a statute for late tenants stipulating excommunication); and Friedman, *Jewish Polygyny,* 242–45 (excommunication against a polygamous husband, Bodl. MS Heb. d. 76.56, also published in Gil, *A History of Palestine,* 2: doc. 148).
26. Yosef Kaplan, "The Social Functions of the Herem in the Portuguese Jewish Community of Amsterdam in the Seventeenth Century," in *Dutch Jewish History: Proceedings of the Symposium on the History of the Jews in the Netherlands,* ed. Jozeph Michman and Tirtsah Levie (Jerusalem: Tel Aviv University, 1984), 120. Kaplan argues that excommunication is a double-edged sword because it subverts the rabbis' intentions by driving the banned party out of the Jewish community once and for all. The genizah attests to conversion to Islam among excommunicated Jews, and thus Kaplan's theory certainly holds there as well, but what interests me here

is rather how unobserved excommunications in and of themselves weakened rabbinic authority.

27. That the *geonim* were aware of the dangers of overusing the ban is evident in a letter of Solomon ben Judah's successor Daniel ben Azariah (acceded to the gaonate in 1051) to the Fustat *ḥaver* Eli ben Amram, where he instructs him that there is no need to excommunicate a certain teacher whose "stature is less than what would necessitate writing a ban" (Judeo-Arab., *qadaruh aqall mimā yaḥtāj ilā kitāb bi-ḥaramih*). T-S Box Misc. 25.132r and 139, second fragment, ll. 4–5, first published in Goitein, *Palestinian Jewry in Early Islamic and Crusader Times in Light of Geniza Documents* (Hebrew) (Jerusalem: Ben-Zvi Institute, 1980), 183–85, cited in this connection in Gil, *A History of Palestine,* 1: sec. 757.
28. Support for this point might be mustered from studies of excommunication as a form of word-magic. See especially Lester Little, *Benedictine Maledictions: Liturgical Cursing in Romanesque France* (Ithaca: Cornell University Press, 1993). In medieval Judaism excommunications were also sometimes accompanied by magical curses: the Cairo Genizah has preserved four formularies and one actual written ban from eleventh- and twelfth-century Egypt that are similar to curses found in Egyptian magical papyri and Mesopotamian incantation bowls. See Gershon Weiss, "Shetar Herem—Excommunication Formulary: Five Documents from the Cairo Geniza," *Gratz College Annual of Jewish Studies* 6 (1977): 98–120, and compare with the texts in Joseph Naveh and Shaul Shaked, *Amulets and Magic Bowls: Aramaic Incantations of Late Antiquity* (Jerusalem: Magnes Press, Hebrew University; Leiden: distributed by Brill, 1985); Naveh and Shaked, *Magic Spells and Formulae: Aramaic Incantations of Late Antiquity* (Jerusalem: Magnes Press, Hebrew University, 1993); and Lawrence H. Schiffman and Michael D. Swartz, *Hebrew and Aramaic Incantation Texts from the Cairo Genizah: Selected Texts from Taylor-Schechter Box K1* (Sheffield: JSOT Press, 1992).
29. On illness as an excuse for delays in correspondence and business-related travel, see Goitein, *A Mediterranean Society,* 5:103–16.
30. T-S Misc 35.11 (Hebrew). First edition in Mann, *Text and Studies,* 1:315–16 (see also his comments on 310–11); second in Gil, *A History of Palestine,* 2: doc. 85. In my translations, square brackets enclose reconstructions of textual lacunae, and parentheses contain words I have added to aid the reader's comprehension of the text. For detailed linguistic notes and discussion of textual emendations to all genizah documents cited in this article, see Rustow, "Rabbanite-Karaite relations," chap. 7.
31. T-S 13 J 36.5, in Judeo-Arabic, dated May 7, 1029. First edition: Goitein, "A History of the Palestinian Gaonate" (Hebrew), *Shalem* 1 (1974): 15–51 (ed. with Hebrew trans. 36–44), reprinted with additions in *Palestinian Jewry,* 97–103. Reedited with Hebrew translation in Gil, *A History of Palestine,* 2: doc. 80. The quotation is from verso, lines 20–23. In the letter's continuation Solomon warns his son in no uncertain terms that political caution dictates not involving himself in Karaite-Rabbanite disputes.
32. ENA 2804.12–13 (Hebrew). First edition in Mann, *The Jews in Egypt and in Palestine under the Fatimid Caliphs: A Contribution to Their Political and Communal History, Based Chiefly on Genizah Material Hitherto Unpublished,* 2 vols. (London: Oxford University Press, 1920–22), 2:142–45 (listed there as ENA 2804.8); second in Gil, *A History of Palestine,* 2: doc. 75. T-S 13 J 17.17 (Hebrew). First full edition in Mann,

"A Note on Solomon b. Judah and Some of His Contemporaries," *Jewish Quarterly Review* n.s. 9 (1918–19): 415; second in Gil, *A History of Palestine,* 2: doc. 64.

33. T-S 24.43 (Hebrew): letter of ca. 1025 in which Solomon ha-Kohen ben Yehosef, having been appointed gaon by the curia of the Jerusalem *yeshivah,* solicits confirmation in office from the chancery of the caliph al-Ẓāhir (1021–36). First edition in Goitein, "New sources," 531–32 (doc. 2), with English translation and commentary, 517–23, and facsimile, 534–35. Goitein dated the letter to 1022–24, but Gil has shown that Solomon ha-Kohen ben Yehosef served as gaon for less than a year, in 1025. See also Goitein, *A Mediterranean Society,* 2:16–17.
34. On gossip as social aggression see James C. Scott, *Domination and the Arts of Resistance: Hidden Transcripts* (New Haven: Yale University Press, 1990): 142–44. Scott draws a distinction between gossip and rumor: in his analysis, rumor is supplied anonymously and repeated widely in the absence of reliable information, whereas gossip (whether true or untrue) is generally intended to damage reputations, often of those in power. The rumor I describe here partakes of both categories; I use the term "rumor" without respect to Scott's distinction.
35. See, e.g., Salmon ben Yerūḥīm's *Sefer Milḥamot Adonai* (Book of the Wars of the Lord), ed. I. Davidson (New York: Jewish Theological Seminary, 1934), 36, 41–42; Ze'ev Elkin, "The Karaite version of *Sefer ha-Ḥilluqim bein Benei Ereṣ-Yisrael li-Venei Bavel*" (Hebrew), *Tarbiz* 66 (1996): 101–11, with references to earlier studies.
36. For rabbinic and Karaite texts attributing holiness to the site, see Gil, *A History of Palestine,* 1: sec. 831.
37. Mann, *Texts and Studies,* 1:316n8, and Gil, *A History of Palestine,* 1: sec. 937, identify this "third" as Tobiah ben Daniel.
38. Robert Brody, *The Geonim of Babylonia and the Shaping of Medieval Jewish Culture* (New Haven: Yale University Press, 1998), 96–99. On a general level as well, Saadya extended and bolstered the concept of a divinely revealed Oral Law, as against discretionary scriptural exegesis. For a helpful analysis of the shift in rabbinic thinking that he occasioned, see Jay Harris, *How Do We Know This? Midrash and the Fragmentation of Modern Judaism* (Albany: State University of New York Press, 1995): 76–81.
39. Goitein, *A Mediterranean Society* 2:58–60. Cf. Goitein, "The Local Jewish Community in the Light of the Cairo Geniza Records," *Journal of Jewish Studies* 12 (1961): 144–45, where he points out, on the basis of T-S 13 J 30.5, that the elders were formally appointed.
40. The governor of Jerusalem in 1025 was Abū Naṣr Fatḥ al-Qal'ī, known as Mubārak al-Dawla wa-Sa'īduha ("Blessed and auspicious one of the Realm"); see the sources cited in Thierry Bianquis, *Damas et la Syrie sous la domination fatimide 359–468/969–1076: essai d'interprétation de chroniques arabes médiévales,* 2 vols. (Damascus: Institut français de Damas, 1986), 317n2. I do not know whether he still held this post in 1029.
41. As stated in Cambridge University Library Or. 1080 J45r (Hebrew); see line 5. First edition in Gil, *A History of Palestine,* 2: doc. 182. Gil surmises that Solomon ben Judah married Solomon ha-Kohen's sister, so that his son was cousin to the latter's sons (*A History of Palestine,* 1: sec. 858).
42. Gil, *A History of Palestine,* 1: sec. 863, argues that the three youths were "stubbornly fanatic" in proclaiming the ban, but their motives may have been merely pragmatic in view of the need to appease the crowd.

43. Neither Mann, Goitein, nor Gil identifies the figure referred to in this letter as al-Duzbarī; to Gil's list of the titles al-Duzbarī held should accordingly be added Mu'tazz al-Dawla, "Mighty One of the Realm" (*A History of Palestine,* 1: sec. 384). Gil also notes an inscription preserved in the travel account of Nāṣir Khusraw in which al-Duzbarī is called *layth al-dawla* (lion of the realm); *A History of Palestine,* 1: sec. 593n. For a list of medieval historiographic and biographical sources on al-Duzbarī, see S. M. Stern, *Fāṭimid Decrees: Original Documents from the Fāṭimid Chancery* (London: Faber and Faber, 1964), 30n1. For details on al-Duzbarī's career, and especially his repression of the Jarrāḥid revolt in Palestine in 1024–29, see Gil, *A History of Palestine,* 1: secs. 584–94, and Bianquis, *Damas et la Syrie,* 424–523.
44. On the possibility Abraham ben Solomon ben Judah was spared because of his father's position, see Mann, *Texts and Studies,* 1:311, and Goitein, *A Mediterranean Society,* 5:369.
45. T-S 13 J 33.12 (Hebrew). First edition in Mann, *The Jews in Egypt and in Palestine* 2:155–57 (see earlier citations there); second in Gil, *A History of Palestine,* 2: doc 121. See comments of Mann, *The Jews in Egypt and in Palestine,* 2:380n and 1:139–40; Mann, *Texts and Studies,* 2:63–64; Gil, *A History of Palestine,* 1: secs. 274, 741, 817, 834, 930.
46. Islamic law dictated that daughters inherited half of what their brothers inherited, whereas under Jewish law, daughters would not inherit at all when they had brothers. The genizah attests to Jewish women who pursued inheritance claims in Islamic courts, even though rabbinic authorities frowned upon any action that might compromise *dhimmī* legal autonomy. See Goitein, *A Mediterranean Society,* 2:395–407; Gil, *A History of Palestine,* 1: sec. 274.
47. An allusion to the talmudic dictum associating women with magical practices; BT Sanhedrin 67a.
48. ENA 4010.32 (Judeo-Arabic), first edition in Gil, *A History of Palestine,* 3: doc. 433. On the role of the *parnasim,* see Goitein, *A Mediterranean Society,* 2:77–82.
49. Lines 11–12. Gil suggests that it may have been the Fatimid authorities who broke the chair (*A History of Palestine,* 3:35, notes to doc. 433); Goitein thinks it was the Karaites (*A Mediterranean Society,* 5:369). Until the left side of the letter is found, Goitein's interpretation fits better in the context of the events.
50. T-S 13 J 13.28 + T-S AS 120.62 (Hebrew). First edition in Marmorstein, "Solomon b. Judah and Some of His Contemporaries," *Jewish Quarterly Review* n.s. 8 (1917–18), 21–22; second in Mann, *The Jews in Egypt and in Palestine,* 2:152–55, with partial translation and comments in ibid., 1:136–39; third in Gil, *A History of Palestine,* 2: doc. 90. See also Mann's corrections to Marmorstein's readings and interpretations of the letter in "Note on 'Solomon b. Judah and Some of His Contemporaries,'" *Jewish Quarterly Review* n.s. 9 (1918–19): 409–21 (here, 417–21).
51. Abu l-Qāsim 'Alī ibn Aḥmad al-Jarjarā'ī (d. 1045) was one of the more colorful characters to have held the Fatimid vizierate. While serving in high office under al-Ḥākim, he had both of his hands and forearms cut off for malfeasance; he nonetheless continued to serve under al-Ẓāhir, who appointed him *wāsiṭa* and then *wazīr,* and he continued to serve under al-Mustanṣir until his death. See Paul Walker, *Exploring an Islamic Empire: Fatimid History and Its Sources,* Ismaili Heritage Series 7 (London: I. B. Tauris, 2002): 46, 106–7 (and the sources he cites at 214nn14–16). Gil, *A History of Palestine,* 1: sec 803n (end) has al-Jarjarā'ī's appointment in 1027, but his calculation should be corrected to 1028.

52. 1024: T-S 12.273, in Hebrew. First edition in Bareket, *The Jews of Egypt, 1007–55: On the Basis of the Archive of Ephraim ben Shemariah* (Hebrew) (Jerusalem: Ben-Zvi Institute, 1995), doc. 30. See Gil, *A History of Palestine,* 1: sec. 803n and quotations in Shulamit Sela, "The Headship of the Jews in the Fatimid Empire in Karaite Hands" (Hebrew), in *Mas'at Moshe,* 260n16; see also Bareket, *"Shafrir Miṣrayim": The Jewish Leadership in Fustat in the First Half of the Eleventh Century* (Hebrew) (Tel Aviv: Diaspora Research Institute, Tel Aviv University, 1995), 250. See also T-S 18 J 4.26 (Hebrew); first edition in Mann, *The Jews in Egypt and in Palestine,* 2:139–41; second in Gil, *A History of Palestine,* 2: doc. 47. Gil dates this letter to the end of 1024; see his note to line 26. The letter was begun by Josiah Gaon who was evidently too ill to finish it, and completed by his successor-to-be Solomon ha-Kohen ben Yehosef; Josiah died in March 1025. Spring 1029: T-S 13 J 36.5, in Judeo-Arabic, dated May 7, 1029. First edition: Goitein, "A History of the Palestinian Gaonate" (Hebrew), 15–51 (ed. with Hebrew trans. 36–44), reprinted with additions in *Palestinian Jewry,* 97–103. Reedited with a new Hebrew translation in Gil, *A History of Palestine,* 2: doc. 80. On the situation in Palestine, the Jews of Jerusalem, and the gaon's appeals during this period, see Gil, *A History of Palestine,* 1: secs. 590 and 780.
53. See Gil, *A History of Palestine,* 1: sec. 879 (on Mevorakh); his daughter would eventually marry Nathan ben Abraham, leader of the putsch against Solomon ben Judah in 1038 in which the Karaites emerged as key players (see below, 1, 232–33)—but for the moment the two were still allied.
54. T-S AS 153.12 (top) + T-S 13 J 25.20 (bottom), a writ of agency for the betrothal of a Karaite woman in Tyre, 1026–27 (conjectural). Assaf published the bottom portion of the deed (*Yerushalayim* 1 [1953]: 106–7) but was unaware that the top fragment also existed. Friedman noted the join in *Jewish Marriage in Palestine: A Cairo Genizah Study,* 2 vols. (Tel Aviv: Tel Aviv University, 1980), 1:218n5, but when Gil republished the bottom fragment (*A History of Palestine,* 2: doc. 272), he missed the top one. He later published the top section in his supplement to the latter work (*Te'uda* 7 [1991]: 324–25) and acknowledged Friedman's footnote. Goitein was likely unaware of the top fragment, since in discussing the bottom one he seems unaware that David ben Isaac, whose *kunya* is revealed only in the opening lines of the letter, is the Karaite notable in question (line 6 of the top fragment). Cf. Olszowy-Schlanger, *Karaite Marriage Documents,* 56n95. Goitein is the only one who has transliterated the name of the betrothed correctly into English as Dhukhr (*A Mediterranean Society* 3:57 and 439n39).
55. Rustow, "Rabbanite-Karaite Relations," chap. 3.
56. ENA 4010.32, l. 18 (see above, note 48). But cf. Goitein, *A Mediterranean Society* 5:369, who asserts that the gaon never made it to Damascus. In all probability, Eli ben Ezekiel wrote his letter after the letter from Solomon under discussion, although he describes earlier events, including the arrest of the brothers.
57. Cf. the similar decree issued some time before 1021: T-S Misc. 20.92 (Arabic). First edition in Geoffrey Khan, *Arabic Legal and Administrative Documents in the Cambridge Geniza Collections* (Cambridge: Cambridge University Press, 1993), doc. 115. Evidently the earlier decree fell into desuetude and the later one attempted to revive it.
58. On the Karaite prohibition on consuming pregnant animals, see the tract cited in Gil, *A History of Palestine,* 1: sec. 930, and the additional references he offers there.

59. Arab. *kull ṭā'ifa min al-ṭā'ifatayn min al-rabbānīn wa-l-qarā'iyīn min al-yahūd.* The text is garbled here; perhaps the intermediate phrase was added as an afterthought in further specification.
60. Arab. *kull man yatamadhhab hādhayn al-madhhabayn.*
61. T-S 13 J 7. 29, in Judeo-Arabic, first edited in Goitein, "A Caliph's Decree in Favour of the Rabbinite [*sic*] Jews of Palestine," *Journal of Jewish Studies* 5 (1954): 118–25 (here, 123), with commentary and English translation, which I have altered; republished in Arabic transliteration in Stern, *Fāṭimid Decrees,* 32–33; reedited by Gil, *A History of Palestine,* 2: doc. 310. The text is parallel to that of a decree in favor of the Karaites, the Arabic original of which was preserved in the archives of the Egyptian Karaite community. Richard Gottheil edited the second decree in "A Decree in Favour of the Karaites of Cairo dated 1024 [*sic*]," *Festschrift zu Ehren des Dr. A. Harkavy* (St. Petersburg, 1908): 115–25. S. M. Stern reedited it, but without seeing the original document, in *Fāṭimid Decrees,* 23–26 (see also his comments in introduction, 12–14). Gil dates both decrees to 1034, the first one speculatively (previous scholars had dated it to some time after 1026), and the second on the basis of a photostat of the document at the Jewish National Library in Jerusalem: where Gottheil read A. H. 415 (1024 C.E.), Gil reads A. H. 425 (1034 C.E.) (*A History of Palestine,* 1: sec. 783n and 2:565). The difference between the two dates is not irrelevant to our purposes here: was the decree the *reason* the authorities intervened in 1029 (as Mann and Goitein supposed, surmising that the state of war in Palestine had accounted for the five-year delay in its enforcement), or did it come several years later as the Karaite *response* to the excommunication and the events that followed it (an interpretation that finds support in my reading above)?
62. Mosseri V2 142 (L. 210) (Hebrew). Attribution of authorship is Gil's. First edition in Gil, *A History of Palestine,* 2: doc. 327; see also 1: secs. 801, 937, and n. 77.
63. T-S 13 J 19.16 and T-S 13 J 16.15 (Judeo-Arabic). First edition by Baneth, published posthumously by Gil, in Baneth, "A Letter from Solomon ben Judah, Gaon of the Jerusalem *yeshivah,* to an Anonymous Party in Fustat" (Hebrew), *Studia orientalia memoriae D. H. Baneth dedicata* (Jerusalem: Magnes Press, 1979), Hebrew sec., 1–16, with a facsimile of the first document after page 179 (Hebrew sec.). Second edition in Gil, *A History of Palestine,* 2: doc. 92. Baneth and Gil each prepared Hebrew translations with their editions, although their editions and translations differ from each other in significant ways and neither is clear in every place. Goitein, who called this a "precious but difficult document" (*A Mediterranean Society,* 2:555n43), noted that Baneth stalled for some time in publishing his edition; he had prepared it already in the 1960s but it waited until after his death to see light of day (Goitein, "New sources," 520n30; cf. *A Mediterranean Society,* 5:610n46). Even Solomon's contemporaries had some difficulty understanding the letter: the second shelf-mark refers to a copy written in Fustat in the handwriting of a scribe whom Gil identifies as Ghālib ha-Kohen ben Moses, the son-in-law of Ephraim ben Shemariah; the first copy is in the gaon's hand (Gil, *A History of Palestine,* 2:170; Mann linked the two documents for the first time, *The Jews in Egypt and in Palestine,* 1:146, with partial edition). But Ghālib's copy differs from Solomon's original, evidently because Ghālib himself, though fluent in Judeo-Arabic, did not understand the text entirely (Gil, introduction to Baneth, "A Letter," 1, first

proposed that some of the scribe's emendations were motivated by a faulty understanding of the text).

64. See Mann's edition of al-Qūmisī's text, "A Tract," 283. English translation in Leon Nemoy, "The Pseudo-Qumisian Sermon to the Karaites," *Proceedings of the American Academy for Jewish Research* 43 (1976): 49–105, and in Nemoy, *Karaite Anthology: Excerpts from the Early Literature,* Yale Judaica Series 7 (New Haven: Yale University Press, 1952), 38. See also the later Karaite quotations adduced by Wieder, *The Judean Scrolls and Karaism,* 71–72.
65. For the full connotations of this epithet, see Zvi Ankori, *Karaites in Byzantium: The Formative Years, 970–1100,* Columbia Studies in the Social Sciences 597 (New York: Columbia University Press, 1959), 420, quoting an eleventh-century Byzantine Karaite use of this term, and n. 177; see also his citation at 211n14 of al-Qūmisī's commentary to Dan. 11:35 (which Ankori incorrectly cites as 11:36); Wieder, *The Judean Scrolls and Karaism,* 104–17; and Frank, *Search Scripture Well,* 165–66.
66. Salmon ben Yerūḥīm, *Sefer Milḥamot Adonai* (see above, note 35), 37 l. 47; in English translation, Nemoy, *Karaite Anthology,* 73 (and see 341, note to line 12); Japheth in Frank, *Search Scripture Well,* 165.
67. Al-Qirqisānī, *Kitāb al-anwār wa-l-marāqib,* 5 vols., ed. Leon Nemoy (New York: Alexander Kohut Memorial Foundation, 1939–43), 1:6–14, trans. in Nemoy, *A Karaite Anthology,* 45–53 (cf. idem, "Al-Qirqisānī's Account of the Jewish Sects and Christianity," *Hebrew Union College Annual* 7 [1930]: 324–25, where the passage is truncated); and in Bruno Chiesa and Wilfrid Lockwood, *Ya'qūb al-Qirqisānī on Jewish Sects and Christianity: A Translation of "Kitāb al-anwār," Book I, With Two Introductory Essays* (Frankfurt: Peter Lang, 1984), 99–100.
68. *Sefer Milḥamot Adonai,* 131. Cf. Salo W. Baron, *A Social and Religious History of the Jews,* 2nd ed. (New York: Columbia University Press, 1957), 5:285.
69. See Elliott S. Horowitz, "The Rite to Be Reckless: On the Perpetration and Interpretation of Purim Violence," *Poetics Today* 15 (1994): 9–54.
70. Goitein, *A Mediterranean Society,* 5:369; cf. Gil, *A History of Palestine,* 1: sec. 937n21, and Baneth, "A Letter," 12 (subheading).
71. On Abū 'Alī Muḥsin, see Goitein, "New Sources," 518–20.
72. Goitein, *A Mediterranean Society,* 5:369, offers that it is the Karaites who are being banned here, but this interpretation is difficult to reconcile with the immediate context of the letter.
73. Bodl. MS Heb. c 13.23, in Hebrew. First edition in Poznanski, "Éphraim b. Schemariah," 172–73; reedited by Gil, *A History of Palestine,* 2: doc. 122. See comments of Mann, *The Jews in Egypt and in Palestine,* 1:139; Gil, *A History of Palestine,* 1: sec. 833; and Bareket, *Fustat on the Nile,* 152. (The first part of the letter [lines 1–10] refers to a separate matter; for commentary see Gil, *A History of Palestine,* 1: secs. 749, 804, and Bareket, *Jews of Egypt,* doc. 35.) Gil dates this letter approximately to 1035 (Bareket follows him), but in my opinion it must date to 1030; for details, see Rustow, "Rabbanite-Karaite Relations," 313n92.
74. "Most of those who made the pilgrimage came only for the sake of the dispute": cf. Josephus, *Jewish War,* 2:42: "It was not the customary festival so much as indignation which drew the people in crowds." Cited in Steven Weitzman, "From Feasts into Mourning: The Violence of Early Jewish Festivals," *Journal of Religion* 79 (1999): 546.

75. Mann identifies the figure referred to here as al-Duzbarī (*Jews in Egypt and in Palestine,* 1:136).
76. Cambridge University Library Or. 1080 J45 (Judeo-Arabic), mentioned in Goitein, *A Mediterranean Society,* 1:53n66; 2:16 at n.36, 318n33; Goitein, "New Sources on the Palestinian Gaonate," 511n10; Mark R. Cohen, "New Light on the Conflict over the Palestinian Gaonate, 1038–42, and on Daniel b. Azarya: A Pair of Letters to the Nagid of Qayrawan," *Association for Jewish Studies Review* 1 (1976): 1–37 (here, 2n1); first edition in Gil, *A History of Palestine,* 2: doc. 182. See Olszowy-Schlanger, *Karaite Marriage Documents,* 7n14, with whose compressed analysis I agree; for more details on the geonic schism and the Karaite role in it, see Rustow, "Rabbanite-Karaite Relations," 346–57.
77. ENA 4020.6 (Hebrew and Judeo-Arabic). First edition: Mann, *The Jews in Egypt and in Palestine,* 2:172–73. Second edition: Gil, *A History of Palestine,* 2: doc. 183. Color photograph in Rustow et al., *Scripture and Schism: Samaritan and Karaite Treasures from the Library of the Jewish Theological Seminary* (New York: Jewish Theological Seminary, 2000), 81 (item 34).
78. On theories about the relationship of ritual to the social, see Catherine Bell, *Ritual Theory, Ritual Practice* (New York: Oxford, 1992). On ritual as a reflection of the social order, see Emile Durkheim, *The Elementary Forms of the Religious Life,* trans. J. W. Swain (1915; reprint, New York: Free Press, 1965); Mary Douglas, *Purity and Danger: An Analysis of Concepts of Pollution and Taboo* (1966; New York: Routledge, 1991). On ritual as an attempt to reshape the social order, see Victor Turner, *The Ritual Process* (Chicago: Aldine, 1969). On ritualized violence, see Emmanuel Le Roy Ladurie, *Carnival in Romans: A People's Uprising at Romans, 1579–80,* trans. M. Feeney (New York: Braziller, 1979), and David Nirenberg's analysis of anti-Jewish violence during Holy Week in thirteenth-century Spain, *Communities of Violence: Persecution of Minorities in the Middle Ages* (Princeton: Princeton University Press, 1996), 200–230. For the pilgrimage festivals as a site of Jewish sectarian strife in the Second Temple period, see Jeffrey Rubenstein, "The Sadducees and the Water Libation," *Jewish Quarterly Review* 84 (1994): 417–44; Weitzman, "From Feasts into Mourning." The pilgrimage to Mecca repeatedly served as the site of intensified sectarian conflict, most famously when the Ismāʿīlī followers of Ḥamdān Qarmaṭ swiped the black stone from the great mosque in 930. Finally, Phillippe Buc has recently argued that "there can be no anthropological readings of rituals depicted in medieval texts, but only anthropological readings of medieval textual practices," and indeed, medieval representations of rituals are subject to the same cautions as any historical event evidence for which lies embedded a set of texts preserved either accidentally or deliberately: Buc, *The Dangers of Ritual: Between Early Medieval Texts and Social Scientific Theory* (Princeton: Princeton University Press, 2001), 4. More intriguing is Buc's argument that modern ritual theory operates without awareness of its own intellectual genealogy and theological vestiges; for a parallel argument about vestiges of Christian anti-Judaism embedded in Weberian sociology, see Nirenberg, "The Birth of the Pariah: Jews, Christian Dualism, and Social Science," *Social Research* 70 (2003): 201–36.
79. For details, see Rustow, "Rabbanite-Karaite Relations," chap. 8.

6

Elijah Yerushalmi and Karaite Ambivalence Toward Rabbanite Literature

DANIEL FRANK

The colophon brims with excitement. Eloquent, learned, and cogent, the old text had excited the Karaite pilgrim Elijah ben Baruch, who transcribed it in the Holy City where it had been written, nearly seven hundred years earlier:

> I found it in Jerusalem and copied it, rejoicing as one might over great wealth or at finding great spoil. I said: "Indeed I have become rich, I have found riches for myself!" And I thanked God for all the great good that He granted me, protecting me on my way so that I arrived safely at my destination, the City of Peace. He granted me one benefit after another, causing this *Epistle of Rebuke* to fall into my hand (a work), replete with delightful things. When I saw it, I copied it ardently and thankfully, for I understood his pleasant words and eloquent statements. All who consider them will become wise and will say: "Is there not a very wise sage among the Karaites, 'who knows the interpretation of a thing' (Eccl. 8:1) for all his words are altogether righteous, a word fitly spoken for every manner of wisdom and knowledge." All who behold them will recognize and know that they are true, and will search, seek, and say: "Where are the books of the Karaites that I may delight in them!" Blessed is He who gives wisdom to the wise and knowledge to those who have understanding.[1]

Sahl ben Maṣliaḥ, author of the *Epistle,* had written with a self-assurance unknown to the tiny Karaite community of mid-seventeenth-century Jerusalem that hosted the traveler. But if Elijah ben Baruch found the few families clustered around the ancient synagogue to be impoverished and ignorant, the books he discovered and copied in their library—including Salmon ben Yerūḥīm's *Wars of the Lord*—were a perfect tonic.[2]

Even to modern ears, the strident, querulous tones of these tenth-century texts still jar. Rational argumentation mingles with merciless mockery: rabbinic institutions are decried for their fraudulence, corruption, and oppressiveness; rabbinic law is reviled as a human fabrication; rabbinic lore is dismissed for its foolishness and blasphemy, and rabbinic customs for their rank superstition. Salmon attacks Saadya Gaon—the leading rabbinic authority of his time—without hesitation; Sahl writes forcefully against Saadya's disciple, Jacob ben Samuel. Neither advocates compromise in the contest with rabbinic Judaism.[3]

Already in the eleventh century, however, a more moderate position developed. Nissi ben Noah enjoined Karaite scholars to express themselves carefully in measured words while refraining from obstinacy and insolence; they were, moreover, supposed to become expert in rabbinic literature.[4] Indeed, the last great Karaite scholar of Jerusalem, Jeshuah ben Judah, displayed an impressive knowledge of rabbinic texts, citing passages *in extenso.*[5] Certainly, the motivation for studying the Oral Law was polemical in origin: whether attacking Rabbanism or defending Karaism, a sectarian scholar had better be informed. At the same time, rabbinic literature was too vast and ramified to ignore; among the innumerable dissenting opinions recorded, in fact, not a few may be aligned with Karaite positions. By the late thirteenth century, a Byzantine Karaite, Aaron ben Joseph, would write in the introduction to his Torah commentary:

> In my commentary, I shall not refrain from citing the Mishnah concerning most of the commandments. I do so because it may support [my arguments], or sharpen the reader's mind, or distinguish between [biblical] expressions, or prove to be correct, or teach something of which the masses are ignorant. For the words [of the sages] are not entirely without value. . . . This is no credit to the Rabbanites, since most of their statements are the words of our ancestors. [Therefore], we have not discarded them all, but only those that lack scriptural support or contradict Scripture.[6]

Indeed, the commentaries of Aaron ben Joseph mark a new stage in Karaite literature.[7]

As the writings of Maimonides and Abraham Ibn Ezra became popular in the Eastern Mediterranean during the thirteenth and fourteenth centuries, the Karaites of Byzantium began to study them with deep interest. The sectarians' library had largely consisted of Hebrew translations and epitomes of Arabic works composed in tenth- and eleventh-century Jerusalem; there were also a few original works.[8] Composed in an artificial, abstruse, and frequently unintelligible language, these books were grounded in a Mutazilite worldview. The Karaism they expounded had become thoroughly outmoded.[9] In contrast, Sefardic scholarship seemed accessible and up-to-date: the language was a lucid—even elegant—Hebrew, and the underlying speculative system philosophical. Rationalistic and philologically precise, the Sefardic approach to biblical exegesis eschewed homiletics and fanciful *aggadot* in favor of contextual explanation (*peshat*). Ibn Ezra, moreover, frequently cited Karaite authorities, and not always with disapproval.[10] It should come as no surprise, then, that Aaron ben Joseph modeled his own commentaries on those of Ibn Ezra. His successor, Aaron ben Elijah of Nicomedia (d. 1369), went further, composing a Karaite *Guide,* a code, and Torah commentary.[11] The two Aarons drew extensively upon Rabbanite writings—especially exegetical and grammatical works—citing Rashi, Ibn Janaḥ, David Kimḥi, Naḥmanides, and Samuel Ibn Tibbon among others.[12] At the same time, they did not discard their Karaite heritage, but attempted a synthesis.

The essential disagreement between Karaite and Rabbanite Judaism is epistemological, revolving around the status of the Oral Law. Consequently, Karaites and Rabbanites differ primarily over practical (halakhic) issues, rather than theoretical (philosophical) ones. For the two Aarons, this meant preserving the legal positions that define Karaism in the face of fierce Rabbanite critiques, such as Ibn Ezra's comments on passages in Exodus and Leviticus.[13] Theology, however, was a different matter. Their education and a certain chauvinism may have predisposed them to the Mutazilite kalâm of Yūsuf al-Baṣīr and Jeshuah ben Judah (both eleventh century), but there was nothing preventing their borrowing Neoplatonic and Aristotelian notions from Maimonides in fashioning their own speculative systems.[14] As exegetes, moreover, they both found the rationalistic way the Sefardim approached narrative passages to be congenial.[15]

The fifteenth century saw a remarkable rapprochement between Karaite and Rabbanite scholars in Byzantium and Turkey.[16] On the Rabbanite side, such noted teachers as Enoch Tsaporta, Moses Kapsali, and in particular Mordecai Komtino readily offered Karaite students instruction in a number of disciplines, both secular and sacred. This display of good will was contingent, of course, upon the sectarians' good behavior: they were not to profane the festivals publicly on the days they were being celebrated by the Rabbanites and they were to refrain from disparaging Rabbanite authorities, living and dead. On the Karaite side, we may note the profound respect accorded by Elijah Bashyachi, Caleb Afendopolo, and Judah Gibbor to their Rabbanite teacher Komtino.[17] Perhaps even more significantly, members of the Bashyachi family instituted several halakhic reforms that brought Karaite practice closer to Rabbanite norms; these included commencing the lectionary cycle in Tishrei and permitting the use of lamps on the Sabbath.[18] The cordial relationships that Rabbanite and Karaite intellectuals maintained with each other did not, however, prevent them from continuing their debates. When all was said and done, Komtino regarded Karaism as heresy, while conservative Karaites like Abraham Bali and Joseph ben Moses Beghi held the rabbanizing Bashyachi reforms to be unacceptable innovations.[19]

Karaite literature from Turkey during the late fifteenth and early sixteenth century reflects these complicated attitudes. The thorough assimilation of Sefardic Hebrew style and literary norms indicates the depth of the sectarians' immersion in Rabbanite sources.[20] Like his Rabbanite contemporary Elijah ha-Kohen ben Israel Çelebi, Elijah Bashyachi composed a long *qasīda* enumerating the commandments, which was modeled upon Ibn Gabirol's *azharah* "Shemor libbi ma'aneh."[21] His younger contemporary Judah Gibbor surpassed him with a versified Torah commentary titled *Minḥat Yehudah* that runs to 1,912 verses![22] Karaite prose from this period freely uses Tibbonian vocabulary and discusses philosophical notions in Maimonidean terms.[23] On the other hand, since the sectarians were sensitive to charges of heresy, they not only took pains to dissociate their history and teachings from the Sadducees—who denied the resurrection of the dead—but they also proclaimed the soundness and integrity of their own doctrines and practices in the face of rabbinic triumphalism. Caleb Afendopolo (1464–1525), for example, carefully surveys Jewish history in the Second Temple period in order to pinpoint the rift between the two groups. The split occurred, he argues, not in the days of Zadok and Boethus—as the Rabbanites would have it—but rather at the time of Simeon son of Shetaḥ, brother-in-law of (Alexander) Jannaeus: "One sect followed Simeon ben Shetaḥ, since he transmitted to them the tradition that he upheld; they are called Rabbanites. The other sect remained steadfast, following the ways of the first sages and prophets without departing from what is written in Scripture. Retaining the ways of their fathers, they did not cast the yoke of Scripture off their necks."[24] Afendopolo's apologetics responded to Rabbanite hardliners, such as Chief Rabbi Moses Kapsali, who opposed any reconciliation with the "Sadducees" and even issued a ban against teaching them.[25] While this enactment was subsequently rescinded by his successor Elijah Mizraḥi, the sectarians apparently never felt completely secure. As a minority within a minority, they sought to preserve their group identity in the face of disparagement from the rabbinic leadership. And if they wished to appropriate Rabbanite scholarship for their own purposes, they had to guard against assimilation from their own ranks to the dominant Jewish culture. The complex, nuanced stance of these Karaite leaders is exemplified by the writings of an author who lived somewhat later, our enthusiastic copyist Elijah ben Baruch Yerushalmi.

Elijah was an epigone, one of the last in a long line of scholars and teachers that had led the Karaite community in Constantinople for six centuries.[26] The honorific "Yerushalmi" was given by Turkish and Crimean Karaites to those, like Elijah, who had visited the Holy City. As we have seen, he was interested in recovering and disseminating lost Karaite classics—largely a futile enterprise. The sectarians only took to printing in the nineteenth century, and manuscripts were lost to fire or sold to Christian collectors faster than they could be copied.[27] With the Karaite community of Constantinople in severe decline, he emigrated to the Crimea—where he had friends—sometime in the late 1650s or early 1660s.[28] There he remained until 1696, when he journeyed to the Land of Israel with the intention of living out his days in Jerusalem.[29]

Elijah wrote four main works: (1) *Ṣeror ha-Mor* (The Bundle of Myrrh), a super-commentary on Judah Gibbor's *Minḥat Yehudah;*[30] (2) the *Yalqut,* an anthology of Karaite and Rabbanite scholarship;[31] (3) *Asarah Ma'amarot* (Ten Articles), concerning the differences between the Karaites and the Rabbanites;[32] and (4) *Iggeret ha-Viqquaḥ* (The Epistle Concerning the Dispute), relating to a Karaite controversy over ritual slaughter.[33] There are also a few epistles extant and at least one sermon;

several other sermons mentioned in his writings appear to be lost.[34] Elijah's works reflect his commitment to Karaite scholarship and his knowledge of Rabbanite writings. These dual interests seem to have engendered real ambivalence: on the one hand, he cites many Rabbanite authors with respect; on the other, he seeks to rein in his fellow sectarians' enthusiasm for Rabbanite literature. Perhaps not surprisingly, bursts of temper occasionally tinge his prose.[35]

Elijah's catholic tastes are immediately apparent from his introduction to *Ṣeror ha-Mor:* in commenting on the poetic style of Judah Gibbor's *Minḥat Yehudah,* he refers to passages in Solomon Ibn Verga's *Shevet Yehudah* and Azariah de' Rossi's *Me'or Einayim.*[36] Shortly thereafter, in discussing Judah Gibbor's exposition of Karaite dogma, he refers to the creeds of Maimonides, Isaac Abarbanel, and Joseph Albo, according each Rabbanite authority the honorific *ha-kevod rav . . . zikhro li-verakhah.*[37]

Even more striking, however, is his *Yalqut,* an annotated miscellany drawn primarily from Rabbanite texts. Realizing the value and difficulty of the teachings, statements, and phrases he has collected, Elijah explicates them for his fellow Karaites in a series of short essays, each a few hundred words in length. He pronounces himself amazed that the book comprises precisely sixty-one essays, corresponding in number to the Mishnah's tractates, and takes this apparent coincidence as a sign of divine approbation. According to Elijah, the study of Rabbanite teachings is obligatory, since most of them are ultimately of Karaite origin. Rabbanite literature becomes, therefore, a repository which must be carefully scrutinized for Karaite teachings:

> Most of the statements (treated here) were made by the sages of the Mishnah and the Talmud, although it is in no way customary for our people to read the[se works]. For if they do not [even] read Karaite books thoroughly, how much the more so Rabbanite books? And not having read them, they are unfamiliar with their words and do not understand obscure statements, though someone who reads and ponders them will know their meaning. It is wrong to disparage those who read [them], since they mostly contain the words of our ancestors. Rabbi Nissi ben Noah actually required our people to study the Mishnah and the Talmud, and Rabbi Aaron [ben Joseph] stated in the introduction to his book . . . "This does not redound to the glory of the Rabbanites, since most of their statements are [really] the words of our ancestors."[38]

The Maimonidean nature of the argument is striking: just as *Guide of the Perplexed* asserts that philosophy was originally a Jewish discipline that was taught esoterically by the ancient rabbis, the *Yalqut* proclaims that most of those philosophical teachings originated with the Karaites.[39] Drawing upon Azariah de' Rossi's *Me'or Einayim,* Elijah even claims Philo—"who lived before the composition of the Mishnah and Talmud and wrote many books"—for the Karaites![40]

Of the sixty-one essays, the first forty-six cover notions and phrases that are either specifically Rabbanite or are common to both communities. The final fifteen, on the other hand, relate specifically to Karaite literature.[41] Perhaps a dozen of the first forty-six explain basic philosophical terms: "Active Intellect" (No. 2); "Hylic Intellect" and "Acquired Intellect" (No. 3); "Sphere of the Intellect" (No. 5); "On the Creation of Attributes" (No. 14); "Negative Attributes" (No. 15); "Man the Microcosm" (No. 31); and "Atomism" (No. 33). Most of the essays, however, explicate aggadic statements, some of which had been invested with philosophical significance by Maimonides: "the angel is the third part of the world" (No. 6);[42] "Great is the power of the prophets; for they liken a form to its creator" (No. 17).[43] The apologetic motivation is clear from the outset. At the conclusion of his opening essay, on the Ineffable Name, Elijah excuses himself for his prolixity, pleading noble intentions:

> [It was] our desire to benefit both ourselves and others who seek pleasing words. We have also seen that scholars wish to know [this matter] and that they try their hardest to prepare words of insight. Moreover, the Rabbanites boast and exult that they know the meaning of the Ineffable Name, and they mock the Karaite scholars, saying that they are destitute and devoid of all knowledge. And they ask us [lit. "them"] the meaning of the Ineffable Name and its significance. Therefore, I was obliged to take upon myself the investigation of this matter in order to silence those who speak impudently about us.[44]

Interestingly, although his discussions are clearly based upon Rabbanite texts, Elijah often passes over his sources in silence.[45] In his second essay, for example, his identification of the Active Intellect with the angel Gabriel is clearly based upon *Kuzari* 1:87 and Judah Moscato's comment in *Qol Yehudah*—works he cites explicitly elsewhere. Here no sources are given.[46] Elsewhere, however, he does not hesitate to refer his readers to

Maimonides: "Our master Moses ben Maimon of blessed memory expostulated at length [on this subject] in his *Guide of the Perplexed.* Whoever wishes to know the details of these matters should consult it and satisfy his thirst. Enough for now."[47] A product of the sectarian encounter with Rabbanite scholarship, the *Yalqut* presents a Karaism that has not only absorbed Maimonidean concepts and terminology but has also laid claim to talmudic dicta. For the most part, the author adopts the conciliatory posture that Byzantine Karaites had been taking toward Rabbanite Judaism for over two centuries. Where he can, he tries to show that the older, Mutazilite writings of Yūsuf al-Baṣīr (Joseph ha-Ro'eh) and Jeshuah ben Judah are compatible with the modern science of the Rabbanites.[48] But he also distances himself from certain theories that they espoused—such as atomism, which he damns by association with the Muslim Mutazilites and the Epicureans.[49]

From a passing reference to Shabbatai Zvi, we may date the *Yalqut* sometime after 1666, when Elijah was already settled in the Crimea.[50] The local readership was not especially sophisticated, and the work was intended to broaden their education. But the Rabbanite works in which Elijah had immersed himself were dangerous, and as a responsible leader, he could not risk the seduction of impressionable Karaite youths. If Ibn Ezra and Maimonides had written classics, they also showed the utmost contempt for Karaite teachings. Impressed by Ibn Ezra's exegetical astuteness, a Karaite student might also accept his dismissal of "Sadducean" *halakhah.* To counter this threat, a second work was needed, one that would conclusively demonstrate the Karaite truth.

In the introduction to his short polemical tract, *Sefer Asarah Ma'amarot al Ḥilluqei ha-Rabbanim la-Qara'im* (Ten Articles on the Differences Between the Rabbanites and the Karaites), Elijah Yerushalmi depicts the intellectual vulnerability of his contemporaries:

> Elijah said: I have seen some of our people who are not well informed casting doubt on the words of the true scholars who follow what is inscribed in the true Scripture, our scholars and men of understanding who enlighten us with their wisdom, the Karaite scholars of blessed memory. And I have seen that there are some from among the masses of the people who do not know the way of the Law and are unacquainted with its path; nor do they have the capacity to navigate the words of the scholars and discuss them, to understand insights and grasp the truth of a matter. Their lack of

> understanding and comprehension compounded by the small measure of faith that they possess, so that truth is concealed from them and the real nature of religious obligation is hidden from their eyes. Moreover, heresy [*minut*] has sprouted upon their foreheads as a consequence of their association with the Rabbanites: they have followed a portion of the [Rabbanites'] teachings and, in neglecting the works of our scholars, have satisfied themselves with alien wisdom,[51] studying their books and *midrashim* and their other teachings which are not good, for they contradict the *peshat.* All this befell them, since some of our people are rash, vain, and ill informed in scholarly matters—not having settled in a place suitable for perfect meditation upon God's Law, so that they might fully understand its secrets.[52]

He had, in short, encountered certain ignorant Karaites who were expressing doubts about their own intellectual and spiritual heritage. Their incomprehension of Karaite texts and their general intellectual incapacity were coupled with a lack of faith. Their association with Rabbanites, moreover, had led them to the heresy of Rabbanite Judaism. Abandoning the Karaite classics, they have occupied themselves with midrashic works that "are not good for they contradict the *peshat.*" Indeed, the situation in Elijah's day was not really any different than it had been over a century and a half previously, when Shabbatai ben Elijah Pravado sought to counter the pernicious influence of Rabbanism by disseminating a monumental code he had rescued from oblivion.[53] The work in question—the twelfth-century *Eshkol ha-Kofer* of Judah Hadassi—is both comprehensive and decisive in its demonstration of Rabbanite error. It is, however, a scholarly work intended for advanced students who have plenty of time. But today, says Elijah Yerushalmi, people have neither the leisure nor the learning to work their way through such long texts in the quest for truth. Consequently, he has composed a concise work aimed at instructing good students, strengthening their faith, developing their discernment, and demonstrating to them the truth of Karaite teachings: "I have prepared some short articles—ten in number—for qualified students to strengthen their faith and teach them understanding, to inform and proclaim to all our people, who are too stubborn to heed the teaching of our scholars and their interpretations, that the interpretations of our scholars, of blessed memory, are altogether righteous."[54] Since some of his contemporaries have, moreover, turned their backs on the works of their ancestors, he has adopted a new strategy for proving to them the validity of Karaite interpretation:

> [I will show them] as well how our opponents themselves acknowledged the statements of the Karaites and their interpretations. Even though those very statements constitute the essence of the schism and controversy, they [the Rabbanites] unashamedly conceded [the truth of the Karaites' position]. Those who acknowledge the statements and interpretation of the Karaite scholars, moreover, are the greatest of their scholars, the leaders of their people, by whose words they [all] live.[55]

This last point—that the greatest Rabbanite scholars have conceded the truth of Karaite teachings—conclusively demonstrates the Karaite truth, and should strengthen the faith of those who are still wavering.

In essence, the Rabbanite error lies in their alteration of the Law. Their tradition [*qabbalah*] contradicts the words of the Torah and confutes the Divine Lawgiver's intention.[56] Their claim, moreover, that the tradition constitutes the authoritative explication of Scripture is unfounded, for it is impossible that two contradictory statements both be true. They themselves even concede the falseness of this contention but, in order to maintain their position, they assert it all the same. And no liar, Elijah reminds us, will ever be reliable, for a lie is never anything but a lie![57] Divine intercession, however, has led some of these Rabbanites to acknowledge the truth, despite themselves: "The Lord God of truth has prompted some of them to admit the truth so that it would be revealed, even though they did not all acknowledge it. One would concede a certain point while another would concede something else. In this way, each would acknowledge one point, so that when all are joined, the words of the Karaites are confirmed, proven, and verified."[58] Since every such act of self-incrimination is "as valuable as one hundred witnesses,"[59] it is appropriate to cite them in turn so that everyone will know on which side the truth resides.

Elijah's polemical strategy, therefore, depends upon several claims. First, he asserts that *peshat* is the ideal toward which all true exegetes—Rabbanites and Karaites alike—strive. *Peshat,* accordingly, corresponds to truth. Second, he argues that the most eminent Rabbanite scholars realized that the oral tradition flies in the face of *peshat* and actually acknowledged the truth of Karaite interpretations. These concessions, moreover, occurred precisely in the most sensitive contexts, namely the *halakhic* passages that effectively define the two groups. Finally—and most significantly—Elijah charges these same Rabbanite scholars with disingenuousness; although they admit the rectitude of Karaite interpretations, they persist, nevertheless, in propounding traditional rabbinic *halakhah* and in disparaging the sectarians. They do this, of course, in order to preserve the authority of the Rabbanite tradition (*qabbalah*) within their community.[60]

This argument goes back to Elijah Bashyachi, who first articulated a new Karaite approach to the classics of Andalusian scholarship. Ibn Ezra, he explained, had been the disciple of Japheth ben Eli. Like his Karaite master, he was a great exegete who followed the way of *peshat.* In composing his commentaries, however, he employed artifices in order to conceal certain teachings from all but a discerning scholarly elite. Ibn Ezra's derogatory remarks concerning the Karaites were, according to Bashyachi, intended for popular consumption. In reality, however, Ibn Ezra was putting up a smoke screen: his real sympathies lay with the Karaites, as a sensitive, intelligent reader would discover.[61]

Following Bashyachi's lead, Elijah Yerushalmi quickly singles out three Rabbanites as witnesses to the Karaite *peshat:* Solomon Sharvit ha-Zahav—a fifteenth-century Byzantine whose works enjoyed a certain local popularity;[62] Maimonides; and Ibn Ezra. It is, of course, the two Andalusians who furnish Elijah with most of his material. Maimonides, he feels, achieved a certain stature among the Rabbanites because he evaluated rabbinic statements critically with an eye to eliminating contradictions.[63] But Ibn Ezra's excellence can be traced to his education—by a Karaite master:

> Another of their greatest scholars was Ibn Ezra, most of whose interpretations accord with the *peshat.* This was entirely due to his associating with the Karaites, for he was the disciple of the great and formidable scholar, our teacher Japheth [ben Eli][64] of blessed memory. By virtue of his being the Master's disciple, he became learned and succeeded in following the paths of the righteous and the just. He was careful to pursue the *peshat,* although he strayed from the true path in a few matters that he was forced to accept. For had he denied all [rabbinic interpretations], he would have been accounted an unbeliever. Therefore, at the beginning of his commentary, he praises their words and rambles on [only] making his intention

> known covertly and by means of hints. In his pursuit of the *peshat*, Ibn Ezra admitted more than did others. In many places he denied the tradition of his [Rabbanite] teachers and contradicted their words, interpreting [Scripture] in accordance with Karaite exegesis. Through this exegetical impartiality, he fulfilled the condition he had imposed upon himself at the beginning of his commentary. Now I shall cite his statements in connection with all the specifics of [these] matters so that [his] intention will be known.[65]

Elijah now proceeds to his evidence. The "Ten Articles" constitute a catalogue of halakhic issues that divide the Karaite and Rabbanite camps. These include laws relating to the festivals, forbidden foods, sexual relations, torts, and the calendar—in short, issues relating to every area of Jewish praxis. Elijah introduces each subject by citing the biblical verse or verses upon which the particular *halakhah* is grounded. Next, he offers the Karaite interpretation of that text, emphasizing that this reading represents the *peshat* and conforms with Karaite practice. Then, he sketches the Rabbanite *halakhah*, pointing out that it in no way corresponds to the *peshat* interpretation. "Now, you can see," he writes at one juncture, "how they draw things out at will, interpreting biblical passages in an implausible fashion in order to claim scriptural support for their practices. In truth, however, not one of the[ir practices] accords with what the *peshat* teaches, though the *peshat* of this passage is as plain as day."[66]

It is always at this point that Elijah introduces his star witnesses, Ibn Ezra or Maimonides: "Now Ibn Ezra admitted [the correctness of] our interpretation and denied the interpretation of his [Rabbanite] predecessors"; "Maimonides conceded this point as well in his *Guide of the Perplexed*."[67] The passages cited by Elijah, interestingly, represent a small corpus of well-known cruxes. The rationalistic principles of Andalusian philological exegesis apparently led both Maimonides and Ibn Ezra to explicate certain biblical laws according to their plain meaning (*peshuto*). In *Guide* III:41, for example, Maimonides treats the *lex talionis* literally. The phrases, "As he has done, it shall be done to him" (*ka-asher yitten mum ba-adam ken yinnaten bo*) and "an eye for an eye" (*ayin taḥat ayin*)[68] signify that a person who has deprived another of a member should suffer the same deprivation. "Do not trouble yourself, however," says Maimonides, "that in such cases we actually impose a monetary fine. For my intention here is to set forth the meaning of the verses and not the meaning of the Talmudic explanation."[69] Now, while this passage troubled some of Maimonides' commentators, such as Moses Narboni and Shem Tov, it pleased Karaite scholars who believed that it vindicated their literal interpretation of the *lex talionis.* Indeed, Maimonides' comments were already cited in the fourteenth century by Aaron ben Elijah as proof that the Rabbanites lacked scriptural support for their legislation.[70] Three centuries later, Elijah Yerushalmi had a stock of such passages at his disposal.[71]

If Elijah Bashyachi was the first to discern and explain Ibn Ezra's duplicity, it was Elijah Yerushalmi who finally fashioned the argument and evidence into a structured, coherent, polemic.[72] His primary goal was not to deflect Karaites from studying Rabbanite writings, but rather to temper their enthusiasm, lest they be persuaded to adopt rabbinic *halakhah.* His own fascination with classical and medieval Rabbanite literature was rooted in a centuries-old Byzantine Karaite curriculum that accorded the works of Ibn Ezra, Maimonides, Judah Halevi, and other Sefardim a place of honor.[73] As a scholar and teacher, he tried to perpetuate the intellectual tradition that he had inherited. If he delighted in copying out the harsh, self-assured polemics of Salmon ben Yeruḥîm and Sahl ben Maṣliaḥ, the pleasure was probably but fleeting. Neither work seems to have left its mark on him or, indeed, on any other later Karaite author.[74] Reading Sahl's *Epistle* in Jerusalem may have been thrilling, but the reality of Karaite intellectual life in the Crimea must have been sobering: in a place "where there is no *yeshivah* in which to meet and discuss fine points of law,"[75] he could only try to promote the course of study he himself had pursued, with all its eclecticism and ambivalence.

Appendix: Dating *Sefer ha-Yalqut* and *Sefer Asarah Ma'amarot*

Neither the *Yalqut* nor *Asarah Ma'amarot* is dated, but it is possible at the very least to suggest a relative chronology and, more important, to establish that both works were completed in the Crimea. As has been noted, Elijah refers to Shabbatai Zvi in the *Yalqut;* the work was completed, therefore, sometime after 1666.[76] *Asarah Ma'amarot* may be tentatively dated to 1659 on the basis of the following evidence:

Oxford Bodleian MS Opp. Add. 4to, 121 is a codex copied in two similar Karaite hands.[77] In addition to Elijah Yerushalmi's *Asarah Ma'marot,* the volume also contains Caleb Afendopolo's *Asarah Ma'marot,* Elijah Afeda Beghi's *Hilkhot Sheḥitah,* some poems by the latter, and a number of short Rabbanite texts.[78] There are two colophons by the scribe Jacob ben Mordecai, the first of which includes the date 1679.[79] Elijah Yerushalmi's *Asarah Ma'marot* (fols. 157a–170b) follows the second colophon and was copied by the second scribe, who added a column of editorial comments on certain folios. One comment (fol. 165a) begins with the abbreviation א״א ריב״ם יצ״ו; a parallel manuscript, Cambridge University Library (CUL) Add. 1743, expands this to אדוני אבי רבנו יעקב בן מרדכי יצ״ו "my father and master, our teacher Jacob ben Mordecai, may his Rock and Redeemer protect him"). The Oxford manuscript is, therefore, the work of a father and son, and the son—Mordecai ben Jacob—is the author of the editorial comments and additions.[80] These interventions, in fact, infuriated Elijah Yerushalmi, who composed an angry open letter, rebuking Mordecai; a later copy is preserved in CUL Add. 1743, fols. 25a–30a. At one point (fol. 27a), Elijah states that he had composed *Asarah Ma'amarot* twenty years earlier and had showed the work to five Karaite elders whom he names; at least three of them—Moses Halevi ben Elijah Halevi, Jacob ben Mordecai, and Isaac Pasha—are known to have been based in the Crimea.

An approximate dating for *Asarah Ma'amarot* may be established on the basis of the following three assumptions: First, it is probable that Mordecai ben Jacob copied his portion of the Oxford manuscript shortly after his father had completed the portion dated 1679. Both paper and ink are uniform and the volume has every appearance of having been produced jointly and in uninterrupted fashion. Second, since the Crimean Karaites maintained close contacts with each other, it is quite likely that Elijah saw either this copy or a similar one soon after Mordecai ben Jacob had prepared it. And third, Elijah very probably dashed off his open letter to Mordecai without delay. We would suggest, therefore, that *Asarah Ma'amarot* was completed ca. 1659, probably around the time of Elijah's immigration to the Crimea.[81]

Notes

I am most grateful to Professors Daniel J. Lasker, Sid Z. Leiman, and Adena Tanenbaum for their helpful comments.

1. S. Pinsker, *Lickute Kadmoniot* (Wien, 1860), Appendices, 25.
2. On Elijah's activities as a copyist in Jerusalem see S. Poznanski, "Karäische Kopisten und Besitzer von Handschriften," *Zeitschrift für hebraeische Bibliographie* 19 (1916): 84–85, no. 30. At the time of his pilgrimage, there were perhaps only twenty

Karaites in Jerusalem; see J. Mann, *Texts and Studies: Karaitica* (Philadelphia: Jewish Publication Society, 1935), 2:322 and n. 10.

3. Salmon's polemic was published by I. Davidson, *The Book of the Wars of the Lord* (New York: Jewish Theological Seminary, 1934), excerpt in Leon Nemoy, *Karaite Anthology* (New Haven: Yale University Press, 1952), 69–82. On Elijah's colophon, see Davidson, *The Book of the Wars of the Lord,* 7, and esp. J. Bardach, *Mazkir li-Venei Reshef* (Vienna, 1869), 37, for his vituperations against Saadya. For Sahl's *Epistle,* see Pinsker, Appendices, 24–43; Nemoy, *Karaite Anthology,* 109–22; Nemoy, "The Epistle of Sahl Ben Masliah," *Proceedings of the American Academy for Jewish Research* 38–39 (1970–71): 145–77. On both works, see also S. Poznanski, "Karaite Miscellanies," *Jewish Quarterly Review* o.s. 8 (1895–96): 684–91; and Poznanski, "The Karaite Literary Opponents of Saadiah Gaon in the Tenth Century," *Jewish Quarterly Review* 18 (1905–6): 209–50, esp. 220–21, 242–49.
4. Pinsker, *Lickute Kadmoniot,* Appendices, 13, lines 2–5. See L. Nemoy, "Nissi Ben Noah's Quasi-Commentary on the Decalogue," *Jewish Quarterly Review* n.s. 73 (1983): 307–48, esp. 340–41, 347. As Nemoy makes clear, the precise period of Nissi's activity remains conjectural.
5. See H. Ben-Shammai, "Yeshuah ben Yehudah—A Characterization of a Karaite Scholar of Jerusalem in the Eleventh Century" (Hebrew), *Pe'amim* 32 (1987): 9–17; O. Tirosh-Becker, "Preliminary Studies in Rabbinic Quotations Embedded in the Pentateuch Commentaries of the Karaite Scholar Yeshu'a Ben-Yehuda" (Hebrew), *Massorot* 5–6 (1991): 313–40; Tirosh-Becker, "Linguistic Study of a Rabbinic Quotation Embedded in a Karaite Commentary on Exodus," in *Studies in Mishnaic Hebrew* [Scripta Hierosolymitana, 37], ed. Moshe Bar-Asher (Jerusalem: Magnes Press, 1998), 380–407.
6. Aaron ben Joseph, *Sefer ha-Mivḥar* (Gözlöw, 1835), vol. 1, fol. 9a. Aaron explains that Jeshuah ben Judah's conversance with rabbinic sources made him cognizant of their value; he also refers to Nissi ben Noah's injunction. See also Z. Ankori, *Karaites in Byzantium* (New York: Columbia University Press, 1959), 241.
7. See D. J. Lasker, "Aaron ben Joseph and the Transformation of Karaite Thought," in *Torah and Wisdom . . . Essays in Honor of Arthur Hyman,* ed. Ruth Link-Salinger (New York: Shengold, 1992), 121–28, and D. Frank, "Karaite Exegetical and Halakhic Literature in Byzantium," in *Karaite Judaism: A Guide to Its History and Literary Sources,* ed. M. Polliack (Leiden: Brill, 2003), 536–41.
8. Ankori, *Karaites in Byzantium,* 415–52.
9. On Byzantine Karaite Hebrew, see A. Maman, "Karaite Hebrew," in *Karaite Judaism,* 485–503; A. Maman, "Ha-Ivrit shel ha-Qara'im," *Weekly Newsletter of the Academy of the Hebrew Language* 8 (December 1989), 2–8; S. Hopkins, "Arabic Elements in the Hebrew of the Byzantine Karaites," in *Genizah Research After Ninety Years,* ed. J. Blau and S. C. Reif (Cambridge: Cambridge University Press, 1992), 93–99. Aaron ben Joseph complained about the translators' Hebrew; see *Sefer Mivḥar Yesharim* (Gözlöw, 1834), 2a. On the Mutazilism of the older Karaite thinkers, see D. E. Sklare, "Yūsuf al-Baṣīr: Theological Aspects of His Halakhic Works," in *The Jews of Medieval Islam: Community, Society, and Identity,* ed. D. Frank (Leiden: Brill, 1995), 249–70.
10. For Ibn Ezra's citation of Karaite authorities, see E. Z. Melammed, *Bible Commentators* (Hebrew), 2nd ed. (Jerusalem: Magnes Press, 1978), 1:676–78; A. Weiser, ed.,

Peirushei ha-Torah le-Rabbeinu Avraham Ibn Ezra (Jerusalem: Mossad Harav Kook, 1976), vol. 1, introduction, 59–71.

11. See I. Husik, *A History of Medieval Jewish Philosophy* (Philadelphia: Jewish Publication Society, 1940), chap. 16; D. Frank, "Ibn Ezra and the Karaite Exegetes Aaron ben Joseph and Aaron ben Elijah," in *Abraham Ibn Ezra and His Age,* ed. F. Díaz Esteban (Madrid: Asociación Española de Orientalistas, 1990), 99–107; D. Frank, "The Religious Philosophy of the Karaite Aaron b. Elijah: The Problem of Divine Justice" (Ph.D. diss., Harvard University, 1991); and D. J. Lasker, "Maimonides' Influence on Karaite Theories of Prophecy and Law," *Maimonidean Studies* (1990): 99–115.
12. D. Frank, "The Religious Philosophy of the Karaite Aaron b. Elijah," xxxviii–xlvi, and D. J. Lasker, "Byzantine Karaite Thought," in *Karaite Judaism,* 505–28, esp. 508–20.
13. On Ibn Ezra's polemics against Karaism, see note 10 above and P. R. Weis, "Abraham Ibn Ezra and the Karaites in the Halakhah" (Hebrew), *Melilah* 1 (1944): 35–53; 2 (1946): 121–34; 3–4 (1950): 188–203. On two occasions, Ibn Ezra records debates he held with "Sadducees," i.e., Karaites; see the Shorter Commentary on Exodus 35:3 and the Commentary on Leviticus 7:23–27.
14. On this synthesis see the following articles by Daniel J. Lasker: "The Destiny of Man in Karaite Philosophy" (Hebrew), *Da'at* 12 (1984): 5–13; "Nature and Science According to Aaron ben Elijah, the Karaite" (Hebrew), *Da'at* 17 (1986): 33–42; "Maimonides' Influence on Karaite Theories of Prophecy and Law"; and "Aaron ben Joseph and the Transformation of Karaite Thought."
15. There are, of course, instances in which Rabbanite champions of *peshat,* such as Ibn Ezra and Mordecai Komtino, accept traditional, midrashic interpretations; not surprisingly, the Karaites reject such readings. See, e.g., the treatment of Genesis 35:22 discussed in J.-C. Attias, *Le commentaire biblique: Mordekhai Komtino ou l'herméneutique du dialogue* (Paris: Cerf, 1991), 64, and Attias, "Intellectual Leadership: Rabbanite-Karaite Relations in Constantinople as Seen through the Works and Activity of Mordekhai Komtino in the Fifteenth Century," in *Ottoman and Turkish Jewry: Community and Leadership,* ed. A. Rodrigue (Bloomington: Indiana University Press, 1992), 75.
16. See S. Assaf, "Le-Toledot ha-Qara'im be-Arṣot ha-Mizraḥ," *Be-ohalei Ya'aqov* (Jerusalem, 1943), 190–96 (181–222).
17. Attias, *Le commentaire biblique,* 87–89. On the Karaite curriculum that emerged from these contacts, see B. Walfish, "Karaite Education in the Middle Ages," in *Dor le-Dor* 5 (1992): 1–25 (Eng. sec.). The main source for our period is Elijah Bashyachi, *Adderet Eliyahu* (Odessa, 1870), fols. 83d–85b. See also the texts collected by S. Assaf, *Meqorot le-Toledot ha-Ḥinukh be-Yisrael,* ed. S. Glick, 4 vols. (New York and Jerusalem: Jewish Theological Seminary, 2001–6), 2: 595–625.
18. Z. Ankori, "Beit Bashyachi ve-taqqanotav," in Elijah Bashyachi, *Sefer ha-Miṣvot . . . Adderet Eliyahu* (Israel: Ha-Mo'aṣah ha-Arṣit shel Adat ha-Yehudim ha-Qara'im be-Yisra'el, 1966), 1–16.
19. See Attias, *Le commentaire biblique,* chap. 2, and Mann, *Texts and Studies,* 2: 294–315.
20. Interestingly, Bashyachi also appreciated the Sefardic mode of chanting the Scriptures; see *Adderet Eliyahu,* 168, col. a, lines 3–5. On the impact of the Iberian exiles in general, see J. Hacker, "The Intellectual Activity of the Jews of the Ottoman

Empire During the Sixteenth and Seventeenth Centuries," in *Jewish Thought in the Seventeenth Century*, ed. I. Twersky and B. Septimus (Cambridge, Mass.: Harvard University Press, 1987), 95–135, esp. 133–35.

21. On Çelebi and his *azharah* "Avarekh le-el nora," see L. J. Weinberger, *Jewish Hymnography: A Literary History* (Oxford: Littman Library, 1998), 371, 376–77, and Weinberger, *Rabbanite and Karaite Liturgical Poetry in South-Eastern Europe* (Cincinnati: Hebrew Union College Press, 1991), 389–406. On Bashyachi and his "Meliṣat ha-miṣvot" see *Jewish Hymnography*, 411, 413–15, and *Rabbanite and Karaite Liturgical Poetry*, 601–12.
22. Philip E. Miller, "At the Twilight of Byzantine Karaism: The Anachronism of Judah Gibbor" (Ph.D. diss., New York University, 1984), esp. 53–75. For the text, see *Seder ha-Tefillot ke-Minhag ha-Qara'im* (Vilna, 1890; reprint, Ramlah, 1971), 1:342–95.
23. See, e.g., the works of Judah Gibbor discussed by Miller, "At the Twilight." Judah drew upon the likes of Maimonides, Ibn Ezra, Naḥmanides, and Baḥya ben Asher both directly and indirectly, since his later Karaite sources—notably the two Aarons—were themselves heavily influenced by the Spanish Rabbanites.
24. Caleb Afendopolo, *Asarah Ma-'amarot*, ed. Yoseph El-Gamil (Ramlah: Mekhon Tif'eret Yosef, 5760/1999), 20–29, esp. 26; see also 153–58 on resurrection. On these passages, see S. Poznanski, "Introduction," *Zecher Caddikim* (Warszawa, 1920), esp. 34–35; and Fred Astren, *Karaite Judaism and Historical Understanding* (Columbia: University of South Carolina Press, 2004), 232–40. Zadok and Boethus were disciples of Antigonus of Sokho; see J. Goldin, *The Fathers according to Rabbi Nathan* (New Haven: Yale University Press, 1955), 39. Maimonides, among others, had traced the Karaites back to the Sadducees, the followers of Zadok; see his *Commentary* on Avot 1:3, *Pirqei Avot im Peirush . . . Rabbeinu Mosheh Ben Maimon ve-'im Peirush Naḥalat Avot* (Jerusalem: Mishpaḥat Zilberman, 1970), 54–55.
25. See Attias, *Le commentaire biblique*, 67–89, esp. 70–72, and Attias, "Intellectual Leadership," 67–86, esp. 76–80.
26. See the brief bio-bibliographic note by the eighteenth-century Polish Karaite Simḥah Isaac Lucki, *Ner Ṣaddiqim* (1750), in Mann, *Texts and Studies*, 2:1427. See also *Encyclopaedia Judaica* (Berlin) 6:498–99 and *Encyclopaedia Judaica* 6:646. For further information see D. Frank, "Elijah b. Baruch Yerushalmi and the Karaite Controversy Concerning Ritual Slaughter in the Seventeenth Century" (Hebrew), *Pe'amim* 89 (2001): 21–50, and D. Frank, "A Karaite Sheḥitah Controversy in the Seventeenth Century," in *Be'erot Yitzhak: Studies in Memory of Isadore Twersky*, ed. Jay M. Harris (Cambridge, Mass.: Harvard Center for Jewish Studies), 69–97.
27. See Mann, *Texts and Studies*, 2:1426, and Frank, "A Karaite Sheḥitah Controversy," 71nn5–7.
28. See Frank, "A Karaite Sheḥitah Controversy," 96, 103. His Crimean friends included the traveler Moses Halevi ben Elijah Halevi Yerushalmi, who stayed with him in Constantinople in 1654; see J. Gurland, *Neue Denkmäler der jüdischen Literatur* (*Ginzei Yisra'el be-St. Peterburg*) (Lyck, 1866), 1:31 (31–43), reprinted in A. Yaari, *Mas'ot Ereṣ Yisra'el* (Tel Aviv, 1946), 306 (305–23).
29. See St. Petersburg, Institute of Oriental Studies [henceforth SP, IOS], MS B471/8, Elijah's account of his final pilgrimage. We do not know when he died, but Abraham ben Josiah's *Emunah Omen* (1712) refers to him with the formulaic blessing for the deceased.

30. For manuscripts, see SP, IOS, MS B304 and MS C134, and Moscow Günzburg MS 924. Judah Gibbor's *Minḥat Yehudah* was completed in 1502, not 1602 as given in Mann, *Texts and Studies,* 2:1471n72. Published edition: *Sefer Ṣeror ha-Mor le-ha-Rav Eliyahu ben Barukh Yerushalmi,* 5 vols., ed. Yoseph El-Gamil (Ashdod: Mekhon Tif'eret Yosef, 2004). All translations from Elijah Yerushalmi's works have been made directly from manuscripts. References to printed editions are provided for the sake of convenience.
31. For manuscripts, see SP, IOS, MS A219 and MS B415 and Russian National Library, MS Evr. II A0002; and Cambridge University Library [henceforth CUL] MS Heb. Add. 1743/3. Published edition: *Sefer ha-Yalqut le-ha-Rav Eliyahu ben Barukh Yerushalmi,* ed. Yoseph El-Gamil (Ashdod: Mekhon Tif'eret Yosef, 2002).
32. For manuscripts, see SP, IOS MS B192/4, MS B159, and MS B330; CUL MS Heb. Add. 1743/1–2; and Oxford Bodleian MS Opp. Add. 4to, 121 (N. 2386/5). Published edition: *Sefer Asarah Ma'amarot la-Ḥakham Eliyahu Ben Barukh Yerushalmi,* ed. Yoseph El-Gamil (Ashdod: Mekhon Tif'eret Yosef, 2005).
33. For manuscripts, see SP, IOS MSS A83 and B332 and CUL MS Heb. Add. 1743, fols. 88a–117a. This text is the focus of Frank, "A Karaite Sheḥitah Controversy" and Frank, "Elijah b. Baruch Yerushalmi and the Karaite Sheḥitah Controversy."
34. See CUL MS Heb. Add. 1743, fols. 25a–30a, for the epistle to Mordecai ben Jacob appended to *Asarah Ma'amarot* and fols. 117b–124a for the letter to Isaac Pasha ben Moses Pasha. In the *Yalqut,* chap. 3, he refers to a eulogy for his father (SP, IOS, MS B415, fol. 9a) and in *Iggeret ha-Viqquaḥ* he refers to a eulogy for his teacher Joseph Maruli (CUL MS Heb. Add. 1743, fol. 112a); neither is extant. For a wedding sermon see SP, IOS, MS A217/2, fols. 24a–26a.
35. This was noted by Poznanski with respect to Elijah's attacks on Saadya; see "The Karaite Literary Opponents," *Jewish Quarterly Review* 20 (1908): 224 and n. 2 referring to Bardach, *Mazkir li-Venei Reshef,* 37. For striking examples in *Asarah Ma'amarot* see the comments concerning Judah Moscato, Oxford Bod. MS Opp. Add. 4to, fols. 164a–165b.
36. See SP, IOS, MS C134, fol. 19 = El-Gamil ed., 17–18.
37. Ibid., fols. 21b–22a = El-Gamil ed., 27.
38. SP, IOS, MS B415, fol. 2b = CUL MS Heb. Add. 1743, fol. 32b = El-Gamil ed., 20–21. The authorities invoked—Nissi ben Noah and Aaron ben Joseph—are, of course, familiar; see above, notes 4 and 6.
39. Cf. Moses Maimonides, *The Guide of the Perplexed,* I:71, trans. Shlomo Pines (Chicago: University of Chicago Press, 1963), 175–76.
40. See SP, IOS, MS B415, fol. 3a = CUL MS Heb. Add. 1743, fol. 33a = El-Gamil ed., 21–22. Elijah is referring to Azariah de' Rossi, *Me'or Einayim,* "Imrei binah," chaps. 3–6, ed. D. Cassel (Vilna, 1866), 90–129, esp. chap. 5, 117–19. As Daniel J. Lasker has reminded me, Bernard Revel noted certain affinities between Karaite and Philonic *halakhah;* see *The Karaite Halakhah and Its Relation to Sadducean, Samaritan and Philonian Halakhah* (Philadelphia: Dropsie College, 1913). Joanna Weinberg has observed that "the rare (and usually indirect) references to Philo in Jewish literature are almost entirely to be found in Karaite writings"; see "The Quest for Philo in Sixteenth-Century Jewish Historiography," in *Jewish History: Essays in Honour of Chimen Abramsky,* ed. A. Rapoport-Albert and S. J. Zipperstein (London: Peter Halban, 1988), 164 and 180n15.

41. SP, IOS, MS B415, fol. 4b = CUL MS Heb. Add. 1743, fol. 34b = El-Gamil ed., 12–14.
42. Genesis Rabbah 68:12. See Maimonides, *Guide* II:10, p. 273; Maimonides, *Mishneh Torah,* "Yesodei ha-Torah," 2:3.
43. Genesis Rabbah 27:1. See Maimonides, *Guide* I:46, p. 103.
44. SP, IOS, MS B415, fol. 7a = El-Gamil ed., 29. One of Elijah's main sources for this essay is Aaron ben Elijah's *Eṣ Ḥayyim,* chaps. 73–74, ed. F. Delitzsch (Leipzig, 1841), 90–93.
45. It goes without saying that this tendency limits the work's usefulness, since it presupposes that the phrases and terms retain their meanings wherever they are used.
46. SP, IOS, MS B415, fol. 7b–8b = El-Gamil ed., 31–34. Cf. Judah Halevi, *Sefer ha-Kuzari* 1:87 (Warsaw, 1880), 1:104–5 and *Qol Yehudah* ad loc.
47. Essay No. 8 on matter, form, and privation; see SP, IOS, MS B415, fols. 11b–12a = El-Gamil ed. 51–52.
48. E.g., Essay No. 15 on Positive and Negative Attributes; see SP, IOS, MS B415, fols. 16b–17b = El-Gamil ed., 75–78.
49. Essay No. 33, SP, IOS, MS B415, fols. 32b–33a = El-Gamil ed., 149–51. On Atomism in Karaite thought, see H. Ben-Shammai, "Studies in Karaite Atomism," *Jerusalem Studies in Arabic and Islam* 6 (1985): 243–97, esp. 280–85; Lasker, "Nature and Science," 40–42 and n. 57.
50. See Essay No. 34, SP, IOS, MS B415, fol. 34a = El-Gamil ed., 155: *ve-Shabbetai Ṣevi ha-ba la-rabbanim hayah mitpa'er be-zo ha-ḥokhmah ve-hayah mithallel she-hayah lo koaḥ le-sha'er meimei ha-yam* ("And Shabbatai Zvi who came to the Rabbanites used to boast of [his knowledge of] this science [i.e., geometry], bragging that he was able to calculate the [volume of the] waters of the sea"). The date of Elijah's immigration can be fixed more or less from his epistle to Isaac Pasha ben Moses Pasha; see CUL MS Heb. Add. 1743, fols. 117b–124a, and Frank, "A Karaite Sheḥitah Controversy," 96n102.
51. Allusion to Isaiah 2:6; cf. David Kimḥi ad loc.
52. Oxford Bodleian MS Opp. Add. 4to, 121, fol. 157a = El-Gamil ed., 11–12.
53. On Shabbatai Pravado and his role in restoring *Eshkol ha-Kofer* to the Karaite community see P. F. Frankl, "Karäische Studien (neue Folge)," *Monatsschrift für Geschichte und Wissenschaft des Judentums* 31 (1882): 270–71 (268–75), and S. B. Bowman, *The Jews of Byzantium, 1204–1453* (Tuscaloosa: University of Alabama Press, 1985), 323–24, doc. 148.
54. Oxford Bodleian MS Opp. Add. 4to, 121, fol. 157b, lines 6–8 = El-Gamil ed., 13.
55. Ibid., fol. 157b, lines 8–11 = El-Gamil ed., 13–14.
56. Ibid., fol. 157b, lines 25–29 = El-Gamil ed., 15.
57. Ibid., fols. 157b, line 29–158a, line 3 = El-Gamil ed., 15.
58. Ibid., fol. 158a, lines 4–8 = El-Gamil ed., 15.
59. Ibid., fol. 158a, lines 9–10 = El-Gamil ed., 16.
60. On the medieval rabbinic definition of *peshat* and its relation to *derash* in halakhic contexts, see D. Weiss Halivni, *Peshat and Derash: Plain and Applied Meaning in Rabbinic Exegesis* (New York: Oxford University Press, 1991), 79–88, 168–73; Y. Maori, "The Approach of Classical Jewish Exegetes to *Peshat* and *Derash* and Its Implications for the Teaching of Bible Today," *Tradition* 21:3 (1984): 40–53; and M. I. Lockshin, "Tradition or Context: Two Exegetes Struggle

with Peshat," in *From Ancient Israel to Modern Judaism . . . Essays in Honor of Marvin Fox,* ed. J. Neusner et al. (Atlanta: Scholars Press, 1989), 2:173–86.

61. See Z. Ankori, "Elijah Bashyachi: An Inquiry into His Traditions Concerning the Beginnings of Karaism in Byzantium" (Hebrew) *Tarbiz* 25 (1955–56): 60–63, 196–99 (44–65, 183–201). For Maimonides' influence on later Byzantine Karaite thought see notes 11 and 14 above.
62. See Bowman, *The Jews of Byzantium,* 147.
63. Oxford Bodleian MS Opp. Add. 4to, 121, fol. 158a, lines 14–15 = El-Gamil ed., 16.
64. Japheth ben Eli was active during the tenth century. As it happens, Elijah had originally written "Yeshu'ah"—i.e., Jeshuah ben Judah (mid-eleventh century)—but the copyist Mordecai ben Jacob altered the text. Mordecai's editorial interventions elicited a furious response from Elijah; see CUL MS Heb. Add. 1743, fols. 24a–25a, and the appendix to this chapter. Of course, Ibn Ezra could not literally have been the disciple of either Japheth or Jeshuah. But he was familiar with their commentaries, which he cites with some frequency. In general, Andalusian Bible commentaries owe a great deal in form, outlook, and approach to the Karaite works composed in the East during the tenth and eleventh centuries; see D. Frank, *Search Scripture Well: Karaite Exegetes and the Origins of the Jewish Bible Commentary in the Islamic East* (Leiden: Brill, 2004), esp. 248–57.
65. Oxford Bodleian MS Opp. Add. 4to, 121, fol. 158a, lines 15–25 = El-Gamil ed., 16–17.
66. Ibid., fols. 159b, line 28–160a, line 3 = El-Gamil ed., 24. The catalogue of halakhic differences between Rabbanite and Karaite *halakhah* constitutes a recognizable genre. See, e.g., L. Nemoy, "Elijah ben Abraham and His Tract against the Rabbanites," *Hebrew Union College Annual* 51 (1980): 63–87; Nemoy, "Ibn Kammūnah's Treatise on the Differences Between the Rabbanites and the Karaites," *Jewish Quarterly Review* 63 (1972–73): 97–135, 222–46; and Mann, *Texts and Studies,* 2:1433, referring to Solomon b. Aaron's *Leḥem She'arim.*
67. See, e.g., Oxford Bodleian MS Opp. Add. 4to, 121, fol. 160a, lines 3–4 = El-Gamil ed., 24 (Ibn Ezra), and fol. 166b, line 25 = El-Gamil ed., 61 (Maimonides). He also cites Moses Naḥmanides (fol. 160a, 161a = El-Gamil ed., 24, 32), Isaac Abarbanel (fol. 163a = El-Gamil ed., 43–44), Baḥya ben Asher (fols. 163b, 168b = El-Gamil ed., 46, 48), Rashi (fol. 163b = El-Gamil ed., 46), Judah Halevi's *Kuzari* (fol. 163b = El-Gamil ed., 47), Judah Moscato (fols. 164a–165b = El-Gamil ed., 49–51), Moses Kapuṣato (fol. 165b = El-Gamil ed., 57), Moses Narboni (fol. 167ab = El-Gamil ed., 61–63), and Shem Tov ben Joseph ben Shem Tov (fol. 167ab = El-Gamil ed., 63–64).
68. Leviticus 24:19–20.
69. Maimonides, *Guide of the Perplexed* III:41 (Warsaw, 1872), fol. 52b (my translation of the Hebrew; cf. Chicago edition, trans. Pines, p. 558). On this passage see D. Novak, "*Lex Talionis:* A Maimonidean Perspective on Scripture, Tradition, and Reason," *S'vara* 2:1 (1991): 61–64, and Weiss Halivni, *Peshat and Derash,* 85–86. Within the Babylonian-Andalusian tradition of rabbinic scholarship there was a disjunction between exegesis and legislation. Rejecting the authority of *midrash halakhah,* these scholars insisted that Jewish Law in its entirety derives from the oral tradition. See J. M. Harris, *How Do We Know This?* (Albany: State University of New York Press, 1995), chap. 4, esp. 82–85.
70. See Aaron ben Elijah, *Sefer Gan Eden* (Gözlöw, 1866), "Dinei mumim," fol. 179d.

71. Elijah devotes Article Eight to the *lex talionis* (fols. 166a–168a = El-Gamil ed., 59–66), as well as the comments of Narboni and Shem Tov ad loc. (167a = El-Gamil ed., 61–64).

72. The same type of polemic can be found as well in at least two later works, Abraham ben Josiah's *Sefer Emunah Omen* (1712) and *Sefer Apiryon Asah Lo* of Solomon ben Jedidiah Aaron of Troki (d. 1745). On Abraham ben Josiah, see S. Poznanski, "Ha-Qara'i Avraham Ben Yoshiyahu Yerushalmi," *Ha-Goren* 8 (1912): 58–75, esp. 61–62 on the *lex talionis*. In *Sefer Apiryon Asah Lo*, part 2, chap. 34 (Ramlah: Mekhon Tif'eret Yosef, 2000), 2:641–45, Solomon ben Aaron addresses Ibn Ezra's sophistry (*hitḥakmut*). (This is the long version of the text published by A. Neubauer, *Aus der Petersburger Bibliothek* [Leipzig, 1866].) On the author, see Mann, *Texts and Studies* 2:740–41. As late as 1880, a Karaite scholar in Istanbul, Solomon Jedidiah ben Eliezer Afeda Kohen, composed a polemic against Ibn Ezra; see *Sefer Divrei Rivot*, ed. Y. El-Gamil (Ashdod: Mekhon Tif'eret Yosef, 2003).

73. For his sketch of the secular curriculum and its seven sciences—logic, arithmetic, astronomy, geometry, music, physics, and metaphysics—see the *Yalqut*, Essay No. 34, SP, IOS MS B415, 33a–34a = El-Gamil ed., 153–59.

74. It is true that he lashes out at Saadya in *Asarah Ma'amarot* (Oxford Bodleian MS Opp. Add. 4to, 121, fol. 159a = El-Gamil ed., 19), but the Gaon was really no more than a bugbear, known only at second-hand from Ibn Ezra's citations (fol. 161a = El-Gamil ed., 29), and, of course, Salmon b. Yerûḥim's *Wars of the Lord*, which Elijah had copied (above n. 3).

75. "Letter to Isaac Pasha ben Moses Pasha," CUL MS Heb. Add. 1743, fol. 118a, lines 24–26.

76. See note 50 above.

77. This is based upon personal observation but is not noted in the catalogues.

78. For a description see A. Neubauer, *Catalogue of the Hebrew Manuscripts in the Bodleian Library* (Oxford: Clarendon Press, 1886), No. 2386, and cf. M. Steinschneider, "Literarische Beilage: Karaitische Handschriften," *Hebraeische Bibliographie* 11 (1871): 10–12, no. 7. For a plate see S. Birnbaum, *The Hebrew Scripts* (London: Palaeographa, 1954–57), no. 392.

79. Fol. 122a, where the date is given as 2 Sivan 5439. In the second colophon (fol. 148a) the date has been erased. On Jacob ben Mordecai, see S. Poznanski, "Karäische Kopisten und Besitzer von Handschriften," *Zeitschrift für hebraeische Bibliographie* 19 (1916): 88, no. 56; Poznanski, "Nachtrag," *Zeitschrift für hebraeische Bibliographie* 20 (1917): 79–83; A. Firkovich, *Avnei Zikkaron* (Vilna, 1872), 111–12, no. 402.

80. Mordecai ben Jacob was also an active copyist; see Poznanski, "Karäische Kopisten und Besitzer von Handschriften," 80, no. 6. See also M. L. Wilensky, "Rabbi Elijah Afeda Baghi and the Karaite Community of Jerusalem," *Proceedings of the American Academy for Jewish Research* 40 (1972): 112–13 and nn. 17–19.

81. On this dating, see Frank, "A Karaite Sheḥitah Controversy," 96n102.

II

Jews, Conversos, and Heretics in the Early Modern Period

7

From the Dossiers of the Inquisition

Crypto-Jewish Attacks on Ecclesiastical Authority

MIRIAM BODIAN

Introduction

A Portuguese student at the University of Salamanca in the 1630s, no doubt a converso, made a remarkable statement during a private conversation with a young theologian—a statement that was later repeated to the Inquisition. The two were discussing what they felt to be the impossibility of believing in a God who existed in three persons (as the doctrine of the Trinity would have it); in a God who was also man (as the doctrine of the incarnation would have it); and in a God who was present in the host (as the doctrine of transubstantiation would have it). But how could they allow themselves to doubt the teachings of the Church? Boldly and ingeniously, the student argued that Scripture itself taught that men possessed a right to independent judgment in theological matters, and he cited the verse "Be not like the horse, or the mule, which have no understanding" (Ps. 32:9). As his companion later explained, this meant "that God said we need not subjugate our reasoning, in the manner of a horse or a mule, to things that seem impossible to the mind."[1]

By the seventeenth century, in a way that parallels developments in some sectarian Protestant circles and may reflect the survival of *alumbrado* attitudes in the Peninsula, certain crypto-Jews were stubbornly claiming for themselves the right to interpret Scripture according to their own lights.[2] They rejected, like the radical sectarians, the Church's claim to exclusive authority over the interpretation of Scripture. But in rejecting the exclusive authority of an elite in theological matters, they laid out a set of ideas that implied a potential conflict with rabbinic authority as well, within the context of Jewish life outside the Peninsula. I should stress the word "potential." Even those few crypto-Jews who managed to gain limited access to post-biblical Jewish literature did not have a grasp of how authority was exercised in a Jewish community.[3] In fact, some of them may well have projected onto normative Jewish life the freedom they enjoyed in the crypto-Jewish underground.

It is not clear to me at this point how common it was in crypto-Jewish circles to reject ecclesiastical authority in principle. I am only beginning to explore the evidence. Some of the evidence has been seen by other scholars and passed over without comment, implying that it was of no particular interest. This reflects a tendency among scholars to construct the world of the crypto-Jew as one defined by a polar struggle between Catholic and Jewish belief systems. To be sure, a crypto-Jewish attack on ecclesiastical authority *was* an attack on Catholicism. But the structure of the conflict, and the sources of support available to the crypto-Jew, had wider implications for his or her religious outlook. The radical, scripturally based anti-clerical thinking we will examine among certain crypto-Jews could easily be transferred to the Jewish sphere and turned against rabbinic authority, as the case of Uriel da Costa appears to demonstrate.

The fact that crypto-Jews exercised a good deal of independence in their religious speculation and behavior is not in itself revealing. Living in an environment in which Jewish traditions could not be transmitted in writing (and in which even verbal communication was risky), a sophisticated crypto-Jew was bound to elaborate on the meager oral lore he or she knew. There was no norm against which to measure such elaborations, no institutionalized authority to impose discipline, no mechanism to control the dissemination of unorthodox ideas. Under these conditions, a certain freedom of innovation was inevitable. What I want to examine is not this general situation, but rather specific notions crypto-Jews expressed about religious coercion, censorship, human reason, and religious autonomy.

Admittedly, the evidence I have collected is not representative. I have gathered it from the Inquisition dossiers of several outstanding *dogmatistas pertinaces* (pertinacious dogmatizers)—that is, learned, Bible-reading "judaizers" who were able to engage in disputations with orthodox Catholic inquisitors and theologians for months and even years without losing confidence in their beliefs. (Such an ordeal in itself no doubt strengthened the sense of religious autonomy.) These dogmatizers were, however, widely scattered geographically, indicating that ideas like theirs were not limited to a certain circle. Let us look at the evidence from four cases that reflect particularly well-developed arguments refuting Church authority, all of which would be used, in time, against rabbinic authority.

Luis Carvajal

The first case is that of the converso Luis Carvajal the younger. Though this figure is well known to scholars, his remarkable teachings have not been critically examined.[4] This is not entirely surprising. Scholars have tended to identify judaizing martyrs with a generalized idea of "Judaism"—just as the Inquisition and Jewish contemporaries did. Their accounts have thus tended to obscure rather than highlight the novel aspects of the martyrs' thinking.

Let us reconsider the evidence. Carvajal was involved in a judaizing circle in the New Kingdom of León (in what is today Mexico) in the 1580s, led by a university-educated physician of Portuguese converso origins. The latter, Manuel de Morales, taught a rather unusual creed. In contrast to the more prevalent orally transmitted, ancestral traditions of Iberian judaizing,[5] the teachings of Morales placed a unique value on written texts. In particular, he taught the members of his circle to rely on a literal reading of key biblical proof texts to "see for themselves" the falsifications of the Church. For this, he provided his students with hand-copied booklets of critical texts prohibited by the Inquisition: crypto-Jewish prayers and hymns in Spanish, and, to a few, a complete Spanish translation of Deuteronomy.[6]

Carvajal's reading of Scripture was literalist and activist. In contrast to the rabbinic approach to Scripture, he assumed the existence of a self-evident "true" reading of the text, accessible to anyone. It was this "transparency" of Scripture that permitted him to attack Church authority with utter confidence. For him, verses such as "All his commandments are sure. They stand fast for ever and ever" (Ps. 111:7–8), or "You shall not add to the word which I command you, neither shall you diminish from it" (Deut. 4:2), constituted empirical proof, as it were, that Christianity was in error.[7] To argue in the face of such verses that the Law of Moses was no longer valid, he argued, was as if to say that the sky had fallen or the sun ceased to shine.[8] The Church was trying to prove "that snow is not white and that there are no nights, only days."[9]

Carvajal's sense of being immediately subject to Scripture and Scripture alone is striking. That he was not simply reiterating what he learned from his mentor is clear from events that occurred after Morales's departure for Europe in 1584. In this period Carvajal managed to buy a printed copy of the Vulgate from a cleric in the mining town of Pánuco, and this purchase allowed him to study the entire canon of Jewish Scripture for the first time. In his autobiography, written in the third person (like other sixteenth-century spiritual memoirs), he recorded a dramatic moment during his first reading of the book of Genesis. "In the course of his assiduous reading [of this Bible] in the solitude [of Pánuco]," he wrote, "he came to understand many divine mysteries; and one day he happened to read chapter 17 of Genesis where the Lord commanded Abraham to circumcise himself." The passionate young Carvajal was struck by "those words that said that the soul who went uncircumcised would be blotted out of the book of the living."[10] This awful prospect led him to find a place where he could conceal himself, and, "with burning desire to be inscribed in the book of life, which is impossible without this holy sacrament [*este sacramento santo*]," he circumcised himself with scissors. What is noteworthy about this incident is the way Carvajal, who was certainly cognizant of the precept of circumcision, was moved to action by his independent discovery of the authentic written source.

Also noteworthy is the flourish of interpretive boldness with which Carvajal concludes the telling of the story. He was concerned that his self-circumcision was slightly imperfect. In reassuring himself that it would be acceptable to God, he turned to a passage elsewhere in Scripture, namely to the words of Solomon in II Chronicles 6:7–9. "It was in the heart of David my father," says Solomon, "to build a house for the name of the Lord God of Yisra'el. But the Lord said to David my father, Since it was in thy heart to build a house for my name, *thou didst well in that it was in thy heart* [emphasis mine]. Yet thou shalt not build the house; but thy son who shall come out of thy loins, he shall build the house for my name." Carvajal interpreted this passage as conveying a general teaching, namely that God credited a person for having the intention to perform a precept, even if he or she was not actually able to carry it out.[11]

This teaching itself was not a novel one in the converso world. On the contrary, there is evidence that many crypto-Jews believed that the intention to observe the Law of Moses, in itself, was sufficient for one's salvation.[12] What is striking in Carvajal's account is his citation of a scriptural "proof text" for this notion. Whether he had "discovered" the passage from Chronicles independently or had been guided to it by Morales, he derived the authority for this teaching not from the usual orally transmitted lore—which was arguably no more reliable than the traditions of the Church—but from Scripture itself.

Carvajal's confident version of *sola scriptura* was accompanied by considerable contempt for a Church that did not allow its lay members free access to Scripture. This is illustrated in his account of an attempt (together with his brother Balthasar) to convert his brother Gaspar, a Dominican friar and sincere Catholic. According to his account, Luis opened with an innocent question. Was it true, he asked, that God himself inscribed his commandments on the Tablets of the Law? (As a lay person in post-Tridentine Spanish lands, Luis would under ordinary circumstances have had no way to confirm this.) Gaspar responded by opening a Bible (undoubtedly the Vulgate) to the relevant passage in Exodus (presumably 32:15–16), showing it to Luis by way of confirmation. Luis remarked that the Law of Moses must then be the Law one was obliged to obey. To this Gaspar replied that while it had once been the Law, it had been abrogated. This reply gave Luis's brother Balthasar the opportunity to point to a New Testament "proof text" refuting the doctrine of the abrogation of the Law. As he put it, "The Gospels themselves relate that your Crucified One said, 'Do not think that I came here to annul the laws or the prophets and their holy and truthful prophecies!' for thus he said, 'Surely it is an easier thing for the sky or the earth to be absent than for a jot or tittle of his holy law to pass away or be changed.' "[13]

In typical polemical fashion, Luis related that Gaspar was confounded. But when Luis suggested that Balthasar and Gaspar spend a few days studying together, Gaspar declined, explaining, according to Luis, "that his law *forbade him to inquire and to increase his knowledge* [my emphasis]."[14] It seems unlikely that Gaspar actually made this statement. However that may be, the statement is intended to articulate the anxiety about free access to written material underlying Gaspar's thinking. For Luis, the Church's position could be understood only as a response to fear—the fear that free inquiry would reveal that the premises of Catholic belief were false. Judaism, by implication, had nothing to fear.

This was a rather naïve position. It was naïve in its assumption that Catholic teaching rested on such fragile foundations, as well as in its simplistic understanding of the Church's attitude to forbidden knowledge.[15] But it was also naïve in its conception of Judaism as standing in diametrical opposition to Catholicism. Carvajal was apparently unaware of the intricate set of traditions that, shaped and reshaped by the rabbinic elite over generations, served as the authoritative basis for the Jewish interpretation of Scripture. However unwittingly, Carvajal was echoing challenges to clerical authority over the interpretation of Scripture that would lead, eventually, to radical challenges to religious control and authority in both Christian and Jewish societies.

Diogo da Asumpção

A more explicitly radical voice than Carvajal's was that of the Capuchin friar Diogo da Asumpção. Frei Diogo was seized by the Inquisition near Lisbon in 1599. He had fled his monastery and was seeking to flee to the Netherlands or England,[16] having come to the conclusion, as he told the tribunal, that "everything among the friars is a pack of lies, falsehoods, and deceptions." From the outset, he openly rejected key teachings of the Church. But initially he said little to indicate that he was a judaizer. (Indeed, a close reading of his dossier suggests that it was only in prison that he gradually became a committed judaizer.) At the outset, Frei Diogo was primarily driven by anger at a Church that claimed authority to supervise all aspects of spiritual life. He argued that "it was not necessary to petition saints, but only God; and that the popes and councilors did not understand Scripture, creating and following human laws and calling them divine; and that the [holy] orders were not [divinely ordained] orders, nor was the mass a sacrament, nor was the sacrament of communion more than bread . . . nor was a man obligated to confess to another man but only to God, and that everything [else] was the invention of men."[17]

In light of such beliefs it is not surprising that Frei Diogo harbored some regard for Martin Luther, who, he maintained, held that "whoever invented the sacraments was an enemy of Jesus."[18] But although the Reformers had broken with the Catholic Church because they had found it "had no basis," they, too, according to the friar, were perpetrating a fraud. Being illustrious men, they needed followers, so "they fashioned new sects in order to hold onto their fame."[19] That is, the Reformers devised new creeds that were, like Catholicism, human inventions that served their own needs. Moreover, they based these creeds on the Gospels, which the friar believed were authored by mortal (and ignorant) men. These convictions, and his uncompromising nature, apparently drove Frei Diogo eventually to the conclusion that only the Scripture of the Jews was the unadulterated word of God.

Frei Diogo was an unusual judaizer in more ways than one: he appears to have had little or no Jewish blood. (Extensive testimony on this matter was gathered by the Inquisition.) Yet he appears to have had ties to New Christians, perhaps crypto-Jews. By his own admission, he initially approached a New Christian named Gaspar Bocarro for help after fleeing his monastery. (He was rebuffed.) Perhaps more significant is the fact that a group of crypto-Jews in Coimbra founded a confraternity in his honor after his death at the stake in 1603.[20] Unfortunately, however, the specific nature of his contacts with New Christians is unclear. Had crypto-Jewish attacks on the Church reinforced his disillusionment with it? Had he perhaps found common ground with crypto-Jews as a result of his disillusionment, even though he was not a converso or a conventional judaizer? If he had contacts with crypto-Jewish circles, did they offer him the freedom of expression (and support) that he had evidently intended to seek in England or the Netherlands? Or, if he did not have such contacts, did he eventually anchor himself in a judaizing belief system because, under intense pressure, he came to identify with crypto-Jews he had heard of?

These are questions that cannot be addressed until we know more about Frei Diogo's monastery in Castanheira. However, viewed in conjunction with other cases, including the next one we shall discuss, Frei Diogo's case suggests a picture of dovetailing interests—perhaps even mutual succor—between anti-clerical Old Christians and the crypto-Jewish underground in the Peninsula. His judaizing, and the commemoration of it both in Coimbra and in the Western Sefardi Diaspora, hints at the contingent, mutable nature of "crypto-judaizing," the absence of clear boundaries between Old and New Christians in heterodox circles, and the freedom enjoyed by crypto-Jews not only from constricting traditions but also from the rigid socio-ethnic religious boundaries that became an integral part of Portuguese Jewish life outside the Peninsula.

Lope de Vera

In 1639, another cleric from a family that was regarded as Old Christian,[21] Lope de Vera, was seized by the Inquisition as he was competing for a chair in Hebrew at the University of Salamanca (a situation that invited intrigue).[22] Unfortunately, the full Inquisition dossier for Lope de Vera has not survived. We possess only the annual summaries sent to the Suprema during the period of his imprisonment.[23] But it is of considerable significance that Don Lope was competing for a position that was an institutional relic of early-sixteenth-century humanism. His familiarity with the Hebrew Bible and his recognition of the inadequacy of the Vulgate (gained by reading a banned work or banned works of Erasmus) contributed to his doubts about ecclesiastical authority. The Vulgate, he declared at one point, had "more than 10,000 errors."

But equally important were his contacts with heterodox Portuguese conversos studying at Salamanca. Lope de Vera appears to have quickly guessed that the Inquisition had testimony against him from one or more Portuguese converso students. He decided to confess to several highly damaging conversations he had had with these persons, including the conversation mentioned in the opening paragraph of this essay. Certainly these conversations betray his heterodoxy. They do not, however, show that he was a fully committed judaizer.

Interestingly, one of the major witnesses against him depicted him not as a judaizer, but as a rationalist who was weighing the comparative merits of Christianity, Islam, and Judaism. According to this witness, Lope de Vera had told a group of students that Catholicism required belief in "many things that were difficult to believe." He found other religions, he said—in particular Islam and Judaism—"more in conformity with natural reason."

Initially, Lope de Vera sought to minimize his inevitable punishment by feigning repentance. But one senses that he had distanced himself too radically from the outlook and sensibility of the Spanish Church of his day to play the part persuasively over the course of a prolonged imprisonment. After a period of severe illness, he made the fateful decision to cease subjugating himself (if not his reason) to "things that seem impossible to the mind." By a psychic and intellectual process that is unfortunately hidden from us, he emerged a fervent judaizer, resolved to "die in the Law of Moses." Among other uncompromising actions, he circumcised himself in his cell with a chicken bone and renamed himself "Judah Creyente."

Lope de Vera, it would then seem, became a committed judaizer only as a secondary consequence of his adamant rejection of ecclesiastical authority. This is indirectly articulated (albeit from the point of view of a pious Catholic) in a letter written by an inquisitor that later reached Jewish hands in Amsterdam.[24] It reads:

> Innumerable masters and *calificadores* spoke with him, trying by all means to bring him back, judging that at such a tender age, with God's help, it might be permitted to win him back. But it was time wasted, for he told them all that they were ignorant and did not understand the translations [of the Bible], and that all [the translations] were contrary to the true [meaning] of the text. All his trouble came to this unhappy man because of his not paying regard to the excommunication that he incurred by reading prohibited books.

His real crime, that is, was insubordination.

Theologians summoned by the Inquisition made repeated efforts to convince Lope de Vera of the error of his judaizing. But by June 1641, they came to the conclusion that "because of his learning, wickedness, and knowledge of the Hebrew language, his remaining in Christianity would be pernicious for all who came in contact with him," and Don Lope was burned at the stake in 1644. It is paradoxical but perhaps also fitting that Spinoza had heard of Lope de Vera, and mentioned him in a passage on Jewish martyrdom.[25]

Isaac de Castro Tartas

Defiance of the Church in the cases I have sketched above reflects a conviction that it was wrong to deny a person the opportunity to make an independent judgment about the true meaning of Scripture. In their lives as crypto-Jews, or at any rate in their careers as defiant judaizers, all three men experienced an unprecedented freedom to interpret Scripture as they chose. It must have seemed natural to associate that freedom with Judaism itself, since crypto-Jews constituted the only significant opposition to Church authority in Iberian lands. It may well be that this was a key factor in the appeal of crypto-Judaism to figures like Diogo da Asumpção or Lope de Vera, who might have become Protestants or sectarians in other circumstances. One senses that they would not have been gratified to live in a Jewish community in which books were censored and "heretics" banned. It would be wrong to say that these men regarded themselves as entitled to religious autonomy *in principle.* They did not possess the conceptual tools to make and argue such a claim. Nevertheless, their thinking reflects an implicit belief that any educated, reasonable, and sincerely motivated person could discern (or discover) for himself the key to salvation, namely, the truth about Scripture.

This conviction was highly valuable to the small number of educated crypto-Jews who chose a path of martyrdom. It sustained them in a prolonged confrontation with a vastly more powerful adversary. It was not, however, a conviction that could be transferred easily to the context of a normative Jewish community. To be sure, no one arrested and interrogated members of a Jewish community because of unorthodox beliefs (which were not uncommon among ex-conversos). But when ex-conversos openly and persistently attacked the tradition of rabbinic interpretation of Scripture as false—as a few did in early modern Amsterdam—the communal authorities exercised their coercive powers and banned the disseminators of heresy. For rabbinic scholars, a spontaneous, literalist reading of Scripture—one which effectively challenged Christianity and defended certain basic Jewish teachings—was undoubtedly admirable in the "lands of captivity," but was unwelcome in "lands of freedom."

The case of Uriel da Costa is instructive. The attack of this Portuguese ex-converso on the Oral Law, first in 1616 and then in his work *Exame das tradições phariseas* (Examination of Pharisaic Traditions) in 1623, reflected a powerful conviction that a simple reading of Scripture was enough to reveal the human artificiality and fraudulence of the rabbinic tradition. In his words, "Two opposites are incompatible and truth cannot be found in both. Therefore the [oral] tradition which is contrary to the Law must be false if the Law is true."[26] Da Costa, who suffered excommunication and other humiliations in Amsterdam before he committed suicide in 1640, unquestionably shared some of the characteristics of the *dogmatista pertinaz,* and used similar rhetoric. In fact, if his so-called autobiography is to be relied upon, he regarded himself a martyr for the truth—one who was destroyed not by the Inquisition but by the Jewish communal establishment.[27]

But most crypto-Jews were not fervent individualists of the type of the *dogmatistas pertinaces,* and shared an outlook in which group interests were paramount. Once they joined Jewish communities outside the Peninsula they readily accepted the common project of "rejudaization" (and the rhetoric that placed it in the context of a covenantal obligation). This was quite consistent with the Amsterdam Sefardi elite's conception of the community as one defined by God-given, time-honored, ethno-religious boundaries that set the

Jews apart from other peoples. Most Portuguese Jews were sufficiently conditioned to a collective, ethnocentric notion of Judaism to accept this state of affairs, and did not dream of a society arranged otherwise.

Quite fascinating in this light is the Inquisition testimony of a young *dogmatista pertinaz* who happened to have been educated in the Jewish community of Amsterdam.[28] For reasons that are not clear, fate had brought this ex-converso to Portuguese Brazil, where he was arrested for judaizing in 1644 and extradited for trial to Lisbon. In contrast to the other *dogmatistas pertinaces,* Isaac de Castro Tartas possessed a thorough formal education in rabbinic Judaism. He must also have learned much from his uncle, the eminent *ḥakham* Moses Rafael d'Aguilar. If there were any doubts about his adherence to rabbinic law, they would have been dispelled when he was seized in Portuguese Brazil with a pair of *tefillin* in his belongings.

Perhaps because of the unusual nature of the case, the youth was questioned at considerable length over the course of two days on his views about religious authority.[29] It is a fascinating discussion, even viewed through the prism of formulaic inquisitorial discourse.

Isaac de Castro was initially asked "if he knew that he had an obligation [by virtue of his having been baptized] to submit himself to the doctrine that he had been taught by learned and virtuous persons [summoned by the tribunal]." He replied carefully, saying "that he knew he had an obligation to submit to persons who understood matters of faith and Holy Scripture better than he, and that he, the prisoner, did not conduct himself by his own authority alone [*que elle Reo senao governa por si*], but by the same Scriptures whose passages they had cited in his trial, as well as others that he pondered daily. And this was what obligated him." He thus cleverly emphasized what he had in common with his inquisitors. He accepted the same ultimate authority they did, namely Scripture (in his case, minus the New Testament). Further, he accepted the necessity of submitting oneself to learned interpreters of that text. But there is a contentious subtext: a clear implication that he understood Scripture better than his inquisitors. (He was indeed highly knowledgeable, and had the advantage of knowing the Hebrew original.) He continued, declaring that "he had no reason to swerve from his belief [in the Law of Moses], for he had beseeched God with great urgency many times to illumine him; and if he had been headed on an erroneous path, he was certain God would have illumined him and directed him [otherwise, leading him] in the true path of his salvation. And God had not done this." The inquisitor did not follow up with another question, presumably because it was time to draw the audience to a close. But he did respond thus to the prisoner's remarks in a closing admonition:

> It was said to [Isaac de Castro Tartas by the inquisitor] that the prisoner had neither the learning nor the years of study [required], nor was it his profession to spend his time in studying Scripture. And even if he had studied much Latin, it was wrong of him to rely on his own judgment [*faz mal de se fiar de seu juizo*], being obligated to submit to what was said to him by this tribunal so many times . . . and that he should know for certain that his stubbornness and contumacy were bred of the illusions of the demon who is our enemy and tries in every way to condemn our soul.

The audience was over but the matter was not forgotten. When questioning resumed the following day, the inquisitor asked the prisoner if he "believed with a sure conscience that he might conduct himself in matters of belief according to his own judgment and personal opinion, refusing to submit himself to the doctrine and admonitions of this tribunal, as well as to what the theologians summoned by this tribunal have told him."

To this the prisoner replied

> that he would not presume to conduct himself with a sure conscience according to some sect of which he was the sole author. Rather he understood that he could rest secure in conducting himself and believing according to the Law that God, the author of the world, gave to all, especially possessing the faith and doctrine they [the rabbis?] had taught him. And he believed that if he conducted himself according to the spirit of his conscience, he could not offend God. On the contrary, it is actions that are not in conformity with conscience that offend God. And the conscience of the prisoner has in no way been swayed [by the tribunal], but rather moved to do the will of God, and a soul could not be lost for doing the will of God when he had no doubt that the path he followed was certain and true.

This is a reply that warrants close reading. Isaac de Castro's remarks were not casual, but carefully formulated during hours of reflection. He made clear that he was not a religious eccentric. He would not presume to adopt a set of beliefs on his own, independent of any authority. He seems to acknowledge the role of his Jewish teachers, who possessed an authority he could not claim. (The passage is a bit obscure.) Yet it is striking that he did not once, here or elsewhere, invoke the authority of the sages and rabbis. He entirely avoided the traditional, ethnically specific rabbinic rationale for adhering to Jewish law, which he certainly knew and understood, and presumably appreciated in a certain context.

Like the other *dogmatistas,* Isaac de Castro adopted a universalistic conception of the sources of religious authority, one that relied on the exercise of human faculties (reason, conscience) and/or personal illumination by God, rather than submission to a specific institutionalized tradition of authority. It is not entirely clear what the relationship between "conscience" and "illumination" was in his thinking, or how he understood the former term. But he was clearly drawing from an ideological discourse that leveled the polemical field during his interrogation, rendering him fit to defend the Law of Moses despite his lack of rabbinic credentials. This is not to imply that his behavior was dictated merely by calculation. He must surely also have believed what he declared so eloquently. But one wonders whether this intelligent youth recognized that by resorting to the authority of conscience, he was borrowing from a conceptual world that was alien to rabbinic thinking, and that would raise a multitude of challenges for the tradition he was seeking to defend.

Notes

1. Archivo Histórico Nacional, Madrid (henceforth AHN), Inq. de Valladolid, Legajo 2135, No. 17, 25v.
2. On similar claims among the *alumbrados* of Spain, see José Nieto, "The Nonmystical Nature of the Sixteenth-Century Alumbrados of Toledo," in *The Spanish Inquisition and the Inquisitorial Mind,* ed. A. Alcalá (Boulder, Colo.: Social Science Monographs; Highland Lakes, N.J.: Atlantic Research and Publications; [New York]: distributed by Columbia University Press, 1987): 431–56; Nieto, *Juan de Valdés and the Origins of the Spanish and Italian Reformation* (Geneva: Droz, 1970).
3. Y. H. Yerushalmi has ingeniously pointed out the ways in which Isaac Cardoso apparently gleaned knowledge about post-biblical Judaism. See Y. H. Yerushalmi, *From Spanish Court to Italian Ghetto: Isaac Cardoso, A Study in Seventeenth-Century Marranism and Jewish Apologetics* (Seattle: University of Washington Press, 1981), 271–301.
4. See Martin Cohen, *The Martyr: The Story of a Secret Jew and the Mexican Inquisition in the Sixteenth Century* (Philadelphia: Jewish Publication Society, 1973); Seymour Liebman, *The Enlightened: The Writings of Luis de Carvajal, el mozo* (Coral Gables,

Fla.: University of Miami Press, 1967); Alfonso Toro, *La familia Carvajal: estudio histórico sobre los judíos y la Inquisición de la Nueva España en el siglo XVI,* 2 vols. (Mexico City: Editorial Patria, 1944).

5. See Miriam Bodian, *Hebrews of the Portuguese Nation: Conversos and Community in Early Modern Amsterdam* (Bloomington: Indiana University Press, 1997), 36–43, 99–103.
6. In Luis Carvajal's valuable spiritual autobiography, a text he composed after his first arrest (it was seized and preserved by the Inquisition), these hand-copied notebooks crop up repeatedly and we get a sense of their centrality in Carvajal's circle. See *Procesos de Luis de Carvajal (el Mozo),* ed. L. González Obregón (Mexico City: Talleres gráficos de la nación, 1935), 465–66, 475.
7. *Procesos de Luis de Carvajal,* 413.
8. Ibid., 294.
9. Ibid., 415.
10. This is an interesting rendering of Genesis 17:14.
11. *Procesos de Luis de Carvajal,* 465.
12. See Bodian, *Hebrews of the Portuguese Nation,* 100–101.
13. A paraphrase of Matthew 5:17–18.
14. *Procesos de Luis de Carvajal,* 472–73.
15. On this topic see Carlo Ginzburg, "The High and the Low: The Theme of Forbidden Knowledge in the 16th and 17th Centuries," in *Clues, Myths, and the Historical Method* (Baltimore: Johns Hopkins University Press, 1989), 60–76.
16. At this time there was only a fledgling Jewish community in the Netherlands, and no openly practicing Jewish community in England. Given this figure's views, it seems possible that he intended to follow in the footsteps of heterodox Iberian monks who fled the Peninsula to join Protestant communities elsewhere in Europe.
17. Arquivo Nacional de Torre do Tombo, Lisbon (henceforth ANTT), Inq. de Lisboa, processo no. 104, fol.208v.
18. Ibid., fol. 5r, and cf. fol. 14v.
19. Ibid.
20. See J. M. de Almeida Saraiva de Carvalho, "The Fellowship of St. Diogo: New Christian Judaisers in Coimbra in the Early Seventeenth Century" (Ph.D. diss., University of Leeds, 1990).
21. There was evidently some testimony indicating that Lope de Vera had a minor degree of Jewish ancestry, but the surviving inquisitorial documents are vague about this. It is interesting that despite his own claims to the tribunal that he was an Old Christian, he was reported to have said to one of the witnesses against him that he "felt great sorrow that *all* his blood was not Jewish, which was the most noble in the world" (my emphasis). This statement appears four times in the summaries; only once does it read "that his blood was not Jewish." Haim Beinart has cited only the latter version of Lope de Vera's statement; see H. Beinart, "The Convert Lope de Vera y Alarcon and His Martyrdom as Judah Creyente" (Hebrew), in *Sefer Yovel li-khevod Aharon Mirski,* ed. Z. Malachi (Lod: Haberman Institute, 1986), 38n28.
22. It would not have been the first time at Salamanca that academic politics had played a role in inquisitorial activity. The scholastic backlash against humanist learning at the University of Salamanca in the second half of the sixteenth century resulted in a

series of inquisitorial trials in the 1570s. Among the theologians tried was the eminent converso Fray Luis de León. On these trials see Henry Charles Lea, *A History of the Inquisition of Spain,* vol. 4 (New York: Macmillan, 1966), 149–68; Miguel de la Pinta Llorente, *Procesos inquisitoriales contra los catedráticos hebraístas de Salamanca: Gaspar de Grajal, Martínez de Cantalapiedra, y Fr. Luis de Leon* (Madrid: Monasterio de el Escorial, 1935); Pinta Llorente, *Proceso criminal contra el hebraísta salmantino Martín Martínez de Cantalapiedra* (Madrid: Instituto Arias Montano, 1946).

23. AHN, Inq. de Valladolid, Legajo 2135, no. 15, fols. 49r–51r; no. 16, fols. 15r–19r; no. 17, fols. 24v–31r; no. 18, 4v–6r, 12v–22r; no. 19, 5v–7r.
24. It was found in the British Museum and published in the 1920s. See L. D. Barnett, "Two Documents of the Inquisition," *Jewish Quarterly Review* n.s. 15 (1924–25): 213–39.
25. See Yosef Hayim Yerushalmi, "Spinoza on the Survival of the Jewish People" (Hebrew), *Proceedings of the Israel Academy of Sciences and Humanities* 6 (1984): 17–19.
26. Uriel da Costa, *Examination of Pharisaic Traditions,* facsimile ed. with translation and introduction by H. P. Salomon and I. S. D. Sassoon (Leiden: Brill, 1993), 55, 271.
27. The work, purportedly written before da Costa committed suicide in 1640, was published by the Dutch theologian Philip van Limborch in 1687. It has been republished by Carl Gebhardt, *Die Schriften des Uriel da Costa* (Amsterdam: M. Hertzberger, 1922), 105–23.
28. ANTT, Inq. de Lisboa, Processo 11550. And see Elias Lipiner, *Izaque de Castro: O mancebo que veio preso do Brasil* (Recife: Fundação Joaquim Nabuco, Editora Massangana, 1992).
29. ANTT, Inq. de Lisboa, Processo 11550, 279r–280v.

8

Regulating Sociability

Rabbinical Authority and Jewish-Christian Interaction in Seventeenth-Century Amsterdam

ADAM SUTCLIFFE

Amsterdam in the seventeenth century was arguably the most dynamic metropolis in Europe. Its population approximately quadrupled over the course of the century, from about 50,000 to over 200,000, stimulated by the undisputed dominance of the city as the key entrepôt of the European and increasingly the global economy.[1] Migrants to Amsterdam were attracted not only by the economic opportunities and enhanced wage levels that the city offered but also by its unique cultural diversity and fluidity. At the beginning of the century migrants from outside the newly constituted Dutch Republic arrived predominantly from the southern Netherlands. After the outbreak of the Thirty Years' War, however, Germany emerged as the leading source of immigrants to Amsterdam, while the Revocation of the Edict of Nantes in 1685 led to an influx of more than 5,000 Huguenots into the city.[2] A small but not insignificant number of migrants also arrived from England, as did, of course, both Sefardic and Ashkenazic Jews, who each numbered about 3,000 in the city by 1700.[3]

Everyday life in this bustling urban setting enabled and even necessitated an unprecedented degree of interaction across multiple boundaries of cultural difference. Other early modern cities—most conspicuously, perhaps, Venice—had been host to notably diverse populations, but in seventeenth-century Amsterdam Flemings, Huguenots, Mennonites, Quakers, Catholics, Sefardic and Ashkenazic Jews, and Blacks from Suriname and other colonial outposts mingled with striking ease among and alongside the native Dutch.[4] The intellectual and political baselines of this culture of diversity were established simultaneously with, and in close relationship to, the determinant phase of the Dutch Revolt against Spain. In the "Great Dutch Toleration Debate" of the late 1620s, the arguments of Remonstrant intellectuals such as Hugo Grotius and Simon Episcopius in favor of religious pluralism prevailed, within Amsterdam at least, over the more conservative Counter-Remonstrant champions of the hegemony of the Dutch Reformed Church.[5] The guiding principles established by this Remonstrant victory reinforced the basic cultural conditions that enabled a unique climate of respectful toleration to flourish in the city.

Amsterdam in the seventeenth century was arguably the first truly cosmopolitan European city, in the sense that its economic and social life was fundamentally shaped by the presence of large numbers of recent arrivals from elsewhere. A very high proportion of the sailors taking ship from the city were foreigners, mostly from Germany or Norway, while seasonal migrants also played an important role in peddling, brick-making, dock work, and in the construction of the many new canals cut in the city over the course of its Golden Age.[6] In the words of a recent historian of the city, by the 1630s "Amsterdam had . . . acquired the dynamics of a city of outsiders."[7] The commercial vigor and maritime transience of the city generated a sense of anonymity in interpersonal relations. "Everyone is so preoccupied with his own profit," wrote René Descartes around 1635, "that I could live here for all my life without ever being noticed by anyone."[8]

However, despite this pragmatic indifference to the private habits of others, Amsterdam was also a place where it was almost impossible to be blind to the multifarious and in some respects nefarious aspects of life in the urban maelstrom. The rituals of prostitution, for example, were inescapably visible to all who had business in the central areas of the city surrounding the docks. As long as certain boundaries of discretion were not too flagrantly transgressed, the sex trade was largely tolerated.[9] Amsterdam's patrician elite and burgeoning bourgeoisie were under no illusions in this respect, as the numerous frank depictions of brothel scenes in seventeenth-century Dutch art vividly testify.[10] Similarly, the presence of a range of national, ethnic, and religious groups in the city was a reality reinforced on a daily basis by myriad visual encounters and routine transactions along Amsterdam's narrow canalside walkways and bridges. The cosmopolitan culture of the city was characterized not simply by a tolerant acceptance of this diversity, but also by a pattern of urban living that necessitated a high degree of awareness of and contact with alien cultures and lifestyles.

The Sefardic community of the city was an early and conspicuous element of this urban mosaic. The initial acceptance of Jewish settlement in the city was itself enabled by the unhesitant pragmatism of Amsterdam's commercial civic culture. While significant restrictions were placed on the initial Sefardic settlement, barring the new arrivals from shopkeeping and established guild-regulated craft industries, their presence encountered little resistance, above all because the Sefardim brought to Amsterdam new streams of commodity trade, in sugar, wood from Brazil, and diamonds from India, all imported via Portugal.[11] Amsterdam almost immediately proved a strikingly welcoming environment for its early Jewish settlers. The detailed, respectful, and elaborate manner in which Jewish customs, buildings, and monuments came to be represented by Dutch artists—most notably the famous depictions by Emmanuel de Witte and Romeyn de Hooge of the grandiose Sefardic synagogue opened in 1675—reflects the proud incorporation of the Sefardim into Amsterdam's cosmopolitan cityscape.[12] However, not only did this cultural embrace have its very real limits but it also posed challenges to the Sefardic community, and to its leadership in particular. The highly visible temptations of Amsterdam's fluid cosmopolitanism continually threatened to erode the efforts by the rabbinate and the lay *parnasim* to enforce the observance of normative Judaism within the Sefardic community.

Most former Marranos arrived in Amsterdam with a theological mindset heavily imbued with Catholic notions of sin and redemption, and also with a profoundly Iberian sense of their ethnic status and separateness.[13] In Holland, however, these assumptions were challenged by contact with contrasting and unfamiliar intellectual currents. Dutch Protestants responded very differently, and with much greater openness and curiosity, to their Jewish neighbors than had the persecutory regimes of the Iberian Peninsula. The steady growth, from the 1620s onward, of the Ashkenazic population in Amsterdam further blurred and problematized the boundaries of Jewishness as understood by the Sefardim. Meanwhile, diversity within the Sefardic community itself, in terms of wealth, religiosity, skin color, and degree of communal affiliation, also heightened the potential for friction and disagreement. The ecumenical openness and economic prosperity of Amsterdam offered the Sefardim immense opportunities, but these same realities caught the community between two opposing intellectual forces. While the establishment of structures of rabbinical and lay authority were central to the project of reestablishing normative Judaism in a population for whom Jewish practices had long been idiosyncratic or extinct, the same Dutch freedoms that enabled this project also enabled individual Jews to choose to dissent from it. Cosmopolitan cultural interaction was both the economic and political sine qua non of Sefardic community life in Amsterdam, and also, from a rabbinical perspective at least, its greatest threat.

The fundamental tensions of Sefardic life in seventeenth-century Amsterdam can all be seen as stemming in essence from the problems and possibilities raised by contact with others. In its precocious modernity Amsterdam presented an environment in which interaction across religious and ethnic boundaries slowly began, in certain circumstances, to corrode the differences on which those boundaries were based. In the medieval and early modern Iberian Peninsula an assumption of difference, and a mutual recognition of cultural separateness, had underpinned relations between Jews, Christians, and Moslems. The introduction of rules of *limpieza de sangre* from the late fifteenth century onward was motivated precisely by the desire among the Spanish aristocracy to reinforce divisions of social hierarchy in racial terms.[14] The Dutch Republic in the seventeenth century was the key crucible in which the universalistic values that most powerfully challenged social divisions first emerged. These ideals, which reached their fullest expression with the French Revolution, were in some sense already implicit in the challenge of Cartesian rationalism, which convulsed Dutch universities in the 1640s. The power of Cartesianism lay in the intellectual reach of its deductive logic, which, despite the attempt of Descartes and his followers to placate their critics by declaring an intellectual firewall between philosophy and theology, nonetheless posed an unmistakable threat to all theologically based dogmas, and also, more subtly, to all rigidly traditional boundaries of social distinction.[15]

These intellectual upheavals emanating from the Dutch universities might have had little impact on the Sefardim of Amsterdam had it not been for the distinctive cosmopolitan environment of the city. The social openness and architectural density of Amsterdam facilitated cultural contact between Jews and Christians, and these contacts inevitably included discussions of theological differences and philosophical controversies. Moreover, many ex-Marranos were particularly likely to take a keen interest in such debates. It has long been acknowledged that the rise of religious doubt, and ultimately of the Enlightenment, was largely a product of sustained intellectual attrition from the clash of competing theologies since the Reformation.[16] If this is the case, then the Sefardim of Amsterdam were a particularly likely source of heresy. Reverting to Judaism in a Protestant environment after centuries of immersion in Catholicism, they were caught between not just two but three radically distinct religious perspectives. The emergence of Cartesian rationalism in the 1640s further heightened the intensity of the intellectual dramas in which philosophically inclined Sefardim could choose to participate. It is not surprising, therefore, that this community was a notable hotbed of dissent, providing a crucial impetus, above all through the conduit of Spinoza, to the development of western secular thought.

The intellectual dynamics of Dutch Sefardic radicalism can be more fully understood when situated within the wider context of Amsterdam's distinctive culture of interactive cosmopolitanism. The influence of Protestantism and Cartesianism on Jewish dissenters (and, concomitantly, the influence of Jewish ideas on non-Jewish Dutch radicals) was not simply transmitted through the moist city air. Intellectual contact arose from social contact—for which the bourgeois public spaces, economic dynamism, and cultural pluralism of the Dutch "New Jerusalem" offered abundant opportunity. The Sefardim were not restricted to settlement in a single area of the city, and the area in which they were most prominent, on and around the Jodenbreestraat, was by no means a ghetto neighborhood. It was a fashionable, newly developed area, popular not only with the Sefardic elite but among other prosperous merchants as well. The Breestraat was also, in the seventeenth century, the center of artistic production. Several painters, most notably Rembrandt, lived in the district, which offered them close proximity to many of their most important and affluent clients.[17] This quarter of the city in particular was an area where Jews and non-Jews mingled openly and easily, fostering a mutual familiarity that was unprecedented in European history.

However, this ease of contact, which was fundamental both to the prosperity and to the rapidly rising cultural confidence of the Sefardic community, was also—at least from a traditionalist perspective—double-edged. The flimsiness and transparency of the boundaries demarcating Jewish spaces and lifestyles in Amsterdam posed a serious threat to the theological and social cohesiveness of the Sefardim. The persistent current of heresy in the community, culminating with Spinoza, was the most blatant symptom of this threat. There were numerous attempts by community leaders to quell external influences toward heterodoxy, both in the form of residual survivals from Iberian Catholicism and new notions percolating in from Protestant groupings in the Dutch Republic. However, rabbis such as Menasseh ben Israel and Saul Levi Morteira were themselves strongly drawn to the excitement of intellectual cross-fertilization. The Sefardic rabbinate and lay *Mahamad* (governing board) were keenly aware of the delicate balance between the pleasures and the perils of cosmopolitan cultural contact. The regulation and policing of the boundaries with the non-Sefardic world was, particularly after the twin shocks in the 1660s of Sabbateanism and Spinozism, their central governmental concern. The destabilizing implications of urban cosmopolitanism, meanwhile, resonated through almost all aspects of community life. The very assumption of fundamental difference, which had hitherto conditioned almost all cultural relations between Jews and non-Jews, was now open to reappraisal and challenge.

Heterodoxy and Identity in the Cosmopolitan City

The collective psychology of the Amsterdam Sefardim, as Miriam Bodian has shown, was extremely particular, based on a complex overlap of Jewish and Iberian patterns of thought. Membership in the "Portuguese nation"—the term the Amsterdam community generally used to described itself—was understood most fundamentally in ethnic terms, heavily influenced by the traditional Iberian notion of *limpieza de sangre* (which, ironically, had taken root in sixteenth-century Spain primarily as a device to exclude Jews), rather than as a specifically religious identity.[18] On arrival in the city, many Marranos possessed only a limited knowledge of Judaism, and religious education was therefore a leading priority of the community leadership.[19] However, this effort was far from straightforward. Many migrants were eager to join a normatively Jewish community, but remained deeply attached to a private theology heavily imbued with Catholic concepts and concerns. Others, however, resisted what they saw as attempts by the community establishment to impose on them a restrictive religious conformity.[20]

The authority of the Amsterdam rabbinate was thus challenged both by informal tendencies toward a Judeo-Catholic syncretism and by a more overt current of theological dissidence. These internal strains were compounded by the indistinct nature of the parameters of the community. A significant number of ex-Marranos living in Amsterdam had no association with the formal institutions of the Sefardic community, and did not, at least in any public sense, identify religiously as Jews. These "non-Jewish Jews" were not subject to the authority of the Sefardic community, and took no notice of community rules such as the interdiction on travel to the Iberian Peninsula, where many of them maintained significant commercial interests.[21] Nonetheless, they were clearly part of the Sefardic community in the cultural sense. Their presence in Amsterdam blurred the outer boundaries of this community and eroded the authority of its leaders, by presenting to other Jews an on-going, visible, and possibly tempting alternative to normative Judaism.

A strikingly large number of anti-Christian theological manuscripts circulated among the seventeenth-century Sefardim, many of them written by leaders of the community in order to allay popular doubts and confusions concerning Judaism, or to boost Jewish pride. This suggests that religious uncertainty was widespread, and that the rabbinate and lay leadership continually found it necessary to offer a concerted and patient response to lay objections. The earliest texts in this genre that circulated in Amsterdam were imported from elsewhere: the *Ḥizzuq Emunah* (Fortification of the Faith), for example—an extremely popular text, which by the early eighteenth century had been translated into Spanish, Portuguese, French, and Dutch—was written in the 1590s by Isaac of Troki, a Lithuanian Karaite.[22] Eliahu Montalto's refutation of the Christian interpretation of the fifty-third chapter of Isaiah—another highly polemical early text that circulated in Amsterdam—was probably written in Venice in the first years of the seventeenth century.[23] Montalto never lived in Amsterdam, but he was buried there, having been brought to the city by his student, Saul Levi Morteira, after his death in Paris in 1616 while serving as the private doctor to Marie de Médicis. These external models, however, were soon followed by several other anti-Christian polemics written in Amsterdam specifically in response to local needs. Morteira himself, in the course of his ensuing rabbinical career in Amsterdam, wrote a number of anti-Christian polemics, energetically tackling key points of theological confrontation between Christianity and Judaism, such as the nature of sin and salvation, the Jewish response to Trinitarianism, and the question of the messiah.[24] His repeated return to this genre of writing suggests that he perceived a continued need to allay doubts and confusions that persisted within the community, and in particular to elucidate the differences between Judaism and Catholicism.

Morteira's polemics, as well as those of other Jewish polemicists, also served as a testament to the cultural pride of the community. Several surviving texts of Jewish controversialist writings from seventeenth-century Amsterdam are volumes of great beauty, lavishly bound and adorned with ornate calligraphy. These elaborate manuscript volumes, it seems reasonable to assume, were not produced and purchased in order to convince Jewish waverers, but rather as a statement of Jewish self-esteem among prosperous community members who considered themselves already fully convinced of the arguments they contained. Nonetheless, it is significant that such texts were chosen as trophy possessions. The cultural confidence of the Amsterdam Sefardim, we can infer, was not enunciated simply as an inwardly oriented assertion of Jewish belief and practice, with little regard for the relationship of Judaism and Jewishness to Gentile beliefs and mores. The Amsterdam Sefardim were, on the contrary, keenly interested in such comparisons. Ownership of a calligraphed volume of Jewish anti-Christian polemics made a statement that a *haggadah* or a *ḥumash* could not: that Judaism was not only a vital culture in its own terms but also a repository of multiple confident and eloquent rebuttals to the objections that had for so long been tirelessly leveled against it by Christians. This assertiveness clearly served to an important extent as a historical riposte to the traumatic memory of the Spanish Inquisition. However, interest in comparisons between religions was also a leading feature of the early Enlightenment, taking grip earliest and most firmly in the cosmopolitan port cities of Holland and England.[25] The relational context in which the Amsterdam Sefardim considered their own culture was also a symptom of this phenomenon.

Morteira's final and seemingly most widely circulated polemical work reflects a particularly striking engagement with Christianity. In his *Tratado de la Verdad de la Ley de Moseh* (1659), Morteira responds not to Catholic but to Protestant and particularly to Calvinist arguments. He critiques Calvin and his followers for their lack of respect for the Mosaic Law. However, this criticism is outweighed by a strong current of enthusiasm in the text for the possibility of an axis of mutual understanding between Judaism and non-Trinitarian Christianity, based on a shared rejection of the idolatry most egregiously represented by Trinitarianism, and on a universal observance of the core Noahide commandments.[26] Unitarianism, Morteira argues, ought to be the logical conclusion of Calvinism. He closely analyzes Calvin's arguments in his *Institutes of the Christian Religion,* praising him for his rejection of the veneration of images. These arguments, Morteira insists, must logically also apply to "invisible images." Calvin's own arguments, even though he himself does not recognize it, thus amount to a refutation of the Trinity.[27]

The intellectual ambition of this text reflects the seriousness with which Morteira engaged with the unfamiliar Protestant theologies he newly encountered in Amsterdam. This was not a theme he bracketed apart from his wider role as a community rabbi: in his surviving sermons he at least twice expounds his positive evaluation of the Reformation.[28] Morteira's final treatise was written at a unique moment in Jewish-Christian relations. The wave of millenarian enthusiasm, enmeshed with many varieties of politico-theological radicalism that swept through English and Dutch Protestantism in the 1650s, influenced the Jewish world, too, and led to an unprecedented openness on both sides to theological collaboration. The most celebrated protagonist in this dialogue was Menasseh ben Israel, whose evocation of a messianic politics of imminent Judeo-Christian intimacy was of crucial importance in securing the de facto readmission of Jewish settlement in England.[29] Richard Popkin's description of Menasseh's interactions with radical Protestants in Amsterdam and London as amounting to an attempt to formulate a "Judeo-Christianity" is, however, overstated.[30] Christian millenarians such as the Amsterdam theologian Petrus Serrarius did indeed anticipate an epochal fusion of Judaism and Christianity: millenarians in both camps, he and some others believed, were awaiting the same imminent event.[31] This conviction in essence amounted to a variation on the traditional theme of the final ushering of the surviving Jewish remnant into the Christian fold. Menasseh, however, did not countenance the extinguishing of Jewish difference, and neither did Morteira: the most ardently reiterated theme of the latter's treatise, encapsulated in its very title, was the enduring majesty and authority of the entirety of the Mosaic Law for Jews.

For mid-century rabbis such as Morteira and Menasseh, intellectual contact with progressive Protestants offered invigorating intellectual stimulation, as well as a context in which to envision an imminent future in which both communities stood to benefit from their improved mutual understanding. It is impossible to trace the precise relationship between Morteira and Menasseh's personal interactions with Protestants and their strikingly optimistic assessments of Protestantism. Petrus Serrarius, however, we know maintained a close friendship with Menasseh ben Israel, while a nucleus of conversionist English Quakers led by the Hebraist Samuel Fisher seems to have found Amsterdam in the 1650s a conducive environment for making amicable contact with Jews.[32] More generally, it seems clear that the dialogue of the 1650s was made possible by the cosmopolitan interactivity of Amsterdam's urban culture, in which friendships of mutual respect could be established across ethnic boundaries. This unprecedentedly fluid and tolerant cultural environment must have struck figures such as Morteira and Menasseh as a stunning contrast to the world most of their community had only recently left behind in Spain. Respectful friendship and intellectual exchange with receptive non-Jews was, it seemed, not merely possible and permissible but the potential starting point for a radical reappraisal of the relationship between Judaism and Christianity.

The restoration of the English monarchy in 1660 dampened the feverishness of Judeo-Christian millenarian expectancy, and the ignominious outcome of the Sabbatean movement six years later brought it virtually to a halt. However, the intellectual interactions of mid-century should not be interpreted as a historical dead end. Although the embarrassment resulting from Shabbatai's conversion to Islam convulsed the Sefardic community, and led to general retreat toward theological conservatism, the social conditions in Amsterdam that so powerfully facilitated exchange between Jews and Christians remained unchanged. In the later seventeenth century—with the notable exception of the "friendly conversation" between Isaac Orobio de Castro and the Remonstrant theologian Phillip van Limborch, which took place in the early 1680s—formal discussion between Jews and Christians on religious matters appears to become less common. However, this should be ascribed not to any estrangement between the two groups, but rather to the rise both of the Early Enlightenment and of the Sefardic elite's visible prosperity and sense of ease in Amsterdam society. Both these factors eroded the significance of set-piece theological debate between Jews and Christians. By the end of the seventeenth century, throughout which Jewish prominence in Amsterdam had been steadily rising, social exchanges between Jews and

Christians, which often brought to the fore questions of religious and cultural difference, had become an almost banal feature of everyday life in the cosmopolitan entrepôt.

The dangers of such routine contact, however, were starkly evident to the Amsterdam rabbinate and lay leadership. The temptations of religious and moral laxity were inevitably heightened in an environment of tolerant social mingling. Ideas drawn from the ferment of Dutch philosophical and theological debates could also readily serve to challenge Jewish orthodoxies. The bitter dispute between the Voetian and Cocceian camps over the allegorical interpretation of Scripture, which raged incessantly in Dutch universities during the middle decades of the century, was in its detailed substance remote from Jewish concerns.[33] However, an awareness of these quarrels must have percolated into the Jewish community, within which, from a rabbinical perspective, any philosophical destabilization of orthodox biblical hermeneutics can only have been a cause for alarm. More specifically, the internal tradition of Jewish heresy in Amsterdam, most powerfully enunciated by Uriel da Costa and by Spinoza, bore witness to the potentially subversive results of contact with non-Jewish philosophy and theology.

Uriel da Costa's *Examination of Pharisaic Traditions* (1623), the earliest heretical work to emerge from Amsterdam, was also probably the most trenchant attack on rabbinical authority written by any Jew in the early modern era. Da Costa rejects *in toto* the notion of an authoritative Oral Law, transmitted and interpreted by rabbis. This belief, he claims, implies that the written law alone is in some way imperfect or inadequate: an implication that he deems scandalously impious.[34] He attacks fundamental tenets of rabbinic law, such as the dietary separation of meat and milk and the wearing of *tefillin* during prayer, on the grounds that they are nowhere mentioned in Scripture, and that the biblical verses invoked to underwrite them ought to be interpreted figuratively, rather than in the narrowly literal sense adopted by the rabbis.[35]

The possible sources of da Costa's arguments have been much debated among scholars. Michael Servetus, Averroës, and Pietro Pomponazzi have all been advanced as conceivable inspirations, particularly for da Costa's rejection of the immortality of the soul, which, he argues, was a falsehood invented by rabbis in order to more effectively discipline their followers with threats of purgatorial torment after death.[36] Whatever the specific texts that da Costa may have read and used, however, it is clear that his personal theology was above all a product of the intensive mix of Catholic, Protestant, and Jewish religious outlooks to which he had been exposed during his formative years. Born in Oporto around 1584, as a young man da Costa had been a devout Catholic, studying canon law at the University of Coimbra. A surge of interest in Judaism, however, seems to have inspired his sudden migration to Amsterdam in 1614.[37] His critique of "Pharisaism" bears the unmistakable traces of his earlier life as a Catholic: this very image, casting the rabbinical tradition as unfeeling, literalistic, and spiritually dead, was a long-standing core assumption of Catholic anti-Judaism. Da Costa's stress on the self-sufficiency of the biblical text, however, strongly suggests a Protestant influence. His argument against rabbinical interpretation exactly echoes the central and much-reiterated Protestant case against papal and priestly interpretive authority. It is beyond doubt that a man of da Costa's intellectual curiosity would swiftly and easily have made use of the possibilities of intellectual engagement with Protestants that the interactive urban culture of Amsterdam made readily available. To understand the emergence of his ideas, we should focus not only on what he may or may not have read but also on the importance of the environment he lived in and the stimulus of the encounters with otherness that Amsterdam offered him.

Despite the vigorous suppression of da Costa's text by the community authorities—all located copies were publicly burned—awareness of his arguments was kept alive within the community, both through oral transmission and by the survival of a detailed refutation of the *Examination* by the Hamburg doctor Samuel da Silva, which included lengthy quotations from da Costa himself.[38] We can be virtually certain that Spinoza, who was eight years old at the time of da Costa's dramatic suicide in 1640, would have been fully aware of his ideas and arguments. Spinoza's own philosophy should itself be seen as the product of cross-fertilizations and clashes between multiple intellectual and religious traditions: Jewish, residual Catholic, Protestant, and Cartesian. Spinoza's expulsion from the Sefardic community fourteen years before the publication of the *Tractatus Theologico-Politicus* in 1670, and the immense scandal that this text generated, led to an immediate tendency, among both Jews and Christians, to discount any Jewish dimension to Spinoza's thought. It is clear, however, that the Jewish philosophical tradition, and Maimonides in particular, was nonetheless an important influence on him.[39] Yirmiyahu Yovel has explored in detail the Marrano dimensions of Spinoza's thought, while the influence on him of Dutch secular philosophy, and above all of Cartesianism, to which he devoted his first published text, is unambiguous.[40] Spinoza's philosophy should thus be seen as the boldest intellectual product of the fecund but disorienting blurring of cultural boundaries that characterized the northern European Sefardic experience.

Spinoza's immense infamy across Europe, particularly following the posthumous publication of his *Ethics* in 1677, was a serious embarrassment to the Amsterdam community. This outcry surrounding his works following soon after the shock of the Sabbatean upheaval, contributed to a wider crisis of Sefardic intellectual and cultural self-confidence in the final third of the seventeenth century, and continuing into the following century. This crisis, however, could from another perspective be seen as a triumph. Jewish acceptance in Dutch society, at least of the more prosperous members of the Sefardic community, had reached an unprecedentedly high ebb. A sense of Jews as markedly distinct and different had certainly not been erased, but never before in European history had this cultural difference been so widely perceived as of so little account. It was precisely this fact, however, that paradoxically fueled the erosion of Sefardic cohesion and communal authority. Rising social integration and economic success ushered in the seductive pressures of assimilation, in response to which the rabbinic and lay leadership fought a persistent uphill battle to reassert the communal boundaries of cohesion and separateness.

Community Authority and Boundaries of Identity

The masterful research of Yosef Kaplan into the social history of the Amsterdam Sefardim has highlighted the continual arduousness of attempts by the community authorities to impose their disciplinary norms. Kaplan's path-breaking work on the profligate use of the *ḥerem* (community ban) by the Sefardic *parnasim* reveals the authorities' central concern with defining, through the use of disciplinary sanctions, the "boundaries of identity" of the community.[41] Myriad forms of contact with non-Sefardim—social, intellectual, economic, and sexual—were repeatedly condemned by the authorities, and punished by the imposition of the *ḥerem*. These strictures, Kaplan shows, were of little ultimate avail. In the eighteenth century, as the temptations of assimilation intensified and the authority of the Sefardic leadership waned, the *ḥerem* was used more limitedly, and was disproportionately imposed on poorer members of the community.[42] This shift reflects the effective surrender of the eighteenth-century community leadership in the face of the powerful temptations of social emulation and integration into elite Amsterdam society. In the early eighteenth century, in keeping with assimilatory trends across Europe, prosperous Jews in Amsterdam were increasingly conforming to mainstream trends in dress and conduct, and showing diminishing respect for Jewish tradition.[43] As community leaders grew decreasingly concerned with circumscribing the boundaries of identity of their well-to-do paymasters and peers, their disciplinary attention became more narrowly focused on major issues of moral conduct, particularly with respect to the behavior of poorer Jews and of women.[44]

A perusal of the disciplinary pronouncements recorded in the community *Livros de Escamoth* (Books of Regulations) for the seventeenth century presents a suggestive picture of the concerns of the community leadership, and reflects the numerous but interrelated fronts on which they struggled to assert the integrity and cultural boundedness of Sefardic life. A small but significant number of ordinances deal directly with issues of intellectual contact between Jews and non-Jews. Other, more mundane issues, however, such as the perennial attempt to stamp out the practice of buying meat from sources other than the Sefardic butcher, nonetheless similarly highlight the porousness of cultural relations in Amsterdam. The sense of Sefardic separateness, on which rabbinical and lay authority was ultimately based, was subjected to gentle erosion by the multiple forms of intercultural interaction enabled by the prosperity and tolerant atmosphere of the city.

From the earliest pronouncements of the first *Mahamad* of the unitary Sefardic community established in 1639, it is clear that disturbances caused by religious disputes with Christians were serious concerns. Rule 38 of the 57 foundational rules of the unified community states that members are forbidden to discuss religion with non-Jews, and in particular to "speak scandalously against their faith," as this risks "disturbing the freedoms we enjoy."[45] This rule was reiterated in the following year,[46] and once again, at great length, in 1677, almost certainly in response to the publication of Spinoza's *Ethics*. This later ordinance forbade both public and private disputes, and imposed the *ḥerem* on offenders.[47] However, the ruling did nothing to impede the participation of one of the most prominent community members, Orobio de Castro, in his "friendly conversation" with Phillip van Limborch in the early years of the 1680s, and Orobio was never punished, let alone banned, for this transgression.[48] While the *Mahamad* was clearly concerned to discourage highly contentious theological arguments between Jews and Christians, polite discussion of intellectual matters, including theology, was by the 1680s a common activity in the self-consciously sophisticated social circles to which members of the Sefardic elite were increasingly gaining access. This may not have been regarded as desirable from the perspective of the rabbinate, but it was exactly what prominent families such as the Belmonte and Nunes da Costa families most wanted—and the community leadership was in no position to stand in their way.

Other early rulings also indicate the eagerness of the *Mahamad* to discourage forms of intercultural contact that they regarded as dangerously intimate. In 1639, the *Mahamad* pronounced against community members entering Christian churches, whether during services or sermons or simply in order to listen to the organ.[49] In the following year an ordinance was issued forbidding the passing on of Jewish religious texts to non-Jews.[50] It can safely be surmised from the specificity of the language of these ordinances that they were drafted in response to actual community practices, which the authorities sought to stamp out. Already by 1640, it seems, religious interaction between Jews and Protestants was widespread enough for the Sefardic leadership to identify it as a serious danger to the integrity of the community. It is extremely unlikely, however, that these edicts had any effect. The cosmopolitan fluidity of life in Amsterdam at mid-century offered ever easier and more abundant opportunities for such encounters to take place.

The high degree of cultural ease between Jews and non-Jews in Amsterdam was reflected in economic and gastronomic interactions, too. In 5405 (1644–45), the *Mahamad* condemned the purchase of bread products from non-Jewish bakeries, whether for personal use or to sell to others.[51] The defense of the monopoly of the Sefardic butcher was apparently one of the most prevalent and vexing community issues: the prohibition against purchasing from Ashkenazic butchers, or from other sources, was reiterated no fewer than twelve times between 1639 and 1708.[52] This matter was to an important degree fiscal in nature. The *Mahamad* was concerned to extirpate evasion of the community tax on kosher meat, which made the Sefardic butcher significantly more expensive than his potential competitors serving the Ashkenazic community.[53] However, an important cultural issue was at stake here too. The erosion of commitment to the community's public standards of *kashrut* signified at a very material, everyday level the lack of commitment among many Sefardim to maintaining the symbolic boundaries of their identity. It is clear from the wording of a number of the edicts that the

Mahamad was acting not only to stamp out use of the Ashkenazic butcher but also the practice by some community members of purchasing meat from altogether non-Jewish sources.[54]

The regulation of public social interaction with non-Jews was also a persistent concern of the Sefardic community authorities. In 1655 the *Mahamad* pronounced against members of the community gathering with non-Jews on the "Lions' Bridge," on both Saturdays and Sundays. This behavior, the *Mahamad* warned, could provoke scandals that would "damage our nation."[55] Thirty years later the *ḥerem* was declared for those of the community guilty of "insolence" either in taverns or in the streets of the city. Such rowdy miscreants, it was implied, endangered the security of the whole community, which, the edict reminded, was only present in Amsterdam thanks to "the benevolence of the very noble and magnificent magistrates of this city."[56] The fact that these pronouncements were considered necessary, but only rather vaguely specified the transgressions they sought to discourage, corroborates the general impression that by the later seventeenth century social contact between Jews and non-Jews was a routine occurrence. The authorities sought in general to discourage all overly intimate or high-spirited conviviality with non-Jews. Their overriding practical concern, however, was with the reputation of the community. Behavior that might provoke resentment, ridicule, or scandal was vigorously condemned. Elite social life, mostly taking place in private homes, was thus largely ignored by the *Mahamad.* Younger and poorer Sefardim, who were more likely to gather in taverns or on the streets, were more closely scrutinized.

The approach of the community leadership to sexual transgressions also reflected a high level of respect for privacy. Cases of adultery during the seventeenth century are recorded obliquely in the community records, and were handled with discretion.[57] Lotte van de Pol's study of prostitution in early modern Amsterdam has shown that, while Sefardim were only very seldom commercially involved in the sex trade, they appear relatively often in court records as the clients of more up-market "chamber prostitutes," for whom they not infrequently figured among the most generous regular clients.[58] Sexual intercourse between Jewish men and Christian women, specifically including prostitutes, had been forbidden by the Amsterdam burgomasters in 1616. Because of this, and also perhaps because the richer Sefardim were willing and able to offer significant bribes in return for leniency, Jewish men were apprehended with disproportionate frequency while visiting the city's brothels.[59] The

Jewish community authorities seem to have ignored this issue, which they would in any case have been largely powerless to control. Private vices, when conducted discreetly, caused little outcry in seventeenth-century Amsterdam. Rather than risk attracting attention to relations between Sefardic men and Dutch prostitutes that were both adulterous and illegal, it seemed more prudent for the *Mahamad* to look the other way.

Perhaps the most surprising of the regulations established by the new *Mahamad* in 1639 is the severe admonition, on pain of the *ḥerem*, against the unlicensed circumcision of non-Jews.[60] This ordinance was reiterated more than once. In 1650, the *Mahamad* revised this *Escama*, specifying the *ḥerem* as the punishment for the circumcision of Blacks or mulattos;[61] in 1676 the *Mahamad* repeated that it was forbidden to circumcise those who were not members of the "Spanish and Portuguese Nation."[62] The Sefardim of Amsterdam regarded circumcision as the most sacred and symbolically powerful marker of community membership, often imbuing the ritual with mystical and distinctly heterodox salvific powers.[63] Circumcision was seen by both Jews and non-Jews as marking the sharpest and most irreversible divide between the two religious worlds. The regulation of this practice was thus fundamental to the definition of the outer boundaries of the community. The city regulations of 1616 also explicitly forbade Jewish attempts to convert or to circumcise Christians, and rare instances of such conversions, for example of the Dutch woman who married the Sefardic broker Jan Cardoso in 1649, provoked widespread horror and alarm.[64] Community ordinances regarding circumcision were clearly designed to prevent such events, and to allay Dutch anxieties, fantastical though they were, regarding Jewish proselytism.

A more everyday issue, however, was the status of non-whites in the Amsterdam community. A number of Black servants and slaves, brought to Amsterdam from Dutch Brazil, Suriname, Curaçao, or elsewhere in the Caribbean, served in the wealthier households of the Sefardim. The dictates of *halakhah* traditionally required the circumcision of male slaves: this was based on a clear assertion in Genesis, upheld, elucidated, and in certain cases restricted in a wide range of medieval rabbinic responsa.[65] In seventeenth-century Amsterdam, however (as well as in England and the Caribbean), this practice steadily declined. In contrast to Sefardic communities in the eastern Mediterranean, where community leaders and rabbis sought to discourage incipient slackness in the observance of this commandment, the Amsterdam authorities actively encouraged its abrogation, culminating in 1650 with their outright banning of the practice.[66] The conversion and circumcision of Blacks did not altogether cease: Jonathan Schorsch has identified at least seven Blacks or mulattos buried in the community cemetery between 1680 and 1716.[67] However, from the 1640s onward there was an unmistakable trend to mark Jewishness apart from Blackness.

The exclusion of non-whites from participation in the life of the Sefardic community took many forms. An ordinance of 1644 asserted, in protection of the "reputation and good government" of the community, that circumcised Black Jews could not be called to the Torah.[68] In 1647, the *Mahamad* marked apart a separate, less prestigious area of the cemetery for the burial of Blacks and mulattos.[69] In 1658, mulatto boys, as well as all other non-Sefardim, were excluded from study at the Amsterdam *yeshivah*, Ets Haim.[70] An unmistakable strain of color-conscious racial prejudice is evident in these ordinances. The concern of the Sefardim to reinforce boundaries of ethnic purity should, however, be understood within the wider context of the changing social status of the community. As the more prosperous and acculturated Sefardim established an increasingly confident and widely accepted profile in the social life of the city, so they sought to mark themselves apart from those of lesser status. This concern with social distinction fueled the widespread disdain of the Sefardim toward their Ashkenazic brethren;[71] it also led to a decline in acceptance of Blacks as members of the Sefardic community. Early modern Amsterdam was nonetheless to some degree a place of greater freedom and cultural openness for the Blacks associated with the Sefardic community. Their terms of employment, while largely opaque to historians, were surely better in Amsterdam, where slavery was not recognized, than in the colonies. However, the increasingly racialized understanding of Sefardic self-identity stands as a stark reminder that, while some social barriers were broken down by the dynamic cosmopolitanism of Amsterdam, other divisions were maintained and even reinforced.

Ambivalent Cosmopolitans?

The account by the Italian émigré writer Gregorio Leti of his associations with the Amsterdam Sefardic elite of the final two decades of the seventeenth century paints a vivid picture of the highly visible grandeur in which the most prosperous families of the community lived. Leti describes the Sefardic community as a whole in unreservedly laudatory terms: their synagogue, he notes, "is like an aristocratic seat, of sophisticated people, almost all civil, well dressed, rich and impressive."[72] He is most fascinated by the richest of the Sefardim, such as Jeronimo Nunes da Costa and Baron Manuel de Belmonte, respectively the effective representatives in Amsterdam of the Portuguese and the Spanish crowns. Leti stresses, however, that both these men were also valuable promoters of the interests of the United Provinces.[73] Their cosmopolitanism, in Leti's eyes, is reflected not only in their plural cultural identities and national loyalties but also in their generous cultural hospitality. Foreign visitors, and writers such as Leti in particular, were regular guests at the grandest Sefardic households. They there took part in what Jonathan Israel has described as "a highly intricate and richly cosmopolitan cultural ritual," in which visitors marveled not only at the splendor of their hosts but also at the erudite and wide-ranging intellectual interests that they cultivated.[74] In some ways prefiguring the Berlin salons at the beginning of the nineteenth century, the Sefardic aristocracy of Amsterdam used both their financial and cultural resources in order to establish their acceptance and significance in the social life of the city. Their distinctive brand of hospitality eloquently celebrated the cosmopolitan values of curiosity, elegance, and cultural exchange. Their wholehearted embrace of these values was intimately related to their own specifically hybrid Sefardic identity; but they were also, in their own minds at least, giving expression to the cosmopolitan spirit of Amsterdam as a whole.

The Sefardic plutocrats were committed patrons of literary production within the Dutch Sefardic community. These literary works themselves, however, were often to a large extent oriented toward a general Iberian reading public, rather than to a specifically Jewish audience. Leading seventeenth-century Dutch Sefardic writers, such as Daniel Levi de Barrios and Joseph Penso de la Vega, typically wrote in two different modes. When writing on general themes they published under secular versions of their names and elegantly reproduced the elaborate genre requirements of the Spanish baroque, while eschewing any explicitly Jewish literary features (although their texts sometimes retained implicit Hebraic or kabbalistic overtones).[75] The writings of de Barrios, for example, who styled himself Don Miguel de Barrios when writing for a wider public, reflect an intricate and in some ways unstable authorial identity, balancing Jewish, Iberian, and self-consciously universalist strands.[76]

A similarly subtle interweaving of Jewish and Iberian sensibilities can be discerned in the dramatic literature of the period. Biblical themes were extremely popular among Sefardic dramatists, who crafted these plays in close accordance with the norms of Spanish Golden Age drama, while also inflecting them with a discreet but distinct Jewish flavor.[77] Dutch Sefardic taste in art was also only very lightly colored by specifically Jewish concerns. Biblical scenes were popular with Sefardic collectors, but they were just as popular among Dutch Calvinists, and in general Sefardic art collections were broadly similar to those of Dutch non-Jews of similar wealth and status.[78] The Sefardic embrace of cosmopolitanism in Amsterdam touched all facets of their cultural life. As consumers of literature and art they in no sense set aside their Jewish identity, but neither did they highlight it. Rather, in a manner not altogether unlike much later generations of Jews in Berlin or New York, they keenly adopted the wider cultural values of Iberia and Holland, discreetly imbuing them with their particular interests and sensibilities.

Daniel Swetschinski has recently characterized the Portuguese Jews of seventeenth-century Amsterdam as "reluctant cosmopolitans." There was an inescapable tension, he argues, between their particularistic forging of a new, distinctively Portuguese Jewish identity, and their universalistic, cosmopolitan striving for religious and cultural harmony.[79] This analysis captures much of the essence of the internally split nature of Sefardic self-perception in Amsterdam and other northern European centers at the end of the early modern era. The desire to be distinctive, and therefore also to some extent separate, strained insistently against the contrary desire to take full advantage of the cosmopolitan possibilities offered in these unprecedentedly interactive urban environments. By the end of the seventeenth century the Sefardic economic and cultural elite showed little sign of inner torment over this issue: the pleasures of social acceptance were extremely seductive, and seemed to be compatible with a refashioned, "braided" sense of Jewish identity.[80] From a rabbinical perspective, however, this issue was more sharply problematic. The rise of Jewish cosmopolitanism indubitably undermined rabbinic authority, as more and more facets of Jewish life migrated to physical spaces and cultural contexts over which the rabbinate had little or no influence. The Jewish search for a new balance between exclusiveness and tolerance was, then, by no means an exclusively Ashkenazic affair. The insights of Jacob Katz's pathbreaking but indubitably Germanocentric study on this topic begin to look significantly different once the significance of the Sefardic experience in Amsterdam and elsewhere is taken into account.[81]

In their at once ardent and hesitant cosmopolitanism, the Sefardim of Amsterdam developed a distinctive urban identity that is extremely difficult to define, but also, from the perspective of our own era, uncannily familiar. In an environment more accepting of cultural difference than any other European city in the seventeenth century, the Amsterdam Sefardim pioneered the exploration of modes of Jewish living in close and friendly contact with the non-Jewish world. The new forms of Jewish identity made possible in this context were both exhilarating and precarious. The historical experience of this community precociously highlighted a paradox that stands at the core of modern city life. While the dynamism of cosmopolitan urban interchange is predicated on contact across cultural difference, this very contact readily erodes the differences that create the cosmopolitanism in the first place.

Notes

1. Leonardo Benevolo, *The European City* (Oxford: Blackwell, 1993), 135. On the economic significance of Amsterdam see Jonathan Israel, *Dutch Primacy in World Trade, 1585–1740* (Oxford: Oxford University Press, 1989).
2. Jonathan Israel, *The Dutch Republic: Its Rise, Greatness and Fall* (Oxford: Oxford University Press, 1995), 328–31, 629.
3. Ibid., 330; Jonathan Israel, *European Jewry in the Age of Mercantilism, 1550–1750,* 3rd ed. (London: Littman Library, 1998), 198.
4. On the Black presence in Amsterdam see Alison Blakely, *Blacks in the Dutch World: The Evolution of Racial Imagery in a Modern Society* (Bloomington: Indiana University Press, 1993), esp. 225–27.
5. Israel, *Dutch Republic,* 499–505; Israel, "The Intellectual Debate about Toleration in the Dutch Republic," in *The Emergence of Tolerance in the Dutch Republic,* ed. C. Berkvens-Stevelinck, J. I. Israel, and G. H. M. Posthumus Meyjes (Leiden: Brill, 1997), 3–35. For the enduring influence of these principles into the eighteenth century, see Ernestine van der Wall, "Toleration and Enlightenment in the Dutch Republic," in *Toleration in Enlightenment Europe,* ed. Ole Peter Grell and Roy Porter (Cambridge: Cambridge University Press, 2000), 114–32.
6. Saskia Sassen, *Guests and Aliens* (New York: New Press, 1999), 10–11.
7. Geert Mak, *Amsterdam* (Cambridge, Mass.: Harvard University Press, 2000), 100.
8. Ibid.
9. Lotte van de Pol, *Het Amsterdams hoerdom: Prostitutie in de zeventiende en achtiende eeuw* (Amsterdam: Wereldbibliotheek, 1996), 94–95.
10. See Simon Schama, *The Embarrassment of Riches: An Interpretation of Dutch Culture in the Golden Age* (New York: Knopf, 1987), 430–80.
11. Israel, *European Jewry,* 51–53.
12. See Richard I. Cohen, *Jewish Icons: Art and Society in Modern Europe* (Berkeley: University of California Press, 1998), 34–43; Simon Schama, "A Different Jerusalem: The Jews in Rembrandt's Amsterdam," in *The Jews in the Age of Rembrandt,* ed. Susan W. Morgenstein and Ruth E. Levine (Rockville, Md.: Judaic Museum, 1981), 3–17.

13. See Miriam Bodian, *Hebrews of the Portuguese Nation* (Bloomington: Indiana University Press, 1997), 85–95; Yosef Kaplan, "The Self-Definition of the Sephardi Jews of Western Europe and Their Relation to the Alien and the Stranger," in *An Alternative Path to Modernity* (Leiden: Brill, 2000), 51–77, esp. 55–56.
14. See Henry Kamen, *The Spanish Inquisition: A Historical Revision* (New Haven: Yale University Press, 1997), 230–54.
15. For an extended argument based largely on this starting point, see Stephen Toulmin, *Cosmopolis: The Hidden Agenda of Modernity* (Chicago: University of Chicago Press, 1992).
16. This is powerfully argued, for the Early Enlightenment period, in Alan Charles Kors, *Atheism in France 1650–1729: The Orthodox Sources of Disbelief* (Princeton: Princeton University Press, 1990).
17. Mak, *Amsterdam,* 109–10; Michael Zell, *Reframing Rembrandt: Jews and the Christian Image in Seventeenth-Century Amsterdam* (Berkeley: University of California Press, 2002), 43.
18. Bodian, *Hebrews,* esp. 76–95; Gerard Nahon, "Amsterdam, Metropole Occidentale des Sepharades au XVIIe Siècle," *Cahiers Spinoza* 3 (1980): 15–50; Daniel M. Swetschinski, *Reluctant Cosmopolitans: The Portuguese Jews of Seventeenth-Century Amsterdam* (London: Littman, 2000), 278–314.
19. See Yosef Hayim Yerushalmi, "The Re-Education of Marranos in the Seventeenth Century," Third Annual Rabbi Louis Feinberg Memorial Lecture (Cincinnati: Judaic Studies Program, University of Cincinnati, 1980).
20. See Yosef Kaplan, "From Apostasy to Return to Judaism: The Portuguese Jews in Amsterdam," in *Binah, Volume 1: Studies in Jewish History,* ed. Joseph Dan (New York: Praeger, 1988).
21. See Yosef Kaplan, "The Travels of Portuguese Jews from Amsterdam to the 'Lands of Idolatry,'" in *Jews and Conversos: Studies in Society and the Inquisition,* ed. Kaplan (Jerusalem: Magnes Press, 1985), 197–224.
22. For the dates and locations of these translations, see L. Fuks and R. G. Fuks-Mansfeld, *Hebrew and Judaic Manuscripts in Amsterdam Public Collections* (Leiden: Brill, 1975).
23. Israel, *European Jewry,* 84–85; Ralph Melnick, *From Polemics to Apologetics: Jewish-Christian Rapprochement in Seventeenth Century Amsterdam* (Assen: Van Gorcum, 1981), 24–28.
24. See Melnick, *Polemics,* 29–32; Marc Saperstein, *"Your Voice Like a Ram's Horn": Themes and Texts in Traditional Jewish Preaching* (Cincinnati: Hebrew Union College Press, 1996), 118–25.
25. The most notable example of this genre is Bernard Picart's immensely successful *Cérémonies et coutumes religieuses de tous les peuples du monde* (Amsterdam, 1723). On this text see Cohen, *Jewish Icons,* 43–52.
26. See H. P. Salomon, ed., *Tratado de verdade da lei de Moisés* (Braga: Barbosa & Xavier, 1988), esp. 1261–64.
27. Saul Levi Morteira, *Providencia de Dios con Ysrael y Verdad de la Ley de Moseh,* Bibliotheca Rosenthaliana, Amsterdam, HS 542, esp. §40.
28. Marc Saperstein, "History as Homiletics: The Use of Historical Memory in the Sermons of Saul Levi Morteira," in *Jewish History and Jewish Memory,* ed. Elisheva Carlebach, John M. Efron, and David N. Meyers (Hanover, N.H.: Brandeis University Press, 1998), 123, 126.

29. See David S. Katz, *Philo-Semitism and the Readmission of the Jews to England, 1603–55* (Oxford: Clarendon, 1982); Harold Fisch, "The Messianic Politics of Menasseh ben Israel," in *Menasseh ben Israel and His World,* ed. Yosef Kaplan, Henry Méchoulan, and Richard H. Popkin (Leiden: Brill, 1996), 23–40.
30. R. H. Popkin, "Some Aspects of Jewish-Christian Theological Interchanges in Holland and England, 1640–1700," in *Jewish-Christian Relations in the Seventeenth Century,* ed. J. van den Berg and Ernestine G. E. van der Wall (Dordrecht: Kluwer, 1988), 24.
31. Ernestine G. E. van der Wall, "The Amsterdam Millenarian Petrus Serrarius (1600–1669) and the Anglo-Dutch Circle of Philo-Judaists," in *Jewish-Christian Relations,* 73–94.
32. Ernestine G. E. van der Wall, "Petrus Serrarius and Menasseh ben Israel," in *Menasseh,* 176–79; Richard H. Popkin, "Spinoza and the Conversion of the Jews," in *Spinoza's Political and Theological Thought,* ed. C. De Deugd (Amsterdam: North-Holland, 1984), 171–83.
33. On this dispute see Israel, *Dutch Republic,* 660–69.
34. Uriel da Costa, *Examination of Pharisaic Traditions* (1623), trans. and ed. H. P. Salomon and I. S. D. Sassoon (Leiden: Brill, 1993), 271–72.
35. Ibid., esp. 290–93, 298–99.
36. See H. P. Salomon and I. S. D. Sassoon, introduction to da Costa, *Examination,* 38ff.
37. Swetschinski, *Reluctant Cosmopolitans,* 266–67; I. S. Révah, "La religion d'Uriel da Costa, Marrane de Porto," *Revue de l'histoire des religions* 161 (1962): 45–76.
38. Samuel da Silva, "Treatise on the Immortality of the Soul," trans. H. P. Salomon and I. S. D. Sassoon, in da Costa, *Examination,* 427–551.
39. See Warren Zev Harvey, "A Portrait of Spinoza as a Maimonidean," *Journal of the History of Philosophy* 19, 2 (1981): 151–72.
40. Yirmiyahu Yovel, *Spinoza and Other Heretics: The Marrano of Reason* (Princeton: Princeton University Press, 1989); Baruch Spinoza, *The Principles of Cartesian Philosophy* (1663), trans. Samuel Shirley (Indianapolis: Hackett, 1998).
41. Yosef Kaplan, "The Social Functions of the Herem," in *Alternative Path,* 108–42.
42. Kaplan, "Deviance and Excommunication in the Eighteenth Century," ibid., 143–52.
43. See Israel, *European Jewry,* 210–11.
44. See Kaplan, "The Threat of Eros in Eighteenth-Century Sephardi Amsterdam," in *Alternative Path,* 280–300.
45. *Compendio de escamoth* (1728), Gemeentelijke Archiefdienst Amsterdam, Archieven der Portugees-Israëlitische Gemeente te Amsterdam, vol. 22, 16.
46. *Escamoth* A, fol. 73 / *Compendio de escamoth,* 27.
47. *Escamoth* A, fol. 765 / *Compendio,* 22.
48. See Yosef Kaplan, *From Christianity to Judaism: The Story of Isaac Orobio de Castro* (London: Littman, 1989), 278.
49. *Escamoth* A, fol. 27 / *Compendio,* 27.
50. *Escamoth* A, fol. 86 / *Compendio,* 27.
51. *Escamoth* A, fol. 185 / *Compendio,* 77.
52. Swetschinski, *Reluctant Cosmopolitans,* 199.
53. Ibid.
54. See, for example, *Escamoth* A, fol. 15 / *Compendio,* 79; *Escamoth* B, fol. 101 / *Compendio,* 84.

55. *Escamoth* A, fol. 320 / *Compendio,* 60.
56. *Escamoth* B, fol. 92 / *Compendio,* 60–61.
57. Kaplan, "Threat of Eros," 284–85.
58. Van de Pol, *Amsterdams hoerdom,* 134–36.
59. Ibid.; Swetschinski, *Reluctant Cosmopolitans,* 14, 217–18.
60. *Compendio,* 16.
61. *Escamoth* A, fol. 281 / *Compendio,* 28.
62. *Escamoth* A, fol. 742 / *Compendio,* 42.
63. Bodian, *Hebrews,* 97–99, 112–13.
64. Ibid., 60–62; Swetschinski, *Reluctant Cosmopolitans,* 237–38.
65. Genesis 17:12–13. See Jonathan Schorsch, "Jews and Blacks in the Early Modern Mediterranean and Atlantic Worlds, 1450–1800" (Ph.D. diss., University of California, Berkeley, 2000), 226–37, 246–57.
66. Ibid., 477–95.
67. Ibid., 269–73.
68. *Escamoth* A, fol. 173 / *Compendio,* 42.
69. *Escamoth* A, fol. 224 / *Compendio,* 35.
70. Schorsch, *Jews and Blacks,* 528–30. See also Schorsch, *Jews and Blacks in the Early Modern World* (New York: Cambridge University Press, 2004).
71. See Gordon M. Weiner, "Sephardic Philo- and Anti-Semitism in the Early Modern Era: The Jewish Adoption of Christian Attitudes," in *Jewish Christians and Christian Jews,* ed. G. M. Weiner and R. H. Popkin (Dordrecht: Kluwer, 1994), 189–209.
72. Gregorio Leti, *Il ceremoniale historico e politico,* 6 vols. (Amsterdam, 1685), 5:734, cited in Jonathan I. Israel, "Gregorio Leti (1631–1701) and the Dutch Sephardi Élite at the Close of the Seventeenth Century," in *Conflicts of Empires: Spain, the Low Countries and the Struggle for World Supremacy 1585–1713* (London: Hambledon, 1997), 373–90, 379.
73. Israel, "Gregorio Leti," 380–82.
74. Ibid., 384–89, esp. 387.
75. Harm den Boer and Jonathan I. Israel, "William III and the Glorious Revolution in the Eyes of Amsterdam Sephardi Writers: The Reactions of Miguel de Barrios, Joseph Penso de la Vega, and Manuel de Leão," in *The Anglo-Dutch Moment: Essays on the Glorious Revolution and Its World Impact,* ed. Jonathan I. Israel (Cambridge: Cambridge University Press, 1991), 439–61, esp. 442–44.
76. Ibid., 444–51.
77. See Haydee Litovsky, *Sephardic Playwrights of the Seventeenth and Eighteenth Centuries in Amsterdam* (Lanham, Md.: University Press of America, 1991), 113–45.
78. Zell, *Reframing Rembrandt,* 7–32.
79. Swetschinski, *Reluctant Cosmopolitans,* esp. 315–23.
80. I borrow this term from Natalie Zemon Davis's forthcoming study, *Braided Histories.*
81. See Jacob Katz, *Exclusiveness and Tolerance: Studies in Jewish-Gentile Relations in Medieval and Modern Times* (Oxford: Oxford University Press, 1961).

9

The Treatment of "Heretical Views" in the Sermons of Saul Levi Morteira of Amsterdam

MARC SAPERSTEIN

This paper is an attempt to characterize the skeptical or "heretical" views that challenged one of the great Jewish communities of early modern Europe from the perspective of the rabbinic establishment. The source materials to be examined are the sermons of the distinguished rabbi in Amsterdam, Saul Levi Morteira, whose rabbinic tenure in that community spanned the excommunications of Uriel da Costa, Juan de Prado, and Baruch Spinoza. The experience of these individuals is generally understood by most modern scholars to represent a dramatically new phenomenon: the "Marrano heresy" or "Marrano heterodoxy" that threatened to undermine the foundations of traditional Jewish life in the Sefardic Diaspora, and informed the skepticism that challenged religious doctrine in wider circles of European society.[1] But did the rabbis themselves who were combating and trying to control these challenges recognize them as something new? Or did they understand and present them as contemporary manifestations of a familiar pattern in Jewish life? How did they evaluate the danger of these threats? Where did they seek guidance in responding to them? These are some of the questions on which our sources may shed some light.

Material from this essay in a somewhat revised form, without the Hebrew text in the notes, was incorporated into chapter 6 of my *Exile in Amsterdam*, published by Hebrew Union College Press in 2005.

As I have written extensively elsewhere about these sermons focusing on other issues, there is no need to describe them at length here. Suffice it to say that the extant sermons of Saul Levi Morteira are accessible in two forms. First is the printed text of fifty sermons on the weekly Torah lesson, published at Amsterdam in 1645 and again at Warsaw—with the omission of anti-Christian polemical material due to the Russian censors—in 1902 and 1912. The second is the manuscripts of some 550 different sermons, written by Morteira in Hebrew between the years 1616 and 1657, currently in the Rabbinical Seminary of Budapest. These have come to the attention of the wider scholarly world only in the last fifteen years or so, after microfilms first arrived at the Institute for Microfilmed Hebrew Manuscripts in Jerusalem.[2]

When, back in 1989, I first confronted this massive amount of new source material by this talented rabbi of such an important community, I thought that there might be hidden away in the dense and difficult writing a kind of "smoking gun": a sermon in which Morteira defended the excommunication of his former student Baruch ben Michael—who undoubtedly heard many of the sermons delivered as he was growing up—and addressed directly and explicitly the doctrines for which he was expelled from the community. There is no such sermon in the extant texts. Indeed, there are very few that can be dated to the 1650s; as Morteira grew older, he characteristically borrowed more from his own writings, repeating and revising sermons he had delivered some years before. It would have been more likely to find sermons explicitly attacking Uriel da Costa, as the texts dating from the 1620s are more numerous than for any other decade. Here too the extant material may disappoint. While the names of many members of the community are recorded in the manuscripts, Uriel does not appear to be one of them.

This is certainly not because Morteira was so aloof as to take no interest in these figures or their eccentric views. His lost book on the immortality of the soul seems to have been a direct response to da Costa's arguments against this principle.[3] His signature appears on the writ of excommunication of Juan de Prado, along with that of his colleague Isaac Aboab, and he was directly involved in the process that led to the severe condemnations of Prado and Spinoza.[4] It is, of course, possible that among the hundreds of sermons that remain lost, there is one or more that may some day be found that addresses these individuals explicitly. But I doubt this, for several reasons.

First, while da Costa was not officially excommunicated in Amsterdam, a meeting of the rabbinic and lay leadership of the community on May 15, 1623, decided that he be excluded on the basis of prior excommunications in Hamburg and Venice. After the publication of his *Examination of the Pharisaic Traditions,* he was banished from the city. While reconciled with the community for a few years following his mother's funeral, new accusations got him in trouble once again. It may well have been that, especially during the years when his ban was considered to be in effect, it was considered inappropriate even to mention his name in public. Samuel da Silva, writing a refutation of da Costa's chapters denying the immortality of the soul, never mentions the name of his adversary.[5]

But beyond this, characteristics of the sermon genre would naturally reinforce reticence. Especially when delivered by a preacher who has served in the same congregation over an extended period of time, the sermon is a mode of discourse intended for a community of acquaintances. The preacher knows those who are listening to him, and he knows what they know. There is no need to state or explain a significant community event in detail; it may be assumed that all of the listeners are aware of the unarticulated reference. If there has been a notorious public scandal, it is unnecessary to mention the name or to dwell at length about the particulars; only the most obtuse in the congregation will fail to recognize a pointed yet non-explicit allusion. Indeed, allowing the members of the congregation themselves to draw this connection between what is said and what is meant may itself be an important rhetorical technique, making the listeners active participants in the condemnation rather than passive recipients of an explicit message. For a good preacher, the subtlety of allusion may be more effective than the bluntness of direct attack. This allusiveness on the verbal level may be underlined by elements of the delivery: a pause or slowing of pace, an intensification of voice, a glance directed toward the offending parties.

A second characteristic of the sermon genre, not unconnected with this allusiveness, is the convention that preachers will anchor their message in the classical texts of the tradition, especially the Pentateuch and the canonical works of the sages. It is not enough to condemn behavior of the present; the preacher will want to make clear why it is unacceptable through recourse to the texts accepted as authoritative by at least the great majority of the community. More than this, it will frequently be useful for the preacher to demonstrate how the offensive behavior is neither unprecedented nor unimagined in the past, but was itself foreshadowed or prophesied in the sacred texts.

This leaves, however, a serious methodological problem for historians who attempt to deduce allusions to contemporary events in discussions of personalities or occurrences of the distant past. That preachers and commentators will sometimes communicate a message about the present when speaking about the familiar passages from the Bible does not title us to conclude that this is always the case. The assumption of contemporary resonance without adequate justification can lead us astray. What markers or pointers can reassure us in concluding that allusions to the present are intended, and would have been understood by the listeners? Let us see how Morteira addresses the issue of "heretical views."

Morteira's sermons on this topic are clustered around two sections of the Torah. The first—perhaps somewhat surprisingly—is the lesson *Tazria,* specifically the first verses of the thirteenth chapter of Leviticus. These verses, describing in precise detail the priestly responsibilities toward handling various afflictions of the skin are, of course, a serious challenge to any preacher who wants to anchor a message of interest to his listeners in the *parashah,* for the verses seem totally irrelevant to the experience of most members of post-exilic Jewish communities. The homiletical challenge is even more pronounced for Morteira, who followed a self-imposed discipline of using each successive verse of the *parashah* as the theme (*nosé*) for his sermon year after year. The way out of this quandary, already adumbrated by the sages, is to transcend the simple meaning of the verses, pertaining to physical affliction, by presenting a message both linked to the text and more germane to the needs of the present.

We see this approach in his sermon on Leviticus 13:10, delivered in the early spring of 1640. After his introductory paragraph, he continues, "The path we have trodden in all the sermons we have delivered on the previous verses of this *parashah* is based on the accepted truth taught us by the Sages: that these blemishes and sicknesses [of the skin] allude to blemishes and sicknesses of the soul. We have seen this in several of their statements. . . . We will proceed on this same path in our present sermon, for it is appropriate with regard to these afflictions to learn what is unknown from what is explicit."[6] After setting out the underlying principle for the homiletical exposition of the verses, he continues to apply them more specifically.

> Thus, in the esoteric mode [*al derekh ha-remez*], it seems to me that these three afflictions are in their names a signal for us about three

> kinds of affliction found in the soul: three kinds of heretics [*kofrim*] who diverge from the path of faith of God's Torah. They are the ones mentioned at the beginning of the *parashah* [in Lev. 13:2]. The first are the philosophers, who follow the path of logical deduction, deriving from it what they apprehend and nothing else. . . . The second are those who accept the divine Torah, and have commandments and deeds intended for the service of God, but whose Teaching has been falsified, attributed to God although it is not [from God]. . . . The third are those from among the children of Israel, who boast that they observe the Torah of our rabbi Moses, but who diverge from some of its principles and roots, such as the Karaites and those like them.[7]

The first category is clearly the pagan philosophers, whom Morteira considers to be essentially atheistic, denying judgment and Judge;[8] the second is the Christians and Muslims (see below). It is the third category, composed of Jews who accept the Torah in principle, that is of concern to us.

A second cluster of sermons in which the topic of heresy arises is less surprising: they come in lessons from the Book of Numbers dealing with the uprising of Korah. In a sermon on Numbers 16:17, dating from the mid-1640s, we find the same tri-partite classification, undoubtedly taken over from the Leviticus sermons: "Now there are three categories of those who arise against the divine Torah at various times. The first are those who deny the divinity of the Torah. The second are those who accept the divinity of the Torah but who claim that their religion is superior to ours. The third are those who accept our religion but who deny one part of it. Now the first are the philosophers; the second are the new religions, such as the Christians and Ishmaelites. The third are such as the Karaites and Boethusians."[9] Alongside this three-fold classification, Morteira employs a distinction between two categories. I would like to look in greater detail at part of a single sermon, delivered in the 1640s, to see how he weaves together material from the Bible and the rabbinic literature to drive home a clear message about heresy in the Jewish community.

Destructive forces, Morteira tells us, can be of two kinds: external or internal, from without or within. This applies in the world of nature, but it also applies in the realm of religion: "It has already occurred that some of the religions have been damaged and destroyed, either because of the multiplicity of doctrines about its fundamental principles held by its adherents, leading to damage and division into many different groups, or because another people stood up against the first religion and annihilated it, destroying it with force, compelling the adherents of the first religion to accept a different one."[10] At this point, Morteira introduces two prominent biblical characters from this section of the Torah, whom he uses as typological prefigurations of subsequent challenges.[11] The first is Balaam, who represents "those from the outside, not from the Jewish people, who have arisen against the divine Torah and the prophecies." Here Morteira is concerned with Christian polemical attacks, and he spends considerable energy in this sermon, as elsewhere in his preaching, outlining the falsifications in Christian anti-Jewish arguments. But that is not our subject here.[12] After dealing with the external threat, he moves on to the internal threat of sectarianism, which is more dangerous than the challenges from without. The prototype prefiguring this challenge from within is Korah and his associates.

When we turn to the actual substance of the heretical views discussed by Morteira in his sermons, we find two focal issues, neither of which has any more relevance to the biblical model than Christian arguments actually pertain to Balaam. The first is the immortality of the soul. Morteira had been concerned with this from the beginning of his career, and he wrote what was apparently a massive treatise covering all kinds of questions relating to the soul, from its origins to its eschatological destiny.[13] It was a subject central to the bitter controversy over Uriel da Costa,[14] a subject to which he kept returning in his sermons. To take just one example, here is a passage from a sermon on Korah, delivered probably in the late 1640s:

> Regarding the soul, there is a false and pernicious view pertaining to its essence. Some have said that its origin is material, and that it is nothing more than potential, and that it may become divine-like as a result of human effort and wisdom. Now this is extremely destructive, radically undermining the excellence and dignity of the soul. It is also against the Torah, which states, "He breathed into his nostrils a living soul" (Gen. 2:7), testifying that it came from God, not through an intermediary.
>
> As a result of this pernicious view, they have sunk appallingly, stage by stage. First, they diminished the dignity of the human being, no longer believing that the human being is exalted above all other created things, although the Torah affirms that all others were

created for his sake. . . . For it makes no sense that something that is in its origin totally material at its core can be the purpose of created things so precious and exalted—an assertion that raises no problem at all if we assume that the soul is derived from the highest spiritual essences. . . . After this, from the same cause, were those who rejected God's individual providence [over human beings], for this is based on the premise of the preciousness of each human soul. That is what makes the human being more exalted than all other species, for which divine providence pertains only to the species in general. If we posit that the human soul is originally material, people would believe that the human species has nothing but general providence, like the other species.

Descending even further than this are others who rejected the immortality of the soul and the resurrection of the dead. For they cannot imagine or believe that there is a certain subject that, for some reason, changes its essence from one extreme to the other, as is the change from potential to reality, and from material to spiritual. The last sect is the cursed sect of the Sadducees, who denied all spiritual reward and punishment, as Maimonides wrote about them in his comment on the Mishnah "Antigonus of Sokho" [M. Avot 1:3]. Because they did not dare to reveal this view to the masses, for it would have turned all against them, they rejected the [rabbinic] tradition, and also the principle of resurrection of the dead. Having rejected this principle, they tried to find arguments and support from the Torah to establish their view, as do all the heretics, who interpret the Torah illegitimately.[15]

On the surface, Morteira is speaking about events in the past, the spread of sectarianism at the beginning of the Christian era. He attributes this to a materialistic conception of the soul, which diminishes the distinctiveness of the human being and leads inexorably to more and more extreme denials of widely accepted Jewish beliefs: individual providence, the immortality of the soul, and the resurrection of the dead. This process is linked with Maimonides' explanation of the origins of sectarianism, although that explanation relies not on the philosophical implications of a particular doctrine of the soul but on students' misunderstanding of a statement about reward by one of the early sages. There is no explicit application to anything in the present. But given the furor over the issue of the soul in this particular community, would those seated in the congregation not have heard an allusion to da Costa? Let us look at the points where this resonance might have been apparent to the listeners.

First, the proof text in this passage, Genesis 2:7 ("He breathed into his nostrils a living soul") was a major issue of contention between da Costa and da Silva in their bitter polemic of 1623–24. Da Silva, like Morteira, insisted this verse meant that the soul was "insufflated into man by God Himself," and therefore of special dignity. Da Costa argued that the same verse showed that "the vital spirit breathed into Adam was the animal soul," namely, "that vital spirit which animates the individual, and which is contained in the blood."[16]

Second, Morteira's complaint that "they diminished the dignity of the human being, no longer believing that the human being is exalted above all other created things, as the Torah affirms," echoes the formulation of da Costa, although it may not precisely report his view. Da Costa had written that "there is no difference between the soul of an animal and the soul of a human being other than that man's soul is rational and the beast's is devoid of reason." "Man has no pre-eminence over a beast as regards permanence, for all is vanity." "Beasts and man have the same spirit."[17]

Third, Morteira states that this position leads to the repugnant conclusion of rejecting the immortality of the soul and the resurrection of the dead.[18] Everyone undoubtedly knew that the main thrust of da Costa's discussion of the soul in his *Examination* was the explicit denial of its immortality. Much of this discussion was based on an analysis of biblical verses; perhaps even more controversial and offensive was his concluding section on the "false and pernicious consequences" of the traditional belief, a passage to which we shall return.

Finally, Morteira refers to the Sadducees as the "cursed sect" that was guilty of holding this heretical doctrine. At least some of the listeners may well have recalled that the image of the Sadducees was another issue in the conflict of 1623–24. Da Silva stated that "the Sadducees were founded by that depraved individual, Ṣadok, who was moved by passionate hatred and insubordination to abandon his master Antigonos and who, surrounding himself with a gang of dissolutes, stirred them up by his false preaching against the Pharisees." Da Costa took up the challenge, and replied by defending Ṣadok, with whom he seems to have identified personally: "If denying immortality was his sole malice and obstinacy, he must have been one of the most truthful men in the world. The Sadducees, far from being vile and depraved were, as Josephus says, the noblest members of the nation." He concluded by insisting that this is not just a matter of the distant past: "nor is their sect extinct, for there are many of them alive today."[19] For all these reasons, the passage seems to have been intended to resonate with memories and issues much more immediate than the early rabbinic period.

The second major area of heretical challenge addressed by Morteira was the Oral Law. In the sermon where he juxtaposed Balaam and Korah as prototypes of external and internal challenges to the integrity of Jewish faith, he points to the Oral Law as the aspect of Judaism most vulnerable to attack. "Korah and his cohorts subverted the tradition," a reading certainly not obvious from the biblical text but useful for a broader point, applying to others:

> As for all those who arose from among the Jewish people to dispute the Jewish religion, they did not dare to dispute about the written Law. Had they done this, they would have left the category of the Jewish people and would no longer have been considered as part of our nation; thus no one would have paid them any heed. Rather, when they sought to introduce contention and strife, they did so regarding the words of tradition and the interpretation of the Law that was given orally, for this is the most vulnerable part, having no support in a written record. They therefore thought they could destroy the Torah through the breach of this wall, for certainly without the Oral Law, the Written Law would be sundered into a thousand torahs according to the large number of opinions, and everyone make of it whatever he wanted.[20]

At this point he returns to categories of heresy, resorting to the famous Mishnah from Tractate Sanhedrin that he had used as the opening dictum of his sermon:

> The breaches they wanted to make in this wall are those enumerated by the Sages in our Mishnah mentioning those who have no portion in the world to come. Now the first is the group that says, "Resurrection of the dead is not in the Torah." This is the group that wants to confound the Torah by minimizing its reward. Not daring to touch it directly, they tried to weaken its power by diminishing its rewards and limiting it to perishable, destructible things, that which we can actually see. They sought to make us despair of the great eternal future rewards on the truth of which many martyrs

> gave up their lives for the sanctification of God's name, exchanging the perishable for the eternal.
>
> This was certainly the sect of Dathan and Abiram, who denied future things, saying, "Is it not enough that you brought us from a land flowing with milk and honey. . . . You have not even brought us to a land flowing with milk and honey" (Num. 16:13–14). They meant by this, "Why should we lose the benefits we can actually see for benefits promised in the future about which we know nothing?" Now just as the Sages said that whoever denies the resurrection of the dead will have no portion in the resurrection of the dead [BT Sanhedrin 90a], so these went down below while still alive, and were buried while living, and did not see the goodness of [the land of] Israel.[21]

This passage could, of course, pertain to the second century with its martyrs to Roman oppression, but it certainly would not be without resonance for a congregation, many of whose relatives had died at the hands of the Portuguese Inquisition. Uriel da Costa had indeed maintained that the future rewards and punishments promised by the Jewish tradition were an illusion, that the only real and assured good and evil were those of the present that we can perceive, and that these are sufficient to inspire moral behavior. Listeners may have recalled that one of the more scandalous and offensive statements by da Costa had been that martyrdom was not desired by God, who does not reward those who accept torture or death to avoid committing idolatry; it was therefore a waste of life.[22] We cannot date this sermon precisely, but it would have been delivered fairly close to the celebrated martyrdom of Isaac de Castro Tartas in December 1647, to whom Morteira devoted a public eulogy.[23]

It is the second category, however, that is more pertinent to us at this point:

> Now the second group is that which says, "The Torah does not come from Heaven." In my view, the principal intent here is about one who denies tradition, and says that the entire Torah is what is written, and there is no additional Torah given orally from Heaven. . . . Thus the sages said there in a bearaita explaining this Mishnah [BT Sanhedrin 99a], "Even if one says that the entire Torah is from Heaven except for one a fortiori argument or one argument from analogy, he is included in the verse, 'because he despised the

> word of the Lord'" [Num. 15:31]. The nature of this second group can be seen in the entire community which rose up the following day against Moses and Aaron and said, "You two have brought death upon the Lord's people" [Num. 17:6]: of your own devising you placed before them the obstacle of the test of the incense; it was not revealed from Heaven [cf. Num. 16:17, 35].
>
> Now their punishment was through the plague, and they saw by their own experience that without tradition, the Torah cannot be sustained. For if their working assumption is that the Torah was without tradition, it would multiply into a thousand torahs, as we have said; or they would give it fabricated interpretations that they had agreed upon. In this way, they learned by experience that tradition preserves the Torah.
>
> Thus they were tried through the plague that came upon them, for the incense, about which they said, "You have brought death upon the Lord's people" [Num. 17:6], is what saved them, as it is written, "Take the fire pan, [and put on it fire from the altar; add incense and take it quickly to the community and make expiation for them]. . . . He stood between the dead and the living until the plague was checked" [Num. 17:11, 13].[24]

The challenge to the Oral Law began many centuries in the past. But as is the case with immortality of the soul, it was hotly disputed in the seventeenth century by skeptics within the Jewish community who claimed that it was an invention of the rabbis—both in antiquity and at present—not an authoritative interpretation of the Torah, not part of the divine revelation transmitted intact from antiquity. This was a critical claim of the *Qol Sakhal,* as well as of Uriel da Costa (beginning with his 1616 *Propostas contra a tradição*), and others. Virtually every defender of Judaism felt constrained to respond to this charge; the accusation that tests imposed upon the people were the invention of the rabbis would certainly have been resonant.[25]

There is a third category mentioned in the Mishnah, the *apiqoros,* explained in the Gemara as pertaining to showing blatant disrespect for a scholar. The preacher continues:

> This sect, which would not dare to attack the Torah, shows contempt for those who study it and slander them, so that as a consequence their words will be scorned and the Torah will be scorned, for if they truly loved the Torah, they would be protective of those who study

> it. This is the very nature of Korah: in order to wage war against the Torah, they waged war against Moses and Aaron, saying, "All the community are holy, all of them, and the Lord is in their midst. Why then do you raise yourselves up to lord it over us?" [Num. 16:3]. This shows their need to degrade the tradition of these men; [we see this] also from the words of Moses, when he said, "I have not taken the ass of any one of them, nor have I wronged any one of them" [Num. 16:15]. Thus we see what they said: that they slandered Moses and Aaron, because they were greedy, with a burning passion for money. Indeed they were punished with fire [Num. 16:35], in accordance with their pride, for the highest kind of insolence of all was within them [?], burning feverishly with the lust for power, and with fire they were burnt.[26]

By the end of this sermon, Morteira's homiletical artistry has once again become clear. After dividing the challenges to religion into external and internal, and discussing the external (Christian) threats prefigured by Balaam, he divides the internal threats into three subcategories: those who reject the immortality of the soul and the future spiritual rewards beyond death, those who reject the Oral Law as divine revelation, and those who reject the rabbis as authoritative expositors of Torah. These are associated with three categories of heretics specified in the rabbinic dictum cited at the beginning of the sermon: those who deny resurrection, the Oral Law, and the *apiqoros* (interpreted in the Gemara as one who scorns the rabbinic scholar). Furthermore, each is associated with one of the groups that arose against Moses in the context of Korah's rebellion: Korah the Levite and his company of 250, the Reubenites Dathan and Abiram, and the "entire community," which rebukes Moses following the death of the rebels. Finally, they are associated with the three kinds of death recounted in the story and recapitulated in the theme verse of the sermon from the lesson *Pinḥas* (Num. 26:10): being swallowed alive by the earth, being burnt by fire, and being afflicted by plague, each one of which is said to fit the specific heresy it punished. The three heresies are also associated with past (tradition), present (rabbinic scholars), and future (spiritual rewards).

Yet with all this artistry, the question of contemporary resonance remains. For the entire structure could be construed as applying just to history: the Bible and subsequent events in the rabbinic period typified by the challenge of the Sadducees. There is one component of the sermon, however, not as yet mentioned, which provides a leitmotif connecting the various themes anchored in exegesis and history and emphasizing their ongoing relevance. This is the element expressed in the last word of the theme verse, *le-nes* (Num. 26:10), taken up at the very beginning of the sermon: "This word, *nes,* which in rabbinic usage always has the meaning of miracles and marvelous things that transcend the logic of nature, in biblical usage means something exalted, like this banner that is high and lofty [perhaps pointing to a banner in the synagogue?]. Its meaning is similar to 'as a sign (of)' [cf. Num. 17:3, Ibn Ezra], which is how Onkelos translated it here."[27] Morteira continues to suggest a subtle difference between the two words: *ot* is used for a visible sign, while *nes* applies to something purely intellectual. This is then applied, toward the end of the introduction, as a general principle pertaining to God's treatment of those who rebelled against His will: "God visited great judgments against them, openly and publicly, so that they might be a sign for the rebellious, and a signal for future generations, that this is what will happen to all like them. Every one of these matters comes to teach a lesson about some specific topic relating to the worship of God and the observance of His Torah. And this is as a paradigm of them all: 'They became an example' [Num. 26:10], namely, in the hearts of those who followed, that this is what would happen to all who corrupt as they did."[28] This formulation removes the discussion from an archaic past; it signals a typological reading of the biblical narrative, situating it as a warning for future generations, presumably including the present.[29]

This methodological principle is not limited to the introductory section of the sermon. Morteira returns to it again and again, as if it were the most important message he wanted the listeners to internalize and remember. In order to feel the force of this repetition, we need to cite his formulations as they reappear. Here he is making the transition from external challenges represented by Balaam to internal challenges represented by Korah:

> Just as God showed a signal through the case of Balaam about those who arise against the divine Torah and prophecies from the outside, not from the children of Israel, so he showed another signal and prototype revealing what would be the characteristic of those who rise up against it from the people of the Torah, as did Korah and all his cohort. In his case, and in our theme verse [Num. 26:10], and its context and component parts we may clearly see all the characteristics of

> [*inyenei*] of these sects and their devices and their fate, "and they became an example" and a signal and a prototype that this happened to them and would happen to all who are like them.[30]

Then, after he first explains the three categories in Korah's rebellion, each one destroyed by a different punishment stated in the theme verse, he continues, "and all of them were an example and a signal of what was to come."[31] In case the message might not be clear, after a discussion that reemphasizes the danger of the attack against tradition from within, he states, "Not alone do we learn from the characteristics of these sectarian groups, but also those who carry forward their controversies in every generation, who have acted in the same way, and whose punishment was measure for measure. And so it will happen to all who are like them. 'And they became an example' and a prototype for others."[32] Finally, in his characteristic recapitulation at the very end of the sermon, Morteira returns once again to this phrase: "These were precisely what were mentioned in our Mishnah, they are the ones mentioned in our theme verse who sought to destroy our Torah with regard to all three times, past, present, and future: past with regard to tradition, future with regard to the spiritual reward, present in delegitimizing the rabbis. And all of them were punished measure for measure, and have no share in the world to come, 'and they became an example' and a prototype for all who are like them."[33]

On the printed page, these recurrences of the phrase ending the theme verse ("they became an example") with its expansion ("and a signal and prototype for the future," or "for all like them") blend into the surrounding paragraph with nothing to distinguish them. In oral delivery, we can be sure that these words would have been emphasized and highlighted to stand out from the rest of the discourse. From the beginning of the sermon to the end, the recurring leitmotif is intended to trumpet a message to the listeners: the biblical and rabbinic examples of heresy are not something that belong to the distant past but a warning for the present, and the punishments recorded or promised for expressions of heresy in the past are very much applicable, potentially, to those in the audience.

Did Morteira intend specific allusions to Uriel da Costa's denial of the immortality of the soul and rejection of the authority of the Oral Law? Were his warnings about punishment measure for measure intended to evoke associations with the da Costa suicide in 1640, within a decade of the time the sermon was delivered? For his homiletical purpose, the specifics of an actual individual are not critical. The text of the sermon suggests that he wanted the listeners to think not of da Costa, but of themselves. They were the ones potentially being prefigured by Korah and warned by his catastrophic end and that of his cohorts. If they harbored doubts about the spiritual reward and punishment of the soul, or about the divine revelation of the Oral Law, or about the authority of the rabbis in their community or elsewhere, they had better take to mind the fate of those who "became an example."

A second point in conclusion. No matter what contemporary historians may conclude, Morteira apparently did not conceive of the heretical views circulating in his community as something new or unprecedented. At least this is not the way he presented them from the pulpit. In this he differed from the rhetorical strategy of rabbis in other contexts—for example, the opponents of philosophical study in the thirteenth and early fourteenth centuries, and the opponents of Ḥasidism in the late eighteenth century—who spoke of the doctrines and behavior they were combating as unheard of, something their ancestors never imagined.[34] To the contrary, through his typological mode of reading and preaching about the Bible, Morteira presents the phenomenon of doctrinal challenge to tradition as an ancient and recurring threat to the Jewish people. The threat is serious—more so than that which comes from Christian polemicists. Yet it is familiar.

Finally, one does not detect a sense of fear that the heretical challenges are a rising tide, a wave that may succeed in undermining the foundations of traditional Jewish faith. To be sure, in some of his sermons dealing with excesses of Jewish behavior, including those using a typological model, the preacher expresses deep discouragement about the possibility of resisting successfully what he perceives as powerful social forces.[35] Here, however, the model leads to the belief that God has encoded into the structure of history these periodic challenges from within the Jewish people, and that God will providentially punish the heretics and ensure the purity of the true faith. It is this assurance with which Morteira concludes his sermon, moving on from the bleak punishment in the theme verse to encouragement about the next generation, drawing from both the story of Korah and the metaphor of affliction of the skin from Leviticus: "But the children of Korah did not die" (Num. 26:11). "This teaches that God has not agreed to allow this leprosy to spread even in a single house, for He purified it immediately, putting the sinners to death and saving those who were good, so that the Torah would always remain standing as it should, until that time when all peoples will confess it, with the coming of our righteous Messiah, quickly and in our days. Amen."[36] Here the biblical verse, stating that the children of Korah remained uncontaminated by the heresy of their father, might seem to be in tension with the contemporary reality, where it was a younger generation causing the problems. Yet it is a conclusion of confidence in the future, promising his listeners the ultimate vindication if they will identify not with Korah and his cohorts, but with the younger generation that kept the faith.

This conclusion, however, while grounded in an invocation of God's providential concern for the Jewish people (a major theme of Morteira's preaching throughout his career),[37] does not imply a quietistic acceptance of whatever may happen, relying on God to take care of matters. Just as Moses had to respond energetically to suppress the challenge initiated by Korah, so Morteira recognized the need for decisive action on the part of the Amsterdam leadership—both rabbis and *Mahamad*—in specific cases of defiance. Allusions in sermons were not enough. Alongside this edification and reassurance, the contemporary leaders were prepared to act to bring about the punishment deserved by those who did not accept their authority, with the most powerful weapons at their disposal.

Notes

1. See I. S. Révah, *Spinoza et le Dr. Juan de Prado* (Paris: Mouton, 1959), 13ff. ("Les tendances heterodoxes dans la communauté judéo-portugaise d'Amsterdam au xviie siècle"); Révah, "L'hérésie marrane dans l'Europe catholique du 15e au 18e siècle," in *Hérésies et sociétés dans l'Europe pre-industrielle,* ed. Jacques le-Goff (Paris: Mouton, 1968), 327–37, with discussion on 338–39; Joseph Kaplan, *From Christianity to Judaism: The Story of Isaac Orobio de Castro* (Oxford: Oxford University Press, 1989), 162–63; Richard H. Popkin, "Jewish Anti-Christian Arguments as a Source of Irreligion from the Seventeenth to the Early Nineteenth Century," in *Atheism from the Reformation to the Enlightenment,* ed. Michael Hunter and David Wooten (Oxford: Clarendon Press, 1992), 159–81, esp. 176–80; Yirmiyahu Yovel, *Spinoza and Other Heretics: The Marrano of Reason* (Princeton: Princeton University Press, 1989), 40–54; Miriam Bodian, *Hebrews of the Portuguese Nation: Conversos and Community in Early Modern Amsterdam* (Bloomington: Indiana University Press, 1997), 117–18; Daniel M. Swetschinski, *Reluctant Cosmopolitans: The Portuguese Jews of Seventeenth-Century Amsterdam* (Oxford: Littman Library, 2000), 259–74; and sources listed in Joseph Davis, "The *Ten Questions* of Eliezer Eilburg and the Problem of Jewish Unbelief in the 16th Century," *Jewish Quarterly Review* 91 (2001): 326n107. Compare the suggestion of Shalom Rosenberg, "Emunat Ḥakhamim," in *Jewish Thought in the Seventeenth Century,* ed. Isadore Twersky and Bernard

Cooperman (Cambridge, Mass.: Harvard University Press, 1987), 313, that in addition to the Marrano background, the Protestant context is important in explaining the spread of "heretical" thinking.

2. On the manuscripts, see my article "The Manuscript/s of Morteira's Sermons," in *Studies in Jewish Manuscripts,* ed. Joseph Dan and Klaus Herrmann (Tübingen: Mohr Siebeck, 1999), 171–98, and the fuller treatment in my *Exile in Amsterdam: Saul Levi Morteira's Sermons to a Congregation of "New Jews"* (Cincinnati: Hebrew Union College Press, 2005).
3. On this work, see my "Saul Levi Morteira's Treatise on the Immortality of the Soul," *Studia Rosenthaliana* 25 (1991): 131–48.
4. See Kaplan, *From Christianity to Judaism,* 139–42, and Yovel, *Spinoza and Other Heretics,* 71–73, on the investigation of Prado; H. P. Salomon, "La vraie excommunication de Spinoza," in *Forum litterarum,* ed. Hans Bots and Maximiliaan Kerkhof (Amsterdam and Maarssen: APA—Holland University Press, 1984), 181–99; Uriel da Costa, *Examination of the Pharisaic Traditions,* ed. H. P. Salomon and I. S. D. Sassoon (Leiden: Brill, 1993), 16. For an early account of Morteira's role in the excommunication of his student, Spinoza, see Jean-Maximilien Lucas, *La Vie De Feu Monsieur De Spinosa* (1673), in *The Oldest Biography of Spinoza,* ed. A. Wolf (London: Allen and Unwin, 1927), 44–56.
5. Da Costa, *Examination,* 16–22, 429 (where da Silva says he will avoid specifying the name out of respect to other members of his family). Menasseh ben Israel, who cites the same chapters in his book on the soul, similarly refrains from writing da Costa's name (*Examination,* 49).
6. Budapest Rabbinical Seminary MS 12 (henceforth: MS) 1:41v, *Tazria,* Lev. 13:10, 1640:

   הדרך אשר דרכנו בכל הדרושים אשר דרשנו בפרשה זאת בפסוקים הקודמים הוא על המוסכם אשר למדנו ז״ל על היות המומים והחולאים האלה רומזים למומי וחולאי הנפש, כמו שראינו בכמה ממאמריהם . . . על הדרך הזה נלך בדרושנו זה כי היא הנכונה בנגעים אלו ללמוד סתם מן המפורש.

   The allegorical interpretation of the kinds of skin affliction in Leviticus 13 as different forms of heresy was a staple of medieval Christian preaching: see Saul Brody, *The Disease of the Soul: Leprosy in Medieval Literature* (Ithaca: Cornell University Press, 1974), especially 126–27; cf. 136–40; Katherine Ludwig Jansen, *The Making of the Magdalen: Preaching and Popular Devotion in the Later Middle Ages* (Princeton: Princeton University Press, 2000), 173–74.
7. MS 1:41v, *Tazria,* Lev. 13:10, 1640:

   ואם כן על דרך הרמז נ״ל [נראה לי] כי ג׳ נגעים הללו בשמותיהם היו לנו לסימן לג׳ מיני נגעים אשר נמצאו בנפש ג׳ מינים מן הכופרים אשר יטו מני אורח אמונת תורת האקלים והם אותם אשר נזכרו בתחלת הפרשה. הא׳ הם הפילוסופים אשר יתנהגו דרך ההקש והסברא . . .
   הב׳ הם אשר יודו בתורת אלקים ויהיה להם מצוות ומעשים מכוונים לעבודת האלקים אולם תורתם היא מזויפת, מיוחסת לאלקים ואיננה . . . הג׳ הם אותם אשר מבני ישראל המה ויתפארו בהיותם שומרים תורת משה רבנו אולם יטו מקצת מעיקריה ושרשיה כמו הקראים וכיוצא בהם . . .

   On "Karaites" as a code term for those in the contemporary Amsterdam community who denied the Oral Law, see Joseph Kaplan, "'Karaites' in Early-Eighteenth-Century Amsterdam," in *Sceptics, Millenarians and Jews,* ed. David S. Katz and Jonathan I. Israel (Leiden: Brill, 1990), 196–236. Several years later, Morteira recapitulated the same classification: "We shall briefly review what we explained on previous verses: we said that the afflictions of the body teach about afflictions of the soul, and among these afflictions, we found three types of corrupted belief, corresponding to the three kinds of physical affliction" (MS 1:39v, *Tazria,* Lev. 13:13).

8. Morteira's attitude toward philosophy is a complex matter that cannot be discussed in detail here. Juan de Prado accused Morteira of stating that "a man who is a philosopher is wicked" (Yovel, *Spinoza and Other Heretics,* 73; cf. 84), but I have not found such a formulation in his written works. He does indeed condemn radical philosophical views in his sermons. For example, discussing the implications of the doctrine that the world existed from eternity (MS 1:3r, *Va-Yiqra,* Lev. 1:10, early 1630s):

כי בהניח ח״ו [חס ושלום] הקדמות וישער היות הי״ת [ה׳ יתברך] פועל בהכרח כפעולות השמש את אורו והאש את חומו המה יקצצו בכל מעלותיו י״ת חכמתו ויכולתו ורצונו, כי מאחר שהוא פועל בטבע מהיכן תראה חכמתו אחרי כי כל סדר פעולותיו הנוראות הן מוטבעות ומוגבלות בטבע, עליהם אין להוסיף ומהם אין לגרוע . . . ואם כן יהרס בזה מעלת אלקות ויבטל כל תורה כי התורה תמשך מן ההשגחה והמוכרח לא ישגיח, ויתבטלו הניסים כי הנס שינוי הטבע והמוכרח אין בידו לשנות דבר ותבטל כל עבודה ויראת אלקים כי מה בצע לעבוד את המוכרח אם לא יתן ולא יוסיף ולא ישכיר ולא יעניש מאחר שנתבטלה היכולת חלילה.

Whether this is a theoretical criticism of doctrines known from the distant past or a response to a kind of proto-Spinozist identification of God with nature actually held within the community is not at all clear. Yet even most defenders of philosophical study in Judaism condemned such radical views. Morteira is to be classified with the moderate rationalists rather than with the extreme opponents of philosophy; he cites Jewish philosophers (Maimonides, Gersonides, Albo, Abraham Shalom) approvingly in his sermons, and even structures one of his sermons on the ten "categories" of Aristotle.

9. MS 1:87r, *Qoraḥ,* Num. 16:17:

והנה הקמים נגד אמיתת התורה האלקית הם כפי מחלקה ג׳ מינים והם היו בזמנים שונים. הא׳ אותם אשר יכחישו כל תורה אלקית. והב׳ אשר יודו תורה אלקית אולם יקדימו דתם לדתינו, והג׳ הם אותם אשר יודו דתינו אולם יכחישו חלק מחלקיה. והנה הראשונים הם הפילוסופים והשניים הדתות החדשות כנוצרים וישמעאלים והג׳ הם כקראים וביתוסים.

Morteira goes on to comment that in all of these cases, the opponents of the Torah, through divine providence, were never united to the point where they would present a perilous challenge, but were always divided among themselves.

10. MS 1:93r, *Pinḥas,* Num. 26:10:

דבר ידוע הוא כי הענינים הנפסדים הנה ימשך הפסדם או מסיבה פנימית או מסיבה חיצונית . . . כבר יקרה גם כן בדתות אשר כמה וכמה נהרסו ונפסדו או מסיבת רוב הדעות אשר נפלו בין מחזיקים בענין עיקריה עד אשר נפסדה הדת ונחלקה למחלוקות רבות או מסיבת עם אחר אשר עמד על הדת הראשונה ובטלה והפסידה בכחו והכריח מחזיקי הראשונה לקבל את זאת . . .

11. Compare his use of Balaam in the sermon on *Balaq* published in *Giv'at Sha'ul* (Amsterdam 1645, 64b, Warsaw 1912, 120b: several long polemical passages were removed from the Warsaw edition without any indication by the editor). On Morteira's use of typological interpretation in his sermons, see my article "Jewish Typological Exegesis after Nahmanides," reprinted in Saperstein, *"Your Voice Like a Ram's Horn"* (Cincinnati: Hebrew Union College Press, 1996), chap. 3, 30–33.

12. For a full discussion of the citation and responses to Christian polemical attacks against Judaism in Morteira's sermons, see my "Christianity, Christians, and 'New Christians' in the Sermons of Saul Levi Morteira," *Hebrew Union College Annual* 70–71 (1999–2000): 329–84.
13. See the article cited above in note 3.
14. See on this, recently, Talya Fishman, *Shaking the Pillars of Exile: "Voice of a Fool," an Early Modern Jewish Critique of Rabbinic Culture* (Stanford: Stanford University Press, 1997), 57–58; and Salomon's edition of da Costa's *Examination.*
15. MS 2:258r–259r, *Qoraḥ,* Num. 16:18:

והנה בענין הנשמה נמצא דעת הכזב ורע בענין מהותה כי אמרו שתחילתה מן החומר והיא הכנה לבד ומתוך מעשה האדם וחכמתו תעשה אלקית. והנה זאת הריסה גדולה וחולשה נמרצת ביקר הנשמה ומעלתה ונגד התורה המעידה ויפח באפיו נשמת חיים (בר׳ ב ז), כי מאת ה׳ היתה לא ע״י אמצעי.
והנה מסיבת דעת הרע הזה ירדו פלאים מדרגה אחר מדרגה ונפלו במוקשים רבים. תחלה בהמעיטו מעלת האדם ולא האמינו היותה מעולה משאר הנבראים, כאשר העידה התורה כי כולם נבראו בשבילו . . . כי לא יסבול הדעת כי דבר אשר מתחלתו כולו חומרי יסדה תכלית לנבראים כל כך יקרים ומעולים מה שלא יקשה כלל אם נניח נשמתו מן העליונים הרוחניים.
ואחרי כן מסיבה זו נמצאו מי שכפר בהשגחה פרטית כי היא מאומתת ומקויימת מצד יוקר נשמת כל איש ואיש אשר על כן נתעלה על כל המינים אשר ישגיח ה׳ בכללותם, ואם נשים נשמתו בהתחלה חומרית הנה לא יאמינו במינו אלא השגחה כוללת, כשאר המינים.
ירדו עוד מזה אחרים וכפרו בהשארות הנפש ובתחיית המתים כי לא יכלו לסבול ולהאמין שימצא נושא מה אשר בסיבה מה ישנה את מהותו מן הקצה אל הקצה כאשר הוא מן ההכנה אל המציאות ומן החומרי אל הרוחני. והנה הכת הזאת האחרונה היתה כת הארורה של הצדוקים כי כפרו בכל גמול ועונש רוחני כמו שכתב עליהם הרמב״ם ז״ל בפירוש למשנת אנטיגונוס איש סוכו. וכפי שלא העיזו לגלות הדעת הזה להמון כי זה ירחיק הקיבוץ הנה כפרו בקבלה וכן בעיקר תחיית המתים. והנה כאשר כפרו בעיקר הזה בקשו להם טענות וחיזוקים מן התורה לקיימו כאשר יעשו כל הכופרים המגלים פנים בתורה שלא כהלכה.

16. Da Costa, *Examination,* 451, cf. 479–82 (da Silva); 321–22, 311 (da Costa).
17. Da Costa, *Examination,* 311, 321. Some years after this sermon was delivered, Orobio de Castro cited Juan de Prado referring to a Dr. Cardoso, who maintained that the human soul is no different from that of the animal, and therefore mortal; see Yosef Hayim Yerushalmi, *From Spanish Court to Italian Ghetto* (New York: Columbia University Press, 1971), 252. Yerushalmi believes that this could not have been Isaac Cardoso, who defended the traditional doctrine of immortality (253–56).
18. For a sixteenth-century Jewish challenge to resurrection, see Davis, "The *Ten Questions* of Eliezer Eilburg," 313–14. For heretical denial of immortality and resurrection in the Christian context, see Carlo Ginzburg, *The Cheese and the Worms: The Cosmos of a Sixteenth-Century Miller* (New York: Penguin, 1982), 47, 72–76, 119, 123–24, 128.
19. Da Costa, *Examination,* 515 (da Silva), 347 (da Costa).
20. MS 1:94r, *Pinḥas,* Num. 26:10:

והנה כל אשר קמו מעם בני ישראל לחלוק על הדת לא מלאם לבם לחלוק על תורה בכתב כי בזה הנה כבר יצא מכלל בני ישראל ולא יחשב מעמנו וכפי זה ישמעו דבריו. אולם כאשר רצו להכניס המריבה והקטטה הוא בדברי הקבלה ופירוש התורה הנתונה על פה באשר היא החלק החלש ממנ׳ אשר אין לה מסעד בכתב, ויסברו להרוס את התורה בפריצת חומה זו כי בודאי לולי תורה שבע״פ [שבעל פה] הנה תורה שבכתב תחלק לאלף תורות כפי רבוי הדעות, איש כל הישר בעיניו יעשה ממנה.

21. MS 1:94r–v, *Pinḥas,* Num. 26:10:

והפריצות אשר רצו לפרוץ בחומה זו הם אותם שמנו ז״ל במשנתנו הקודמת אשר אין להם חלק לעה״ב [לעולם הבא] ורק המה עניני שלשת הכתות האלה.
והנה הראשונה היא האומר אין תחיית המתים מן התורה, והנה זו היא הכת אשר רצתה לערבב אם התורה בהמעיט שכרה כי כאשר לא מלאם לבם לגשת אליה הנה בקשו להחליש כחה בהשפיל שכרה ולהגבילו בעניניים כלים ונפסדים והם ההווין לעינינו ויבקשו ליאש את לבנו מן העתידות הנצחיות והגדולות אשר עליהם ועל אמיתם מסרו כמה וכמה קדושים את עצמם על קדושת ה׳ להחליף את הכלה בנצחי וימאסו כל טובות העולם הזה. הלא זאת בעינה היתה כת דתן ואבירם, אשר כחשו בעתידות ואמרו, המעט כי העליתנו מארץ זבת חלב ודבש [...] אף לא אל ארץ זבת חלב ודבש הביאתנו (במ׳ טז יג־יד), ר״ל למה נאבד הטובות אשר לעינינו בשביל הטובות המיועדות העתידות אשר לא ידענו?
והנה כמו שאז״ל שמי שכופר בתחיית המתים לא יהיה לו חלק בתחיית המתי׳ כן אלו ירדו חיים מטה ונקברו בחייהם ולא ראו בטובת ישראל.

Note the totally different homiletical use of Dathan and Abiram as a model for those Portuguese immigrants who long to return to the "lands of idolatry" in MS 1:83v, *Qoraḥ,* Num. 16:14, 1638, cited in my "Christianity, Christians, and 'New Christians,'" 380–81.

22. On the illusory character of future rewards, see da Costa, *Examination,* 342–43 and cf. 529; on martyrdom, see 409–11; cf. 342: "Others stupidly offered their souls to cruel martyrdom. Vainly and without cause these wasteful and foolish people surrendered and discarded that life so highly valued by the ancient patriarchs." Cf. also *Examination,* 563, from da Costa's *Exemplar.* Immanuel Aboab identified martyrdom as one of the topics that proved the need for an Oral Law: *Nomologia* I, 14; *Be-ma'avaq al erkah shel torah,* trans. and ed. Moises Orfali (Jerusalem: Ben Zvi Institute, 1997), 101–4.
23. Cecil Roth, *A History of the Marranos* (Philadelphia: Jewish Publication Society, 1959), 157–58; Yerushalmi, *From Spanish Court to Italian Ghetto,* 398; Bodian, *Hebrews of the Portuguese Nation,* 82–83.
24. MS 1:94v, *Pinḥas,* Num. 26:10:

והנה השנית היא האומר אין תורה מן השמים. ולפי דעתי שעיקר הכונה בזה הוא הכופר בקבלה ואומר כי כל התורה היא מה שבכתב ואין עוד תורה שניתנה על פה מן השמים . . .
וכן אז״ל שם בברייתא בפי׳ משנה זו ואפי׳ אומר כל התורה כולה מן השמים חוץ מק״ו [מקל וחומר] זה מג״ש [מגזירה שוה] זו, זה הוא כי דבר ה׳ בזה (במ׳ טו לא).
זאת היא הכת השנית אשר ענינה נראה בעדה כולה אשר קמה ממחרת על משה ועל אהרן ואמרו אתם המיתם את עם ה׳ (במ׳ יז ו) אתם מלבכם נתתם לפניהם מכשול נסיון הקטרת לא היה מן השמים.
והנה היה עונשם במגפה וראו בנסיון כי לולי הקבלה לא תתקיים התורה שאם יניחו ביד כאלו התורה בלתי קבלה תרבה לאלף תורות כמו שאמרנו או יתנו לה פירושי׳ בדוים מוסכמים מהם ובזה ינסו בנסיון כי הקבלה שמירת התורה. וכן ניסו אלו במגפה אשר באה עליהם, כי הקטרת אשר עליו אמרו אתם המיתם את עם ה׳ (במ׳ יז ו) הוא אשר הצילם כדכתיב, קח את המחתה וכו׳ (במ׳ יז יא) ויעמוד בין המתים ובין החיים ותעצר המגפה (במ׳ יז יג).

25. Fishman, *Shaking the Pillars of Exile,* 49, and index s.v. Oral Torah; Moises Orfali, introduction to Immanuel Aboab, *Be-ma'avaq al erkah shel torah,* 22–27.
26. MS 1:94v, *Pinḥas,* Num. 26:10 (fully annotated translation of this entire sermon is in my *Exile in Amsterdam*):

והכת הזאת באשר לא ימלאם לבם לנגוע בתורה הנה מבזים לומדיה ומוציאין עליהם לעז כדי שממילא יתבזו דבריהם ותתבזה התורה, שאם היו מחבבין את התורה היו מחפין על לומדיה. זה עצמו היה ענין קרח אשר ללחום כנגד התורה נלחמו כנגד משה ואהרון ואמרו כל העדה כולם קדושים ובתוכם ה׳

ומדוע תתנשאו כי תשתרר עלינו (במ׳ טז ג, יג) ר״ל צריך להשפיל מסרת אלו, ומדברי משה כאשר אמר לא חמור א׳ מהם נשאתי ולא הרעותי את אחד מהם (במ׳ טד טו). ראינו מה היו דבריהם כי היו מוציאין עליהם לעז להיותם חמדנים ולהוטים אחר הממון, אמנם נענשו באש כפי גאותם, כי הזד [?] היותר גבוה מכולם היו בקרבם קודחי אש לתאות השררה ובאש נשרפו.

27. MS 1:93r, *Pinḥas,* Num. 26:10:

המילה הזאת נס אעפ״י שבאה תמיד בדברי רז״ל על הניסים והנפלאות היוצאים מההקש הטבעי הנה בדברי התורה באה על ענין הרוממות כנס הזה שהוא גבוה ונשא, והנה ענינו הוא כמו לאות וכן תרגם אונקלוס [במ׳ כו י] והוון לאת. . . .

Cf. the discussion of the semantic issues among medieval grammarians, focusing more on the verb than the noun, in Albert van der Heide, "Banner, Miracle, Trial? Medieval Hebrew Lexicography Between Facts and Faith," in *Hebrew Scholarship and the Medieval World,* ed. Nicholas de Lange (Cambridge: Cambridge University Press, 2001), 92–106.

28. MS 1:93r, *Pinḥas,* Num. 26:10:

ויעש ה׳ בהם שפטים גדולים גלוים ומפורסמים כדי שיהיו לאות לבני מרי ולנסיון לדורות כי כן יקרה לכל כיוצא בהם וכל א׳ וא׳ מן הענינים ההמה היה ללמוד ולמוסר לענין פרטי בעבודות ה׳ ושמירת תורתו והנה זאת כדמות בנין אב לכולם כמו שנ׳ ויהיו לנס ר״ל בלבות הבאים כי כן יקרה לכל מי שיקלקל כהם. . . .

29. See above, note 11.
30. MS 1:93r, *Pinḥas,* Num. 26:10:

והנה כמו שהראה הי״ת הנסיון בזה בענין בלעם על הקמים נגד התורה האלקית והנבואות אשר הם חוצה לה ולא מבני ישראל המה, כן הורה נסיון ודוגמא אחרת איך יהיה ענין הקמים נגדה מבני עמה כשעשה קרח וכל עדתו אשר בענינם ובפסוק נושאנו ומקומו וחלקיו נר׳ בבירור כל עניני הכתות האלו ותחבולותיהם וסופם ויהיו לנס לנסיון ולדוגמא כי כן קרה להם ויקרה לכל כיוצא בהם. . . .

31. Ibid., 94r: וכולם היו לנס ולנסיון להבא.
32. Ibid., 94r:

ולא זו בלבד נר׳ מעניני הכתות האלה אלא גם כן נושאי מחלוקותם בכל דור ודור אשר עשו כל כיוצא בהם והיה עונשם מדה כנגד מדה כפי חטאתם וכן יקרה לכל כיוצא בהם ויהיו לנס ולדוגמא לזולתם.

33. Ibid., 94v:

אלו ממש הנזכרים במשנתנו הן המה הנזכרים בפסוק נושאנו אשר יבקשו להרוס את התורה כנגד שלושת הזמנים עבר הווה עתיד עבר בקבלה עתיד בשכר הרוחני הווה בפסול את החכמים וכולם נענשים מדה כנגד מדה ואין להם חלק לעה״ב ויהיו לנס ולנסיון ולדוגמא לכל כיוצא בהם.

34. This rhetorical mode might be traced through the polemical use of the verse "new ones, who came but lately, whom your fathers did not know" (Deut. 32:17). See, for example, in the context of opposition to philosophy in the thirteenth and early fourteenth century: Judah Alfahar in "Iggerot Qena'ot," (*Qoveṣ Teshuvot ha-Rambam ve-Iggerotav,* part 3 [Leipzig, 1859], 3 col. a middle), and the formulation in the second *ḥerem* of Rashba (*Teshuvot* [Benei Beraq, 1958], 1:152a): "Has anything like this evil thing ever been heard since the day when the earth was spread to its borders?" The Deuteronomy verse similarly became a leitmotif for the later opponents of Ḥasidism: see Mordecai Wilensky, *Ḥasidim u-Mitnagdim,* 2 vols. (Jerusalem: Mossad Bialik, 1970), 1:103–4 (*Ḥerem* of Vilna, 1781, 123, 138; *Ḥerem* of

Cracow, 1786), and also 2:57: "new Torah," 1:45 and 2:57: "new customs," 2:145, 154: "new way."

35. See, especially, the conclusion of his 1623 sermon titled *Qin'at Am,* "The People's Envy," translated in my *Jewish Preaching, 1200–1800* (New Haven: Yale University Press, 1989), especially 285.

36. MS 1:94v, *Pinḥas,* Num. 26:10:

    אמנם בני קרח לא מתו (במ׳ כו יא), להורות כי לא הסכים הי״ת שתתפשט הצרעת הזאת אפי׳ בבית אחד כי מיד טהרו והמית את החוטאים והציל את הטובים ותשאר תמיד התורה על מתכונתה עד אשר יודוה עמים כולם (ע״פ תה׳ סז ו) בביאת משיח צדקנו במהרה בימינו אמן.

37. See, for example, his Sabbath of Repentance sermon on Deuteronomy 32:12, delivered in the early 1630s and included in the 1645 edition of *Giv'at Sha'ul;* this text is fully translated and annotated in my *Exile in Amsterdam.*

10

Spinoza and the Rabbis

Immortality on the Amstel

STEVEN NADLER

On July 27, 1656 (the sixth of Av, 5416, by the Jewish calender), the following proclamation was read in Hebrew from in front of the Holy Ark in the crowded synagogue of the Portuguese-Jewish community of Amsterdam:

> The *Senhores* of the *ma'amad* [the congregation's lay governing board] having long known of the evil opinions and acts of Baruch de Spinoza, have endeavored by various means and promises, to turn him from his evil ways. But having failed to make him mend his wicked ways, and, on the contrary, daily receiving more and more serious information about the abominable heresies which he practiced and taught and about his monstrous deeds, and having for this numerous trustworthy witnesses who have deposed and born witness to this effect in the presence of the said Espinoza, they became convinced of the truth of this matter; and after all of this has been investigated in the presence of the honorable *ḥakhamim* ["wise men," or rabbis] they have decided, with their consent, that the said Espinoza should be excommunicated and expelled from the people of Israel. By decree of the angels and by the command of the holy men, we excommunicate, expel, curse, and damn Baruch de Espinoza, with the consent of God, Blessed be He, and with the consent of the entire holy congregation, and in front of these holy scrolls with the 613 precepts which are written therein; cursing him

> with the excommunication with which Joshua banned Jericho and with the curse which Elisha cursed the boys and with all the castigations which are written in the Book of the Law. Cursed be he by day and cursed be he by night; cursed be he when he lies down and cursed be he when he rises up. Cursed be he when he goes out and cursed be he when he comes in. The Lord will not spare him, but then the anger of the Lord and his jealousy shall smoke against that man, and all the curses that are written in this book shall lie upon him, and the Lord shall blot out his name from under heaven. And the Lord shall separate him unto evil out of all the tribes of Israel, according to all the curses of the covenant that are written in this book of the law. But you that cleave unto the Lord your God are alive every one of you this day.

The document concludes with the warning that "no one should communicate with him, neither in writing, nor accord him any favor nor stay with him under the same roof nor [come] within four cubits in his vicinity; nor shall he read any treatise composed or written by him." A Portuguese version of the proclamation was later entered into the community's record books.[1]

We do not know for certain why Spinoza was punished with such extreme prejudice. That the punishment came from his own community—from the congregation that had nurtured and educated him, and that held his family in such high esteem[2]—only adds to the mystery. Neither the *ḥerem* itself nor any document from within the community tells us exactly what his "evil opinions and acts [*más opinioins e obras*]" were supposed to have been, nor what "abominable heresies [*horrendas heregias*]" or "monstrous deeds [*ynormes obras*]" he is alleged to have practiced and taught. He had not yet published anything, nor (as far as we know) even composed any treatise. Spinoza never refers to this period of his life in his extant letters, and thus does not himself offer his correspondents (or us) any clues as to why he was expelled.[3] All we know with certainty is that Spinoza received, from the *parnasim* composing the community's leadership in 1656, a *ḥerem* like no other in the period. It was never rescinded.

And yet, is it not *obvious* why Spinoza was excommunicated? Anyone who has read his major writings, the *Ethics* and the *Theological-Political Treatise,* will wonder what could possibly be the mystery here. If Spinoza was, around the time of his *ḥerem,* uttering even a small selection of the audacious opinions that appear in these mature treatises, there can be no wonder that he was severely punished by his congregation. Can there truly be any question as to why one of history's boldest and most radical thinkers was banned from his synagogue as a young man?

In fact, two documents from the period give us something tangible on which to base our speculations. In a chronology of the events leading up to the *ḥerem,* Maximilien Lucas, Spinoza's earliest biographer, tells us that there was much talk in the congregation about Spinoza's opinions; people, especially the rabbis, were curious about what the young man, known for his intelligence, was thinking. As Lucas tells it, "Among those most eager to associate with him there were two young men who, professing to be his most intimate friends, begged him to tell them his real views. They promised him that whatever his opinions were, he had nothing to fear on their part, for their curiosity had no other end than to clear up their own doubts."[4] They suggested, trying to draw Spinoza out, that if one read Moses and the prophets closely, then one would be led to the conclusion that the soul is not immortal and that God is material. "How does it appear to you?" they asked Spinoza. "Does God have a body? Is the soul immortal?" After some hesitation, Spinoza took the bait.

> I confess, said [Spinoza], that since nothing is to be found in the Bible about the non-material or incorporeal, there is nothing objectionable in believing that God is a body. All the more so since, as the Prophet says, God is great, and it is impossible to comprehend greatness without extension and, therefore, without body. As for spirits, it is certain that Scripture does not say that these are real and permanent substances, but mere phantoms, called angels because God makes use of them to declare his will; they are of such kind that the angels and all other kinds of spirits are invisible only because their matter is very fine and diaphanous, so that it can only be seen as one sees phantoms in a mirror, in a dream, or in the night.

As for the human soul, Spinoza reportedly replied that "whenever Scripture speaks of it, the word 'soul' is used simply to express life, or anything that is living. It would be useless to search for any passage in support of its immortality. As for the contrary view, it may be seen in a hundred places, and nothing is so easy as to prove it."

Then there is the report of Brother Tomas Solano y Robles. Brother Tomas was an Augustinian monk who was in Madrid in 1659, right after a voyage that had taken him through Amsterdam in late 1658. The Spanish Inquisitors were interested in what was going on among the former Marranos now living in northern Europe, most of whom had once been in its domain or still had converso relatives back in Iberia. They interviewed the friar, as well as another traveler to the Netherlands, Captain Miguel Pérez de Maltranilla, who had stayed in the same house in Amsterdam, and at the same time, as Brother Tomas. Both men claimed that in Amsterdam they had met Spinoza and Juan de Prado, a fellow recipient of a *ḥerem,* who were apparently keeping each other company after their respective banishments. The two apostates told Brother Tomas that they had been observant of Jewish law but "changed their mind," and that they were expelled from the synagogue because of their views on God, the soul, and the law. They had, in the eyes of the congregation, "reached the point of atheism."[5] According to Tomas's deposition, they were saying that the soul was not immortal, that the Law was "not true [*no hera verdadera*]," and that there was no God except in a "philosophical" sense.[6] Maltranilla confirms that, according to Spinoza and Prado, "the law . . . was false [*falsa*]."[7]

Now we know from his later writings that Spinoza denied both the conception of a providential God—the God of Abraham, Isaac, and Jacob—and the revelation of the Torah to Moses by God. He also rejected the continued validity of the Law for contemporary (i.e., seventeenth-century) Jews. These documents suggest that these opinions—opinions that would clearly be disturbing to the rabbis of a seventeenth-century congregation—were already being expressed by him around the time of his *ḥerem.* It is perfectly understandable why the utterance of such views would bring upon one harsh sanctions.

What strikes me as curious, however, is the role reportedly played in Spinoza's ban by the third issue found in these reports: that is, the issue of the immortality of the soul. I see no reason to question the reliability of these accounts in this regard. As I show, there can be no doubt that this issue did in fact play an important role in the decision to punish Spinoza. Moreover, there is absolutely no question in my mind that Spinoza did indeed deny the personal immortality of the soul. First of all, this is (I, at least, would insist) perfectly clear from his account of the eternity of the mind in part 5 of the *Ethics.* He says there that there may indeed be an eternal aspect to the human mind. Indeed, he argues, there are two eternal aspects, corresponding both to the mind as the idea of the essence of the body and to the acquisition in this lifetime of adequate ideas and intuitive understanding through the "third kind of knowledge." But, he is arguing, in no way should these be construed as the postmortem survival of a personal self. Second, the denial of immortality is central to Spinoza's moral and political project. Virtue, he insists, is rewarded by happiness, well-being, and peace of mind in this life; not by the distribution of eternal rewards in some afterlife. Moreover, Spinoza believes that many historical and contemporary political problems—including the downfall of the Israelite kingdom and the current predicament of the Dutch Republic (in the 1660s)—have their source in the usurpation of political power by ecclesiastical authorities. These religious leaders secure their power, both over the state and over our personal lives, by manipulating our passions—especially the emotions of hope and fear. They are able to do this and keep us in line by holding out the carrot and stick of eternal reward and eternal punishment. I believe that Spinoza thought that the best way to undercut the ecclesiastical press for power was to kill it at its roots, by eliminating the foundational belief to which they appealed in their use of our hopes and fears, namely, the belief in the immortality of the soul.[8]

But now here is what I find curious. Let us say that Spinoza did deny the personal immortality of the soul. Nonetheless, the question of immortality is a metaphysical issue. It is a matter not of law or *halakhah,* but of philosophical speculation, and thus belongs to the tradition of *aggadah.* There is no Jewish dogma on this question; there is nothing that a Jew *must* believe about the fate of the soul after death. There is not even a Jewish doctrine. The Torah is pretty much silent on the issue. The rest of Hebrew Scripture contains various hints and suggestions, especially in its later books, but there is nothing definite to be found there. And there is no single and normative account of the immortality of the soul in the rabbinic literature. What there is, in the Talmud, the *midrashim,* and elsewhere, are numerous, sometimes reconcilable but more often contradictory viewpoints expressed by authoritative figures, indeed whole schools of thought, on the nature of the soul and what happens to it (or, in some cases, what does *not* happen to it) when a person dies. There is a good deal of divergence—and outright disputation—in the opinions of the rabbis and sages over what the soul is and whether it perishes along with the body or enjoys a separate existence after the end of this life. Some of these opinions involve fairly substantial accounts of immortality and the world to come; others represent an outright denial of personal immortality.

What is clear to me is that, for the most part, this is a question on which one was granted a good deal of latitude. Ordinarily, there is nothing specific that a Jew needs to believe about the fate of the soul after death.

The problem is that things were not ordinary in Jewish Amsterdam in the 1650s. In short, the immortality of the soul was simply the wrong issue to pick on in that community at that time.

The question of what happens to a person after he or she dies was very important for the Sefardic Jews of Amsterdam, perhaps more so than for many other Jewish communities in Europe. Given their personal and communal history and social background, these one-time conversos or descendents of conversos took very seriously the issues surrounding the postmortem fate of the soul. Part of the reason for this has to do with their common origins in a Catholic environment. Many members of the community, including its rabbis and leaders, were raised (at least nominally) as Catholics and educated in Catholic institutions. The Judaism they may have drunk from in secret—and to which they turned overtly in Amsterdam—was undoubtedly influenced by the dogma of its oppressively Christian surroundings, devoted to a strong eschatology, with an emphasis on immortality and eternal reward and punishment.

But there is a more immediate and concrete set of considerations that I want to focus on here.

Many members of Amsterdam's Portuguese-Jewish community had relatives, close friends, and business associates still living (at least outwardly) as Catholics in Spain. The situation of these people caught between two religions was as precarious and potentially dangerous as ever. The Inquisition had not slackened in its efforts to root out heresy. It was still on the lookout for crypto-Jews among its "New Christians," and even the most sincere of the converted had to worry about suspicion and betrayal. The Amsterdam Jews were sensitive to the plight of their brethren in Iberia. One of the community's regulations explicitly forbade its members from sending letters or other types of communication (such as business orders) containing any mention of or reference to the Jewish religion to people in Spain; it was feared that such a letter would jeopardize its recipient, most likely someone of converso descent, by putting them under suspicion of being a secret Judaizer.

Indeed, the concern of the Amsterdammers extended well beyond the safety and well-being of the Iberians in *this* life. They seem to have been worried, as well, about what would become of the souls of their relatives and friends in Spain and Portugal after they died. These were, after all, people who were committing two of the most serious sins a Jew can commit: denying their Jewishness and, by participating in the Catholic mass, engaging in an activity that in Jewish eyes was considered idolatry. Maimonides concedes that there are many occasions when a Jew, under the threat of death, may violate one or another of the Torah's commandments. In such circumstances—if the law is a minor one, for example, or the transgression occurs in private and not in the presence of ten Jewish males—it is preferable to break Jewish law rather than be killed. Martyrdom is not always a virtue. But if one is called upon to renounce the Torah itself or to violate its central and most important commandments, such as that forbidding murder or the worship of idols, then "one should sacrifice his life rather than transgress."[9] Later Sefardic emigrés, thinking about their apostate relatives, would have seen a clear lesson here for those living under the oppressive dominion of the Inquisition. Rabbi Joseph Karo, the author of the *Shulḥan Arukh* and, like Maimonides, an authority of special importance to Sefardim, claims that it is permitted, even preferable, to sacrifice your life in order to observe the Torah even in minor matters. Even if one is not required to choose death over disobedience, it is nonetheless, he notes, a sanctification of God's name to do so.[10]

The question in the minds of Amsterdam's Jews, then, must have been the following: What will happen to the souls of our apostate relatives and friends? Yes, they are suffering torment now in their denial of the faith. But will they find permanent rest from their torments in the hereafter? The Mishnah promises that "all of Israel will have a share in the world to come."[11] But the same chapter also notes that certain sinners will be denied a place therein. Have the conversos of Iberia forfeited their right to a place in *olam ha-ba* because of their continued renunciation of the Torah? Do they even belong to "Israel"? Will they suffer eternal punishment for their sin?

This question was so important to the Amsterdam Sefardic Jews, in fact, that it almost led to a schism within the community.[12] In the early 1630s, a number of individuals had taken to proclaiming that every Jew will, as a matter both of right and of fact, eventually enjoy a portion of eternal happiness in the world to come. They took the Talmud's words literally and insisted (apparently very vocally) that no Jew will ever suffer eternal punishment. Even if one has committed the most serious of sins, simply by virtue of being Jewish one is still guaranteed a place in paradise. They were, of course, worried about the theological and eschatological status of their converso relatives in Spain and Portugal. The thesis of the unconditional, ultimate salvation of all Jewish souls would be attractive to Marranos and former Marranos, since it meant that even those Jews who were still practicing Catholicism in the old country would be guaranteed a place in *olam ha-ba*.

Rabbi Saul Levi Morteira—the chief rabbi of the congregation—was not at all pleased by this. Of course, he did not deny that the Talmud contains the statement that it does. But does it follow that whoever belongs by descent to the nation of Israel, no matter how grave his sins and no matter how long he remains a sinner without repentance, is promised an eventual portion in the world to come—the ultimate reward—and thus will not suffer eternal punishment for his sins? In Morteira's mind, such a view could lead only to wanton licentiousness; there would be nothing to fear, long-term and before God, on account of one's misdeeds. The views of the "young rebels," he also argued, were contrary to classic rabbinic opinion, which clearly excludes certain types of sinner from *olam ha-ba*. According to Morteira, when the sages claim that every Israelite will have a portion in the world to come, the term "Israelite" refers only to a righteous person, not simply to any Jew whatsoever. And someone who has failed to follow the laws of the Torah, and who has openly denied the principles of the faith, is no righteous person and will be eternally punished for his transgressions. There is no guarantee that just because a person has a Jewish soul he can avoid eternal punishment in hell for his sins.[13]

Morteira's response only inflamed the passions of his opponents. In early 1635, his sermons at the Beth Jacob synagogue were being disrupted by young hotheads who took offense at his claim that "the wicked who commit grave sins and die without repentance do incur eternal punishment." These "immature disciples" were not, it seems, acting on their own. Rabbi Isaac Aboab, of the Beth Israel congregation, supported them in their views, and was probably even their inspiration and instigator (or, as Morteira preferred to put it, their "corruptor"). Pretty quickly the two rabbis themselves were clashing on the issue, much to the dismay of their respective congregants. The debate was a reflection of the ethnic and intellectual differences between the two most important and powerful rabbis in Amsterdam in the seventeenth century. Rabbi Aboab had been born a New Christian in Portugal in 1605. He had a rather mystic bent, more so than the other rabbis in the community, and a deep interest in Kabbalah. In this respect, he could not have been more unlike Morteira, who was inclined toward a rationalistic or philosophical approach to religion. Moreover, unlike Aboab, Morteira was an Ashkenazic Jew, and thus neither he nor his family ever went through the Marrano experience. Although he lived out his life among the former conversos of Amsterdam and preached to them in fluent Portuguese, it is easy to imagine his lack of empathy with what the members of his congregation (or their ancestors) had been through, and perhaps his impatience with their loose and unorthodox approach to some Jewish beliefs and practices.[14]

Morteira's opponents asked the leaders of the community to issue an injunction forbidding Morteira from preaching the doctrine of eternal punishment. Such a doctrine, they insisted, came dangerously close to Christian beliefs on reward and punishment, and would therefore discourage conversos from returning to the Jewish fold.[15]

The matter was too big for the relatively young community to handle by itself, especially since it involved a question of orthodoxy, something on which the community's leaders were perhaps still educating themselves. As on so many other questions, they turned to Venice and asked the leading rabbis of the older, more established Sefardic community there to rule on the dispute. Morteira and his opponents submitted their respective pleas, with Morteira marshaling a great deal of textual evidence—from the Bible and the Talmud, as well as from Jewish philosophers such as Maimonides—to argue for the doctrine of eternal punishment for unrepentant sinners, even if they are Jews. To the Venetian rabbis, it seemed a very delicate tactical matter. They hesitated to bring it up officially before their *bet din*, in part because they did not want it to seem as though the question of eternal punishment was a difficult one to answer and for which there were good reasons on both sides; this would only confuse lay people. Their initial recommendation was that the leaders of the Amsterdam community try to find a way to settle it amongst themselves, mainly by persuading Aboab to set an example for his younger protegés—if indeed they were simply following his directions—and publicly renounce his opinion. It appears that this approach did not work, and so the Venetians wrote to Aboab himself, in early 1636, appealing to him, in gentle and flattering but firm terms, to be reasonable and abandon an opinion that is explicitly denied by the sages of the Talmud and other rabbinical authorities.[16]

The letter from the Venetians did not have its desired effect. In response, Aboab composed, in 1636, a treatise titled *Nishmat Ḥayyim* (The Breath of Life). In the treatise, he directly addresses the question: "Is there eternal punishment of souls or not? And what did our rabbis, of blessed memory, intend by saying 'The following have no share in the world to come'?" He insists that the true answers to these questions are to be found in Kabbalah, not in philosophy or the Talmud (as Morteira had argued); and that the kabbalistic texts show authoritatively, if not clearly to the uninitiated, that *all* Jewish souls ultimately receive salvation. No matter what sins a Jew may have committed (or continues to commit), he or she will eventually enjoy the eternal bliss that is their right as members of the nation of Israel. The doctrine of eternal punishment is inconsistent with the notion of an infinitely merciful God. All things, we are told, eventually return to God, and this is no less true of the human soul than of anything else. While the Talmud does seem at times to speak of eternal punishment, its words need to be carefully interpreted. For example, when we are told that certain classes of sinners will "descend to hell [*gehinnom*] and are punished there for generation after generation,"[17] the phrase "generation after generation [*le-dorei dorot*]" must not be understood to mean "eternally," but rather only until the coming of the messiah.[18] When the sages insist that "the following [sinners] shall have no portion in the world to come," what they mean, Aboab claims, is not that their souls will never be admitted to paradise. The Talmud is in fact saying one of two things: either *olam ha-ba* refers to the period of the general resurrection of bodies, and the claim means only that the bodies of sinners will not be resurrected at that time; or *olam ha-ba* refers, as usual, to the spiritual hereafter, and the claim means that *within* the world to come there will be a separation of the souls of sinners from the souls of the righteous, with the latter enjoying their own special realm in paradise.[19] On neither interpretation of the talmudic passage is it the case that the souls of sinners are permanently excluded from eternal bliss.

Aboab says that many souls will, as a result of their sins, have to go through a painful process of purification before they can be admitted to paradise. What he has in mind, following the tradition of Lurianic Kabbalah, is a series of transmigrations, whereby the soul of the sinner will be reincarnated a number of times in different kinds of creatures, slowly working its way back to a human form. This journey will effect a *tiqqun,* or healing, for the soul. Morteira had grudgingly admitted the possibility of such a transmigration, or *gilgul;* but he limited it to a maximum of three journeys: "If in the end integrity is not achieved, the wicked will finally be cut off."[20] Aboab, on the other hand, claims that it may take as many as a thousand such transformations for a soul to be sufficiently prepared, and that in the end it will always have its desired effect. Moreover, it is a remedy available to *every* Jewish soul. Righteous or sinners, they all still belonged to Israel: "All Israelites are a single body and their soul is hewn from the place of Unity." The messiah will come only when all souls are pure enough for the world to come.[21]

Given the background of the overwhelming majority of the Jews in Amsterdam's Portuguese community, there is no question that many of them were sympathetic to Aboab's views. On the other hand, Venice's rabbis, whom they regarded with great respect, had made their own opinion on this matter quite clear: Morteira was right, Aboab was wrong.

The debate over eternal punishment was one of the most serious internal crises faced by the community in the period. It had lasting repercussions for the careers of the rabbis involved and for the organizational structure of Amsterdam's Sefardim. But the episode is also important for showing how important the doctrine of the immortality of the soul was for the Amsterdam Jewish community in the seventeenth century. For despite the deep, even irreconcilable differences between Morteira and Aboab, there is a fundamental assumption that is essential to both of their positions: the soul *is* immortal, in a very personal sense. In Aboab's view, there is an eternal reward guaranteed to every Jewish soul after death. This would obviously require a robust doctrine of individual immortality. Aboab, in fact, argues at length that the annihilation of the soul is—not just in fact, but in principle as well—impossible.[22] He cites numerous authorities, especially the late medieval philosopher Naḥmanides, in support of the soul's natural incorruptibility and immortality. Because it is immaterial, the soul is not subject to the decay and disintegration that besets the material body.

On the face of it, Morteira's view of eternal punishment might not seem to require the natural and personal immortality of the soul. Following one reading of Maimonides' doctrine, he could have argued simply that the souls of sinners will be "cut off," *karet,* and that the punishment of sin is death. The eternal punishment he is arguing for could be understood as nothing but the final non-attainment of happiness. But Morteira makes it perfectly clear that he has something stronger in mind. Sinners will not simply fail to sustain a happy life, but after death their souls will positively suffer eternally for their wrongs. The righteous, on the other hand, will enjoy everlasting bliss. Being "cut off" or denied a portion in *olam ha-ba* means, for Morteira, an eternal presence in hell for an immortal soul, with *gehinnom* organized into various levels for different degrees of sin.

Both sides of the debate were thus strongly committed to a robust doctrine of personal immortality. They differed only in what they understood to be the nature of eternal reward and punishment, not on the basic fact that there was compensation and retribution in the afterlife. One can easily imagine, in fact, that the Dutch Sefardim generally, solicitous as they were of the eternal fate of those members of Israel still compelled to live as Christians in Iberia, were very sensitive to the question of immortality, and would not have been tolerant of one who would deny altogether a future life in the hereafter. The Portuguese Jews of Amsterdam would no doubt respond very seriously to any attempt to deny outright the foundational doctrine upon which the positions of both Aboab and Morteira rested.

As a matter of fact, in the 1620s, a heretic of questionable emotional stability had given them just the right opportunity to do so.

In 1616, Uriel da Costa, an erstwhile member of the Amsterdam community but now living in Hamburg, published his *Propostas contra a tradição,* a set of ten theses attacking, among other things, the validity of the Oral Law (the Talmud) and demonstrating "the vanity and invalidity of the traditions and ordinances of the Pharisees." He was also plagued by some doubts about the immortality of the soul and an eternal life in the hereafter. To make his point, da Costa sent the work to the rabbis in Venice for their edification.

The point was received. Venice responded to da Costa's broadside with a *ḥerem,* pronounced against him on August 14, 1618, by Rabbi Leon Modena, who had been Rabbi Morteira's teacher. Modena condemned those "who contradict the words of our sages and who, notwithstanding the gaze of Israel, destroy above all the fences around the Torah, claiming that all the words of our sages are incoherent and calling stupid all those who believe in these words."[23] Modena's judgment would have great force in Hamburg and Amsterdam, given the mentoring relationship that existed between the Venetian congregation and those communities.

Da Costa was also put under a ban in Hamburg. Before returning to Amsterdam a short time afterward, where he continued to propound his views, he had apparently decided to give more systematic vent to his ideas on the Oral Law and, especially, on immortality. By 1623, he had composed a spirited critique of the Jewish religion, which, when finally published in Amsterdam in 1624, bore the title *Examination of the Pharisaic Traditions.* Among the objects of his attack are the rite of circumcision and the use of various articles of Jewish ritual, including phylacteries (*tefillin*), prayer shawls (*tallitot*), and the attachment of *mezuzot* to doorposts. The single issue which receives the greatest amount of attention, however, is the immortality of the soul.

Da Costa tells the reader that the thesis of the immortality of the soul has caused him a good deal of trouble for quite some time. The doctrine of eternal reward and punishment, in both its Jewish and (earlier in his life) Christian versions, was a source of great anxiety to him, and he apparently left the Catholic religion because the fear of eternal damnation tormented him.[24] "Certainty eluded me and the means to attain that eternal life, which I had been indoctrinated to believe in as the ultimate goal of human existence seemed out of reach. . . . In truth, the most distressful and wretched time in my life was when I believed that eternal bliss or misery awaited man and that according to his works he would earn that bliss or that misery."[25] Relief came only when he realized the true nature of the soul and, thus, its mortality.

The soul, da Costa claims, is not like "a damsel housed in our bodies," capable of departing upon death. Rather, the soul is a part of the body. It is a vital spirit in the blood and is that which is responsible for animating an individual. In this respect, the human soul is no different from the soul of any other living creature. The only distinguishing feature of the human soul is its rationality. "There is no difference between the soul of an animal and the soul of a human being other than that a man's soul is rational and the beast's is devoid of reason."[26] The origin of the soul in a person lies in a completely natural process. There is no special act by God creating the soul as a thing distinct from the body. It is engendered, like any other part of a human being's biological makeup, by procreation. It follows, da Costa argues, that the human soul is essentially and naturally mortal. Because it is a part of the body, when the body dies so does the soul.[27]

In addition to this philosophical argument for the soul's mortality, da Costa marshals a good deal of evidence from the Jewish textual tradition. Nowhere, da Costa insists in opposition to the exegetical arguments of his opponents, does the Torah explicitly say that the soul is immortal. "The first proof is an *argumentum ex silentio:* the Law nowhere indicates that the human soul is immortal or that another life, whether of punishment or glory, awaits it." In fact, the entire lesson of the Bible—the message of its stories, moral lessons, and epic events—is that "once he is dead, nothing remains of a man, neither does he ever return to life."[28] Nor does the immortality of the soul constitute the proper way to understand the manner in which the human being is created "in the image of God." Immortality is essentially a divine, not a human quality, and cannot belong to a creature.[29]

Once the truth about human mortality is accepted, a good number of "errors and evils" generated by the belief in immortality will disappear. "Since one absurdity leads to another and one error gives birth to many, this erroneous opinion or, rather, delusion concerning the immortality of the soul has such numerous offspring that it will not be easy to exhibit them all." Because of this doctrine, people recite endless prayers and supplications for the dead, make useless and wasteful offerings to God, and practice "countless silly superstitions at funerals." In expectation of some greater good in the hereafter, people despise the goods and evils of this world. They ignore their material well-being and engage in destructive acts of self-mortification, sometimes going so far as to offer themselves for martyrdom. All of this is not only intrinsically unreasonable but well beyond the bounds of what the Law demands in worship of God.[30]

Da Costa's treatise holds back nothing, and he is unforgiving in his indictment of the belief in immortality. Many of his charges about the doctrine will reappear in Spinoza's own thinking on immortality and how it is used by ecclesiastics to manipulate the passions of people.[31] Spinoza may possibly have read da Costa's treatise at some point, although it seems unlikely: the Amsterdam authorities—Jewish and Gentile—did everything they could to try to ensure that no one had the opportunity to see it. He surely heard about its contents, however.[32]

Before da Costa could publish the work, there appeared in Amsterdam, in 1623, a refutation of his views. The author was Samuel da Silva, a medical doctor living in Hamburg who had managed to get a hold of parts of da Costa's manuscript. Da Silva's book, the *Tratado da immortalidade da alma,* focuses (as the title suggests) on the immortality of the soul, and was most likely commissioned by the Amsterdam Jewish authorities, in whose domain da Costa was again living. He employs a variety of logical and textual arguments to counter da Costa's theses, although it is, on the whole, a fairly amateurish job.[33] Still, there can be no doubt that his treatise captures the spirit of reaction to da Costa's attack upon a cherished doctrine, one that the Amsterdam Jews considered to be of the utmost importance.

Alerted by the leaders of the Hamburg congregation, the Amsterdam community was clearly alarmed by the heretic's return to their city. And the seriousness with which they regarded da Costa's denial of immortality is testified by the trouble they went to in sponsoring da Silva's retort. They added their own response, on May 15, 1623, in the form of a *ḥerem*.[34]

As if that were not enough—and this makes it only more clear that the real issue in da Costa's case was his denial of immortality—Rabbi Morteira decided to take things into his own hands and compose a direct response to da Costa's views on the soul.[35] Unfortunately, Morteira's handiwork, a treatise that in extant references bears alternately the titles "The Immortality of the Soul" (*Sha'arut ha-Nefesh*) and "The Soul of Man" (*Nefesh Adam*), is long lost. One scholar, however, has been able to reconstruct, on the basis of a number of references to the treatise in Morteira's sermons, the likely content of the 1623–24 work, which Morteira (for some reason) never published.[36]

The treatise, devoted primarily to "proofs from Scripture and reason for the immortality of the soul" (according to one contemporary description),[37] apparently contained a defense of the view that there is a storehouse of souls in heaven, all of which were created by God at the beginning of time. Morteira thereby rejects the view that God creates a soul only on the occasion when it is needed to animate a particular body. It is only after this treasury is empty and all of its souls have been sent into the bodies created to receive them that the messiah will come. Sometime after that point, the bodies of the dead will be resurrected and reunited with their souls, and the latter will be judged for their righteousness or wickedness. And there should be no doubt that the ultimate fate allotted to each soul is an eternal one. Morteira, more than ten years before his conflict with Aboab, thus demonstrates a concern for defending the eternality of punishment. But the heart of the treatise is a discussion of the nature of the "rational soul [*ha-nefesh ha-sikhlit*]" itself. The soul, Morteira insists, is "eternal and immortal," and his presentation contains scriptural and philosophical demonstrations to this effect (although none of them are extant).

In the face of this onslaught—da Silva's vituperative polemic, yet another *ḥerem,* and Morteira's treatise—da Costa was defiant. He went ahead and published his *Examination of Pharisaic Traditions*—at the same Dutch publisher that produced da Silva's work!—including in it a lengthy response to da Silva's attack. This was too much for the Amsterdam Jewish leaders. As da Costa himself tells the story, "No sooner had [my book] appeared in print than the senators and rulers of the Jews agreed to lodge a complaint against me before the public magistrate, setting forth that I had published a book to disprove the immortality of the soul, and that with a view to subvert not only the Jewish but also the Christian religion. Upon this information I was apprehended and sent to prison."[38] His incarceration ended after ten days, when his brothers bailed him out. Either the municipal magistrates or the Jewish governors had also ordered that all copies of da Costa's book be burned publicly.[39] The community leaders had only one final regret: that, because of the absence of an Inquisition in the Netherlands, they could not condemn da Costa to death.[40]

This was only the beginning of a recurring cycle of offense, punishment, repentance, and reconciliation that would characterize da Costa's relationship with the Amsterdam congregations for the next fifteen years. Eventually, it all became too much for poor Uriel to bear. In 1640, after being stripped, publicly whipped, and forced to lie prostrate at the synagogue's doorway while the entire Talmud Torah congregation walked out over his body, he went home and shot himself in the head.

The message was loud and clear. The Jewish community of Amsterdam would not tolerate anyone denying the immortality of the soul. Those who do attempt to undermine the doctrine, especially in a public and prejudiced manner, will be dealt with severely. And it is clear from da Costa's own testimony above that, at least in his mind (and we have no reason to suspect that he was under any illusions about this), his major offense was his denial of immortality.

But the controversy over da Costa's views on immortality took place in the early 1620s. Spinoza's own *ḥerem* would not occur for another thirty years. Is there any reason to think that the immortality of the soul remained an important and sensitive issue to the rabbis and lay leaders of the Amsterdam Sefardic community well into the 1650s?

Spinoza was not the only person who was both banned by the community in the 1650s and (allegedly) denying the soul's immortality. We have seen that Juan de Prado, with whom Spinoza kept company after their respective punishments, was likewise said to have claimed in conversation with Brother Tomas Solano in 1658 "that the soul dies with the body." There can be little doubt that this opinion was one of the reasons behind his ban. In January of that year, in fact, the congregation's governing board, suspecting that Prado—who had apologized in 1656 for the error of his ways and reconciled with the community—was reverting to his old heresies, started to compile a dossier on him. They took a deposition from one Jacob Monsanto, who alleged that, having mentioned to his teacher Prado his own faith in the doctrine of eternal reward and punishment ("Is it not one of [Maimonides'] thirteen articles?"), Prado replied to the effect that he did not share that belief, given the lack of evidence in favor of an afterlife: "Up until now, no one has ever come back from the other world to ask for our assistance."[41] Monsanto's testimony, along with that of others, was sufficient to convince the board that a second *ḥerem* was in order. Some years later, now living outside Amsterdam and responding to a written attack by his erstwhile friend, Isaac Orobio de Castro, Prado asserted that he had never denied the immortality of the soul, but few have found his profession of innocence convincing.[42]

Then there is the case of Prado's friend Daniel Ribera, a convert to Judaism who moved to Amsterdam sometime between 1653 and 1655 and who was teaching in one of its schools. Ribera seems to have been a bit of a troublemaker, and was said to be, like Prado, mocking Jewish rituals. Of great concern to the board was the accusation by one of his students, Isaac Pacheco, that Ribera was proclaiming "that the soul dies together with the body."[43] Ribera, too, would probably have received a *ḥerem* had he not skipped town when he learned that the community's leaders were putting together a file on his opinions and behavior.[44]

This shows that there was no more tolerance for the denial of the immortality of the soul in the period around Spinoza's ban than there was in da Costa's time. Given the makeup and mindset of the community's religious leadership, however, this should not be at all surprising.

In Amsterdam in the seventeenth century, and especially from the time of the union of the three original congregations in 1639 through the expulsion of Spinoza in 1656 and up to the building of the Great Synagogue (Esnoga) in 1675, four rabbis stand out both for their learning and personality and, more important, for their authority within and influence upon the community.[45] They were, without question, the spiritual and intellectual leaders of the community. Other rabbis came and went, some merely as visitors, but these four *ḥakhamim* were a relatively continuous[46] and highly prominent (if not always cooperative and amicable) presence among the Amsterdam Sefardim. And it is a most telling fact that every single one of these rabbis wrote a treatise defending the immortality of the soul.

Aboab's *Nishmat Ḥayyim,* from 1636, was composed in different circumstances from the other works, since it was directed not at a denial of the doctrine of immortality but at a fellow rabbi's views on eternal punishment. Aboab defended the immortality of the soul as an essential part of his plan to argue for every Jew's being guaranteed a rightful place in the world to come. Morteira's treatise on immortality was written in 1624. But we also know that the immortality and eschatological fate of the soul was a prominent theme in many of his later sermons. In fact, a homily on the Torah portion *Va-Yelekh* is devoted mainly to discussing the nature of the soul, its union with the body, and its immortality.[47]

Rabbi Moses Raphael d'Aguilar, raised and educated in Amsterdam, joined the Amsterdam rabbinate in 1639. He was once Morteira's pupil, and he himself served as a teacher and mentor to many of the community's lay leaders.[48] (He took over teaching Talmud in the community school's sixth level from Menasseh ben Israel, who had replaced Aboab; the seventh, highest level was taught by Morteira.) Among his many writings, D'Aguilar composed his own *Tratado da immortalidade da alma.* Like his colleagues, he argues on a rational and scriptural basis that the soul is an immaterial and incorruptible substance that survives the death of the body and that will be the recipient of divine reward and punishment in the afterlife.

And then there is Menasseh ben Israel, the unhappy rabbi. Poor Menasseh felt that he never received the respect that he deserved. He was right. Ranked low in the hierarchy of the community's rabbis, stuck teaching in the elementary school, given fewer rabbinical duties than the others, and provided with the lowest salary, the learned and cosmopolitan Menasseh was treated as a second-class rabbi. He was forced to supplement his income by engaging in mercantile dealings, which he found insulting. "At present, in complete disregard of my personal dignity, I am engaged in trade. . . . What else is there for me to do?"[49] Ironically, he was also the rabbi best known to Gentiles in Europe. He had far-flung intellectual and commercial contacts, and was internationally celebrated as a printer and bookseller, as well as the most prominent Jewish apologist of his time.

In 1636, Menasseh published his *On the Resurrection of the Dead.* Though the main purpose of the book was to combat those "Sadducees"—an "abominably perverse sect"—who denied that the bodies of the dead would be resurrected and reunited with their souls at the end of time, the book's subtitle emphasizes the fact that the work also contains a proof of individual immortality: "In which, contrary to the Sadducees, is demonstrated the immortality of the soul." Menasseh's immediate target may have been Uriel da Costa,[50] although the book's scriptural, philosophical, and kabbalistic arguments clearly had an independent import greater than any role they played in a particular polemic. Menasseh, in an argument that follows well-established Jewish and Gentile tradition, endorses the opinion of Maimonides: "What you wanted to know, that is, what is the soul, is something about which the books of the Greek sages have already spoken. All agree: the soul is form, not matter; and thus when the body dies, the soul does not die but stays in its place like an immobile angel, and it enjoys and sees in the light of the world what is the world to come."[51] In 1651, Menasseh published his own *Nishmat Ḥayyim.* It is a long book on the nature of the soul, its temporary union with the body in this life, and, through its intellectual and spiritual union with God, its immortality. It was Menasseh's first book in Hebrew, and he clearly believed that it would provide him with a reputation in the world of Jewish learning equal to that which he already had earned among Gentile scholars.[52]

When Spinoza was put under a ban in 1656, all four of these men—each of whom had written substantially on the *immortalidade da alma*—were still the community's rabbis.[53] Despite their differences in background, temperament, knowledge, and intellectual persuasion—Morteira was a philosophical rationalist, Aboab a mystical kabbalist, d'Aguilar a stodgy scholastic, and Menasseh a confirmed messianist—all of them were deeply committed to a rigorous understanding of personal immortality, and all of them had argued strenuously in writing for their views.

Clearly, part of the importance of the question of immortality for these rabbis lay in the fact that they saw it as intimately connected to other, more obviously central elements of the Jewish faith. As Kasher and Biderman show in their thorough study of the issues surrounding Spinoza's *ḥerem,* Morteira and Menasseh had a tendency to lump together the three doctrines that appear to have played a role in Spinoza's ban: the truth of the Torah, the existence of a providential God, and the immortality of the soul.[54] Menasseh, in fact, explicitly saw the doctrine of immortality as fundamental for the other tenets:

> On this belief in the immortality of the soul depend, learned reader, the major foundations and the principles of religion, namely, the existence of God, the divine origin of the Torah, and reward and punishment. For if you say that the soul dies with the body, this precludes reward and punishment. And if there are no reward and punishment and divine providence, then the existence of God is precluded. And if God does not exist and there is no reward and punishment, what is the purpose of the divine Torah and the toil of observing the precepts? Therefore, the threefold cord is not quickly broken.[55]

For Menasseh, denying the immortality of the soul is the first step down the slippery slope of denying the Jewish faith. Like Maimonides before them, he, Morteira, Aboab, and d'Aguilar believed the immortality of the soul to be one of the "grand principles" of Judaism.

The denial of personal immortality is an important element in Spinoza's philosophy, and especially his moral thought, his views on religion, and his broader social and political project. And it is practically certain that Spinoza was denying the immortality of the soul around the time of his *ḥerem;* we have credible reports that this was one of the three opinions for which he was banned—the other two being the denial of a providential God and the rejection of the validity (or "truth") of the Torah. But then there was the question—and it is a particularly glaring one, in the light of Jewish tradition and the wide maneuvering room usually provided therein for thinking on metaphysical matters—as to *why* a denial of the immortality of the soul should contribute to one's earning an excommunication. Now that we have seen how seriously the rabbis and leaders of the Amsterdam community took the issue of immortality, it should be fairly clear how Spinoza's expression of his views on the matter would have been a particularly aggravating factor in his case. It may possibly have been, in fact, *the* decisive element in the decision to issue Spinoza the harshest writ of *ḥerem* in the community's history.

Jewish Amsterdam in the 1650s was simply the wrong place in which to deny the immortality of the soul.

Notes

1. The Hebrew text is no longer extant, but the Portuguese version is found in the Book of Ordinances (*Livro dos Acordos de Naçao e Ascamot*), in the Municipal Archives of the City of Amsterdam, Archives for the Portuguese Jewish Community in Amsterdam, 334, no. 19, fol. 408. The translation follows that in Asa Kasher

and Shlomo Biderman, "Why Was Spinoza Excommunicated?" in *Sceptics, Millenarians, and Jews*, ed. David S. Katz and Jonathan Israel (Leiden: Brill, 1990), 98–99.

2. That his family was held in high esteem is testified by the fact that his father served in numerous leadership positions in the community, including several terms on the *mahamad* as one of its *parnasim*. In fact, his final term as *parnas* was in 1649–50, just a few years before his son would be banned. See the documents in A. M. Vaz Dias and W. G. Van der Tak, "Spinoza: Merchant and Autodidact," *Studia Rosenthaliana* 16 (1982): 105–71 (130–31).
3. Spinoza's friends, who edited his works and letters for publication immediately after his death, seem to have destroyed all letters that were not of mainly philosophical (as opposed to biographical and personal) interest.
4. J. Freudenthal, *Die Lebensgeschichte Spinoza's in Quellenschriften, Urkunden und Nichtamtlichen* (Leipzig: Verlag Von Veit, 1899), 5.
5. I. S. Révah, *Spinoza et le Dr. Juan de Prado* (Paris: Mouton, 1959), 32–33.
6. The text of Brother Tomas's deposition (ibid., 32) reads as follows:

> He knew both Dr. Prado, a physician, whose first name was Juan but whose Jewish name he did not know, who had studied at Alcala, and a certain de Espinosa, who he thinks was a native of one of the villages of Holland, for he had studied at Leiden and was a good philosopher. These two persons had professed the Law of Moses, and the synagogue had expelled and isolated them because they had reached the point of atheism. And they themselves told the witness that they had been circumcised and that they had observed the law of the Jews, and that they had changed their mind because it seemed to them that the said law was not true and that souls died with their bodies and that there is no God except philosophically. And that is why they were expelled from the synagogue; and, while they regretted the absence of the charity that they used to receive from the synagogue and the communication with other Jews, they were happy to be atheists, since they thought that God exists only philosophically . . . and that souls died with their bodies and that thus they had no need for faith.

7. The original text of Maltranilla's testimony is in ibid., 67.
8. I argue both of these points in greater length in *Spinoza's Heresy: Immortality and the Jewish Mind* (Oxford: Oxford University Press, 2002).
9. "In times of a decree—that is, when a wicked king like Nebuchadnezzar or his like will arise and issue a decree against the Jews to nullify their faith or one of the *miṣvot*—one should sacrifice one's life rather than transgress any of the other *miṣvot* [i.e., the important ones], whether one is compelled to transgress in the midst of ten Jews or one is compelled to transgress merely in the midst of Gentiles" (*Mishneh Torah*, "Hilkhot Yesodei ha-Torah," 5:3), trans. E. Touger (New York: Moznaim Publishing, 1989), 210–12.
10. *Shulḥan Arukh*, Yoreh De'ah 157:1.
11. Mishnah Sanhedrin 10:1.
12. The event, in fact, undoubtedly contributed to the three congregations' decision in 1638 to merge into one Talmud Torah with a ranked cadre of rabbis. The best and most thorough study of the debate over eternal punishment in the 1630s is Alexan-

der Altmann's "Eternality of Punishment: A Theological Controversy within the Amsterdam Rabbinate in the Thirties of the Seventeenth-Century," *Proceedings of the American Academy for Jewish Research* 40 (1972): 1–88. This article contains both a long discussion of the issues around the debate and the three central texts themselves. I am greatly indebted to Altmann's work here for my summary of the debate.

13. See ibid., Text A, lines 103–6.
14. See ibid., 18.
15. Their argument here was rather disingenuous, as their own belief in eternal salvation was no less "Christian" than Morteira's position.
16. Altmann, "Eternality of Punishment," 15.
17. BT Rosh Hashanah 17a.
18. Altmann, "Eternality of Punishment," Text C, sec. 3, lines 25–33.
19. Ibid., Text C, sec. 3, lines 53–156.
20. Ibid., Text A, lines 95–96.
21. Ibid., Text C, sec. 3, lines 1–25.
22. Ibid., Text C, sec. 2, lines 9–47.
23. Carl Gebhardt, ed., *Die Schriften des Uriel da Costa* (Amsterdam: Curis Societatis Spinozanae, 1922), 154f.
24. Ibid., 124.
25. Uriel da Costa, *Examination of the Pharisaic Traditions,* trans. H. P. Salomon and I. S. D. Sassoon (Leiden: Brill, 1993), 343.
26. Ibid., 311.
27. "To the question as to whether the soul of a human being is mortal or immortal, we reply that . . . it must be mortal if it is contained in the blood, as we have ascertained. It is in fact the vital spirit which dies and is extinguished before the human being can expire" (ibid., 312).
28. Ibid., 316.
29. Ibid., 321.
30. Ibid., part 2, chap. 3.
31. It is clear that Harry Wolfson's thesis, that Spinoza composed his views as an effort to combat da Costa's and defend the traditional rabbinic doctrine, is entirely untenable (*The Philosophy of Spinoza,* 2 vols. [Cambridge, Mass.: Harvard University Press, 1934], 2:323–25).
32. The question of da Costa's influence on Spinoza is a contentious one. Révah believes that Spinoza reflected much on da Costa and his ideas; see "Du marranisme au judaisme et au déisme," in *Des Marranes à Spinoza,* ed. H. Méchoulan et al. (Paris: Vrin, 1995). Gebhardt, on the other hand, is more skeptical; see *Die Schriften des Uriel da Costa,* xxxiii–xxxix. See also the discussions by Yirmiyahu Yovel, *Spinoza and Other Heretics: The Marrano of Reason* (Princeton: Princeton University Press, 1989), 42–51; and Gabriel Albiac, *La synagogue vide* (Paris: PUF, 1994), part 2, chap. 1.
33. An English translation of da Silva's treatise is in da Costa, *Examination,* 429–551. For a discussion of the da Silva–da Costa polemic, see Albiac, *La synagogue vide,* 293–300.
34. The following translation is from da Costa, *Examination,* 15: "The *ḥakhamim,* in the presence of delegates from the three Boards of Elders, held meetings with Uriel in the course of which mild and gentle persuasion was applied to bring him back to

the truth. Seeing that through pure obduracy and arrogance he persists in his wickedness and wrong opinions, the delegates from the three boards of elders, together with the boards of wardens and the consent of the *ḥakhamim,* ordained he be excluded as a person already excommunicated [i.e., in Venice and Hamburg] and accursed of God, and that . . . no communication with him is henceforth permitted to anyone except his brothers, who are granted eight days to wind up their affairs with him." (Portuguese Jewish Archives, Municipal Archives of Amsterdam, no. 13, fol. 25–26.)

35. Marc Saperstein has argued, however, that Morteira's treatise was composed not as a response to da Costa, but rather as a "discursive and encyclopedic" treatment of an issue of great importance to Morteira, although "it undoubtedly contained material directly relevant to the da Costa conflict"; see "Saul Levi Morteira's Treatise on the Immortality of the Soul," *Studia Rosenthaliana* 25 (1991): 131–48 (140–41).
36. Ibid.
37. By Shabbetai Bass, *Siftei Yeshenim,* published in Amsterdam in 1680; see Saperstein, "Saul Levi Morteira's Treatise on the Immortality of the Soul," 131.
38. Da Costa, *Exemplar Humanae Vitae,* in *Examination,* 558.
39. At least two copies survived. One of them ended up with the Spanish Grand Inquisitor and was put on the Index in 1632; see Salomon and Sassoon, introduction to da Costa's *Examination,* 17.
40. See da Costa, *Examination,* 18, for a quote from a letter that the Amsterdam Jewish leaders wrote to Rabbi Jacob Halevi in Venice.
41. The text of Monsanto's deposition is in I. S. Révah, "Aux origines de la rupture Spinozienne: Nouveaux documents sur l'incroyance dans la communauté judéo-portugaise d'Amsterdam à l'époque de l'excommunication de Spinoza," *Revue des études juives* 123 (1964): 359–430 (395).
42. See, for example, Révah, *Spinoza et le Dr. Juan de Prado,* 45; and, discussing Prado's response to Monsanto's deposition, "Aux origines de la rupture Spinozienne: Nouveaux documents," 379.
43. Révah, "Aux origines de la rupture Spinozienne: Nouveaux Documents," 402.
44. On Ribera, see Yosef Kaplan, *From Christianity to Judaism: The Story of Isaac Orobio de Castro* (Oxford: Oxford University Press, 1989), 142–45.
45. In addition to Morteira, Aboab, d'Aguilar, and Menasseh, David Pardo was also a member of the Amsterdam rabbinate. But from what I can tell he was not a major intellectual presence in the community, as the others were. In 1639, when the original congregations merged, he was made director of funerals and supervisor of the burial grounds at Ouderkerk.
46. Both Rabbi Aboab and Rabbi d'Aguilar did depart for a time (1642–54) to lead the congregation of expatriates in Recife, Brazil, while Menasseh spent the last two years of his life (1655–57) living in England trying to arrange for the readmission of the Jews into that country.
47. See the collection of his sermons first published in Amsterdam in 1645 by his disciples under the title *Giv'at Sha'ul;* I have used the edition published in Warsaw in 1912. *Va-Yelekh* appears on 288–303. The substance of this sermon has been discussed above in connection with Morteira's 1624 treatise.
48. See Kaplan, *From Christianity to Judaism,* 110–14.

49. Quoted in Cecil Roth, *A Life of Menasseh ben Israel* (Philadelphia: Jewish Publication Society, 1934), 53.
50. Or so Albiac argues; see *La synagogue vide,* 300–325.
51. *De la Resurreccion de los muertos,* quoted in Albiac, *La synagogue vide,* 319.
52. See Roth, *A Life of Menasseh ben Israel,* 97–99. For a recent edition of Menasseh's book, see *Nishmat Ḥayyim* (Jerusalem: Yerid ha-Sefarim, 1995).
53. However, Menasseh was out of the country at the time of Spinoza's *ḥerem,* working for the readmission of the Jews to England.
54. "Why Was Spinoza Excommunicated?" 110–11.
55. Menasseh ben Israel, *Nishmat Ḥayyim,* introduction.

11

The Besht as Spinozist

Abraham Krochmal's Preface to Ha-Ketav ve-ha-Mikhtav

Introduction and Translation

ALLAN NADLER

Part 1: Introduction

Synopsis of Krochmal's Preface

Abraham Krochmal's *reshit davar* (preface) to his work of biblical text-criticism, *Ha-Ketav ve-ha-Mikhtav* (1874), is a preposterous introduction to a serious book.[1] The juxtaposition of this absurdly satirical preface—described disdainfully by Joshua Heschel Schorr, Krochmal's one-time comrade-in-arms in the radical Galician *Haskalah,* as "a vain and stupid tale"—with the sober and highly technical work of biblical criticism that follows is, to my knowledge, without parallel in Hebrew literature. Like so many prefaces to Jewish books since the early medieval period, the preface is intended to provide a rationale for the book's publication and justify its general content. Krochmal's preface begins on a highly defensive note, as he shares with the reader his fears that the radical content of his book, a work of biblical text criticism, would bring censure and even excommunication upon himself from the fanatical rabbis of his day. The fantastic story he goes on to tell is intended to blunt their criticism by recounting the amazing truth about his book's sacred origins. Krochmal claims to have invented nothing himself, as his book is based on a holy manuscript that he had unearthed and whose content reflects traditions that were already known to Moses' successor, Joshua bin Nun. Krochmal recounts the history of the series of revelations and concealments of these textual traditions, culminating in his rediscovery of them in the Podolian town of Miedzyborz, the birthplace of Rabbi Israel Baal Shem Tov (the Besht). Regardless of how shocking and apparently subversive the details of his book might appear to the rabbis of his day, Krochmal insists that he has nothing for which to apologize. Quite the contrary, he ought to be thanked for bringing back to light the authentic and accurate text of the Torah as it was originally revealed to Moses, and correcting the Masoretes' textual corruptions.

Krochmal further claims that he did not arrive at any of the hundreds of emendations to the Masoretic text of the Hebrew Scriptures that make up *Ha-Ketav ve-ha-Mikhtav* on the basis of his own reason and scholarship. Unlike "heretics" such as Abraham Ibn Ezra and his disciples, as well as Baruch Spinoza, who dared to criticize the biblical text on the basis of reason alone, Krochmal insists—both in the preface and on the title page of *Ha-Ketav ve-ha-Mikhtav*—that his book is based entirely on that ancient and holy manuscript that he had unearthed from under a rock in Miedzyborz. Moreover, this manuscript, while comprising the most esoteric teachings of Rabbi Adam, the mysterious mentor of the founder of Ḥasidism, originated with none other than Spinoza. Even the brazen heretic of Amsterdam had no intention of publishing this subversive material and, according to Krochmal's tale, Spinoza burned his own manuscript shortly before his death. Before he did so, however, a copy was secretly made by the famously mysterious Rabbi Adam Baal Shem who, as it turns out, had spent some time studying under Spinoza in Amsterdam. After Spinoza's death, Rabbi Adam left Amsterdam to return to Poland, bringing the manuscript with him. Rabbi Adam then transferred the manuscript to his nameless son who, according to Ḥasidic lore, instructed Rabbi Israel Baal Shem Tov in the deepest secrets of the Kabbalah. Having completed his instruction of the Besht, he passed the manuscript containing Spinoza's teachings to him. The Besht, sensing just how explosive its message was, buried the manuscript under a rock in Miedzyborz where it remained hidden until Abraham Krochmal was epiphanously informed that he was destined by the heavens to disinter and publish its contents. Krochmal overcomes all of the supernatural guardians that had been appointed by the Besht to protect the buried treasure, thereby fulfilling a prophecy hinted at in *Shivḥei ha-Besht,* and redeems the manuscript by publishing it as *Ha-Ketav ve-ha-Mikhtav.*

This remarkable tale carries with it a very dramatic implication: namely, that the most esoteric doctrine of Beshtian Ḥasidism is in fact identical with the radical and religiously subversive biblical criticism advocated by Spinoza in the *Theological-Political Treatise*.[2] Spinoza and the Besht were well aware of the explosiveness of this doctrine and, acting in the spirit of the Spinozan motto, "caute," concealed it. In daring to publish the concealed manuscript containing the details of Spinoza's and the Besht's teachings, the champion of the authentic biblical text is, ironically enough, the radical *maskil* Abraham Krochmal, who acts against dangerous supernatural forces in order to restore the true original text of the Torah to the Jewish people.

This is the general idea of Krochmal's strange preface. It is followed by two pseudepigraphic prefaces, in the form of epistles, allegedly from the disciples of the great medieval exegete Abraham Ibn Ezra and from Baruch Spinoza. The first of these epistles suggests that Ibn Ezra would have advocated the bold emendations to the biblical text contained in *Ha-Ketav ve-ha-Mikhtav*. The students of Ibn Ezra insist that their teacher advocated correcting the biblical text, even when this would lead to a radical reform of halakhic practice.[3] The latter letter, allegedly from Spinoza himself, unapologetically justifies his method of biblical criticism, elucidated in the *Theological-Political Treatise*.

The text of *Ha-Ketav ve-ha-Mikhtav* is followed by a German postscript (or introduction, depending on how one opens the book) that departs dramatically from the tone of the satirical Hebrew preface by offering a passionate defense of the Hebrew Scriptures and polemicising with some of the more radical German biblical critics. In this essay, I focus only on Krochmal's own Hebrew preface, which I have translated and annotated below. The meaning of this tall tale and Krochmal's purpose in inventing it raise a host of themes in modern Jewish intellectual history, ranging from maskilic anti-Ḥasidism to modern Jewish attitudes toward Spinoza. In the discussion that follows I try to parse this bizarre satirical text and decipher its historical and intellectual context by exploring these and other questions that it raises.

Strange Besht-Fellows: Spinoza, Adam Baal Shem, and the Biblical Critics

In describing his "discovery" that the esoteric writings of the mysterious Rabbi Adam Baal Shem—a manuscript which, according to Ḥasidic legend, contained "the deepest secrets of the Torah" and was for that reason buried by the Besht under a rock in Miedzyborz[4]—had actually originated with Baruch Spinoza, Abraham Krochmal excitedly declares: "Besht!—how remarkable a name—one that is virtually the same as that of the Amsterdam philosopher. This cannot possibly be a vain matter."

The connection Krochmal mischievously draws here between Spinoza's and the Besht's respective teachings was, it may be argued, not entirely original. By Krochmal's day, numerous Spinozists—particularly in Germany—had developed elaborate analogies between Spinozan pantheistic philosophy and earlier kabbalistic traditions.[5] Moreover, in the century after Krochmal wrote his preface, many Jewish writers—from Salomon Rubin to Joseph Klausner—connected Spinozism, medieval Jewish Neoplatonism, and Beshtian Ḥasidism. But Krochmal's identification of those teachings as Spinoza's biblical criticism found mainly in the *Theological-Political Treatise* was unprecedented, and remains uniquely brazen to this day. Krochmal's equation of the secret doctrines imparted to the Besht by the son of Rabbi Adam with what had long been considered by traditional Jews the most offensive of Spinoza's many heretical writings is thus an unexpected and radical twist on a theme that is otherwise not terribly uncommon in the Jewish literature on Spinoza's philosophy.

What is so novel about Krochmal's conception of the thesis connecting Spinozism, Kabbalism, and Beshtian Ḥasidism is that it relates not to the more commonly observed similarities of Spinoza's pantheism—articulated primarily in the *Ethics*—and Ḥasidic panentheism, but rather suggests a fantastic literary-historical connection between the *Shivḥei ha-Besht* and the notorious *Theological-Political Treatise,* a work recently and accurately described by Arthur Hertzberg as "the greatest single attack on Jewish orthodoxy and fundamentalism that was ever written."[6]

It is no accident that the first reference to Spinoza to be found in Jewish literature after his excommunication in 1656 took the form of an attack—published more than a century after the *ḥerem*—on his critical approach to the study of the Bible. In the introduction to a work dedicated to upholding the integrity of the Masoretic biblical text, *Seyag la-Torah* (Frankfurt, 1766), the German-Jewish physician and conservative rationalist scholar Asher Anshel Worms polemicized against the growing tendency in his day of critically questioning the sanctity of the Hebrew Scriptures. He singles out three particularly pernicious practitioners of biblical criticism in the course of his defense of the integrity of the Masoretic text:

> They direct their arrows of mockery at the highest authority; their jeering against the holy never ceases, as day and night they laugh before all the nations at . . . Holy Scripture. Such men are Spinoza, Hobbes, and Edelmann, who travel all about and aggrandize themselves by preaching against all men of good faith—both the circumcised and the uncircumcised—who place their trust in the Holy Scriptures that were inscribed by the finger of God and refuse to depend on their own intellect, insisting rather that reason must yield to the words of the living and eternal God.[7]

Worms goes on to say that it was precisely the heresy of men such as Spinoza, Hobbes, and Edelmann that aroused him to come to the defense of the Bible by publishing *Seyag la-Torah*. It is important to note that this book was published just one year before the death of Johann Christian Edelmann (1698–1767), arguably the most radical German Spinozist of the eighteenth century. Edelmann openly claimed to have been "inspired" to reject Christianity in its entirety as the direct result of having read the *Theological-Political Treatise*. Some sixteen years before Worms published his book, Edelmann's heretical writings—in particular his bold rejection of the authority of the Bible, *Moses mit aufgedeckten Angesichte* (Moses' Face Revealed), and his scandalous "confession" against revealed religion, *Glaubens-Bekentniss*—had been consigned to the flames in an elaborate public ceremony in Frankfort. Jonathan Israel describes the dramatic event:

> On May 9, 1750, seventy guards and eight drummers formed up around a prepared square pile of birchwood. As the entire magistracy and city government looked on, the commission's condemnation of Edelmann's publications and radical doctrines was read out to the assembled crowd. The writing and publication of godless and blasphemous books was strictly forbidden, the people were reminded, and the present spectacle was intended to serve as an example to others. After a fanfare, the bonfire was lit and nearly 1,000 confiscated copies of various of his writings were consigned to the flames.[8]

Worms, who took great pride in his medical education and philosophical enlightenment, and who was particularly sensitive about the image of the Jews in German society, joined his moderately enlightened Christian colleagues in rejecting utterly the radical Spinozism and anti-biblicism of Edelmann and other Spinozists. *Seyag la-Torah* was a seminal, highly celebrated, and even plagiarized work.[9] As it turns out, however, despite his bitter protest against the biblical criticism of Spinoza and Edelmann, Worms did include some of his own suggested emendations to the work of the Masoretes in *Seyag la-Torah,* thus pioneering a conservative form of lower biblical criticism in Hebrew scholarship.

The most important eighteenth-century Jewish response to developments in German biblical scholarship was, of course, Moses Mendelssohn's German translation of and commentary to the Pentateuch, *Netivot ha-Shalom,* which appeared between 1780 and 1783. While Mendelssohn's purposes in publishing *Netivot ha-Shalom* were complex, one of the central intentions of the work was to reestablish the sacrosanct integrity of the Masoretic text. This goal was made evident in the lengthy programmatic introduction to the translation *Or la-Netivah,* published separately fourteen years after *Seyag la-Torah,* in which Mendelssohn declared:

> In order that our lives not be hanging on the hairbreadth of conjecture or the thread of reflection alone, our Sages decreed for us the Masorah and erected a fence for the Torah and for the commandments, for decrees and laws, in order that we not grope like the blind in the dark. This being the case, we should not move from their paved way to chart a path of life without the honest scales and balances of truth, following the conjectures and deliberations of a grammarian or editor taken from his own mind. We do not live from the mouth of [such an emendator] but from that which our trustworthy masters of the Masorah transmitted to us.[10]

Krochmal's *Ha-Ketav ve-ha-Mikhtav* engages in precisely the kind of biblical criticism against which Mendelssohn so passionately warned. It also serves indirectly to rehabilitate Spinoza's critical method of reading Scripture and his rejection of its Mosaic authorship, both of which Mendelssohn vehemently rejected.[11] It represented the penchant for textual emendations that characterized the radical wing of the *Haskalah* which challenged Mendelssohn's conservatism on the questions of revelation and the authority of both the Masoretes and the talmudic sages. His book, in fact, extends the work that had been initiated more cautiously by Worms a century earlier and continued both by his father, Nachman Krochmal, and by his closest colleague, Joshua Heschel Schorr. The book itself is a very dry work of "lower" biblical criticism, consisting essentially of an extensive list of proposed emendations to the Masoretic text. The format of the book could hardly be more technical: each pair of pages consists of the original Hebrew version of the Masoretic textual verses to be emended along with a German translation, on the left side, and the suggested emendation, again with German translation, on the right. Krochmal adds brief Hebrew commentaries justifying his proposed changes to the Masorah, in footnote form. Unlike the century-earlier *Seyag la-Torah,* Krochmal's book was poorly received, particularly by Schorr, his own friend and teacher, who published a long and scathing review of it in his Hebrew journal, *He-Ḥalutz.*[12] Within a few years, *Ha-Ketav ve-ha-Mikhtav* was all but forgotten, rendered essentially obsolete by the rapid advances in critical biblical scholarship in the late nineteenth century. Unfortunately, Krochmal's far more interesting preface to this book of technical biblical-text criticism—a ribald document that stands, as we have noted, in shocking contrast to the dry, scholarly book that it introduces—was relegated to obscurity along with the rest of the work. A wicked satire on Ḥasidism and a bizarre justification of Spinoza at one and the same time, this text was not even noted by Israel Davidson in his exhaustive bibliography of nineteenth-century Hebrew parodies and satires.[13]

In weaving a fantastic tale about his discovery of the legendary writings of Rabbi Adam, and asserting that his present work of biblical criticism is the authentic transcription of those writings, Krochmal attempts—in a single swoop—to undermine the traditionalism of the Besht, sanctify Spinoza's *Theological-Political Treatise,* and facetiously claim ancient authority for his own radical biblical text-criticism. What is perhaps most intriguing about this text is the novel way in which it connects Spinoza and the Besht. In order to appreciate more fully both the context and the originality of the story Krochmal tells, a general consideration of the tendency in modern Jewish literature to connect Spinoza, the Kabbalah, and Ḥasidism is in order. We begin with the more recent examples of that tendency and work our way back to Abraham Krochmal.

Spinoza, Kabbalah, and Ḥasidism in Later Jewish Literature

At the conclusion of his celebrated memoir *In My Father's Court,* Isaac Bashevis Singer describes the simultaneously shattering and inspiring impact of his discovery—while still a Ḥasidic youth living under his rabbinical father's roof—of Spinoza's philosophy:

> I discovered Stupnicki's book on Spinoza.[14] I remember how father used to say that Spinoza's name should be blotted out, and I knew that Spinoza contended that God was the world and the world was God. My father, I recalled, had said that Spinoza had contributed nothing. There were already the teachings of the Baal Shem Tov, who also identified the world with the Godhead. True, the Baal Shem Tov had lived after Spinoza, but my father argued that Spinoza had drawn from ancient sources. Which no Spinoza disciple would deny.
>
> The Spinoza book created a turmoil in my brain. His concept of God as a substance with infinite attributes . . . fascinated and bewildered me. As I read this book I felt intoxicated, inspired as I had never been. It seemed to me that all of the truths that I had been seeking since early childhood had at last become apparent. Everything was God—Warsaw, Bilgoray, the spider in the attic, the water in the well, the clouds in the sky, and the book on my knees. Everything was divine. . . . I was exalted; everything seemed good. There was no difference between heaven and earth, the most distant star and my red hair. Even my tangled thoughts were divine.[15]

Singer's dramatic account is remarkable on many levels, not least for its description of Spinoza's thought in excited mystical terms that recalls many historical depictions of the initial impact of early Ḥasidic doctrine upon the masses of eastern European Jewry in the late eighteenth century. But what is most surprising—almost comical—is Singer's father's contradictory attitude to Spinoza. On the one hand, he is an evil heretic; on the other, his doctrine is basically the same as the Besht's and "draws" from the ancient wellsprings of the Kabbalah.

Singer's interest in the connection between Spinoza and the kabbalistic tradition endured for many years. In fact, in his subsequent volume of memoirs, Singer related that his very first original writing was a monograph on "Spinoza and the Kabbalah" for which he could not find a publisher and which he eventually discarded with disgust in a dustbin on the streets of Warsaw.[16] Singer's autobiographical reference to the enormous impact on his faith of Spinoza's philosophy and his unpublished manuscript on Spinoza made their way into his later works of fiction. For example, in the semi-autobiographical work *The Certificate* the aspiring young Yiddish writer David Bendiger arrives in Warsaw in 1922 with very few possessions: "In my backpack—among several dirty shirts, handkerchiefs and socks—there were a few manuscripts in Hebrew and in Yiddish, an unfinished novel, an essay on Spinoza and the Cabala, and a miniature collection of what I called 'poems in prose.'"[17] Bendiger's adaptation to life in the big city is slow and difficult and his perceptions of secular Jewish Warsaw are vividly described by Singer throughout this largely autobiographical novel, through "the lens that Spinoza polished."

The nexus between Spinoza's pantheism and Beshtian Ḥasidism is a recurring theme in the twentieth-century Yiddish literature on Spinoza's philosophy, most notably in Sh. Setzer's extensive intellectual biography of the Baal Shem Tov.[18] A. Almi, the Yiddish polemicist and harsh critic of Spinoza's philosophy, also managed—in a rare moment of generosity toward Spinoza—to find significant commonalities shared by the Amsterdam philosopher and the great Ḥasidic master Rabbi Levi Isaac of Berditchev.[19] In his remarkable essay "Utz, Amsterdam un Berditchev," Almi ponders both these similarities and the dialectical tensions between Spinozism and Ḥasidism: "The great man of Amsterdam [Spinoza] sings the very same song to God as the great Berditchever, if somewhat differently accented. For the Berditchever, God is to be found everywhere in the world. For the 'Amsterdamer,' the world is to be found everywhere in God."[20] Ultimately, however, Almi comes to the dramatically subversive conclusion that the faith of Spinoza—whom he suggestively nicknames "Der Amsterdamer"—is even stronger than that of Rabbi Levi Isaac: "Spinoza the pantheistic philosopher is after all, as we have by now seen, more pious than both Job and Rabbi Levi Isaac. . . . For one can have no complaints with Spinoza's God, since there is no expectation of mercy and compassion from Him."[21] Many earlier modern Jewish champions of Spinoza's rehabilitation as a legitimate Jewish philosopher engaged these very issues. In their efforts to recover Spinoza for modern Judaism, they tirelessly found parallels and precedents for Spinoza's philosophy in classical Jewish literature, most notably in the Jewish neo-platonic and mystical traditions. The Galician *maskil* Salomon Rubin, the first and most prolific Hebrew Spinozist, repeatedly drew analogies between the teachings of Spinoza and those of the great medieval Hebrew writers such as Ibn Gabirol and Abraham Ibn Ezra.[22] This predilection for forging an unbroken chain of tradition linking Spinoza to the medieval Jewish philosophical and mystical traditions was also indulged by many of Rubin's contemporaries, such as Abraham Krochmal and Senior Sachs, and became a major trope of early-twentieth-century Hebrew Spinoza scholarship. Writers such as Hillel Zeitlin, Nahum

Sokolow, David Neumark, and Joseph Klausner all tried to incorporate Spinoza's philosophy into the mainstream of Jewish philosophical literature in much the same way as Rubin had done. This tendency in early Jewish Spinoza scholarship generated extensive discussions on the pages of the Hebrew journals of the late nineteenth and early twentieth centuries. Only a small minority of modern Hebrew writers on Spinoza—most notably Samuel David Luzzatto in the nineteenth century and Jacob Klatzkin in the twentieth—resisted this tendency.[23] Emphasizing the radically anti-religious nature of Spinoza's pantheism and critique of Judaism, they argued that his teachings fundamentally challenged the most basic assumptions of medieval Jewish philosophy and mysticism.[24]

The argument for this (very tenuous, in this writer's judgment) connection between Spinoza and medieval Jewish thought remains surprisingly strong in contemporary Jewish scholarship. Israeli scholars such as Zeev Levy, Rivka Horwitz, and Yirmiyahu Yovel have all affirmed the "essential Jewishness" of Spinoza's philosophical system. A recently published volume of Spinoza studies by Western scholars is dedicated almost entirely to this theme and includes numerous articles pointing to the alleged "continuities" between Spinozism and medieval Jewish philosophy and mysticism.[25] In an ironic twist, this Jewish "rehabilitation" of Spinoza, originally most pronounced among eastern European *maskilim,* was fiercely resisted by some of the most prominent early-twentieth-century German-Jewish thinkers, most notably Hermann Cohen and Martin Buber. While much has been written about Cohen's trenchant philosophical critique of Spinoza,[26] it is Buber's far less systematic or negative appraisal that is of particular relevance to the present discussion, since it is to be found in the context of Buber's discussion of what first attracted him to Ḥasidic mysticism.

Martin Buber on Spinoza and the Besht

Buber's essay "Spinoza, Shabbetai Zevi and the Baal-Shem" offers a highly subjective and ahistorical assessment of the relationship between the philosophies that came out of Amsterdam and Miedzyborz. Buber sees in the Besht's teachings a direct response and important corrective to the pantheistic excesses of Spinoza: "The Baal Shem-Tov probably knew nothing of Spinoza; nevertheless he has given the reply to him. In the truth of history one can reply without having heard."[27]

While Buber finds Spinoza's rejection of the medieval mystics' ascetic dualism attractive, he is offended by his rigorous determinism that renders impossible all forms of worship, or—in Buber's terminology—man's "intercourse with God." Buber praises Spinoza as being motivated by the same "primal impulse" that led the biblical prophets to rail against the heathens of their time but who went too far, eliminating a personal God in the course of reuniting the earthly with the divine:

> Not outside the world, but only in the world itself can man find the divine; Spinoza set this thesis in opposition to the bifurcation of life that had become current in his age. He did so out of a primal Jewish impulse; out of a similar impulse there once arose the protest of the prophets against the sacrificial cults that had become independent. But his attack swung beyond this legitimate object. Along with world-free intercourse, all personal intercourse with God became unworthy of belief for him.[28]

Ḥasidism preserved the noblest element of Spinozism, namely its identification of God with the natural universe, but corrected its excesses by transforming the universe into what Buber terms a "sacrament." That is to say, in reuniting the earthly and the divine realms, Ḥasidism rendered the world merely one small part of a God who remains—in dramatic contrast to the *Deus Sive Natura* of Spinoza—both transcendent and providential: "That the Hasidic message may be understood as a reply to Spinoza, even though its speakers and hearers knew nothing of him, arises from the fact that it expressed the confession of Israel in a new manner, through which, in fact it became a reply. . . . Through God's indwelling in the world, the world becomes—in general religious terms—a sacrament."[29] On the one hand, Buber sought to reclaim Spinoza as an authentic Jewish philosopher who responded to the spiritual crisis of his day in a manner analogous to that of the ancient biblical prophets. On the other hand, Buber was clearly repulsed by Spinoza's determinism, his identification of God with mute, unhearing, and unchanging nature. Spinoza's strict pantheism was understandably intolerable for Buber, at the center of whose religious philosophy lay the challenge of man's dialogue with his Creator. While Buber welcomed Spinoza's rejection of the separation of God and the world that was the hallmark of medieval dualistic and ascetic spirituality, he argued that Spinoza took his monism to an unacceptable extreme that essentially reduced God to stone. Ḥasidism represented for Buber the needed correction to Spinoza's excesses, for it struck the correct balance between the otherworldly spirituality of the ascetics and the cold and Godless worldliness of Spinoza. In a remarkable passage, Buber seems to confess that it was Ḥasidism that redeemed his own soul from the faithlessness of Spinozism: "This very teaching of man's being bound with the world in the sight of God, the reply of Hasidism to Spinoza, was the one element through which Hasidism so overpoweringly entered into my life. I early had a premonition, indeed, no matter how I resisted it, that I was inescapably destined to love the world."[30] Buber's early impulse—that he eventually abandoned on the side of the "way to Hasidism"—to reclaim Spinoza (even by those who had fundamental differences with him) as an authentic Jewish thinker by linking him with medieval Jewish neo-platonic and mystical thought had been widespread among modern Jewish thinkers since the late nineteenth century, as we have seen above. This impulse, however, only rarely led enlightened Jewish writers to point to the even more obvious commonalities between Spinoza's pantheistic doctrine and the panentheist teachings of Ḥasidism. The deeply ingrained bias against Ḥasidism among both the *maskilim* and the early practitioners of *Wissenschaft das Judentums* prevented them from going that route. To have seen in Spinozism the seeds of Ḥasidic panentheism would have defeated their purpose of establishing him as a model for a contemporary system of Jewish belief liberated from the ghetto Judaism of which Ḥasidism was, to their lights, the most deplorable example. Nevertheless, there were some prominent *maskilim* in Abraham Krochmal's days and in his native Galicia who did point to the commonalities shared by Spinozism and Ḥasidism. Most notable among them was the first *Haskalah* apologist for Ḥasidism, Eliezer Zweifel.

The Spinoza/Ḥasidism Nexus in the Galician Haskalah

In the course of his passionate defense of Ḥasidism in *Shalom al Yisra'el*, Eliezer Zweifel argued that Ḥasidism's panentheism was in many respects both a popular and purified mystical application of Spinoza's philosophical system. Zweifel devoted an entire section of this book to prove—as that section's heading clearly states—that "pure Beshtianism and pure Spinozism are, at their root, identical systems."[31] Zweifel was responding to his *Haskalah* colleagues' simultaneous rehabilitation of Spinoza and condemnation of Ḥasidism by pointing out that both shared an essential belief, namely pantheistic faith in a perfect God who fills nature with his glory.[32] In fact, the original manuscript of the first volume of *Shalom al Yisra'el* (Zhitomir, 1868) included a poem celebrating this connection between Spinoza and the Besht that Zweifel was pressured to delete from the published edition. According to Abraham Rubenstein, Zweifel's poetic analogy between the doctrines of Spinoza and the Besht "so inflamed the burning rage of the *maskilim* that Zweifel had no choice but to bow to the pressure" to delete the poem.[33] Zweifel finally did allude to it, however, in the fourth part of *Shalom al Yisra'el,* published four years later.[34]

Zweifel's efforts to connect Spinoza with the earlier immanentist doctrines of the Kabbalah and the subsequent panentheist teachings of Ḥasidism were denounced by a number of later *Haskalah* writers. In his passionate defense of Spinoza, *Even ha-Roshah* (Vienna, 1871), although not specifically mentioning Zweifel, Abraham Krochmal was almost certainly reacting at least in part to his predilection to link Spinoza with Ḥasidism. This work—which takes the form of an elaborate imaginary dialogue regarding Spinoza's writings between Krochmal's father, the philosopher Nachman Krochmal, and Rabbi Zevi Hirsch Chajes of Zolkiew—includes the senior Krochmal's strenuous assertion that "Spinoza's system is as far from the Kabbalah as the East is from the West,"[35] with which Chajes, after some debate, eventually and fully concurs.[36] Krochmal was generally hostile to the tendency among many Jewish Spinozists—beginning with Rubin—to connect Spinozism with medieval Jewish philosophy and mysticism. In fact, he appends the pseudepigraphic preface by Spinoza to *Ha-Ketav ve-ha-Mikhtav* with the following endnote that dismisses the apologetic book on Spinoza by Manuel Joel: "Thus declared Abraham [Krochmal]: It would be worthwhile to point out to the Rabbi of Breslau, Doctor Joel, that he might be so good as to [Heb. 'yo'il,' a play on Joel's name] read these words that I have presented from the philosopher of Amsterdam, and he will thus see that the entire book that he published in 1870 about the *Theological-Political Treatise* is null and void."[37] Although there is no literary record of Krochmal's specific response to the publication of *Shalom al Yisra'el,* the pages of the *Haskalah* journals throughout Europe were filled for more than six years after the appearance of the first volume in 1868 with vigorous, mostly negative, responses to Zweifel's book.[38] It is known, moreover, that Krochmal and Zweifel were good friends and remained on cordial terms despite their serious ideological differences. In his diary, Moses

Leib Lilienblum—who considered himself a disciple of Abraham Krochmal—describes the scene of one of his many meetings with his teacher. The occasion was the visit to Odessa of Eliezer Zweifel, who was at the time the head of the Zhitomir Rabbinical Seminary:

> On that day [April 2, 1870] we all sat together in Zweifel's hotel room: Abraham Krochmal, Eliezer Zvi Zweifel, Ts. Shereshevsky,[39] and I. Zweifel's son-in-law [Pesach] Engelstein, joined us as well, in Zweifel's hotel room. We enjoyed delightful and pleasing conversation, exchanging words of the Sages, lofty ideas, penetrating interpretations of rabbinic texts, that were a source of great and heartfelt joy. Rabbi Krochmal revealed great and esoteric matters of universal importance [*devarim ha-omedim be-rumo shel olam*]. This was the first time I experienced such joy since coming here [to Odessa] and I shall always remember it.[40]

Although there is no way of knowing precisely what was discussed during the course of that glorious day in Zweifel's hotel room, the meeting took place less than a year before the publication of Krochmal's work on Spinoza's philosophy, and in the immediate aftermath of the appearance of the first volume of *Shalom al Yisra'el,* which had already created a storm of controversy about Ḥasidism in *Haskalah* circles. Several months before this meeting with Krochmal and Lilienblum, Zweifel had actually published a response to the attacks of the *maskilim* in the Odessa journal *Ha-Melitz*.[41] It is hard to imagine that the conversation did not at some point turn to both Spinoza and Ḥasidism, topics that were then, indeed—in Lilienblum's words—*devarim ha-omedim be-rumo shel olam*—especially in Jewish Odessa.

Krochmal's friendship with Zweifel somehow endured despite their conflicting views of Ḥasidism. There is no evidence that Krochmal ever departed even to the slightest degree from his father's utter disdain for the Ḥasidim. Nachman Krochmal was not only contemptuous of the Ḥasidim and their beliefs, which he regarded as mired in ignorance and superstition; he strenuously warned his son Abraham against the evils of Ḥasidism, most famously in a letter that was included in his opus *Moreh Nevukhei ha-Zeman*. Here the elder Krochmal lists the many evils of Ḥasidism and identifies drunkenness and lethargy as its hallmark characteristics.[42] The depiction in our text of Abraham Krochmal's encounter with the elderly Ḥasid in Miedzyborz, whom he deliberately plies with alcohol in order to get him to identify the rock under which Rabbi Adam's secret manuscript was buried, betrays the enduring influence of this anti-Ḥasidic bias.

In light of Krochmal's deep affection for Spinoza, his hostility to Ḥasidism, and his adamant rejection of any connection between Spinoza's pantheism and the Jewish mystical tradition, the satirical introduction to his work of biblical criticism assumes a truly bizarre character. By asserting that the most sublime and esoteric teachings of the Besht—those received under the tutelage of Rabbi Adam's son and buried under a rock in Miedzyborz—originated with Spinoza, Krochmal intends to demolish several sacred cows with a single stroke of his pen. To begin with, the tale he weaves is clearly intended to mock the *Shivḥei ha-Besht* in the tradition of such classic *Haskalah* satires as Joseph Perl's *Megalleh Temirin*.[43] At the same time—since the hidden manuscript never became public or integrated into the normative Ḥasidic teachings or customs that Krochmal so disdained—this satire in no way compromises Krochmal's championship of Spinoza, to whom he refers with the honorific "our rabbi, Baruch, of blessed memory"[44] and whose knowledge of God he proclaimed to be even greater than that of the patriarch Abraham.[45] Since Ḥasidism never acknowledged or incorporated Spinoza's biblical criticism—far from it—Spinoza remains untainted with all that the *maskilim* found so repulsive in Ḥasidic culture.

Krochmal's satirical use of the legends regarding Rabbi Adam in *Shivḥei ha-Besht* constitutes an assault upon the very source of the Besht's authority. In his study of the literary genre of Ḥasidic tales, Joseph Dan argues that the purpose of the tales regarding Rabbi Adam were no less than "to remove from the Besht the category of being a bastard, to remove him from being (perceived) as one with no father and no teacher."[46] As Emanuel Etkes has most recently demonstrated, the tales about the teachings of Rabbi Adam are intended to compensate for the Besht's apparent lack of scholarly credentials, and to legitimize his teachings by connecting them to a chain of tradition whose sources can be traced back to biblical times.[47] By identifying this tradition with the most heretical ideas in Spinoza's *Theological-Political Treatise*, Krochmal wickedly undermines this basic Ḥasidic enterprise of establishing the religious authority and legitimacy of Beshtian teachings.

Schorr she-Nagaḥ: The Assault on Krochmal in *He-Halutz*

While Krochmal's cordial relationship with Eliezer Zweifel seems to have endured their major differences on Ḥasidism, his very close friendship and literary collaboration with Joshua Heschel Schorr was clearly wrecked beyond repair by the publication of *Ha-Ketav ve-ha-Mikhtav.* Krochmal and Schorr's friendship seems to have dated back to their teen years. According to Ezra Spicehandler, it is likely that they first met when Schorr visited Krochmal's famous father.[48] Abraham Krochmal was a co-founder, along with Isaac Erter, of Schorr's radical Hebrew periodical, *He-Ḥalutz,* and seems to have operated as one of its editors in the early years of its publication.[49] After Schorr, whose writing constituted more than half the contents of the journal, Krochmal was the most prolific contributor to the first four volumes of *He-Ḥalutz* (1852–59). Krochmal's friendship and close collaboration with Schorr began to deteriorate in subsequent years, and by the time Schorr published his devastating review of *Ha-Ketav ve-ha-Mikhtav* in 1877, he had become a mean and paranoid social recluse who used *He-Ḥalutz* primarily as a vehicle with which to lash out at his many real and imagined enemies.[50] But even by Schorr's brutal standards, his review of Krochmal was particularly mean-spirited.

Schorr's assault on *Ha-Ketav ve-ha-Mikhtav* consists of two basic criticisms: plagiarism and stupidity. He charged that the book itself was largely lifted from Schorr's own extensive work of biblical text-criticism that had been published over the years in the pages of *He-Ḥalutz* as well as from other published works. Schorr provides a comprehensive list of Krochmal's alleged plagiarisms and sums them up as follows: "This is the last of his [Krochmal's] emendations, blessed is the last that did not embarrass the first, for his first emendation was taken from *He-Ḥalutz* as was his last one. And the total number of the emendations, which he drew joyously from the wellsprings of *He-Ḥalutz,* comes to one hundred and two, whose symbol [*gematria*] is: *'Va-ye'esham ba-Ba'al'* [and Israel sinned with Baal], or alternately, *'Bala va-yaqi'enu'* [he swallowed and then vomited]."[51] As angered as Schorr was with Krochmal's theft of his scholarship, he reserved his real wrath for the last few pages of his very long and scathing review, where he finally deals with Krochmal's preface. Schorr found this text to be both arrogant and silly, a stupid, self-aggrandizing tale that serves no purpose. Worst of all, however, is the fact that Krochmal involved Spinoza in his self-serving fantasy. Krochmal's plagiarism might be forgiven, but his desecration of Spinoza is viewed by Schorr as an unpardonable offense: "This is the sin that will never be forgiven: namely, that he attached his destructive writings to the great sage and elevated scholar, the most lofty and sublime of them all—Baruch Spinoza, of blessed memory (z"l)."[52] Schorr continued his assault by presenting his facetious theory that Krochmal—a man widely respected for his scholarship and personal integrity—could not possibly have been the author of this shameful and ignorant work. Rather, Schorr speculates, an imposter bent on destroying his reputation was responsible for writing *Ha-Ketav ve-ha-Mikhtav* and attributed the miserable book to Krochmal. Once Schorr succeeds in identifying the criminal responsible for publishing this fraudulent book and attributing it to Krochmal, he trusts that he will be appropriately thanked: "And I certainly expect that my good friend Rabbi A. Krochmal will recognize the favor I did for him by rising to cleanse him of this insult and that he will stir himself to exact retribution from the real author of this booklet who deliberately attached his [Krochmal's] name to it in order to muddy his reputation."[53] Of course, Schorr knew full well that there were no questions about the authorship of the book, especially given the fact that, upon its publication, Krochmal sent him a copy of *Ha-Ketav ve-ha-Mikhtav* with a very cordial inscription.[54]

Having fastidiously documented Krochmal's alleged piracy of his own work, Schorr continues his devastating review with a long list of errors that he found in *Ha-Ketav ve-ha-Mikhtav,* and concludes with the following observation: "He was in such a hurry to finish his work, and so anxious to get it to the printer, in order to benefit the public by 'removing all of Scripture's serpentine and misleading expressions and cumbersome phrases, thereby healing his people and mending its broken spirit,' as he so modestly informed us, that in his urgency and under the burden of this great *miṣvah,* he published in his anthology corrections to Scriptures that he had not studied at all."[55]

Conclusion

Abraham Krochmal's parodic introduction to *Ha-Ketav ve-ha-Mikhtav* is surely one of the strangest and least effective works of *Haskalah* satire. Not only did its bizarre anti-Ḥasidic message fail to resonate in the enlightened Jewish circles of his day but it threatened to undermine the reception of his entirely serious and assiduous work of linear biblical text emendations among Jewish scholars. It remains unclear precisely what Krochmal hoped to achieve, or what message he meant to send, by spinning this far-fetched yarn about the origins of his biblical criticism. There are three disparate themes woven together in this text that never quite coalesce into anything resembling a coherent thesis or argument. On the one hand, Krochmal is poking fun at classic Ḥasidic tales regarding the origins of the teachings of the Besht; on the other hand, he indirectly, and almost certainly unintentionally, seems to grant classical Ḥasidic doctrine some type of legitimacy by connecting it with the earlier teachings of Spinoza. But, in so doing, he also threatens to undermine the originality of his own work.

One of the most stubborn puzzles about this kind of satirical writing is the question of its intended audience. Did he really expect any religious Jews to take seriously his false piety and ludicrous claims that his book was the transcription of the most secret teachings of Rabbi Adam and the Besht, which he discovered under a rock with the help of his use of magical incantations? If he did, why would he then connect those teachings with the universally despised heretic, Spinoza?

In all likelihood, Krochmal wrote his satire for like-minded radical *maskilim,* as an exercise in anti-Ḥasidic satire, and had no expectations that his claims regarding the sources for his biblical criticism might in any way protect him from the ire of the rabbis of his day. Despite its apparent failure to resonate with any Jewish audience, Krochmal's preface is nevertheless of great interest for those concerned with the history of the *Haskalah* generally, as well as the Jewish reception and interpretation of Spinoza in the modern period. For, as we have seen, this strange text touches on numerous themes—most important, the relationship between Spinozism and Ḥasidism—that remained of vital interest to Jewish interpreters of Spinoza for more than a century after Krochmal's death.

Part 2: Translation

Title Page

The Writ and the Letter
To the Torah, Nevi'im, and Ketuvim
The writ is the writing of man and the letter is the word of God
This book is the manuscript that was found hidden under a rock
near the city of Miedzyborz
In the Podolia region of the Country of Ruthenia
To which is added a commentary and brief explanation in German
Completed in the year:
Five Thousand Six Hundred & Thirty Four
By yours truly, the impoverished among the multitude of Israel
A'ben Ha-Kohen Krochmal
Press of Karl Budweiser (Cracow), 1874

Foreword

From the day I graduated from "Mattanah," that is, the Written Torah, to "Nahaliel," the Oral Torah, and from "Nahaliel to Bamoth,"[56] namely, to scholarly and critical studies ranging from the world's creation to the "Mystery of the Chariot," I have always kept before me the words of King Solomon, of blessed memory, the wisest of men: "A healing tongue [language] is the staff of life, but its corruption shatters the spirit" [Proverbs 15:4].

I yearned to heal my people, to mend its broken spirit by examining the writings of its teachers, prophets, and oracles with an eye to removing all of their serpentine and misleading expressions and cumbersome phrases. For these [textual corruptions] have over the course of history—largely as a consequence of scribal errors—become ensconced in our holy writings. Even worse, these mistakes have been deliberately canonized as part of the heritage of the Masoretes, acquiring thereby the status of sanctity. All kinds of protective fences and legal decrees have been established to protect not only the correct original versions but also a large variety of corruptions and mistakes in the [Masoretic] text.

Yet I was fearful of the wrath and fury of religious fanatics, lest they censure me with the authority of Naḥmanides, who—with the bite of a serpent and the hiss of a poisonous snake—pronounced the ban and excommunication on anyone who might dare to correct corrupted texts. I did not want, God forbid, to be denounced as a goring ox; for am I not already a gored ox? I have already been admonished and denounced as a destructive man, despite the fact that I—a son of the true and holy philosopher—have been the victim of all sorts of persecution. As a result, so long as the spirit of life was within me, I was afraid to approach the work of textual emendation; believe me, my brothers and friends, I was terrified! If you do not believe me because you are rather the traditional "believers and sons of believers," you should know that to this day I would not have been able to muster the strength to insult the honor of the Masoretes, whom you consider to be possessed of the divine spirit, were it not, that is, for the remarkable circumstances and events that happened to me, occurrences that I will presently relate to you in order to cleanse my hands, purify me of any dross and launder me of all remnants of guilt.

So hear now my brothers, hear me well and then you will understand me and accept my righteousness. I inherited a family tradition of many generations, going back all the way to the godly philosopher of Amsterdam [Spinoza] that a Jew from Poland came to study with him and when the philosopher inquired about his name he replied: "My master, why do you need to know my name? I go by the name of Adam for I am a human being with the spirit of God within me, no different from all other men." Thus this man found favor in his [Spinoza's] eyes; he became his neophyte in philosophy, drew from the wellsprings of his wisdom and served him just as the prophet Elijah served Ahijah the Shilonite.[57]

It came to pass, when the philosopher's day of death was approaching, he revealed to this man his intent to burn a bundle of his writings on the Holy Scriptures. When Adam heard this he almost fainted and he said to himself: "How can I possibly witness the calamity that will befall my people if this irreplaceable treasure is destroyed?"[58] He then decided to deceive his teacher by copying this entire collection of writings, and he then hid them among his possessions. Following the death of the philosopher he returned to Poland, taking with him a complete copy of these writings.

This story has been handed down to me from Jews hailing from Amsterdam, who brought the printing press from there to my home town of Zolkiew at the command of the mighty and compassionate King Jan [John III] Sobieski, who in his wisdom fled from Austria.[59]

In my youth I made every effort to reinforce this tradition that I had received from solid hands, in such a way that it reached the rabbis Shir[60] and Geiger.[61] This tradition has indeed remained clear and vital in my memory, such that it will never fade.

It then came to pass, several years ago, while I was living in the commercial city of Odessa, I came across a copy of the book, *Shivḥei ha-Besht,* in which I found the story of a certain rock in the town of Miedzyborz, under which the teachings of the ṣaddiq Rabbi Adam were buried by the Besht [Rabbi Israel Baal Shem Tov].[62] I immediately heard a loud voice calling from behind me, overwhelming my ears and proclaiming: "The words of Torah are impoverished in one place, but rich in another. The buried writings referred to here are without a doubt the work of the philosopher of Amsterdam that enlighten the Holy Scriptures, that his apprentice, Rabbi Adam, of blessed memory, copied in order to save them from the flames and brought to Poland. They were then transferred by his son to the Besht who buried them in the crevice of the rock by the city of Miedzyborz since the time was not yet ripe to reveal them."[63]

Now, upon my return from Odessa to Lwow, I happened to pass by the town of Miedzyborz. I said to myself: "The day has indeed come to investigate this matter and to search out the writings of Rabbi Adam that the Besht buried, in the hope that I might find them and be able to distribute them among the sons of Jacob and spread them throughout Israel. I would then cleave to the God of all spirits to know the ways of all souls.[64] The Geigerites will rejoice when I bring to them the words of the Amsterdam philosopher, and the pious will celebrate in the glory of the writings of the Ṣaddiq Rabbi Adam that originated, according to the *Shivḥei ha-Besht,* in the days before Joshua bin Nun."

That is how I reasoned with my own heart, and to the Kloyz of the Besht did I hastily depart. When I arrived there I found an old decrepit man bent over a holy book. I invited him to the tavern and ordered the barkeep to bring him wine. After the old fellow got good and drunk, I asked him to tell me all about the Besht (may his soul rest in the highest heavens), for the more one recounts the merits of the Ṣaddiqim, the more praiseworthy he is. So he responded and told me that he served Rabbi Baruch of Miedzyborz,[65] the grandson of the Besht and also the *rebuker* of Polnoe,[66] of blessed memory. They told him of the miracles and wonders of the Besht, who rests in the Garden of Eden:

> They would overwhelm your two ears were I to relate them to you. But why do I bother you with that which is well known? Rather, let me tell you what else I heard from them: namely, that the rock under which the Besht buried Rabbi Adam's writings was known to them. But since the Besht had appointed four guardians—two sacred and two profane—they had no right to approach that rock of Israel in order to extract these writings. However, at the end of a century following the death of the Besht, and once the hand of 'Nofeṣ' will have been removed for a decade and a half, a descendant of the Besht will come and that rock will be made smooth by another rock [*even be-aven tesotet:* a Hebrew wordplay on the acronym of Krochmal's Hebrew name, Avraham ben Naḥman = *aven*] and he will remove the writings and publish them.

After I had listened intently to these words, I stood trembling and amazed by several matters: 1) 'Besht'—what a remarkable name!—one that is virtually the same as that of the Amsterdam philosopher. This cannot possibly be a vain matter." 2) I recalled that my father and master, of blessed memory, told me the following: I [Nachman

Krochmal], Rabbi Naḥman of Uziran [Yiddish for Jezierzany],[67] and Rabbi Naḥman of Bratslav, the author of *Liqqutei Moharan,* all three of us are called by the same name, Naḥman, for we are blood relatives, unfit to offer legal testimony about each other, on my mother's side. Since it is well known that Rabbi Naḥman of Bratslav is the maternal grandson of the Besht,[68] it turns out that I too am a direct descendant of the Besht. 3) I was flabbergasted to see the words, "at the end of the rule over the Holy People of "Nofeṣ." For this acronym clearly refers to the tormenter of Israel, Tsar Nicholas I.[69] Thus this prophecy does not refer to distant future days, but clearly prophesies regarding the very times in which I live.

Thus I stood in a state of shock for several moments. Immediately thereafter, I rushed to give the old man some cash and I took leave of him in peace, so that I could go outside and inquire of my own heart about what I was to do next. As soon as I went outside, my heart responded that I must neither fear nor be timid about going to that place where I was destined to be in order to find those writings. For it is clear that the prophecy that the old man had just recounted was in fact about me. On the other hand, I worried about what harm might come to me from the four guardians that my ancestor the Besht positioned on the way to that rock, and how they might forcibly block my path. As I was worrying about this, I became suddenly agitated when all four of the watchmen mentioned by the author of the *Shitah Mequbbeṣet* [in his commentary to *Bava Batra,* chap. 2, quoting the Rabad],[70] appeared in my imagination. So I headed to the south, in accordance with the advice of our Sages, "He who wishes to become wise, should go south."[71]

After descending from the town, I beheld before me a wide expanse of land spread beneath my feet, and when I looked up I saw a massive billy-goat, as large as the citadel in the town center, approaching me and he opened his mouth and hissed one hundred times, like one who is bringing evil tidings. I immediately responded and chanted: "More than one hundred [generations] have passed since Amathlai, mother of Abraham and daughter of Karnebo, perished."[72] Then the goat disappeared and slipped away, while my ears heard the shrieks of countless flocks of sheep, proclaiming: "Make way and clear the path to the hidden treasure for the scion of the holy Besht!" So it was that with great energy and spiritual fervor I moved forward. But when I arrived at a distance of about two bowshots from the place,[73] I raised my eyes and I saw before me a huge raven, large as a citadel, with its massive wings spread and covering all of Miedzyborz. Although I was afraid, I declared: "The time has come to destroy the net of Amathlai, daughter of Arbeto, mother of Haman."[74] And like a passing cloud the raven flew away, and as it passed I heard a chorus of hundreds of thousands of ravens singing: "Make way and clear the path for the progeny of our king, the Besht!" So I marched forward cloaked with pride and I climbed the mountain. When I arrived at the summit, I cast my eyes and saw a very wide rushing river gushing in my direction. There was a boat in that river whose masthead reached into the heavens and it was coming at me. The captain was standing over an army of sailors who were rowing, their oars were rising and descending feverishly. I once again was in fear, but I steeled myself and spoke out: "Many seasons have passed since [the death of] Zaphenath daughter of Ar'el, mother of King David." Suddenly that raging river was transformed into a calm brook, its waves disappeared and the ship drifted off like a passing wind. And I heard a chorus of hundreds of thousands of sailors calling out with great aplomb: "Remove all of the barriers and prepare the way for our true captain, the seed of the Besht!" I did not tarry and after I had traveled over a small plot of land I descended into a valley and it was overgrown with a heavy thicket of trees, like the cedars of Lebanon, whose branches were all intertwined so that one could barely see through the thicket. Any reflection of light was absorbed into its darkness such that not even a shoelace of light could penetrate. Then, out of the thicket there emerged a gorgeous young maiden adorned with magnificent radiance and beauty, and she began to approach me. How lovely her footsteps appeared to me as she approached. When she arrived before me she raised her hand to her lips and the sound of her kiss was to my ears as the ringing of a silver bell, as it is written: "Let him kiss me with the kisses of his mouth for my lover's taste is better than fine wine."[75] "Though I was greatly tempted by this maiden, I restrained myself and declared: 'Many ages have gone since the passing of the mother of Samson, Hazellelponi and her sister Nashik.'"[76] As soon as had uttered these words both the forest and the maiden disappeared as if into a vacuum, and I beheld before my eyes a large boulder. Now I did not use any instrument but rather chiseled it away with my bare hands, to fulfill the vision: A rock will be made smooth by another rock ("even be-aven tesotet"). I then found a hole in it and put my hand deep inside and removed a bundle of writings. When I examined the binding in which the writings were kept I saw the following inscription:

> From Adam to my eldest son Israel! These lines of scripts and letters which I send to you via my son and partner in the covenant will make it clear to you that our people Israel follows in her path like blind sheep. Such sinful and routine behavior is the source of her superstitious rebelliousness. Therefore my son, you must be unassuming and God-fearing, walking modestly before your Lord in fulfilling the task that you have set for yourself to liberate the children of Israel from the unclean table. Let therefore these scriptures and letters be for you a sign to call your grandson by the name of Baruch, like the name of my master and teacher from whose hands I have received these writings. May God help you fulfill your task so that all who bless you will be blessed and those who curse you will be cursed, and you will be the blessed redeemer of Israel.

Upon reading these words with a joyous heart and an uplifted spirit my soul cried out: "Alas, the truth of the matter is exactly in accordance with the testimony of the protagonist of this story—whose authority is like that of one hundred witnesses—that it was indeed from his teacher, the philosopher of Amsterdam, that Adam received these writings."

I then hid these writings under my cloak and I did not take them out again until after I had returned home to Lwow. When I opened the writings and began to read them I realized that the section referred to as "ketav" consists of a large selection of scriptural texts as they are now found in our holy books. The section referred to as "mikhtav" consists of the corrected variants of those [corrupted] texts. I thought to myself, "Behold here [proof of] the testimony of the preacher of Polnoe that I found in the book *Shivḥei ha-Besht*, declaring that the writings of Rabbi Adam were already available to Joshua son of Nun. For Moses received the Torah at Sinai and transmitted it to Joshua in a perfectly correct version."

Still, only half of the matter was revealed to me and I did not know it all. For I still did not understand and could not decipher the meaning of the statement by the preacher of Polnoe that the writings of Rabbi Adam had already been revealed, only later to be concealed, four times before the days of the Besht, and they were revealed to him for the fifth time. But then I found among the papers not only an introduction that must have been written by the Amsterdam philosopher but also a short epistle that is titled "an introduction by the students of Rabbi Abraham Ibn Ezra," which I will reproduce below.

So it became crystal clear to me that these scriptural verses are exactly as they were revealed to Moses on Mount Sinai and the version of the text that we have before us now is the precise one that was transmitted to Joshua son of Nun. These writings of Rabbi Adam are nothing more or less than those that were handed to Joshua. However, during the days of mourning for Moses, some of the texts were forgotten until the disciples of Rabbi Abraham Ibn Ezra came along and established them on the basis of their own reasoning. Thus the writings of Rabbi Adam were effectively revealed to them. But they were once again forgotten during the tribulations of the generation that was exiled from Spain. Along came the philosopher from Amsterdam and he restored them from his own heart. Thus were the writings revealed to him for the third time. They were then revealed to Rabbi Adam for the fourth time and to the Besht for the fifth time. Now, as has already been stated, the Besht concealed them by burying them under a rock in the town of Miedzyborz, until I, his descendant, disinterred them in order to present them to you, my distinguished readers.

Having now revealed all of these facts to you, you must know that aside from the depraved ones—that is, the students of Ibn Ezra and the philosopher of Amsterdam—no person has ever dared approach the task of correcting corrupted texts from our holy Scriptures on the basis of his own logic and reason. I therefore assign any and all blame upon them, and I declare that the ban of Naḥmanides will cause his curse to fall upon them. Let their guilt serve as my absolution, and let their sins be my atonement. As for poor me, all I have attempted to do here is bring some measure of benefit and to heal the broken spirit of my people, in accordance with the words of King Solomon. So that I may merit a life of goodness and peace together with all those who endeavor to elevate the prestige of the House of Israel. Amen.

Notes

1. Abraham Krochmal (1817–88), son of the famous pioneer of the Galician *Haskalah* Nachman Krochmal (1785–1840), was one of the most radical *maskilim* of his day and an unusually bold advocate of halakhic reform in eastern Europe. The most extensive treatment of his life and works is Joseph Klausner's biographical essay in *Historyah shel ha-Sifrut ha-Ivrit ha-Ḥadashah: Shi'urim* (Jerusalem: Hebrew University, 1941), vol. 4, 89–118. Unfortunately, Klausner does not deal in any depth with Krochmal's work of biblical criticism, focusing instead on his critique of rabbinic authority. On *Ha-ketav ve-ha-Mikhtav,* see 104–5.

2. Much has been written on Spinoza's biblical criticism. The most recent book on this subject is J. Samuel Preus, *Spinoza and the Irrelevance of Biblical Authority* (Cambridge: Cambridge University Press, 2001), a highly engaging and cogent review of this subject. Unfortunately, Preus does not deal at all with the many Hebrew and Yiddish writings on Spinoza's critique of the Bible.
3. In the latter part of the epistle of the students of Ibn Ezra, Krochmal focuses on the implications of emending the phrase in Exodus 23:19, "You shall not boil a kid in its mother's milk." The basic thrust of his re-reading of this verse is that the entire rabbinic legal tradition mandating the separation of meat and milk is based on a corrupt text. Krochmal seems to have been especially interested in undermining the Jewish dietary laws, by one means or another. Elsewhere in his writings, he challenges the rabbinic laws of ritual slaughter (*sheḥitah*) based again on his independent understanding and reading of the relevant biblical texts. See A. Krochmal, "Koḥah de-heteira," in *Agudat Ma'amarim* (Lemberg: Wajdowicz, 1885), 65–78.
4. On the esoteric teachings of Rabbi Adam and their concealment by the Besht, see *Shivḥei ha-Besht*, ed. Benjamin Mintz (Jerusalem: Yad Binyamin, 1969), 44–52. A rather extensive scholarly discussion has emerged in contemporary Jewish scholarship about both the authenticity of this tale and the identity of Rabbi Adam's mythical manuscript. Gershom Scholem, basing himself on the archival research of Wolf Rabinowitsch in the Stoliner Ḥasidic Genizah, suggested a connection between the manuscript of Rabbi Adam and the Sabbatean work of Rabbi Heshel Zoref; see W. Rabinowitsch, "Manuscripts from an Archive in Stolin" (Hebrew), *Zion* 5, 2 (1940): 125–42 and 244–47, and G. Scholem, "Chapters in Sabbatean Research" (Hebrew), *Zion* 6 (1940): 85–100. The Ḥasidic scholar Yehoshua Mondshine took very strong exception to Scholem's thesis. See *Sefer Shivḥei ha-Besht: Faksimil mi-Ketav Yad etc.* (Hebrew) (Jerusalem: n.p., 1982), introduction, 58–65. On various versions of the relationship between Rabbi Adam's son and the Besht, see Jacob Elbaum, "The Besht and Rabbi Adam" (Hebrew), *Jerusalem Studies in Jewish Folklore* 2 (1983): 66–79. See also the studies on the history and identity of the source text by Chone Shmeruk, "The Tales about Rabbi Adam Baal Shem and Their Versions in Shivḥei Habesht," in *Yiddish Literature in Poland* (Hebrew), 119–39, and Avraham Rubenstein, "The Mentor of Rabbi Israel Baal Shem Tov and the Sources of His Knowledge" (Hebrew), *Tarbiz* 48 (1978/79): 156–58. Recently, the Adam tales have featured in the scholarly dispute between Moshe Rosman and Emanuel Etkes about the reliability of the *Shivḥei ha-Besht* as a historical source. See Etkes, *Ha-Besht: Magyah, Mistiqah, Hanhagah* (Hebrew) (Jerusalem: Merkaz Shazar, 2000), 336–79.
5. On the earliest German philosophical analogies between Spinozism and the Kabbalah, see the discussion of Johann Wachter and Peter Spaeth in Jonathan Israel, *Radical Enlightenment* (Oxford: Oxford University Press, 2001), 645–52. The perception of Ḥasidism as a form of popularized Spinozism was repeated periodically in later German Jewish writings. For a particularly extreme statement of the case in the twentieth century, see the curious monograph by Georg Nador, *Spinoza, Kabbala, Gnosis; Schneur Zalman in Zusammenhang gesetzt* (London: Bina, 1975).
6. Arthur Hertzberg, "End of a Century, Beginning of a Millennium: What Do Such Things Mean To Jews," *Proceedings of the Rabbinical Assembly* 61 (1999): 11.

7. Asher Anshel Worms, *Seyag la-Torah* (Frankfurt am Main, 1766), "Haqdamah Kolelet," 1.
8. Israel, *Radical Enlightenment*, 663.
9. Jacob Heilbronn of Eschwege, in his commentary on the Masorah, *Mevin Ḥiddot* (Amsterdam, 1765), plagiarized entire sections of Worms's work. See the article on Worms by Y. Horowitz in the *Encyclopaedia Judaica*.
10. Cited in Edward Breuer, *The Limits of Enlightenment: Jews, Germans, and the Eighteenth-Century Study of Scripture* (Cambridge, Mass.: Harvard Center for Jewish Studies, 1996), 161. On Mendelssohn's extreme conservatism toward all aspects of the Masoretic text, including its punctuation and diacritics, see chap. 5, esp. 156–67. Unfortunately, Breuer does not place Mendelssohn's work in the context of either earlier or later *Jewish* critics of the Masorah, referring instead almost entirely to the work of German Bible scholars. For a good recent evaluation of Mendelssohn's *Biur*, see Shmuel Feiner, *The Jewish Enlightenment*, trans. Chaya Naor (Philadelphia: University of Pennsylvania Press, 2004), 127–34.
11. On the likelihood that Mendelssohn had Spinoza in mind in his defense of Mosaic authorship, see Breuer, *The Limits of Enlightenment*, 165.
12. See Schorr's review in *He-Ḥalutz* 10 (1877): 103–70.
13. I. Davidson, *Parody in Jewish Literature* (New York: Columbia University Press, 1907).
14. S. I. Stupnitzky, *Borukh Shpinoza: Zayn Filozofie, Bibel-Kritik, Shtotslere un Zayn Bedaytung in der Entviklung fun Mentshlikhn Denken* (Warsaw, 1917).
15. I. B. Singer, *In My Father's Court* (Philadelphia: Jewish Publication Society, 1966), 304–5.
16. See I. B. Singer, *Mayn Tatns Beys-Din Shtub: Hemsheykhim Zamlung*, ed. Chone Shmeruk (Jerusalem: Magnes Press, 1996), 296–306.
17. I. B. Singer, *The Certificate* (New York: Plume, 1993), 1.
18. See Sh. Zetser, *Reb Yisroel Bal-Shem-Tov: Zayn Leben Lehre un Virken*, vol. 3 (New York: Farlag Amerike, 1919), esp. chap. 3, 234–51.
19. See A. Almi, *Spinoza Contra Spinoza* (Buenos Aires: Asociación Pro Cultura Judia, 1963), a scathing critique of both the inherent contradictions in Spinoza's philosophy and a denunciation of Spinoza as an enemy of his people. See also Almi's two essays on Spinoza in *Kheshbn Un Sakhakl* (Buenos Aires: Asociación Pro Cultura Judia, 1959), 301–14.
20. Almi, *Kheshbn Un Sakhakl*, 303.
21. Ibid., 304.
22. Rubin's works on Spinoza are as follows: (1) *Spinoza und Maimonides: ein psichologisch-philosophisches Antitheton* (Ph.D. diss., University of Vienna, 1849); (2) *Moreh Nevukhim he-Ḥadash*, 2 vols. (Vienna, 1856–57); (3) *Teshuvah Niṣaḥat* (Lvov, 1859), a response to the criticisms of Samuel David Luzzatto (Shadal); (4) *Ḥeqer Elo'ah in Torat ha-Adam* (Vienna, 1885), a Hebrew translation of Spinoza's *Ethics* with a lengthy introduction; (5) *Hegyonei Shpinozah al ha-Elohut, ha-Tevel, ve-Nefesh ha-Adam* (Podgorze-Cracow, 1897); (6) *Diqduq Sefat Ever* (Podgorzse-Cracow, 1905), a Hebrew translation of Spinoza's Hebrew grammar with introduction; and (7) *Barukh Shpinozah be-Rigshei Ahavat Elohim* (Amor Dei Intellectualis) (Podgorze-Cracow, 1910).
23. On Shadal's critique of Spinoza, see Rivka Horwitz, "Shadal U-Shpinozah," in *Barukh Shpinozah 300 Shanah le-Moto: Qoveṣ Ma'amarim* (Haifa: Haifa University

Press, 1978), 167–86, and Aryeh Motzkin, "Shpinozah, Luṣato, Filosofyah va-dat," in *Barukh Shpinozah: Qoveṣ Ma'amarim Al Mishnato,* ed. Menaḥem Brinker (Tel Aviv: Mif'alim Universita'iyim, 1978), 135–44. A rich discussion of the debates between Luzzatto and the Galician *maskilim* is to be found in Menaḥem Dorman, *Viqquḥei Shpinozah: ba-Aspaqlarya Yehudir: mi-David Nyeto ad David Ben Guryon* (Tel Aviv: Hakibbutz Hameuchad, 1987), chap. 7, 97–152. For Klatzkin's critique, see *Barukh Shpinozah: Ḥayyav, Sefarav, Shitato* (Leipzig, 1923), 59–88.

24. I am currently writing a book on the history of the rehabilitation of Spinoza in modern Jewish culture that will include several chapters on these Hebrew writers, as well as the treatment of Spinoza in Yiddish literature.
25. Heidi M. Ravven and Lenn E. Goodman, *Jewish Themes in Spinoza's Philosophy* (Albany: State University of New York Press, 2002).
26. For a good summary of Cohen's critique of Spinoza, see Efraim Shmueli, "Biqorto shel Hermann Cohen et Shpinozah," in *Barukh Shpinozah 300 Shanah le-Moto,* 145–54.
27. Martin Buber, *The Origins and Meaning of Hasidism,* ed. and trans. Maurice Freedman (New York: New Horizon Press, 1960), 93.
28. Ibid., 95.
29. Ibid., 97.
30. Ibid., 99.
31. Eliezer Zevi Ha-Kohen Zweifel, *Shalom al Yisra'el,* ed. Avraham Rubenstein (Jerusalem: Bialik Institute, 1972), 2:98.
32. Ibid., 2:98–102. On Zweifel's treatment of Spinoza and Ḥasidism, see Gloria Wiederkehr-Pollack, *Eliezer Zweifel and the Intellectual Defense of Hasidism* (New York: Ktav, 1995), 179–83, and Shmuel Feiner, *Haskalah and History: The Emergence of a Modern Jewish Historical Consciousness* (Oxford: Littman Library, 2002), 312–33.
33. See Rubenstein's introduction to *Shalom al Yisra'el,* 1:22–23.
34. See *Shalom al Yisra'el,* 2:100, sec. 4.
35. Abraham Krochmal, *Even Ha-Roshah* (Vienna, 1871), 49.
36. Ibid., 49–50.
37. The reference is to Manuel Joel, *Spinoza's theologisch-politischer Traktat auf seine Quellen geprueft* (Breslau: Schletter, 1870), which is largely dedicated to establishing affinities between Spinoza's critique of religion and medieval rationalist Jewish philosophy.
38. Many indignant criticisms of *Shalom al Yisra'el* appeared in the *Haskalah* journals almost from the moment of its appearance. The first major critical review of Zweifel's book, by the editor of *Ha-Melitz,* Ḥayyim Zelig Slonimski, appeared within a few months of its publication. See *Ha-Melitz* 8 (1868): 270–345.
39. Shereshevsky was a Hebrew essayist and regular contributor to *Ha-Melitz.* See the entry on Shereshevsky in G. Kressel, *Leksikon ha-Sifrut ha-Ivrit ha-Ḥadashah,* 11:981.
40. Cited by Joseph Klausner in *Historyah shel ha-Sifrut ha-Ivrit ha-Ḥadashah: Shi'urim,* 4:97.
41. "Moda'ah Rabbah," *Ha-Melitz* 9 (Fall 1869): 251–52. For an excellent discussion of the context and significance, in the history of the *Haskalah,* of *Shalom al Yisra'el,* see Shmuel Feiner, "Ha-Mifneh be-ha'arakhat ha-Ḥasidut: Eliezer Zweifel ve-ha-Haskalah ha-Metunah be-Rusyah," in *Ha-Dat ve-ha-Ḥayyim: Tenu'at ha-Haskalah ha-Yehudit be-Mizraḥ Eiropah,* ed. Immanuel Etkes (Jerusalem: Merkaz Shazar, 1993), 336–79.

42. See Naḥman Krochmal, *Moreh Nevukhei ha-Zeman,* ed. Simon Rawidowicz (Waltham, Mass.: Ararat, 1960), letter no. 10, 229.
43. For an excellent summary of *Megalleh Temirin,* see the introduction by Dov Taylor to his English translation of the book: *Joseph Perl's Revealer of Secrets: The First Hebrew Novel* (Boulder, Colo.: Westview, 1997), xix–lxxv.
44. Spinoza is referred to by Krochmal as *Rabbenu Barukh D'Espinoza, z(ikhrono) l(i-verakhah)* on the title page of his polemical defense of Spinozism, *Even Ha-Roshah* (Vienna, 1871).
45. See A. Krochmal, *Iyyun Tefillah* (Lemberg, 1885), 70.
46. See Yosef Dan, *Ha-Sippur Ha-Ḥasidi* (Jerusalem: Keter, 1975), 80.
47. See Etkes's discussion of the Rabbi Adam legends in *Ha-Besht,* 78–83. Etkes concludes that among the chief functions of these tales was "to answer the question: what is the source of the Besht's esoteric knowledge?" (82)
48. See Ezra Spicehandler, "Joshua Heschel Schorr: Maskil and Reformist," *Hebrew Union College Annual* 31 (1960): 187.
49. On the place of Schorr's journal, *He-Ḥalutz,* in the history of the Galician *Haskalah,* see Shmuel Feiner, *Haskalah and History,* 152–56.
50. See Ezra Spicehandler, "Joshua Heschel Schorr—The Mature Years," *Hebrew Union College Annual* 50–51 (1969–70): esp. 18–22.
51. *He-Ḥalutz* 10 (1877): 81.
52. Ibid., 102.
53. Ibid., 103.
54. In his article, "Joshua Heschel Schorr—The Mature Years," Spicehandler claims to have seen this inscription in the copy of *Ha-Ketav ve-ha-Mikhtav* in the collection of the Klau Library at the Hebrew Union College in Cincinnati. Unfortunately, I was unable to find that copy of the book, which is currently listed as missing from the collection.
55. Schorr, *He-Ḥalutz* 10 (1877): 108.
56. A play on the biblical verse: "And from Mattanah to Nahaliel and from Nahaliel to Bamoth" (Num. 21:18).
57. On Ahijah the Shilonite see I Kings 11:29–39. According to the Jewish mystical tradition, Ahijah was one of the seven people whose life spans all of human history. In Ḥasidic lore, Ahijah was the Besht's guide during the latter's mystical ascents. See G. Nigal, "The Teacher and Master of the Besht" (Hebrew), *Sinai* 71 (1972): 150–59.
58. A reference to Esther 8:6.
59. The reference is to the Amsterdam printer Uri ben Aaron Faivesh, who in 1692 established the first Hebrew printing press in Zolkiew. See Bernhard Friedberg, *Toledot Ha-Defus Ha-Ivri Be-Polanyah* (1951), 62ff.
60. Solomon Judah Leib Rapoport of Lemberg (1790–1867), a leading Galician *maskil* and pioneer of critical Jewish scholarship.
61. Abraham Geiger (1810–74), leader of the Reform movement in Germany, leading ideologue, and outstanding scholar of the early *Wissenschaft des Judentums* movement.
62. The tales of how Rabbi Adam's writings were transmitted by his son to the Besht are found in Mintz, *Shivḥei ha-Besht,* 44–52. For the scholarship on this tale, see note 4, above. The motif of hidden writings in Ḥasidic culture became a staple

theme in the *Haskalah* satires and parodies, beginning with Joseph Perl's famous parody *Megalleh Temirin.* On maskilic anti-Ḥasidic satires, see Davidson, *Parody in Jewish Literature,* 60–77. In his extensive bibliography of nineteenth-century Jewish parodies (209–63), Davidson does not refer to Abraham Krochmal at all.

63. The long and convoluted tale of the relationship between the Besht and the son of Rabbi Adam in *Shivḥei ha-Besht* concludes with the following paragraph, which forms much of the basis for Krochmal's satire: "The Besht concealed those writings under a certain rock on a hill. He commanded that rock to open and, when it opened, he placed the writings in it, whereupon it closed up again. He appointed a guard at that place. Now, the rabbi of our community said that he heard the Mokhiaḥ [rebuker] of the holy community of Polnoe declare during his final years: 'I have the power to retrieve the writings from that place because I know exactly where they are. Since however the Besht concealed them, I do not want to take them.' He further declared that the Besht was the fifth person to whom these writings were revealed. He also said that those writings had been in the hands of our Father Abraham, peace upon him, and in the hands of Joshua bin Nun, and the others I do not know" (Mintz ed., 52).
64. A reference to Numbers 27:16–17, in which God describes to Moses his heir's qualifications to lead the Israelites into the land of Israel.
65. Baruch of Miedzyborz (1757–1810), the maternal grandson of the Besht, was the first Ḥasidic *Ṣaddiq* to establish a lavish, royal-style court and as a result the object of several maskilic satires directed against the alleged decadence of "Ṣaddiqism." He is the author of *Buṣina di-Nehora* (Lemberg, 1880), a rich collection of early Ḥasidic teachings.
66. Aryeh Leib (d. 1770), known as the "*Mokhiaḥ* [rebuker] of Polnoe," was one of the first students of the Besht, who as an itinerant preacher spread his teachings throughout Galicia. These teachings are collected in the work *Qol Aryeh* (Koretz, 1798).
67. On the history of the Jewish community of Jezierzany, known in Hebrew as Uziran, see R. Ben-Shem, "Oziran: Qite'ei Historyah Ve-Geógrafyah," in *Sefer Oziran ve-ha-Sevivah* (Jerusalem: Ha-teḥiyah, 1959), 19–30. I have been unable to identify Rabbi Naḥman of Uziran referred to here by Krochmal.
68. Rabbi Naḥman of Bratslav (1772–1811), the founder and only *Ṣaddiq* of the Bratslav sect of Ḥasidism, was the great-grandson of the Besht. His mother, Feyge, was the daughter of the Besht's daughter, Odel.
69. Tsar Nicholas I died in 1855. Krochmal claims to have discovered the buried secret (i.e., the "Mikhtav" section) of his book—which was published in 1874—in 1872, corresponding exactly to the timing in his version of the "prophecy" in *Shivḥei ha-Besht.*
70. *Shitah Mequbbeṣet,* a major synthetic compendium of geonic and medieval rabbinic commentaries to the Talmud based entirely on unpublished manuscripts collected by the author, is the magnum opus of Rabbi Bezalel Ashkenazi (1520–91), a leading rabbi in Egypt, and later chief rabbi of Jerusalem. I could not find any reference to the "four guardians" in the *Shitah Mequbbeṣet* to tractate Bava Qamma. Given the mainly halakhic nature of the work, it seems likely that this is a fictitious reference.
71. BT Bava Batra 25b.
72. Krochmal is apparently reciting a variation of a Hebrew incantation invoking the name of "Amathlai daughter of Karnebo and mother of Abraham" that was recited

before meeting with hostile Gentile authorities. On this incantation, see "Pitḥei Olam" to *Shulḥan Arukh,* Oraḥ Ḥayyim, 114. On the identity of Amathlai, as the legendary name of the mothers of both Abraham and Haman, as well as the other names used by Krochmal subsequently in our text, see BT Bava Batra 91a: "The mother of Abraham was Amathlai, the daughter of Karnebo; the mother of Haman was Amathlai, the daughter of Orabti. . . . The Mother of Samson was Zlelponith, and his sister was Nashyan. How do these names matter? In respect to a reply to the heretics." In utilizing these legendary talmudic names to fend off the guardians of the Besht's manuscript, Krochmal deepens his satire. The Talmud's interest in these names is to refute those heretics who question the integrity of the Bible, and they are invoked by Krochmal to enable him to do just that heretical work.

73. Genesis 22:16.
74. This is yet another variation on the incantation referred to in note 72, above.
75. Song of Songs 1:2.
76. See BT Bava Batra 91a.

III

Sabbateanism and Its Repercussions

12

Toward a Reevaluation of the Relationship between Kabbalah, Sabbateanism, and Heresy

MATT GOLDISH

Gershom Scholem's view of the Sabbatean movement focuses on two premises: that its success was based squarely on its foundations in Lurianic Kabbalah, and that it was deeply heretical. These elements are adumbrated in the title of Scholem's chapter on the movement from his classic work *Major Trends in Jewish Mysticism,* called "Sabbatianism and Mystical Heresy."[1] Scholem discusses several heretical aspects of the movement, all of them connected with specific deeds. One heretical aspect is the Sabbateans' acceptance, even glorification, of Shabbatai Zvi's deliberate ritualized transgressions of Jewish law, called *ma'asim zarim* (strange actions), generally based on kabbalistic reasoning.[2] A second heretical aspect is Nathan of Gaza's doctrine concerning the overturning of the body of *halakhah* in favor of a new Torah, with different stipulations, for the messianic age.[3] The culmination of these two heresies came in Shabbatai's apostasy to Islam, the ultimate "strange action" called for by the messianic dispensation. A third heretical aspect of the movement described by Scholem is the generalized ritual antinomianism practiced by the believers *after* Shabbatai's apostasy.[4]

This third heretical facet of Sabbateanism was by far the most important in Scholem's view: "Sabbatianism as a mystical heresy dates from the moment when the apostasy of Sabbatai Zevi, which was an entirely unforeseen occurrence, opened a gap between the two spheres in the drama of Redemption, the inner one of the soul and that of history."[5] The relationship between these three aspects of heresy is never fully explored by Scholem. What is central for him is that the theology behind all these heresies was couched in terms of the Lurianic Kabbalah; and that the most interesting part of Sabbatean heretical Kabbalah, the radical aspects that make it meaningful in later generations, developed after the apostasy and in response to it.

I suggest that Scholem was correct about the close relationship between Kabbalah, Sabbateanism, and heresy, but that the core of this relationship has less to do with Sabbatean theology than with the larger religious context of the Sabbatean movement.[6] Among the central elements in Sabbateanism's success was the sociological impact of popular myths about the kabbalists, as distinct from the contents of esoteric kabbalistic texts. Heresy was not strictly a result of Sabbateanism, but also a cause—the movement partook in heretical trends that already existed and were well known before 1665–66. This surrounding breakdown of established Jewish faith was itself partially a result of the subversion of traditional authority structures by the popularity of the kabbalists' image.

Scholem and Mystical Heresy; Sasportas and Anti-Rabbinic Heresy

Scholem's insistence on the centrality of heresy in Sabbateanism would appear to find support in the most important contemporary source on the Sabbatean movement in 1665–66, the *Ṣiṣat Novel Ṣevi* (The Wilted Blossom of Zvi) by Ḥakham Jacob Sasportas, the greatest enemy of the movement. Sasportas makes constant comments and references to the heresy of Shabbatai and his prophets. He appears to present precisely the kind of textual evidence Scholem needs for his case—until one examines specifically what Scholem and Sasportas mean by heresy. In the end they are two rather different things.

Scholem's position is that the Kabbalah of Sabbatean theology ruptures the bounds of previous kabbalistic attitudes by justifying a radical new interpretation of the legal principle *miṣvah ha-ba'ah ba-averah,* a commandment performed by means of a transgression, which is of course forbidden. The Sabbateans turned this rule into a positive precept (Scholem's translator renders it "redemption through sin"), advocating ritual antinomianism. Even Shabbatai's apostasy was justified through this principle. The well-known line of development in Scholem's view is as follows. Kabbalah had always carried the seeds of mystical heresy, but they were generally either unrecognizable or obscured by the esoteric language and highly limited circulation of kabbalistic ideas. The expulsion of the Jews from Spain in 1492 changed the entire face of Jewish history. Among its effects was an intense search for meaning in a messianic impulse newly infused with kabbalistic concepts. The immediate result was a wave of messianism in the early sixteenth century, followed by an intellectualized eschatology clothed in the Kabbalah of Rabbi Isaac Luria of Safed. The deep impact of the expulsion, expressed in Lurianic ideas, erupted again when the Sabbateans invested Lurianism with the antinomian hue of their messianic faith.[7]

This perspective fits a larger pattern in Scholem's thought about the relationship between Kabbalah, messianism, and heresy. In the opening paragraphs of his book *Be-Iqveta di-Meshiḥa,* Scholem writes:

> In the annals of Kabbalah we find a phenomenon which repeats itself as if by some invisible rule: If the kabbalists feel strongly and explicitly that the salvation at the end of history is imminent, this feeling is coupled with the appearance of a boldness for innovation in their thought. Their attitude is that, with the approach of redemption, permission is granted to open the heretofore locked gates, now spread wide for them only in the merit of this imminent event. Almost every attempt to dig into new and deeper understandings about the layers of the Infinite or the secret of divinity is accompanied by this awareness, which justifies these authors (at least in their view or that of their followers) when they reveal concepts not found at all in the words of their predecessors.[8]

The real "chutzpah" of the Sabbateans, he continues, by which he means their specific heresy, was not in their messianically charged innovations, but in the actual content of their ideas. The already novel Lurianic Kabbalah, under the impact of imaginative intellects like Nathan of Gaza and Abraham Miguel Cardoso, went beyond the pale of creativity and into the realm of antinomian heresy. Scholem saw this radical trend as a major turning point in Jewish history.

Ḥakham Sasportas, like Scholem, believed the Sabbatean movement was shot through with heresy. But unlike modern Kabbalah scholars, Sasportas essentially lost most of his interest in the movement after the apostasy. He felt that anyone prepared to believe that a Muslim could be the Jewish messiah was indeed a heretic but, more significant, an irrelevant fool. His main attacks on the heresy of Sabbateanism came at the movement's height. Some of them address Shabbatai's "strange actions," but what most concerned him were less the complex theological constructions of apocalyptic antinomianism than seemingly mundane transgressions: the Sabbateans' disrespect for rabbinic tradition and its bearers and their non-traditional exegesis of the Bible, Talmud, Zohar, and Maimonides. These, for him, constituted the dangerous heresy of the movement.[9] Sasportas railed against the grandiose exoteric claims of ordinary believers, while he had only a little to say about the Sabbateans' complex kabbalistic theology.

Sasportas on Sabbatean Heresy

A variety of Sabbatean teachings and activities are referred to by Sasportas as heresies. A few examples highlight how, despite being in the same spectrum in many cases, the anti-rabbinic heresy that bothered Sasportas differs from the mystical heresy with which Scholem was concerned. When Sasportas does deal with what he considers theological aberrations, they are for the most part not kabbalistic per se.

At the beginning of the movement, Sasportas made the following statement to Rabbi Aharon Sarfatti, a believer in Shabbatai. It is part of his response to Nathan of Gaza's original letter to Raphael Joseph Chelebi, in which Nathan lays out his prophetically inspired understanding of the nature of Shabbatai's messianic mission and the series of events to come. Nathan says, among other things, that the Law would be changed in certain ways, and that Shabbatai has the right to judge every person as he pleases, whether that person is in fact guilty or innocent, not excluding Jesus.

Sasportas's prose is very flowery and difficult to translate, but his intent is clear enough:

> I consider this matter a possibility, and though it is an unlikely one, I am not opposed to your prophet. If I said the things [Nathan says] are impossible if they are taken at face value, it is my right, and a truthful response would be to say that some of them are meant as riddles or parables, some are temporary measures for the exigencies of the time, and some are miracles. Indeed, the prophet has not said otherwise. But if you actually take them literally, you have scorned the honor of the prophet, the Oral Law, and the true Kabbalah.[10]

Sasportas is particularly troubled by Nathan's claim that Shabbatai can render the guilty innocent and the innocent guilty, for, he says, "It is impossible to ascribe to God the uprooting of a cornerstone of the religion, which is based on Providence, consequences, and reward and punishment."[11] These are among the beliefs Maimonides lists in his thirteen principles of Jewish dogma, without which a Jew is considered a heretic. Sasportas's ire at this in the Raphael Joseph letter is rivaled by his indignation at the Sabbateans' demand that everyone believe in Nathan and Shabbatai, even without any sign or miracle:

> If one would tell me that somebody who questions the truthfulness of [Nathan's] prophecy *after* he has offered signs and wonders will be lost from the land of the living, he would have spoken well. But *before* confirming it, his messiah has already acquired the power to declare innocence and guilt, etc.! Who would agree with him, and who would listen to him in this matter, to receive a new Torah, God forbid, to move from my [!] faith, or to discard even one iota of it, before it is confirmed? It is impossible![12]

Another matter that concerns Sasportas is the great significance given to mass prophecies by ordinary people at the height of the movement. Here he reproves his student Raphael Supino and all those who give credence to these prodigies. He emphasizes in various places that if God were going to renew prophecy in the world, it would certainly be given to the greatest scholars and holy men, rather than such lowly persons. He then continues on his previous theme, Shabbatai's claim to divine powers of judgment. His argument again is that the believers ignore the authority and tradition of the rabbis and almost deify Shabbatai:

> Your absolute, unquestionable proof to your claims is that all your prophets prophesied about it together and in the same way. Tell me: would you really place your faith in this large group of prophets and prophetesses who are surely fools, or epileptics, or conduits of idiocy? Or would you lead off with that fool from the island of Portafarraio [to show] that it [prophecy] is found there? When he speaks, "his body is paralyzed and he has almost no pulse, something that can't be feigned." And he mutters "Shabbatai Zvi is our king, our savior, the righteous teacher, crowned with the highest crown, he will rule over all the land and the hosts of heaven; and

> Nathan is the prophet, teacher of the salvation of Israel. . . ." May a boiling pot be poured down the throat of this tailor. . . . He [Shabbatai] rules over the upper and lower beings, all the world, every person born of a woman—the king of the world is alive and well! Who would wield his [God's] scepter without His command, as did Moses, Elijah, and others of His prophets? But they will not denounce his [Shabbatai's] mastery, and they recognize him as their lord. Do you not know that even the children of Noah [i.e., all peoples] are warned against a belief in partnership [a co-ruler with God]? Yet it was not enough that they made him a partner in the creation—they also made him a second deity, tearing kingship from the King who is garbed in greatness [God] and giving it to him [Shabbatai], God forbid.[13]

Here, then, we can see some adumbrations of Scholem's mystical and antinomian heresy as it appears later; but Sasportas focuses on the illegitimacy of lay prophets and the ridiculous, heretical message they communicate.

He returns to some of these themes later in the letter, when he rebukes the believers for doing exactly what Scholem describes: offering new explanations of the Torah and Talmud according to their prophetically perceived meaning in the messianic age. "For they showed insolence toward the Sages of the Oral Law, saying they perverted the truth. They even spoke evil of the prophets of truth and righteousness, saying they consider them charlatans who did not understand their own prophecies! They instead support their own seers and prophets of this messiah. I won't even get started about the Amora'im and Ge'onim who followed them, whom they regard as simply a nuisance."[14] A final example is Sasportas's reaction to the thing that surely troubled him most—the fact that the believers in Shabbatai called his opponents "heretics":

> You are further guilty and have opened your mouth to mislead and destroy your place in the land of the living, when you say that "anyone who refuses to believe in this is like one who rejects the Torah of our teacher Moses and the doctrine of resurrection; and he is from the Mixed Multitude [non-Jews who left Egypt with the Israelites]." This was expressed in the letter from your prophet. May a boiling pot and a hot lead bar be thrown in the mouth of one who says this.[15] How can one who does not believe in your messiah—

> before he has performed the deeds of the messiah—be like a denier of the entire Torah? . . . Go ahead and believe in him and reject the whole Torah, while all the Jews and their sages reject *him* and believe in the Torah.[16]

This sampling serves to give the flavor and overall direction of Sasportas's views concerning Sabbatean heresy.

Heresy, Kabbalah, and Sabbatean Research

The difference between the conceptions of heresy propounded by Sasportas and Scholem have far-reaching implications for our understanding of the impact of Sabbateanism on the Jewish world. Scholem believed this movement represents a major break in Jewish history; it was the archetype of his "crisis of tradition in Jewish messianism," even more than Christianity.[17] For Scholem, Shabbatai's conversion to Islam, the complex theology of antinomianism developed to justify it, and the subsequent centrality of "redemption through sin" in Sabbatean thought were cornerstones in the development of a secularizing Jewish worldview that emerged in the *Haskalah* and Reform movements. Sabbateanism was therefore a seminal moment in which deeply buried heretical ideas that had been dormant within Kabbalah burst onto the historical plane, unleashing the winds of heresy in the Jewish mind.

For Sasportas, on the other hand, the heresy of Sabbateanism was not the occasion of a rupture in Jewish life, but part of a rupture that already existed. A central theme in Sasportas's diatribes against the Sabbateans is a fear of the Sabbatean threat to rabbinic authority. He is repeatedly explicit about Sabbateanism's imperilment of the Oral Law and rabbinic tradition. The issues on which he particularly focuses are Shabbatai's ability to render judgment at will, the demand that Nathan and Shabbatai be believed with no corroborating miracle, the mass movement of lay prophecy, and the labeling of non-believers as heretics. None of these is essentially an antinomian kabbalistic heresy, but they all threaten rabbinic courts and the sole power of the rabbinate to mediate God's will to the Jewish people.

Anyone familiar with early modern Jewish life in western Europe will have no trouble placing the crisis of rabbinic authority in its contemporary context. In the seventeenth century there was a widespread feeling that the Oral Law tradition was under siege. The *Qol Sakhal,* the work one scholar called "the *Shulḥan Arukh* of the *apiqorsim*," appeared in the 1620s. The former conversos of Amsterdam, London, and Hamburg were faced with famous heretics like Uriel da Costa, Juan de Prado, Daniel Ribera, and Baruch Spinoza, as well as a host of lesser-known figures. It is perhaps not coincidence that Sasportas had served as rabbi in all of these communities. Until the writings of Spinoza, Thomas Hobbes, and Richard Simon gained wide influence in the eighteenth century, the Jewish community was not yet combating a major peril to the Written Law; but the Oral Law and Kabbalah were barraged with critique. Perhaps even more significant, there was a widespread malaise concerning the observance of rabbinic ordinances all over—in Ashkenaz, Italy, western Europe, and the Ottoman Empire.[18]

Sasportas was clearly seeing the Sabbatean movement in terms of its participation in this wider assault. The nature of Sabbatean claims about the powers of Shabbatai, Nathan, and the other prophets are clearly different from the rationalist heresies of the *Qol Sakhal* or Spinoza. Yet, as previous scholars have occasionally pointed out, these are just different manifestations of an extensive but subtle anti-rabbinic culture, a broad-based undermining of the traditional authority structure in Judaism.[19] This phenomenon has its parallels in the Christian world of the seventeenth century, and it may be regarded as a feature of the so-called "general crisis of the seventeenth century." It is particularly significant, in any case, that Scholem did not place the Sabbatean enterprise of 1665–66 into the context of the Oral Law controversy, though other historians have suggested this general direction. But it *is* the context in which Sasportas placed Sabbatean enthusiasm, and the reason he took it so seriously.

It appears, then, that the heresy with which Sasportas was concerned existed before the Sabbatean movement and prepared the ground for it. The antinomian kabbalism that Scholem saw as the essential heresy, on the other hand, was hardly visible before Shabbatai, but it became a central moving force in Jewish history as a result of his conversion. It is possible, of course, to connect the two forms of heresy by looking at antinomian Kabbalah as an extreme form of anti-rabbinism, but it seems to me there are ultimately significant differences that belie such a linear relationship. The formulations of the specific, kabbalistic antinomianism that fascinated Scholem were often so obscure and esoteric that opponents of the Sabbateans in the next generation, such as Rabbi Moshe Ḥagiz, the Ḥakham Zvi, and Rabbi Jacob Emden, who saw matters as

Sasportas did, often failed to convince their peers that they were seeing Sabbatean heresy in a text before their very eyes.[20] It is indeed possible to trace the effects of this Kabbalah in an entirely different way, as I suggest below. But I think the influence of actual heretical kabbalistic doctrines was minor compared with the wider, exoteric phenomenon of anti-rabbinism and the decline of rabbinic authority in which the Sabbatean movement took part.

The Role of Kabbalah

I return now to the role of Kabbalah in Sabbatean heresy. For Scholem, Lurianic Kabbalah supplied the theological images, terminology, and imagination for the heretical positions of Nathan of Gaza, Abraham Miguel Cardoso, and the movement's other ideologues. A more important role of Kabbalah, however, may have been its corrosion of certain facets of rabbinic authority. That is to say, Kabbalah helped create the crisis of rabbinic power out of which Sasportas believed Sabbateanism grew.

The authority structure of Judaism, like that of Christianity, clearly underwent major changes in the sixteenth and seventeenth centuries. Some of the causes in the two communities were the same and some different.[21] For the Jews, Kabbalah had a major role. Historians of the *Wissenschaft des Judentums* school, particularly Heinrich Graetz, spoke of Kabbalah as a foreign, corrosive element in Judaism. Graetz saw it as a threat to the genuine values of the Jewish tradition because Kabbalah introduced magical and potentially heretical mystical theologies into pure Jewish monotheism. Scholem responded with a dialectical aggrandizement of Kabbalah, insisting that it was as genuinely Jewish as any other part of the tradition. He believed its heresies as well as its more attractive mysteries played an important and positive role in the development of Jewish thought. Both agree, in any case, that Kabbalah contains much potential heresy, though it was deeply buried for many centuries. They also agree that in the early modern period, following the expulsion of the Jews from Spain, and even more in the wake of the great kabbalistic flowering of late-sixteenth-century Safed, Kabbalah became a broadly known and influential force in Jewish life.

Certain, more specific elements about early modern Kabbalah, which affected the traditional authority structure of Judaism, can be linked to the crisis of rabbinic authority in the age of Sabbateanism.

1. *Kabbalistic Elite vs. Rabbinic Elite.* Moshe Idel points out that traditional rabbinic elites were composed of men who stood out for their achievements in Jewish law, exegesis, or homiletics. As the Kabbalah became an increasingly strong force in the Jewish community, the kabbalists came to constitute a new and different kind of elite. The authority of the kabbalist did not generally rest on his deep knowledge of the Talmud, Midrash, and law codes. The wisdom of Kabbalah derived from a separate literature, and often depended on a kind of spiritual talent, imagination, and even prophecy. The term "Kabbalah" itself (meaning something received) did not necessarily refer to wisdom received in tradition from previous generations. Often it meant that which was received directly from heaven through some form of prophecy.

A group of factors coalesced in the sixteenth and seventeenth centuries to bring Kabbalah, or at least the kabbalists, into the popular imagination of Jews. These included a certain common disillusionment with Aristotelian philosophy, and the consequent search for a more personal, intense form of Jewish religiosity after the Spanish Expulsion; a concerted effort by certain kabbalists to spread their mystical teachings abroad (partly to help bring the messiah); and the invention of print, which allowed widespread access to tales of the kabbalists as well as their texts. Along with the popularization of Kabbalah came a new kind of authority. Many of the kabbalists were young. Luria, the most famous example, died at the age of thirty-eight. Most were not famous for their expertise in traditional Jewish sources. Their power in the community rested on reputation, spread through hagiography and general word of mouth, for wonder-working, healing, prognostication, imaginative exegesis of kabbalistic texts, and pure charisma.

The impact of Kabbalah on Sabbateanism thus did not depend on a widespread knowledge of Lurianic doctrines, a state of affairs posited by Scholem and strongly challenged by Idel.[22] It was sufficient that a large number of Jews accepted the reality of kabbalistic authority within Judaism and respected its purveyors, a situation that definitely obtained in 1665–66. This was a large part of the reason that Nathan of Gaza, possessed of a broad reputation as a doctor of the soul (and not a halakhist or exegete) at the age of twenty-two, wielded enough power to raise the curtain of Shabbatai Zvi without becoming a laughingstock. It similarly helps explain how Shabbatai himself, not yet forty years old when the movement began, could be taken seriously as a messianic figure with no credentials as a talmudist, halakhist, exegete, or sage. Shabbatai, like Nathan, had a reputation for spirituality, asceticism, and mastery of kabbalistic writings. Such figures, though they certainly existed earlier, could hardly have been the stuff of an enormous Jewish messianic movement two centuries earlier, before the kabbalistic elite made its inroads in the structure of rabbinic authority.

2. *Pseudepigraphy.* One of the hallmarks of Jewish mystical literature is its penchant for pseudepigraphic pedigrees. The *Sefer Yeṣirah* is attributed to the patriarch Abraham, the *Bahir* to Rabbi Neḥunya ben ha-Kanah, and the Zohar to Rabbi Simeon bar Yoḥai. Unlike most classic pseudepigraphic *midrashim,* these were not books that had been known continually since talmudic times. Yet in no case, including that of the Zohar, was there any significant objection in the community to such attributions. These works even became influential in the formulation of *halakhah,* though this was not without its limits. Kabbalah thus helped condition the Jewish people to the conferral of great authority upon books nobody had ever seen before.

It is this background that can help us understand how Nathan of Gaza, at the beginning of the Sabbatean movement, could produce the most flagrant forgery without raising the notice of anyone except the arch-opponent of the Sabbateans, Rabbi Jacob Sasportas. Nathan claimed to have found certain "ancient" apocalypses predicting Shabbatai's messiahship through divine inspiration:

> It is most amazing to any wise person, this document full of foolishness coming from Gaza [Nathan], and called *The Wisdom of Solomon* [*Ḥokhmat Shelomoh*], which is accepted by you, but not by anyone to whom God has given discernment and understanding. How do you not look in it and see it is full of childish foolishness and confused mixtures of ideas, designed to look mysterious and to scare young children, by saying, "I am Abraham, and after I was shut up for a year I was amazed by the great serpent which thrives under the rivers of Egypt; when would the end of these wonders come? etc. Now a man appeared before me whose appearance was as shiny brass." . . . It is a transgression to waste paper on all this. In any case, the purpose was to fool the masses who will believe anything.[23]

What was patent to Sasportas was obviously not clear to the believers, among whom were some great Torah scholars. Having become accustomed to long-lost kabbalistic treatises appearing from nowhere and wielding very considerable authority, it is not necessarily surprising that the Jews did not immediately attack Nathan's hoax when he presented it.

3. *Flexibility.* Jewish prophetic and messianic ideas have always been relatively flexible and non-dogmatic, but the level of flexibility found in kabbalistic views far outstrips that in other traditional genres. What is true in the *olam ha-asi'ah* may be false in the *olam ha-beri'ah* or *olam ha-yeṣirah.* What is true in this age may be completely different in the messianic age. The mystical interpretation of a biblical or talmudic passage may yield numerous interpretations that have nothing whatsoever to do with the simple meaning of the text. A particularly significant type of flexibility derives from the kabbalistic conception of metempsychosis, especially as it was conceived by the Luria circle. According to this notion, people have multiple souls within them that have rolled over from persons of earlier ages.[24] Only a member of the kabbalistic elite is able to identity to whom these souls previously belonged, and there is nobody to gainsay this knowledge. None of this required any serious familiarity with the Lurianic texts—it could all be learned from popular, published hagiographies and ethical works.

Through the flexibility of Kabbalah, particularly in the matter of soul-roots, the Sabbateans were able to make claims that might otherwise have seemed ludicrous. Scholem and his school have already shown in some detail how Kabbalah was used to support Shabbatai's "strange actions" and other abrogations of commandments or traditions in the movement. Perhaps the way the Sabbateans treated soul-roots is even more significant. Shabbatai and Nathan could claim to be *gilgulim* of Rabbi Isaac Luria and Rabbi Ḥayyim Vital, and at the same time of Rabbi Akiva, the patriarchs, and various other historical figures. These doctrines could also explain how someone without a pedigree relating him by ancestry to King David, the father of the messianic line, could still claim a relationship, even an identity, with David.

4. *Prophecy.* Sabbateanism is riddled with prophecy, from its earliest glimmerings to its very latest forms. The rabbinic view that prophecy stopped after the early Second Commonwealth period is well known, but various forms of prophecy and divination were practiced by the rabbis of the Talmud and those who followed them. In the Middle Ages, though, it is specifically in the circles of mystics and kabbalists that one finds the vast majority of prophetic claims. This tendency mushroomed with the Safed circle of the sixteenth century. A positive

explosion of maggidism, automatic writing, xenoglossia, meetings with the prophet Elijah, dreams, augury, and visitations of the holy spirit littered the spiritual landscape of the Galilee in that period.[25] Thus, by the time Shabbatai Zvi appeared on the scene in the later seventeenth century, the great prevalence of prophecy in his circle did not cause immediate rejection and renunciation, as it might have without the kabbalistic influence. Prophecy rather served to bolster the movement, and to associate the Sabbateans with the Luria circle in the minds of many Jews.

This conception of the influence of Kabbalah on Sabbateanism and its heresy, then, is substantially different than that of Scholem. While Sabbatean theology did rely heavily on images and concepts from Lurianic Kabbalah, particularly after Shabbatai's conversion, I suggest that the myth of the kabbalists and their powers was much more important than their theology, because it unsettled rabbinic authority structures. This was occurring before Sabbateanism erupted and forms a significant part of the fragmentation of rabbinic authority that underlay the movement.

Conclusion

While the heresy inherent in the Sabbatean movement seems to be a point of general agreement, there is a very significant difference between the way Gershom Scholem saw that heresy and the way a contemporary, Rabbi Jacob Sasportas, saw it. For Scholem, whose views are widely accepted today, Sabbatean heresy was a kabbalistic heresy of mystical theology supporting "redemption through sin." As a significant force in Jewish history, this heresy came into being in the wake of Shabbatai's apostasy. For Sasportas the movement was heretical from its very beginning because it spurned traditional rabbinic authority, transgressed talmudic law, and showed a lack of respect for contemporary rabbinic luminaries. This anti-rabbinic heresy was part of a larger movement of anti-rabbinism that had been developing and expanding during the seventeenth century. Sabbateanism was thus more the result of an existing crisis than the inception of a new one. This crisis of rabbinic authority, however, was itself caused partially by the popularity of Kabbalah and kabbalists.

Thus Scholem's edifice of a Sabbatean-kabbalistic-heretical nexus remains intact, but, using Sasportas as a guide, I would argue that Scholem emphasized less critical aspects of this issue while downplaying something more central. Sasportas's approach makes for a less spectacular thesis but one that is easier to sustain. The same crisis of rabbinic authority that fed Sabbatean heresy would go on in the eighteenth century to become a central element in the rise of modern Jewish movements such as Ḥasidism, *Haskalah*, and later, Reform.

Notes

My sincere thanks go to David Malkiel, as well as to Joseph Davis, Lois Dubin, and the anonymous readers for Wayne State University Press for their valuable comments on this paper.

1. Gershom Scholem, *Major Trends in Jewish Mysticism* (New York: Schocken, 1941), 287–324.
2. See Gershom Scholem, *Sabbatai Ṣevi, The Mystical Messiah*, trans. R. J. Z. Werblowsky (Princeton: Princeton University Press, 1973), 807–14 and elsewhere.
3. Ibid., 319–25.
4. Several people have questioned whether antinomianism is the correct term for a state under which Jewish law is generally observed in the traditional fashion, but deliberately broken in specific moments of religious import. I use the term "ritual antinomianism" to distinguish this situation from others in which law is abandoned altogether. One of the press readers suggested a differentiation between ritual antinomianism and symbolic violations of Jewish law (to demonstrate belief that the messianic era had begun), but I confess that I do not entirely understand the purpose of the distinction. In any case, it occurs to me that these divisions among types of antinomianism might have very serious repercussions for Scholem's thesis about the impact of Sabbateanism on the *Haskalah* and Reform movements.
5. Scholem, *Major Trends*, 306.
6. This point and others in this paper are also explored in my book *The Sabbatean Prophets* (Cambridge, Mass.: Harvard University Press, 2004).
7. This trunk of development is fully articulated by Scholem in *Major Trends*, chaps. 7–8, and *The Messianic Idea in Judaism* (New York: Schocken, 1971), chaps. 1–4.
8. Scholem, *Be-Iqveta di-Meshiḥa* (Jerusalem: Tarshish, 1944), 5 (my translation).
9. Scholem, *Sabbatai Ṣevi*, 691, recognizes Sasportas's intuition.
10. Rabbi Jacob Sasportas, *Ṣiṣat Novel Ṣevi*, ed. I. Tishbi (Jerusalem: Bialik Institute, 1954), 33.
11. Ibid., 37.
12. Ibid., 43. On the Sabbateans' manipulation of Maimonides' position on the messiah, see David Berger, "Some Ironic Consequences of Maimonides' Rationalistic Messianism" (Hebrew), *Maimonidean Studies* 2 (1991): 4–6.
13. Sasportas, *Ṣiṣat Novel Ṣevi*, 93.
14. Ibid., 94.
15. The term used is *petilah shel avar*, a term applied in several ways in the Talmud. Here it appears to reflect the meaning in BT Sanhedrin 52a, where it refers to a

burning lead bar being thrown into the mouth of a person being executed by *sereifah,* burning.

16. Sasportas, *Ṣiṣat Novel Ṣevi,* 180.
17. Scholem, "The Crisis of Tradition in Jewish Messianism," in *The Messianic Idea,* 49–77.
18. There is a large literature on converso heresy and anti-rabbinism. See, e.g., Shalom Rosenberg, "Emunat Hakhamim," in *Jewish Thought in the Seventeenth Century,* ed. I. Twersky and B. Septimus (Cambridge, Mass.: Harvard University Press, 1987), 285–341; Uriel da Costa, *Examination of Pharisaic Traditions,* ed. and trans. H. P. Salomon and I. S. D. Sassoon (Leiden: Brill, 1993). On the *Qol Sakhal* and anti-rabbinism see Talya Fishman, *Shaking the Pillars of Exile* (Stanford: Stanford University Press, 1997) and her bibliography there. On Ashkenaz see Joseph Davis, "The *Ten Questions* of Eliezer Eilburg and the Problem of Jewish Unbelief in the Sixteenth Century," *Jewish Quarterly Review* 91 (3–4) (2001): 293–336, and Davis's contribution to this volume. While there is some dissension among scholars concerning laxity of practice at this time, the responsa, some communal records, and other sources seem to me to present sufficient evidence of slackness somewhat beyond the level normal in earlier periods.
19. See, e.g., Rosenberg, "*Emunat Hakhamim,*" 295ff.
20. Professor Joseph Davis has pointed out to me that Leib ben Ozer, the beadle of the Ashkenazi synagogue in Amsterdam, was perfectly able to understand and explain these kabbalistic niceties. I do not believe this was indeed the case concerning the quite complex and subtle aspects one finds, for example, in the work of Neḥemiah Ḥiyya Ḥayon or Solomon Aailion.
21. The literature on the "general crisis" is large and touches on Sabbateanism in various ways; for some ideas about the crisis of authority, see Theodore K. Rabb, *The Struggle for Stability in Early Modern Europe* (New York: Oxford University Press, 1975).
22. See Scholem, *Sabbatai Ṣevi,* part 1; Idel, "'One from a Town, Two from a Clan'—The Diffusion of Lurianic Kabbala and Sabbateanism: A Re-Examination," *Jewish History* 7, no. 2 (1993): 79–104.
23. Sasportas, *Ṣiṣat Novel Ṣevi,* 184–85.
24. The most complete analysis of this system to date is in Menachem Kallus, "Pneumatic Mystical Possession and the Eschatology of the Soul in Lurianic Kabbalah," in *Spirit Possession in Judaism: Cases and Contexts from the Middle Ages to the Present,* ed. M. Goldish (Detroit: Wayne State University Press, 2003), 159–85. In general, see J. H. Chajes, *Between Worlds: Dybbuks, Exorcists, and Early Modern Judaism* (Philadelphia: University of Pennsylvania Press, 2003).
25. See Chajes, *Between Worlds.*

13

Jacob Frank Fabricates a Golem

HARRIS LENOWITZ

Jacob Frank (1726–91) was the most important of the self-proclaimed Jewish messiahs following Shabbatai Zvi (fl. 1666; referred to by Frank as "the First").[1] He made use of Shabbatai's biography, the writings of his prophet, Nathan of Gaza, and those of the various other prophets and groups spawning the Sabbatean enthusiasm. Frank took over what remained of the unified leadership after the death of Barukhya Russo ("the Second"), and, leaving Turkey, established a large following in Poland. Another Sabbatean group, which was quite different from the Polish following in terms of its intimacy with him, continued as Sabbateans in the west, Bohemia and Austria. Frank and his Polish followers led two important disputations against Judaism and its texts, ostensibly on behalf of Christianity. He converted to Catholicism on two different occasions, and was imprisoned for thirteen years in the fortress-shrine of Częstochowa as a religious fraud. He was able to flee westward when Russia invaded Poland, traveling and living as a noble in Bohemia and Austria until his death, when his daughter assumed authority.

Frank was reared in a somewhat haphazard fashion and wandered, doing odd jobs—especially conducting caravans—through the Ottoman Empire. As a youth his adherence to traditional Jewish ways and social structures was virtually non-existent, and his acquaintance with Jewish thought and practice was tenuous. Then, in Izmir and Salonika, and from itinerant preachers of the Dönme (the name by which the various Sabbatean sects were known in Turkey and the Ottoman empire), he learned of the thought and practices of that secret faith, based on the remnants of the teachings of Shabbatai Zvi and his prophets. From then until the end of his life Frank was constantly making his own religion, whether as a variety of Judaism, Islam, or Christianity; whether he was free, a noble, or in prison; whether in Turkey/Walachia or Polish, German, or Bohemian territory.

He began teaching his system of belief and conduct in Iwanie, a small village where he and his following were granted residence by the Polish crown in 1758. What he said in his sessions with the inner circle of his followers, the Brothers and Sisters of the Company, is recorded in the Polish manuscripts of his dicta. In these he relied on images and ideas from other religions and texts, folk traditions, and Jewish texts and practices for materials. The Jewish sources, however, were only introduced insofar as they served him as foils that could be counterposed with both Islamic and Christian texts and ideas.[2] He called the religious objective he sought to inculcate the *Das,* a Hebrew word rendered in the Ashkenazi Hebrew ethnolect that appears frequently in his dicta and represents at different times, or occasionally at the same time, both standard Hebrew *da'at* (knowledge) and *dat* (religion). The word also has associations to the "missing" *sefirah* called *da'at,* the uppermost *sefirah* of the middle column in the tree of the *sefirot;* and it sometimes appears in the expression *Das Edom,* which may mean Christianity or Esau-ism.[3]

Jacob Frank's project, he said, was to make a new sort of human being.[4] Arguably he achieved this. Many of his Polish followers converted away from Jewish thought and practice to Christianity and gained enhanced economic and social status. Zalman Shazar, president of Israel and an eminent Jewish historian, after visiting the site of the Frankist court in Offenbach, noted that Frank's military force (his own escort, actually, and later a youth-training institution, perhaps the first Jewish summer camp) constituted the first Jewish army in Europe. Frank's new model person changed as his own situation changed, as the roles of his listeners changed, and as the hour required. His speeches to them, the dicta (excerpted below), reflect these relationships. It seems possible, though difficult, to calculate roughly the alterations in Frank's new model man as things changed, just as it has been shown possible to write a history of the teachings of Nathan of Gaza that accords with his addressees, his changes in belief, and other changes in his teaching that resulted from Shabbatai Zvi's deeds and communications.[5] The two had similar programs, Nathan speaking for a messiah, Frank as his own prophet: "I will form you. This faith will make you a new creature, liberated from doubt and victorious in battle over a petrified, ineffective, and deceptive community structure and its leadership." A new being, fideist and heterodox, shaped itself in their words and deeds as both idea and performance: a doubt-free authority and authentic divine creature, based in the mythic.

Relying on Frank's words to his followers, I attend to the central theme of the making of the new model human, a theme that runs throughout his long career as messiah. He told his followers what they should be; he told them that he was an example of that; and he told them that although they could not be him, they could be mighty like him. The telling was the making, not unlike the Ḥasidic transformation of exempla taking place at the same time and places. So, too, the idea of joining a group of followers one to another in contemplating the image of the leader for the purpose of uplifting all together is a familiar teaching and practice among Ḥasidic groups. (See below, near dictum 14.)

The manufacture of a golem is a theoretical and intellectual enterprise rather than a material one. Jacob Frank's new model human—the one in whose image he sought to refashion the identities of his followers—was likewise a proposal for bringing such a being to life. Whether he actually made such a golem is the central question addressed here. Scholem's proposition, that Frankism contributed to the creation of Ḥasidism, the *Haskalah,* and the Reform movement, has been discounted by recent scholars, who usually allow for its contribution to Ḥasidism alone. None of these three movements was directly connected to the personages of Frankism—neither to the followers in Poland, the Ukraine, or Podolia, nor to those of Prague and Germany. All three were, it might nevertheless be reasonably contended, parallel contemporaries, co-explorers, not quite on the same trip, perhaps, and at times even locked in icy rivalry with each other. (In the same way, the co-conspirators in the creation of Hebrew fiction, Perl and those who told the tales of the Ba'al Shem Tov [Besht],[6] wrestle with each other while struggling against their common enemy, the clenched fist of rabbinic power.)[7] Jacob Frank was no less audacious than the Baal Shem Tov, no less daring than Moses Mendelssohn, no less intrepid than David Friedlaender. Like them, Frank came closer to actually creating his new Heavens and new Earth and their inhabitant, the Ideal new man, than did Rava and Rav Ze'ira. He succeeded in one particular way where they failed.

Fiat Golem

> Once upon a time, I, by my power, turning air into water, and water again into blood, and solidifying it into flesh, formed a new human creature—a boy—and produced a much nobler work than God the Creator. For He created a man from the earth, but I from air—a far more difficult matter; and again I unmade him and restored him into air, but not until I had placed his picture and image in my bed-chamber, as a proof and memorial of my work.
>
> Simon Magus[8]

Empowered speech being a central matter to him, Moshe Idel notes, "It was the silence of the anthropoid which served as a touchstone of his being a nonhuman entity and thus susceptible of being destroyed by its maker."[9] Frank's golem—himself—talked himself into a reality, an existence, that rang true in the ears of his followers, themselves longing to be free of economic, social, and political oppression. If Frank never quite got his followers what he promised—the majesty of cosmic power, eternal, youthful life free from sickness, giant stature, and the life beyond life; that is, his Ideal Human—then let us recall that not one of the golem makers in that long line descended from the talmudic parable ever physically created a golem. Both their creatures and his creature, theirs of incantation and his of entrancing and enabled narration, were but images of a longing for the unachievable ideal of power without limits.

Strewn throughout the chaos of Frank's dicta, memorializing his unceasing negotiations with his inner circle of followers, are found the *disjecta membra* of the golem. These include information concerning Frank's character and activities as a traditional magus, manipulating alchemical and herbal arcana, and two other dialectics involving the figures of the child and the *prostak* (simpleton) that are related to knowledge and conduct. Each aspect of these topics has its history in Jewish religious thought, a field in which Frank gleaned what was useful to him and came to be not quite the ignoramus others have found him. The creature that he raises up—first in the village of Iwanie, and then in the fortress shrine of Częstochowa, then in Brno near his relatives the Dobrushka-von Schoenfeld family, and finally in Offenbach, first at the castle of the prince of Isenburg and then at the mansion of "Under the Three Swiss" where the manuscripts of his dicta were created—lurches away from control and the norms of the previous societies of his followers, toward the rebellion typical of infantile rage and mutiny against authority and a malevolent destiny. It does so in images that repeat themselves not only in works like David Frischmann's romantic novella of the golem (in *Ba-Midbar*) but also in the colossi of Bialik's *Metei Midbar*.[10] Frank's golem is their kin and its ancestry is biblical (in the sense of the New Testament as well). It is the child of Nimrod; the idol erected upon the Tower of Babel by its presumptuous builders; Esau.

The form of the dialectic is well suited to the creation of an ideal (as opposed to the realization of one)[11] since the energy flows through it in the perpetual motion machine of assertion and counter-assertion, creation and destruction. The first of the dialectics to be explored in this context counterposes knowledge and ignorance in the figure Frank calls the *prostak*. In his employment of this term, the noun (and the adjective to a lesser degree) achieves the creative status of the powerful, life-giving Name,[12] creating itself and its speaker and audience as new beings by speech alone, as in the narrative "Speech of Simon Magus" quoted above. A line of thought from the anonymous *Sefer ha-Ḥayyim* (northern France, ca. 1250) asserts, "Just as the divine creative speech operates on/in the ether, so does the spoken word of holy men, its vapor combining with the air of the world. At once the thing spoken is made."[13]

Furthermore, both the Speech of Simon Magus and the *Sefer ha-Ḥayyim* resemble Frank's socio-political stance as well as his praxis: the Simon Magus pseudepigraph intends to be anti-authoritarian, and the *Sefer ha-Ḥayyim* stands alone, outside the tradition of verbal magic using alphabetic combinations in complex rituals like those employed in Ashkenazi Ḥasidic circles. To this creation-by-naming Frank brought himself as fleshly support. In dictum 33 we hear him say, *I am prostak*.[14] He says further that the power of his speech is beyond that of the speech of authorities:[15] "962. I cannot tell you what confusion there is now in the world. Just as you yourselves see that your understanding is muddled, so all the kings have become confused in their thinking; and I, *prostak*, have been chosen and cast among them as it clearly stands: Before him kings will close their mouths" (Isa. 52:15). Frank's use of the *prostak* includes his physical as well as his mental capacities. He makes himself be physically strong, abnormally so: "35. For security he put that wagon in his yard which was surrounded by a high fence. At midnight I came there with two ladders which, after having tied [them] together, I put against the fence, took the cart weighing 100 *ok* [more than 275 pounds] on my back, carried it over the fence and, having descended the ladder with it I carried it on myself for half a mile, to Roman. . . . This is a second display of my *prostak*-ness." The *prostak* is also a creature that fears nothing: "1157. I was *prostak* and did not even know that verse: *Szama Isruel Adonai Elohaini Adonai eḥet.* Hear, o Israel, our God, one God. And when I was struggling with powerful robbers I yelled out that verse and pronounced that word *aḥet,* one, and then cut off a head." Nevertheless, he can accuse the *prostak* of being a coward: "1189. There was a certain *prostak*; he had a beautiful daughter, his last. A lot of lords came and sought to marry her but he didn't want to give her to them. He fled the town." He proclaims the *prostak* a simpleton.[16] As to his mental capacity: "103. You see me before you, *prostak*. You should have concluded on the basis of that that all laws and teachings will fall. If scholars were needed then they would have sent you one with knowledge of everything." Against this definition he counterposes the same creature's knowledge of traditional literature:

> 804. [They said] the signal has already gone out that a great deal of blood will flow in the world and we want to go and rescue many; only you bless for us the way. I am *prostak,* I replied. I can say no more than this word: Abraham, Isaac, Jacob; and this verse: The angel who delivered me [Genesis 48.16] & & . . . They said to me, we have a book here in which stand blessings. Bless us with this book; we only ask you that you bless us out loud. They gave me the book which was written in large Hebrew letters without dots. They bent their heads and I, after raising my hands above their heads, blessed them. There were beautiful words there, but I do not remember more than two words that were at the end, *Du Jankiew,* "That is Jacob."

The three patriarchs are often taken as one in the Lurianic and post-Lurianic Kabbalah, *Adam ha-Rishon.* The "two words" here are very likely from those passages in the Zohar that enumerate the qualities of Jacob.[17] Zohar 1:60b reads, "The middle one of the fathers of the Chariot, *d'a ya'aqov*"; 1:145b speaks of Jacob as the *sefirah* of *Ḥesed,* linking speech (*dibbur*) to sound (*qol*). Frank, in his character as Jacob, often recites Genesis 27:22, "The voice is the voice of Jacob," a voice stirring other voices throughout the cosmos, a voice more powerful than "the hands of Esau"; and Exodus 26:28, "The middle bar goes from one extreme to the other." Both have a long history of supplied meaning in the rabbinic literature.

The inner dialectic between fearlessness and cowardice and another between stupidity (ignorance of traditional Jewish literature) and dazzling virtuosity are enveloped in the dicta by a major theme of the topic of identity, the opposition of physicality and interiority.

Child

In 1997, in the course of a conversation concerning the dícta and the edition of some of them recently completed by Jan Doktór[18] and their Polish-Jewish context, Professor Chone Shmeruk told me that he was very excited about using those that touched on the figure of the child for a proposed study of child life in the area and period.[19] I mentioned to him that the stories Frank tells of his own childhood would appear to be germane, and that many of them include well-known childhood tales, just as many elements of the three-fold tales he tells contain common folkloric motifs and plots.[20] He said that this was precisely what made them useful to him.[21] Why did Frank employ the figure of the child so frequently?

The figure of the child is a constituent of the cluster of golem motifs.[22] It is one of the images and ideas connected to the homunculus and to the larger theme of the literature concerning the subject of the macranthropos/micranthropos, and more generally the macrocosmos/microcosmos.[23] The golem is both an early human creature of the created world, and huge; as well as the last being created, and small. He is a master God dreads and a servant that lives on condition. Classically, the child is taken to be a "person," even one who has the capacity to prophesy (BT Bava Batra 12b), as well as a non-"person," one who may not be trusted to give tithes (BT Yevamot 113a) or be counted in a quorum for prayer (BT Berakhot 20b–22a). The child is also, of course, the born messiah of Isaiah 9:5, and appears in the Sabbatean amulets written by Rabbi Jonathan Eibeschuetz.[24] (There is, however, no question that the child has a soul, whereas all agree that the golem does not.) Frank makes it clear that his followers, and presumably he as well, do not possess souls, that no one ever has, but that they may come to do so:

> 108. I tell you, people who come forth from earthly seed have no soul yet and their spirit is like that of a beast. And that is what Job

> said, "Through my body I see God,"[25] which means that the Adam whom he created Adam was not whole, but those people who will be worthy to embrace a soul from God himself will be able to see from one end of the world to the other and live forever. Even concerning Jacob no more is [said] than that his spirit became alive—but not [his] soul.[26]

The figure of the child encloses a future that may be entered with divine guidance and sanction. Frank's own childhood and the childhoods of his followers lie in the past; his example constructs redemption for all his followers. They will be the active agents—as he is—and will design their own place in society. Frank will not be what his father was.

The status of the child in the religious society is the fulcrum upon which Frank applies his force. "289. During prayers when ten [adult male Jews] are not present they take a child and put a Bible [i.e., *sefer torah*] in his hands and, due to the fact that he is holding it, the Jews count it as a complete person. Once, having dressed a common Christian boy in my frock, I put the Bible in his hands and he was the tenth for prayers." By forcing the congregation to include a Christian child, Frank demolishes both the prohibition on counting minors and that on Christians (*ovedei kokhavim u-mazalot*) in BT Yevamot 113a. He makes use of the same device the members of the minyan do, converting that which is soulless (inanimate) into a being reckoned as having a (Jewish) soul. In the next text Frank increases the pressure by including "common" (i.e., Christian) girls in religious rituals: "288. I had a band of peasant children of the same age as me, and having gone to the synagogue, took out a trumpet [i.e., shofar] and went with those boys to the Prut [river], and I blew the trumpet with them just as though in the synagogue and there had to be common girls present at this deed." In another dictum Frank makes use of his weakness in his status as a child to overcome the power and wrath of his maker—that is, his father:[27]

> 1240. The Lord narrated: In my youth I stole a lot of money from my father, which the children had coaxed me to do, and I went to play cards with them. In the morning my father got up and, having seen the money fallen scattered on the ground and me not being at home, he went to look for me until he caught up with me in a little room in town. Hearing my voice, he recognized me immediately. The lads closed the door against him but he broke it down with his

> power. The lads hid me under a certain vessel, but he found me. Having gotten me, he beat me powerfully until I closed one eye saying that he had knocked out my eye. I dropped my hand and screamed that he had broken my arm, which, Mother having seen, she began to weep a lot and said to Father, "See what kind of bandit you are. You have made him blind and crippled."

The rebellious son motif mentioned above certainly does have its associations with the episode in the infancy narrative from the book of Luke in which the child Jesus, *not yet a bar miṣvah,* astonishes the rabbis in the Temple with his answers and his questions (Luke 2:40–50). Illustrations of the episode are common in the Christian controversy with Judaism.[28] Consider Frank's tale of himself as a child at the Seder:

> 292. When I was little, I asked Rabbi Leib about Easter,[29] You say that this night is guarded.[30] Nevertheless, during that night many Jews are killed and there are many thefts. Why do you call it guarded? Second, it is a custom with you to put out one glass full of wine for Elijah. Is it likely that he would be able to drink all the glasses of all the Jews who are in existence at the same hour? Third, how are you praising God when you say that he has four sons? Fourth, at such a table and praises, is it proper to mention such abominations as lice, frogs, etc. with those plagues? Fifth, you take Easter bread[31] with horseradish and, putting them together, eat them? If that elder was so stupid and did that, [why] do I have to do that? All this is false, untrue. All, who were sitting at the table wept, recognizing that all these questions were fair.[32]

This is a match for the New Testament tale, as told and as pictured. The child at Passover and his rebellion appears again, a matter of more than a little interest to Shmeruk: "525. When I was young, I saw a book for children in which all the customs were written, and along with it, different portraits, such as Pharaoh bathing in the blood of children, etc. At that, the children and I took a knife and began to stick holes in it—not only what was bad, but everything good that was in there too, so that we put holes in the whole book." Illustrated books are aimed at the unlettered, and especially at children, to teach them religious truths where print cannot. Frank first reconfigures the meanings of the illustration, then uses it to teach—and act out—his truth concerning the exercise of the power of the adult over the innocent child.

What draws me particularly to these images of the vile child (or the *vilde khaye,* the *enfant sauvage*) and the trauma contributing to his *sauvagerie* is not only their association with the micranthropos or the infant/embryo of the classic golem accounts but another motif: the salvation of the era through the agency of empowered innocence. For the "little man" golem we have the following dictum:

> 735. You would also have heard [in a particular chamber in the palace of the Big Brother] the proclamation coming for this world, of [which] it is said, Truly the foundation of that root remains in the earth.[33] For when a branch is cut, even though the leaves on it are still fresh, they will yet wither; but the foundation of the root never rots. In a short time it will begin to sprout and put forth flowers. There you would have known and heard what that *Das* is and the whole road which it is necessary to tread. I cannot now tell you of the foundation of that root. The cutting off of the branches signifies the death of religions, but the foundation of the root remains in the dirt; therefore it will be, "Shake yourself free from the dirt."[34] There grow those gold trees with gold fruits upon them. Those gold trees will also give fruit good for eating and another three things which I cannot reveal. If you ate that fruit, you would know everything. If you could have brought the fruit from those trees and stood guard so that no one could come near it, then all the kingdoms of the world would have been as nothing in your eyes. Now I must go by other means, without Brothers and Sisters. And when I tread all the roads, then that closed room will open and the Big Brother will be astonished at the little man who will be there, at how the power of all powers flows from him. Here the Lord showed the height of one cubit with his holy hand.[35]

In a version of the "Prophecy of Isaiah" fragments,[36] we also come upon the following: "This is that burden that the Lord himself determined and decreed upon the entirety of the kingdom. 'For everything from the beginning of the world to the end was shown to me,' said the Lord, 'in the form of a man. I demanded further that it be shown to me in miniature so that I might carry out this holy *misterium magnum* in life size.' "[37]

Another tale describes Frank's battle with the water monster, an image that associates Frank with the legends of Shabbatai Zvi and the biblical monster enemies—titans of chaos—Rahab, Tannin, Leviathan, and their companions.

> 453. In my youth there was found in the Prut a *som* [the large European catfish, the wels], a fish that lay in the depths. Some children and I were bathing in that river and that *som* breathed in and pulled several people down and swallowed them. Only their robes were cast up on the shore of the Prut. Once my friends and I bathed near that deep spot and we felt that a spirit/breath began to pull us down. However, there was among us a wise lad who said, There surely must be here either a witch or a fish which draws us to it with its breath. Not far from there lay a great tree with branches and that youth advised me to grab one branch of that tree. When I did, everybody grabbed me and so I saved them all. Afterwards many people pulled out that fish and in it were found many children which it had swallowed. And so it is with you: there was not one among you who could give that good advice, how to escape from the mouth that swallows.

It is clear from the reference to *She'ol* (the hell-mouth) that Frank is aware of the primal depths in which he sets this struggle—along the lines of Isaiah 5:14—intending it to be understood so. And perhaps the tale rests on that of Shabbatai Zvi and his near drowning off Izmir in 1660. Scholem remarks that "the hymns [for the Sabbateans' day of 'Purim'] interpret the event as a symbol for the rising of the messiah's soul from the depth of the abyss. . . . One hymn states that he was drowned in the sea, but that he arose from the abyss and beheld the 'crooked serpent.' "[38] In his notes to this Scholem takes us to the Shabbatean hymnal[39] and explains the reference to the event as interpreted among the Dönme. He cites hymn 133, which has Shabbatai Zvi wrestling the dog, and the celebration of his victory in the sectarian "Purim." Scholem also cites a hymn from another Dönme liturgical text with the lines: "He (*he/vav/alef*)[40] is the light hid away, the crooked serpent he did slay."[41] Additional occurrences of the conquest of this monstrous dog/serpent in the hymnal are to be found in hymns 70, 88, 117, and 123f.: " 'You shall die' is now halted / the snake he has slain" and "He has halted that snake." Scholem brings associations with "oriental hymns" where Jesus fights a serpent in the waters of the Jordan. He suggests a source for them in the "Hymn of the Pearl."

The ancient Near Eastern and biblical sources stand behind this later version.[42] In the texts mentioned—from Zvi, from the later Sabbateans, and from Frank—the theme of salvific acts protrudes. In the case of Frank at least, the savior is a child, a component of Frank's golem montage. Of course, this is long before the versions of the tale of the golem that include that motif (Yudel Rosenberg's in 1909, and Chayim Bloch's in 1920),[43] which both Idel and Scholem find innovative in this respect. The theme does come to predominate in these later versions and their literary descendants, such as Jerry Siegel and Joe Shuster's 1938 creation, Superman. Since the child/golem savior appears in the Frank dicta, it should be noted—without straying from the motif into that of the child genius or into non-Jewish sources—that the motif of a creature made in order to do some task for its makers, a somewhat rough and strong being, a hardy servant, is to be found from the earliest accounts to the latest in Jewish literature, and it emerges here.[44]

Mobs, too, are associated with the salvific or hardy golem. Frankenstein's creature, at whose residence a mob congregates, is the best-known example. Mobs form around Frank at a couple of points. In dictum 52 he mentions that while he was a youngster in Bucharest he took violent action against a military commander, and that the populace, led by the aga and his soldiers, a crowd of over 700 people, gathered where he was staying and threatened him. He rushed out, beat them all up, and drove them off.

The second mob leads me to the next golem feature. It is an account related to Frank's last domicile, his court at Under the Three Swiss, a mansion belonging to the princes of Isenburg in Offenbach to which he moved after staying some time in their abandoned palace. Alexander Kraushar writes that when Frank moved into these refurbished quarters in Offenbach, at the corner of Frankfurt and Canal streets, among other outbuildings there was to be found "an extensive laboratory, the object of extreme interest to the locals."[45]

Magus

> I am ashamed to confess that I too belonged among his admirers. I considered him to be not only a sage and the reincarnation of the soul of Shabbatai, *but also as one who could perform magic.*
>
> Jacob Golinski to the king of Poland,
> in a letter of denunciation received
> at the Chancellery, September 7, 1776[46]

Kraushar writes that "wonderworking played no small role in the system of Frank's deeds. The various acts of witchcraft carried out by the master and his daughter included feats of delusion concerning the existence of a certain herb that, when smeared on iron, would turn it to gold; and there was 'a certain thing' that would give eternal life, to come to which 'a maiden' was required."[47] (This statement introduces a series of magical and alchemical performances by Frank in chapter 6.) Kraushar also writes that "[Frank's] words and ideas bedazzled his listener's minds with a flood of Hebrew, Greek, and Chaldean words and borrowings from white magic."[48] I have touched on Frank's performative speech[49] and would like to turn now to some related matters concerning techniques associated with the science of creation, chrysopoeia, the *aurum potabile,* and herbalism.

In the following dictum Frank makes his sales pitch: "280. I bought 200 *ok.* of *neun brüder blut*.[50] Everybody laughed at me. I bought some cinnabar for it and, having mixed it, I made powder out of it. And when any sick person came, then I gave them that. Everyone was cured by it, and just whatever I did, God made successful in my hands[51] so that everybody called me Doctor. Only thereafter did I abandon that thing."

This medicinal herb is also known as dragon's blood, *Daemonorops draco* (several species), and was imported continuously in several varieties into Europe from the East since Pliny's times. The name "Nine Brothers Blood" seems to come from another of the plant's names, "Two Brothers Blood," which relates to a Hindu myth associated with the plant on the island of Socotra. The myth, related to the battle between Brahma (an elephant) and Shiva (a giant cobra), has it that the liquid is blood extracted from a dragon which has just sucked all the blood from an elephant that, falling upon the dragon, crushes it to death. Its use as a medicine did not decline until the mid-nineteenth century. The tree from which the sap is extracted grows on both the east and west coasts of Africa. The drops of its sap are red (and thick) so that the potion "with the cinnabar" is intended to recall, perhaps, Frank's punning associations of Edom and Hebrew *udom* (*adom,* red), themselves a feature of midrash, early and late. The change of number, from two brothers to nine, may have been influenced by the poem "The Death of Mother Yugovich," one of the two most famous Yugoslav epics. The poem tells of the war between the Serbs and the Turks in which Mother Yugovich's nine sons die in battle on the Kosovo Plain. Alternately, the change may have occurred via Frank's informant or because Frank himself inadvertently crossed into the structures of magic spells, in which nine is frequently employed as a magic number (by itself or as the beginning or end of a counting series using all single-digit numerals).

Cinnabar, the bright red ore of mercury sulfide also known as "Dragon's Blood," gets its name from a common pair of Indo (-European) roots that come together in a Persian word, *zinjafr,* which is the ancestor of "zangwill" and "ginger" and the name of the island off east Africa, south of Socotra, Zanzibar. In alchemy, cinnabar represents the hardened habits and terrestrial marriages of soul and spirit that must be broken by the process known as calcination (disintegration by heat). The dragon in flames is a symbol of that process. Frank is an inheritor of all this lore, one who often turns toward the dragon, the tree, and the serpent; and also, making use of barely known and powerful "medicines," one who seeks to shatter his followers' practices and psychologies and then to make them one.

He may have given up on that particular salver, as he says, but Frank never left off the trade. In the *Chronicle* we read this entry: "108. September 2, 1785 the Lord sent a letter to the Company with information about the drops of gold, that these were the cure for every illness." Another dictum, also quite late, is spoken during one of Frank's last periods of illness:

> 2123. Like those drops of gold water, one who wishes to drink must first become such that all the power of man be weakened and fall away from him, so that nearly no power stay in him, and the least stirring of the old completely give way before the new. At that time, that gold water helps and gives him new power and life.[52] And so I must take on myself all the pains and plagues and completely bear the troubles until thereafter the good God renews and rejuvenates my years like the eagle rejuvenates;[53] I will be powerful and healthy forever.

Frank was an herbalist and knew some chemistry in addition, as may be seen in the first of the dicta above (280) and in other dicta where herbs serve medicinal purposes as well. In some others, the herb is used as a topic in three different ways: the herb as the subject of tales Frank tells; in practical and symbolic herbalism; and as the mystic herb. Since he adds little to the folk-tales and legends of the first category, I will disregard it here and proceed to the second category.

Frank's acquaintance with herbal lore included ways of using herbs to cure and harm, as they are understood in the science of affinities, from which both naturopathy and homeopathy descend. In the following dictum he speaks of an herbal compound that has an affinity for precious metal. He employs an acid in the labor of unearthing the treasure and then sets out to poison his partners.

> 53. In Bucharest, during my youth, six peasants came to me showing me a drill, smeared with some special herbs, which had such a property that wherever it was put in the ground and whenever it would be touched by metal there, it would bring it to the surface immediately. They said, "We have located a treasure in a certain place. Come with us. Since you are strong, you will help us to get it out and we shall divide it with you." "Fine." I agreed to it. We went. Having come to a certain mountain we began to dig in it and carry the soil on our shoulders to the water. So, having come to the bottom of the hill with what we had dug up, we noticed an iron door barred with a fearful lock. We had with us *scheidwasser,*[54] files and all the other tools necessary for this and so we filed away, but still a piece remained. Since we were very tired I proposed to them that we leave the completion of our plan till the morning. So it was. We went home. Having arrived, I thought to myself, Why should I share this treasure with them? I will make use of a trick. I took two lead flasks, both exactly the same. The one in the right hand I filled with pure vodka, [in] the other, in the left, I mixed the vodka with poison, planning to keep the first one for myself and to treat them with the second.

The tale proclaims Frank's constant victory over his foes. (Later in the dictum we learn that a seer, an old woman, tells Frank that his plan is no good and that his partners intend to murder him with their plot before he can execute his own. The moral of this tale has to do with his craftiness and his fortune. The hag is in a line with his own grandmother, a powerful astrologer able to turn away witches, according to her grandson [dictum 44].)

At times, in the process of indoctrinating his listeners, Frank merely repeats what he has heard of the science: "389. There was a certain rich man in Bucharest. He was given a certain herb so that he became crazy. He played the violin extraordinarily. Having purchased a new violin, he broke it into pieces and glued it together so that its voice/sound[55] might be heard from far away." Here one finds the herbalism turned back to parable at the end of the dictum. (One notes that drops of "dragon's blood" are used in glazing the wood of violins.) For Frank, that which has been broken and mended is stronger than that which has not undergone the process of remaking. In another dictum the herbal world serves him as analog to the process of converting the bitter, that which is unpleasant and yet powerful, to a substance of enduring worth:

> 833. In Bucharest there are two sorts of herbs called *Tron;*[56] from it they make salad to eat. One is cheap, the other expensive; for one cup one must pay ½ ducat. Both are the same color. The only thing that distinguishes them is that the expensive one has a far better odor. Likewise, when salt is added to the common *Tron* and it is squeezed, it is crushed and [the flavor] gets lost; but the good one, even though it is salted and squeezed, its force comes out so that one cannot eat it on account of its sharpness. Only when they add olive oil to it and good vinegar is it consolidated and comes back to its first color, as if just picked from the garden; and it comes back to its first strength. Its effect is to very much increase the appetite for food.

Here, at the end, Frank touches on his own eating disorders, specifically his lack of appetite as he aged. In a final example of this genre, Frank sets out the symbol of the thread (from the kabbalistic background of the *ḥuta daqiqa,* the thread left extended from the uncreated world, stretching into the lower one) and hooks his followers to it through the one (himself) that has gotten hold of it: "497. There is a certain herb which has this attribute, that he who carries it will not be hurt by any weapon; and not only he himself, but also several thousands of those who hold on to him by a thread, then nothing will hurt any of them."

Elsewhere the dicta are concerned with truly magic herbs and herbs related to magic processes, not only elixirs but also universal symbols of Frank's theology.[57] He seeks to gain the magic herbs from his Big Brother, in whose kingdom grow plants of power:

> 414. . . . Likewise, I would ask for an herb from his country which would have the power to renew years. I would not want to do that so that men's rejuvenation would be to the 15th but only to the 20th year. Also I would ask him for a well which would have the power such that if a one-hundred year old man would bathe in it he would become rejuvenated.

115. I told you in Iwanie that there is a certain herb in the earth which cannot be pulled up except in silence. King Solomon said that also, "A time to speak, a time to be silent." [Eccl. 3:7]

Solomon, given his connections to magic in legend, was a natural stand-in for Frank and here is connected to a legendary magic herb. (There is more than one candidate for the "herb," but in this context I think the mandrake root is the likeliest.) One of this sort of herbal tale is particularly interesting, bringing in an important new element:

636. We must try hard and labor that we might come to the good thing as it is written, *Jugaiti umocoso* [!][58]—"work hard and you will find." Just so Jacob said, *Hoisi beiom acholani haurew boekerech [!] beloilo watida[r] [!] szenosi meenoi*[59]—"By day heat made me miserable and cold by night and sleep was taken from my eyes," just as we may see how a good gardener takes constant care of precious roses and waters them and sets them in the sun for warmth and then they grow lovely; but how when he does not give them attention they dry up. I said to you, I have planted a vineyard of you and wanted to work hard so you all might be of good seed; what could I do when you did not wish it? For even though you saw me do things which were strange and bitter in your eyes, you know that it must be bitter at first and thereafter, sweet; and that after the light, darkness comes, and then through the darkness may be seen light. We need to go to the darkness in which is light. *Same de chai gonus besame demause*[60]—the herb of life is hidden in that of death. But you went off by yourselves, [to] that darkness where there is no brightness.

Here we encounter the herb of (eternal) life which, as always in the dicta, is hidden within that of death, together with a citation (which I have been unable to find so far) and a familiar figure, the good gardener (Pol., *ogrodnik*). This figure is so familiar from Ḥasidic parabolic genres—including the tales of Rabbi Naḥman—that it is one of the lexical items selected by Joseph Perl for the dictionary of that dialect appended to his novel, *Megalleh Temirin*.[61] In dictum 78 we learn that there is in fact no death herb there; that it only seems so to people's eyes.

It seems that by applying the skills he possesses as spellbinder-*cum*-alchemist-*cum* herbalist, Frank can make his new people by talking the new self into existence before their eyes and just beyond their grasp. First he sets out the goal: they must become like him—in every way indistinguishable from him: "14. When still in Iwanie the Lord was saying, I shall beg the Holy Lord not to let me be pockmarked and you, if you will be good and entire, then we shall all sit together at a round table and you will all be completely similar to me in every way[62] so that it will be impossible to differentiate you even by a single hair. And whenever one of you goes out then [people] will always say that this one is the Holy Lord himself."[63] They must draw near to his own image in themselves so they may be fit to change. He will help: "2170. I wanted to make you pure clear gold; now you are only like copper. I must scrape you well so that I will at least be able to gild you. 700. Likewise concerning Daniel it stands[64] that God sent an angel to him, that, that was his own form.[65] And so here. First everyone must come to that form that fear will fall upon the animals, then a higher thing may dwell on him. They do not put precious things like gold on trashy things, but gold may be put on copper or brass." Here the image of plating is sufficiently well understood that it is able to serve as the vehicle for the more distant achievement.

They must learn the science of making gold: "1013. On the 10th of October [17][84],[66] the Lord, being dressed in white, said, If I saw of you at least that you had achieved the wisdom of making gold, then I would say nothing to you. And that is what I said to Rabbi Issohar and Mardocheusz. I will not believe of you that you are chosen, unless I see that wisdom from you. I tell you, if you had followed me in wholeness, then that wisdom would also not have been hidden from you, and you would have lacked no wisdom." He will test them. "566. First you ought to have tested [to learn] if you are able to make gold with your own understanding; thereafter you could have carried out other things." They will then become the incorruptible, eternally bright metal themselves, not just in part, but altogether—a golden golem. But this will not happen if they cannot or will not change: "2234. The 1st of December [17]83. I saw that I was refining silver and gold in a crucible and everything came out pure, only I threw out the dross from on top." If they can learn and change then it will be:

> 86. Every man is tied by a thread to his fortune, with only this difference, that one is [tied by] a simple, woolen thread; and another, whose fortune is great, is tied to it by a golden thread: he who is of pure gold from head to foot—not as it was with Nebuchadnezzar, where only the head was golden,[67] but wholly gold; that one stands before God, without him it is not possible to come to God himself.

> He has the power of just looking at a man [made] of earth and changing him to pure gold as he is himself, and those who will be worthy to come to this, that they may be transformed into [gold], such [people] will be able to come to this, that God himself will be able to look at them and give them eternal life. But in no way can God look at people [made of] earth since they are subject to decay; I wanted to lead you away from the name of Israel, since that name has no fortune,[68] and tie that golden thread to you, but you have entwined it with a woolen thread. N.B. In Częstochowa in a dream the Lord once saw himself completely gold, even his hair, nails *etc.* were pure gold.

The God that Frank mentions here is not simply the good God that has never been in this world, but an amalgam of those qualities present and familiar—including the very texts that tell of his own nature—to his listeners and those potentially there. I think that in general it is better to consider Frank as another in the line of those who sought the union of contraries[69] than to set him altogether in the camp of the "Gnostics."

In any case, it is, as with other golem-making, with the power over creation and destruction that Frank demonstrates, through his qualifications as magus and speaker-out, *Ausspracher,* that he gets the golem made. He does this against the background of a number of different performers. These include the tale-tellers in the Turkish tea houses, of course, but it is the other *spielers,* the *darshanim* and the other Jewish preachers that are his counters. He, an anti-rabbi, makes an anti-golem. But, if I may say so, he knows much more about himself and what he is doing than he needs to know. Twice he brings us this stunning image of self-making, self-seeing: "2212. The 20th of October, 1785: I saw as if I had on my hand a gold ring. It fell from my hand on a mirror and broke it into small pieces. Then I turned the mirror over on the other side. It also shone, and a ring also fell from my hand and broke it. The Lord interpreted: 'My assistance hastens to come.'"

I have sought to demonstrate that Frank, using traditional materia, made a golem, that is, he made new identities up for himself and his followers. Conversely, I hope that what has appeared is something unsaid so far about the whole matter of golem-making: the objective—since no golem is ever really made—of the exercise may be, as Idel has proposed, making the golem-maker, demonstrating or gaining the power of creation, becoming godlike. In the process all the characters of the relationship change: Heaven is brought to earth. But more to the point, other figures, powerful politicians dominating the society and applying its norms, are uncreated, the rabbinic structure among them, the secular authorities among them. The golem rescues the golem makers (the teller and the listeners). And even though the crowd is gathered outside the laboratory, outside the palace, in faith and hope, and even though they call for the creature's blood and that of its maker—and the 700 actually win this battle—in Prague and in Offenbach and in Jerusalem, the creature and some of those the creature has created remains free, to be made again, and the struggle to be fought again has been advanced in the society. The muscle Jew of Max Nordau, for example, and the *metei midbar* of Ḥayyim Naḥman Bialik join Frank's golem among the lines from Shazar's visit to Offenbach as he looks upon their military exercises. He is attendant to the words of the gatekeeper who re-creates for him the "'campaigns' that once took place here, fought out by the children of kabbalists and end-reckoners, the secret-sharers in their chambers, whose hands have now learned war; shield and spear, horse and rider become their holy vessels."

Notes

1. This name, Frank, had been attached to him as an appellative—meaning either a Jew of the Ottoman Empire (in Europe) or a European Jew (in Turkey)—and he took it as his last name when he converted to Christianity.
2. The major works on the life of Frank and the history of the movement are H. Skimborowicz, *The Life, Death and Teachings of Jacob Joseph Frank* (Polish) (Warsaw, 1866), a journalistic account (from the popular *Tygodnik Illustrowany*); H. Graetz, *Frank and the Frankists: The History of a Sect* (German) (Breslau, 1868), based on Rabbi Y. Emden's polemic materials, particularly those in *Torat ha-Kana'ut* and *Sefer Shimush;* Z. L. Sulima, *The History of Frank and the Frankists* (Polish) (Cracow, 1893), which, though quite inaccurate, served S. Dubnow as his principal source for his article in the *Jewish Encyclopedia;* A. Kraushar, *Frank and the Polish Frankists, 2 vols.* (Polish) (Cracow, 1895), vol. 1 appearing in Hebrew, trans. N. Sokolow (Warsaw, 1895), and recently in English in a poor translation, revised and with a cranky introduction by Herbert Levy, as *Jacob Frank: The End to the Shabbatean Heresy* (Lanham, Md.: University Press of America, 2001); M. Balaban, *Towards a History of the Frankist Movement* (Hebrew) (Tel Aviv: Devir, 1934); P. Arnsberg, *From Podolia to Offenbach: The Jewish Holy Army of Jacob Frank* (German) (Offenbach: Offenbacher Geschichstverein, 1965); G. Scholem, s.v. "Frank, Jacob, and the Frankists," in *Encyclopaedia Judaica* (1972); A. Mandel, *The Militant Messiah* (Atlantic Highlands, N.J.: Humanities Press, 1979); J. Doktór, *Jacob Frank and His Doctrine against the Background of the Crisis of Traditional Polish Jewry of the Eighteenth Century* (Polish) (Warsaw, 1991). Two edited volumes of essays—related to conferences held in Cracow and Jerusalem—some of which are

devoted to Frankism, have appeared: M. Galas, ed., *Jewish Spirituality in Poland* (Polish) (Cracow, 2000), and R. Elior, ed., *The Sabbatian Movement and Its Aftermath: Messianism, Sabbatianism and Frankism,* Jerusalem Studies in Jewish Thought 17 (Hebrew and English) (Jerusalem: Hebrew University, 2001). The annual *Polin* 15 (2002), ed. Antony Polonsky, is devoted to Jewish religious life in Poland, 1500–1800, and contains several contributions on the topic of Frankism. This is not the place for a detailed assessment of the large literature on Frankism, including the many essays and book chapters that touch on it; it is of very mixed quality. Happily, several Polish scholars, including Galas, Pawel Maciejko, and Doktór, have entered the lists. Klaus S. Davidowicz has published a brief introductory work for German readers, *Jakob Frank, der Messias aus dem Ghetto* (Frankfurt am Main: Peter Lang, 1998). Pawel Maciejko's doctoral dissertation at Oxford, "The Development of the Religious Teachings of Jacob Frank" (2004), is groundbreaking in terms of the new material he has investigated, and attentive not only to the history itself, but to its reception. Editions: Jan Doktór has recently published the material from the Lublin manuscript as *Various Notes, Events, Deeds and Anecdotes of the Lord* (Warsaw, 1996); and the material from the Biblioteka Jagiellonska, as *The Book [sic!] of the Words of the Lord* (Warsaw, 1997), with an introduction and notes. In addition to a number of essays, book chapters, encyclopedia entries, and so forth by the present author, the edited and annotated English translation of the dicta (from the manuscripts) is available at www.languages.utah.edu/kabbalah. See the *Errata* to Doktór's editions therein.

3. A full treatment of the concept of *Das* in the dicta is beyond the scope of this essay. It ceases to appear in the manuscripts at dictum 1200, having been a major topic in some thirty dicta. Frank clearly describes the ambiguity in 227 ("Das is two words") (where I have a long note about its deployment); it is "among the sefirot" in 236; "knowledge" in 256. Entering into its secret life one gains new clothes and a new name (373); women—the Sisters of Frank's inner circle—and especially one woman, play important parts in it (434), as do children (961) and, in a second, later entry into *Das* all the Jews together with the Brothers and Sisters who have failed to achieve its level previously make it in (1199). Frank makes adjustments in its meaning as "[secret] religion" and in its relationship to conversion to Christianity, particularly in 319, 516, 711, and 624 that no doubt relate to concerns among the inner circle.
4. This paper uses gender neutral language in regard to the creature Frank proposes, though his attention to "a new sort of female" is infrequent (only in dictum 434 of the materials discussed here is it brought out in so many words). Nevertheless, the Sabbatean tradition sounds a note of redemption for women from the time of Shabbatai Zvi himself through that of Frank. See 54f. and 58 of *Ṣippiyot Shav' shel ha-Yehudim Kefi she-Nitgalu bi-Demuto shel Shabbetai Ṣevi* (the Hebrew translation [Jerusalem: Merkaz Dinur, 1998] of Thomas Coenen, *Ydele verwachtinge der Joden* [Amsterdam: Joannes van den Bergh, 1669]).
5. Such an approach has underpinned the rich contributions made in the work of Avraham Elqayam on Nathan's writings from the time of his doctoral thesis, "The Mystery of Faith in the Writings of Nathan of Gaza" (Hebrew University, 1993), to the present.
6. Y. Dan, *Ha-Sippur ha-Ḥasidi* (Jerusalem: Keter, 1975), 36ff., esp. 38.
7. Cf. Matt Goldish's chapter in this volume.

8. In M. Idel, *Golem* (Albany: State University of New York Press, 1990), 5 and nn. 10–12.
9. Ibid., 4.
10. D. Frischmann, "*Ha-Golem*" (Warsaw, 1909), in *Ba-Midbar* (Berlin, 1923); H. N. Bialik, "Metei Midbar" (1902).
11. Cf. Mario Vargas-Llosa's utterly self-destructive arch-dialectician in *The Real Life of Alejandro Mayta* (Barcelona, 1984; English, New York: Farrar, Straus, and Giroux, 1986).
12. Frank never uses the Hebrew word *golem*. His use of Hebrew was restricted to citations from Hebrew literature. The golem-making based on the *Sefer Yeṣirah* and associated with letter combinations in Hebrew was not in his interest. Nor does the Yiddish *goylem* appear. Given the word's long tradition, he would not so call the new being he creates of himself. Moreover, the Sabbatean usage—perhaps even that of the Dönme—connects the term to a highly abstract concept, the lower, unconstructed *tehiru*. (Cf. Gershom Scholem, *Sabbatai Ṣevi* [Princeton: Princeton University Press, 1973], 301, 305, 109, 311; H. Wirszubski, "The Shabbatean Theology of Nathan of Gaza," *Kneset* 8 [1943–44]: 217, n. 4.) It is worth noting nevertheless that one of the poems in *Sefer Shirot ve-Tishbaḥot shel ha-Shabta'im*, ed. M. Attias and G. Scholem (Tel Aviv, 1947), 72, speaks of this realm as "his golem" (*su golem*), the unformed body of the messiah Shabbatai Zvi. Another poem (93) says that the golem is that of Amira, one of the by-names of Zvi.
13. Idel, *Golem*, 89f. and nn. ad loc.
14. The translations of the dicta from A. Kraushar, *Frank i frankiści polsci*, 2 vols. (Cracow, 1895), and from the other Polish manuscripts (Cracow: Biblioteka Jagiellońska), 6968, 6969/1/2/3; Lublin Biblioteka Publiczna (2118), are mine. The few presented here constitute about one-fifth of those where the word *prostak* occurs in those manuscripts, about one-quarter of those on the topic of "child," and about one-fifth of those mentioning gold or herbal materia. (With one or two exceptions—each noted—none of the dicta as presented in Kraushar—including the recent translation edited by H. Levy [*Jacob Frank*]—or in the translations in the Scholem archives are reliable or employed.) It is difficult to say whether dicta that are sequential are related to a common theme, or to the variations on the theme explored here (*prostak*, child, magus), or whether they were uttered at the same or sequential sessions. Further, it matters little whether Frank actually did all the things he said he did in the dicta. The telling of the tales was certainly ritualized behavior, and acts described in them—such as the exchange of feces for the spices in the *besamim* container used in the *havdalah* ritual in dictum 295—seem to have been both ritually done and ritually related, and even to have been trans-cultural. Cf. the same substitution tale told by Christian children with the censer as its focus.
15. I have employed the same symbols that appear in the manuscripts to set off editorial interpolations, often notes concerning Frank's performance, and retained all other peculiarities of the sigla used in the manuscripts.
16. Mishnah Avot 5:7 defines the golem as the opposite of the *ḥakham*. The distinctions pertain to the scholarly society. The text and commentaries distinguish the golem as a simpleton, unrestrained in speaking to/against a sage, interruptive, one who says what he wants to say without regard to whether it is accepted law, refuses to

admit his ignorance and is always right; as opposed to "the *ḥakham* who does not speak before one who is more *ḥakham* than he or older than he." See S. Hurwitz, ed. *Maḥzor Vitry,* 2:541 (Nuremberg, 1923).

17. The word *Du,* Yiddish for "you," is less likely than the Aramaic *da'* = "this/that." My preferred reading would include both these possibilities—Frank frequently makes both intra- and inter-language puns. Thus, "You are Jacob, the one spoken of." Jacob's blessing over Joseph's sons, though not referenced by the words themselves, is recalled in Frank's raising his hands (Gen. 48:14).
18. *Księga [sic!] Słów Pańskich,* 2 vols. (Warsaw: Semper, 1997).
19. See his treatment of dictum 525, discussed below, in *Teksty Drugy* 6, 36 (1995).
20. H. Lenowitz, "The Three-fold Tales of Jacob Frank," Proceedings of the Ninth World Congress of Jewish Studies, C. 117–24; A. Sela, "A Study in One Three-fold Tale of Jacob Frank" (Master's thesis, University of Utah, 1988).
21. Shmeruk was probably referring to his pleasure at finding—against some critics—evidence of printed *haggadot,* in dictum 525. See his discussion in n. 15, and the text of the dictum below.
22. The child, the *yanuqa,* is likewise a potent figuration of mystic apprehension in Zohar 3:186a ff. The work that I have found most helpful in learning about medieval/early modern childhood is C. Heywood, *A History of Childhood* (Malden, Mass.: Polity Press, 2001). I. G. Marcus, *Rituals of Childhood* (New Haven: Yale University Press, 1996), though it deals with the imagination of childhood in one Jewish society, has only occasional and inverse applicability to Frank's childhood in his societies.
23. A. Debus, *Man and Nature in the Renaissance* (Cambridge: Cambridge University Press, 1978), provides an introduction and overview of this symbol-structure, esp. 12f., 26f. J. Godwin, *Robert Fludd* (Boulder, Colo.: Shambhala Press, 1979), adds interesting material and illustrations.
24. S. Z. Leiman and S. Schwarzfuchs, "New Evidence on the Emden-Eibeschuetz Controversy: The Amulets from Metz," *Revue des études juives* 165 (2006): 229–49.
25. Job 19:26.
26. Cf. Genesis 32:31. Other dicta on this include 112, 205, 153 (with a characteristic self-contradiction), 338, 369; 517:

> I went on one road and you on another road, as it clearly stands, *Zadikim ielkhu bo* [Hos. 14:10]—The righteous will walk upon it. How could you say that man has a soul on this cursed earth? 578. No man in the world has yet had a soul, not even the First or the Second. Not any of the Patriarchs, the pillars of the world, have had souls, for a soul cannot come from any other than God himself; and from one other place. At that time the worlds will be stable and he who possesses a soul then will also be eternally stable and will be able to see from one end of the world to the other and more and more and higher, as was said above. For at the creation of Adam three things were deficient and where there is deficiency there can be no stability. And that is precisely what is written, *Eiszer boro Elohim laisos* [Gen. 2:4]—God created so that he could do, which means, in order that thereafter he might make man without a deficiency. We can see it clearly, When children ask their father for bread, does he give them a stone instead? [Luke 11:11]. [Dr. Pawel Maciejko has pointed out to me that there is substantial evidence that Frank possessed Yiddish translations of the New Testament.] Just

so, you see that there exist honest, God-fearing men, and we see that even though they ask God for bread yet they get none. [Ps. 36:25 and the Grace after Meals.] Where is the love of the father for his own children? And further, how is it proper for a father to kill his children? From which it follows that the true God himself has had no part in the present creation. Therefore, all the vessels have been broken until now, for he who created them broke them himself so that they might come out purer and finer, and that, that is what stands, *Wehanfilim hoiu be-orez*—There were *Nephilim* in the world. And they were already called *Nephilim* because of their falling and being cast down from greatness. Therefore it cannot be that there has been a soul in such a coarse and lowly flesh as is now. I wanted to lead you to a certain place where you could first bathe and cleanse yourself so that you might have the strength to receive a soul. And now you cannot reach that degree, so that you might be worthy to come to Esau.

27. In general, Frank does not picture his relations with either his father or mother as anything other than fond ones. On the mystic plane, both parents present good and evil aspects, though the figure of the mother naturally lends itself to identification with his image of the Shekhinah/the Maiden. Both seem to have exercised authority and dealt out punishments as well as rewards and gifts. In several dicta he does tell about being separated from his father from necessity, and living with his mother as late as the age of thirteen. As a child he shows himself leading an independent life, associating himself more closely with youth gangs, accessing their codes and taking the lead role. He seems to have begun working—rather than following traditional Jewish educational patterns—shortly afterward, though not as an apprentice.
28. See H. Schreckenberg, *The Jews in Christian Art* (New York: Continuum, 1996), 21f. and the references there.
29. Pol., *Pascha.* Most Jewish terms are translated to their Christian cognates in the dicta.
30. In Hebrew, *leil shimurim.*
31. I.e., matzah.
32. All the matters mentioned appear in the *haggadah.* Oddly, Frank is not acting in an entirely improper fashion here, since children and others are encouraged to ask questions in order that the tale of the exodus from Egypt may be elaborated.
33. Daniel 4:20.
34. Manuscript 6968 adds the Hebrew, *Hissnaari meofor,* from Isa. 52:2.
35. The "little man" here has wandered a truly long way even from his previous appearance in Sabbatean literature, in Nathan of Gaza's "Vision of Rabbi Avraham," not to say from his first appearance in BT Mo'ed Katan 18a (text and notes in Scholem, *Shabbatai Ṣevi,* 224 ff.)
36. This fragment is preserved only in Kraushar, *Jacob Frank and the Polish Frankists,* 2:213.
37. P. Ariés, *Centuries of Childhood* (New York: Knopf, 1962), whatever its faults, was the first work to present the art phenomenon of the child depicted as a man on a smaller scale as evidence for the early, pervasive social construction of the child itself in Europe.
38. Scholem, *Sabbatai Ṣevi,* 145.
39. See note 11, above. The clothing motif in Frank's tale may itself invert the same motif in the hymns where Shabbatai's clothing—left upon the beach?—seems to have been stolen.

40. A name for the *sefirah Keter,* "hidden away." See, e.g., Zohar 365b.
41. See *Sabbatian Hymns,* 136n1, citing JTS MS Adler 492, trans. M. Attias.
42. The theme continues to be of interest to biblical scholars but the basic material is gathered already in T. Gaster, *Myth, Legend and Custom in the Old Testament* (New York: Harper and Row, 1969), 2:575f., 787f.
43. Yudl Rosenberg, *Nifla'ot ha-Maharal 'im ha-Golem* (Lvov, 1909); Chayim Bloch, *Der Prager Golem* (Berlin, 1920), in English as *The Golem* (Vienna: n.p., 1925).
44. See Gershom Scholem, *Kabbalah* (New York: Quadrangle, 1974), 351–54.
45. Kraushar, *Jacob Frank and the Polish Frankists,* 2:103.
46. Ibid., 2:24 (emphasis added). Golinski was rabbi of Gliniany and among those baptized on September 24, 1759.
47. Ibid., 2:72.
48. Ibid., 2:183f.
49. Above, and in a paper, "*Mischsprache* as a Feature of Late Shabbatean Literature," given at the Sixth International Congress of Misgav Yerushalayim on the Languages and Literature of the Jews of Sefarad and the Orient, June 2000 (now included in my essay "Leaving Turkey: The Dönme Comes to Poland" in *Kabbalah: Journal for the Study of Jewish Mystical Texts and History* 8 [2003]: 65–113). It is possible that alchemical images and tales were among the sources Frank drew on for his own stories. It is no easy matter, however, to determine from which direction they might be coming to him. The rose-among-thorns image in dicta 340 and others, for example, may begin with the biblical passage (Song 2:2); but it has a long history of interpretation and reinterpretation. Zohar 1:1a could be a more apposite source. Yet given Frank's involvement with Freemasonry, could the engraving of a rose encircled by thorns, for example, and the motto *difficilia quae pulchra* in an illustration from, perhaps, D. de Planis Campy, *L'ouverture de l'escolle* (Paris, 1633), itself descended from the Song and its tradition, have been a further or more immediate stimulus? The question may bear directly on the elaborate tale of two princes that is dictum 2186, when considering Beroalde de Verville's *Voyage des princes fortunez* (Paris, 1610) and in its background the *Hypnerotomachia Poliphilii.*
50. I would like to thank an anonymous reader for the stimulus to learn more about this plant, and my colleagues Catherine and Ken Rockwell for getting me started with the entry that identifies this plant's two names in H. L. Gerth van Wijk, *Dictionary of Plant Names* (The Hague: Martinus Nijhoff, 1909–16), 2:1049. See G. Lyons, "In Search of Dragons," *Cactus and Succulent Journal* 44 (1974): 267–82.
51. Genesis 39:6, of Joseph.
52. Kraushar, *Jacob Frank and the Polish Frankists,* 2:84.
53. Psalms 103:5.
54. German, an acid.
55. Polish *gtos* (as here) means "voice," and "sound" less commonly (cf. Heb., *qol*); *dźwięk,* "sound." The theme of the voice/sound (of Jacob) causing other voices/sounds to join with it and bringing about change in the upper *sefirot* can be found in several passages in the Zohar; 3:38b and 99b–100a associate this verse (Gen. 27:22, "the voice is the voice of Jacob, but the hands are the hands of Esau") with the sounding of the shofar on Rosh Hashanah, for example. See also Zohar 1:74a, 151a, 246b. The general principle of the Zohar (3:31b) is that "through an action below an action above is aroused."

56. Perhaps basil.
57. See the magic deed in the following *Chronicle* entry, replete with mystery and the uniting of the broken world.

    99. In 1780 the Lord did the following deed.

    A secret act

    The Lord went to the woods to the Paradise and there the day before he gave an order to split down the middle a little oak that was growing facing the sun and whose branches were bent towards the sun. The next day he himself went out towards the dawn and ordered Franciszek Szymanowski and Dębowski to spread out that little oak and the Lord trod upon it three times with his right foot, always coming towards it from the right side. The Lord did this deed three times. The first time was the 26th of June; the 2nd, the 7th of March and the 21st 1780. The Lord said that that act was to repair the *bruch* [break, disaster]. Thereafter the Lord ordered to take a rock in the left hand, and after lighting a fire, to throw the rock at the roots of the little oak and entwine the little oak with twigs and to go away from there. This act he repeated, every time with a young oak.

58. Cf. Jeremiah 45:3, in BT Megillah 6b.
59. Cf. Genesis 31:40. The reading of the Hebrew as *va-tidar* for *va-tidad* suggests an error in the transcription of the Hebrew script rather than an oral/aural one.
60. I have not located the source of this saying; cf. BT Shabbat 88b and BT Yoma 72b.
61. Joseph Perl, *Megalleh Temirin* (Vienna, 1819).
62. Manuscript 6968 lacks *we wszystkim* (in every way).
63. The first occurrence of "the Holy Lord" here might refer to the "unknown Good God"; the second, to Frank himself (cf. "the Lord"), who was in fact heavily pockmarked.
64. Manuscript 6968 + Heb: *Eloho szolach malucho.*
65. Daniel 6:23; cf. dictum 324.
66. Written [17]94, clearly an error.
67. Daniel 2:38.
68. BT Shabbat 156a. Frank, on the basis of a rabbinic statement (which he takes to mean the virtual reverse of what was intended; see the talmudic passage), explains that the struggle that resulted in the change of Jacob's name in the Bible led to the captivity of Israel in Egypt.
69. As in dictum 1402 (only in Kraushar, *Jacob Frank and the Polish Frankists,* 2:88), where he describes the union of the Brothers and Sisters of the Company with their parallels in the world of the Big Brother as the "uniting of fire and water."

14

When a Rabbi Is Accused of Heresy

The Stance of Rabbi Jacob Joshua Falk in the Emden-Eibeschuetz Controversy

SID Z. LEIMAN

Introduction

Rabbi Jacob Joshua Falk was born in Cracow in 1681. A distinguished talmudist of noble lineage, he succeeded Rabbi Zvi Hirsch Ashkenazi (d. 1718) as Chief Rabbi of Lwow in 1718. Large numbers of students were attracted to his *yeshivah* in Lvov, and later to his *yeshivot* in Berlin, Metz, and Frankfurt. In 1739 at Amsterdam, the first volume of his magnum opus, *Penei Yehoshu'a,* appeared in print. A running commentary on the Talmud—largely defending Rashi against the strictures of Tosafot—it is studied to this day in all *yeshivot.* Falk served as Chief Rabbi of Frankfurt from 1742 until 1753. He was seventy years old—and serving in Frankfurt—when the Emden-Eibeschuetz controversy erupted in 1751. At the time, he was generally recognized as the *zeqan ha-dor,* the senior and most authoritative rabbi in an age of rabbinic titans.[1]

Strangely, Falk's stance in the Emden-Eibeschuetz controversy has been largely neglected by modern scholarship. Except for the brief comments by Graetz,[2] Kahana,[3] and others[4] in their general accounts of the controversy, no book, monograph, or scholarly study has focused specifically on Falk's role. Some key issues that need to be addressed include the following: What were Falk's objectives in his struggle against Eibeschuetz? What means did he employ in order to obtain those objectives? Specifically, what strategies did Falk employ in waging the war against Eibeschuetz? Did Falk succeed? These issues—at least in the published literature—have never been raised, much less resolved. Indeed, the very framing of the questions is intended to set an agenda for scholars to pursue. Precisely because this is a pioneering investigation, whatever is said here is provisional at best. Moreover, due to constraints of time and space, the scope of this investigation is necessarily narrow and limited. Should others be stimulated to broaden and deepen the investigation, *ve-hayah zeh sekhari* (let that be my reward).

The Controversy

The Emden-Eibeschuetz controversy erupted on Thursday, February 4, 1751, when Rabbi Jacob Emden (d. 1776) announced at a private synagogue service held in his home that an amulet ascribed to the Chief Rabbi could only have been written by a secret believer in the false messiah, Shabbatai Zvi. The Chief Rabbi, Rabbi Jonathan Eibeschuetz (d. 1764), was a renowned talmudist who had served with distinction as rabbi, teacher, and preacher in Prague and Metz, prior to his assuming the post of Chief Rabbi of the triple community of Altona, Hamburg, and Wandsbeck in September 1750. Emden's announcement initiated what was perhaps the most explosive rabbinic controversy in the last three hundred years. The controversy would involve not only the leading rabbis of the eighteenth century, such as Ezekiel Landau (d. 1793) of Prague[5] and Elijah b. Solomon (d. 1797) of Vilna,[6] but also Christian scholars and foreign governments.[7] The controversy was widely reported in the newspaper and periodical literature of the time,[8] and continues to be a rich topic of investigation for modern scholarship.

Eibeschuetz, a distinguished kabbalist, wrote amulets to help ward off evil spirits, to protect those in danger—especially pregnant women—and to heal the sick. Indeed, as early as 1743, while serving as Chief Rabbi of Metz, he was widely known as a *ba'al shem*, a master of the secrets of the Kabbalah who wrote amulets.[9] In Metz itself, and throughout the surrounding Jewish communities of Alsace-Lorraine, Eibeschuetz wrote amulets. When he left Metz in 1750 and made his way northward through the Rhineland, he wrote and sold amulets in the various Jewish communities on the Rhine, including several in Frankfurt. Upon his arrival in Altona (which then belonged to the Kingdom of Denmark) and Hamburg (a free city in Germany) in September 1750, he had barely unpacked his bags when rumors were rife about the new Chief Rabbi's Sabbatean leanings. Apparently, some of the amulets written in Frankfurt were shown to leading rabbinic scholars in that city, who immediately designated them as Sabbatean in character. Letters from Frankfurt were sent to private individuals in Altona and Hamburg, warning them about the heretical leanings of their new Chief Rabbi. When these rumors came to Eibeschuetz's attention, he dismissed the charges as a recycling by his enemies of similar charges leveled against him in the 1720s. Eibeschuetz claimed they were false charges then, as they were now. Nonetheless, several members of the triple community were now alerted to a potential problem, and they decided to monitor Eibeschuetz's amulets to the extent possible. It did not take long before an amulet written by Eibeschuetz in Hamburg fell into their hands. It appeared to them to be Sabbatean in character, and they eventually consulted with Emden, who concurred. The Chief Rabbi denied that he wrote the amulet in question. The triple community was once again rife with rumors. Matters came to a head when Emden was summoned to a meeting with representatives of the Jewish council of the triple community in Altona on Tuesday, February 2, 1751. A second meeting was scheduled for the following Thursday; it never convened. Emden realized at the first meeting that he was going up against a stacked deck of cards; the triple community was intent on vindicating its Chief Rabbi. And so Emden decided to go public on that fateful Thursday morning. The scheduled meeting, of course, was canceled. The next day, Friday, the Jewish council officially disbanded the private synagogue service that had convened in Emden's home for almost twenty years. Shortly thereafter, Emden was placed under house arrest; all social contact with Emden was banned. He was notified that within six months he would have to leave Altona permanently. That very Friday, Emden's last day as a free citizen in Altona, he managed to send out letters to several of the leading rabbinic authorities of the time. Each received a synopsis of the events that had occurred—similar to the summary presented here—and an urgent plea for aid. One of the letters was addressed to Rabbi Jacob Joshua Falk of Frankfurt.[10]

Options in the Controversy

What to do about Eibeschuetz was the prime issue for most of European Jewry in 1751. For many, the issue was one of establishing Eibeschuetz's innocence or guilt. Evidence needed to be gathered, examined, and weighed by a rabbinic court, after which a decision would be rendered and the matter laid to rest once and for all. This was not the case for Emden, Landau, Falk, and others. Their minds were made up early in the fray: Eibeschuetz was guilty.[11] The key issue for them was establishing a strategy. How do you bring Eibeschuetz down without destroying rabbinic Judaism in the process? How do you depose, arguably, the leading talmudist (certainly so in number of students) of the eighteenth century—who will surely turn to his disciples in a moment of need—without risking a civil war whose devastating effects may in fact lead to victory for the forces of Sabbateanism? A variety of options needed to be considered, none of them particularly pleasant.

Option A: The Emden Approach

Emden opted for confrontation with Eibeschuetz from the beginning to the end of the controversy. His single-minded goal was to "defrock" and depose Eibeschuetz. For Emden, Eibeschuetz—even if he repented—could never again serve as rabbi, *darshan* (preacher), or *rosh yeshivah* (head of a talmudic academy).[12] A rabbi who is simultaneously a confirmed Sabbatean can never again be trusted to hold public office. The means toward attaining the goal was sustained and unrelenting frontal attack. The scandal was to be kept in the headlines at all times. Any means could be used to bring Eibeschuetz down: yellow journalism, slander, protests, informing the governmental authorities, and, of course, the wielding of rabbinic power. Emden placed Eibeschuetz under the ban, as well as Eibeschuetz's family and his disciples. Emden accused any rabbi who wrote a letter in defense of Eibeschuetz of either being a Sabbatean or an acceptor of bribes.

Emden, however, was his own worst enemy. He kept tripping over himself. Among his more egregious claims: Eibeschuetz was an *am ha-areṣ* (ignoramus), and he, Emden, was a better public preacher than Eibeschuetz.[13] These and other ridiculous claims led to total loss of credibility on Emden's part. They did more to shore up Eibeschuetz's innocence than anything Eibeschuetz could have claimed on his own behalf. Emden was a loose cannon, to say the least. Sober-minded rabbis distanced themselves from him.

Option B: The Landau Approach

Two rabbis, Ezekiel Landau and Mordecai of Duesseldorf (d. 1770), foresaw much that would transpire.[14] Early on, they warned the anti-Eibeschuetz forces that any frontal attack on Eibeschuetz was doomed to failure. They stressed that Eibeschuetz was articulate, bold, and influential in governmental circles. He could not be defeated. He could, however, be neutralized. The only strategy worth pursuing was a strategy of neutralization. All rabbis in Europe would be asked to sign a general ban against any and all forms of Sabbatean belief. Eibeschuetz, as one of the leading *gedolei ha-dor* (rabbinic authorities of the era), would be among the first rabbis asked to sign the ban. Given the present set of circumstances, this would be an offer he could not refuse. Indeed, given the accusations that had been leveled against him, even more could be demanded of him. He must publicly denounce belief in Shabbatai Zvi, and in any and all Sabbatean writings, especially those Sabbatean writings ascribed to Eibeschuetz himself. He must agree to withdraw all his amulets from circulation, and to never write amulets again. The rationale here was simple: once Eibeschuetz was cleansed of Sabbatean connections, he would be identified publicly only by his Torah teaching, which was great indeed. What he really believed in the deep recesses of his heart was a matter between Eibeschuetz and God. This was a brilliant approach; it also provided Eibeschuetz with a graceful exit from the controversy. It failed only because Emden and, more importantly, Falk were relentless in their pursuit of Eibeschuetz.

Option C: The Falk Approach

The most distinguished member of the anti-Eibeschuetz forces was neither Emden, nor Rabbi Samuel Hilman Heilprin (d. 1765) of Metz,[15] nor Rabbi Aryeh Leib (d. 1755) of Amsterdam.[16] While they led the battle against Eibeschuetz in its opening stages, they eventually gave way to Rabbi Jacob Joshua Falk of Frankfurt. From April 1751 until his death on January 16, 1756, Falk directed the campaign against Eibeschuetz. A clever strategist, he began by forging a coalition of German rabbis. The goal was to isolate Eibeschuetz, and then force him to appear before a Jewish court of law. There, he would either be vindicated or found guilty. If found guilty, he could be rehabilitated—meaning that Eibeschuetz would be given the opportunity to repent, to express genuine regret for the sins of his past, and to accept upon himself the penance prescribed by the court. If rehabilitated, he could serve once more as Chief Rabbi, *darshan,* and *rosh yeshivah.* If defrocked, he could never again serve as rabbi, preacher, or teacher anywhere in the world.

Falk's approach was a principled one. It was predicated on the principle that there can be no duplicity in a *gadol be-yisrael* (rabbinic authority). A *gadol be-yisrael* who is also a secret Sabbatean must either be rehabilitated or defrocked. Falk, in effect, distanced himself from the Emden approach, which offered no possibility of rehabilitation on the part of Eibeschuetz, even as he distanced himself from the Landau approach, which—by focusing on outer form rather than inner conviction—did not require genuine repentance on the part of Eibeschuetz.

Eibeschuetz, for his part, rejected the Emden approach out of hand. He welcomed the Landau approach and implemented all its stipulations with alacrity.[17] With regard to the Falk approach, he apparently was in no hurry to make a court appearance. Instead, he chose to engage in a battle of wits against Falk and his rabbinic coalition.

The rationale for Falk's position was poignantly argued in a broadside published by Rabbi Aryeh Leib of Amsterdam in 1752.[18] It was a public response to a group of rabbis who defended Eibeschuetz by explaining away the amulets, and who expressed concern for the *kevod ha-torah* (honor accorded to the Torah learning) of rabbinic scholars and the *ḥillul ha-Shem* (profaning of the name of God) if the controversy would be allowed to continue. Every word of the broadside against Eibeschuetz's defenders was approved by Falk, who as commander-in-chief of the anti-Eibeschuetz forces made a point of editing every broadside before it could be published.[19]

The text reads in part:

ידעתי גם ידעתי שחכמים גדולים כמותם יודעים האמת לאמתו, אך שהם רוצים בתקנתו, אמנם תקנתם גופו והדרתו ולא תקנתם רוחו ונשמתו, לא כן אנחנו, אנו רוצים בתקנתו תיקון נפשו ונשמתו, וישב על כסא כבודו וגדולתו, אך בשובו מרשעתו ויודה על האמת ויקבל עליו שלא ישוב לכסלתו, ואז טוב לו אחרית דבר מראשיתו, וזה הוא כל מגמת כונתינו להעמיד הדת על תלה ולהיות לכלנו שפה אחת ודברים אחדים, לייחד ולקדש שמו הגדול הנערץ בקדושתו .... סוף דבר חכמים ונבונים כמותם יודעים ומבינים תוכן הענינים, אך שרוצים לחוס עליו, ומלבשיט הענין שעושים לשם שמים שלא להרבות מחלוקת בישראל ומפני חלול השם.

I know well that great scholars such as yourselves know the truth of the matter. You even want to rehabilitate him. But you have rehabilitated his body and outer appearance, not his spirit and soul. Not so for us. We want to rehabilitate his spirit and soul. Let him retain his seat of glory and greatness, but only if he turns from his wickedness, admits the truth, and resolves never to return to his folly. Then the end of the matter will be better for him than its beginning. This is our only concern: to reestablish our Faith on its mound, so that we all share one language and the same words, in order to unify and

> sanctify the Great Name of the One held in awe due to His sanctity. . . . The bottom line: scholars such as yourselves know full well the essence of the matter. But you wish to take pity on him, and you cover up the matter by claiming that what you do is for the sake of Heaven, in order to contain divisiveness in Israel and prevent the desecration of [God's] Name.

Falk's Role in the Controversy

Long before the outbreak of the controversy, Falk was known for his ability to battle and contain Sabbateanism. In 1722, while serving as rabbi of Lvov, he excommunicated all Sabbateans in a public ceremony.[20] In 1725, he presided over judicial proceedings that allowed penitent Sabbateans to return to normative Judaism. One of the penitents, a distinguished rabbi, informed Falk as follows:

> גיבט איין עצה, וואש טוט מען איך וויש בידיעה ברורה דש ר׳ יונתן איזט ראש לכולם.
>
> Please provide advice: What shall we do? I know with certainty that Reb Yonasan [Eibeschuetz] is the head of all of them [the Sabbateans].[21]

Falk, then, had reason to suspect Eibeschuetz as early as 1725. In that same year, the leading rabbis (including David Oppenheim[22] [d. 1736] of Prague, Ezekiel Katzenellenbogen[23] [d. 1749] of Altona, and Jacob Cohen Poppers[24] [d. 1740] of Frankfurt) established a policy that all Sabbateans had to be either rehabilitated or excommunicated. With regard to those Sabbateans who opted for rehabilitation, the policy was that they could be rehabilitated only in the presence of three *geonei ereṣ rabbanim mefursamim* (master talmudists who are also prominent rabbis).[25] Falk applied this policy to Eibeschuetz. Not only would Eibeschuetz have to appear in a Jewish court of law; it would have to be in a court consisting of three distinguished *geonim*—and presided over by none other than Falk himself.[26]

It is one matter to have a policy; it is quite another matter to implement it. Initially, Falk refused to enter the fray. He refused to respond to Emden's urgent plea at the start of the controversy (see above).[27] Doubtless, he understood it was a no-win situation. After several months of disarray, which saw virtually all the rabbis in Europe under excommunication (for supporting either Emden or Eibeschuetz), calls came from all quarters that Falk, as *zeqan ha-dor* and a tried and tested Sabbatean-buster, end the stalemate and restore order.[28] His strategy was one of diplomacy, resolve, and gradual escalation of rabbinic power, as necessary. In brief, he did the following over a five-year period:

1. He sent private messages (via third parties) to Eibeschuetz, asking that Eibeschuetz contact him. Eibeschuetz did not respond.[29]

2. He published a missive, calling for the accused party to appear before a rabbinic court. He deliberately made no mention of Eibeschuetz's name in this public missive. Eibeschuetz did not respond.[30]

3. He addressed a private message directly to Eibeschuetz, asking that Eibeschuetz contact him. Eibeschuetz did not respond.[31]

4. In the summer of 1751, Falk printed as a broadside his private message addressed directly to Eibeschuetz. The letter indicated for all to see that if Eibeschuetz were to refuse to appear before a rabbinic court, Falk would rally rabbis the world over and appropriate action would follow.[32]

With this public threat, Falk finally caught Eibeschuetz's attention. What followed was a battle of titans—Falk and Eibeschuetz—which ended only with Falk's death in 1756.

At the height of the controversy, on Second Adar 6, 5513 (March 12, 1753), with Eibeschuetz still refusing to appear in a court of Jewish law, Falk called for Eibeschuetz to be defrocked. He did so in a letter addressed to the *keṣinim, parnasim, u-manhigim* (lay leadership) of Altona, Hamburg, and Wandsbeck.[33] The letter, published here for the first time, reads:

וורמיישא יום ב׳ ויו אדר שני תקי״ג לפ״ק

אליכם אישים חכמי חרשים שלומכן יסגא לחדא, ה״ה האלופים רוזנים קצינים
פרנסים ומנהיגים בג׳ קהלות אה״ו יע״א.
ולכבוד הדיינים המופלגים וכל לומדי התורה וליחידי סגולה היראים והחרדים
לדבר ה׳, דברי שלום ואמת.
הנה מראשית כזאת הודעתי אתכם זה כמה פעמים ליסר ולהוכיח אתכם על אודות
האב״ד שלכם הנקרא ר׳ יונתן אייבשיץ, שהסית והדיח את רבים מבני עמינו
מאמונתינו האמתית ומהדת המאושר לאמונה הכוזבת ולהדת המשוקץ והמגועל,
והיא האמונה והדת של שק״צי צבי ימ״ש ונימח זכורו, שכבר נשתקע שמו ואבד זכרו
מן העולם. זה יותר משלושים שנה על ידינו במדינת פולין, שהוחרמו ונתנדו בשנת
תפ״ב לפ״ק בק״ק זאלקווי ע״י שבעה רבנים ושבעה שופרות וכבוי נרות בחרם הגדול
הכתוב בס׳ כל בו, ועל כל פרק ופרק חדש וחדש מזל ומזל תקעו שברים ותרועה, וכל
העם בקיבוץ גדול ותינוקות של בית רבן ענו אחריהן אמן, ויזעקו אל אלקים בקול

גדול ובכי גדולה עד למרום, וכמה וכמה פושעים וחטאים מכת הארורה הזאת עמדו אתנו על הבמה, וגם המה התוודו על עוונם בבכי ובזעקה גדולה ומרה ואמרו כזאת וכזאת עשינו, כפי סדור הנוסחא שסדרנו, ולאחר יציאת מבהכנ"ס י"ז בתמוז בשתא ההיא הוכרחו לנהוג בעצמם דיני אבלות ונידוי שבעה ושלושים ככל דיני המנודה ואבל, זולת שאר עונשין ונזיפות אשר יצא מאתנו ז' הרבנים, ואנא ברישא, שהייתי אב"ד דק"ק לבוב והגליל בעת ההיא. וכמו כן נעשה בכמה ק"ק שבמדינות פולין ע"י המנוח הגאון המפורסם בתורה וחסידות מוהר"ר אלעזר זלה"ה שהיה אב"ד בק"ק אמשטרדם, ומשם נסע לארץ הקדושה מנוחתו כבוד. וגם הרב המאה"ג הגאון המפורסם מוהר"ר אריה ליב נר"ן אב"ד דק"ק אמשטרדם החזיקו על ידינו בכל מקומות ממשלתם.

ובשנת תפ"ה החזיקו על ידינו שלשה מוסדי ארץ במדינות אשכנז, ה"ה הרב המנוח הגאון המפורסם מוהר"ר יעקב כהן זלה"ה שהיה אב"ד בקהילת פפד"מ, והמנוח הגאון המפורסם מו"ה יחזקאל זלה"ה שהיה מרא אתרא דלכון, והגאון המנוח מוהר"ר אברהם זלה"ה שהיה אב"ד בקהילת אמשטרדם. ומימים ההם והלאה שקטה הארץ קצת במדינות פולין ובמדינות אשכנז כמבואר הכל באר היטב בקונטרס הנדפס מחדש הנקרא חויא דרבנן. ולא נשאר מכת הרשעים ארורים שמחזיקים באמונת הש"ץ ודתו ימ"ש כ"א מעט מזעיר שעשו מעשיהם בחשאי, ואחר הדלת והמזוזה שמו זכרונם, עד שבא האב"ד שלכם והחזיר הטומאה ישנה ליושנה כטומאה רצוצה שבוקעת ועולה, עד שקבץ בער"ה כמה וכמה תלמידים שאינם הגונים לאין מספר שהחזיקו על ידו, וכמעט שיצא דבריהם בפומבי ולא היה כח ביד גדולי הדור לעונשם על ככה כל זמן שלא היה בירור גמור, עד שזה לערך עשר שנים נתגלה לי הדבר ע"י תכריך מחבילות של שטרי הדיוטות וספרי מינות שהיה בין אב"ד שלכם הנ"ל ובין ליבל פרוסטיץ ימ"ש, ודברי אפיקורסות ומינות שלא נמצא כמוהם לרעה מיום הוסדה הארץ, ובתוכם נזכר הקונטרס ואבוא היום אל העיון, וכל זה מסר לידי הגאב"ד דק"ק פיורדא ה"ה מוהר"ר דוד שטרויס נר"ו שהיה אז אחד מדייני מומחה בק"ק פפ"ד, זולת מה שהגיד לי פא"פ ע"י כמה ברורים שר' יונתן הנזכר לא נמצא מין ואפיקורס כמוהו, וכמו כן הגיד לי בשנה דאשתקיד, כדברים האלה הגיד לי פא"פ הרב הגאון הישיש מו"ה משה נר"ו אב"ד דמדינת מאגענצא, וגם הגאון אב"ד במדינת שוואבאך ה"ה מוהר"ר העשיל נר"ו, מלבד מה שהריצו אגרותיהם אל הרבנים מוהר"ר דוד ומוהר"ר העשיל הנ"ל באלו הימים.

ותכריך גדול של שטרות מסר לידי הרב המופלג מוהר"ר נפתלי הירץ נר"ו אב"ד בקהילת מערגטום והגלילות, ממה שהגיע לידו מכתבי המנוח הגאון המפורסם מוהר"ר יעקב כהן זלה"ה שהיה אב"ד בקהילת פפ"ד.

וכל זה היה בתחילת ביאת האב"ד שלכם לקהילת מיץ, שקלקל שם ג"כ בעניני התפילין בחה"מ, ושאר דברים כיוצא באלו, עד שעוררתי עליו בקול גדול הגאון המנוח מו"ה יחזקאל זלה"ה שהיה מרא אתרא דלכון, ולגאון המפורסם מוהר"ר אריה ליב נר"ו אב"ד בקהילת אמשטרדם, ולשארי רבנים, והשיבו לי בכתבם ששניהם לדבר אחד נתכוונו לאמר שבקי לרוויא דמנפשיה נפלי, כולי האי ואולי יתבררו הדברים בבירור יותר גמור, ומאז החזרתי כמה כתבים מהנ"ל למרי קמאי. ולכן כאשר האב"ד שלכם ראה שלא מיחו בידו גדולי הדור החזיק בטומאתו ואמר מי

אדון לי מאחר שנתקיימו לו הבטחות ליב פרוסטיץ ימ״ש, שהבטיח אותו שנתגלה לו בחזיון לילה משיח שלהם שק״צי צבי ואמר לו שבעת כאשר יתגדל שם ר׳ יונתן למעלה אזי מתוך כך יתגדל שם ש״ץ ימ״ש, ואז יתהפכו שמותיו ויקרא צבי שק״צי, כאשר נמצא בכתבים הנזכרים ע״פ עדים ברורים שנגבו בכמה בתי דינין במדינות מעהרין, ה״ה הגאון המנוח המפורסם מוהר״ר יששכר בעריש י״ץ אב״ד דק״ק ניקלשבורג והגאון המפורסם מוהר״ר הילמן נר״ו שהיה אב״ד בקהילת קרעמזיר בעת ההיא, וגלל כן נמצא בכמה קמיעות בתחילתן כתב שק״צי צבי ובסוף כתב צבי שק״צי. וגלל כן ג״כ התחיל ר׳ יונתן הנ״ל לעשות יותר בפומבי להקל בד׳ תעניות ולכתוב כמה וכמה קמיעות לאין מספר, שכולם כתובים על שם ש״ץ ימ״ש. ובתוכם כתב בפירוש יתגדל ויתקדש בבתי הבי בעולם, והרבה מינות ואפיקורסות כיוצא באלו, אלא שבכל זה עדיין לא נתגלו הדברים על בורין מאחר שהקמיעות תפורין בנרתיקן ומכוסין, עד שזה לערך שלשה שנים נתגלה ענין הקמיעות בבירור גמור, שע״י שנפתח אחת מהן נפתחו כולם, ונמצאו בכולן דברי שקוצים וגילולים מינות ואפיקורסות, וע״כ כתבתי לו אג״ש המתחיל בחרוז השוכן בשמי מרומים, שכבר נדפס מחדש דברי האגרת לבדו, וגם מה שנדפסו כמה וכמה קמיעות בכרך קטן, ואף שעיקר הדפוס לא נעשה על ידי, מ״מ הקמיעות ההם ברור כשמש שיוצאין מתחת ידו וביחודאותן חמשה קמיעות המקוימים משתי נאמני הקהילה בקהילת מיץ, מלבד כמה וכמה קמיעות שכתב בקהילת פפ״ד מידי עברו דרך שם, וכולן כאחד מקרא בלתי טהור שנזכר בהם שם התועב ש״ץ ימ״ש, ועל כל אלה הוכחתיו בתוכחת מגולה באג״ש הנזכר, ולא השבני דבר או חצי דבר.

נמצא שעניני הקמיעות אינן אלא גילוי מלתא בעלמא, שנתגלה עונו ונתגלה קץ וזמן לזמר עריץ ולהכרית החוחים והקוצים המינים והאפיקורסים הנוטים אחר אמונת ש״ץ ודתו ימ״ש, עד שבאמת משום כך נתפרסמו עניני הקונטרס ואבוא היום אל העיון וחיבור אילת אהבים של שיר השירים וכוונות תקיעות שופר וכוונות מגילת אסתר שכולם חיבור אחד לטומאה וכולם מלאים חרופים וגדופים ממש כפירת כל התורה כולה, כאשר נתגלה לי זה עשר שנים ע״י הרב הגאון מוהר״ר חיים כהן אב״ד דק״ק לבוב, ועכשיו נתברר יותר ע״י כמה וכמה רבנים מובהקים במדינות פולין שנתאספו יחד ביומא דשוקא בק״ק בראד בחודש חשון העבר, ולכן יצאנו לקראתו בכתבים הקודמים בשנה דאשתקד וגם עתה מקרוב להודיע לכם מה שעשינו בענין זה נעשה הכל בהסכמות ממש כל רבני אשכנז ופולין. הלא זה הדבר אשר דברנו שהאב״ד שלכם הטה את לב המלך ושריו באומרו שרוב הקהילות והלומדים עומדים על צדו, ובאמת לא נמצא אפילו שנים או שלשה גרגרים מרבנים מובהקים שיעמדו על צדו, כ״א רבים מהאספסוף מכת הארורה הנזכרים הנגררים אחריו, ומהם רבים שהמה ממיודעיו וממשפחתו כאשר כתבתי באריכות, שכבר הגיע השעה להודפו ולרודפו עד חובה, לולי שעשינו לכבוד המלכות ה״ה המלך האדיר והחסיד יר״ה, שכל כוונתו ומגמתו להשתיק הריב ולעשות שלום בגבולכם, ולכן כתבתי שגם אנו פותחין לו בשלום להזהירו עוד בהתראה אחרונה ע״י מיודעיו או ע״י נאמני הקהילה. וכהיום שהגיע לעינו, שכבר נעשה המעשה שנמסר לו ההתראה ע״י שני נאטאריוס ומתוך תשובתו ניכר שעדיין עמד במרדו ואינו משגיח כלל לדברי חכמי גאוני דורינו,

לכן אנחנו עומדים על דעתינו ולדברינו כמו שכתבתי, שכללו של דבר הכל הולך אחר החתום ולמדין משטה אחרונה שכל זמן שלא יקבל עליו האב״ד שלכם לקיים מה שנפסק עליו ולשוב בתשובה שלימה רצויה וברורה, הרי הוא כא׳ מהמינין והאפיקורסין לכל דבר, כמבואר בכתבים הקודמים מאתנו, ויש בכלל זה שהוא מוחרם ומנודה ומובדל ומופרש מכל קדושת ישראל, ואין צריך לומר שיוסר המצנפת הטהור מעל ראשו להורות שום דבר הנוגע באיסור והיתר ולדרוש ברבים ובכל דברים השייכים לנימוסי הדת שלנו, רק שלא יחרימו אותו בפירסום בפועל בלתי רשיון משרי ויועצי המלך, וכ״ש שלא יעשו אותו כלה לדחותו על שעה א׳ בשתי ידים, וכולי האי ואולי יכניע את ערפו הקשה לטוב לו כל הימים, לעקור מקום קביעת מקומו מקהלתכם וילך עם כל בני ביתו כמאן דביש ליה בהאי מתא אזל למתא אחריתא, ששינוי המקום יגרום לשוב בתשובה שלימה כמ״ש הרמב״ם ז״ל בהל׳ תשובה, וגם בכל מקומות אשר יקבע מקום דירתו יקבל ויאסר על עצמו שלא לנהוג שום רבנות ועניני הוראה על כמה וכמה שנים אשר יורו לו חכמי גאוני דורינו, וכשיקבל עליו כנ״ל חלילה לכם לעשות לו שום דבר ביזוי, וכ״ש שלא לשלוח בו יד, והלואי שיצא מעצמו לזמן הנראה בעיניכם, שהוא מההכרח לצאת מקהלתכם, ואם יהי׳ מהצורך ליתן לו צדה לדרך איזה סך קצוב, וכ״ש מהשכירות והכנסות שמגיע לו עד כלות משך ימי שטר הרבנות, ובכל זה נכנסנו עמו הרבה לפנים משורת הדין כיון דבר אוריין ובר אבוהן הוא.

אמנם על אלו המכעיסים מאנשי זרוע שבקהילתכם שאפילו בפתחו של גהינם אינן חוזרין בתשובה מחמת איזה ניצוח שלהם ומחמת אונאות ממון, ועי״כ גורמין המחלוקת בקהילתכם ובשאר קהילות כאשר עשו עד הנה, הללו אין להם כפרה כלל, ועל קצינים פרנסים ומנהיגים והאלופים הדיינים שבקהילתכם מוטל להתרות בהם עוד הפעם, שאם לא ישובו מדרכם הרעה יחרימו אותן בפועל ולעשות בהם שפטים גדולים כראוי ונכון בעיניהם, ואף לקונסם בקנס עצום ומסוים חצי למלך יר״ה וחצי לאיזה דבר טוב וכשתתנהגו ככל הדברים האלה הרי אתם מופקעים מהחרמות ושמתות ונידוים, וכ״ש אותן אנשים שהיו מצדו להתגבר במחלוקת וע״י גזרתינו חזרו בתשובה להכיר את בוראם, וגם המה מופקעים מכל החרמות ושמתות ונידוים שיצאו מפי גאוני דורינו בכל משך שנים שעברו, וכל הקללות והארורים יתהפכו לברכה אי קיימי בהמנותייהו ולא יחזרו לסורם ח״ו, ויקבלו תשובה שלימה לפני המקום כל אחד לפי ענינו כאשר יורו להם דייני ולומדי קהילתכם את הדרך אשר ילכו בה, ולא בדרך כפיה ח״ו כ״א לצאת י״ח שמים. ומעתה תתנהגו בשלום אהבה ואחוה וריעות והראשונות לא תזכרנה עוד, ירב לכם הרבה זכויות שזכיתם לכם, שעל ידכם תתבטל ותתעקר הטומאה רצוה של ש״ץ ימ״ש, ומה רב טוב הצפון לכם לצדיקים, וכ״ש לבעלי תשובה דעבדי תשובה מעלי ושכרכם יהיה כפול מן השמים, וה׳ ישלח ברכה והצלחה באסמיכם ובכל משלח ידכם עד ביאת הגואל צדק שיבוא במהרה בימינו אמן.

כ״ד החותם לכבוד המקום ולכבוד תורתנו הקדושה ולטובת כל אחינו בני ישראל, ובהסכמת גאוני חכמי דורינו, הצעיר יעקב יושע קראקא, פה ק״ק ורמייזא, ומצפה לתשועת ה׳ להוציא מחשבה לפועל לשבת בא״י תוב״א.

Worms, Monday, 6 Second Adar, 5513

To the wise lay leaders of the triple community, Altona, Hamburg, and Wandsbeck, may God protect it, and may he grant you increased well-being, and to the distinguished judges and all the Torah scholars, and to those exceptional individuals who fear the word of God, words of peace and truth.

I have previously warned you on many occasions regarding your Chief Rabbi, who is called Rabbi Jonathan Eibeschuetz, and who has enticed and led astray many Jews from the true faith to the false and abominable belief, the religion of Shabbatai Zvi, may his name and apparition be blotted out. His name has already receded and his memory has been blotted out from the world.

More than thirty years have passed since we placed [all Sabbateans] under the ban in Zolkiew, Poland, in the year 1722, in the presence of seven rabbis with seven ram's horns, and by means of extinguishing candles, as is prescribed for the great ban in *Sefer Kol Bo*.[34] At the end of each paragraph of the text used in the ceremony, and at the mention of each month and sign of the zodiac, they sounded the ram's horn. All the Jews gathered in large numbers, and the school children responded "Amen." They cried out to God in a loud voice, even unto the heavens. Many of the sinners from the accursed sect stood with us on the platform. They too confessed their sins, crying out loudly and bitterly, saying, "Such and such have we done," according to the fixed text that we formulated. When we left the synagogue on the seventeenth day of Tammuz in that year, we required the penitents to practice the law of mourning and of being placed under the ban, whether for seven or thirty days, aside from the other punishments meted out by us, the seven rabbis. I presided [over the ceremonies], serving at the time as Chief Rabbi of Lwow and environs. Similar action was taken in various communities throughout Poland by the late Gaon, renowned for his Torah and piety, Rabbi Eleazar, who [later] served as Chief Rabbi of Amsterdam.[35] From there he traveled to the Holy Land, where he rests in peace.[36] So too the distinguished Gaon, Rabbi Aryeh Leib, [the present] Chief Rabbi of Amsterdam, took similar action in the communities under his control.[37]

In 1725, three "pillars of the earth" in Germany took similar action. They were the late renowned Gaon, Rabbi Jacob Kohen, Chief Rabbi of Frankfurt;[38] the late renowned Gaon, Rabbi Ezekiel, who served as your Chief Rabbi;[39] and the late Gaon, Rabbi Abraham,

Chief Rabbi of Amsterdam.[40] From then on, the Jewish communities of Poland and Germany found some respite [from the Sabbatean threat]. All this is recorded explicitly in the recently reprinted broadside called *Ḥivya de-Rabbanan*.[41] Only a few members of the accursed sect remained who still believed in Shabbatai Zvi and his teaching, a small number who practiced their deeds in secret, behind closed doors. That is, until your Chief Rabbi came and restored the old impurity, causing it to rise once again. He gathered together unworthy disciples who supported him. They almost went public, yet the rabbinic leaders of the generation could not punish them as long as the evidence was less than clear. Approximately ten years ago, however, it was all revealed to me when I discovered a cache of letters and heretical manuscripts that formed the correspondence between your Chief Rabbi and Leibel Prosstitz [*sic*],[42] may his name be blotted out. These were heretical works without parallel since the world was created. Mentioned in these writings was the [heretical] tract, *Va-Avo ha-Yom el ha-Iyyun*.[43] All this was given over to me by the Chief Rabbi of Fuerth, Rabbi David Strauss,[44] who at the time served as a judge on the rabbinic court of Frankfurt. This, aside from what he told me orally, based on much investigation, that there is no other heretic the like of Rabbi Jonathan. So too he informed me last year. I heard similar comments, face to face, from the elderly Gaon, Rabbi Moses, Chief Rabbi of Mayence,[45] and from the Gaon, Rabbi Heschel, Chief Rabbi of Schwabach.[46] This, aside from letters sent at that time to the above mentioned Rabbi David and Rabbi Heschel. Moreover, the distinguished Rabbi Naftali Hertz of Mergentheim[47] presented me with a large cache of letters that he had gotten from the archive of his father-in-law, the late renowned Gaon, Rabbi Jacob Kohen, who served as Chief Rabbi of Frankfurt.

All this took place at the start of your Chief Rabbi's tenure in Metz, where he fouled up with regard to the wearing of *tefillin* on *ḥol ha-mo'ed* and other such issues.[48] I complained bitterly to the late Gaon Rabbi Ezekiel, who was your Rabbi, and to the renowned Gaon, Rabbi Aryeh Leib, Chief Rabbi of Amsterdam, and to other rabbis, calling for a protest on their part. They replied in writing, both coming to the same conclusion: "Leave a drunkard to his own devices, he will fall by himself."[49] Would that were to happen; if not, perhaps more persuasive evidence will come to light. At that time, I returned much of the written material to its original owner.

When your Chief Rabbi saw that no protest came forth from the leading rabbis of the generation, he became firm in his impurity, saying, "Who can lord it over me?" Moreover, [he believed that] the predictions of Leib Prosstitz, may his name be blotted out, came true. Leib assured Rabbi Jonathan that their Messiah, Shabbatai Zvi, had appeared to him in a vision at night. The Messiah informed him that when Rabbi Jonathan's name would become great on high, the Messiah's name would also become great, at which point his name will be reversed, and he will be called Zvi Shabbatai. So according to the above mentioned writings,[50] as attested by trustworthy witnesses whose testimony was recorded in the Jewish courts of Moravia, under the aegis of the late renowned Gaon, Rabbi Issachar Berish, Chief Rabbi of Nikolsburg,[51] and the renowned Gaon, Rabbi Hilman, who at the time was Chief Rabbi of Kremsier.[52] That is why some [of his] amulets open with Shabbatai Zvi and close with Zvi Shabbatai. [Due to the lack of rabbinic protest,] Rabbi Jonathan began to go more public [with Sabbatean practices], treating lightly the four fasts and writing countless amulets, all invoking the name of Shabbatai Zvi, may his name be blotted out. In them he wrote explicitly, "May the name of BBTY HBY[53] become great and sanctified in the world," and other such heresies. But none of this became open knowledge because the amulets were sewn into their cover and hidden away [from the naked eye]. Some three years ago the matter of the amulets became open knowledge when one of the amulets was opened, which led to all the amulets being opened. Abomination, filth, and heresy were found in all of them. So I addressed a "letter of peace" to him, beginning with the words, "He who resides in the heavens on high."[54] It has recently been published separately [as a broadside].[55] So too many of the amulets have been published in a small pamphlet[56]—even though I had nothing to do with its publication—and it is clear as the sun that he wrote them. This is especially true regarding the five amulets notarized by the two official notaries of the Jewish community of Metz.[57] Aside from this, he wrote numerous amulets as he passed through the Jewish community of Frankfurt. All of them contain impure texts and invoke the abominable Shabbatai Zvi, may his name be blotted out. Regarding all this, I chastised him in the above mentioned "letter of peace." He replied with neither a word nor half a word.

It is evident, then, that the amulets merely make public what was always known. His sins have been revealed, [and] so too the time has come to extirpate the wicked and to cut off the thorns and thistles, i.e., the heretics who believe in Shabbatai Zvi and his teaching. Truthfully, due to the amulets, the existence of the treatises titled *Va-Avo ha-Yom el ha-Iyyun, Ayyelet Ahavim* on Song of Songs, *Kavvanot Teqi'ot Shofar,* and *Kavvanot Megillat Ester* became public knowledge.[58] They combine to form a single book of impurity. All these treatises are replete with blasphemy, a denial of the Torah in its entirety. All this was already revealed to me some ten years ago by the Gaon, Rabbi Ḥayyim Kohen, Chief Rabbi of Lwow.[59] Now it has become even clearer on the basis of the discussion of numerous distinguished rabbis in Poland, who convened on market day, last Ḥeshvan, in Brody.[60] Therefore, we confronted him with our earlier missives sent out last year, and now again more recently, making sure to inform you that whatever we have done in this matter was done with the full consent of all the rabbis in Germany and Poland. We have already informed you that your Chief Rabbi misled the King and his officers when he claimed that the majority of Jewish communities and Jewish scholars support him. In fact, not even two or three distinguished rabbis support him. His supporters come from the masses who are members of the accursed sect, many being associates of his and members of his family. I have written about this at length. The time has come to run him out of the community. We are restrained only by the honor due the Crown, the mighty and pious King, may his glory increase.[61] His only concern has been to contain the controversy and to restore peace in your community. That is why I wrote that our opening position [to Rabbi Jonathan] was one of peace, issuing him a final warning via his associates or the communal authorities.

He has now seen our summons and warning, and the deed is done, for two notaries delivered it to him. From his response, it is evident that he is still a rebel, and is not concerned at all about the words of the wise Geonim of our generation. We therefore stand by our decision and words, as already recorded. The rule is: all follows the closing section, and one learns from the last line. So long as your Chief Rabbi refuses to follow the legal decision that was rendered regarding him, and so long as he does not genuinely repent, he is considered a heretic for all purposes, as spelled out in our writings. This includes: he is placed under the ban, and separated from all that is holy in Israel. There is no need to mention that the holy headdress will be removed from his head. He is banned from deciding any issue of Jewish law pertaining to what is prohibited or permitted. He may not preach in public or participate in any matter pertaining to Jewish law and practice. He may not, however, be banned in a public ceremony, until proper authorization from the royal authorities is obtained. He surely may not be forcibly removed from office. Would that this works! Perhaps he will bend his stiff neck for his own eternal benefit, and will leave your community, moving away together with his entire family. For one who fares poorly in one place should move away to another; the change of place will lead him to genuine repentance, as Maimonides has written in "Hilkhot Teshuvah."[62] Wherever he settles, he must vow and agree not to serve as a rabbi or decisor of Jewish law for as many years as the rabbis of our generation determine. Once he agrees to the above, he may not be abused in any manner, and certainly not harmed physically. Would that he leaves of his own accord, within a time frame acceptable to you! It is essential that he leave your community. If it is necessary to provide him with provisions for his journey, this should be done. Certainly, he should receive whatever monies are owed him for the remainder of his rabbinic contract. Regarding all these matters, we have ruled leniently, and not applied the letter of the law, for he is a rabbinic scholar and of noble lineage.

Regarding those hot-headed members of the community who are prone to using strong-arm tactics either to assure victory or for monetary gain—who would not repent even when faced by the gates of hell—and thereby incite controversy in your community and in other communities as well, there is no atonement whatsoever for them. It is incumbent upon the communal officials and the judges of your community to warn them once again that if they refuse to abandon their wicked ways, they will be placed under the ban. The communal officials can punish them severely as they see fit. They can be fined a huge sum of money, half of which will be turned over to the King, and half of which will be designated for some useful purpose. When you act according to these guidelines, all previous bans issued against you will become null and void. This applies even more so to all supporters of Rabbi Jonathan during the controversy who, due to the instructions we have issued, repent and recognize their Creator. All previous bans issued against them in past years by the great rabbis of our generation are null and void. All the curses shall be transformed into blessings, but only if they remain faithful and do not revert to their sinful ways, and if they repent fully before God, each according to his situation and according to the instructions he receives from the judges and scholars of your community. Repentance, of course, cannot be forced upon anyone. It can only be done in order to fulfill the will of Heaven.

I beseech you to practice the ways of peace, love, and friendship. The earlier sins will no longer be recalled. May your increased merit enable you to annul and extirpate the impurity of Shabbatai Zvi. How great is the reward stored away for the righteous! How much more so will be the reward for those who genuinely repent! Your reward from Heaven will be doubled. May God fill your storehouses—and whatever you undertake—with blessing and success. May He continue to do so until the righteous redeemer appears, soon, in our time, Amen.

These are the words of the one who signs in honor of God, and in honor of the holy Torah, and for the benefit of our brethren the children of Israel, and with the support of the wise Geonim of our generation, the young one, Jacob Joshua of Cracow, here in Worms, awaiting God's salvation, who is in the process of implementing his goal of settling in the land of Israel.

Conclusion

Did Falk succeed? Much, of course, depends on how one defines success. Personally, Falk paid dearly for his efforts to bring down Eibeschuetz. He was deposed from the rabbinate of Frankfurt and spent his last years as a layman, wandering between Mannheim, Worms, and Offenbach, where he died in 1756.[63] On the communal front, it would also appear that Falk failed. The goal was either to rehabilitate or defrock Eibeschuetz. Neither event occurred. Eibeschuetz never appeared before a Jewish court of law, so no rehabilitation took place. In 1753, he took his case (without making a personal appearance) before the Council of the Four Lands in Jaroslaw and was vindicated by a large plurality.[64] In 1756, he was reelected as Chief Rabbi of Altona, Hamburg, and Wandsbeck by an even greater plurality than in his first candidacy. He died in 1764 as Chief Rabbi of the triple community, and was buried with full honors in the rabbinic section of Altona's Koenigstrasse cemetery. Eulogies were delivered in his honor in Altona and Prague, if not the world over.[65]

Falk failed largely because he was following a script designed in 1725 by master talmudists who were also prominent rabbis, so that they could lord it over lesser rabbis and laymen who were tainted by

Sabbateanism. But Eibeschuetz was not a lesser rabbi; indeed, he was perhaps the most prominent of the master talmudists. No one could lord it over him. Eibeschuetz was clever: precisely because Falk was following a script, Eibeschuetz anticipated every move he made, and was always one step ahead, outmaneuvering and outflanking him—at least for a while.

In this battle of heavyweights, neither could knock out his opponent. Eibeschuetz perhaps won on points, but he won only the battle. Hounded by Falk, Eibeschuetz was discredited and isolated from almost all the rabbis in Germany and from most Sabbateans. Students no longer flocked to his lectures. No new offers came his way, and Eibeschuetz died lonely and defeated. Sabbateanism would never again pose a real threat to rabbinic Judaism.[66] Falk had won the war.

Notes

1. On Falk, see M. Horovitz, *Frankfurter Rabbinen*, ed. J. Unna (Jerusalem: n.p., 1969), 126–66. Significant material was omitted from the Hebrew edition: רבני פרנקפורט (Jerusalem: Mossad Harav Kook, 1972), 90–118. See also D. L. Zinz, עטרת יהושע (Bilgoraj, 1936; photo-offset, New York, 1982).
2. H. Graetz, *Geschichte der Juden*, 3rd ed. (Leipzig, 1897), 10:332–97 and notes.
3. D. Kahana, תולדות המקובלים השבתאים והחסידים (Tel Aviv, 1926), 2:23–54 and appendices.
4. See, e.g., S. P. Rabbinowitz's revised Hebrew version of Graetz's *Geschichte der Juden*, דברי ימי ישראל, (Warsaw, 1899), 8:455–528, 614–36.
5. See S. Leiman, "When a Rabbi Is Accused of Heresy: R. Ezekiel Landau's Attitude Toward R. Jonathan Eibeschuetz in the Emden-Eibeschuetz Controversy," in *From Ancient Israel to Modern Judaism: Essays in Honor of Marvin Fox*, ed. J. Neusner et al. (Atlanta: Scholars Press, 1989), 3:179–94.
6. See S. Leiman, "When a Rabbi Is Accused of Heresy: The Stance of the Gaon of Vilna in the Emden-Eibeschuetz Controversy," in מאה שערים (Studies in Memory of Isadore Twersky), ed. E. Fleischer et al. (Jerusalem: Magnes Press, 2001), 251–63.
7. See, e.g., B. Brilling, "Das Erste Gedicht auf Einen Deutschen Rabbiner aus dem Jahre 1752," *Bulletin des Leo Baeck Instituts* 11 (1968): 38–47. Cf. the studies by C. Anton, S. J. Baumgarten, D. F. Megerlin, and J. F. Zachariae reprinted in *Period Documents Concerning the Emden-Eibeschuetz Controversy*, ed. B. Ogorek (Brooklyn: n.p., 1992).
8. See, e.g., J. S. E. F. v. Bernstorff, "Nachricht von der den Juden zu Hamburg und Altona entstandenen und nunmehr geendigten Streitigkeit: ob der itzige Oberrabbi von dem ehemaligen falschen Messias der Juden Sabbathai Zebhi ein Anhaenger sey?" in *Anhang zu den Actis Historico-Ecclesiasticis* 17 (1754): 997–1031. Cf. the gazette accounts reprinted in B. Ogorek, *Period Documents*.
9. See מעשה נורא זכה ברורה (Detmold, 1743), reprinted in G. Nigal, סיפורי דיבוק בספרות ישראל (Jerusalem: R. Mass, 1983), 107–14.

10. J. Emden, ויקם עדות ביעקב (Altona, 1755–56), 4a–9a; Emden, התאבקות (Altona, 1769), 10a–23a. Cf. J. Eibeschuetz, לוחת עדות (Altona, 1755; photo-offset, Jerusalem, 1966), introduction.
11. That Emden considered Eibeschuetz guilty from the start requires no documentation (beyond the references listed in the previous note). For Landau, see Leiman, "When a Rabbi . . . R. Ezekiel Landau." For Falk, see below.
12. J. Emden, עקיצת עקרב (Altona, 1753), 19b.
13. For Eibeschuetz as *am ha-areṣ* (ignoramus), see J. Emden, שבירת לוחות האון (Altona, 1756), 16b, 38b. For Emden as preacher, see his מגילת ספר, ed. Kahana (Warsaw, 1897), 101, 112; cf. ויקם עדות ביעקב, 13b.
14. For Landau, see Leiman, "When a Rabbi . . . R. Ezekiel Landau." For Rabbi Mordecai of Duesseldorf, see שפת אמת ולשון זהורית (Altona [actually Amsterdam], 1752; photo-offset, Jerusalem, 1971), 59–60. A short biography of Rabbi Mordecai of Duesseldorf appears in *Encyclopaedia Judaica* (Jerusalem, 1971), vol. 7, col. 1175.
15. Rabbi Samuel Hilman Heilprin served as rabbi of Kremsier in Moravia from 1720 to 1726. In 1751, he succeeded Rabbi Jonathan Eibeschuetz as Chief Rabbi of Metz, serving in that post until his death. On Heilprin, see A. Cahen, "Le Rabbinat de Metz," *Revue des études juives* 12 (1886): 289–94. Cf. L. Loewenstein, *Geschichte der Juden in der Kurpfalz* (Frankfurt, 1895), 198–201.
16. Rabbi Aryeh Leib b. Saul served as rabbi of Dukla, Rzeszow, and Glogau. In 1740, he succeeded Rabbi Eleazar b. Samuel as Ashkenazic Chief Rabbi of Amsterdam. See Z. H. Horowitz, לתולדות הקהילות בפולין (Jerusalem: Mossad Harav Kook, 1978), 202–23.
17. For Emden's testimony that Eibeschuetz refused to write amulets after the controversy began, see עקיצת עקרב, 5a.
18. The original broadside is preserved in various public and private collections. It was also printed in שפת אמת ולשון זהורית (the first edition is without pagination), end pages. It was inadvertently omitted from the Jerusalem reprint of 1971 (which was based on a faulty original).
19. See Falk's letter to Rabbi Aryeh Leib of Amsterdam, dated 8 Second Adar, 5513 (March 14, 1753), in J. Emden, פתח עינים (Altona, 1756), 13b–14b.
20. See Falk's letter published below. Cf. J. Emden, תורת הקנאות (Altona, 1752), 34a.
21. J. Praeger, גחלי אש (Bodleian Library manuscript Michael 106), 1: fol. 70a. Cf. G. Scholem, "ברוכיה ראש השבתאים בשאלוניקי," ציון 6 (1941): 193n55 (reissued in G. Scholem, מחקרי שבתאות, ed. and annotated by Y. Liebes [Tel Aviv: Am Oved, 1991], 376n186).
22. Rabbi David Oppenheim, famous bibliophile, served as Chief Rabbi of Nikolsburg (1689–1702) and Prague (1703–36). See Y. K. Duschinsky, תולדות הגאון ר' דוד אופנהיימער (Budapest, 1922); cf. his "Rabbi David Oppenheimer," *Jewish Quarterly Review* n.s. 20 (1929–30): 217–47.
23. Rabbi Ezekiel Katzenellenbogen served as Chief Rabbi of Altona, Hamburg, and Wandsbeck from 1713 until his death. See E. Duckesz, אוה למושב (Cracow, 1903), 21–29.
24. Rabbi Jacob Cohen Poppers served as Chief Rabbi of Frankfurt from 1718 until his death. See Horovitz, *Frankfurter Rabbinen*, 117–24 (Hebrew edition, 84–89).
25. Since the Sabbatean heresy was characterized by duplicity, one could never be certain that a Sabbatean's repentance was genuine. Hence the need for safeguards,

such as a Jewish court consisting of distinguished *geonim.* See Y. D. Wilhelm and G. Scholem, "כרוזי 'חויא דרבנך' נגד כת שבתי צבי", קרית ספר 30 (1955): 99–104. See esp. 104:

> ופן ואולי תשובותיהם רמי' איזט עושה מעשה נח"ש, ע"כ אין תשובתו רצוי' ומקובלת ביז ער ווערט זיין תשובה מקבל זיין בפני שלושה גאוני ארץ רבנים מפורסמים, דש רעכטי תשובה חקירה ודרישה האבין אויב פיו ולבו שווים זיין.

> Lest their repentance be an act of deceit, in the manner of Neḥemiah Ḥayon, no one's act of repentance will be accepted as genuine until he appears before three talmudic masters who are also prominent rabbis. They—by means of interrogation—will determine whether what he says is what he believes and, hence, whether his repentance is genuine.

26. Early in the fray, Falk demanded that Eibeschuetz appear before a rabbinic court consisting of three distinguished *ge'onei ereṣ.* Only when Eibeschuetz's delaying tactics became evident did Falk insist that he must sit on, and preside over, the court. Doubtless, Falk felt that only he would be in a position to grill Eibeschuetz and determine the genuineness of his repentance. Certainly, Falk's colleagues were persuaded that only he had the requisite fortitude, expertise, and wisdom that it would take to contain Eibeschuetz.
27. So Emden, התאבקות, 23a.
28. See, e.g., Landau's letter of 1752, in J. Praeger, גחלי אש, 2: fol. 129a. Cf. Rabbi Mordecai of Duesseldorf's letter referred to above, note 14.
29. שפת אמת ולשון זהורית, 57.
30. Ibid., 30, 34–35.
31. Ibid., 57–58.
32. The broadside is available in public and private collections. For the text, see ibid. Cf. Eibeschuetz, לוחת עדות, introduction (in the Jerusalem 1966 ed., 4).
33. The text appears in J. Praeger, גחלי אש, 2: fol. 169a–173a.
34. ספר כל בו (New York, 1946), 98b, §139.
35. The reference is to Rabbi Eleazar b. Samuel (d. 1742), who served as rabbi of Brody from 1714 to 1734, and as Ashkenazic Chief Rabbi of Amsterdam from 1735 to 1740. See E. Katzman, "הגאון החסיד ר' אלעזר רוקח זצ"ל אב"ד בראד ואמשטרדם", *Perspective* 3 (1976): 61–72. For the concluding portion of Katzman's essay, see כל ספרי ר' אלעזר רוקח (Benei Beraq: Y. Heilprin, 1983), 1:29–40.
36. On his pilgrimage to the land of Israel, see Y. Bartal, "עליית ר' אלעזר מאמשטרדם לארץ ישראל בשנת תק"א (1740)", in מחקרים על תולדות יהדות הולנד, 4 (1985): 7–25, ed. Y. Michman.
37. See above, note 16.
38. See above, note 24.
39. See above, note 23.
40. Rabbi Abraham b. Judah Berliner served as Ashkenazic Chief Rabbi of Amsterdam from 1716 to 1730. Cf. M. H. Gans, *Memorbook,* trans. A. P. Pomerans (Baarn, 1977), 165.
41. The broadside was first issued in 1725, then reissued (in part) in Altona in 1752. For the text of the original broadside, see Wilhelm and Scholem, "כרוזי 'חויא דרבנך' נגד כת שבתי צבי". The 1752 reissue appeared in a broadside titled למען דעת.

42. On the Sabbatean prophet Judah Leib b. Jacob Prossnitz (d. ca. 1730), see the biographical entry by Gershom Scholem in *Encyclopaedia Judaica* 13:1240–42. Cf. Y. Liebes, סוד האמונה השבתאית (Jerusalem: Mossad Bialik, 1995), 70–76 and notes.
43. The anonymous theosophical Sabbatean treatise often ascribed to Rabbi Jonathan Eibeschuetz is more accurately titled *Va-Avo ha-Yom el ha-Ayin, apud* Genesis 24:42. On the treatise and its author, see Liebes, סוד האמונה השבתאית, esp. 344n85.
44. Rabbi David Strauss (d. 1762) served as Chief Rabbi of Fuerth from 1748 until his death. See L. Loewenstein, "Zur Geschichte der Juden in Fuerth," *Jahrbuch der Jüdisch-Literarischen Gesellschaft* 6 (1908): 187–90.
45. The reference is to Rabbi Moses Brandeis, who served as Chief Rabbi of Mainz from 1733 until his death in 1767. See L. Loewenstein, "Zur Geschichte der Rabbiner in Mainz," *Jahrbuch der Jüdisch-Literarischen Gesellschaft* 3 (1905): 228–31; cf. L. Rakow, ed., ספר זכרון קרן ישראל (London: n.p., 2000), 63–65. See Brandeis's חידושי רבי משה חריף (Jerusalem: Mekhon Yerushalayim, 1987).
46. The reference is to Rabbi Joshua Heschel b. Rabbi Aaron Moses Ezekiel, who served as Chief Rabbi of Schwabach from 1749 until his death in 1770. See D. L. Zinz, גדולת יהונתן (Piotrkow, 1930–34), 289; cf. B. Z. Ophir, ed., *Pinkas ha-Kehillot: Germany-Bavaria* (Jerusalem: Yad Vashem, 1972), 364.
47. Rabbi Naftali Hirsch Katzenellenbogen (d. 1800) served as Chief Rabbi of Mergentheim (1741–63). See Loewenstein, *Geschichte der Juden in der Kurpfalz*, 240–43.
48. See Zinz, גדולת יהונתן, 134 and 283.
49. BT Shabbat 32a.
50. See Praeger, גחלי אש, 1: fol. 58a.
51. Rabbi Issachar Baer Eskeles (d. 1753) served as Chief Rabbi of Moravia and Hungary, administering both offices from Nikolsburg and Vienna. On Eskeles, see Loewenstein, "Zur Geschichte der Rabbiner in Mainz," 226–27.
52. See above, note 15. Doubtless, Falk is referring to a document signed by Rabbi Issachar Baer and Rabbi Samuel Hilman Heilprin, whose text is preserved in Praeger, גחלי אש, 1:fols. 59b–60a.
53. In *atbash* code—in which *alef* becomes *tav, bet* becomes *shin,* and so forth—BBTY HBY = SBTY ZBY, i.e., Shabbatai Zvi.
54. The letter, dated 11 Sivan, 5511 (June 4, 1751), appears in שפת אמת ולשון זהורית, 56–58.
55. The letter first appeared in print as a broadside in Amsterdam, 1751. Its appearance in print was a matter of contention between Eibeschuetz and Falk. Eibeschuetz claimed that it appeared in print even before he received it. See his לוחת עדות (Jerusalem, 1966), 4. Falk explained that it was printed without his permission. See שפת אמת ולשון זהורית, 62.
56. שפת אמת ולשון זהורית (Amsterdam, 1752).
57. See S. Leiman and S. Schwarzfuchs, "New Evidence on the Emden-Eibeschuetz Controversy: The Amulets From Metz," *Revue des études juives* 165 (2006): 229–49.
58. All the treatises listed were ascribed to Rabbi Jonathan Eibeschuetz. Their titles became public knowledge due to various broadsides published during the controversy. See, e.g., the addendum to the letter of Rabbi Ezekiel Landau, circulated in August 1752 and published in the broadside אספקלריה המאירה (Altona, 1753).

59. Rabbi Ḥayyim ha-Kohen Rapoport (d. 1771) served as Chief Rabbi of Lwow from 1740 until his death. See S. Buber, אנשי שם (Cracow, 1895), 69–72.
60. Landau alludes to a rabbinic conference that convened in 1752 on market day in Brody. See Emden, פתח עינים, 7b. Falk may be referring to the proclamation issued by a rabbinical group that convened in Brody in 1752. The proclamation, printed in אספקלריה המאירה, lists by title the various heretical works ascribed to Eibeschuetz. The proclamation, however, is dated Ellul (August) 1752, whereas Falk dates the meeting to Ḥeshvan (October) 1752.
61. Altona in 1753 belonged to the kingdom of Denmark, whose ruler, Frederick V, reigned as king of Denmark and Norway from 1746 to 1766.
62. Maimonides, *Mishneh Torah,* "Hilkhot Teshuvah" 2:4.
63. See Zinz, עטרת יהושע, 15–25.
64. See L. Lewin, "Die Synode und die Emden-Eibenschuetz'sche Fehde 1751–56," in his *Neue Materialien zur Geschichte der Vierlaendersynode* (Frankfurt, 1916), 50–66.
65. For the eulogy in Altona (by Rabbi Isaiah Breslau), see Emden, התאבקות, 111a. For the eulogies in Prague (by Rabbi Ezekiel Landau, Rabbi Zeraḥ Eidlitz, and others), see E. Landau, דרושי הצל"ח (Warsaw, 1884), 92–93, and Z. Eidlitz, אור לישרים (Budapest, 1942), 27–41. Emden's claim, loc. cit., that no eulogies were delivered outside of Altona and Prague, cannot be taken seriously. See, e.g., Rabbi Mordecai b. Samuel, שער המלך (Amsterdam, 1774), vol. 2, gate 5, chap. 7.
66. I.e., after Eibeschuetz's death in 1764. Due to its affirmation of the blood libel, followed by mass conversion to Christianity in 1759, much of the Frankist branch of the Sabbatean heresy lost whatever credibility it may once have had in rabbinic circles.

Contributors

Miriam Bodian (Ph.D., Hebrew University) is Professor of Jewish History at Touro College. Her research deals with the conversos and other areas in early modern Jewish history. She is the author of *Hebrews of the Portuguese Nation: Conversos and Community in Early Modern Amsterdam* (1997) and *Dying in the Law of Moses: Crypto-Jewish Martyrdom in the Iberian World* (forthcoming).

Joseph M. Davis (Ph.D., Harvard) is Associate Professor of Jewish Thought at Gratz College. He is the author of *Yom-Tov Lipmann Heller: Portrait of a Seventeenth Century Rabbi* (2004) and other studies on the intellectual culture of medieval and early modern Ashkenazic Jews.

Daniel Frank (Ph.D., Harvard) is Associate Professor of Near Eastern Languages and Cultures at the Ohio State University. His publications include *Search Scripture Well: Karaite Exegetes and the Origins of the Jewish Bible Commentary in the Islamic East* (2004), an edited volume, *The Jews of Medieval Islam: Community, Society, and Identity* (1995), and other studies devoted to Karaite Judaism and medieval Jewish biblical exegesis.

Matt Goldish (Ph.D., Hebrew University) is Melton Professor of Jewish History at the Ohio State University. He has published *Judaism in the Theology of Sir Isaac Newton* (1998) and *The Sabbatean Prophets* (2004), as well as studies on Sefardic history and Jewish messianism.

Ephraim Kanarfogel (Ph.D., Yeshiva University) is Ivry Professor of Jewish History at Yeshiva University. His research deals with the intellectual and social history of medieval European Jewry. His publications include *Jewish Education and Society in the High Middle Ages*

(1992) and *Peering through the Lattices: Mystical, Magical, and Pietistic Dimensions in the Tosafist Period* (2000).

Menachem Kellner (Ph.D., Washington University) is Professor of Jewish Thought at the University of Haifa. His research centers on medieval Jewish philosophy and modern Jewish thought. His most recent books include an English translation of Maimonides' *Book of Love* (Mishneh Torah, vol. 2) (2004), *Must a Jew Believe Anything?* (2nd ed., 2006), and *Maimonides' Confrontation with Mysticism* (2006).

Sid Z. Leiman (Ph.D., University of Pennsylvania) is Professor of Jewish History and Literature at Brooklyn College, City University of New York. He is the author of *The Canonization of Hebrew Scripture* (2nd ed., 1991), as well as many studies of the biblical canon, eighteenth-century rabbinic schism, and late Sabbateanism.

Harris Lenowitz (Ph.D., University of Texas) is Professor of Hebrew at the University of Utah. His recent work focuses on the history of Jewish messiahs and messianism. His publications include *The Jewish Messiahs, From the Galilee to Crown Heights* (1998) and a complete English translation of Jacob Frank's *Dicta,* available on the worldwide web.

Allan Nadler (Ph.D., Harvard) is Professor of Jewish Studies at Drew University. His research concerns modern Jewish thought in Eastern Europe. His publications include *Faith of the Mithnagdim: Rabbinic Responses to Hasidic Rapture* (1997), *The Hasidim in America* (1995), and *The Heretic as Hero: Spinoza in the Modern Jewish Imagination* (forthcoming).

Steven Nadler (Ph.D., Columbia University) is Professor of Philosophy and Max and Frieda Weinstein/Bascom Professor of Jewish Studies at the University of Wisconsin-Madison. His work focuses on the history of early modern philosophy. His recent books include *Spinoza: A Life* (1999), *Spinoza's Heresy: Immortality and the Jewish Mind* (2002), *Rembrandt's Jews* (2003), and *Spinoza's Ethics: An Introduction* (2006).

Marina Rustow (Ph.D., Columbia) is Assistant Professor of History and Jewish Studies at Emory University. Her work focuses on the political culture of the tenth- and eleventh-century Near East, rabbinic leadership, and documents from the Cairo Geniza. She is author of *Toward a History of Jewish Heresy: Rabbanites and Qaraites in Medieval Egypt and Syria* (Cornell University Press, forthcoming).

Marc Saperstein (Ph.D., Harvard) is Principal of the Leo Baeck College Center for Jewish Education in London, on extended leave from the George Washington University. His books include *Jewish Preaching, 1200–1800* (1989), *"Your Voice Like a Ram's Horn"* (1996), and *Exile in Amsterdam* (2005). He is the leading authority on the history of the Jewish sermon.

Adam Sutcliffe (Ph.D. Cambridge, 1998) is Lecturer in Early Modern European History at King's College London. His work focuses on the role of Jews in eighteenth-century European thought. He is the author of *Judaism and Enlightenment* (2003) and other studies.

Adena Tanenbaum (Ph.D., Harvard) is Associate Professor of Near Eastern Languages and Cultures at the Ohio State University. She is the author of *The Contemplative Soul: Hebrew Poetry and Philosophical Theory in Medieval Spain* (2002) and other studies. Her research focuses on medieval Jewish intellectual history with an emphasis on literary works from Islamic lands.

Index